FUZZY CONTROLLERS, THEORY AND APPLICATIONS

Edited by **Teodor Lucian Grigorie**

Fuzzy Controllers, Theory and Applications
Edited by Teodor Lucian Grigorie

Published by InTech
Janeza Trdine 9, 51000 Rijeka, Croatia

Publishing Process Manager Ana Nikolic

Technical Editor Teodora Smiljanic

Cover Designer InTech Design Team

Additional hard copies can be obtained from orders@intechopen.com

Fuzzy Controllers, Theory and Applications, Edited by Teodor Lucian Grigorie
p. cm.
ISBN 978-953-307-543-3

For EU product safety concerns:
IN TECH d.o.o., Prolaz Marije Krucifikse Kozulić 3, 51000 Rijeka, Croatia,
info@intechopen.com or visit our website at intechopen.com.

Meet the editor

Teodor Lucian Grigorie was born in 1975 in Craiova, Romania where he received the BsC and MsC in Aerospace Engineering from the Faculty of Electrical Engineering, University of Craiova in 1998 and 1999, respectively. In 2006 he obtained the PhD at the Faculty of Aerospace Engineering, Politehnica University of Bucharest in Aerospace Engineering field. From 1998 to 2005 he worked as assistant professor at Avionics Division of University of Craiova, while from 2005 to 2009 he was senior lecturer in inertial navigation systems at the same institution. Since 2009 he has been associate professor at the Avionics Division of University of Craiova. Between May 2008 and February 2009 he was postdoctoral fellow at the University of Quebec, Canada, institution wherewith he collaborates in research projects since 2002. He authored or co-authored 2 books and more than 100 papers in journals and conference proceedings of international and domestic scientific events. His research activities concern navigation systems, miniaturized inertial sensors, aircraft's board equipments, automatic control systems (including intelligent control systems), and morphing aircraft structures. He participated in 9 research projects with the Romanian Ministry of Education and Science, and in 7 international research projects with University of Quebec, Ecole de Technologie Superieure en Montreal, Canada.

Contents

Preface

Global technologies evolution triggered increasing complexity of applications developed both in industry and in the scientific research fields. Thus, many researchers concentrated their efforts on providing simple and easy control algorithms to cope with the increasing complexity of the controlled systems. The main challenge of a control designer is how to find a formal way to convert the knowledge and experience of a system operator into a well designed control algorithm. From other point of view, the control design method should allow a full flexibility in the control surface adjusting, taking into account that the systems involved in practice are generally complex, strongly nonlinear and often with poorly defined dynamics. If a conventional control methodology based on linear system theory is used, a linearised model of the nonlinear system should be previously developed. Because the validity of the linearised model is limited in a range around the operating point, any guarantee of good performance can't be provided by the obtained controller. As a consequence, to have a satisfactory control of a complex nonlinear system, a nonlinear controller should be developed. On the other way, if the controlled system is difficult to be precisely described by conventional mathematical relations, hence the design of a controller using classical analytical methods would be totally impractical. With such systems is motivated the interest in using a control designed by an operator on the base of its years-long experience and knowledge about static and dynamic characteristics of the system; the controller is known as Fuzzy Logic Controller (FLC). FLCs are based on fuzzy logic theory developed by L. Zadeh. By using multivalent fuzzy logic, linguistic expressions in antecedent and consequent parts of IF-THEN rules describing the operator's actions can be efficaciously converted into a fully-structured control algorithm suitable for microcomputer implementation or implementation with specially designed fuzzy processors. In contrast with traditional linear and nonlinear control theory, a FLC is not based on a mathematical model, and provides a certain level of artificial intelligence to the conventional controllers.

Trying to meet the requirements in the field, present book deals with some studies of control systems based on fuzzy logic both in terms of optimization of existing controllers, as well as that of determining the optimal design techniques for new controllers. Developments made in some of the book chapters can also serve to acquaint the reader, eager to further deepening, with the complex problem of fuzzy logic control systems. The book is divided into seventeen chapters that treat different fuzzy control architectures both in terms of the theoretical design and in terms of comparative validation studies in various applications, numerically simulated or experimentally developed.

A very interesting idea regarding the hardware implementation of fuzzy controllers is exposed in Chapter 1. The study shows that for a sufficient wide set of applications, fuzzy controllers can be implemented as rather simple CMOS devices, which can be used in embedded systems or as an IP core. Starting from the deterministic character of the fuzzy controller device, for which one and only one value of the output analogue variable corresponds to each value combination of the input analogue variables, it results that the fuzzy controller should realize an analogue function. So, the proposed methodology is oriented to hardware implementation of fuzzy controllers as analogue devices, and is based on the searching for simple basic multi-valued functions, which would present a complete functional basis in the multi-valued logic and could be efficiently implemented by CMOS technology. It is shown that all parts of fuzzy controllers can be effectively implemented on the basis of summing amplifiers with saturation.

In Chapter 2 a robust fuzzy control design based on gain and phase margins specifications for nonlinear systems in the continuous time domain is proposed. A mathematical formulation based on Takagi-Sugeno fuzzy model structure as well as the parallel distributed compensation strategy is presented. Analytical formulas are deduced for the sub-controllers parameters in the robust fuzzy controller rules base, according to the fuzzy model parameters of the fuzzy model plant to be controlled. Also, one axiom and two theorems are proposed in order to guarantee the robust stability, and the derived results for the necessary and sufficient conditions for the fuzzy controller design are presented. The proposed method validation is made through numerical simulation for a one-link robotic manipulator.

Chapter 3 focuses on adaptive fuzzy modelling and control for non-linear systems using interval reasoning and differential evolution. As an introduction, a systematic design method of extended fuzzy logic system (EFLS) for engineering applications is presented. The EFLS is implemented to solve the inverse kinematic modelling problem of a two-joint robotic arm which cannot be well modelled by the typical fuzzy methods. Under the presented framework of EFLS, the adaptive fuzzy control system is designed to deal with the uncertainties from complex dynamics of control plant by integrating the global optimization method: Differential Evolution (DE). The main difference in this adaptive control system is the defuzzification part. For dealing with the variable control target and solving the nonlinear optimization performance, the crisp outputs are derived from the interval of outputs of subsystems by the DE optimization method. The adaptive fuzzy control system is designed for a typical nonlinear quarter car active suspension system, and the obtained results confirm that the control performance is improved, while the design process is more flexible than other methods.

Chapter 4 proposes a new approach to improve the local and global approximation and modelling capability of Takagi-Sugeno (T-S) fuzzy model, and to design an optimal fuzzy controller. The approach is based on an iterative method using the extended Kalman filter, and can be considered as a generalized version of T-S fuzzy identification method with optimized performance in estimating nonlinear functions. The main aims are the obtaining of high function approximation accuracy and the fast convergence. To validate the proposed methodology, the stabilizing and balancing of swing up of an inverted pendulum are performed.

The design of a robust $H\infty$ fuzzy controller for a class of uncertain fuzzy systems is performed in Chapter 5. Firstly, this class of uncertain nonlinear systems is approximated by a Takagi-Sugeno fuzzy model. After that, based on a linear matrix inequalities (LMI) approach, is developed a technique for designing robust $H\infty$ fuzzy state-feedback and output feedback controllers such that the L2-gain of the mapping from the exogenous input noise to the regulated output is less than a prescribed value. The LMI-based approach is used to derive sufficient conditions for the existence of a robust $H\infty$ fuzzy controller in terms of a family of LMIs. The fuzzy controller design validation is made through numerical simulation for a problem of the chaotic Lorenz system.

Chapter 6 presents affine-type fuzzy tracking-controllers to trace a moving-target and a model-following-target, respectively. Although a linear type T-S fuzzy system is very popular, and has been successfully applied to various fields, the affine type system is more preferred for computation-intelligent (neural-fuzzy-evolution) modelling as a system is too complex to be described. To compensate the target-variation and to respond to the rule-consequence singleton, two differential equations are derived and then integrated into an extra-action to achieve adaptive-tracking. Both designed closed-loop tracking systems are demonstrated to be globally stable by using a Lyapunov-based stability analysis.

Chapter 7 proposes a simplified implementation of the type-2 fuzzy systems (T2FLS). The proposed architecture of Type-2 FLS uses four embedded Type-1 FLSs and is an alternative to the type-reduction method. To assess the ability of the proposed implementation to handle uncertainties, a numerical comparative analysis of the type-1 fuzzy systems (T1FLS) and type-2 fuzzy systems (T2FLS) proposed architecture for a greenhouse climate control problem is made. The obtained T2FLS architecture provides a smoother control surface and a greater ability to detect and treat the measurement and modelling uncertainties in the controlled system with the aid of a genetic algorithm. It also achieved a dramatic reduction in computational complexity without sacrificing performance compared to its equivalent type-2 FLS with type-reduction method. The proposed T2FLS is easy to implement using MATLAB® Fuzzy Logic Toolbox™ and it does not require more than the basic knowledge of T1FLS.

In Chapter 8 a model-free self-learning fuzzy controller is proposed to control the molten steel level of strip casting process monitoring. The quality of strip casting process depends on many process parameters, such as molten steel level in the tundish, solidification position and roll gap. Their relationships are complex and the strip casting process has the properties of nonlinear uncertainty and time-varying characteristics. Hence, it is difficult to establish an accurate process model for designing a model-based controller to monitor the strip quality. The proposed fuzzy controller has on-line learning ability and the rule tables can be modified automatically and continuously for responding to the system's nonlinear and time-varying behaviours. In addition, the adopted control strategy can monitor the molten steel at the preset desired level without overshooting effectively to guarantee the steel strip casting quality.

Chapter 9 proposes an interesting application of fuzzy logic controllers, for maximum power point tracking for a grid-connected photovoltaic system. In this way, a controller for a solid state inverter in a single phase grid-connected photovoltaic system is derived. The maximum power point tracking algorithm is improved by means a short circuit current estimator based on a Takagi-Sugeno (T-S) fuzzy model. Finally, simpler linear controllers are used to achieve the maximum power point where the reference is imposed by the short circuit current estimator.

Chapter 10 presents a way for optimal tuning of proportional-integral fuzzy controllers, providing a scheme for obtaining optimum values of fuzzy membership function's slope. As application for the proposed method validation, the control of the BLDC motor drive system is chosen.

Another interesting application of fuzzy control theory is described in Chapter 11, which shows an efficient controller that improves the operating characteristics of an atomic force microscope (AFM) by increasing the bandwidth of the feedback controller, thereby allowing for faster scan rates and higher resolutions. For closed-loop feedback control of an AFM probe two controllers are designed: 1) based on conventional fuzzy Mamdani control theory; and 2) based on the introduction of a fuzzy controller to a PD controller to tune online the PD gains resulting in a hybrid PD-fuzzy controller. Also, a comparative analysis of the results of these controllers and a baseline a high-gain PD controller is realised.

Chapter 12 deals with an application of the fuzzy controllers in autonomic computing systems, the proposed objectives of the authors being to minimize response time by maximizing system utilization and also to maximize the profit of an e-commerce system by maximizing system utilization. In this way, two fuzzy controllers are designed and implemented: 1) for minimizing the response-time by optimizing the value of max-requests, and 2) for maximizing the profit by optimizing the value of max-requests.

In Chapter 13, a type-2 fuzzy controller is proposed to control both the left and right drive wheel of a nonholonomic automatic guided vehicle (AGV) for the wall following. The proposed controller is especially suitable for the AGV using a sonar system to measure the distance between the AGV and the wall. The inevitable noise problem in AGV's sonar-based distance measuring scheme is resolved by using type-2 fuzzy sets to define the distance measurements. An experimental comparative study of a nonholonomic automatic guided vehicle (AGV) for the wall following with the proposed type-2 fuzzy controller and with a type-1 fuzzy controller is realised.

The application presented in Chapter 14 focuses on the development of a new morphing mechanism using smart materials such as Shape Memory Alloy (SMA) as actuators and fuzzy logic techniques. Two important applications of the fuzzy logic technique are highlighted in this work: the identification of a model for a system starting from some experimental input-output data, and the automatic control of a system. In this way, in this morphing application two directions are developed: smart material actuator modelling and actuation lines' control. Based on a neuro-fuzzy network and using numerical values resulted from the SMA experimental testing (forces, currents, temperatures and elongations), an empirical model is developed for the SMA actuators. The second application of fuzzy-logic techniques in this project (actuation lines' control) supposes the design of an SMA actuators' controller starting from the developed SMA actuators' model. A fuzzy PD architecture is chosen for the controller. In its design, numerical simulations of the open loop morphing wing integrated system, based on a SMA neuro-fuzzy model, are performed. A bench test and a wind tunnel test are conducted as subsequent validation methods.

Chapter 15 presents the use of fuzzy-control to model the control behaviour of a human pilot during a high and a low gain flight task. The concrete realization of the fuzzy-sets as a mathematical representation of the linguistic terms is depended from the variations of the individual human control behaviour. In both approaches the developed cognitive pilot model reproduced well the characteristics of the human pilot and it could be pointed out that the cognitive pilot models fulfil the requirements of the according flight task; the measurements and the control commands of the pilot models and the human pilot are very similar in magnitude and trend; the control behaviour of the cognitive pilot models are based on the control strategy of the human pilot; the cognitive pilot models commands induce a similar aircraft reaction as the human pilot.

Chapter 16 of the book deals with the acquisition and chaos-entropy analysis of individuality and proficiency of human operator's skill using a fuzzy controller. As a demonstrative application the stabilizing control of an inverted pendulum by a human operator is chosen. It is demonstrated that the fuzzy controller identified from the measured time series data for each trial for each human operator clearly exhibited the human-generated decision-making characteristics, exhibiting chaos and a large amount of disorder. Also, it is shown that the estimated number of degrees of freedom of motion increases and the estimated amount of disorder decreases with the increase in proficiency in the fuzzy control simulation. The study clarifies that a simple fuzzy controller can be very useful for identifying the individuality and proficiency of a human operator when stabilizing an unstable system.

In Chapter 17 fuzzy logic dead-zone compensation with a linear controller for tracking of mobile manipulators is developed. The proposed design procedure results in a kinematic tracking loop with an adaptive fuzzy logic system in the feed forward loop for dead-zone compensation. The proposed control scheme is shown to be asymptotically stable through theoretical proof and numerical simulation.

Through the subject matter and through the inter and multidisciplinary content, this book is addressed mainly to the researchers, doctoral students and students interested in developing new applications of intelligent control, but also to the people who want to become familiar with the control concepts based on fuzzy techniques. Bibliographic resources used to perform the work include books and articles of present interest in the field, published in prestigious journals and publishing houses, and websites dedicated to various applications of fuzzy control. Its structure and the presented studies include the book in the category of those that make a direct connection between theoretical developments and practical applications, thereby constituting a real support for the specialists in artificial intelligence, modelling and control fields.

Teodor Lucian Grigorie, PhD
Avionics Division,
Faculty of Electrical Engineering,
University of Craiova,
Craiova,
Romania

Part 1

Fuzzy Controllers: Theoretical Design and Numerical Simulation Validation

1

Hardware Implementation of Fuzzy Controllers

Victor Varshavsky, Viacheslav Marakhovsky[1],
Ilya Levin[2] and Hiroshi Saito[3]
[1]*St. Petersburg State Politechnical University*
[2]*Tel Aviv University*
[3]*The University of Aizu*
[1]*Russian Federation*
[2]*Israel*
[3]*Japan*

1. Introduction

Fuzzy logic control is a methodology bridging *artificial intelligence* and traditional *control theory*. This methodology is usually applied in the only cases when accuracy is not of high necessity or importance. On the other hand, as it is stated in (TI SPRA028, Jan.1993), "Fuzzy Logic can address complex control problems, such as robotic arm movement, chemical or manufacturing process control, antiskids braking systems or automobile transmission control with more precision and accuracy, in many cases, than traditional control techniques … . Fuzzy Logic is a methodology for expressing operational laws of a system in linguistic terms instead of mathematical equations."

Wide spread of the fuzzy control and high effectiveness of its applications in a great extend is determined by formalization opportunities of necessary behavior of a controller as a "fuzzy" (flexible) representation. This representation usually is formulated in the form of logical (fuzzy) rules under linguistic variables of a type "If A then B".

The Fuzzy Logic methodology (Yager & Zadeh, 1992; Klir & Yuan, 1996) comprises three phases:

1. The *fuzzification* is a transformation of analog (continuous) input variables to linguistic ones, e.g., transformation of temperature into the terms *cool*, *warm*, *hot* or transformation of speed into the terms *negative big* (*NB*), *negative small* (*NS*), *zero* (*Z*)", *positive small* (*PS*), *positive big* (*PB*). Such transformation is realized by introduction of so-called *membership functions*, which define both a range of value and a degree of membership. For linguistic variables it is important not only which membership function a variable belongs to, but also a relative degree (weight) to which it is a member. A variable can have a weighted membership in several membership functions at the same time.
2. The *fuzzy inference* maps input linguistic variables onto output linguistic variables on the base a system of fuzzy rules of the type "IF A THEN B" For instance: "IF the temperature is *worm* THEN the speed is *Positive Small* (*PS*)" or "IF the speed is *Negative Big* (*NB*) THEN force is *ZERO*". Since input linguistic variables are weighted, the output linguistic variables can be obtained weighted as well. Traditional fuzzy logic approach comprises Mamdani- type and Sugeno-type inference methods. The Mamdani-type

method is more intuitive and assumes the output variables as a fuzzy set. Fuzzy rules in it contain a *fuzzy precondition* part (after IF) and a *fuzzy consequence* part (after THEN). The Sugeno-type method expects the output variables to be singletons or dealing with consequents that are equations. So it is better suited for mathematical analysis, nonlinear system modeling and interpolation.

3. In the *defuzzification* phase, the weighted values of output linguistic variables obtained as a result of fuzzy inference have to be transformed to analogue (continuous) variables. This procedure is also based on membership functions. Two major methods are used for defuzzification:

- The *maximum* defuzzification method, wherein an output value is determined by the linguistic variable with the maximum weight;
- The *centroid* calculation defuzzification method, wherein an output value is determined by the weighted influence of all the active output membership functions.

As a rule, or at least in a great part of applications, a fuzzy controller is a transformer of input analog signals into an analog output signal. A linguistic variable is a *subjective* characteristic of an input analog variable, values of which are transformed on bases of given membership functions into a set of weighted values of corresponding linguistic variables. This procedure is called a fuzzification and it contains as its composite part the analog-digital transformation.

A set of combinations of weighted linguistic variables corresponds to each value combination of input analog variables. On bases of a system of fuzzy inference rules it is possible to receive the set of weighted output linguistic variables. Using these variables and their membership functions, with help of one of well known defuzzification methods it is possible to form values of the analog output variable. The defuzzification procedure also includes digital-analog transformation.

At present the most wide-spread way of fuzzy logic control implementation is using the programmable fuzzy controllers, which are available on the market together with the means of computer aided programming (e.g. Motorola's 8-bit 68HC11 and 16-bit 68HC12 microcontrollers or specialized fuzzy processors of Siemens 80C517/80C535 families). However, in spite of the implementation evidence and fuzzy controllers' accessibility this approach to controller implementation possesses some disadvantages, e.g. such as high cost and low throughput (that is especially important when fuzzy control in the control contour is used) etc.

This work shows that for a sufficient wide set of applications, fuzzy controllers can be implemented as rather simple CMOS devices, which can be used in embedded systems or as an IP core. What is the basic idea of the proposal?

A fuzzy controller is a deterministic device, for which one and only one value of the output analog variable corresponds to each value combination of the input analog variables. It means that the fuzzy controller should realize an analog function $Y = f(x_1, x_2, ..., x_n)$. It should be noticed that in suppressing majority of publications on fuzzy controllers, this function is given as a response surface and practically without exception this surface has a piecewise linear form.

There are two important questions:

1. How to transit from a standard specification of a fuzzy logic function to the specification of corresponding analog function?
2. How to transit from an analog function specification and/or from a standard specification of a fuzzy logic function to corresponding CMOS implementation?

First of all, let us address to membership functions. In most cases (Yager & Zadeh, 1992; Marks II, 1994; Klir & Yuan, 1996) , membership functions have a triangle or trapeze form (see Fig. 1).

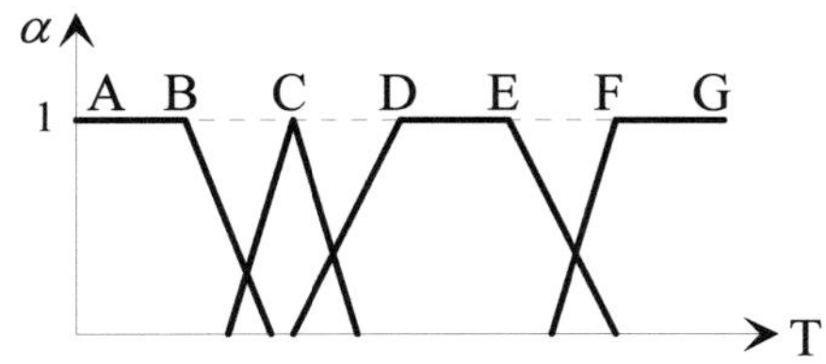

Fig. 1. Types of membership functions.

In Fig. 1 linguistic points (variables) A and B are *cold*, C is *fresh*, D and E are *worm*, F and G are *hot*. These points determine the connection of the linguistic variables with values of the analog variable T (T is *temperature*). Relatively to these points and similar points for other analog input variables we can compose a table of fuzzy rules connecting combinations of input linguistic variables with output linguistic variables.

On bases of membership functions we can put into accordance to the input and output linguistic variables a set of integer numbers splitting by appropriate way all diapason of changing of corresponding analog variables. Then the table of fuzzy rules will to determine by obvious way the function of multi-valued logic, values of which define the digit representation of the output linguistic variable on chosen value combinations of multi-valued input variables. In other words, according to our concept, for a broad class of fuzzy controller specifications it is possible to construct corresponding tables connecting input and output membership functions. Frequently membership functions evenly divide the ranges of output variables' variations. If it is not so, the membership functions can be brought to even scale by increasing the number of gradations or, as it will be shown later, by introducing a certain equalization procedure for logical levels. Therefore, specification tables represent nothing but tables determining a specific multi-valued logical function. And what is more, for a number of implementations it is possible to neglect weighting and determining input linguistic variables and simply to use continuous-valued variables.

The above idea was in the focus of our research. We dealt with searching for simple basic multi-valued functions, which, from the one hand, would present a complete functional basis in the multi-valued logic, and from the other hand, could be efficiently implemented by CMOS technology.

2. Hardware implementation of fuzzy controllers

2.1 Summing amplifier as a multi-valued logical element

Summing amplifier's behavior, accurate to the members of the infinitesimal order that is determined by the amplifier's gain factor in disconnected condition (Fig. 2), is described as follows:

$$V_{out} = \begin{cases} V_{dd} & \text{if } \sum\limits_{j=1}^{n} \dfrac{R_0}{R_j}\left(V_j - \dfrac{V_{dd}}{2}\right) \le -\dfrac{V_{dd}}{2} \\ \dfrac{V_{dd}}{2} - \sum\limits_{j=1}^{n} \dfrac{R_0}{R_j}\left(V_j - \dfrac{V_{dd}}{2}\right) & \text{if } \dfrac{V_{dd}}{2} > \sum\limits_{j=1}^{n} \dfrac{R_0}{R_j}\left(V_j - \dfrac{V_{dd}}{2}\right) > -\dfrac{V_{dd}}{2} \\ 0 & \text{if } \dfrac{V_{dd}}{2} \le \sum\limits_{j=1}^{n} \dfrac{R_0}{R_j}\left(V_j - \dfrac{V_{dd}}{2}\right) \end{cases} \quad (1)$$

where V_{dd} is the supply voltage, V_j is the voltage on j^{th} input, R_j is the resistance of jth input, R_0 is the feedback resistance, and $V_{dd}/2$ is the midpoint of the supply voltage.

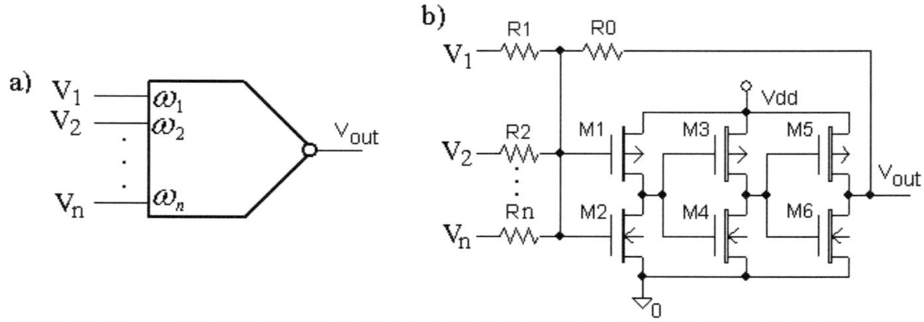

Fig. 2. Summing amplifier: a) general designation, b) CMOS implementation using symmetrical invertors.

Dependence of V_{out} on $\sum_{j=1}^{n} \frac{R_0}{R_j} \cdot (V_j - \frac{V_{dd}}{2})$ is shown in Fig. 3 (a).

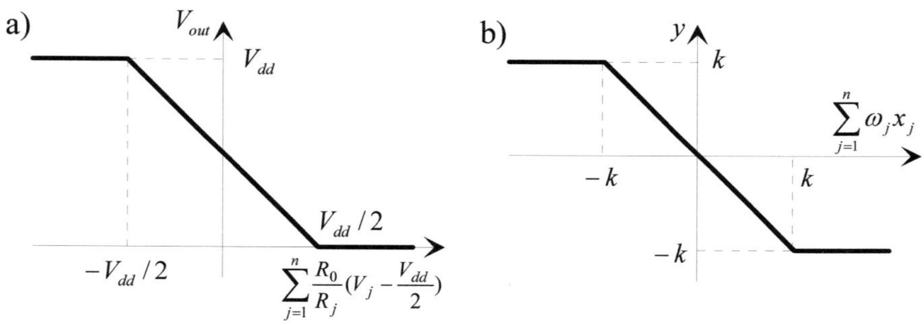

Fig. 3. Summing amplifier's behavior: a) within voltage coordinates; b) within multi-valued variable coordinates.

Let us split the source voltage V_{dd} on $m = 2k+1$ voltage levels. Then replacing the input voltages $V_j - V_{dd}/2$ by m-valued logical variables $x_j = (2V_j - V_{dd})k/V_{dd}$ and the output voltage V_{out} by m-valued variable y and designating $R_0/R_j = \omega_j$ the system (1) can be represented as (2).

$$y(X) = S(\sum_{j=1}^{n} \omega_j \cdot x_j) = \begin{cases} +k & \text{if } \sum_{j=1}^{n} \omega_j \cdot x_j \le -k \\ -\sum_{j=1}^{n} \omega_j \cdot x_j & \text{if } k > \sum_{j=1}^{n} \omega_j \cdot x_j > -k \\ -k & \text{if } \sum_{j=1}^{n} \omega_j \cdot x_j \ge +k \end{cases} \tag{2}$$

Graphical view of (2) is shown in Fig.3 (b).

Later on, we will call the functional element, whose behavior is determined by the system (2), a multi-valued threshold element. When $\omega_j = 1$, $j = 1, 2, 3,$, we will call it a majority element and designate as $maj(x_1, x_2, x_3)$.

2.2 Functional completeness of the threshold element

The basic operation (or a set of basic operations) is called functionally completed in arbitrary-valued logic, if any function of this logic can be represented as superposition of the basic operations.

There are some known functionally complete sets of functions. It is clear, that for proving the functional completeness of a certain new function it is sufficient to show that every function of the known functionally complete set can be represented as a superposition of the considered function. One of functionally complete functions in m-valued logic is the Webb's function (Post, 1921):

$$w(x,y) = [\max(x,y)+1]_{\mathrm{mod}\, m}\,. \tag{3}$$

Therefore, for proving functional completeness of the threshold operation in multi-valued logic it is sufficient to show how the Webb's function can be represented through this operation (Varshavsky et al., 2003, 2004).

First, let us represent the function $\max(x_1, x_2)$ by threshold functions. To do this let us consider the function $f_a(x)$, such as

$$f_a(x) = \max(x,a) = \begin{cases} a & \text{if} \quad a \geq x \\ x & \text{if} \quad x > a \end{cases}, \quad |x| \leq k, \ \ |a| \leq k. \tag{4}$$

The diagram of this function is shown in Fig. 4(a). The $-maj(x,-a,-k)$ function diagram is shown in Fig. 4(b). Actually, as far as $x < a$, $x - a - k < -k$ and $-maj(x,-a,-k) = -k$. Note that for all values of x,

$$f_a(x) = -maj(x,-a,-k) + a + k$$

as it follows from Fig.4, hence

$$f_a(x) = -maj(-maj(x,-a,-k),a,k)\,. \tag{5}$$

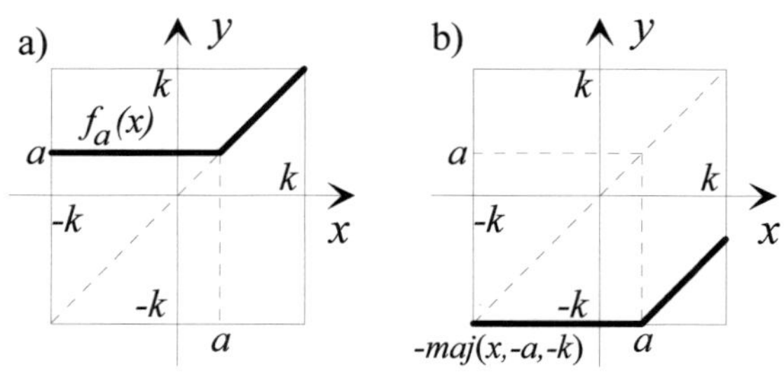

Fig. 4. Diagrams of the functions a) $f_a(x)$ and b) $-maj(x,-a,-k)$.

Taking into consideration

$$-maj(a,b,c) = maj(-a,-b,-c),$$

it follows from (5) that

$$\max(x_1,x_2) = maj(maj(x_1,-x_2,-k),-x_2,-k)\ . \tag{6}$$

Now let us consider the representation of the function $y = (x+1)_{\mathrm{mod}m}$, $x \geq 0$, $0 \leq y \leq m-1$ through threshold functions. First of all we designate $m = 2k+1$ and change the beginning of coordinates so that the function will have a form $y = (x+k+1)_{\mathrm{mod}(2k+1)} - k$, $x \geq -k$, $-k \leq y \leq +k$. To implement this function on threshold elements let us turn to the sequence of pictures in Fig. 5.

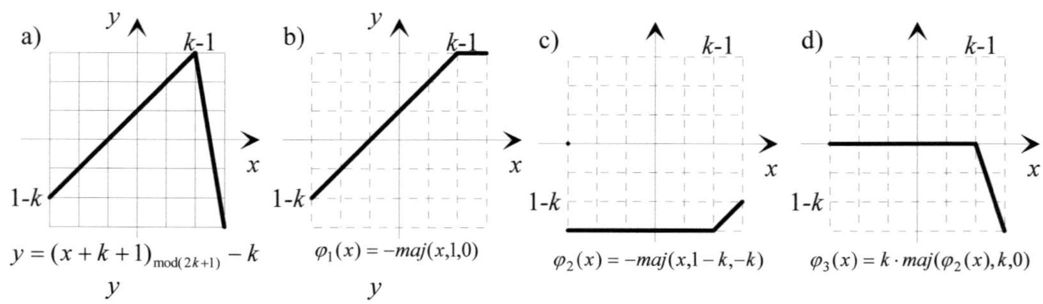

Fig. 5. Implementation of the function $y = (x+k+1)_{\mathrm{mod}(2k+1)} - k$.

It is easy to see that

$$(x+k+1)_{\mathrm{mod}(2k+1)} - k = \phi_1(x) + 2\varphi_3(x)$$

and obviously, this function can also be implemented on threshold elements as

$$y = maj(maj(x,1,0), k \cdot maj(maj(x,1-k,-k),-k,0), k \cdot maj(maj(x,1-k,-k),-k,0)).$$

Hence, the functional completeness of the summing amplifier in arbitrary-valued logic is shown. The proof procedure of functional completeness naturally does not give information about methods of effective synthesis. Some methods of a circuit design in the proposed basis will be developed later.

2.3 Fuzzy devices as multi-valued and analog circuits

Conventional implementation of fuzzy devices usually has the structure shown in Fig. 6. Analog variables $X = \{x_1,x_2,\ldots,x_n\}$ enter the fuzzy device input. Fuzzifier converts a set of analog variables x_j into sets of weighted linguistic (digital) variables $A = \{a_1,a_2,\ldots,a_n\}$.

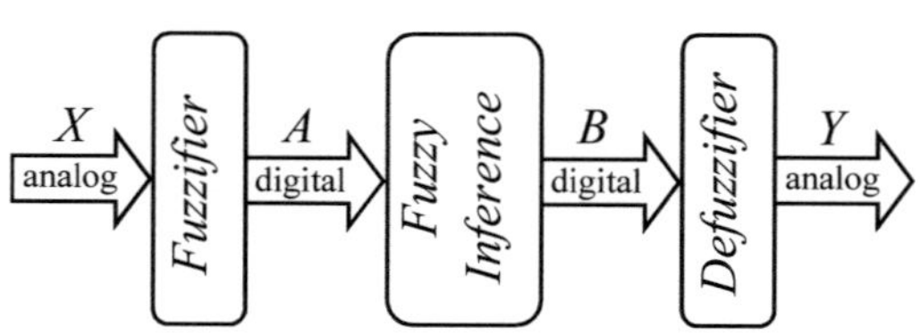

Fig. 6. Conventional structure of a fuzzy device implementation.

Fuzzy Inference block generates based on the fuzzy rules a set of weighted linguistic variables values $B = \{b_1,b_2,\ldots,b_k\}$.

Defuzzifier converts sets of weighted linguistic (digital) variables $B = \{b_1,b_2,...,b_k\}$ into a set of output analog variables $Y = \{y_1,y_2,...,y_k\}$.
As a rule, fuzzifier and defuzzifier include AD and DA (analog-digital and digital-analog) converters and are implemented on both levels (hardware and software). Fuzzy inference is usually implemented on the level of microprocessor software.
It is easy to see that each set of values of output analog variables unambiguously corresponds to some set of input analog variable values; hence a fuzzy device could be specified as a functional analog of a signal converter

$$Y(X) = \{y_1(X), y_2(X),..., y_k(X)\}$$

and its output Y determines a system of n-dimensional surfaces. In cases of sufficient simple membership functions (in known publications such functions are in majority), for fuzzy controller implementations as analog devices it is sufficient to provide a piecewise-linear approximation between a couples of points calculated as adjacent values of a multi-valued logic function.
Let $m = 2k+1$ linguistic variables a_j ($a_j \in A$) correspond to values of analog variable x_j ($xj \in X$). Then basing on a system of fuzzy rules, we can specify a system of m-valued logic functions, as follows:

$$B(A) = \{b_1(A), b_2(A),..., b_k(A)\} . \tag{7}$$

Note that most publications describing fuzzy controllers contain tables specifying fuzzy controllers' behaviour as (7) and a plenty of publications contain piecewise-linear approximations of the corresponding surfaces.
The apparent conclusion can be made from the things mentioned above: if a fuzzy controller is represented as (7), it can be implemented as superposition of multi-valued threshold elements. In this case, owing linear behavior of the threshold element in the zone between the saturation levels ((2) and Fig. 3(b)), natural piecewise linear approximation appears between the discrete points of specification.
In the last subsection of this section some illustrations will be given to show that for a number of real applications the offered approach can provides simple and efficient circuits of controllers.

2.4 Fuzzy controller implementations as circuits from threshold elements

2.4.1 Example 1

Let us consider the example, which is taken from (Kandel & Zedeh, 1993, pp. 81 – 86): "Design of a Rule-Based Fuzzy Controller for the Pitch Axis of an Unmanned Research Vehicle".
The fuzzy control rules for the considered device depend on the error value $e = ref - output$ and changing of error $ce = \frac{old\,e - new\,e}{sampling\ period}$. Fuzzifier gives seven linguistic variables for each of input analog variables (NB - negative big; NM - negative middle; NS - negative small; ZO - zero; PS - positive small; PM - positive middle; PB - positive big). The output has the same seven gradations. Corresponding 49 fuzzy rules are represented in Table 1.
Let us split evenly the source voltage (e.g. 3.5V) onto seven logical levels corresponding to linguistic levels and enumerate them with integer numbers from -3 to +3. Then Table 2 will represent Table 1 as the function of seven-valued logic.

e								
ce		NB	NM	NS	ZO	PS	PM	PB
	NB	ZO	PS	PM	PB	PB	PB	PB
	NM	NS	ZO	PS	PM	PB	PB	PB
	NS	NM	NS	ZO	PS	PM	PB	PB
	ZO	NB	NM	NS	ZO	PS	PM	PB
	PS	NB	NB	NM	NS	ZO	PS	PM
	PM	NB	NB	NB	NM	NS	ZO	PS
	PB	NB	NB	NB	NB	NM	NS	ZO

Table 1. Table of Fuzzy Rules.

It is seen from Table 2 that the function is symmetric with respect to "North-West - South-East" diagonal and its values can be calculated as $e - ce$. This dependency is shown in Fig. 7.

	e							
ce	0	-3	-2	-1	0	1	2	3
	-3	0	1	2	3	3	3	3
	-2	-1	0	1	2	3	3	3
	-1	-2	-1	0	1	2	3	3
	0	-3	-2	-1	0	1	2	3
	1	-3	-3	-2	-1	0	1	2
	2	-3	-3	-3	-2	-1	0	1
	3	-3	-3	-3	-3	-2	-1	0

Table 2. The Seven-Valued Function.

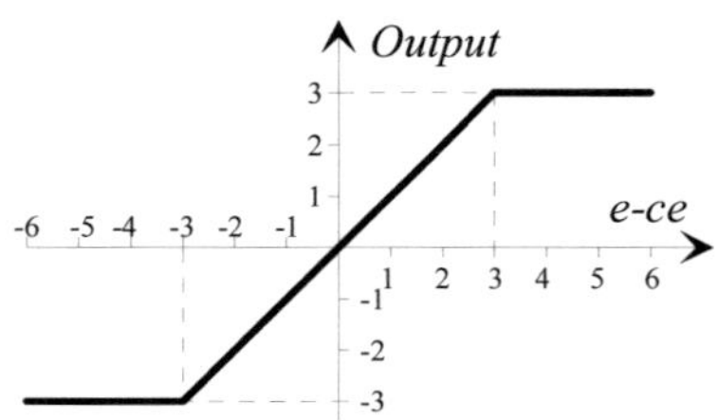

Fig. 7. Graphical representation of the function specified by Table 2.

It apparently follows from comparison of Fig. 3 (b) and Fig. 7 that in order to reproduce the function specified by Table 2 it is sufficient to have one two-input summing amplifier and one one-input amplifier that will be called inverter.

Note that inversion of logic variables lying within $-k \div +k$ interval is the operation of diametric negation $\overline{x} = -x$; the operation $V_{out} = V_{dd} - V_{in}$ corresponds to it in the terms of summing amplifier's input and output voltages. Thus CMOS circuit containing 12 transistors and 5 resistors, which implements our function, is shown in Fig. 8.

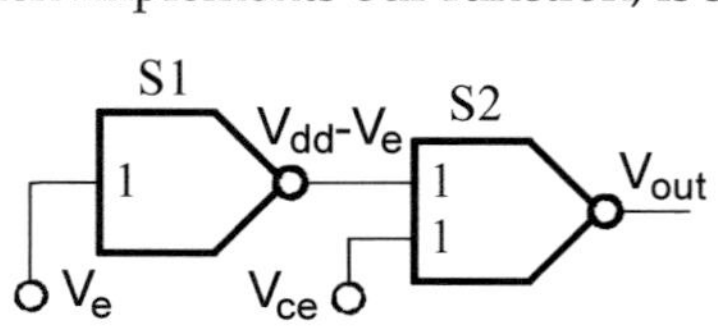

Fig. 8. Implementation of the fuzzy controller specified by Table 2.

2.4.2 Example 2

This example is taken from (Kandel & Zedeh, 1993, pp. 168 - 172): "Manipulator for Man-Robot Cooperation (Control Method of Manipulator/Vehicle System with Fuzzy Inference)". In the considered example the experimental manipulator has two force/torque sensors. One of them is the operational force sensor F_h; the other is "the environmental force sensor" ω. Each of input and output variables of the manipulator controller is represented with three linguistic variables - S (small), M (middle) and B (big). The controller has five fuzzy rules, as it follows:

If $\omega = S$ then $Output = B;$
If $\omega = B$ then $Output = S;$
If $\omega = M$ and $F_h = S$ then $Output =$ S;
If $\omega = M$ and $F_h = M$ then $Output = M;$
If $\omega = M$ and $F_h = B$ then $Output = B.$

The controller *Output* is three-valued logic function specified in Table 3.

		F_h		
		–1	0	+1
ω	–1	+1	+1	+1
	0	–1	0	+1
	+1	–1	–1	–1

Table 3. The ternary function.

It can be simply proved by trivial substitution that $Output = maj(2\omega, -F_h, 0)$ and CMOS implementation coincides with the circuit shown in Fig. 8, if make substitutions $V_e = V_{F_h}$, $V_{ce} = V_\omega$ and change the weight of the input V_ω to 2.

2.4.3 Example 3. Fuzzy controller for washing machine

This example is taken from Aptronix Incorporated (http://www.aptronix.com/fuzzynet).

A. Controller specification

Input variables:
Dirtiness of clothes: Large (L), Medium (M), and Small (S);
Type of dirtiness: Greasy (G), Medium (M), and Not Greasy (NG).
Output variable is *washing time* (minutes): *Very Long* (*VL*), *Long* (L), *Medium* (M), *Short* (S), and *Very Short* (*VS*). *Fuzzy rules* are represented in Table 4.

Wash. time		*Dirtiness of clothes*		
		S	*M*	*L*
Type of dirt.	*NG*	*VS*	*S*	*M*
	M	*M*	*M*	*L*
	G	*L*	*L*	*VL*

Table 4. Matrix of linguistic variables.

According to our approach Table 4 can be transformed into the table of multi-valued logic variables (Table 5).

Wash. time		Dirtiness of clothes (Y)		
		–2	0	+2
Type of dirt. (X)	–2	–2	–1	0
	0	0	0	+1
	+2	+1	+1	+2

Table 5. Matrix of multi-valued variables.

In this table the output variable *Wash. time* has 5 logical levels but input variables *X* and *Y* have only three. Because of change ranges of the output and input variables should be the same in the Table 5 logical levels of input variables *X* and *Y* are –2, 0, and +2.

B. Functional decomposition

Let us represent the washing time matrix as a sum of two matrices:

$$\begin{array}{ccc} \text{Wash time} & \varphi_1 & \varphi_2 \\ \begin{vmatrix} -2 & -1 & 0 \\ 0 & 0 & +1 \\ +1 & +1 & +2 \end{vmatrix} = & \begin{vmatrix} -1 & -1 & 0 \\ 0 & 0 & +1 \\ +1 & +1 & +2 \end{vmatrix} + & \begin{vmatrix} -1 & 0 & 0 \\ 0 & 0 & 0 \\ 0 & 0 & 0 \end{vmatrix} \end{array} \tag{8}$$

or (*Wash. time*) = $S(-\varphi_1-\varphi_2)$ were *S* is the function of summing amplifier with saturation. Let us take into consideration a function of one variable

$$\varphi_3(Y) = S(0.5\cdot Y-2) = \begin{vmatrix}+2 & +2 & +1\end{vmatrix}. \tag{9}$$

In (9) *Y* corresponds to the *dirtiness of clothes* and varies from -2 to +2 as follows

$$Y = \begin{vmatrix}-2 & 0 & +2\end{vmatrix}.$$

Now the following intermediate sum is introduced:

$$\varphi_3(Y)-0.5\cdot X-2 = \begin{vmatrix} +1 & +1 & 0 \\ 0 & 0 & -1 \\ -1 & -1 & -2 \end{vmatrix} = -\varphi_1. \tag{10}$$

Here *X* corresponds to the *type of dirtiness* and varies also from -2 to 2 as follows

$$X = \begin{vmatrix} -2 \\ 0 \\ +2 \end{vmatrix}.$$

From (8) and (10) it is easy to see that (10) is $-\varphi_1$ and

$$(\textit{Wash. time}) = S(\varphi_3(Y)-0.5\cdot X-2-\varphi_2).$$

Now let us introduce the function:

$$\varphi_4(X,Y) = S(X+Y+4) = \begin{vmatrix} 0-2-2 \\ -2-2-2 \\ -2-2-2 \end{vmatrix} \tag{11}$$

and form the second intermediate sum:

$$0.5 \cdot \varphi_4(X,Y) + 1 = \begin{vmatrix} +1 & 0 & 0 \\ 0 & 0 & 0 \\ 0 & 0 & 0 \end{vmatrix} = -\varphi_2\,. \tag{12}$$

Finally

$$\begin{aligned} (\textit{Wash time}) &= S[\varphi_3(Y) - 0.5 \cdot X - 1 + 0.5\varphi_4(X,Y)] = \\ &S_4[S_1(0.5Y-2) + 0.5S_2(X+Y+4) + 0.5S_3(X) - 1]\,. \end{aligned} \tag{13}$$

In Fig. 9 the CMOS implementation of the expression (13) is presented. The circuit is implemented as the superposition of four multi-valued threshold elements.

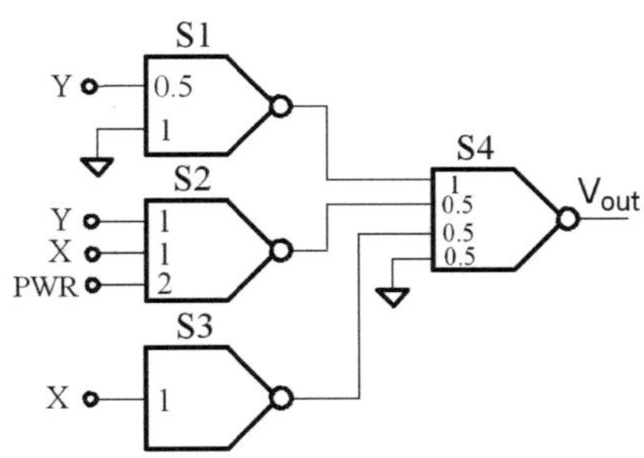

Fig. 9. CMOS implementation of fuzzy controller for washing machine.

The result of the SPICE simulation of the circuit in Fig. 9 is shown in Fig. 10 in the form of response surface.

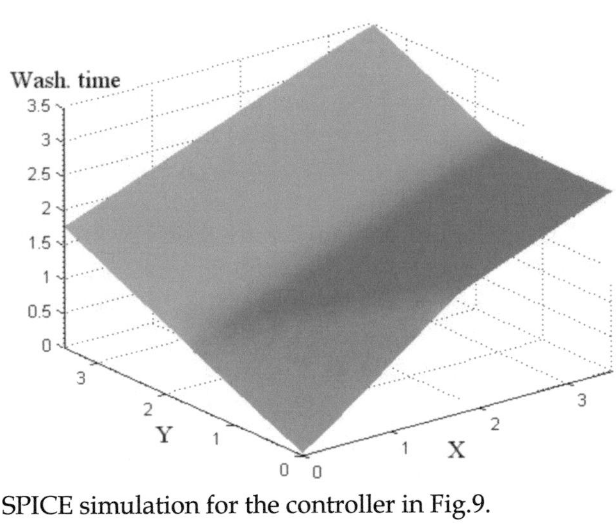

Fig. 10. Results of SPICE simulation for the controller in Fig.9.

In Fig. 10 all variables are represented in voltages. The correspondence of logical values to voltages is shown in Table 6. It is easy to see that the controller output signal represented by the surface in Fig. 10 has linear approximation between adjacent logical levels.

-2	-1	0	1	2
0V	0.875V	1.75V	2.625V	3.5V

Table 6. Correspondence voltages to logical levels.

3. Universal method of implementing fuzzy inference rules

It was shown in 2.2 and (Varshavsky et al., 2003) that a summing amplifier with saturation is a functionally complete element in any multi-valued logic (of an arbitrary value). Thus it may serve as a basis for hardware implementation of fuzzy devices.

The study subject is design techniques for analog CMOS circuits implementing fuzzy controller multi-valued functions.

Without departing from the general character of the study, let us suppose that the logic has odd value $m = 2k+1$. Let's also assume that $X = \{x_1, x_2, \dots, x_n\}$, $-k \le x_j \le +k$, , is a set of input multi-valued variables and $y = F(X)$ is the output variable. Then for a function of multi-valued logic it is possible to build an analog of the Shannon's decomposition in the binary logic:

$$y_i = F_i(X) = \bigcup_{\alpha=-k}^{+k} [\text{if } x_j = \alpha \text{ then } y = F(x_j = \alpha, X \setminus x_j)]. \qquad (14)$$

Equation (14) can be further expanded so that it would be possible to build an realizing circuit using the variables exclusion method. To this effect, we need a sub-circuit implementing the function:

$$\text{if } \; Z = A \quad \text{then } \; y = F(Z = A, X \setminus Z) \qquad (15)$$

where $Z \subset X$ and A is a value combination of the variable set Z.[1]

Having a basic element (sub-circuit realizing (15)), we can implement a fuzzy device directly according to the system of fuzzy rules. However, note that equations (14) and (15) represent multi-valued functions in a piecewise-constant manner. An example of a 7-valued function is given in Fig. 11(a).

Taking into account fuzzification and defuzzification procedures in fuzzy logic, corresponding multi-valued logic function should has at least piecewise-linear approximation between adjacent logical levels. Fig. 11(b) gives an example of such a representation of the function with evenly distributed logical values of the input and the output in the range of corresponding voltages.

[1] It is possible to add **else** in (15) that can be defined by circuit requirements.

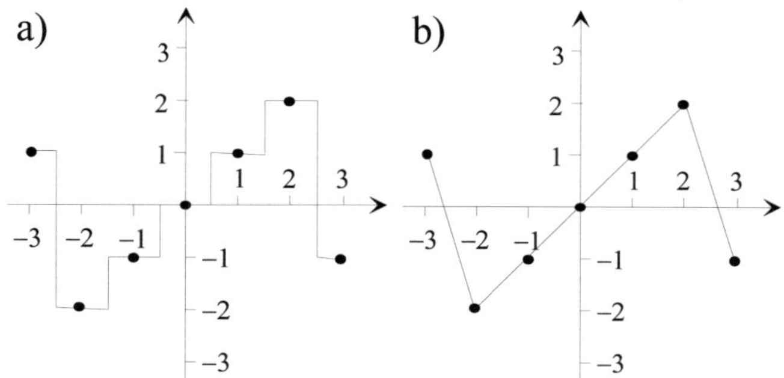

Fig. 11. Example of a seven-valued function: a) piecewise-constant representation; b) piecewise-linear representation.

3.1 Masking inputs of summing amplifiers

Let us rewrite the definition (2) of the inverting summing amplifier with saturation in the following form:

$$S(A\cdot X;\beta)=\begin{cases}+k & \text{if } \sum_{i=1}^{n}\alpha_i\cdot x_i+\beta\le -k\\ -\sum_{i=1}^{n}\alpha_i\cdot x_i-\beta & \text{if } +k>\sum_{i=1}^{n}\alpha_i\cdot x_i+\beta>-k\\ -k & \text{if } +k\le\sum_{i=1}^{n}\alpha_i\cdot x_i+\beta\end{cases} \tag{16}$$

where $A = \{\alpha_1,\alpha_2,...,\alpha_n\}$ is a set of weight coefficients, $X = \{x_1,x_2,...,x_n\}$ is a set of analog or multi-valued variables, β is a constant symbolizing a threshold, and $\pm k$ is a saturation value (in the case of m-valued logic, $m = 2k+1$).

Let us introduce a masking function $M_\alpha(x)$ by the next way:

$$M_\alpha(x)=\begin{cases}+k & \text{if } x\le\alpha-1\\ k(\alpha-x) & \text{if } \alpha-1<x<\alpha+1\\ -k & \text{if } \alpha+1\le x\end{cases} \tag{17}$$

where α ($-k \le \alpha \le +k$) is a fixed value of the variable x. It can be easily seen that when $x = \alpha$, $M_\alpha(x) = 0$. Fig. 12 illustrates an example of the function $M_{-1}(x)$ for $m = 7$.

Taking into account that the source voltage V_{dd} has the logical value equal to $+k$ and the ground potential V_{gnd} has the logical value equal to $-k$, the mask-function can be easily implemented on bases of summing amplifier as

$$M_\alpha(x)=\begin{cases}S(kx-\alpha\cdot V_{dd}) & \text{if } \alpha<0\\ S(kx) & \text{if } \alpha=0\\ S(kx+\alpha\cdot V_{gnd}) & \text{if } \alpha>0\end{cases} \tag{18}$$

where x ($V_{gnd} \le x \le V_{dd}$) is measured in voltages.

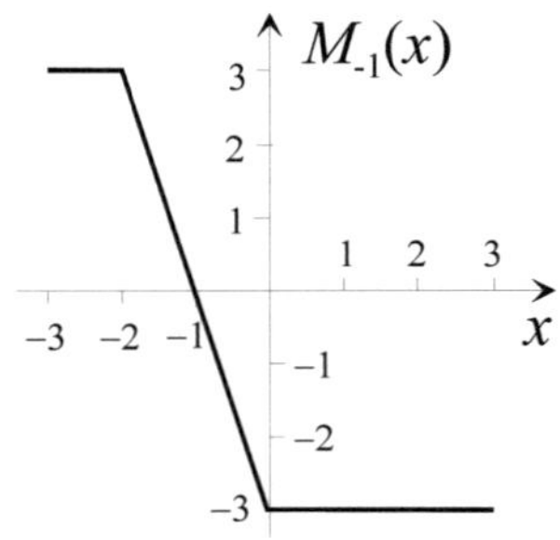

Fig. 12. $M_{-1}(x)$ diagram for $m = 7$.

Using the mask-function $M_\alpha(x)$ it is possible to implement the rule

$$\text{if } x = \alpha \text{ then } y = F(x = \alpha, Y) \text{ else } y = 0, \tag{19}$$

which extracts the value of the function $F(x = \alpha, Y)$ in the point $x = \alpha$, using the circuit from summing amplifiers shown in Fig. 13.

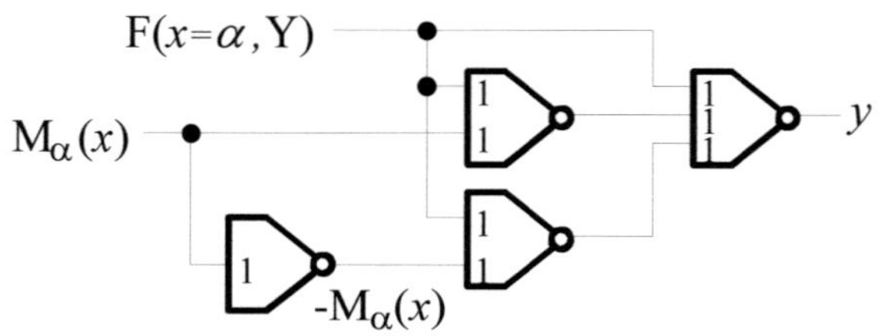

Fig. 13. Implementation of the rule (19).

This implementation can be written in analytical form as

$$y = S\{S[M_\alpha(x) + F(x = \alpha, Y)] + S[S(M_\alpha(x)) + F(x = \alpha, Y)] + F(x = \alpha, Y)\}. \tag{20}$$

For example, in the case when $\alpha = -1$, $F(x = -1, Y) = 2$, and $m = 7$, the behavior of the circuit in Fig.13 can be represented by Fig.14.

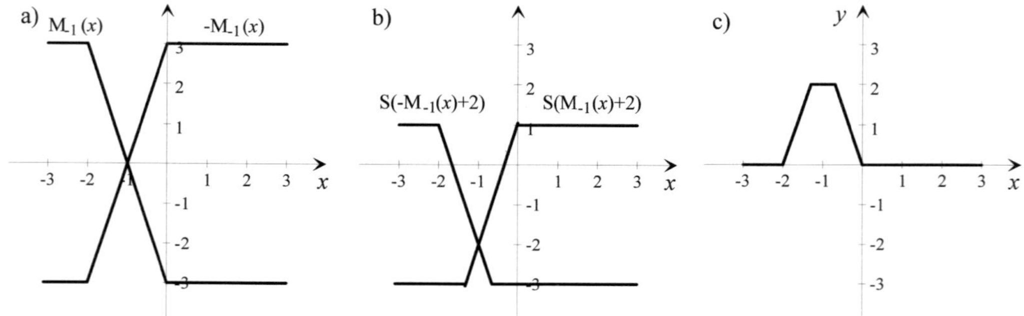

Fig. 14. Implementation example of the rule (19).

Analyzing the implementation of the rule (19) it is possible to see that in it the condition $x = \alpha$ is realized as the condition $M_\alpha(x) = 0$.

3.2 Mask-functions of other types

To decrease the number of variables, which an m-valued logical function depends on, by one using the analog of Shannon's decomposition (14) we need to implement m rules of the type (19) and to find m components $F(x = \alpha, Y)$, $-k \le \alpha \le +k$, of the decomposition. Sometimes the number of rules can be reduced, if the function $F(x,Y)$ doesn't change on some interval of changing logical values of the variable x. A single rule can correspond to such interval of the variable x and the conditional part of this rule can have one of three forms: $\alpha \le x \le \beta$, $x \le \beta$, $\alpha \le x$ where $-k \le \alpha < \beta \le +k$. For the condition $\alpha \le x \le \beta$ let us construct the following mask-function:

$$M_{\alpha,\beta}(x) = \begin{cases} +k, & \text{if } \ x \ge \beta + 1 \\ -M_{\alpha-1}(x) - M_{\beta+1}(x), & \text{if } \ \alpha - 1 < x < \beta + 1 \\ -k, & \text{if } \ x \le \alpha - 1 \end{cases} \tag{21}$$

It is easy to see (Fig. 15(b)) that on the interval $\alpha \le x \le \beta$ this function takes the value 0.
In the case when $\alpha = -k$ or $\beta = k$, this mask-function will have one of the forms:

$$M_{-k,\beta}(x) = \begin{cases} +k, & \text{if } \ x \ge \beta + 1 \\ +k - M_{\beta+1}(x), & \text{if } \ x < \beta + 1 \end{cases} \quad \text{or} \tag{22}$$

$$M_{\alpha,+k}(x) = \begin{cases} -\mathrm{M}_{\alpha\text{-}1}(x) - k, & \text{if } \ \alpha - 1 < x \\ -k, & \text{if } \ x \le \alpha - 1 \end{cases} \tag{23}$$

and represents conditions $x \le \beta$ or $\alpha \le x$ respectively.
Mask-functions (21), (22), and (23) can be implemented on bases of summing amplifiers as

$$M_{\alpha,\beta}(x) = S[M_{\alpha-1}(x) + M_{\beta+1}(x)]\,, \tag{24}$$

$$M_{-k,\beta}(x) = S[V_{gnd} + M_{\beta+1}(x)]\,, \tag{25}$$

$$M_{\alpha,k}(x) = S[M_{\alpha-1}(x) + V_{dd}]\,. \tag{26}$$

Let us look how the masking can be performed for a wider scope of the variable changes, such as:

$$\text{if } \alpha \le x \le \beta \text{ then } y = F(\alpha \le x \le \beta, Y) = \Phi(Y) \text{ else } y = 0. \tag{27}$$

Using the mask-function $M_{\alpha,\beta}(x)$ it is possible to transform the rule (27) into the following form:

$$\text{if } M_{\alpha,\beta}(x) = 0 \text{ then } y = F(\alpha \le x \le \beta, Y) = \ \Phi(Y) \ \text{ else } \ y = 0. \tag{28}$$

The rule (28) can be implemented with the circuit shown in Fig. 13, if to change in it the inputs $M_\alpha(x)$ and $F(x = \alpha, Y)$ with the inputs $M_{\alpha,\beta}(x)$ and $\Phi(Y)$ respectively. This implementation is represented analytically as

$$y = S\{S[M_{\lambda,\delta}(x) + \Phi(Y)] + S[S(M_{\lambda,\delta}(x)) + \Phi(Y)] + \Phi(Y)\}. \tag{29}$$

The sequence of pictures in Fig. 15 illustrates the implementation of the rule

$$\text{if } -2 \le x \le +1 \text{ then } y = -2 \text{ else } y = 0$$

for the case of ($m = 9$)-valued logic.

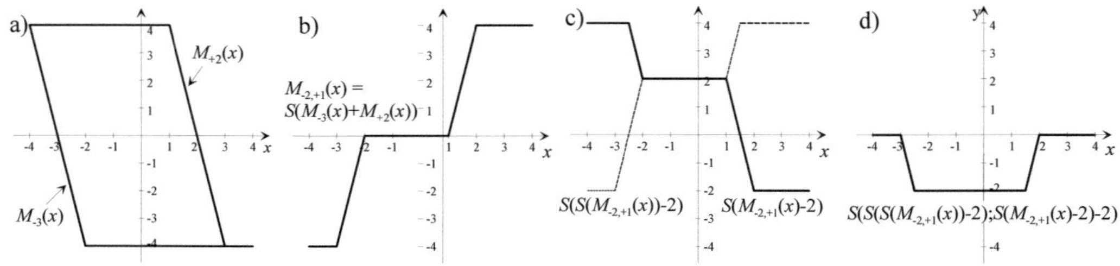

Fig. 15. Example of mask-functions application.

3.3 An application example of interval masking

For further explanation of the matter discussed in 3.2, let us recall an example from (Marks II, 1994, pp. 123 – 128) "*A Fuzzy Logic Force Controller for a Stepper Motor Robot*".

The fuzzy controller implements the function of two analog variables: *position error* and *force error*, which will be designate as x and y respectively. Each of the variables x and y is represented with 7 linguistic variables: NL, NM, NS, ZE, PS, PM, PL, and their membership functions are shown in Fig. 16.

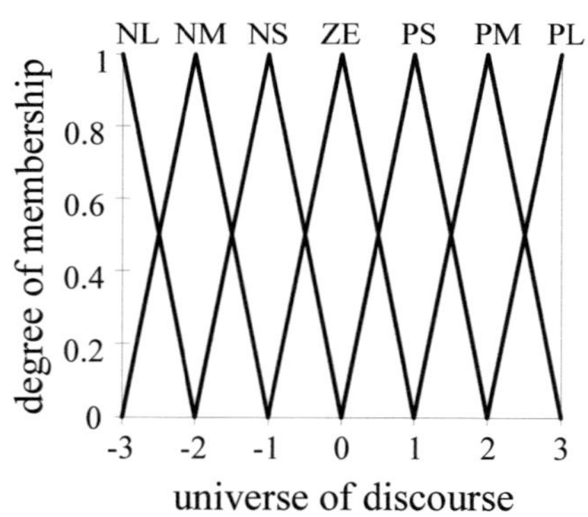

Fig. 16. Fuzzy sets for *force error* and *position error* inputs.

The Inference Engine Rule Matrix for the output linguistic variable from the cited work looks as it is shown in Table 7.

Let us transform the Table 7 into the Table 8 taking into account that we are going to produce fuzzy inference calculating values of the corresponding multi-valued logic function.

Table 8 comprises only two different columns defining two functions depending on the variable *force error* (Table 9).

Fig. 17 illustrates graphs of these functions. It is easy to see that the function $F_1(y)$ looks like mask-function $M_{-1,1}(y)$ but has different slops of the lines. By analogy with (17), (18), (21), (24), Fig. 15(a), and Fig. 15(b), it is possible to construct the function $F_1(y)$ in accordance with graphics in Fig. 18.

		position error (x)						
		NL	NM	NS	ZE	PS	PM	PL
force error (y)	NL	NM	NL	NL	NL	NL	NL	NM
	NM	NS	NM	NM	NM	NM	NM	NS
	NS	ZE	NS	NS	NS	NS	NS	ZE
	ZE	ZE	ZE	ZE	ZE	ZE	ZE	ZE
	PS	ZE	PS	PS	PS	PS	PS	ZE
	PM	PS	PM	PM	PM	PM	PM	PS
	PL	PM	PL	PL	PL	PL	PL	PM

Table 7. Rule matrix of the inference engine.

		position error (x)						
		-3	-2	-1	0	1	2	3
force error (y)	-3	-2	-3	-3	-3	-3	-3	-2
	-2	-1	-2	-2	-2	-2	-2	-1
	-1	0	-1	-1	-1	-1	-1	0
	0	0	0	0	0	0	0	0
	1	0	1	1	1	1	1	0
	2	1	2	2	2	2	2	1
	3	2	3	3	3	3	3	2

Table 8. Matrix of the multi-valued logic function.

	force error (y)						
	-3	-2	-1	0	1	2	3
$F_1(y)$	-2	-1	0	0	0	1	2
$F_2(y)$	-3	-2	-1	0	1	2	3

Table 9. Two different functions of the *force error.*

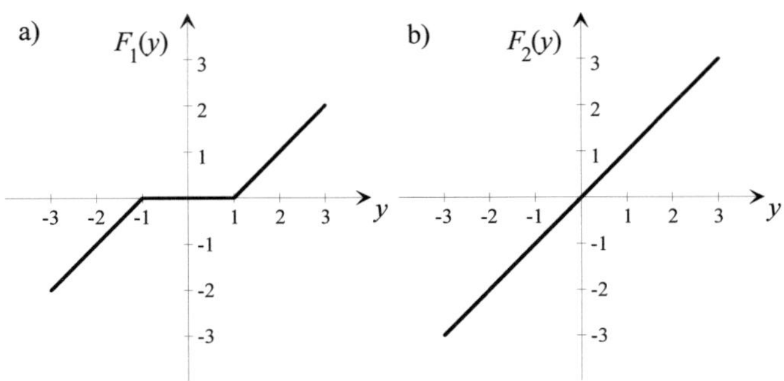

Fig. 17. Components of the function defined by Table 8 and decomposed relative to variable x.

As a result, the functions $F_1(y)$ and $F_2(y)$ can be implemented as

$$F_1(y) = S_3[\tfrac{2}{3}S_2(\tfrac{3}{2}y + \tfrac{3}{2}V_{gnd}) + \tfrac{2}{3}S_1(\tfrac{3}{2}y + \tfrac{3}{2}V_{dd})],\ \ F_2(y) = y. \quad (30)$$

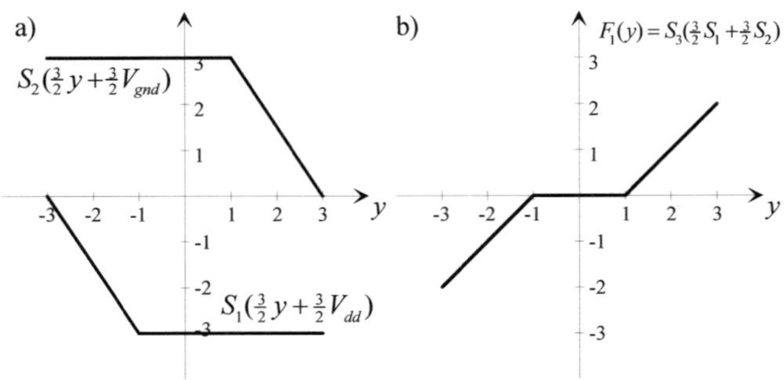

Fig. 18. Constructing of the function $F_1(y)$.

It is seen from the Table 7 and Table 8 that the behaviour of the controller's output in the decomposition by variable x has the form:

$$\text{if } NM \le x \le PM \text{ then } Output = F_2(y) \text{ else } Output = F_1(y); \text{ or}$$

$$\text{if } -2 \le x \le +2 \text{ then } Output = F_2(y) \text{ else } Output = F_1(y). \quad (31)$$

It is possible to split the rule (31) into two rules and represent them as:

$$\text{if } M_{-2,+2}(x) = 0 \text{ then } Output = F_2(y) \text{ else } Output = 0; \quad (32)$$

$$\text{if } M_{-2,+2}(x) \ne 0 \text{ then } Output = 0 \text{ else } Output = F_1(y). \quad (33)$$

The rule (32) can be implemented in accordance with (29) and (30) and (24) as

$$\begin{cases} M_{-2,+2}(x) = S_4(M_{-3}(x) + M_{+3}(x)), \\ -M_{-2,+2}(x) = S_5(M_{-2,+2}(x)), \\ \Phi_1 = S_{11}\{S_6[M_{-2,+2}(x) + F_2(y)] + S_7[-M_{-2,+2}(x) + F_2(y)] + F_2(y)\}. \end{cases}$$

It is easy to check that the rule (33) can be implemented in accordance with the structural scheme shown in Fig. 13, in which the output amplifier has the weight equal to 2 of the input $F_1(y)$:

$$\Phi_2 = -S_{10}\{S_9[M_{-2,+2}(x) + F_1(y)] + S_8[-M_{-2,+2}(x) + F_1(y)] + 2F_1(y)\}.$$

Finally the output of the controller can be calculated as

$$Output = \Phi_1 + \Phi_2 .$$

For producing this summation it is possible to use summing amplifier S_{11}

$$Output = S_{11}(-\Phi_1; -\Phi_2).$$

Fig. 19 illustrates the structural scheme of the controller implementation with elements containing designations of input weights.

The controller circuit has been constructed from three-stage push-pull CMOS operational amplifiers with 1-MegOhm resistors in the feedback (Fig. 2(b)). It's functioning has been checked with SPICE simulation (MSIM 8). MOSIS BSIM3v3.1, level 7 model of 0.4μm transistors has been used. In this paper, all other SPICE simulation experiments with designed circuits of controllers have been executed under the same conditions.

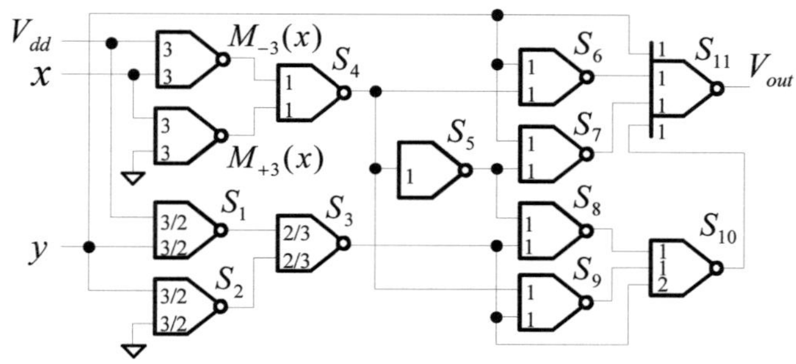

Fig. 19. Structural diagram of the controller.

In the experiments with the controller presented in Fig. 19, source voltage was 3.5V, input variable x changed linearly from 0V to 3.5V, input variable y changed discreetly in accordance with its logical values and kept constant value within one cycle of x changing. For the controller constructed from 3-stage elements results of SPICE simulation are shown in Fig. 20. It is possible to see that the functioning of the controller is correct (logical values of the circuit output depend on the logical values of the input variables in accordance with Table 7 and 8).

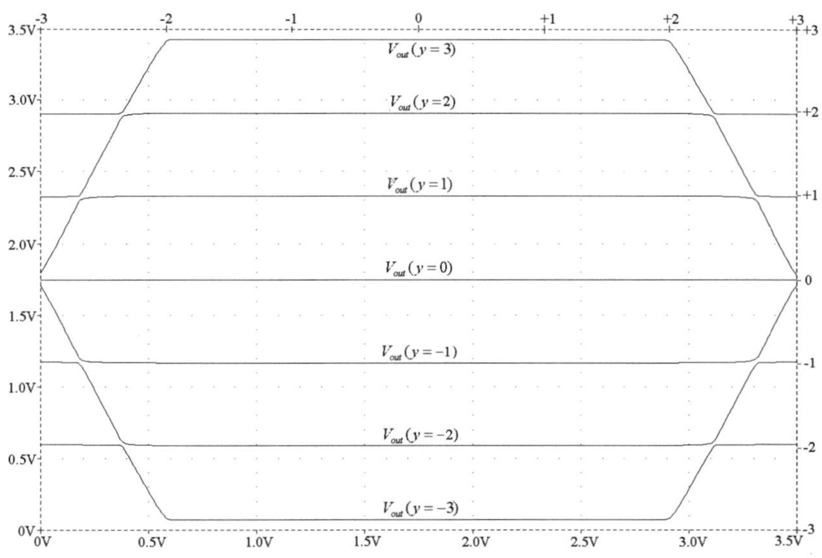

Fig. 20. SPICE simulation results for the controller constructed from 3-stage summing amplifiers.

4. Particular methods of fuzzy inference implementation

The universal method of implementing multi-valued logic functions proposed in the previous section can be always used but often can give inappropriate results due to its

universality. For this reason some particular design methods for fuzzy inference part of controllers were developed. These methods utilize specific properties of certain multi-valued logical function descriptions corresponding to sets of fuzzy inference rules.
According to the approach described above, an initial set of fuzzy rules is represented in the form of a matrix or matrices defining multi-valued logical functions. As a rule these matrices cannot be directly implemented. They must be decomposed into component matrices with relatively simple configuration of elements allocation, for which rather simple implementations can be find. The topologies of valuable elements inside of such component matrices can be specified as symmetrical, diagonal, matrixes with linear configurations of elements, with elements located along rows and columns, matrices containing single valuable element, and others.
The best way to introduce particular design methods is to show possible matrix decomposition into a set of implementable matrices on bases of a real design example.
Let us take the description of the rather complex fuzzy controller from the patent (Kimura & Kawawa, 1993) of Toyota Motors Corporation. The controller calculates a regeneration time decision coefficient R on the base on a differential pressure coefficient K_p and total fuel consumption Q_f. The set of fuzzy rules in terms of linguistic variables is represented in Table 10. Transformations of the input and output analog signals are performed in accordance with corresponding membership functions.

		K_p						
		NB	NM	NS	ZO	PS	PM	PB
Q_f	NB	NB	NB	NM	NS	ZO	PB	PB
	NM	NB	NM	NS	NS	ZO	PB	PB
	NS	NM	NM	NS	ZO	ZO	PS	PB
	ZO	NM	NS	ZO	ZO	PS	PM	PB
	PS	NS	ZO	ZO	PS	PS	PM	PB
	PM	ZO	ZO	PS	PM	PM	PM	PB
	PB	PS	PS	PM	PM	PM	PB	PB

Table 10. Fuzzy rules for regeneration time decision coefficient R.

Analysis of the membership functions in (Kimura & Kawawa, 1993) of linguistic variables representing input and output analog signals shows that the linguistic variables having maximum weight are evenly distributed within the change ranges of corresponding analog signals. It means that without losing the accuracy of representation, these linguistic variables can be replaced with logical values as it is shown in Table 11.

x\y	-3	-2	-1	0	1	2	3
-3	-3	-3	-1	-1	0	3	3
-2	-3	-2	-1	-1	0	3	3
-1	-2	-2	-1	0	0	1	3
0	-2	-1	0	0	1	2	3
1	-1	0	0	1	1	2	3
2	0	0	1	2	2	2	3
3	1	1	2	2	2	3	3

Table 11. The 7-valued logical function

In this table, signals Q_f and K_p are changed with 7-valued logic variables x and y respectively.

4.1 Extracting a symmetrical component matrix

Let the Table 11 of the controller is represented as initial matrix M, which, in its turn, can be represented as sum of two component matrixes (M_1 and M_2).

$$\overset{M}{\begin{vmatrix} -3 & -3 & -2 & -1 & \pm 0 & +3 & +3 \\ -3 & -2 & -1 & -1 & \pm 0 & +3 & +3 \\ -2 & -2 & -1 & \pm 0 & \pm 0 & +1 & +3 \\ -2 & -1 & \pm 0 & \pm 0 & +1 & +2 & +3 \\ -1 & \pm 0 & \pm 0 & +1 & +1 & +2 & +3 \\ \pm 0 & \pm 0 & +1 & +2 & +2 & +2 & +3 \\ +1 & +1 & +2 & +2 & +2 & +3 & +3 \end{vmatrix}} = \overset{M_1}{\begin{vmatrix} -3 & -3 & -2 & -2 & -1 & \pm 0 & \pm 0 \\ -3 & -2 & -2 & -1 & \pm 0 & \pm 0 & +1 \\ -2 & -2 & -1 & \pm 0 & \pm 0 & +1 & +1 \\ -2 & -1 & \pm 0 & \pm 0 & +1 & +1 & +2 \\ -1 & \pm 0 & \pm 0 & +1 & +1 & +2 & +2 \\ \pm 0 & \pm 0 & +1 & +1 & +2 & +2 & +3 \\ \pm 0 & +1 & +1 & +2 & +2 & +3 & +3 \end{vmatrix}} + \overset{M_2}{\begin{vmatrix} \le 0 & \le 0 & \pm 0 & +1 & +1 & +3 & +3 \\ \le 0 & \pm 0 & +1 & \pm 0 & \pm 0 & +3 & \ge 2 \\ \pm 0 & \pm 0 & \pm 0 & \pm 0 & \pm 0 & \pm 0 & \ge 2 \\ \pm 0 & \pm 0 & \pm 0 & \pm 0 & \pm 0 & +1 & \ge 1 \\ \pm 0 & \pm 0 & \pm 0 & \pm 0 & \pm 0 & \pm 0 & \ge 1 \\ \pm 0 & \pm 0 & \pm 0 & +1 & \pm 0 & \pm 0 & \ge 0 \\ +1 & \pm 0 & +1 & \pm 0 & \pm 0 & \ge 0 & \ge 0 \end{vmatrix}}$$

Matrix M_1 corresponds to a symmetrical component and M_2 corresponds to nonsymmetrical residual component.

Matrix M_1 is symmetrical relative to the side diagonal. Its components can be represented as a function $f_1(z)$ of one variable $z = (x+y)/2$. After performing the linear approximation between adjacent logical levels this function will has the form shown in Fig. 21.

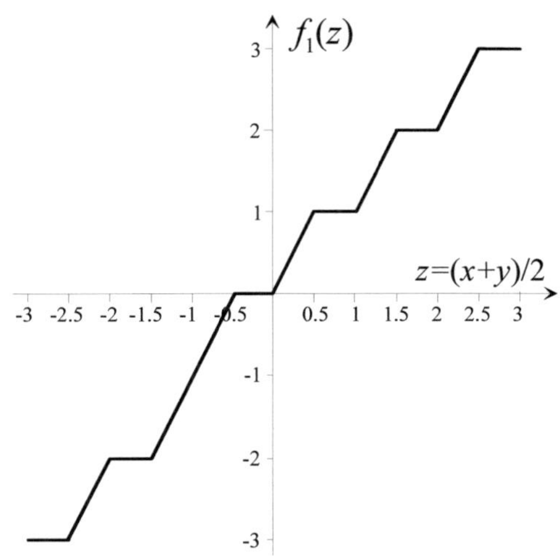

Fig. 21. Graph of the function $f_1(z)$.

To implement the function $f_1(z)$ let us represent it as a sum of 5 subfunctions $\alpha_j(z)$ shown in Fig. 22(a). It is easy to see, that

$$f_1(z) = \sum_{j=1}^{5} \alpha_j(z) \,. \tag{34}$$

Let us consider formation of $\alpha_j(z)$ using summing amplifiers on the example of $\alpha_1(z)$. For this let us address to Fig. 22(b).

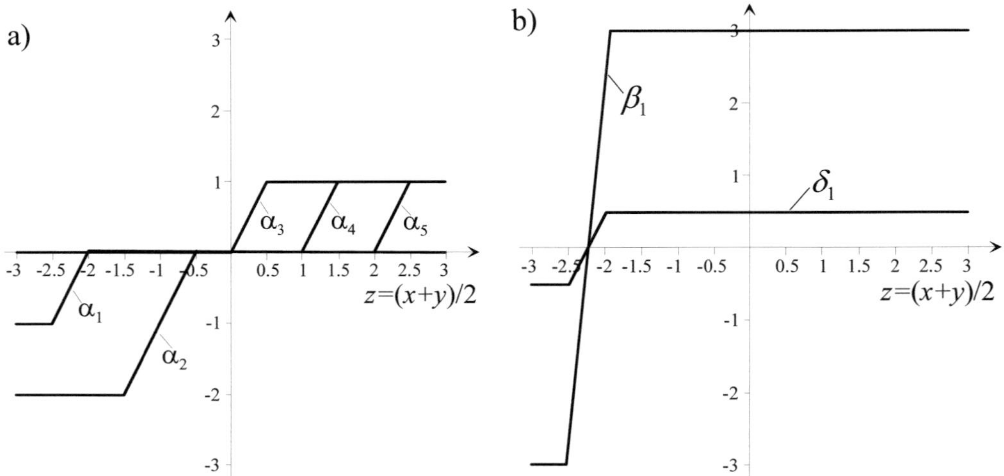

Fig. 22. a) Five components of the function $f_1(z)$; b) Representation of the function $\alpha_1(z)$.

The function $\beta_1(z)$ in Fig. 22(b) can be implemented as $\beta_1(z) = -S(k_1 \cdot z + a_1)$. For $z = -2.25$, $\beta_1 = 0$ then $a_1 = 2.25k_1$. Taken into account that $k_1 = 6/0.5 = 12$, we receive $a_1 = 27$ and

$$\beta_1(x,y) = -S(6x+6y+27)\,,\ \delta_1(x,y) = \tfrac{1}{6}\beta_1(x,y)\,.$$

Finally

$$\alpha_1(x,y) = \delta_1(x,y) - 0.5 = \tfrac{1}{6}\cdot\beta_1(x,y) - 0.5\,. \tag{35}$$

In the same way it is possible to find

$$\begin{aligned}
\alpha_2(x,y) &= \tfrac{1}{3}\beta_2(x,y) - 1 = \ -\tfrac{1}{3}S(3x+3y+6) - 1;\\
\alpha_3(x,y) &= \tfrac{1}{6}\beta_3(x,y) + 0.5 = -\tfrac{1}{6}S(6x+6y-3) + 0.5;\\
\alpha_4(x,y) &= \tfrac{1}{6}\beta_4(x,y) + 0.5 = \ -\tfrac{1}{6}S(6x+6y-15) + 0.5;\\
\alpha_5(x,y) &= \tfrac{1}{6}\beta_5(x,y) + 0.5 = \ -\tfrac{1}{6}S(6x+\cdot y-27) + 0.5.
\end{aligned} \tag{36}$$

The function $f_1(z)$ can be calculated in accordance with (34) on one summing amplifier. Finally taking into account mutual compensation of constants, we have

$$f_1(x,y) = S\{-\tfrac{1}{6}\cdot[\beta_1(x,y) + 2\cdot\beta_2(x,y) + \beta_3(x,y) + \beta_4(x,y) + \beta_5(x,y)]\}. \tag{37}$$

Thus, the implementation of the function $f_1(x, y)$, which represents the matrix M_1, consists of six summing amplifiers.

4.2 Extracting a matrix with elements separated by a line

This method is applicable for realization of matrices composed from two types of elements, which can be separated with a line. After extracting the symmetrical component the residual matrix is M_2.

$$
\begin{array}{ccccc}
M_2 & & M_3 & & M_4 \\
\left|\begin{matrix}
\le 0 & \le 0 & 0 & +1 & +1 & +3 & +3 \\
\le 0 & 0 & +1 & 0 & 0 & +3 & \ge 2 \\
0 & 0 & 0 & 0 & 0 & 0 & \ge 2 \\
0 & 0 & 0 & 0 & 0 & +1 & \ge 1 \\
0 & 0 & 0 & 0 & 0 & 0 & \ge 1 \\
0 & 0 & 0 & +1 & 0 & 0 & \ge 0 \\
+1 & 0 & +1 & 0 & 0 & \ge 0 & \ge 0
\end{matrix}\right|
& = &
\left|\begin{matrix}
0 & 0 & 0 & 0 & 0 & +3 & +3 \\
0 & 0 & 0 & 0 & 0 & +3 & +3 \\
0 & 0 & 0 & 0 & 0 & 0 & +3 \\
0 & 0 & 0 & 0 & 0 & 0 & +3 \\
0 & 0 & 0 & 0 & 0 & 0 & +3 \\
0 & 0 & 0 & 0 & 0 & 0 & 0 \\
0 & 0 & 0 & 0 & 0 & 0 & 0
\end{matrix}\right|
& + &
\left|\begin{matrix}
\le 0 & \le 0 & 0 & +1 & +1 & \ge 0 & \ge 0 \\
\le 0 & 0 & +1 & 0 & 0 & \ge 0 & \ge 0 \\
0 & 0 & 0 & 0 & 0 & 0 & \ge 0 \\
0 & 0 & 0 & 0 & 0 & +1 & \ge 0 \\
0 & 0 & 0 & 0 & 0 & 0 & \ge 0 \\
0 & 0 & 0 & +1 & 0 & 0 & \ge 0 \\
+1 & 0 & +1 & 0 & 0 & \ge 0 & \ge 0
\end{matrix}\right|
\end{array}
$$

This matrix has some elements of types $\le a$ and $\ge b$. This means that instead of values a and b of the elements it is possible to substitute any logical value less than a and more than b respectively. Let us split the matrix M_2 in two matrices (M_3 and M_4) and try to implement the matrix M_3. The matrix M_4 is a new residual matrix.

Let us address to Fig. 23. It is easy to see that the matrix M_3 consists of elements with two different values, which can be separated with help of two parallel lines: $x - 3y + 8 = 0$ and $x - 3y + 8 = 1$. A new variable is introduced

$$w = x - 3y + 8\,. \tag{38}$$

Value of the variable w in the point with coordinates (x, y) is proportional to the distance of this point from the line. In all points lying on and up of the line, $w \le 0$, and in all points lying on and down of the dashed line $(x - 3y + 7 = 0)$, $w \ge 1$.

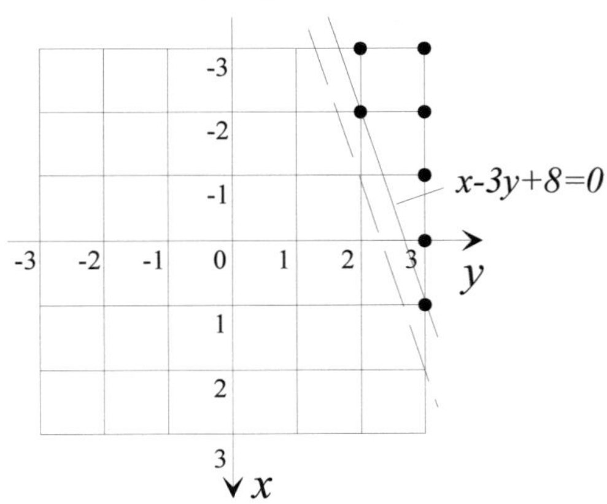

Fig. 23. Separating valuable elements of the matrix M_3.

It is easy to see, that the matrix M_3 representing the function $f_2(x, y)$ can be implemented as

$$f_2(x,y) = S\{S[3(-x+3y-8)]-3\}\,. \tag{39}$$

In this implementation all valuable matrix elements are equal to "3".

4.3 Extracting a matrix with rectangular configuration of valuable elements

Let us introduce a *Pyramid Function* that is the function, which corresponds to a matrix with a single valuable element and represents a rule of the type

$$\text{if } (x=a)\,\&\,(y=b) \text{ then } f(x,y)=c \text{ else } f(x,y)=0. \tag{40}$$

This function is shown in Fig. 24.

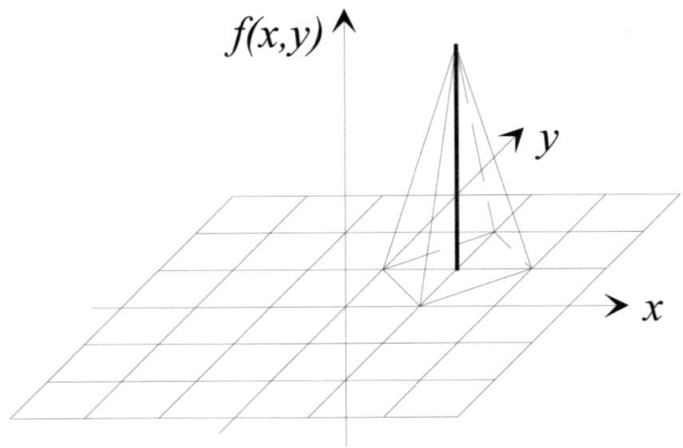

Fig. 24. A pyramid function.

The *Pyramid Function* has some fixed value c ($-k \le c \ne 0 \le +k$) at the point (a, b) and at the rest of the space bordered by points neighboring to (a, b) this function is zero. The transition from c to zero is linear. Neighborhood is defined by coordinate increments $\Delta_x = \pm 1$ and $\Delta_y = \pm 1$.
Let's turn to Fig. 25 to construct the pyramid function.

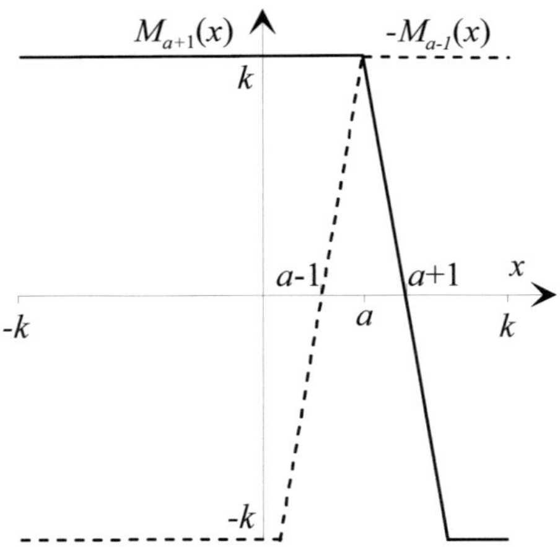

Fig. 25. Component functions of the pyramid projection onto the flat $y = b$; $c = k$.

The figure shows two component mask-functions $M_{a+1}(x)$ and $-M_{a-1}(x)$ those are implemented for $(2k+1)$-valued logic ($-k \le x \le +k$) as:

$$\begin{aligned} M_{a+1}(x) &= S[k\cdot(x-a-1)], \\ -M_{a-1}(x) &= S[k\cdot(-x+a-1)]. \end{aligned} \tag{41}$$

Similarly component functions of the pyramid projection onto the flat $x = a$ for the case $c = k$ can be constructed as:

$$\begin{aligned} M_{b+1}(y) &= S[k \cdot (y-b-1)], \\ -M_{b-1}(y) &= S[k \cdot (-y+b-1)]. \end{aligned} \tag{42}$$

It is easy to check that the function

$$\gamma(x) = S[M_{a+1}(x) - M_{a-1}(x) - 2k] \tag{43}$$

has the form shown in Fig. 26; $\gamma(x)$ equals to "0" when $x = a$ and equals to "+k" for all other integer argument values.

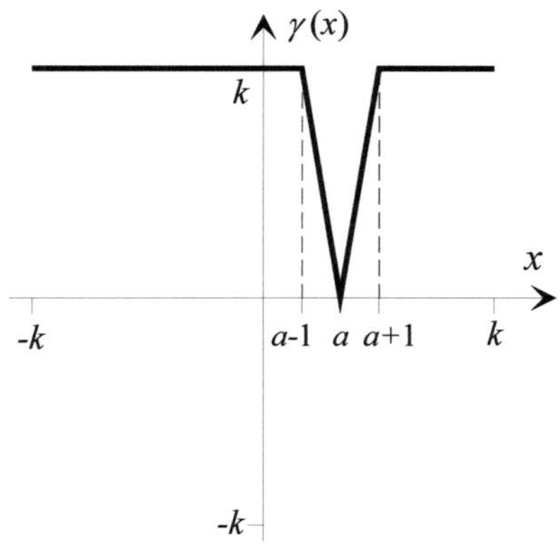

Fig. 26. Graph of the function $\gamma(x)$.

In a similar manner, we can construct the following function of 2 variables:

$$\gamma(x,y) = S[M_{a+1}(x) - M_{a-1}(x) + M_{b+1}(y) - M_{b-1}(y) - 4k]. \tag{44}$$

The function $\gamma(x, y)$ equals to "0" when $(x = a)\&(y = b)$ and equals to "+k " for all other matrix points.

Now it is easy to construct the pyramid function with height "c" presented in Fig. 25:

$$f(x,y) = \frac{c}{k} S[\gamma(x,y) - k]. \tag{45}$$

A pyramid of an arbitrary height is obtained by simple input gain factor scaling of the next amplifier. The pyramid sign can be elementarily changed at the stage of component mask-function constructions.

We anticipate some complications in the case when it is needed to receive good "sewing" pyramids with already implemented functions. The pyramid function $f(x, y)$ (45) of Fig. 24 type has intersections with the flats $y = \{b, b \pm 5, b \pm 1\}$ and with the flats $x = \{a, a \pm 0.5, a \pm 1\}$ shown in Fig. 27.

When "sewing" a pyramid function with other functions to get monotonous piece-linear approximation between adjacent logical values the view of the pyramid function by each of its coordinate can be changed to one of variants shown in Fig. 29.

To construct a pyramid function with graphs by coordinates x and y of the Fig. 28(a) type (center trapeze), it is sufficient to substitute in the functions (41) - (45) instead of original variables x, y new variables $z = x + y$, $w = x - y$ and instead of points a, b points $c = a + b$, $d = a - b$ respectively.

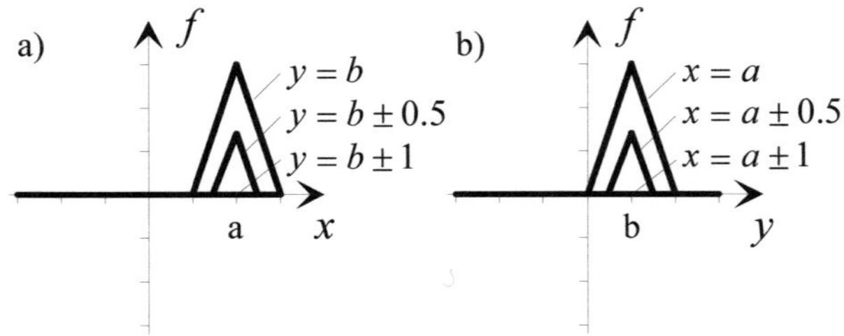

Fig. 27. Graph of the pyramid function a) by coordinate x and b) by coordinate y.

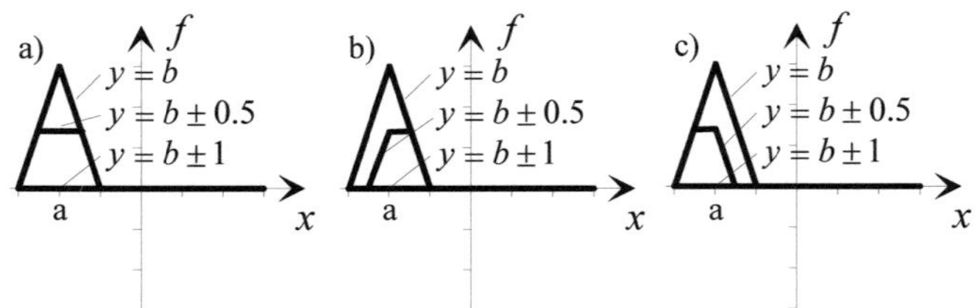

Fig. 28. Possible graphs of a pyramid function by one of coordinates: a) center trapeze, b) right trapeze, c) left trapeze.

It means the transition to the pyramid function shown in Fig. 29, which is implemented by analogy with (41) - (45) as

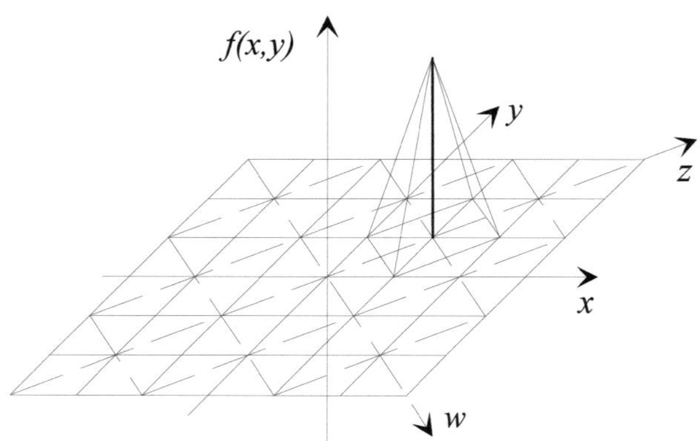

Fig. 29. A pyramid in coordinates $z = x + y$ and $w = x - y$.

$$\begin{aligned} f(x,y) = S\{S[S(k(x+y-a-b-1)) + S(k(-x-y+a+b-1)) + \\ S(k(x-y-a+b-1)) + S(k(-x+y+a-b-1)) - 4k] - k\}. \end{aligned} \tag{46}$$

For implementing a function that has graphs along one of its variables (e.g. x) of the right trapeze type (Fig. 28(b)), let us introduce two intermediate functions $\phi\,[x,\xi(y)]$ and $\psi\,[x,\xi(y)]$ shown in Fig.30.
It is easy to check that these intermediate functions can be implemented as

$$\begin{aligned} \varphi[x,\xi(y)] = S[M_{a-1}(x) + 2k - \xi(y)], \\ \psi[x,\xi(y)] = S[-M_a(x) - 2k - \xi(y)]. \end{aligned} \tag{47}$$

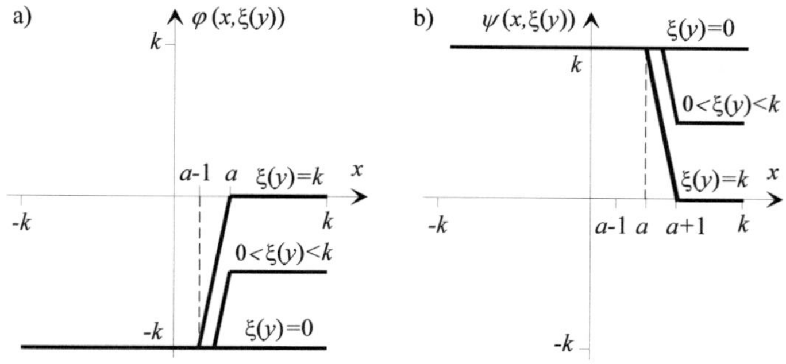

Fig. 30. Intermediate functions a) $\varphi\ [x,\xi(y)]$, b) $\psi\ [x,\xi(y)]$.

The function $f(x,y)=\varphi[x,\xi(y)]+\psi[x,\xi(y)]$ has the right-hand trapeze form along the axis x (Fig. 28(b)). If the function $\xi(y)$ has a triangle form, $\xi(b)=\pm k$, and $\xi(y<b-1)=\xi(y>b+1)=0$, the function $f(x, y)$ is a pyramid function.
For implementing a function that has graphs along the axis x of the left trapeze type (Fig. 28(c)), two intermediate functions $\varphi[x,\xi(y)]$ and $\psi\ [x,\xi(y)]$ shown in Fig. 31 are introduced.

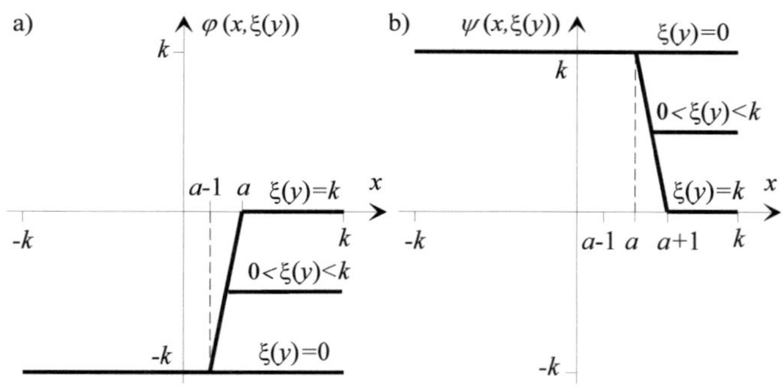

Fig. 31. Intermediate functions a) $\varphi[x,\xi(y)]$, b) $\psi\ [x,\xi(y)]$.

These functions are implemented as

$$\varphi[x,\xi(y)]=S[M_a(x)+2k-\xi(y)]-2k+\xi(y),$$
$$\psi[x,\xi(y)]=S[-M_{a+1}(x)-2k-\xi(y)]+2k-\xi(y).$$

Then the function

$$f(x,y)=\varphi[x,\xi(y)]+\psi[x,\xi(y)]=S[M_a(x) +2k-\xi(y)]+S[-M_{a+1}(x)-2k-\xi(y)] \tag{48}$$

has the form of the left trapeze type along the axis x shown in fig. 28(c).
The pyramid function approach is not limited to rules with point condition (40) and may be extended to rules with interval condition of the type

$$\text{if } (a_1 \le x \le a_2 \text{ and } b_1 \le y \le b_2) \text{ then} f(x,y)=k \text{ else } f(x,y)=0. \tag{49}$$

Interval conditions can be implemented by simple changing constants in mask-functions. The rule (49) represents matrices with rectangular configurations of valuable elements. Such matrices can be implemented as truncated pyramids.
Note that the function similar to (44) may be constructed for an arbitrary number of variables. Implementation of a pyramid function of two variables requires 6 amplifiers. Introducing each additional variable requires two additional amplifiers.

4.4 Extracting a matrix with valuable elements laying on a diagonal

Let us split the matrix M_4 on two matrices (M_5 and M_6) and try to implement the matrix M_5. Matrix M_6 is the next residual matrix.

$$\overset{M_4}{\begin{vmatrix} \le 0 & \le 0 & 0 & +1 & +1 & \ge 0 & \ge 0 \\ \le 0 & 0 & +1 & 0 & 0 & \ge 0 & \ge 0 \\ 0 & 0 & 0 & 0 & 0 & 0 & \ge 0 \\ 0 & 0 & 0 & 0 & 0 & +1 & \ge 0 \\ 0 & 0 & 0 & 0 & 0 & 0 & \ge 0 \\ 0 & 0 & 0 & +1 & 0 & 0 & \ge 0 \\ +1 & 0 & +1 & 0 & 0 & \ge 0 & \ge 0 \end{vmatrix}} = \overset{M_5}{\begin{vmatrix} 0 & 0 & 0 & 0 & 0 & 0 & 0 \\ 0 & 0 & 0 & 0 & 0 & 0 & 0 \\ 0 & 0 & 0 & 0 & 0 & 0 & +1 \\ 0 & 0 & 0 & 0 & 0 & +1 & 0 \\ 0 & 0 & 0 & 0 & 0 & 0 & 0 \\ 0 & 0 & 0 & +1 & 0 & 0 & 0 \\ 0 & 0 & +1 & 0 & 0 & 0 & 0 \end{vmatrix}} + \overset{M_6}{\begin{vmatrix} \le 0 & \le 0 & 0 & +1 & +1 & \ge 0 & \ge 0 \\ \le 0 & 0 & +1 & 0 & 0 & \ge 0 & \ge 0 \\ 0 & 0 & 0 & 0 & 0 & 0 & \ge 0 \\ 0 & 0 & 0 & 0 & 0 & 0 & \ge 0 \\ 0 & 0 & 0 & 0 & 0 & 0 & \ge 0 \\ 0 & 0 & 0 & 0 & 0 & 0 & \ge 0 \\ +1 & 0 & 0 & 0 & 0 & \ge 0 & \ge 0 \end{vmatrix}}$$

In its turn, the matrix M_5 can be composed from two matrices

$$\frac{1}{3}\overset{M_{51}}{\begin{vmatrix} 0 & 0 & 0 & 0 & 0 & 0 & 0 \\ 0 & 0 & 0 & 0 & 0 & 0 & 0 \\ 0 & 0 & 0 & 0 & 0 & 0 & +3 \\ 0 & 0 & 0 & 0 & 0 & +3 & 0 \\ 0 & 0 & 0 & 0 & +3 & 0 & 0 \\ 0 & 0 & 0 & +3 & 0 & 0 & 0 \\ 0 & 0 & +3 & 0 & 0 & 0 & 0 \end{vmatrix}} + \frac{1}{3}\overset{M_{52}}{\begin{vmatrix} 0 & 0 & 0 & 0 & 0 & 0 & 0 \\ 0 & 0 & 0 & 0 & 0 & 0 & 0 \\ 0 & 0 & 0 & 0 & 0 & 0 & 0 \\ 0 & 0 & 0 & 0 & 0 & 0 & 0 \\ 0 & 0 & 0 & 0 & -3 & 0 & 0 \\ 0 & 0 & 0 & 0 & 0 & 0 & 0 \\ 0 & 0 & 0 & 0 & 0 & 0 & 0 \end{vmatrix}}$$

and represented as the sum of corresponding functions

$$f_3(x,y) = \tfrac{1}{3}[f_{31}(x,y) + f_{32}(x,y)] .$$

In the matrix M_{51}, elements with the value "+3" lay on the line $x + y - 2 = 0$. This matrix can be described by the function of one variable $f_{31}(z = x + y)$, which is defined by the rule

$$\text{if } z = 2 \text{ then } f_{31}(z) = 3 \text{ else } f_{31}(z) = 0.$$

The function $f_{31}(z)$ can be constructed as it is shown in Fig. 32.
It is easy to see from this figure that

$$f_{31}(z) = \alpha_6(z) + 3, \quad \alpha_6(z) = S[\beta_6(z) + \delta_6(z) + 6], \quad \beta_6(z) = S(3z - 3), \quad \delta_6(z) = S(-3z + 9).$$

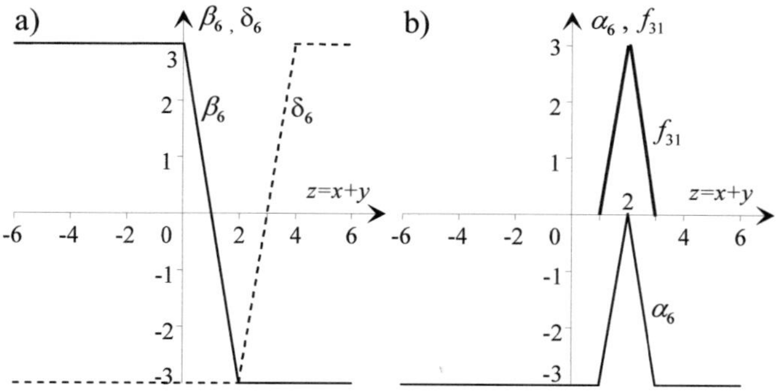

Fig. 32. Functional representations of the matrixes M_5.

For good "sewing" the function f_{32} with f_{31} and the function f_3 with f_1 the function f_{32} has to be implemented as pyramid function of variables $z = (x + y)/2$ and $w = (x - y)/2$ as it is shown in Fig. 29. Substitution of the variables z and w in formula (46) instead of $x + y$ and $x - y$ respectively, $a = +1$, $b = +1$, $k = 3$, and changing the sign of the function gives

$$f_{32}(z,w) = S\{S[\beta_6(z) + \delta_6(z) + \beta_7(w) + \delta_7(w) + 12] + 3\}$$

where $\beta_6(z)$, $\delta_6(z)$ are already implemented and

$$\beta_7(w) = S(3w + 3), \quad \delta_7(w) = S(-3w + 3).$$

Finally, the function $f_3(x, y)$ corresponding to the matrix M_5 can be implemented as

$$f_3(x,y) = \tfrac{1}{3}S\{\beta_6(x,y) + \delta_6(x,y) + S[\beta_6(x,y) + \delta_6(x,y) + \beta_7(x,y) + \delta_7(x,y) + 12] + 9\} + 1 \quad (50)$$

where

$$\beta_6(x,y) = S(3x + 3y - 3), \quad \delta_6(x,y) = S(-3x - 3y + 9),$$
$$\beta_7(x,y) = S(3x - 3y + 3), \quad \delta_7(-3x + 3y + 3).$$

4.5 Implementation of the matrix M_6

Let us split the matrix M_6 on two matrices (M_7 and M_8) and try to implement the matrix M_7. The new residual matrix is M_8, all elements of which are defined.
The matrix M_7

$$\overset{M_6}{\begin{vmatrix} \le 0 & \le 0 & 0 & +1 & +1 & \ge 0 & \ge 0 \\ \le 0 & 0 & +1 & 0 & 0 & \ge 0 & \ge 0 \\ 0 & 0 & 0 & 0 & 0 & 0 & \ge 0 \\ 0 & 0 & 0 & 0 & 0 & 0 & \ge 0 \\ 0 & 0 & 0 & 0 & 0 & 0 & \ge 0 \\ 0 & 0 & 0 & 0 & 0 & 0 & \ge 0 \\ +1 & 0 & 0 & 0 & 0 & \ge 0 & \ge 0 \end{vmatrix}} = \overset{M_7}{\begin{vmatrix} 0 & 0 & 0 & +1 & +1 & +1 & +1 \\ 0 & 0 & 0 & 0 & 0 & 0 & 0 \\ 0 & 0 & 0 & 0 & 0 & 0 & 0 \\ 0 & 0 & 0 & 0 & 0 & 0 & 0 \\ 0 & 0 & 0 & 0 & 0 & 0 & 0 \\ 0 & 0 & 0 & 0 & 0 & 0 & 0 \\ 0 & 0 & 0 & 0 & 0 & 0 & 0 \end{vmatrix}} + \overset{M_8}{\begin{vmatrix} 0 & 0 & 0 & 0 & 0 & 0 & 0 \\ 0 & 0 & +1 & 0 & 0 & 0 & 0 \\ 0 & 0 & 0 & 0 & 0 & 0 & 0 \\ 0 & 0 & 0 & 0 & 0 & 0 & 0 \\ 0 & 0 & 0 & 0 & 0 & 0 & 0 \\ 0 & 0 & 0 & 0 & 0 & 0 & 0 \\ +1 & 0 & 0 & 0 & 0 & 0 & 0 \end{vmatrix}}$$

has one rectangular component and can be represented as the function $f_4(x, y)$ that is defined by the rule

$$\text{if } (x = -3\,)\&(y \geq 0\,) \text{ then } f_4(x,y) = 1 \text{ else } f_4(x,y) = 0.$$

By analogy with constructing formulas (41) – (45) let us compose two auxiliary functions: $\gamma_1(x)$ for the condition $x = -3$ and $\gamma_1(y)$ for the condition $y \geq 0$. These functions are represented in Fig. 33 and can be constructed as

$$\gamma_1(x) = S[-M_{-3}(x)], \quad \gamma_1(y) = S[M_{-1}(y) + 3]\,.$$

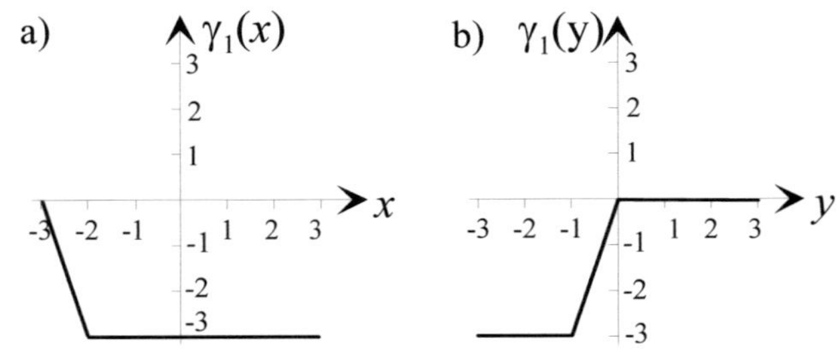

Fig. 33. Two auxiliary functions: a) $\gamma_1(x)$ for the condition $x = -3$ and b) $\gamma_1(y)$ for the condition $y \geq 0$.

Based on the functions $\gamma_1(x)$ and $\gamma_1(y)$ it is possible to construct the function of two variables

$$\gamma_1(x,y) = S[-M_{-3}(x) + M_{-1}(y) + 3].$$

Taking into account that for $k = 3$

$$-M_{-3}(x) = S(-3x - 9), \quad M_{-1}(y) = S(3y + 3)$$

it is not difficult to find

$$f_4(x,y) = \tfrac{1}{3} S[S(-3x - 9) + S(3y + 3) + 3] + 1\,. \tag{51}$$

The residual matrix M_8 has only two nonzero elements with coordinates ($x = +3$, $y = -3$) and ($x = -2$, $y = -1$). Let us designate the functions, with help of which the controller function can be corrected in these points, as f_5 and f_6 respectively. Depending on coordinates of a valuable element and conditions of good "sewing" its function with already implemented fragments different implementation methods can be used.

The function $f_5(x, y)$ is equal to 0 everywhere except the point ($x = +3$, $y = -3$), at which $f_5(x, y) = 1$. For monotonic piecewise-linear connection of this function with the function $f_1(x, y)$, graphs of the function $f_5(x, y)$ along each of its arguments must have the form of Fig. 28(a) or (b). The function $f_5(x, y)$ can be implemented as pyramid function in accordance with (46) but the following approach, which is shown in Fig. 34, gives better implementation.

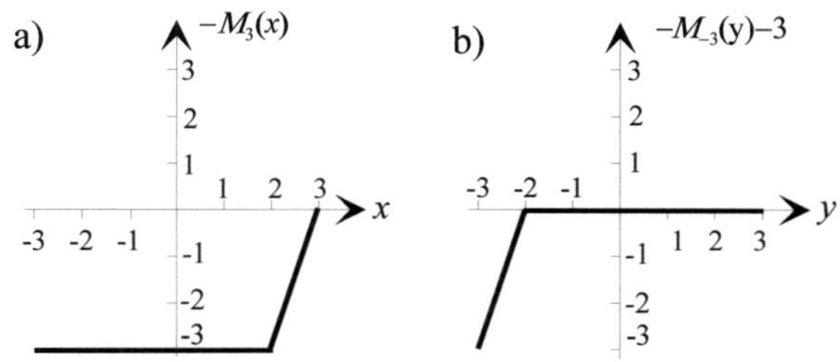

Fig. 34. Auxiliary functions: a) $-M_3(x)$ and b) $-M_3(y) - 3$.

Now it is not difficult to construct the function

$$f_5(x,y) = \tfrac{1}{3}\{S[-M_{-3}(y) - 3 - M_3(x)] - M_3(x)\}$$

and finally the function f_5 is implemented as

$$f_5(x,y) = \tfrac{1}{3}S[S(-3y-9) + S(-3x+9) - 3] + \tfrac{1}{3}S(-3x+9). \quad (52)$$

As experiments showed, the monotonic piecewise-linear approximation between the logical level in the point (-2,-1) and logical levels in the adjacent points of the functions $f_1(x, y)$ and $f_4(x, y)$ will be obtained, if the pyramid function f_6 in the point (-2,-1) is implemented in accordance with the formula (46).

$$f_6(x,y) = \tfrac{1}{3}S\{S[S(3x+3y+6) + S(-3x-3y-12) + S(3x-3y) + S(-3x+3y-6) - 12] - 3\}.$$

After some transformations providing the possibility to save one summing amplifier this function looks as follows

$$f_6(x,y) = \tfrac{1}{3}S[S(-3x-3y-6) + S(3x+3y+12) + S(-3x+3y) + S(3x-3y+6) + 12] + 1. \quad (53)$$

4.6 Implementation of the controller

Correctness of the designed controller and its functioning has been checked with SPICE simulation (MSIM 8). In simulation experiments MOSIS BSIM3v3.1 level 7 models of 0.4μm transistors have been used.

As building blocks for the controller circuit two types of summing amplifiers were used (ordinary and powerful). They are built on the basis of three-stage push-pull CMOS operational amplifier[2] with 1.5-MegOhm resistor in the feedback. Examples of such summing amplifiers are shown in Fig. 35. Transistors in this figure are marked with two numbers, which designate transistor dimensions (length and width).

---

[2]The operational amplifier of this type ii the simplest and is chosen only with the purpose of simplifying SPUCE simulation.

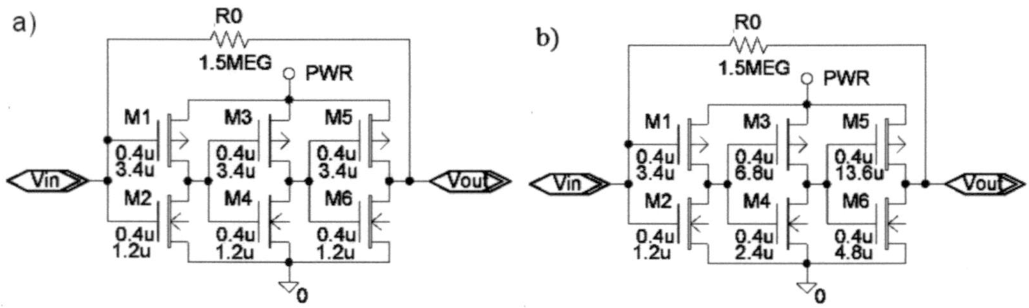

Fig. 35. Operational amplifier with feedback: a) ordinary, b) powerful.

The controller schematic for experiments is represented in Fig. 36. Two powerful elements PHS1 and PHS2 of the controller produce signals -y and -x respectively. Other elements are ordinary.

Analytical description of the controller schematic can be derived on bases of the function implementations (35) – (37), (39), (50) – (53) and has the following form

$$
\begin{aligned}
f_1(x,y) &= S_9[\tfrac{1}{6}S_3(6x+6y+27)+\ \tfrac{1}{3}S_4(3x+3y+6)+\tfrac{1}{6}S_5(6x+6y-3)+\\
&\quad \tfrac{1}{6}S_6(6x+6y-15)+\tfrac{1}{6}S_7(6x+6y-27)];\\
f_2(x,y) &= S_9(S_8(-3x+9y-24)-3);\\
f_3(x,y) &= \tfrac{1}{3}S_{12}\{S_{10}(3x+3y-3)+\ S_{11}(-3x-3y+9)+S_{15}[S_{10}(3x+3y-3)+\\
&\quad S_{11}(-3x-3y+9)+S_{14}(3x-3y+3)+S_{13}(-3x+3y+3)+12]+9\}+1;\\
f_4(x,y) &= \tfrac{1}{3}S_{18}[S_{16}(-3x-9)+S_{17}(3y+3)+3]+1;\\
f_5(x,y) &= \tfrac{1}{3}S_{21}[S_{19}(-3x+9)+S_{20}(-3y-9)-3]+\tfrac{1}{3}S_{19}(-3x-9);\\
f_6(x,y) &= \tfrac{1}{3}S_{26}[S_{23}(-3x-3y-6)+\ S_{22}(3x+3y+12)+S_{25}(-3x+3y)+\\
&\quad S_{24}(3x-3y+6)+12]+1;\\
F(x,y) &= \sum_{j=1}^{6} f_j(x,y) = S_{28}[S_{27}(S_9+\tfrac{1}{3}S_{12}+\ \tfrac{1}{3}S_{18}+\tfrac{1}{3}S_{19}+\tfrac{1}{3}S_{21}+\tfrac{1}{3}S_{26}+3)].
\end{aligned}
$$

Enumeration of summing amplifiers in this description corresponds to enumeration of elements in the controller circuit. The controller contains 28 amplifiers and 86 resistors. Resistor values have been calculated as $R_j = R_0 / w_j$ where w_j is logical weight of the jth element input signal.

In experiments, source voltage was 3.5V. Input variable x changed linearly from 0V to 3.5V, input variable y changed discreetly and kept constant value within one cycle of x changing.

The voltage range was evenly divided onto seven logical levels so that the logical levels "-3" and "+3" corresponded to voltages V_{gnd} and V_{dd} respectively.

Results of SPICE simulation of the controller schematic are represented in Fig. 37. This figure has been constructed by using GNUplot and illustrates the response surface in the coordinates X, Y. Analyzing the surface it is possible to conclude that the functioning of the controller is correct because of logical values of the circuit output depend on the logical values of the input variables in accordance with the Table 11.

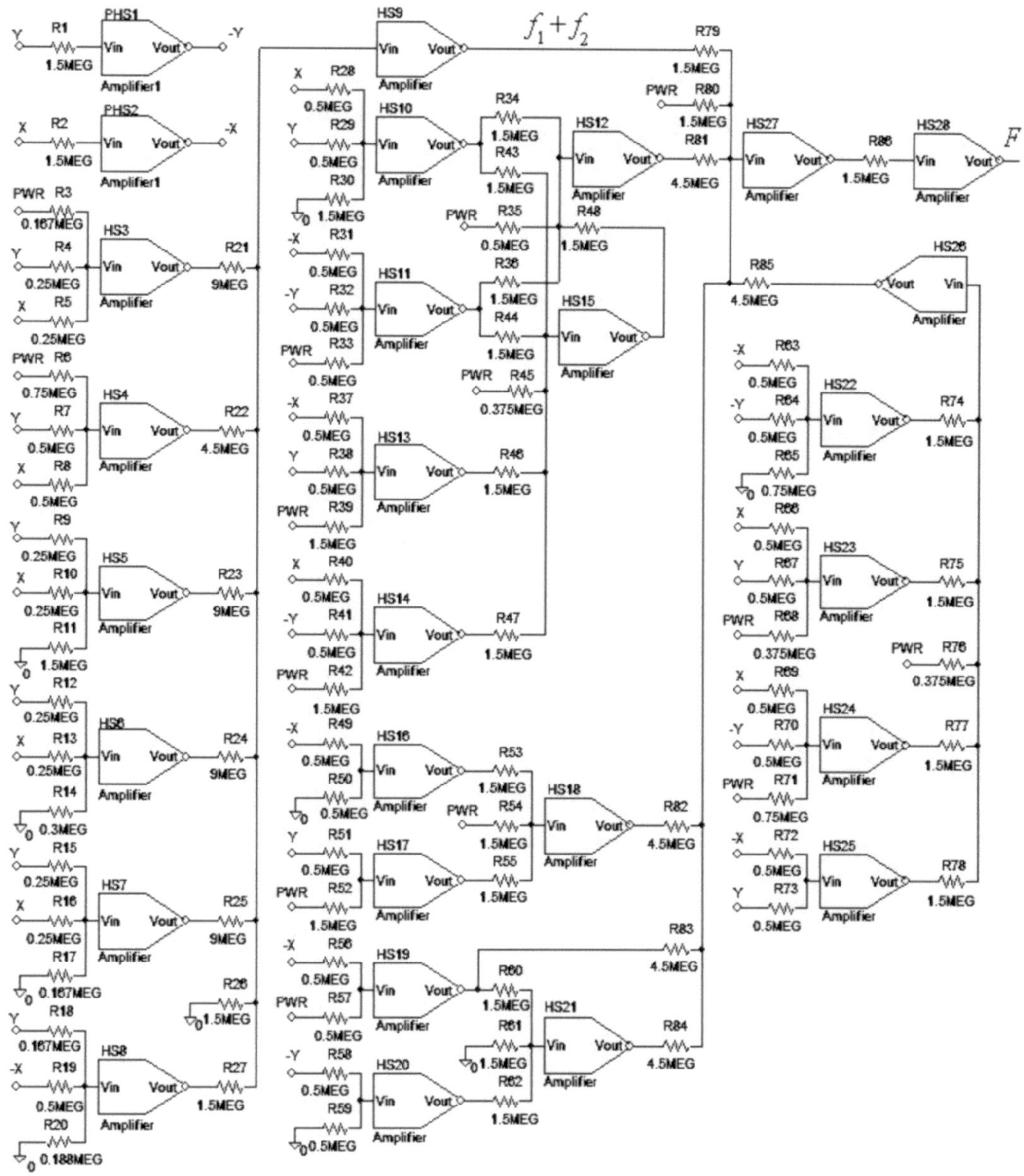

Fig. 36. The controller schematic for experiment.

Moreover, the controller output signal has monotonic piecewise-linear approximation between adjacent logical levels. Thus the designed controller can be used as an analog device, which has analog inputs and produces an analog output signal.

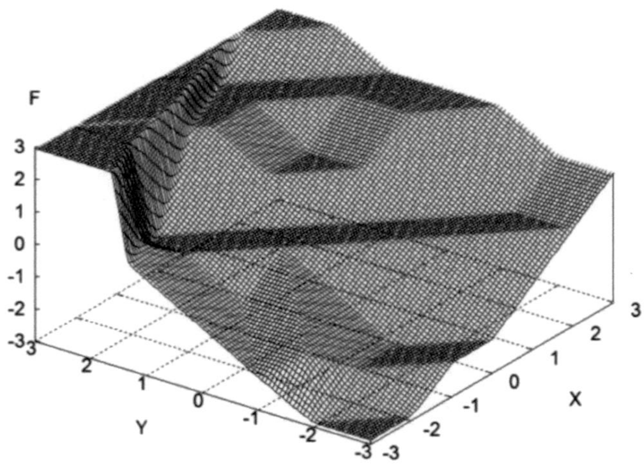

Fig. 37. The response surface of the controller.

5. Transformation of analog signals into multi-valued logic variables

In previous sections functions of multi-valued logic were specified by tables of fuzzy rules over linguistic variables. It was implicitly assumed that values of analog signals, which corresponded to linguistic variables, were evenly distributed in the range of voltages representing analog signals. Otherwise by artificial means the number of linguistic variables can be increased that leads to growing the implementation complexity.

In this section a procedure of transforming input analog variables into multiple-valued logic variables with evenly distributed logical levels is suggested. This procedure in some sense is analogous to the procedure of fuzzification in fuzzy controllers. Because of using a fuzzy control description for implementation of controllers as multi-valued logical functions the same term "fuzzification" for the suggested procedure of logical levels equalization for input variables will be used.

The same procedure is supposed to be used when output multi-valued variables with evenly distributed logical levels demand backward transformation to an analog form with not evenly distributed voltages corresponding to logical levels. In this case the term "defuzzification procedure" will be applied.

5.1 Fuzzification procedures

Let us examine more attentively the fuzzification procedure for the case of linear membership functions or membership functions, which sufficiently simply can be represented as piecewise-linear, and propose sufficiently simple universal method. Here the standard determination of a membership function is used. The membership function determines the weight of the corresponding linguistic variable b for each value of an analog variable X:

$$w_b = F(b, X); \ 0 \le w_b \le 1 .$$

The simplest example of membership functions is given in Fig. 38.

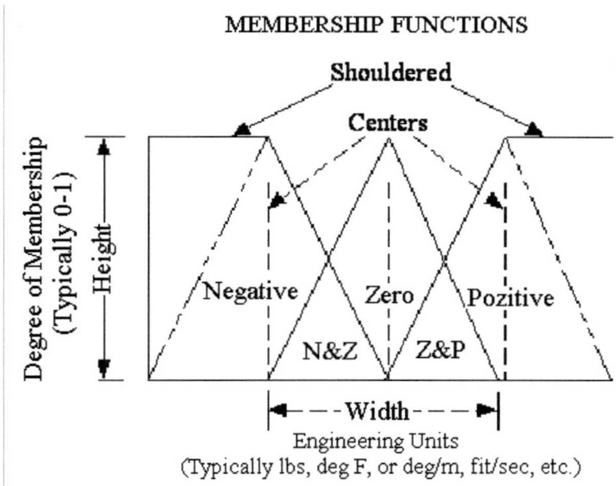

Fig. 38. The simplest type of membership functions.

“The membership function is a graphical representation of the magnitude of participation of each input. It associates a weighting with each of the inputs that are processed, define functional overlap between inputs, and ultimately determines an output response. The rules use the input membership values as weighting factors to determine their influence on the fuzzy output sets of the final output conclusion. Once the functions are inferred, scaled, and combined, they are defuzzified into a crisp output which drives the system. There are different memberships functions associated with each input and output response. Some features to note are:

SHAPE - triangular is common, but bell, trapezoidal, haversine and, exponential have been used (More complex functions are possible but require greater computing overhead to implement.);

HEIGHT or magnitude (usually normalized to 1);

WIDTH (of the base of function);

SHOULDERING (locks height at maximum if an outer function. Shouldered functions evaluate as 1.0 past their center);

CENTER points (center of the member function shape);

OVERLAP (N&Z, Z&P, typically about 50% of width but can be less)”.[3]

Fig.38 illustrates the features of the triangular membership function, which is used in the following example.

The procedure of fuzzification and constructing corresponding diagram is examined on an example of the Container Crane fuzzy Controller, membership functions for which are given in Fig. 39.[4]

It is assumed, without disrupting the generality of reasoning, that with changing the *angle* within the limits $(-90^\circ \div +90^\circ)$ and the *distance* in the limits (-10 ÷ +30) *yards* the corresponding analog voltages vary within the range $(0\div3.5)V$. The source voltage of the controller circuit is also 3.5V.

[3] Citation is taken from “Fuzzy Logic - an Introduction”, part 4, by Steven D. Kaehler, http://www.seattlerobotics.org/encoder/mar98/fuz/fl_part4.html

[1] http://www.fuzzytech.com/e/e_a_pdf.html

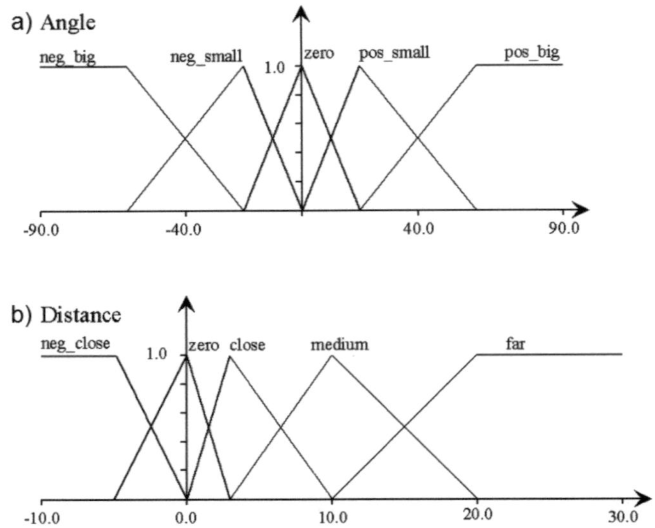

Fig. 39. Membership functions for the Container Crane Fuzzy Controller: a) for the *angle* and b) for the *distance*.

Table 12 determines the function of fuzzification for the piecewise-linear membership functions of the variable *angle* shown in Fig. 39(a). It contains linguistic variables, corresponding to them angle values and voltages, and also logical values evenly distributed within the voltage range. Linearity the membership functions gives the possibility to connect the points of logical values by straight lines. The corresponding fuzzification (equalization) function is given in Fig. 40(a). In this figure the variations of voltages from the average (equilibrium) point of summing amplifier are plotted along the axes.

neg_big	neg_small	zero	pos_small	pos_big
-90°÷-60° (0÷0.58) V	-20° 1.361 V	0° 1.75 V	20° 2.139 V	60°÷90° (2.917÷3.5) V
-2 0 V	-1 0.875 V	0 1.75 V	+1 2.625 V	+2 3.5 V

Table 12. Angle membership functions.

For implementation of the function $V_{out} = F_1(V_{in})$ shown in Fig. 40(a) three auxiliary functions should be introduced. These functions are represented in Fig. 40(b). Their sum with saturation on the levels ± 1.75 V determines the fuzzificated input function for the controller fuzzy inference part, which, as it has been already proved in previous sections, can be implemented as a multi-valued logic function.

In Fig. 40(b) the angle α and functions φ_j (α) are represented in positive and negative voltages. These component functions and the fuzzifier output function $F_1(\alpha)$ can be implemented by the following way:

$$\begin{aligned}&\varphi_1(\alpha) = -0.5S(4.5\alpha);\quad \varphi_2(\alpha) = -S(1.125\alpha + 2.19);\quad \varphi_3(\alpha) = -S(1.125\alpha - 2.19);\\ &F_1(\alpha) = S(-\varphi_1(\alpha) - \varphi_2(\alpha) - \varphi_3(\alpha)) = S(\tfrac{1}{2}S(4.5\alpha) + S(1.125\alpha + 2.19) + S(1.125\alpha - 2.19)).\end{aligned} \tag{54}$$

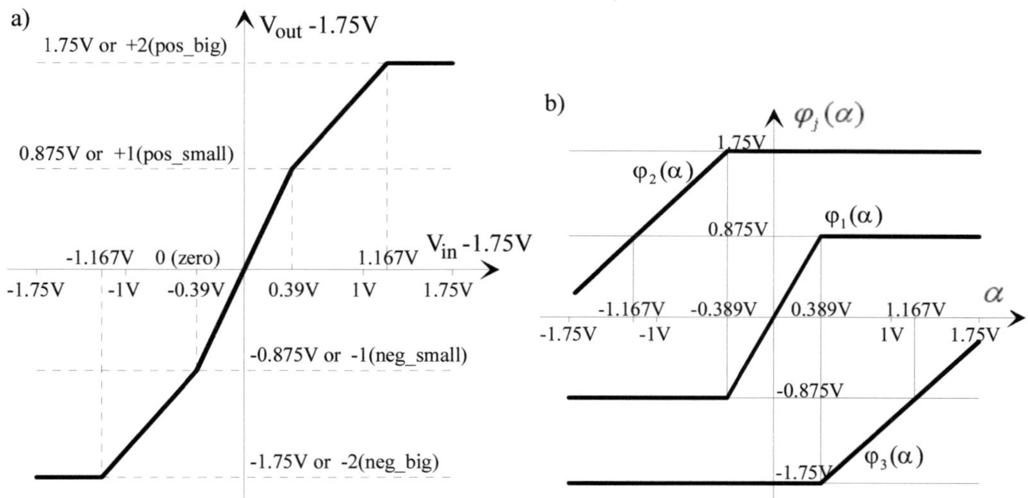

Fig. 40. a) Piecewise-linear function for fuzzification of the variable *angle;*
b) Component functions for the function represented in (a).

Now let us show how to construct and implement the fuzzification function for the input variable *distance*. As can be inferred from Fig. 40(b), the membership functions are characterized, first, by asymmetry of the measured distance ((-10 ÷ +30) yards) and, second, by the explicit asymmetry of the linguistic variable positions along the distance axis. It assumed that the complete range of the measured distance corresponds to the complete range of the supply voltages ($0V \div 3.5V$) or ($-1.75V \div +1.75V$) in deviations from the middle point of amplifiers. For this case, the fuzzification function is determined by Table 13.

neg_close	zero	close	medium	far
≤ -5 yards $\leq 0.4375V$	0 yards $0.875V$	3 yards $1{,}1375V$	10 yards $1.75V$	≥ 20 yards $\geq 2.625V$
-2 $0V$	-1 $0.875V$	0 $1.75V$	+1 $2.625V$	+2 $3.5V$

Table 13. Distance membership functions

In this table the linguistic variable *close* corresponds to value "log.0" and the linguistic variable *zero* corresponds to the value "log.-1". The balance point of the amplifier input voltage corresponds to linguistic variable *medium*.

Corresponding function $V_{out}(V_{in}) = F_2(V_{in})$ is given in Fig. 41. For implementation of this function it is necessary to realize four auxiliary functions, whose sum with saturation on the levels $\pm 1.75V$ will give the desired result. The auxiliary functions are given in Fig.42. Their values and value of the variable d (*distance*) are represented in negative and positive voltages.

The ways of forming the component functions given in Fig.42 and the function $F_2(d)$ are shown below:

$$\begin{aligned}
&\psi_1(d) = -S(2d+3.5); \quad \psi_2(d) = -0.25S(13.6d+10.14);\\
&\psi_3(d) = -0.25S(5.67d+1.75); \quad \psi_4(d) = -S(d-1.75);\\
&F_2(d) = S(-\psi_1(d)-\psi_2(d)-\psi_3(d)-\psi_4(d)) =\\
&S[S(2d+3.5)+0.25S(13.6d+10.14)+\ 0.25S(5.67d+1.75)+S(d-1.75)].
\end{aligned} \tag{55}$$

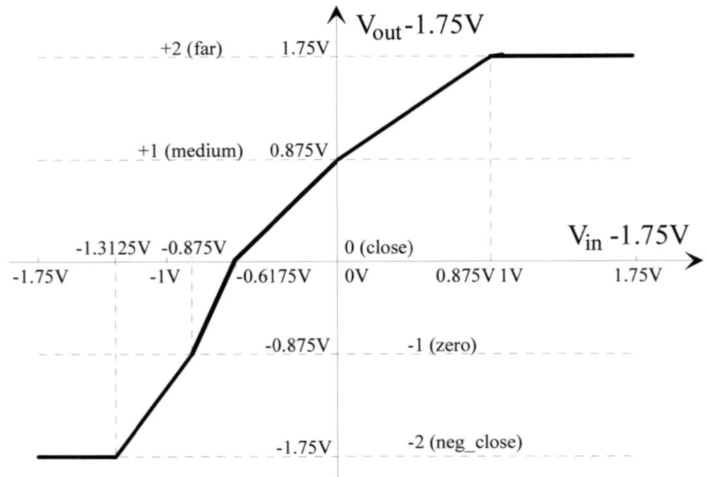

Fig. 41. Piecewise-linear fuzzifications function for the variable *distance*.

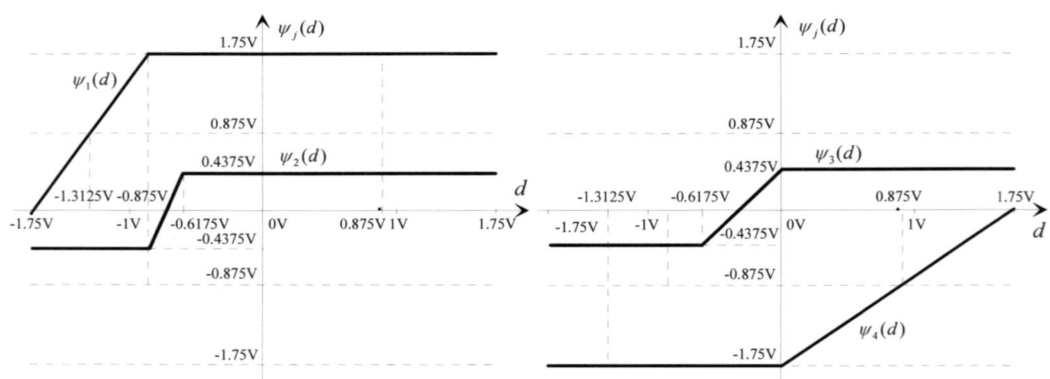

Fig. 42. Component functions for the function represented in Fig.41.

5.2 Fuzzifier implementations 5.2

For the completion of the fuzzifier design it only remains to determine the values of the input resistances of summing amplifiers and to conduct SPICE simulation for checking correctness of the implementations (54) and (55). These implementations are represented graphically in Fig.43(a) and Fig.43(b) respectively. Their schematics, which have been used for SPICE simulations, are shown in Fig.44 (a) and Fig.44 (b).

Summing amplifiers used in the schematics are constructed on the bases of three-stage push-pull CMOS operational amplifier in accordance with Fig.35(a).

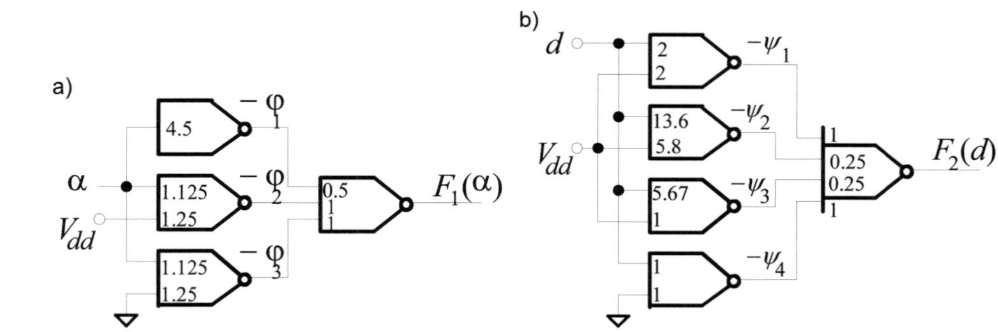

Fig. 43. Fuzzifiers of the variables a) *angle* and b) *distance*.

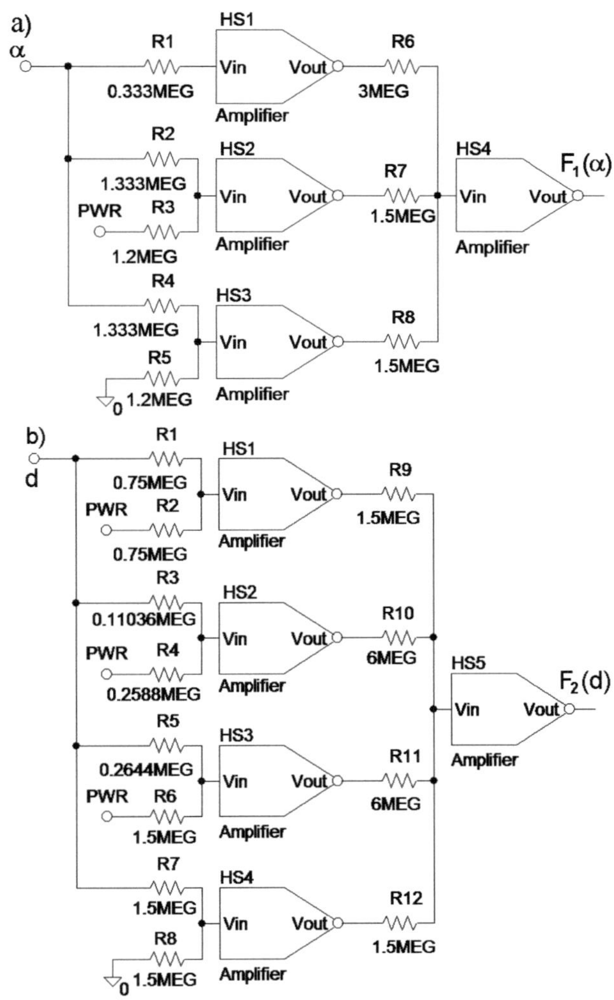

Fig. 44. Fuzzifier schematics a) for the *angle* and b) for the *distance*.

Results of SPICE simulation of the fuzzifiers for variables *angle* and *distance* are shown in Fig. 45.

It is easy to see that the simulation plots are exactly the same as it is required for fuzzification of the input variables *angle* (Fig.40(a)) and *distance* (Fig.41). This proves the correctness of the fuzzifier implementations.

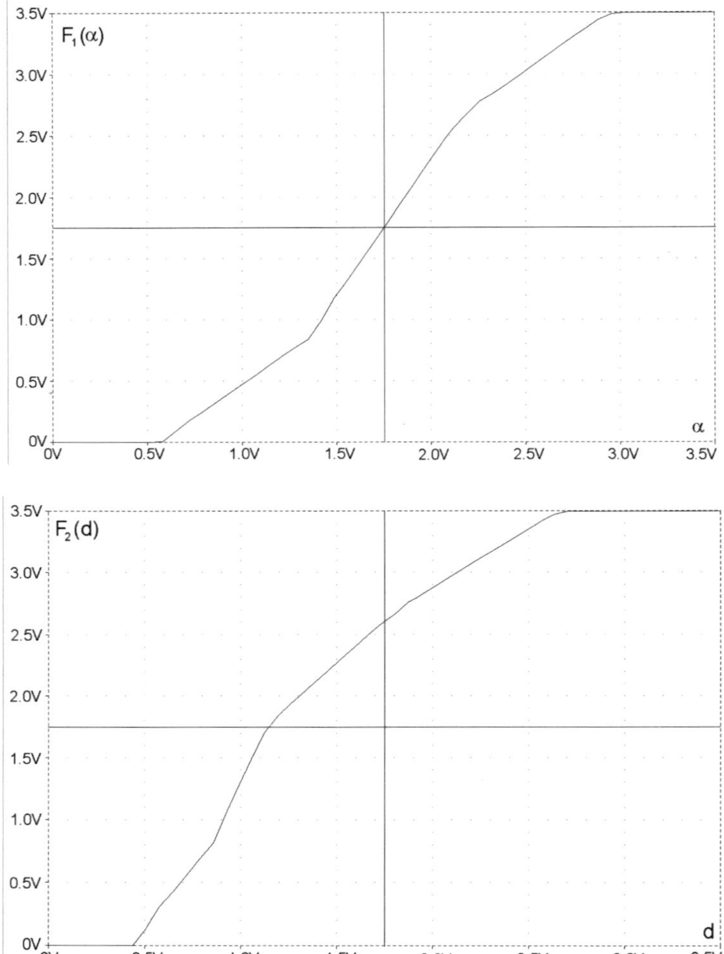

Fig. 45. Outputs of the fuzzifiers (shown in Fig.44) derived by SPICE simulation.

It should be noted that in the case of software implementation of the fuzzification and defuzzification functions, their component functions may be chosen not only piecewise-linear but providing any reasonable approximations.

6. Conclusion

Thus, it was shown that all parts of fuzzy controllers can be effectively implemented on bases of summing amplifiers with saturation in accordance with the proposed methodology.

This methodology is oriented to hardware implementation of fuzzy controllers as analog devices. Certainly the traditional approach to implementation of fuzzy controllers provides more accurate control and gives better approximation extracted levels in comparison with suggested. But in many cases our approach gives so simple circuits of controllers that their implementation on the base of standard processors looks rather redundant. Moreover, hardware implementation have advantages of better response time and reliability, low power consumption, smaller die area, etc. It should be noticed that the methodology also admits software implementation of the controllers by means of simulation using the summation operation with restrictions.

In all examples of controllers presented in the paper, the push-pull summing amplifier containing three CMOS invertors is used. Obviously this amplifier circuit is the simplest among operational amplifiers of other types but unfortunately it has the worst characteristics. It was chosen only by two reasons: first, to simplify SPICE simulation of designed controllers and second, to show that using even such primitive and imperfect building block gives rather appropriate characteristics of designed controllers. Certainly in real projects of controllers it is better to use another types of operational amplifiers, e.g., a differential amplifier.

Someone may object that summing amplifiers in all examples of controllers designed with help of suggested methodology contain resistors of large values and it is very difficult to implement these resistors in CMOS VLSI technology. Indeed it is correct. In our case p-well resistors (1-10K Ohms/sq.) or pinch resistors (5-20K Ohms/sq.) can be used. These resistors are compatible with CMOS technology but occupy very large die area, possess bad accuracy, and have big temperature and voltage coefficients. By these reasons the possibility of creating a dynamical model of the summing amplifier with saturation using capacitors instead of resistors has been considered. This consideration gave positive results and perhaps will be published in the future.

The proposed methodology has been applied for designing several devices specified as fuzzy controllers, showed high efficiency and gave very economical implementations. Techniques of synthesizing fuzzy devices in the offered base should get further developing and problems of implementability under the conditions of real production should be resolved in the nearest future.

7. References

TI SPRA028 (1993). Implementation of Fuzzy Logic Selected Applications, Texas Instruments, January.

Yager, R.R. & Zadeh, L.A. (Ed.) (1992). *An Introduction to Fuzzy Logic Applications in Intelligent Systems,* Kluwer International Series in Engineering and Computer Science, 165, Jan., 356 p.

Klir, G.J.; Yuan B. & Zadeh L.A. (Ed.) (1996). *Fuzzy Sets, Fuzzy Logic, and Fuzzy Systems,* (Advances in Fuzzy Systems - Applications and Theory), World Scientific Pub Co.; Vol. 6, 826 p.

Marks II, R.J. (Ed.) (1994). *Fuzzy Logic Technology and Applications,* IEEE Technology Update Series, Selected Conference Papers, 575 p.

Varshavsky, V.; Marakhovsky, V.; Levin, I. & Kravchenko, N. (2003). Summing Amplifier as a Multi-Valued Logical Element for Fuzzy Control, *WSEAS Transactions on Circuit and Systems*, Issue 3, Vol. 2, pp. 625 - 631.

Varshavsky, V.; Levin, I.; Marakhovsky, V.; Ruderman, A. & Kravchenko, (2004). CMOS Fuzzy Decision Diagram Implementation, *WSEAS Transactions on Systems*, Issue 2, Vol. 3, pp. 615 - 620.

Post E. (1921). Introduction to a general theory of elementary propositions, *Amer. J. Math.*, 43, pp. 163 - 185.

Kandel, A. & Zadeh, L.A. (Ed.) (1993). *Fuzzy Control Systems*, CRC Press LLC, pp. 81 - 86, pp. 168 - 172.

Kimura, K. & Kawawa, T. (1993). *Exhaust Emission Control Device for Internal Combustion Engine*, Toyota Motor Corp., Patent of Japan No. 05-312020.

Dualibe, C.; M. Verleysen, M. & Jespers, P.G.A. (2003). *Design of Analog Fuzzy Logic Controllers in CMOS Technologie*s, Kluver Academic Publishers.

Varshavsky, V.; Marakhovsky, V.; Levin, I. & Kravchenko, N. (2004). Functionally Complete Element for Fuzzy Control Hardware Implementation, *47th IEEE Midwest Symposium on Circuits and Systems*, Hiroshima, Japan, Vol. 3, July, pp. 263 – 266.

Varshavsky, V.; Marakhovsky, V.; Levin, I. & Kravchenko, N. (2004). Fuzzy Controller CMOS Implementation, *WSEAS Transactions on Circuits and Systems*, Issue 9, Vol. 3, November, pp.1762 – 1769.

Varshavsky, V.; Marakhovsky, V. & Levin, I. (2005). CMOS Fuzzification Circuits for Linear Membership Functions, *WSEAS Transactions on Systems*, Issue 4, Vol. 4, April, pp. 238 - 243.

Varshavsky, V.; Marakhovsky, V. & Levin, I. (2005). CMOS Fuzzification Circuits for Linear Membership Functions, *WSEAS Transactions on Systems*, Issue 4, Vol. 4, April 2005, pp.238 - 243.

2

Takagi-Sugeno Fuzzy Control Based on Robust Stability Specifications

Joabe A. Silva[1] and Ginalber L. O. Serra[2]
[1]*Federal Institute of Education, Science and Technology - IFMA*
MSc Program in Electrical Engineering - PPGE/UFMA, São Luís-MA
[2]*Federal Institute of Education, Science and Technology-IFMA*
Department of Electrical Engineering - DEE, São Luís-MA
Brazil

1. Introduction

In the design of modern and classical control systems, the first step is establish a suitable mathematical model to describe the behavior of the controlled plant (Takagi & Sugeno, 1985; Ying et al., 1990). However, in practical situations, such a requirement is not feasible because in practical control systems the plants are always nonlinear systems, which makes this task analytically unfeasible for complex systems (Cetin & Demir, 2008; Dong et al., 2009; Park et al., 2007; Pelladra et al., 2009). This fact has motivated the use of fuzzy logic in the development of fuzzy model based control systems. In this context, The Fuzzy Systems have been widely used due to flexibility of its structure to incorporate linguistic information (knowledge expert) with numerical information (sensors and actuators measurements), as well as its functional efficiency as universal approximator capable of treat adequately uncertainties, parametric variations and nonlinearity of the plant to be controlled (Castro-Sitiriche et al., 2008; Cetin & Demir, 2008; Cheng et al., 2009; Ibrahim, 2003; Mishra et al., 2000; Park et al., 2007; Wen-Xu et al., 2009). Modeling is the task that simplifies a real system or complex reality with the aim of easing its understanding. In this sense, an effective approach to the identification of complex nonlinear systems is to partition the available data into subsets and approximate each subset by simple model. Fuzzy Clustering can be used as a tool to obtain a partitioning of experimental data where the transitions between the subsets are gradual rather than abrupt. The potential of fuzzy clustering algorithms to reveal the underlying structures in data can be exploited, not only for classification and pattern recognition in the available data, but also for the reduction of complexity in modeling and identification. One of the major applications of the model is the design of a controller for the true system. The ultimate goal of a control-system is to build a system that will work in the real environment. Since the real environment may change with time (parametric variations and nonlinearity) or operating conditions may vary (noise and disturbance), the control system must be able to withstand these variations (Petros & Sun, 1996). This fact has motivated, since 1980's, the proposal of new methodologies for design of robust controllers. In this context, fuzzy systems have been widely used in robust controllers design (Barton, 2004; Serra & Boturra, 2006; Silva & Serra, 2009; Tanaka & Sugeno, 1993; Zhan, 2010). In this paper a robust fuzzy control design based on gain and phase margins specifications for nonlinear systems, in the continuous time domain, is proposed. A mathematical formulation based on Takagi-Sugeno fuzzy model structure as well as the PDC strategy is presented. Analytical formulas are deduced for the sub-controllers parameters, in the robust fuzzy controller rules base, according to the fuzzy model parameters of the fuzzy model plant to be controlled. Results for the necessary and sufficient conditions for the fuzzy controller design, from the proposed robust methodology, with one axiom and two theorems are presented. Simulation results, based on robust methodology, for a single link robotic manipulator are presented. The paper is organized as follows: In section II, it is introduced firstly the preliminary concepts fot the proposal methodology; secondly the the robust fuzzy control design and tuning formulas, based on gain and phase margins specifications, as well as the robust stability analysis of the fuzzy controller, are proposed in section III. Finally, Simulation results and conclusions are drawn in sections IV and V, repectively.

2. Preliminary concepts

In this section, some importants concepts to development the proposal methodology are presented.

2.1 Takagi-Sugeno fuzzy inference systems

The TS fuzzy model, originally proposed by Takagi and Sugeno (Takagi & Sugeno, 1985), is composed of a fuzzy **IF-THEN** rule base that partitions a space - usually called the *universe of discourse* - into fuzzy regions described by the *antecedents*. The *consequent* of each rule i is a simple functional expression of model inputs and that all fuzzy terms are monotonic functions. In this case, specifically, the TS fuzzy model can be regarded as a mapping from the antecedent (input) space to a convex region (polytope) in the local sub-models space into the consequent, defined by the variants consequents parameters of the plant to be controlled. This property simplifies the analysis of the TS fuzzy model in a context of robust time-variant and linear system for design of controllers with desired characteristics of the closed loop control system or stability analysis.

The $i|^{[i=1,2,\ldots,l]}$-th TS rule, without loss of generality, the following structure:

$$R^{(i)}: \text{ IF } \tilde{x}_1 \text{ is } F^i_{j|\tilde{x}_1} \text{ AND } \cdots \text{ AND } \tilde{x}_n \text{ is } F^i_{j|\tilde{x}_n} \text{ THEN } \tilde{y}_i = f_i\left(\tilde{\mathbf{x}}\right) \tag{1}$$

where

$$\tilde{\mathbf{x}}^T = [\tilde{x}_1, \tilde{x}_2, \cdots, \tilde{x}_n],$$
$$\tilde{\mathbf{y}}^T = [\tilde{y}_1, \tilde{y}_2, \cdots, \tilde{y}_n],$$

l is the number of fuzzy **IF-THEN** rules. The vector $\tilde{\mathbf{x}} \in \Re^n$ contains the antecedent linguistic variables. Each linguistic variable has its own universe of discourse $U_{\tilde{x}_1}, \cdots, U_{\tilde{x}_n}$ partitioned by fuzzy sets representing the linguistic terms. The variable $\tilde{x}_t|^{[t=1,2,\ldots,n]}$ belongs to the fuzzy set $F^i_{j|\tilde{x}_t}$ with a value $\mu^i_{F_{j|\tilde{x}_t}}$ defined by a membership function $\mu^i_{\tilde{x}_t}: \Re \rightarrow [0,1]$, with $\mu^i_{F_{j|\tilde{x}_t}} \in \mu^i_{F_{1|\tilde{x}_t}}, \mu^i_{F_{2|\tilde{x}_t}}, \mu^i_{F_{3|\tilde{x}_t}}, \ldots, \mu^i_{F_{p_{\tilde{x}_t}|\tilde{x}_t}}$, where $p_{\tilde{x}_t}$ is the number of partitions of the universe of discourse associated to the linguistic variable $\tilde{\mathbf{x}}$. The activation degree of h_i for the rule i, is given by:

$$h_i\left(\tilde{\mathbf{x}}\right) = \mu^i_{F_{j|\tilde{x}_1^*}} \otimes \mu^i_{F_{j|\tilde{x}_2^*}} \otimes \cdots \mu^i_{F_{j|\tilde{x}_n^*}} \tag{2}$$

where $\tilde{x}_t^*$ is some point in $U_{\tilde{x}_t}$. The normalized activation degree for the rule i, is given by:

$$\gamma_i(\tilde{\mathbf{x}}) = \frac{h_i(\tilde{\mathbf{x}})}{\sum_{\lambda=1}^{l} h_\lambda(\tilde{\mathbf{x}})} \tag{3}$$

where it is assumed that

$$\sum_{\lambda=1}^{l} h_\lambda(\tilde{\mathbf{x}}) > 0,$$

$$h_\lambda(\tilde{\mathbf{x}}) \geq 0, \quad i = 1, 2, \cdots, l$$

And, this normalization implies that

$$\sum_{i=1}^{l} \gamma_i(\tilde{\mathbf{x}}) = 1 \tag{4}$$

The TS fuzzy model response is a weighted sum of the consequent parameters, i.e., a convex linear combination of the local functions (models) f_i, which reads

$$f_i(\tilde{\mathbf{x}}) = \sum_{i=1}^{l} \gamma_i(\tilde{\mathbf{x}}) f_i(\tilde{\mathbf{x}}) \tag{5}$$

Each linear component $f_i(\tilde{\mathbf{x}})$ is called a *subsystem*. This model can be seen as a Linear Parameters Varying (LPV) System (Balas et al., 1997; Shamma & Athans, 1991). This property simplifies the analysis of the TS fuzzy model in a context of robust time-variant and linear system for design of controllers with desired characteristics of the closed loop control system or stability analysis.

2.2 Fuzzy model based control design steps

The design of a controller that can alter or modify the behavior and response of an unknown plant to meet certain perfomance requirements can be a tedious and challenging problem in many control applications. The plant inputs u are processed to produce several plant outputs y that represent the measured output response of the plant. The control design task is to choose the input u so that the output response $y(t)$ satisfies certain given performance requirements. Because the plant process is usually complex, i.e., it may consist of various mechanical, electronic, hydraulic parts, etc., the appropriate choise of u is in general straightforward. The control design steps often followed by most control engineers in choosing the input u are explained below.

2.2.1 Modeling

The task os the control engineer in this step is to undestand the processing mechanism of the plant, which takes a given input signal $u(t)$ and produces the output response $y(t)$, to the point that he or she can describe it in the form of some mathematical equations. These equations constitute the mathematical model of the plant. An exact plant model should produce the same output response as the plant, provided the input to the model and initial conditions are exactly the same as those of the plant. The complexity of most physical plants, however, makes the development of such an exact model unwarranted or even impossible. But even if the exact plant model becomes available, its dimension is likely to be infinite, and its description nonlinear or time time varying to the point that its usefulness from the control design viewpoint is minimal or none. This makes the task of modeling even more difficult and challenging, because the control engineer has to came up with a mathematical model that describes accurately the input/output behavior of the plant and yet is simple enough to be used for control design purposes. A simple model usually leads to a simple controller that is easier to understand and implement, and often more reliable for practical purposes. A simple model usually leads to a simple controller that is easier to understand and implement, and often more reliable for practical purposes.

A plant model may be developed by using physical laws or by processing the plant input/output (I/O) data obtained by performing various experiments. Such a model, however, mat still be complicated enough from the control design viewpoint and further simplifications may be necessary. Some of the approaches often used to obtain a simplified model are:

(a) Linearization around operating points;

(b) Model order reduction techniques;

(c) Fuzzy Clustering.

In approach (a) the plant is approximated by a linear model that is valid around a given operating point. Different operating points may lead to several different linear models that are used as plant models. Linearization is achieved by using Taylor's series expansion and approximation, fitting of experimental data to a linear model, etc.

In approach (b) small effects and phenomena outside the frequency range of interest are neglected leading to a lower order and simpler plant model.

In approach (c), used in this work, the fuzzy clustering algorithms are used to construct fuzzy models from experimental data. Among the most popular methods are the following: *Fuzzy C - Means (FCM), Gustafson - Kessel (GK)* and *Fuzzy Maximum Likelihood Estimates (FLME) algorithms*. All these algorithms share the following definitions.

A ***cluster*** is a group of objects that are more similar to another than to members of other clusters (Bezdek, 1981; Jain & Dubes, 1988). The term *"similarity"* should be understood as mathematical similarity, measure in some well-define sense. In metric spaces, similarity is often defined by means of a distance norm. Distance can be measure from a data vector to some cluster prototypical (center). Data can reveal clusters of different geometric shapes, sizes and densities. While clusters can be characterized as linear and nonlinear subspaces of the data space.

The objective of clustering is to partition the data set Z into c clusters. Assume that c is known, based on priori knowledge. The ***fuzzy partition*** de Z can be defined as a family of subsets $\{A_i|1 \leq i \leq c\} \subset P(Z)$, with the following properties:

$$\bigcup_{i=1}^{c} A_i = Z \tag{6}$$

$$A_i \cap A_j = 0 \tag{7}$$

$$0 \subset A_i \subset Z_i \tag{8}$$

Equation 6 means that the subsets A_i collectively contain all the data in Z. The subsets must be disjoint, as stated by 7, and none off than is empty nor contains all the data in Z, as stated by 8.

In terms of *membership functions,* μ_{A_i} is the membership function of A_i. To simplifly the notation, in this work we use μ_{ik} instead $\mu_i(z_k)$. The cxN matrix $\mathbf{U} = [\mu_{ik}]$ represents a fuzzy partitioning space if and only if:

$$M_{fc} = \left\{ \mathbf{U} \in \Re^{cxN} | \mu_{ik} \in [0,1], \forall i,k; \sum_{i=1}^{c} \mu_{ik} = 1, \forall k; 0 < \sum_{k=1}^{N} \mu_{ik} < N, \forall i \right\} \tag{9}$$

The i-th row of the fuzzy partition matrix $\mathbf{U}$ contains values of the i-th membership function of the fuzzy subset A_i of Z.

The clustering algorithms optimizes an initial set of centroids by minimizing a ***cost function*** J in an iterative process. Such function is usually formulated as:

$$\mathbf{J}(\mathbf{Z};\mathbf{U},\mathbf{V},\mathbf{A}) = \sum_{i=1}^{c}\sum_{k=1}^{N} \mu_{ik}^{m} D_{ikA_i}^{2} \tag{10}$$

where, $\mathbf{Z} = \{z_1, z_2, \cdots, z_N\}$ is a finite data set. $\mathbf{U} = [\mu_{ik}] \in M_{fc}$ is a fuzzy partition of $\mathbf{Z}$. $\mathbf{V} = \{\mathbf{v}_1, \mathbf{v}_2, \cdots, \mathbf{v}_c\}, \mathbf{v}_i \in \Re^n$, is a vector of cluster prototypes (centers). $\mathbf{A}$ denote a c-tuple of the norm-induting matrices: $\mathbf{A} = (\mathbf{A}_1, \mathbf{A}_2, \cdots, \mathbf{A}_c)$. $D_{ik\mathbf{A}_i}^2$ is a squared inner-product distance norm. $m \in [1, \infty)$ is a weighting exponent which determines the fuzziness of the resulting clusters.

The clustering algorithms differ in the choice of the norm distance. The ***norm metric*** influences the clustering criterion by changing the measure of dissimilarity. The Euclidean norm induces hiperspherical clusters. It's characterizes the ***FCM*** *algorithm,* where norm-inducing matrix $\mathbf{A}_{i_{FCM}}$ is equal to identity matrix ($\mathbf{A}_{i_{FCM}} = \mathbf{I}$), this strictly imposes a circular shape to all clusters. The Euclidean Norm is given by:

$$D_{ik_{FCM}}^2 = (z_k - v_i)^T \mathbf{A}_{i_{FCM}} (z_k - v_i) \tag{11}$$

An adaptative distance norm, in order to detect clusters of different geometrical shapes in one data set, characterizes the ***GK*** *algorithm*:

$$D_{ik_{GK}}^2 = (z_k - v_i)^T \mathbf{A}_{i_{GK}} (z_k - v_i) \tag{12}$$

In this algorithm, each cluster has its own norm-inducing matrix $\mathbf{A}_{i_{GK}}$, where each cluster to adapt the distance norm to the local topological structure of the data set. $\mathbf{A}_{i_{GK}}$ is given by:

$$\mathbf{A}_{i_{GK}} = [\rho_i det(\mathbf{F}_i)]^{1/n} \mathbf{F}_i^{-1}, \tag{13}$$

where ρ_i is cluster volume, usually fixed in one. n is data dimension. $\mathbf{F}_i$ is the *fuzzy covariance matrix* of the i-th cluster defined by:

$$\mathbf{F}_i = \frac{\sum_{k=1}^{N} (\mu_{ik})^m (z_k - v_i)(z_k - v_i)^T}{\sum_{k=1}^{N} (\mu_{ik})^m} \tag{14}$$

The eigenstructure of the cluster covariance matrix provides information about the shape and orientation cluster. The ratio of the hyperellipsoid axes is given by the ratio of the square roots of the eigenvalues of $\mathbf{F}_i$. The directions of the axes are given by the eigenvectores of $\mathbf{F}_i$. The eigenvector corresponding to the smallest eigenvalue determines the normal to the hyperplane, and can be used to compute optimal local linear models from the covariance matrix.

The *fuzzy maximum likelihood estimates* (**FLME**) *algorithms* employs a distance norm based on maximum lekelihood estimates:

$$D_{ik_{FLME}} = \frac{\left[det\mathbf{G}_{i_{FLME}}\right]^{1/2}}{P_i} exp\left[\frac{1}{2}(z_k - v_i)^T \mathbf{F}_{i_{FLME}}^{-1}(z_k - v_i)\right] \tag{15}$$

Note that, contrary to the GK algorithm, this distance norm involves an exponential term and thus decreases faster than the inner-product norm. $\mathbf{F}_{i_{FLME}}$ denotes the fuzzy covariance matrix of the i-th cluster, given by equation 14. When m is equal 1, we have a strict algorithm FLME. If m is greater than 1, we have a *extended algorithm FLME*, or *Gath-Geva (GG) algorithm*. P_i is the prior probability of selecting cluster i, given by:

$$\mathbf{P}_i = \frac{1}{N}\sum_{k=1}^{N}(\mu_{ik})^m \tag{16}$$

Gath and Geva (Gath & Geva, 1989) reported that the FLME algorithm is able to detect clusters of varying shapes, sizes and densities. This is because the cluster covariance matrix is used in conjuncion with an "exponential" distance, and the clusters are not constrained in volume. The system identification procedure is illustrated in the Figure 1 below.

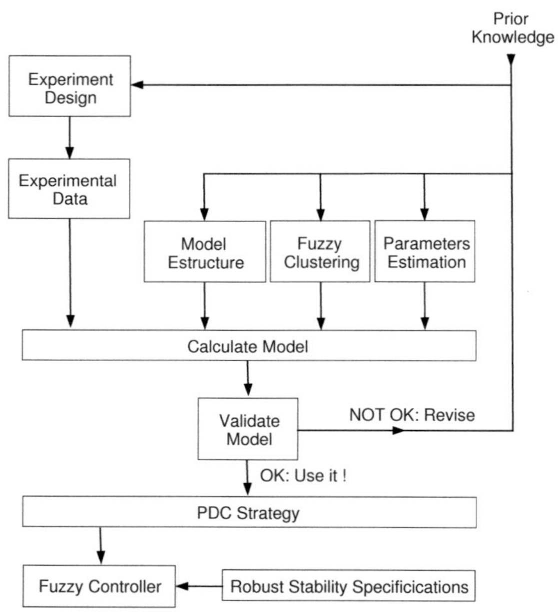

Fig. 1. The control system diagram

The fuzzy clustering algorithms can be used to approximate a set of experimental data by local linear models. Each of these models is represented by a fuzzy subset in the data set available for identification. In order to obtain a model useful for controller design, an additional step must be applied to generate a model independent of the identification data. Such a model can be represented either as a rule base. Each cluster obtained by clustering algorithms of the identification data set can be regarded as a local linear approximation of the regression hypersurface. The global model can be conveniently represented as a set affine Takagi-Sugeno

(TS) rules, can decribed in equation 1. The antecedent fuzzy sets can be computed analitically in the antecedent product space, or can be extracted from the fuzzy partition matriz by projections.
The consequent parameters are estimated from the data using the weighted least-squares method. Where, the identification data and the membership degrees of the fuzzy partition are arranged in the following matrices:

$$X = \begin{bmatrix} x_1^T \\ x_2^T \\ \vdots \\ x_N^T \end{bmatrix}, \qquad y = \begin{bmatrix} y_1 \\ y_2 \\ \vdots \\ y_N \end{bmatrix}, \qquad \Omega_i = \begin{bmatrix} \mu_{i1} & 0 & \cdots & 0 \\ 0 & \mu_{i1} & \cdots & 0 \\ \vdots & \vdots & \ddots & \vdots \\ 0 & 0 & \cdots & \mu_{iN} \end{bmatrix} \tag{17}$$

The consequent parameters of the rule belonging to the i-th cluster, depending of the model identification structure, are concatenated into a single parameter vector, θ_i, for example:

$$\theta_i = \left[a_i^T, b_i^T\right] \tag{18}$$

X_{reg} gives the extended regressor matrix, depending too of the model identification structure. Assuming that each cluster represents a local linear model of the system, the consequent parameter vectors θ_i, $i = 1, 2, \cdots, c$, can be estimated independently by the weighted least-squares method. The membership degrees μ_{ik} of the fuzzy partition serve as the weights expressing the relevance of the data pair (x_k, y_k) to that local model. If the columns of X_{reg} are linearly independent and $\mu_{ik} > 0$ for $1 \leq k \leq N$, then

$$\theta_i = \left[X_{reg}^T \Omega_i X_{reg}\right]^{-1} X_{reg}^T \Omega_i y \tag{19}$$

Since that,

$$\tilde{y}_k = f_i\left(x_k; \theta_i\right) \tag{20}$$

where the functions f_i are parameterized by $\theta_i \in \Re^{p_i}$. We have,

$$\tilde{y}\left(\tilde{\mathbf{x}}\right) = \frac{\sum_{i=1}^{l} h_i\left(\tilde{\mathbf{x}}\right) \tilde{y}_i}{\sum_{i=1}^{l} h_i\left(\tilde{\mathbf{x}}\right)} \tag{21}$$

2.2.2 Controller design

Once a model of the plant is available, one can proceed with the controller design. The controller is designed to meet the performance requirements for the plant model. If the model is a good approximation of the plant, one would hope that the controller performance for the plant model to be close to that achieved when the same controller is applied to the plant. In this sence, the robust stability control problem is to find a control law which maintains system response and error signals within prescribed tolerances despite the effects of parametric variations on the plant. In this paper a robust fuzzy control design based on gain and phase margins specifications for nonlinear systems, in the continuous time domain, is proposed. A mathematical formulation based on Takagi-Sugeno fuzzy model structure as well as the PDC strategy is presented. Analytical formulas are deduced for the sub-controllers parameters, in the robust fuzzy controller rules base, according to the fuzzy model parameters of the fuzzy model plant to be controlled.

2.2.3 Implementation

In this step, a controller designed in previous step, which is shown to meet performance requirements for the plant model and is robust with respect possible plant model disturbances, is ready to be applied to the unknow plant. The implementation can be done using a digital computer, all though in some applications analog computers may be used too. Issue such as the type of computer available, the type of inference devices between the computer and the plant, software tools, etc., need to be considered priori. Computer speed and accuracy limitations may put constraints complexity of the complexity of the controller that may force the control engineer to go back to previous step or even first step to come up with a simpler controller without violating the performance requirements.
Another important aspect of implementation is the final adjustment or as often called the tuning, of the controller to improve performance be compensating for the plant model disturbances that are not accounted for during the design process. Tuning is often done by trial and error, and depends very much on the experience and intuition of control engineer. In this work, the adjusts are done based on gain and phase margin especifications.

2.3 Gain and phase margins especifications

A successfully designed control system should be always able to maintain stability and performance level in spite of disturbances in system dynamics and/or in the working environment to a certain degree. Gain margin and phase margin have always served as important measures of robustness. It is also known from classical control that phase margin is related to the damping of the system, and can therefore also serve as a performance measure (Franklin et al., 1986). Controller designs to satisfy gain margin and phase margin (GPM) criteria are not new (Franklin et al., 1986; Ogata, 2002).
The **Phase Margin** is that amount of additional phase lag at the gain crossover frequency required to bring the system to the verge of instability. The gain crossover frequency is the frequency at which $|G(j\omega)|$, the magnitude of the open-loop transfer function, is unity. The phase margin ϕ_m is 180° plus the phase angle $\angle G(j\omega)$ of the open-loop transfer function at the gain crossover frequency, or:

$$\phi_m = \angle G(j\omega) + \pi \tag{22}$$

The phase margin is positive for $\phi_m > 0$ and negative for $\phi_m < 0$. For a minimum-phase system[1] to be stable, the phase margin must be positive.
The **Gain Margin** is the reciprocal of the magnitude $|G(j\omega)|$ at the frequency at which the phase angle is $-180°$. Defining the phase crossover frequency ω_p, to be the frequency at which the phase angle of the open-loop transfer function equals $-180°$ gives the gain margin A_m:

$$A_m = \frac{1}{|G(j\omega_g)|} \tag{23}$$

The gain margin expressed in decibels is positive if A_m, is greater than unity and negative if A_m is smaller than unity. Thus, a positive gain margin (in decibels) means that the system is stable, and a negative gain margin (in decibels) means that the system is unstable. For a stable minimum-phase system, the gain margin indicates how much the gain can be increased

[1] Transfer functions having neither poles nor zeros in the right-half s plane are *minimum-phase* transfer functions, whereas those having poles and/or zeros in the right-half s plane are *nonminimum-phase* transfer functions

before the system becomes unstable. For an unstable system, the gain margin is indicative of how much the gain must be decreased to make the system stable. For a minimum-phase system, both the phase and gain margins must be positive for the system to be stable. Negative margins indicate instability. Proper phase and gain margins ensure us against variations in the system components and are specified for definite positive values. The two values bound the behavior of the closed-loop system near the resonant frequency. For satisfactory performance, the phase margin should be between 30° and 60°, and the gain margin should be greater than 6 dB. With these values, a minimum-phase system has guaranteed stability, even if the openloop gain and time constants of the components vary to a certain extent. Although the phase and gain margins give only rough estimates of the effective damping ratio of the closed-loop system, they do offer a convenient means for designing control systems or adjusting the gain constants of systems. the Figure 2 shows the gain and phase margins for two different systems.

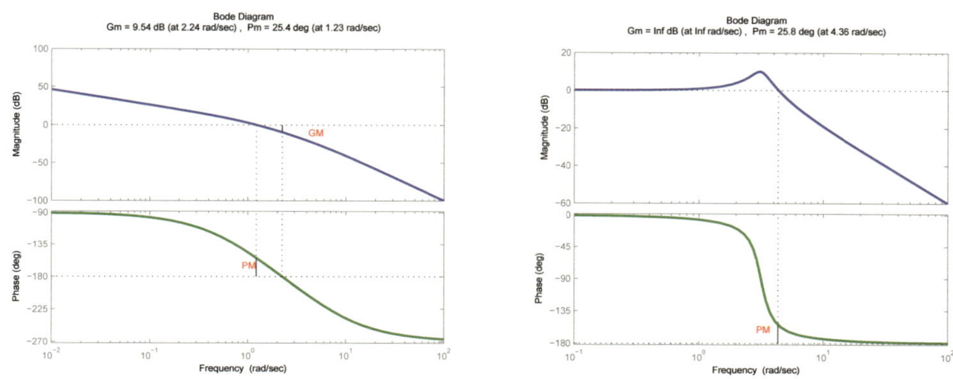

(a) $G_1 = 10/s(s+1)(s+5)$ (b) $G_2 = 10/(s^2+s+10)$

Fig. 2. The phase (9.54dB) and gain (25.4dB) margins of the system $10/s(s+1)(s+5)$ is showed in (a). The phase (25.8dB) and gain (inf.) margins of the system $10/(s^2+s+10)$ is showed in (b). Note that the gain margin of a first or second-order system is infinite since the polar plots for such systems do not cross the negative real axis.

For minimum-phase systems, the magnitude and phase characteristics of the openloop transfer function are definitely related. The requirement that the phase margin be between 30° and 60° means that in a Bode diagram the slope of the log-magnitude curve at the gain crossover frequency should be more gradual than -40 dB/decade. In most practical cases, a slope of -20 dB/decade is desirable at the gain crossover frequency for stability. If it is -40 dB/decade, the systems could be either stable or unstable. (Even if the system is stable, however, the phase margin is small.) If the slope at the gain crossover frequency is -60 dB/decade or steeper, the system is most likely unstable.
Denote the process and the controller transfer function by $G_p(s)$ and $G_c(s)$, and the specified gain and phase margins by A_m and ϕ_m, respectively. The formulas for gain margin and phase margin are as follows:

$$arg\left[G_c(j\omega_p)G_p(j\omega_p)\right] = -\pi \tag{24}$$

$$A_m = \frac{1}{\left|G_c(j\omega_p)G_p(j\omega_p)\right|} \tag{25}$$

$$\left|G_c(j\omega_g)G_p(j\omega_g)\right| = 1 \tag{26}$$

$$\phi_m = arg\left[G_c(j\omega_g)G_p(j\omega_g)\right] + \pi \tag{27}$$

where the gain margin is defined by Eqs. 24 and 25, and the phase margin by Eqs. 26 and 27. The frequency ω_p at which the Nyquist curve has a phase of $-\pi$ is known in classical terminology as the phase crossover frequency, and the frequency ω_g at which the Nyquist curve has an amplitude of 1 as the gain crossover frequency.

2.4 Parallel Distributed Compesation (PDC) strategy

The history of the so-called parallel distributed compensation (PDC) began with a model-based design procedure proposed by Wang (Wang et al., 1995). The PDC offers a procedure to design a fuzzy controller from a given T-S fuzzy model. To realize the PDC, a controlled plant is first represented by a T-S fuzzy model. In the PDC design, each control rule is designed from the corresponding rule of a T-S fuzzy model. The designed fuzzy controller shares the same fuzzy sets with the fuzzy model in the premise parts. The Figure 3 shows the concept of PDC design.

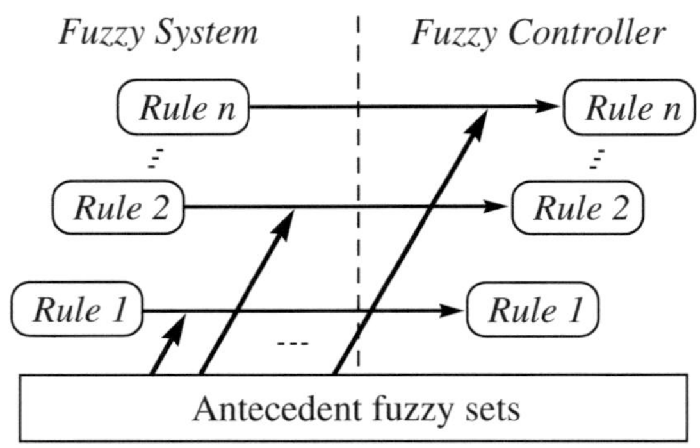

Fig. 3. In the PDC strategy, the fuzzy controller shares the same fuzzy sets with the fuzzy system.

In this paper is presented an fuzzy robust model based control scheme from the TS fuzzy model structure, the PDC strategy and gain and phase margins robust specifications. In the proposed methodology, the fuzzy controller parameters, with TS structure, are obtained through analytical formulas from the definition of gain and phase margins specifications. The robust fuzzy controller designed and the TS fuzzy model of the plant model to be controlled shares the same fuzzy sets, in the antecedents. In the fuzzy inference engine the sub-controller is selected based on the plant dynamic behavior and the gain and phase margins robust specifications. The dynamic system class under analysis for the fuzzy control design structure of the robust control is proposed with the objective to obtain the above robustness characteristics, from generalized analytical formulas.

3. Robust fuzzy control based on gain and phase margins especifications

In this section, the robust fuzzy control methodology based on gain and phase margins especifications are presented.

3.1 TS fuzzy dynamic model

The TS fuzzy inference system for a second-order plant, $G_p(s)$,presents in the $i|^{[i=1,2,\ldots,l]}$-th rule, without loss of generality, the following structure:

$$R^{(i)}: \quad IF \;\; \tilde{\tau} \;\text{is}\; F^i_{k|\tilde{\tau}} \;\; AND \;\; \tilde{\tau}' \;\text{is}\; G^i_{k|\tau'} \;\; AND \;\; \tilde{K}_p \;\text{is}\; H^i_{k|\tilde{K}_p}$$

$$\text{THEN} \;\; G^i_p(s) = \frac{K^i_p}{(1+s\tau^i)(1+s\tau'^i)} e^{-sL} \tag{28}$$

The time constants $\tilde{\tau}$ and $\tilde{\tau'}$, where $\tilde{\tau} \geq \tilde{\tau}'$, and the gain $\tilde{K}_p$, represent the linguistic variables of the antecedent. The activation degree of h_i for the rule i, is given by:

$$h_i\left(\tilde{\tau}, \tilde{\tau'}, \tilde{K}_p\right) = \mu^i_{F_{k|\tilde{\tau}^*}} \otimes \mu^i_{G_{k|\tilde{\tau}'^*}} \otimes \mu^i_{H_{k|\tilde{K}^*_p}} \tag{29}$$

The normalized activation degree for the rule i, is given by:

$$\gamma_i\left(\tilde{\tau}, \tilde{\tau}', \tilde{K}_p\right) = \frac{h_i\left(\tilde{\tau}, \tilde{\tau}', \tilde{K}_p\right)}{\sum\limits_{\lambda=1}^{l} h_\lambda\left(\tilde{\tau}, \tilde{\tau}', \tilde{K}_p\right)} \tag{30}$$

And, this normalization implies

$$\sum_{i=1}^{l} \gamma_i\left(\tilde{\tau}, \tilde{\tau}', \tilde{K}_p\right) = 1 \tag{31}$$

Therefore, the TS fuzzy model, $G^i_p(s)$, of the plant is a weighted sum of second order linear sub-models, as follow:

$$G_p\left(s, \tilde{\tau}, \tilde{\tau'}, \tilde{K}_p\right) = \sum_{i=1}^{l} \gamma_i\left(\tilde{\tau}, \tilde{\tau'}, \tilde{K}_p\right) \frac{K^i_p}{(1+s\tau^i)(1+s\tau'^i)} e^{-sL} \tag{32}$$

3.2 TS robust fuzzy controller

The TS fuzzy inference system proposed for the fuzzy controller, $G_c(s)$, whereas the definition of parallel distributed compensation, presents in the $j|^{[j=1,2,\ldots,l]}$ -th rule, without loss of generality, is given by:

$$R^{(j)}: \quad IF \;\; \tilde{\tau} \;\text{is}\; F^j_{k|\tilde{\tau}} \;\; AND \;\; \tilde{\tau}' \;\text{is}\; G^j_{k|\tau'} \;\; AND \;\; \tilde{K}_p \;\text{is}\; H^j_{k|\tilde{K}_p}$$

$$\text{THEN} \;\; G^j_c(s) = \frac{K^j_c\left(1+sT^j_I\right)\left(1+sT^j_D\right)}{sT^j_I} \tag{33}$$

The activation degree h_j for the rule j, is given by:

$$h_j\left(\tilde{\tau},\tilde{\tau}',\tilde{K}_p\right) = \mu^j_{F_{k|\tilde{\tau}^*}} \otimes \mu^j_{G_{k|\tilde{\tau}'^*}} \otimes \mu^j_{H_{k|\tilde{K}_p^*}} \tag{34}$$

where $\tilde{\tau}^*$, $\tilde{\tau}'^*$ and $\tilde{K}_p^*$ are some point in $U_{\tilde{\tau}}, U_{\tilde{\tau}'}$ and $U_{\tilde{K}_p}$, respectively. The normalized activation degree for the rule j, is given by:

$$\gamma_j\left(\tilde{\tau},\tilde{\tau}',\tilde{K}_p\right) = \frac{h_j\left(\tilde{\tau},\tilde{\tau}',\tilde{K}_p\right)}{\sum\limits_{\lambda=1}^{l} h_\lambda\left(\tilde{\tau},\tilde{\tau}',\tilde{K}_p\right)} \tag{35}$$

And, this normalization implies

$$\sum_{j=1}^{l} \gamma_j\left(\tilde{\tau},\tilde{\tau}',\tilde{K}_p\right) = 1 \tag{36}$$

Therefore, the TS fuzzy model for the fuzzy controller, $G_c\left(\tilde{\tau},\tilde{\tau}',\tilde{K}_p,s\right)$, is a weighted sum of the local fuzzy sub-controllers, as follows:

$$G_c\left(s,\tilde{\tau},\tilde{\tau}',\tilde{K}_p\right) = \sum_{i=1}^{l} \gamma_j\left(\tilde{\tau},\tilde{\tau}',\tilde{K}_p\right) \frac{K_c^j\left(1+sT_I^j\right)\left(1+sT_D^j\right)}{sT_I^j} \tag{37}$$

The compensated open-loop fuzzy model (Figure 4), according to the PDC strategy, with the controller and the plant, from the equations 32 and 37, respectively, is

$$G_p(s)G_c(s) = \sum_{j=1}^{l}\sum_{i=1}^{l} \gamma_j\left(\tilde{\tau},\tilde{\tau}',\tilde{K}_p\right)\gamma_i\left(\tilde{\tau},\tilde{\tau}',\tilde{K}_p\right) \times \tag{38}$$

$$\times \frac{K_c^j K_p^i\left(1+sT_I^j\right)\left(1+sT_D^j\right)}{sT_I^j\left(1+s\tau^i\right)\left(1+s\tau'^i\right)} e^{-sL}$$

3.3 Robust stability based on gain and phase margins

Denote the process and the controller transfer function by $G_p(s)$ and $G_c(s)$, and the specified gain and phase margins by A_m and ϕ_m, respectively, as defined previously in the Section 2.3. The formulas for gain margin and phase margin, in the fuzzy context, are as follows::

$$arg\left[G_c(\tilde{\tau},\tilde{\tau}',\tilde{K}_p,j\omega_p)G_p(\tilde{\tau},\tilde{K}_p,j\omega_p)\right] = -\pi \tag{39}$$

$$A_m = \frac{1}{\left|G_c(\tilde{\tau},\tilde{\tau}',\tilde{K}_p,j\omega_p)G_p(\tilde{\tau},\tilde{K}_p,j\omega_p)\right|} \tag{40}$$

$$\left|G_c(\tilde{\tau},\tilde{K}_p,j\omega_g)G_p(\tilde{\tau},\tilde{\tau}',\tilde{K}_p,j\omega_g)\right| = 1 \tag{41}$$

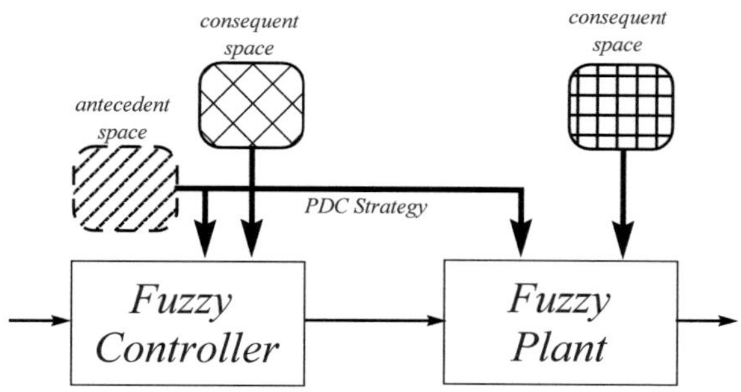

Fig. 4. Controller and plant fuzzy model in open-loop share the same fuzzy sets in the antecedent space.

$$\phi_m = arg\left[G_c(\tilde{\tau}, \tilde{K}_p, j\omega_g)G_p(\tilde{\tau}, \tilde{\tau}', \tilde{K}_p, j\omega_g)\right] + \pi \tag{42}$$

Replacing the equation 38 in 39-42, it has:

$$l\left[\sum_{i=1}^{l}\left(\arctan\left(\omega_p T_I^i\right) - \arctan\left(\omega_p \tau^i\right)\right) - \frac{\pi}{2} - \omega_g L\ \right] = -\pi \tag{43}$$

$$A_m = \frac{1}{\sum_{j=1}^{l}\sum_{i=1}^{l}\gamma_j\left(\tilde{\tau}, \tilde{\tau}', \tilde{K}_p\right)\gamma_i\left(\tilde{\tau}, \tilde{\tau}', \tilde{K}_p\right)\left(\frac{K_c^j K_p^i}{\omega_p T_I^j}\right)\left(\sqrt{\frac{\left(\omega_p T_I^j\right)^2 + 1}{\left(\omega_p \tau^i\right)^2 + 1}}\right)} \tag{44}$$

$$\sum_{j=1}^{l}\sum_{i=1}^{l}\gamma_j\left(\tilde{\tau}, \tilde{\tau}', \tilde{K}_p\right)\gamma_i\left(\tilde{\tau}, \tilde{\tau}', \tilde{K}_p\right)\left(\frac{K_c^j K_p^i}{\omega_g T_I^j}\right)\left(\sqrt{\frac{\left(\omega_g T_I^j\right)^2 + 1}{\left(\omega_g \tau^i\right)^2 + 1}}\right) = 1 \tag{45}$$

$$\phi_m = l\left[\sum_{i=1}^{l}\left(\arctan\left(\omega_g T_I^i\right) - \arctan\left(\omega_g \tau^i\right)\right) - \frac{\pi}{2} - \omega_p L\right] + \pi \tag{46}$$

For a given linear sub-model, $G^i(s, \tilde{K}_p^i, \tilde{\tau}^i, \tilde{\tau}'^i)$, and gain and phase margins specifications (A_m, ϕ_m), the Equations 43-46 can be used to determine the parameters of the PID sub-controllers, $G_c^j(s, K_c^j, T_I^j, T_D^j)$. Therefore, using the approximation of arctan function in the case $|x| > 1$, the Equations 44 and 45 are given by:

$$\sum_{j=1}^{l}\sum_{i=1}^{l}\gamma_j\left(\tilde{\tau}, \tilde{\tau}', \tilde{K}_p\right)\gamma_i\left(\tilde{\tau}, \tilde{\tau}', \tilde{K}_p\right)\frac{A_m}{\omega_p}\left(\frac{K_c^j K_p^i}{\tau^i}\right) = 1 \tag{47}$$

$$\sum_{j=1}^{l}\sum_{i=1}^{l}\gamma_j\left(\tilde{\tau}, \tilde{\tau}', \tilde{K}_p\right)\gamma_i\left(\tilde{\tau}, \tilde{\tau}', \tilde{K}_p\right)\left(\frac{K_c^j K_p^i}{\omega_g \tau^i}\right) = 1 \tag{48}$$

respectively. Using the same approach, the Equations 43 and 46 are given by:

$$l\left[\sum_{i=1}^{l}\left(\frac{\pi}{4\omega_p\tau^i}-\frac{\pi}{\omega_p T_I^i}-\frac{\pi}{2}-\omega_p L\right)\right]=-\pi \tag{49}$$

$$\phi_m=l\left[\sum_{i=1}^{l}\left(\frac{\pi}{4\omega_g\tau^i}-\frac{\pi}{\omega_g T_I^i}-\frac{\pi}{2}-\omega_g L\right)\right]+\pi \tag{50}$$

respectively. Therefore, the analytical solution for the tuning of the PID sub-controllers parameters, $G_c^j(s)\Big|^{[i=1,2,\ldots,l]}$, according to Equations 47-50, is given by

$$T_D^j=\tau'^i \tag{51}$$

$$\begin{bmatrix} \sum_{i=1}^{l}\gamma_i\left(\tilde{\tau},\tilde{\tau}',\tilde{K}_p\right)\left(\frac{K_p^i}{\tau^i}\right) & \cdots & \sum_{i=1}^{l}\gamma_i\left(\tilde{\tau},\tilde{\tau}',\tilde{K}_p\right)\left(\frac{K_p^i}{\tau^i}\right) \\ \sum_{i=1}^{l}\gamma_i\left(\tilde{\tau},\tilde{\tau}',\tilde{K}_p\right)\left(\frac{K_p^i}{\tau^i}\right) & \cdots & \sum_{i=1}^{l}\gamma_i\left(\tilde{\tau},\tilde{\tau}',\tilde{K}_p\right)\left(\frac{K_p^i}{\tau^i}\right) \end{bmatrix}\times$$

$$\times\begin{bmatrix} \gamma_1\left(\tilde{\tau},\tilde{\tau}',\tilde{K}_p\right) & \cdots & 0 \\ \vdots & \ddots & \vdots \\ 0 & \cdots & \gamma_l\left(\tilde{\tau},\tilde{\tau}',\tilde{K}_p\right) \end{bmatrix}\begin{bmatrix} K_c^1 \\ \vdots \\ K_c^l \end{bmatrix}=\begin{bmatrix} \frac{\omega_p}{A_m} \\ \omega_g \end{bmatrix} \tag{52}$$

and

$$\begin{bmatrix} l\frac{\pi}{\omega_p} & \cdots & l\frac{\pi}{\omega_p} \\ l\frac{\pi}{\omega_g} & \cdots & l\frac{\pi}{\omega_g} \end{bmatrix}\begin{bmatrix} \left(T_I^1\right)^{-1} \\ \vdots \\ \left(T_I^l\right)^{-1} \end{bmatrix}=\begin{bmatrix} l\left\{\sum_{i=1}^{l}\left(\frac{\pi}{4\omega_p\tau^i}\right)-\frac{\pi}{2}-\omega_p L\right\}+\pi \\ l\left\{\sum_{i=1}^{l}\left(\frac{\pi}{4\omega_g\tau^i}\right)-\frac{\pi}{2}-\omega_g L\right\}-\phi_m+\pi \end{bmatrix} \tag{53}$$

where ω_p is given by:

$$\omega_p=\frac{A_m\phi_m+\frac{1}{2}\pi A_m(A_m-1)}{(A_m^2-1)L} \tag{54}$$

3.3.1 Robust stability analysis

For the design of robust fuzzy PID controller, from Equations 51-53, respectively, based on the gain and phase margins specifications, the following Axiom and Theorems are proposed:

Axiom: *The linear sub-models,* $G_p^i(s)\left|^{[i=1,2,\ldots,l]}\right.$*, of the plant, are necessarily of minimum phase, i.e., all poles of the characteristic equation are placed in the left half-plane of the complex plane.*

Theorem 1: Each robust PID sub-controller, $G_c^j(s)\left|^{[j=1,2,\ldots,l]}\right.$, guarantee the gain and phase margins specifications for the linear sub-model, $G_p^i(s)\left|^{[i=1,2,\ldots,l]}\right.$ with $i = j$, of the plant to be controlled.

Proof: The normalized activation degree, in a given operating point, on the rules base of the robust PID fuzzy controller, satisfies the following condition:

$$\sum_{i=1}^{l} \gamma_j\left(\tilde{\tau},\tilde{\tau}',\tilde{K}_p\right) = 1 \tag{55}$$

The total normalized activation degree, for a simple p-th rule activated, as defined in the equation 4, is given by

$$\gamma_p\left(\tilde{\tau},\tilde{\tau}',\tilde{K}_p\right) = 1 \tag{56}$$

Based on the Parallel Distributed Compensation strategy, it has

$$\begin{bmatrix} \gamma_p\left(\tilde{\tau},\tilde{\tau}',\tilde{K}_p\right)\left(\frac{K_p^p}{\tau^p}\right) & \cdots & \gamma_p\left(\tilde{\tau},\tilde{\tau}',\tilde{K}_p\right)\left(\frac{K_p^p}{\tau^p}\right) \\ \\ \gamma_p\left(\tilde{\tau},\tilde{\tau}',\tilde{K}_p\right)\left(\frac{K_p^p}{\tau^p}\right) & \cdots & \gamma_p\left(\tilde{\tau},\tilde{\tau}',\tilde{K}_p\right)\left(\frac{K_p^p}{\tau^p}\right) \end{bmatrix} \times$$

$$\times \begin{bmatrix} 0 & 0 & \ldots & 0 \\ 0 & \gamma_1\left(\tilde{\tau},\tilde{\tau}',\tilde{K}_p\right) & \ldots & 0 \\ 0 & 0 & \ldots & 0 \\ \vdots & \vdots & \ddots & \vdots \\ 0 & 0 & \ldots & 0 \end{bmatrix} \begin{bmatrix} 0 \\ K_c^p \\ 0 \\ \vdots \\ 0 \end{bmatrix} = \begin{bmatrix} \frac{\omega_p}{A_m} \\ \\ \omega_g \end{bmatrix} \tag{57}$$

Solving the Equation 57 for K_c, it has

$$\gamma_p\left(\tilde{\tau},\tilde{\tau}',\tilde{K}_p\right)\left(\frac{K_p^p}{\tau^p}\right)\gamma_p\left(\tilde{\tau},\tilde{\tau}',\tilde{K}_p\right)\left(K_c^p\right) = \frac{\omega_p}{A_m} \tag{58}$$

and

$$\gamma_p\left(\tilde{\tau},\tilde{\tau}',\tilde{K}_p\right)\left(\frac{K_p^p}{\tau^p}\right)\gamma_p\left(\tilde{\tau},\tilde{\tau}',\tilde{K}_p\right)\left(K_c^p\right) = \omega_g \tag{59}$$

Isolating K_c^p, the Equation 58, is given by:

$$K_c^p = \left(\frac{\tau^p}{K_p^p}\right)\left(\frac{\omega_p}{A_m}\right)\left(\frac{1}{\gamma_p\left(\tilde{\tau},\tilde{\tau}',\tilde{K}_p\right)^2}\right) \tag{60}$$

To obtain the parameter T_I^p, in a given time, as defined previously, it has:

$$\begin{bmatrix} l\frac{\pi}{\omega_p} \dots l\frac{\pi}{\omega_p} \\ l\frac{\pi}{\omega_g} \dots l\frac{\pi}{\omega_g} \end{bmatrix} \begin{bmatrix} 0 \\ \left(T_I^p\right)^{-1} \\ \vdots \\ 0 \end{bmatrix} = \begin{bmatrix} l\left(\frac{\pi}{4\omega_p\tau^p} - \frac{\pi}{2} - \omega_p L\right) + \pi \\ l\left(\frac{\pi}{4\omega_g\tau^p} - \frac{\pi}{2} - \omega_g L\right) + \pi - \phi_m \end{bmatrix} \tag{61}$$

which results in

$$\left(\frac{\pi}{4\omega_p\tau^p} - \frac{\pi}{2} - \omega_p L\right) + \pi \tag{62}$$

and

$$l\frac{\pi}{\omega_g}\frac{1}{T_I^p} = l\left(\frac{\pi}{4\omega_g\tau^p} - \frac{\pi}{2} - \omega_g L\right) + \pi - \phi_m \tag{63}$$

Isolating ϕ_m, the Equation 63, is given by:

$$\phi_m = l\left(\frac{\pi}{4\omega_g\tau^p} - \frac{\pi}{\omega_g}\frac{1}{T_I^p} - \frac{\pi}{2} - \omega_g L\right) + \pi \tag{64}$$

and,

$$\gamma_p\left(\tilde{\tau},\tilde{\tau}',\tilde{K}_p\right)\gamma_p\left(\tilde{\tau},\tilde{\tau}',\tilde{K}_p\right)\left(\frac{K_p^p A_m}{\tau^p\omega_p}\right) \times$$

$$\left(\frac{\tau^p\omega_p}{K_p^p A_m}\right)\left(\frac{1}{\gamma_p\left(\tilde{\tau},\tilde{\tau}',\tilde{K}_p\right)\gamma_p\left(\tilde{\tau},\tilde{\tau}',\tilde{K}_p\right)}\right) = 1 \tag{65}$$

and

$$A_m = A_m \tag{66}$$

Assuming, in a given time, the total activation of a simple rule p, as defined previously, in Equation 35, we have:

$$\phi_m = l\left(\frac{\pi}{4\omega_g\tau^p} - \frac{\pi}{\omega_g T_I^p} - \frac{\pi}{2} - \omega_g L\right) + \pi \tag{67}$$

Comparing the Equation 67 with 64, it has

$$\phi_m = \phi_m \tag{68}$$

From those analysis, the robust fuzzy PID controller guarantee the gain and phase margins specifications for the plant to be controlled.

Theorem 2: Each robust PID sub-controller, $G_c^j(s)\Big|^{[j=1,2,\ldots,l]}$, guarantee the stability for all linear sub-models, $G_p^i(s)\Big|^{[i=1,2,\ldots,l]}$, of the non-linear plant to be controlled.

Proof: The closed-loop transfer function is given by:

$$G_{MF}\left(s,\tilde{\tau},\tilde{\tau}',\tilde{K}_p\right) = \sum_{j=1}^{l}\sum_{i=1}^{l}\gamma_j\left(\tilde{\tau},\tilde{\tau}',\tilde{K}_p\right)\gamma_i\left(\tilde{\tau},\tilde{\tau}',\tilde{K}_p\right)\frac{K_c^j K_p^i\left(1+sT_I^j\right)e^{-sL}}{\left[sT_I^j\left(1+s\tau^i\right)+K_c^j K_p^i\left(1+sT_I^j\right)\right]} \tag{69}$$

For the stability condition, the characteristic equation of the closed-loop transfer function, given in Equation 69, must have roots (poles) in the left half-plane of the complex plane (negative real part). Therefore, it has

$$\sum_{i=1}^{l}\sum_{j=1}^{l}\gamma_i\left(\tilde{\tau},\tilde{\tau}',\tilde{K}_p\right)\gamma_j\left(\tilde{\tau},\tilde{\tau}',\tilde{K}_p\right)\left[sT_I^j\left(1+s\tau^i\right)+ +K_p^i K_c^j\left(1+sT_I^j\right)\right]=0 \tag{70}$$

$$\sum_{i=1}^{l}\sum_{j=1}^{l}\gamma_i\left(\tilde{\tau},\tilde{\tau}',\tilde{K}_p\right)\gamma_j\left(\tilde{\tau},\tilde{\tau}',\tilde{K}_p\right)\left[\tau^i T_I^j s^2+ +\left(T_I^j+K_p^i K_c^j T_I^j\right)s+\left(K_p^i K_c^j\right)\right]=0$$

By application of the Routh Stability Criterion Franklin et al. (1986) in 69, it has

$$\begin{array}{c|cc} s^2 & \tau^i T_I^j & K_p^i K_c^j \\ s^1 & (T_I^j + K_p^i K_c^j T_I^j) & 0 \\ s^0 & K_p^i K_c^j & \end{array} \tag{71}$$

And, it is necessary that all terms of the first column are positive:

$$\tau^i T_I^j > 0 \tag{72}$$

$$(T_I^j + K_p^i K_c^j T_I^j) > 0 \tag{73}$$

$$K_p^i K_c^j > 0 \tag{74}$$

Since the parameters of the stable sub-models of the plant to be controlled (τ^i, τ'^i e K_p^i), according to **Axiom**, are positive as well as the gain and phase margins specifications (A_m e ϕ_m), from Equations 51-53, the values of the robust fuzzy PID controller parameters (K_c^j, T_I^j, T_D^j) are positive. Therefore, the inequalities, in Equations 72-74, are satisfied, and each robust PID sub-controller guarantee the stability for all sub-models of the plant to be controlled.

4. Computational results

This section describes the experimental results of the robust fuzzy control method in this paper.

4.1 Dynamic system description

To illustrate the proposed robust fuzzy control method in this paper, a simulation example is carried out for a one-link robotic manipulator showed in Figure 5. The dinamic equation of the one-link robotic manipulator is given by:

$$ml^2\ddot{\theta} + d\dot{\theta} + mglsin(\theta) = u \tag{75}$$

with,

$m = 1kg$, payload,
$l = 1m$, length of link,
$g = 9.81m/s^2$, gravitational constant,
$d = 1kgm^2/s$, damping factor,
u =control variable (kgm^2/s^2).

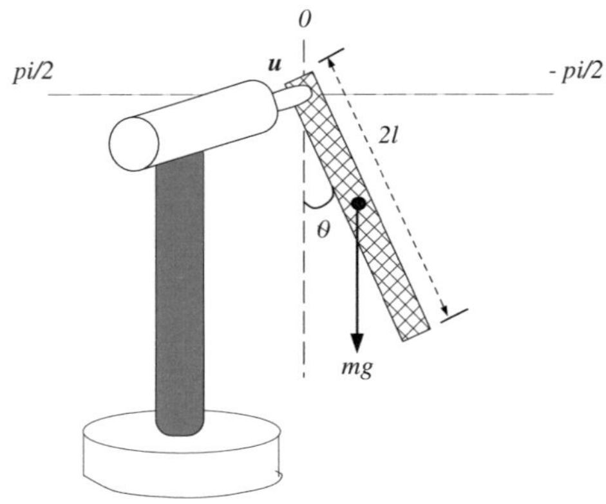

Fig. 5. One-link robotic manipulator.

This process has as input the torque, and as output the robotic manipulator angular position, denoted by θ.

4.2 Data collection

Several simulations were performed to collect suitable identification and validation data. The input of the system were excited with chirp signal. The left plots in Figure 6 show the input signal and the right plot shows the corresponding output.

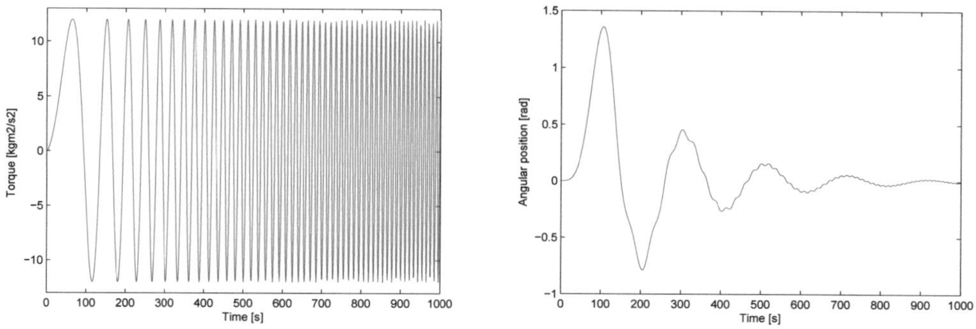

Fig. 6. Identification data set

4.3 Takagi-Sugeno fuzzy model

Based on the prior knowledge about the process, a second-order structure in transfer function terms was selected, resulting in TS rules of the following form:

$$\textbf{IF} \quad \tilde{\theta}(t) \quad \textbf{is} \quad A^i_{k|\tilde{\theta}} \quad \textbf{THEN} \quad G^i_p(s) = \frac{b^i}{s^2 + a^i_1 s + a^i_2} e^{-sL} \tag{76}$$

where $\tilde{\theta}(t)$ is the angular position at the time t. The membership functions of the antecedent linguistic term $A^i_{k|\tilde{\theta}}$, as well as the consequent parameters b^i, a^i_1 and a^i_2 were estimated from the data by fuzzy clustering, as described in subsection 2.2.1.

First the data matrix $\mathbf{Z}$ is formed, which contains the regressors $u(t), \dot{\theta}(t)$ and $\ddot{\theta}(t)$:

$$\mathbf{Z} = \begin{bmatrix} u(1) & \dot{\theta}(1) & \ddot{\theta}(1) \\ u(2) & \dot{\theta}(2) & \ddot{\theta}(2) \\ \vdots & \vdots & \vdots \\ u(t-1) & \dot{\theta}(t-1) & \ddot{\theta}(t-1) \end{bmatrix} \tag{77}$$

All the clustering algorithms, described in this paper, was applied to the data, but the GK algorithm has selected. We choose the fuzzification factor $m = 2$ and the termination criterion $\epsilon = 0.001$. The clusters number varied from 2 to 5. Due the lower mean square error or MSE obtained for five clusters, as show in Figure 8, the following data classification and clustering, as show in Figure 7, is obtained.

Each obtained cluster corresponds to one rule of the TS fuzzy model. The antecedent membership degrees are directly obtained in the product space of the antecedent variable, and the consequent parameters are estimated by weighted least-squares method. Using the identification method based on fuzzy clustering, the following five TS rules, to plant model, were extracted from identification data:

$$\textit{Rule } 1: \quad \textbf{IF} \quad \tilde{\theta}(t) \quad \textbf{is} \quad A^1_{k|\tilde{\theta}} \quad \textbf{THEN} \quad G^1_p(s) = \frac{1.001}{s^2 + 1.014s + 9.464} e^{-0.1s}$$

$$\textit{Rule } 2: \quad \textbf{IF} \quad \tilde{\theta}(t) \quad \textbf{is} \quad A^2_{k|\tilde{\theta}} \quad \textbf{THEN} \quad G^2_p(s) = \frac{0.998}{s^2 + 1.002s + 9.125} e^{-0.1s}$$

$$Rule\ 3: \quad \textbf{IF} \quad \tilde{\theta}(t) \quad \textbf{is} \quad A^3_{k|\tilde{\theta}} \quad \textbf{THEN} \quad G^3_p(s) = \frac{0.892}{s^2 + 0.706s + 7.828} e^{-0.1s}$$

$$Rule\ 4: \quad \textbf{IF} \quad \tilde{\theta}(t) \quad \textbf{is} \quad A^4_{k|\tilde{\theta}} \quad \textbf{THEN} \quad G^4_p(s) = \frac{0.999}{s^2 + 1.023s + 9.389} e^{-0.1s}$$

$$Rule\ 5: \quad \textbf{IF} \quad \tilde{\theta}(t) \quad \textbf{is} \quad A^5_{k|\tilde{\theta}} \quad \textbf{THEN} \quad G^5_p(s) = \frac{0.998}{s^2 + 0.991s + 9.342} e^{-0.1s}$$

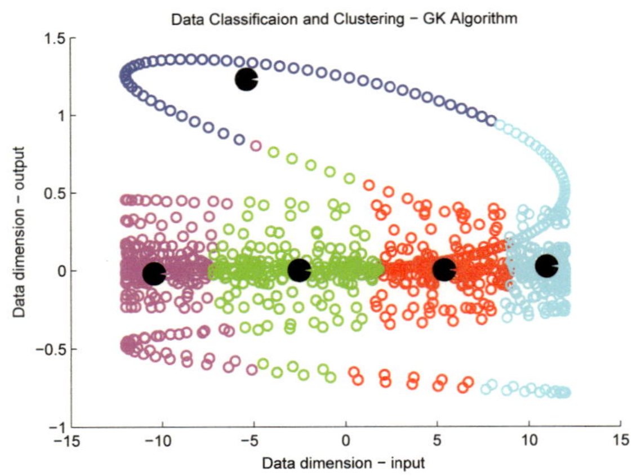

Fig. 7. The dark dots represents the obtained clusters and data classification. Each cluster represents the estimated local sub-models.

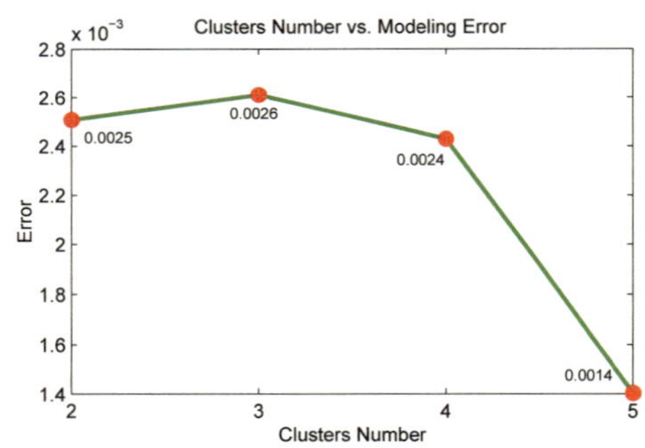

Fig. 8. Modeling error vs. clusters number.

Validation was performed on a different data set than the one used for identification. From Figure 9 one can see that the TS model follows the process output with a reasonable accuracy.

4.4 Robust fuzzy control based on gain and phase margins

Based on the PDC strategy, each control rule in the robust fuzzy controller rules base is designed from the corresponding rule of the TS fuzzy model. The designed fuzzy controller shares the same fuzzy sets with the fuzzy model in the premise parts. The robust fuzzy controller rule base is:

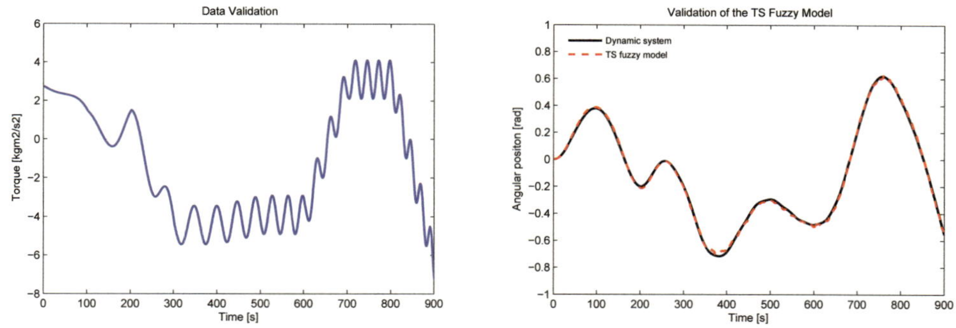

Fig. 9. Validation of the TS fuzzy model. Solid line: dynamic system, dashed line: TS fuzzy model.

$$Rule\ 1: \quad \textbf{IF} \quad \tilde{\theta}(t) \quad \textbf{is} \quad A^{1}_{k|\tilde{\theta}} \quad \textbf{THEN} \quad G^{1}_{c}(s) = \frac{0.647s^2 + 3.292s + 3.979}{0.507s}$$

$$Rule\ 2: \quad \textbf{IF} \quad \tilde{\theta}(t) \quad \textbf{is} \quad A^{2}_{k|\tilde{\theta}} \quad \textbf{THEN} \quad G^{2}_{c}(s) = \frac{0.643s^2 + 3.258s + 3.939}{0.500s}$$

$$Rule\ 3: \quad \textbf{IF} \quad \tilde{\theta}(t) \quad \textbf{is} \quad A^{3}_{k|\tilde{\theta}} \quad \textbf{THEN} \quad G^{3}_{c}(s) = \frac{0.389s^2 + 2.199s + 3.107}{0.353s}$$

$$Rule\ 4: \quad \textbf{IF} \quad \tilde{\theta}(t) \quad \textbf{is} \quad A^{4}_{k|\tilde{\theta}} \quad \textbf{THEN} \quad G^{4}_{c}(s) = \frac{0.662s^2 + 3.349s + 4.019}{0.511s}$$

$$Rule\ 5: \quad \textbf{IF} \quad \tilde{\theta}(t) \quad \textbf{is} \quad A^{5}_{k|\tilde{\theta}} \quad \textbf{THEN} \quad G^{5}_{c}(s) = \frac{0.624s^2 + 3.190s + 3.898}{0.495s}$$

For robust fuzzy controller design, different gain margins and phase margins are specified for the model of robotic manipulator plus dead-time in Table 1. Observed that among the gain and phase margins specifications obtained (marked by *), to $A_m = 2$ and $\phi_m = 45$, and $A_m = 3$ and $\phi_m = 60$ the phase margin is quite close to the specified ones. The largest error occurred for gain margin. The dead-time process is 0.1s and the Padé approximation order is 2.

Specified		**Resultant**	
A_m	ϕ_m	A_m^*	ϕ_m^*
6.02	45	12.62	48.86
9.54	45	12.9	20.23
13.98	45	13.8	36.58
9.54	60	13.7	60.28
13.98	60	14.1	66.30

Table 1. Gain and phase margins obtained from the especifications.

The Figure 10 shows the results obtained with the fuzzy robust controller based on gain and phase margins specifications plus the TS fuzzy model. As well as the gain and phase margins resulting.

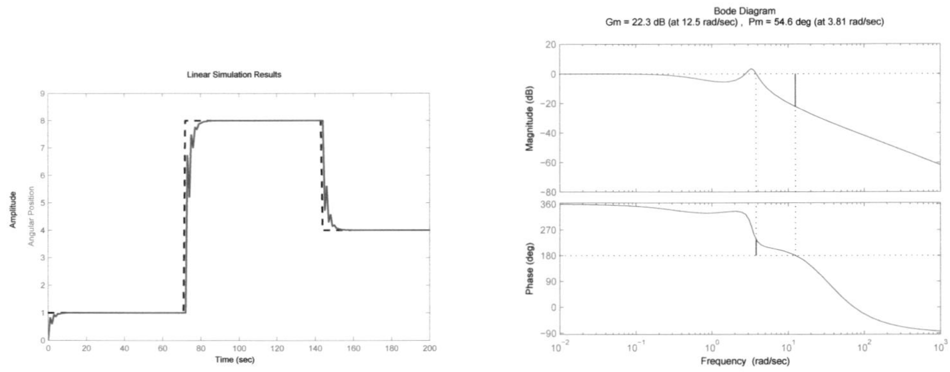

Fig. 10. Performance of the robust fuzzy controller based on the gain and phase margins specifications. The dashed line is the reference and the solid line is the robotic manipulator model with the robust fuzzy controller.

5. Conclusion

This paper presented a proposal for analysis and design of robust fuzzy control, for non-linear systems based on gain and phase margins specifications. From the proposed analysis and design, it has the following final remarks:

- The TS fuzzy model, due to the flexibility to incorporate in its structure the linear sub-models of the non-linear plant made possible, via PDC strategy, the design of robust fuzzy sub-controllers;
- The proposed Axiom and Theorems guaranteed the robust stability, since all formulation and analysis were made in the frequency domain, based on gain and phase margins specifications;
- As noted, the identification method based on fuzzy clustering is effective for modeling the robotic manipulator;
- The proposed robust fuzzy controller, based on gain and phase margins specifications, guarantees the stability of the obtained model as observed.

6. Acknowledgment

The authors thank National Council of Scientific and Technological Development (CNPq) for financial support of this research.

7. References

Balas, G., Fialho, I., Lee, L., Nablantoglu, V., Packard, A., W. Tan, E. Wenhoff, G. W. & Wu, F. (1997). *Theory and Application of Linear Parameter Varying Control Techniques*, 1997 ACC Workshop notes.

Barton, Z. (2004). Robust control in a multimachine power system using adaptive neuro-fuzzy stabilisers, *IEE Proceedings on Generation, Transmission and Distribution* 115: 261–267.

Bezdek, J. (1981). *Pattern Recognition with Fuzzy Objective Function*, New York.

Castro-Sitiriche, M., Rubaai, A. & Ofoli, A. (2008). Design and implementation of parallel fuzzy pid controller for high-performance brushless motor drives: An integrated environment for rapid control prototyping, *IEEE Transactions on Industry Applications* 44(7): 1090–1098.

Cetin, S. & Demir, O. (2008). Fuzzy pid controller with coupled rules for a nonlinear quarter car model, *Proceedings of World Academy of Science, Engineering and Technology*, Vol. 31, pp. 238–241.

Cheng, X., Lei, Z. & Junqiu, Y. (2009). Fuzzy pid controller for wind turbines, *Second International Conference on Intelligent Networks and Intelligent Systems*, pp. 74–77.

Dong, J., Wang, Y. & Yang, G.-H. (2009). Control synthesis of continuous-time t-s fuzzy systems with local nonlinear models, *Systems, Man, and Cybernetics, Part B: Cybernetics, IEEE Transactions on* 39(5): 1245–1258.

Franklin, G., Powell, J. D. & Baeini, A. (1986). *Feedback control of dynamic systems*, Addison-Wesley.

Gath, I. & Geva, A. (1989). Unsupervised optimal fuzzy clustering, *IEEE Trans. Pattern Analysis and Machine Intelligence* 7: 773–781.

Ibrahim, A. (2003). *Fuzzy Logic for Embedded Systems Applications*, Elsevier Science, USA.

Jain, A. & Dubes, R. (1988). *Algorithms for Clustering Data*, Prentice Hall.

Mishra, S., Dash, P. & Panda, G. (2000). Ts-fuzzy controller for upfc in a multimachine power system, *Generation, Transmission and Distribution, IEE Proceedings-* 147(1): 15–22.

Ogata, K. (2002). *Modern Control Engineering*, 4th edn, Prentice-Hall, NJ.

Park, J., Oh, C., Bang, H. & Tahk, M. (2007). *An experimental study on attitude control of spacecraft using fuzzy controller*, Dept. of Aerospace Engineering, Korea, Advanced Institute of Science and Technology.

Pelladra, P., Apkarian, P. & Tuan, H. (2009). Missile autopilot design via a multi-channel lft/lpv control method, *International Journal Robust and Nonlinear Control* 12(1): 1–20.

Petros, A. & Sun, J. (1996). *Robust Adaptive Control*, PTR Prentice-Hall.

Serra, G. & Boturra, C. (2006). Genetic approach for neural scheduling of multiobjective fuzzy pi controllers, *International Symposium on Evolving Fuzzy Systems*, pp. 274–279.

Shamma, J. & Athans, M. (1991). Guaranteed properties of gain scheduled control for linear parameter varying plants, *Automatica* 27: 559–564.

Silva, J. & Serra, G. (2009). Gain-scheduled takagi-sugeno fuzzy pi control methodology for lpv systems, *2009 IEEE International Symposium on Computational Intelligence in Robotics and Automation (CIRA)*, pp. 222–227.

Takagi, T. & Sugeno, M. (1985). Fuzzy identification of systems and its applications to modeling and control, *Proceedings of the IEEE Transactions on Systems, Man and Cybernetics*, Vol. 15, pp. 116–132.

Tanaka, K. & Sugeno, M. (1993). Concept of stability margin of fuzzy systems and design of robust fuzzy controller, *2nd IEEE International Conference on Fuzzy Systems*, Vol. 1, pp. 29–34.

Wang, H., Tanaka, K. & Griffin, M. (1995). Parallel distributed compensation of nonlinear systems by takagi-sugeno fuzzy model, *5th IEEE International Conference on Fuzzy Systems*, Vol. 2, pp. 531–538.

Wen-Xu, Y., Zhi-Cheng, J. & Jin, H. (2009). Shunt active power filter line current control based on t-s fuzzy model, *4th IEEE Conference on Industrial Electronics and Applications, 2009*, pp. 2241 –2246.

Ying, H., Siler, W. & Buckley, J. (1990). Fuzzy control theory: a nonlinear case, *Automatica* 26: 513–520.

Zhan, X. (2010). Robust iterative learning control for nonlinear system based on t-s model, *2010 Chinese Control and Decision Conference (CCDC)* pp. 2115–2119.

3

Adaptive Fuzzy Modelling and Control for Non-Linear Systems Using Interval Reasoning and Differential Evolution

Jiangtao Cao[1], Ping Li[1] and Honghai Liu[2]
[1]*Liaoning Shihua University,*
[2]*University of Portsmouth*
[1]*China*
[2]*United Kingdom*

1. Introduction

Fuzzy systems have been developed to a major scientific domain since fuzzy set theory was introduced by Zadeh about four decades ago (Zadeh, 1965). There are certain particular properties of fuzzy systems that offer them better performance for specific applications. In general, fuzzy systems are suitable for uncertain or approximate reasoning, allow decision making with estimated values under incomplete information and represent descriptive or qualitative expressions which are easily incorporated with symbolic statements (Klir & Folger, 1987). However, under the general framework of typical fuzzy systems, some kinds of uncertainty cannot be handled, particularly in practical applications (Mendel & John, 2002; Ross, 2004; Hagras, 2004). Therefore, further flexibility can be obtained by considering the uncertainty in fuzzy systems which occur from qualitative knowledge and stochastic information.

As mentioned in (Mendel & John, 2002; Hagras, 2004; Liu & Li, 2005a), most of uncertainties in fuzzy systems can be embodied by the information of fuzzy membership functions. In order to expand fuzzy systems to solve more complex uncertainty, some novel methods have been proposed during recent decade. Type-2 fuzzy logic system (T2FLS) was proposed to model and control further uncertainties in typical fuzzy systems by using the secondary fuzzy membership functions (Karnik & Liang, 1999; Liang & Mendel, 2000a). The T2FLS was originally inspired by the fact that the typical FLS limits introducing uncertain factors from linguistic rules through predefined membership functions. The type-2 fuzzy methods can be roughly described that their fuzzy sets are further defined by the typical fuzzy membership functions, i.e., the membership degree of belonging for each element of these sets are fuzzy sets, not a crisp number (Liang & Mendel, 2000b; Karnik & Mendel, 2001; Wu & Mendel, 2009). In comparison with the typical FLS, a type-2 FLS has the two-fold advantages as follows. Firstly, it has the capability of directly handling the uncertain factors of fuzzy rules caused by expert experience or linguistic description. Secondly, it is efficient to employ a

[0]:Supported by Program for Liaoning Science and Technology Innovative Research Team in University(2007T103,LT2010058), the Program for Liaoning Excellent Talents in University(2008RC32) and a full PhD scholarship at University of Portsmouth, UK.

type-2 FLS to cope with scenarios in which it is difficult or impossible to determine an exact membership function and related measurement of uncertainties. These strengths have made researchers consider type-2 FLS as the preference for real-world applications (Sepúlveda et al., 2007; Astudillo et al., 2007).

From the viewpoint of real-time application, many researchers use interval type-2 fuzzy sets to solve the computational complexity of general type-2 fuzzy sets and have brought some application results(Wu & Mendel, 2002; Julio & Alberto, 2007). However, the computational expense on type reduction of type-2 FLS also is a bottleneck to use an type-2 FLS for real-time control applications(Mendel, 2007). Some new alternative ways have been provided to reduce the computational expense and to promote the applications (Castro et al., 2008; Hagras, 2008; Nie & Tan, 2008; Cao et al., 2008). Up to now, how to design an efficient type-2 FLS with less calculation and strong adaptive ability to overcome uncertainty of industrial control is still an open question.

By introducing the probabilistic information into fuzzy membership functions, the Probabilistic Fuzzy Logic Systems (PFLS) were established to handle stochastic uncertainties which occurred in complex plant dynamics (Liu & Li, 2005a;b). The mathematical expectation of fuzzy output centroid was calculated to perform defuzzification of PFLS. In spite of many research results, the problem of systematic handling uncertainty of fuzzy system has not yet been completely resolved.

In this paper, firstly, a systematic design method of extended fuzzy logic system (EFLS) is represented for engineering applications based on our previous research(Cao et al., 2009). By introducing the degree of uncertainty in membership functions, the EFLS can not only make use of typical fuzzy system which has been well developed, but also can expand its capability of handling uncertainty in complex circumstance. In the EFLS, the process is similar to conventional fuzzy system which includes fuzzification, inference engine and defuzzification. But in each part of this process, the operation methods are different. In the fuzzification, the EFLS uses the interval membership functions which are generated from typical membership functions. The inference engine is separated into two parts which perform fuzzy reasoning on inner and outer fuzzy subsystems, respectively. In the defuzzification, the outputs are calculated by weighted outputs of subsystems with novel adaptive optimal algorithm and feedback structure.

Secondly, under the above framework of EFLS, the adaptive fuzzy control system is designed to deal with the uncertainties from complex dynamics of control plant by integrating the global optimization method : Differential Evolution(DE). The main difference in this adaptive control system is the defuzzification part. For dealing with the variable control target and solving the nonlinear optimization performance, the crisp outputs are derived from the interval of outputs of subsystems by the DE optimization method. For evaluating the framework of EFLS, it is applied on the inverse kinematics modelling problem of a two-joint robotic arm. The adaptive fuzzy control system is implemented on a typical nonlinear quarter car active suspension system.

The paper is organized as follows. In Section 2 the interval fuzzy membership functions with degree of uncertainty are addressed. A systematic design method based on interval fuzzy membership functions and adaptive optimal algorithm is represented in Section 3. The novel adaptive fuzzy control system with DE method is designed in Section 4. Simulations on the two-joint robotic arm and the quarter car active suspension system are investigated in Section 5, finally the paper is concluded with concluding remarks and future work in Section 6.

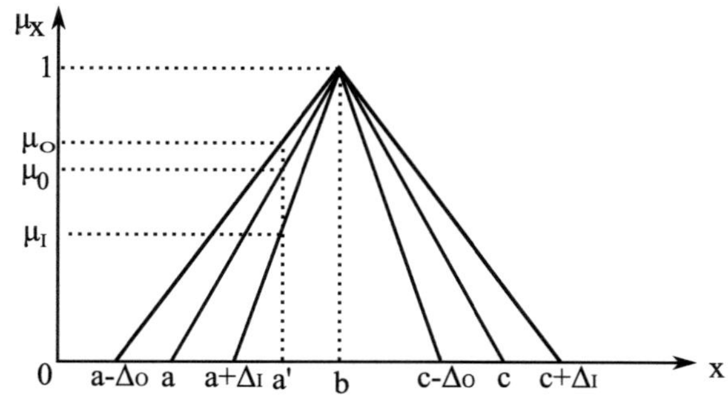

Fig. 1. Degree of uncertainty in fuzzy membership function

2. Interval fuzzy membership function generation methods

Although fuzzy systems have been used in different scientific and engineering applications, the phenomenon of uncertainty in typical fuzzy systems has been studied and some novel methods have been proposed to cover more uncertainties. Type-2 fuzzy methods expanded the typical fuzzy systems by a secondary membership function. The PFLS methods proposed the probabilistic fuzzy membership functions to represent the stochastic uncertainty in fuzzy systems. However, it is still a difficult task to completely solve all problems caused by uncertainty in fuzzy systems.

Generally, there are three types of uncertainty which mainly occur in conventional fuzzy methods. First type is uncertainty due to variability of inputs and/or model parameters. Second type is uncertainty due to understanding of linguistic knowledge and quantification of fuzzy rules. Third type is uncertainty due to unknown process and/or unmodelled dynamics. In this section, by introducing the degree of uncertainty in fuzzy membership function, interval membership function generation method is proposed to build proper membership functions for covering possible uncertain information.

2.1 Degree of uncertainty in fuzzy membership function

Considering the natural property of uncertainty, there are many different methods to quantitatively describe it. Generally, there are three kinds of methods to quantify uncertainty. One is margin of uncertainty which is stated by giving a range of values around true value. The other is standard deviation of estimate value by repeating measurement enough times. The third one is fuzzy presentation by fuzzy sets and fuzzy rules. The second method has been used in PFLS and the third method was used in type-2 fuzzy systems. Here, the first method is used to define a margin of uncertainty for membership function which is called degree of uncertainty in fuzzy membership function. In this paper, the degree of uncertainty is used to describe possible uncertainty which is inherent in fuzzy membership functions.

As an example, a triangle membership function with degree of uncertainty is shown in Fig.1. For implementation, the center triangle membership function can be presented as $[a,b,c]$. It is deduced by expert knowledge or any training methods of fuzzy membership function. With degree of uncertainty, the proposed fuzzy membership function belongs to a bounded region which the outer and inner boundaries of membership function can be presented as $[a-\Delta_O,b,c+\Delta_O]$ and $[a+\Delta_I,b,c-\Delta_I]$. Here,$\Delta_O$ and Δ_I are defined as bounded values of uncertainty in fuzzy membership function and their values can be adaptive tuned by proposed method in Section 3. The inner and outer degrees of uncertainty are defined in equation 1.

$$\alpha = \frac{\Delta_O}{\Delta_O + \Delta_I}, \beta = \frac{\Delta_I}{\Delta_O + \Delta_I} \tag{1}$$

With the membership function $[a,b,c]$, the membership grade of crisp input a' is μ_0. However, with proposed interval membership function, the membership grade belongs to an interval domain $[\mu_I, \mu_O]$. The exact grade will depend on the bounded uncertainty and the proposed fuzzy system in Section 3.

2.2 Interval fuzzy membership functions

The proposed method simply uses an appropriate predefined typical fuzzy membership functions, such as triangular, trapezoidal, Gaussian, or S functions, to expand to the interval fuzzy membership functions with the degree of uncertainty. The following is an example of triangular membership function which can be expanded to interval membership function from typical membership function.
The typical triangular fuzzy membership function is

$$\mu(x;a,b,c) = \begin{cases} 0 & x \le a \\ \frac{x-a}{b-a} & a \le x \le b \\ \frac{c-x}{c-b} & b \le x \le c \\ 0 & x \le c \end{cases} \tag{2}$$

Based on the above fuzzy membership function, with the defined degree of uncertainty in Section 2.1, the interval fuzzy membership function can be represented as below.

$$\mu\left(x;a,b,c\right) = \begin{cases} 0 & x \le a - \Delta_O \\ \frac{x-a+\Delta_O}{b-a+\Delta_O} & a - \Delta_O \le x \le a + \Delta_I \\ \left[\frac{x-a-\Delta_I}{b-a-\Delta_I}, \frac{x-a+\Delta_O}{b-a+\Delta_O}\right] & a + \Delta_I \le x \le b \\ \left[\frac{c-\Delta_I-x}{c-\Delta_I-b}, \frac{c+\Delta_O-x}{c+\Delta_O-b}\right] & b \le x \le c - \Delta_I \\ \frac{c+\Delta_O-x}{c+\Delta_O-b} & c - \Delta_I \le x \le c + \Delta_O \\ 0 & x \ge c + \Delta_O \end{cases} \tag{3}$$

3. Systematic design of extended fuzzy logic system

A framework of EFLS for fuzzy modelling is proposed as Fig. 2. Similar to the typical FLS (Ross, 2004), the EFLS still has operations of fuzzification, inference engine and defuzzification. Different with the typical FLS, the EFLS uses the interval fuzzy membership functions which can be generated from typical fuzzy membership function. Thus the membership grade for the crisp input belongs to an interval which aims to expand the typical fuzzy sets to cover more uncertain information in practical applications. Considering the computational cost, the inference engine of EFLS is separated into two parts and the reasoning results are presented by two typical boundary FLSs. With the fuzzy interval reasoning results, a novel adaptive algorithm is established to transfer them into expected crisp output.

3.1 Fuzzification of EFLS

Considering a T-S fuzzy model represented as the general form:
$R^{(k)}$: IF z_1 is F_1^k and z_2 is F_2^k, ..., and z_m is F_m^k, THEN $x(t+1)$ is $g^k(X,U)$, here, $k \in K := 1,2,\ldots,n$

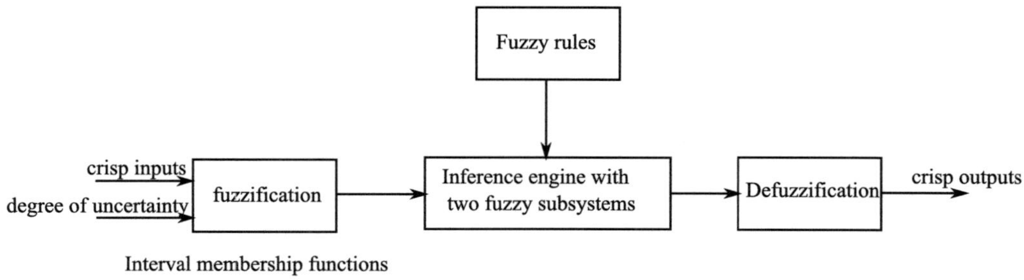

Fig. 2. The framework of interval fuzzy logic system

Here R^k denotes the kth fuzzy rule, n denotes the number of fuzzy rules, m denotes the number of input variables, $F_j^k(j = 1,2,\ldots,m) = (F_j^k(inner), F_j^k(outer))$ denote the proposed interval fuzzy sets as shown in Section 2, $z(t) := [z_1, z_2, \ldots, z_m]$ denote measurable variables, $x(t) \in \Re^n$ denotes the state vector, $u(t) \in \Re^p$ denotes the input vector, and the T-S consequent term g_i^k is defined in equation 4.

$$g^k(X,U;\theta^k) = A_k x(t) + B_k u(t) \\ k \in K := 1,2,\ldots,n \tag{4}$$

where A_k and B_k are the parameter matrices of the kth local model.
Different with other fuzzy systems, the fuzzification of EFLS requires the predefined outer and inner degrees of uncertainty in fuzzy membership functions, that is α, β which can be defined by expert knowledge or the measurement data and predicted error boundary. These degrees of uncertainty are used to present the possible uncertainty due to the understanding of linguistic knowledge or unknowing system dynamic in fuzzy system. The structure of fuzzification is shown in Fig. 3. And all the degrees can be self-tuned by proposed adaptive algorithm in Section 3.3.
Based on these degrees of uncertainty and typical fuzzy sets, a crisp input variable is transferred into two fuzzy membership grades which belong to an interval region. From practice viewpoint, a bounded region of fuzzy membership grade will be more flexible to cover uncertain information.

3.2 Inference engine in EFLS

With the proposed fuzzification, each crisp input variable is changed to fuzzy value which relates to two fuzzy membership grades in a bounded fuzzy set. The fuzzy inference engine is separated into two parts to perform fuzzy reasoning on the inner boundary fuzzy subsystem S_{inner} and the outer boundary fuzzy subsystem S_{outer} as shown in Fig. 4. With the fixed fuzzy membership functions $F_j^k(inner)$ and $F_j^k(outer)$, typical fuzzy inference engines are used to perform fuzzy reasoning with the same fuzzy rules. However, since the degree of

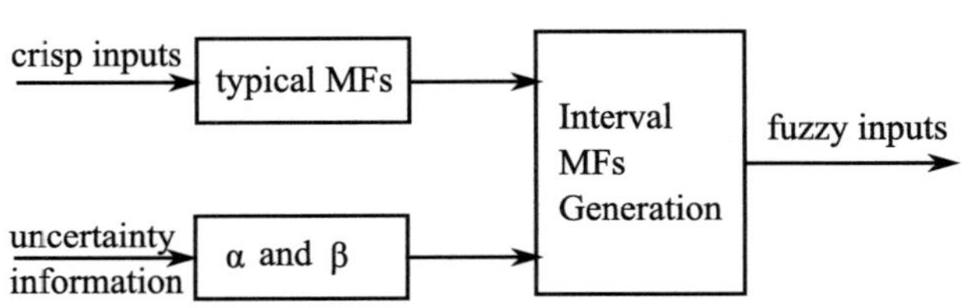

Fig. 3. The interval membership functions(MFs) generation

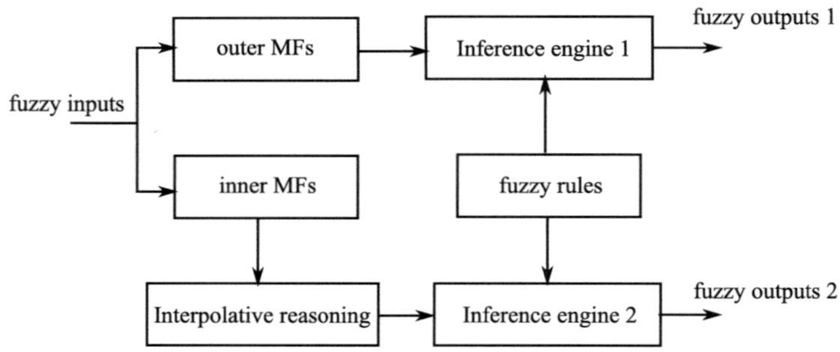

Fig. 4. The inference engine of EFLS

uncertainty is tuned in real time, the inner boundary fuzzy subsystem possibly becomes a sparse fuzzy rule-based system. That's means, for some inputs, their fuzzy sets are not defined or their fuzzy membership grade can't covered by neighbourhood membership functions. In order to deal with these problems, there have been many fuzzy interpolative reasoning methods for the sparse fuzzy systems (Baranyi et al., 2004; Huang & Shen, 2006; Lee & Chen, 2008). Considering the overlapping phenomenon in the inner boundary fuzzy subsystem, the method in (Lee & Chen, 2008) is used.
With the fuzzy rules in Section 3.1, the firing strength of the kth rule can be described as:

$$\mu_k^I = \mu_{F_1^k}^I * \mu_{F_2^k}^I * \cdots * \mu_{F_i^k}^{I(*)} * \cdots * \mu_{F_m^k}^I \geq 0 \tag{5a}$$

$$\mu_k^O = \mu_{F_1^k}^O * \mu_{F_2^k}^O * \cdots * \mu_{F_m^k}^O \geq 0 \tag{5b}$$

in which $\mu_k^I \in [0,1]$ and $\mu_k^O \in [0,1]$ denote the inner and outer grades of membership governed by the inner and outer fuzzy membership functions, respectively. Furthermore, $\mu_{F_i^k}^{I(*)}$ denotes the interpolative grade by the interpolative reasoning method. The fuzzy inference logic employs the max-min product to operate the fuzzy rules. The reasoning results are two fuzzy values which are deduced from two fuzzy subsystems.

3.3 Defuzzification and adaptive algorithm

The centroid calculation is used to obtain crisp outputs from two fuzzy reasoning results by typical defuzzification. Each crisp output corresponds to one bounded fuzzy subsystem. The two boundary outputs can be written as

$$\begin{aligned} x^I(t+1) &= \frac{\sum_{k=1}^{n} \mu_k^I [A_k x(t) + B_k u(t)]}{\sum_{k=1}^{n} \mu_k^I} \\ &= \sum_{k=1}^{n} h_k^I [A_k x(t) + B_k u(t)] \end{aligned} \tag{6a}$$

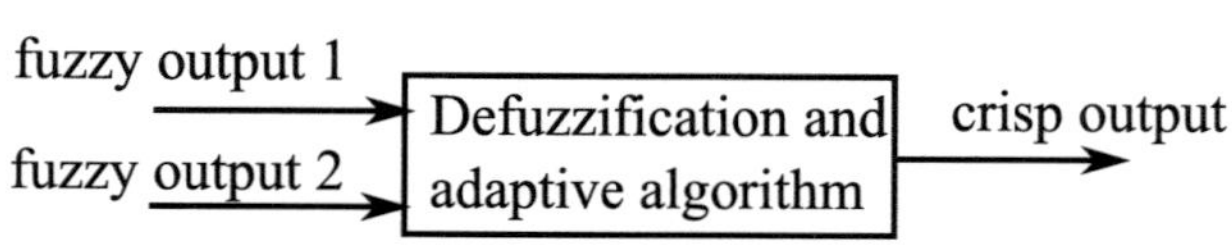

Fig. 5. The defuzzification of EFLS

$$x^O(t+1) = \frac{\sum_{k=1}^{n} \mu_k^O [A_k x(t) + B_k u(t)]}{\sum_{k=1}^{n} \mu_k^O} = \sum_{k=1}^{n} h_k^O [A_k x(t) + B_k u(t)] \tag{6b}$$

where

$$h_k^I = \frac{\mu_k^I}{\sum_{k=1}^{n} \mu_k^I}, h_k^O = \frac{\mu_k^O}{\sum_{k=1}^{n} \mu_k^O} \tag{7}$$

And,

$$\begin{array}{l} h_k^I \geq 0, h_k^O \geq 0, k = 1, 2, \cdots, n \\ \sum_{i=1}^{n} h_k^I = 1, \sum_{i=1}^{n} h_k^O = 1 \end{array} \tag{8}$$

For interpreting the uncertain information inherent in these two subsystems, an adaptive algorithm is established to get final crisp outputs. The algorithm can be presented as follows. Let $y_I = x^I(t+1)$ and $y_O = x^O(t+1)$,

$$e_O = y^* - y_O, e_I = y^* - y_I \tag{9}$$

here, y^* is the reference value, measurement value or objective function for system modelling. Let $\tilde{e}_I = |e_I|$ and $\tilde{e}_O = |e_O|$, the crisp output of EFLS is

$$y = f(y_O, y_I) = \frac{\tilde{e}_O}{\tilde{e}_O + \tilde{e}_I} y_I + \frac{\tilde{e}_I}{\tilde{e}_O + \tilde{e}_I} y_O \tag{10}$$

The system error is

$$e = y^* - y \tag{11}$$

In order to tune the degree of uncertainty to deal with uncertainties, the adaptive algorithm is presented as follows.
If the condition is

$$e_O e_I < 0, and, \tilde{e}_O > \tilde{e}_I \tag{12}$$

then the inner degree of uncertainty is kept as the same, and the outer degree of uncertainty will be tuned as

$$\alpha = (1 - \Delta\alpha)\alpha \tag{13}$$

here,

$$\Delta\alpha = \eta_O \cdot \frac{\tilde{e}_O}{\tilde{e}_O + \tilde{e}_I} \tag{14}$$

and η_O is the tuning factor for the outer subsystem. If the condition is

$$e_O e_I < 0, and, \tilde{e}_O < \tilde{e}_I \tag{15}$$

then the outer degree of uncertainty is kept as the same, and the inner degree of uncertainty will be tuned as

$$\beta = (1 - \Delta\beta)\beta \tag{16}$$

here,

$$\Delta\beta = \eta_I \cdot \frac{\tilde{e}_I}{\tilde{e}_O + \tilde{e}_I} \tag{17}$$

and η_I is the tuning factor for the inner subsystem. If the condition is

$$e_O e_I > 0, and, \tilde{e}_O > \tilde{e}_I \tag{18}$$

then the outer degree of uncertainty is kept as the same, and the inner degree of uncertainty will be tuned as

$$\beta = (1 + \Delta\beta)\beta \tag{19}$$

here, $\Delta\beta$ can be solved by equation 17.
If the condition is

$$e_O e_I > 0, and, \tilde{e}_O < \tilde{e}_I \tag{20}$$

then the inner degree of uncertainty is kept as the same, and the outer degree of uncertainty will be tuned as

$$\alpha = (1 + \Delta\alpha)\alpha \tag{21}$$

here, $\Delta\alpha$ can be solved by equation 14.
Once the outer and inner degree of uncertainty are tuned to new values, by solving the equation 1, the new values of Δ_O and Δ_I are obtained. Then the new bounded region for uncertainty is rebuilt.

3.4 Systematic design of EFLS

With the information of section 3.1-3.3, a systematic procedure is obtained to design the EFLS for system modelling.

- Step 1) Determine the state variables, their typical fuzzy membership functions and fuzzy rules.
- Step 2) Define the degrees of uncertainty in membership functions and build the interval membership functions for all the input variables by equations 1-3.
- Step 3) Obtain the input and output data of modelled process.
- Step 4) Calculate the fuzzy reasoning results by equation 10 and the system error by equation 11.
- Step 5) Perform on-line adaptive algorithm to update the degree of uncertainty by equations 12-21. Then back to the second step to rebuild the interval membership functions and recalculate the system outputs. Recycle this process until that system error reduces to an expected region.

4. Adaptive fuzzy control system

With the above systematic design of EFLS, a novel general framework of interval fuzzy reasoning system has been built. From the point of control system design, by implementing the DE to optimize the control performance on the interval reasoning results, an adaptive control structure is proposed in this section.

4.1 Design of the adaptive control system

Based on the reasoning results from subsystems as equations 6a- 6b, the further optimization process can be designed to find the optimal values which satisfy the required control performance. This adaptive control structure aims to rebuild the switching routes between the local subsystems.

With the proposed adaptive control structure, the crisp outputs of the control system can be recalculated as,

$$\underline{u}_c^* = \min\left\{x^I(t), x^O(t)\right\} \tag{22a}$$

$$\overline{u}_c^* = \max\left\{x^I(t), x^O(t)\right\} \tag{22b}$$

$$\begin{aligned} &\Gamma = f(\tilde{u}(t)) \\ &\tilde{u}(t) \in (\underline{u}_c^* + \Delta u_c^*, \underline{u}_c^* + 2\Delta u_c^*, \cdots, \overline{u}_c^*) \end{aligned} \tag{22c}$$

$$\Delta u_c^* = \frac{\overline{u}_c^* - \underline{u}_c^*}{n} \tag{23}$$

where $x^I(t)$ and $x^O(t)$ can be calculated from equations 6a and 6b, n denotes the re-sampling number, Γ denotes the further optimization goal, f is defined as a performance function of the system with variable $\tilde{u}(t)$. The control output $\tilde{u}(t)$ can be solved from equation 22c by the global optimization algorithm: DE algorithm. For clearly showing the details of optimal process, the DE method is represented in Section 4.2.

4.2 Differential evolution algorithms

DE method, recently proposed by Storn (Storn & Price, 1997), is one kind of evolutionary algorithms(EAs) which are a class of direct search algorithms. The main advantage of DE method is to converge fast and to avoid being trapped by local minim. It has been applied to several engineering problems in different areas(Storn, 1999; Abbass, 2002; Price et al., 2005; Brest et al., 2006). The main difference between the DE method and other EAs is the mutation scheme that makes DE self adaptive the selection process. In DE algorithms, all solutions have the same chance of being selected as parents without dependence of their fitness value. DE algorithm employs a greedy selection process: The better one of new solution and its parent wins the competition providing significant advantage of converging performance over other EAs (Karaboga et al., 2004).

As a population based algorithm, DE algorithms uses the similar operators as the genetic algorithms: crossover, mutation and selection. The main difference is that genetic algorithms rely on crossover while DE algorithm relies on mutation operation. The DE algorithm also uses a non-uniform crossover that can take child vector parameters from one parent more often than it does from others. By using the components of the existing population members to construct trial vectors, the crossover operator efficiently shuffles information about successful combinations, enabling the search for a better solution space.

The main steps of the DE algorithm is given below(Karaboga et al., 2004):

- *Initialization*
- *Evaluation*
- **Repeat**

    Mutation

    Recombination

    Evaluation

    Selection

- **Until**(termination criteria are met)

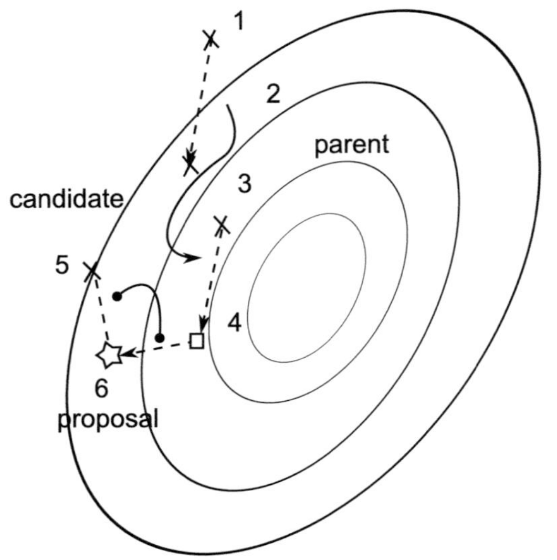

Fig. 6. Obtaining a new proposal in DE algorithm (Karaboga et al., 2004)

4.2.1 Mutation

For each target vector$x_{i,G}$, a mutant vector is produced by

$$u_{i,G+1} = x_{i,G} + K \cdot (x_{r1,G} - x_{i,G}) + F \cdot (x_{r2,G} - x_{r3,G}) \tag{24}$$

where $i, r1, r2, r3 \in 1, 2, \cdots, NP$ are randomly chosen and must be different from each other. In 24, F is the scaling factor which has an effect on the difference vector $(x_{r2,G} - x_{r3,G})$, K is the combination factor.

4.2.2 Crossover

The parent vector is mixed with the mutated vector to produce a trial vector $u_{ji,G+1}$ as below.

$$u_{ji,G+1} = \begin{cases} v_{ji,G+1} \text{if}(rnd_j \leq CR)\text{or} j = rn_i \\ q_{ji,G} \text{if}(rnd_j > CR)\text{and} j \neq rn_i \end{cases} \tag{25}$$

where $j = 1, 2, \cdots, D$; $r_j \in [0,1]$ is the random number; CR is crossover constant $\in [0,1]$ and $rn_i \in (1, 2, \cdots, D)$ is the randomly chosen index.

4.2.3 Selection

All solutions in the population have the same chance of being selected as parents without dependence of their fitness value. The child produced after the mutation and crossover operations is evaluated. Then, the performance of the child vector and its parent is compared and the better one is selected. If the parent is still better, it is retained in the population.

Figure6 shows DE algorithm process in detail. The difference between two population members (1,2) is added to a third population member(3). The result (4) is subject to the crossover with the candidate for replacement (5) to obtain a proposal (6). The proposal is evaluated and replaces the candidate if it is found to be better.

4.3 Systematic design of adaptive fuzzy control system

With the above information, the systematic control procedure of proposed method is obtained as follows.

- Step 1) Determine all the state variables, their typical fuzzy MFs and fuzzy rules.
- Step 2) Define the degrees of uncertainty in membership functions and build the interval membership functions for all the input variables by equations 1-3.
- Step 3) With the control plant and required control aims, design the optimization task and the related parameters for the DE algorithm.
- Step 4) Obtain the system inputs, the interval outputs are calculated with the proposed EFLS by equations 5a- 6b.
- Step 5) Calculate the fuzzy control outputs by further optimization structure with equations 22a - 23.
- Step 5) Perform the control outputs on the plant, the system inputs are updated and the system performance in further optimization part are also recalculated.
- Step 6) Return to the Step 4) to do the next interval fuzzy reasoning. Recycle this process until the expected system performance is obtained.

In comparison with the existed type-2 fuzzy control systems and PFLS, the proposed structure build a more general framework to represent the fuzzy modelling and control process. Under the proposed structure, the crisp output of the EFLS and the related control system represent two-fold information. One is the fuzzy rules which are extracted from expert knowledge or industrial experience. The other is the further optimal goal which is required by practical issues or is impossible to be combined into the fuzzy rules. With the optimization algorithms, the control performance will be improved and the optimal goal can be flexibly designed. For the purpose of evaluating the proposed structure, a inverse kinematics modelling of a two-joint robotic arm and a case study on a non-linear quart-vehicle active suspension system are presented in Section 5.

5. Simulations

5.1 Modelling by EFLS

In order to demonstrate the performance of proposed EFLS, the numerical simulations have been carried out on the inverse kinematics modelling of a two-joint robotic arm (Gan et al., 2005). The model of robotic arm is presented in Fig. 7.

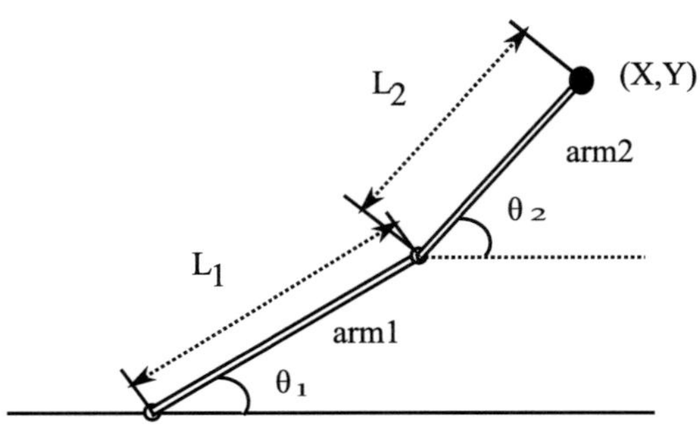

Fig. 7. The two-joint robotic arm with two angles

l	S_1	S_2	S_3
B_1	1	4	7
B_2	2	5	8
B_3	3	6	9

Table 1. The Antecedents of Fuzzy Rules

The inverse kinematics modelling is a typical problem in robotics. In a two-dimensional input space, with a two-joint robotic arm and the desired location, the problem reduces to find the angles between arms. For simple structures of the two-joint robotic arm, its dynamics is described as the following dynamical equations:

$$c_1 = \frac{x^2 + y^2 - L_1^2 - L_2^2}{2L_1L_2} \tag{26a}$$

$$c_2 = \sqrt{1 - c_1^2}, c_3 = L_1 + L_2c_1, c_4 = L_2c_2 \tag{26b}$$

$$\theta_1 = \arctan\frac{Y}{X} - \arctan\frac{c_4}{c_3} \tag{26c}$$

$$\theta_2 = \arctan\frac{c_2}{c_1} \tag{26d}$$

where, X, Y are the desired location, θ_1 and θ_2 are the corresponded angles as shown in Fig.7. The parameters are chosen as: $L_1 = 8$ and $L_2 = 5$.
With the fuzzy toolbox of MATLAB, the typical fuzzy system for this inverse kinematics problem is established which membership functions have been decided by hybrid neuro-fuzzy learning algorithm. Based on this typical fuzzy system, the proposed EFLS is designed. The inputs are the desired locations which are presented by the data pair (X,Y). Their typical membership functions are shown in Fig. 8 and Fig.9. The original uncertain margins are chosen as $\Delta_I = 0.4$ and $\Delta_O = 0.4$. The outputs are two angles. By the T-S fuzzy model, the fuzzy rules are described as:
$R^{(l)}$: IF X is S_p^l, and Y is B_q^l, THEN $\theta_1 = c_1^l X + c_2^l Y + c_3^l$, $\theta_2 = d_1^l X + d_2^l Y + d_3^l$, here, $l = 1,2,\ldots,9$, $p = 1,2,3$ and $q = 1,2,3$.
The antecedents are shown in TABLE 3 and the consequents are shown in TABLE 2.
The true values of angles are solved from equations 26a-26d. The predicted angles are obtained by the typical fuzzy system and the proposed EFLS, respectively. The comparisons of modelling results are performed by the error of predicted angles. For evaluating performance of the proposed EFLS, the inverse kinematics with or without noise are modelled and the predicted errors of two angles are shown in Fig.10-Fig.13.
According to the comparison of modelling errors in Fig.10 and Fig. 11, the proposed EFLS improved typical FLS to obtain better non-linear model of inverse kinematics. Also Fig.12 and Fig.13 both showed that robust and adaptive ability of the proposed EFLS was stronger than the typical FLS.
The simulation results have demonstrated the proposed EFLS can deal well with non-linear model and expanded the typical fuzzy system to handle uncertainty in complex circumstance.

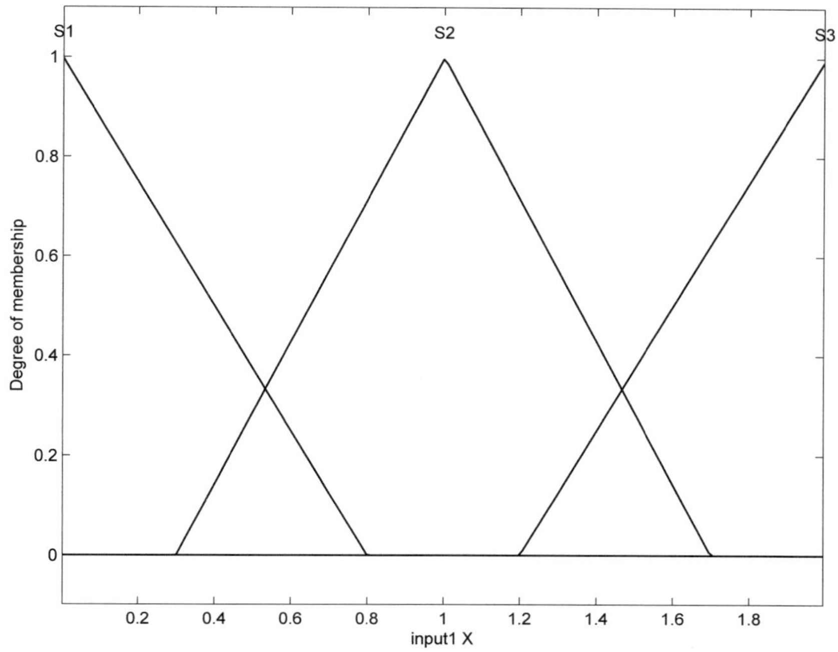

Fig. 8. The fuzzy membership functions of input X

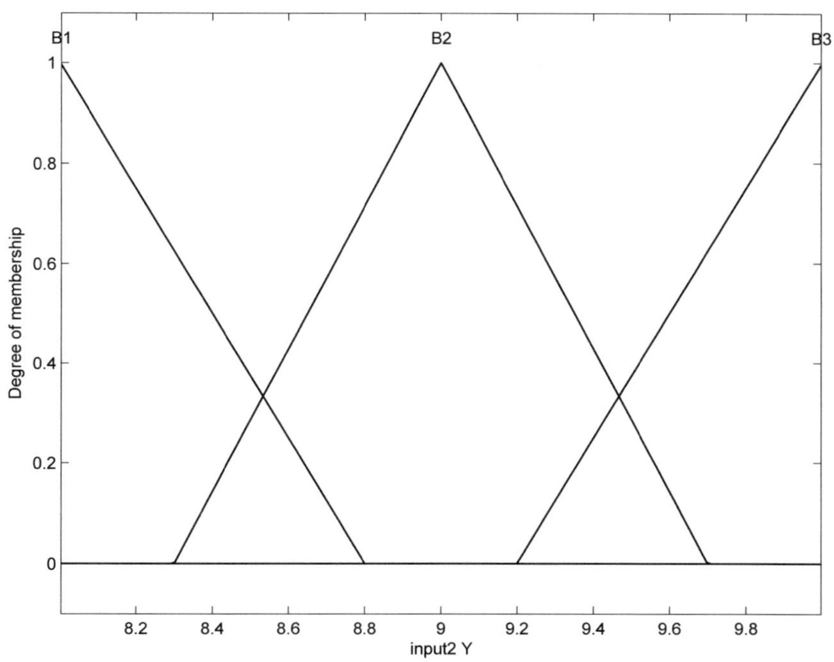

Fig. 9. The fuzzy membership functions of input Y

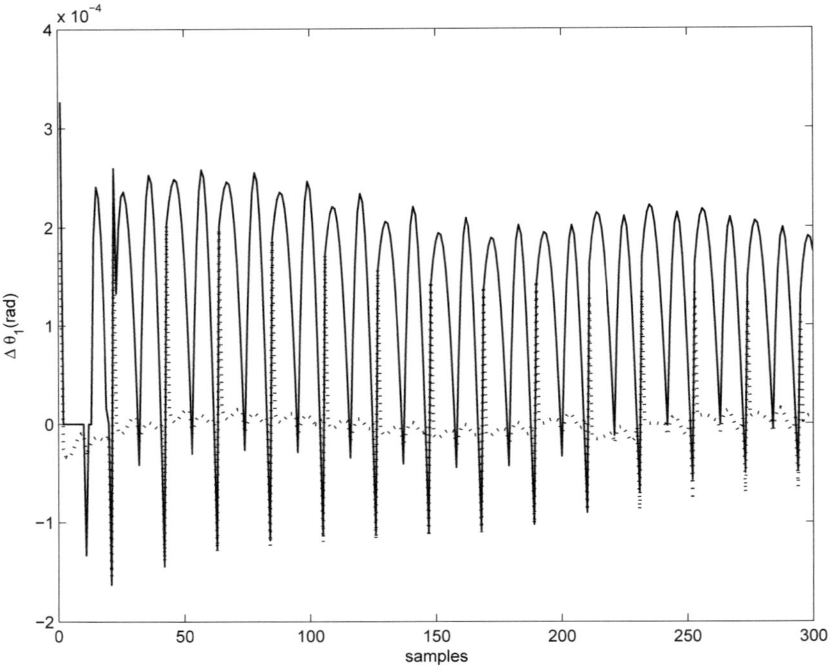

Fig. 10. The angle error of θ_1 by typical FLS(solid line) and EFLS(dot line)

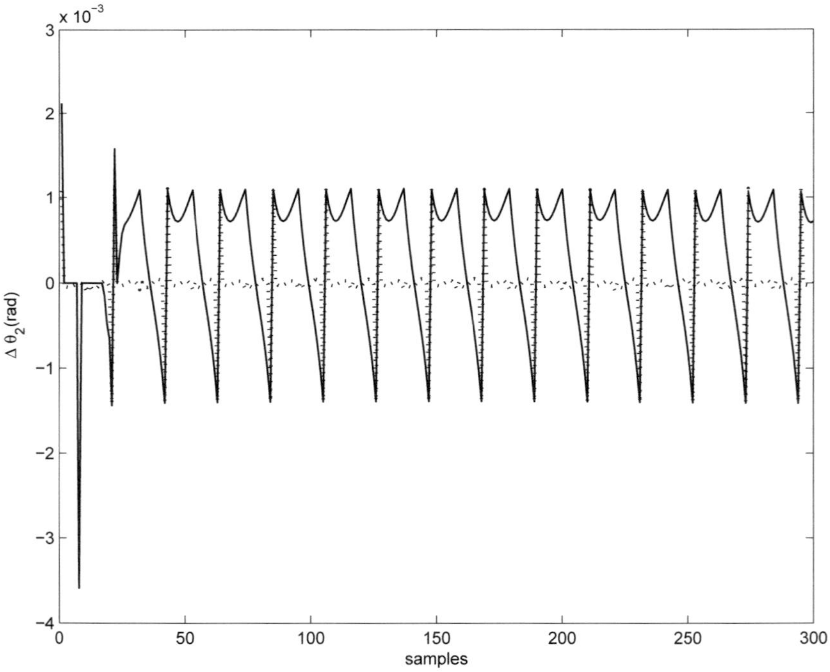

Fig. 11. The angle error of θ_2 by typical FLS(solid line) and EFLS(dot line)

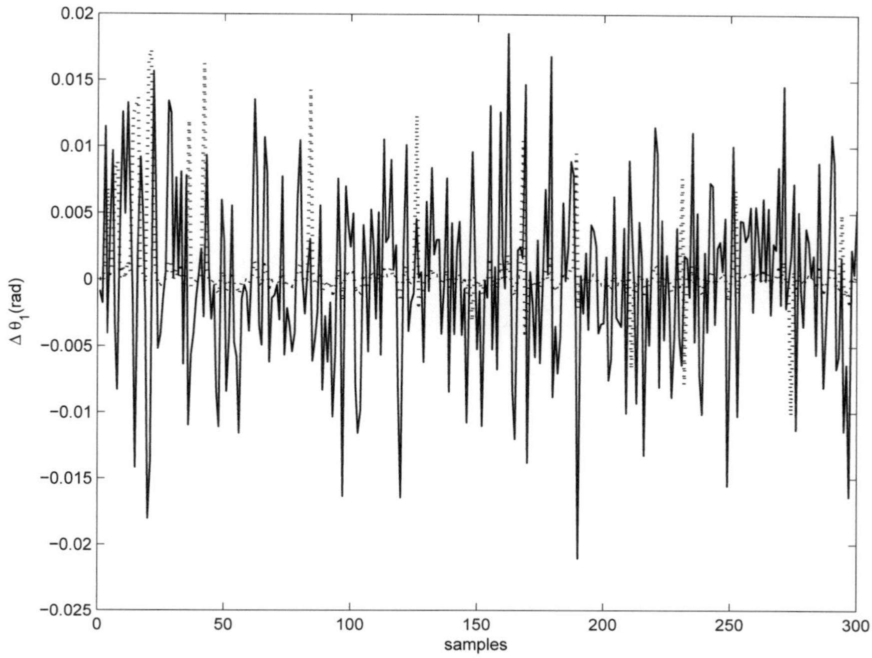

Fig. 12. The angle error of θ_1 by type-1 FLS(solid line) and EFLS(dot line) with random noise

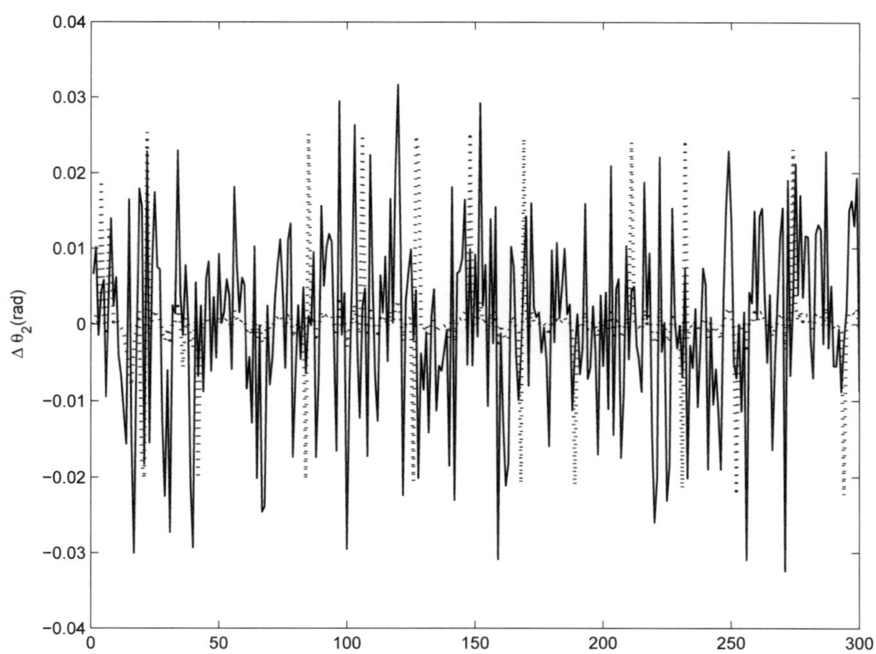

Fig. 13. The angle error of θ_2 by type-1 FLS(solid line) and EFLS(dot line) with random noise

l	c_1^l	c_2^l	c_3^l	d_1^l	d_2^l	d_3^l
1	-0.12	0.09	0.16	-0.01	0.19	0.36
2	-0.11	0.11	0.03	-0.01	0.18	0.03
3	-0.09	0.12	-0.11	-0.01	0.17	-0.26
4	-0.12	0.09	0.14	-0.03	0.19	0.35
5	-0.10	0.11	0.03	-0.03	0.18	0.28
6	-0.09	0.12	-0.10	-0.02	0.17	-0.26
7	-0.11	0.10	0.13	-0.04	0.19	0.35
8	-0.09	0.11	0.02	-0.04	0.19	0.03
9	-0.09	0.11	-0.09	-0.04	0.17	-0.25

Table 2. The Consequents of Fuzzy Rules

5.2 Control by the adaptive fuzzy control system and DE

For evaluating the performance of proposed adaptive fuzzy control system, the numerical simulations have been carried out on a quarter vehicle active suspension system as shown in Fig. 14 whose mathematical model was given in (Cao et al., 2008). Parameters of the model are provided in Table 3, partly from (Taghirad & Esmailzadeh, 1998).
The vehicle body velocities (*i.e.*, $\dot{z}_b$, $\dot{z}_w$), displacements (*i.e.*, z_b and z_w) are chosen as input variables, the actuator forces (*i.e.*, f_a is output variables. The original MFs of the inputs and outputs are provided in Fig. 15. Here, N means negative, Z means zero, P means positive. These typical MFs are used to build the interval fuzzy MFs by the method in section 2. With the assumption that the amplitude of uncertainty will not extend the one fifth of original variable, the original values of α and β are 0.2. Considering the balance between the convergence speed and stability of adaptive algorithm, the tuning factors (*i.e.*, η_I and η_O) are both 0.9. For simplicity, the MFs of outputs are chosen as typical MFs which are shown in Fig. 16. Here,

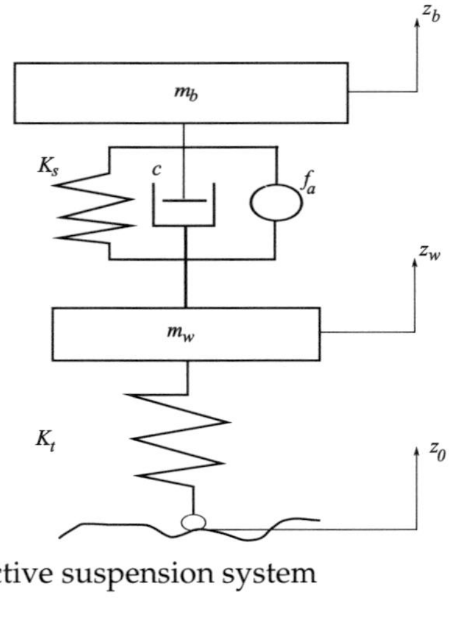

Fig. 14. The quarter vehicle active suspension system

$m_b(Kg)$	$m_w(Kg)$	k_{s0} (N)	k_{s1} (N/m)
1494.4	120.04	-136	70502
k_{s2} (Ns/m)	k_{s3} (N/m^3)	c_1 (Ns/m)	c_2 (Ns/m)
-10865	104	1290	426

Table 3. The Parameters of Quarter Vehicle Active Suspension

NB means negative big, NS means negative small, PS means positive small, PB means positive big. Since the main task is to improve the ride comfort by reducing the body acceleration, the reference variable y^* is defined as the body acceleration, the value is equal to zero. The vehicle speed is 20 m/s.

For evaluation propose, a passive suspension system and a typical FLC are also designed to compare with the proposed approach. The MFs for typical FLC are the original MFs in Fig. 15-Fig. 16.

According to the International Standardization Organization (ISO) classification using the Power Spectral Density (PSD), the class average and poor road surfaces are used as random road inputs, where their road roughness are 6.4×10^{-5} m^3/cycle and 2.56×10^{-4} m^3/cycle, respectively.

Here, two kinds of performance criteria are used to evaluate the vehicle suspension system. One is the root mean square (RMS) value which presents the vehicle ride comfort and handling performance from time domain(Hrovat, 1997). Another is the ride index of body vibration which focus on the ride comfort from frequency weighted vibrating accelerations(2631-1, 1997).

Average Road	VA(m/s^2)	TD (m)
Passive	4.5211×10^{-4}	1.2010×10^{-6}
FLC	4.1460×10^{-4}	2.1465×10^{-7}
Proposed method	4.0032×10^{-4}	1.8423×10^{-7}
Poor Road	VA(m/s^2)	TD (m)
Passive	2.4216×10^{-3}	3.1087×10^{-5}
FLC	1.5671×10^{-3}	1.6233×10^{-6}
Proposed method	1.3211×10^{-3}	1.4213×10^{-6}

[a]VA: Vehicle Accelerations, TD: Tyre Deflections

Table 4. The RMS Values Comparison of Body Accelerations with nominal mass m_b

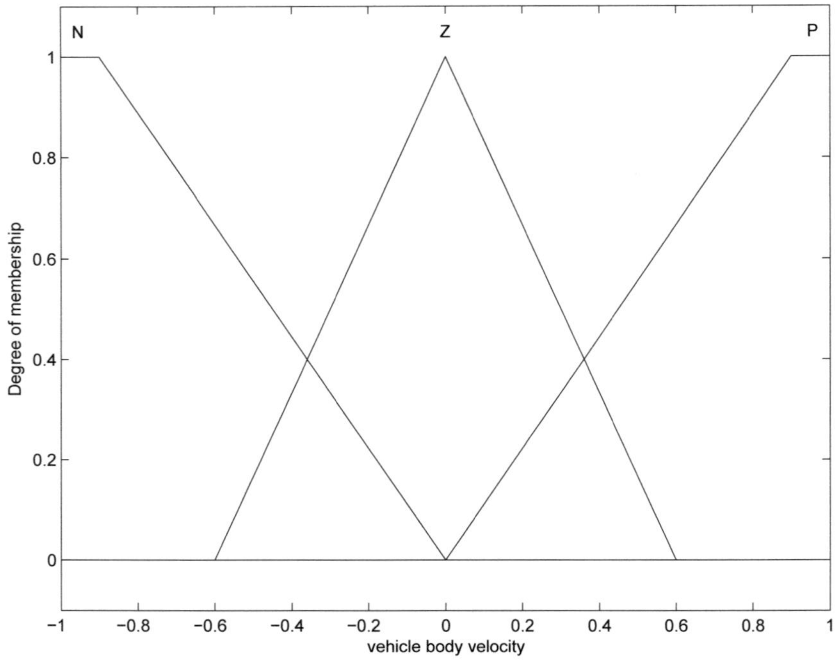

(a) Membership functions of the vehicle body velocities, $\dot{z}_b$

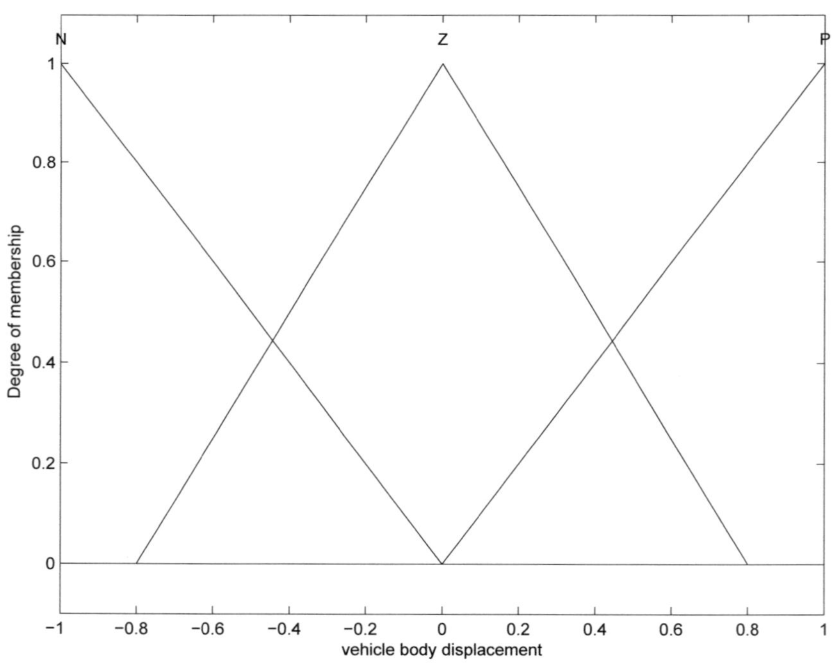

(b) MFs of displacements of the vehicle body, z_b

Fig. 15. Fuzzy membership functions of the input variables

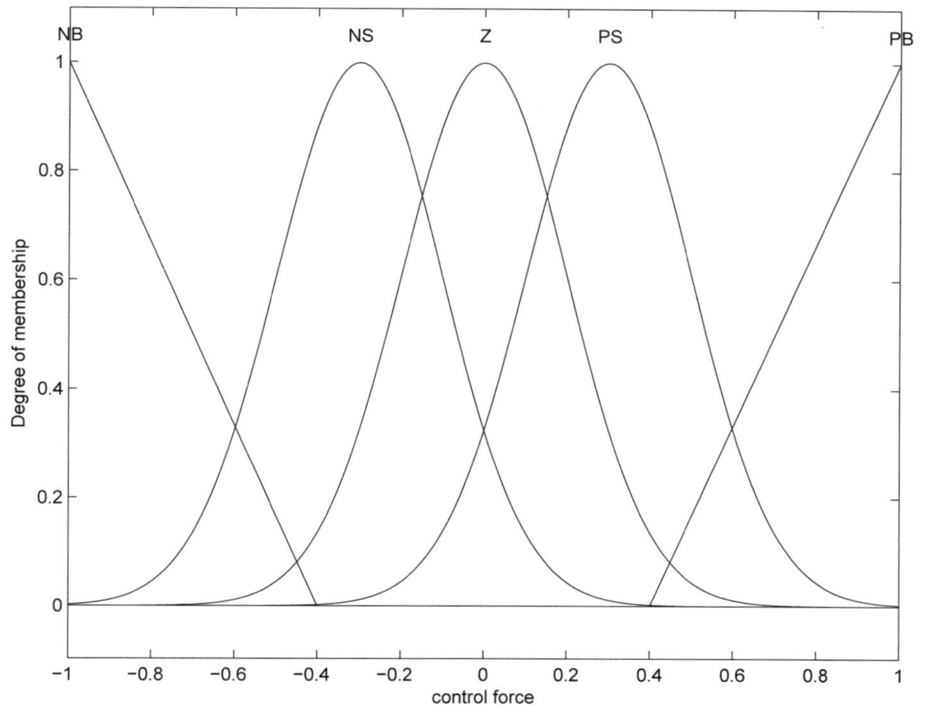

Fig. 16. Membership functions of control forces, f_a

The comparison of RMS values with nominal vehicle body mass m_b are shown in Table 4. With additional $\pm 20\%$ changes of vehicle body mass, the RMS value comparisons are shown in Table 5 and Tabel 6.

Regarding to the RMS accelerations of the vehicle body , the proposed method has achieved better performance on ride comfort than the other two methods. Furthermore, with the comparison of tyre deflections, vehicle handling performance has been improved by proposed method.

6. Concluding remarks

A novel extended fuzzy logic system has been built in this paper. With the interval fuzzy reasoning and adaptive tuning rules, the proposed structure generated a more general framework to cover the uncertain information of complex dynamic systems. Based on this framework, integrating with the DE algorithm, an adaptive fuzzy control system was designed to improve the control performance by using the further optimization process. The EFLS was implemented to solve the inverse kinematic modelling problem of a two-joint robotic arm which can not be well modelled by the typical fuzzy methods. The simulation results verified the EFLS can not only obtain more precise model, but also has potential capability to handle the high level uncertain information due to the understanding of linguistic knowledge and the quantification of fuzzy rules. Furthermore, an adaptive fuzzy control system was designed for a typical complex non-linear system: quarter-vehicle active suspension system. The control performance was improved and the design process was more flexible than other existed methods.

Average Road	VA(m/s^2)	TD (m)
Passive	4.7160×10^{-4}	1.4145×10^{-6}
FLC	4.2312×10^{-4}	2.3254×10^{-7}
Proposed method	4.012×10^{-4}	1.9744×10^{-7}
Poor Road	VA(m/s^2)	TD (m)
Passive	2.5764×10^{-3}	3.7677×10^{-5}
FLC	1.6070×10^{-3}	2.0001×10^{-6}
Proposed method	1.4912×10^{-3}	1.8231×10^{-6}

Table 5. The RMS Values Comparison of Body Accelerations with (1+20%) m_b

Average Road	VA(m/s^2)	TD (m)
Passive	4.3762×10^{-4}	6.8341×10^{-7}
FLC	4.1579×10^{-4}	2.0502×10^{-7}
Proposed method	3.6352×10^{-4}	1.2133×10^{-7}
Poor Road	VA(m/s^2)	TD (m)
Passive	2.1945×10^{-3}	3.0046×10^{-5}
FLC	1.5071×10^{-3}	1.4907×10^{-6}
Proposed method	1.2958×10^{-3}	1.2877×10^{-6}

Table 6. The RMS Values Comparison of Body Accelerations with (1-20%) m_b

Future work has been targeted to address the theory analysis of proposed framework, especially the convergence of adaptive algorithm and impact assessment of uncertainty. Besides, the stability of closed-loop control system should be analyzed.

7. References

2631-1, I. (1997). Mechanical vibrations and shock - evaluation of human exposure to whole-body vibration part 1: general requirements, *International Standardization Organization* .

Abbass, H. (2002). The self-adaptive pareto differential evolution algorithm, *Congress on Evolutionary Computation (CEC2002)*, Vol. 1, Citeseer, pp. 831–836.

Astudillo, L., Castillo, O. & Aguilar, L. (2007). Intelligent Control for a Perturbed Autonomous Wheeled Mobile Robot: a Type-2 Fuzzy Logic Approach, *Journal of Nonlinear Studies* 14(3): 37–48.

Baranyi, P., Koczy, L. & Gedeon, T. (2004). A generalized concept for fuzzy rule interpolation, *Fuzzy Systems, IEEE Transactions on* 12(6): 820–837.

Brest, J., Greiner, S., Boskovic, B., Mernik, M. & Zumer, V. (2006). Self-adapting control parameters in differential evolution: A comparative study on numerical benchmark problems, *IEEE Transactions on Evolutionary Computation* 10(6): 646–657.

Cao, J., Li, P. & Liu, H. (2009). An extended fuzzy logic system for uncertainty modelling, *FUZZ-IEEE 2009*, Korea, pp. 888–893.

Cao, J., Liu, H., Li, P. & Brown, D. (2008). Adaptive fuzzy logic controller for vehicle active suspensions with interval type-2 fuzzy membership functions, *FUZZ-IEEE 2008*, Hong Kong, pp. 83–89.

Castro, J., Castillo, O. & Melin, P. (2008). Intelligent control using an interval type-2 fuzzy neural network with a hybrid learning algorithm, *FUZZ-IEEE 2008*, Hong Kong, pp. 893–900.

Gan, J., Oyama, E., Rosales, E. & Hu, H. (2005). A complete analytical solution to the inverse kinematics of the Pioneer 2 robotic arm, *Robotica* 23(01): 123–129.

Hagras, H. (2004). A hierarchical type-2 fuzzy logic control architecture for autonomous mobile robots, *Fuzzy Systems, IEEE Transactions on* 12(4): 524–539.

Hagras, H. (2008). Developing a type-2 flc through embedded type-1 flcs, *FUZZ-IEEE 2008*, Hong Kong, pp. 148–155.

Hrovat, D. (1997). Survey of advanced suspension developments and related optimal control applications, *Automatica* 33(10): 1781–1817.

Huang, Z. & Shen, Q. (2006). Fuzzy interpolative reasoning via scale and move transformations, *Fuzzy Systems, IEEE Transactions on* 14(2): 340.

Julio, R. & Alberto, V. (2007). Calculating functions of interval type-2 fuzzy numbers for fault current analysis, *IEEE Transactions on Fuzzy Systems* 15(1): 31–40.

Karaboga, D., Okdem, S. & Simple, A. (2004). A Simple and Global Optimization Algorithm for Engineering Problems: Differential Evolution Algorithm, *Turk J Elec Engin* 12(1).

Karnik, N. & Liang, J. (1999). Type-2 fuzzy logic systems, *Fuzzy Systems, IEEE Transactions on* 7(6): 643–658.

Karnik, N. & Mendel, J. (2001). Centroid of a type-2 fuzzy set, *Information Sciences* 132(1-4): 195–220.

Klir, G. & Folger, T. (1987). *Fuzzy sets, uncertainty, and information*, Prentice-Hall, Inc. Upper Saddle River, NJ, USA.

Lee, L. & Chen, S. (2008). Fuzzy interpolative reasoning for sparse fuzzy rule-based systems based on the ranking values of fuzzy sets, *Expert Systems With Applications* 35(3): 850–864.

Liang, Q. & Mendel, J. (2000a). Interval type-2 fuzzy logic systems: theory and design, *Fuzzy Systems, IEEE Transactions on* 8(5): 535–550.

Liang, Q. & Mendel, J. (2000b). Interval type-2 fuzzy logic systems: theory and design, *Fuzzy Systems, IEEE Transactions on* 8(5): 535–550.

Liu, Z. & Li, H. (2005a). A probabilistic fuzzy logic system for modeling and control, *Fuzzy Systems, IEEE Transactions on* 13(6): 848–859.

Liu, Z. & Li, H. (2005b). A probabilistic fuzzy logic system for uncertainty modeling, *Systems, Man and Cybernetics, 2005 IEEE International Conference on*, Vol. 4.

Mendel, J. (2007). New results about the centroid of an interval type-2 fuzzy set, including the centroid of a fuzzy granule, *Infromation Sciences* 117: 360–377.

Mendel, J. & John, R. (2002). Type-2 fuzzy sets made simple, *Fuzzy Systems, IEEE Transactions on* 10(2): 117–127.

Nie, M. & Tan, W. (2008). Towards an efficient type-reduction method for interval type-2 fuzzy logic systems, *FUZZ-IEEE 2008*, Hong Kong, pp. 1425–1432.

Price, K., Storn, R. & Lampinen, J. (2005). *Differential evolution*, Springer.

Ross, T. (2004). *Fuzzy logic with engineering applications*, Wiley.

Sepúlveda, R., Castillo, O., Melin, P., Rodríguez-Díaz, A. & Montiel, O. (2007). Experimental Study of Intelligent Controllers Under Uncertainty Using Type-1 and Type-2 Fuzzy Logic, *Information Sciences* 177(10): 2023–2048.

Storn, R. (1999). System design by constraint adaptation and differential evolution, *IEEE Transactions on Evolutionary Computation* 3(1): 22–34.

Storn, R. & Price, K. (1997). Differential Evolution - a Simple and Efficient Heuristic for Global Optimization over Continuous Spaces, *Journal of Global Optimization* 11(1): 341–359.

Taghirad, H. & Esmailzadeh, E. (1998). Automobile passenger comfort assured through LQG/LQR active suspension, *Journal of Vibration and Control* 4(5): 603–618.

Wu, D. & Mendel, J. (2009). A comparative study of ranking methods, similarity measures and uncertainty measures for interval type-2 fuzzy sets, *Information Sciences* 179(8): 1169–1192.

Wu, H. & Mendel, J. (2002). Uncertainty bounds and their use in the design of interval type-2 fuzzy logic systems, *Fuzzy Systems, IEEE Transactions on* 10(5): 622–639.

Zadeh, L. (1965). Fuzzy sets, *Information and Control* 8(3): 338–353.

4

Extended Kalman Filter for the Estimation and Fuzzy Optimal Control of Takagi-Sugeno Model

Agustín Jiménez, Basil M.Al-Hadithi and Fernando Matía
Intelligent Control Group, Universidad Politecnica de Madrid
Spain

1. Introduction

This chapter is aimed at improving the local and global approximation and modelling capability of Takagi-Sugeno (T-S) fuzzy model and the design of an optimal fuzzy controller. The main aim is obtaining high function approximation accuracy and fast convergence. The approach developed here can be considered as a generalized version of T-S fuzzy identification method with optimized performance in estimating nonlinear functions. We propose an iterative method by applying the extended Kalman filter. We show that the Kalman filter is an effective tool in the estimation of T-S fuzzy model. It is a powerful mathematical tool for stochastic estimation from noisy environment. It has various applications in optimizing fuzzy systems. For example, it has been used to extract fuzzy rules from a given rule base (Wang, L. & Yen, J. (1998)) and to optimize the output function parameters of T-S fuzzy systems (Ramaswamy, P.; Edwards, R. R. & Lee, K. (1993)). For linear systems with white noise and measurement noise, the Kalman filter is known to be an optimal estimator. For nonlinear dynamic systems with coloured noise, the Kalman filter can be extended by linearizing the system around the current parameter estimates. This algorithm updates parameters in a way that is consistent with all previously measured data and generally converges in a few iterations. In this chapter, we describe how the extended Kalman filter can be applied to fuzzy system optimization. Fuzzy logic has been used to compute the gains of a bank of parallel Kalman filters in order to combine their outputs (Hsiao, C. (1999)). Fuzzy logic has also been used to tune the parameters of a Kalman filter (Kobayashi, K.; Cheok, K. & Watanabe, K.(1995).).

A fuzzy controller (FC) based Linear Quadratic Regulator (LQR) is then proposed in order to show the effectiveness of the estimation method developed here in control applications. An Illustrative example of a highly nonlinear system is chosen to evaluate the robustness and remarkable performance of the proposed method. The main idea is to design a supervisory fuzzy controller capable to adjust the controller parameters in order to obtain the desired response. The reason behind this scheme is to combine the best features of fuzzy control and those of the optimal LQR.

In control design, it is often of interest to design a controller to fulfil, in an optimal form, certain performance criteria and constraints in addition to stability. The theme of optimal control addresses this aspect of control system design. For linear systems, the problem of designing optimal controllers reduces to solving algebraic Riccati equations, which are usually easy to solve and detailed literature of their solutions can be found in many references. Nevertheless, for nonlinear systems, the optimization problem reduces to the so-called Hamilton-Jacobi (HJ) equations, which are nonlinear partial differential equations. Different from their counterparts for linear systems, HJ equations are usually difficult to solve both numerically and analytically. Improvements have also been carried out on the numerical solution of the approximated solution of HJ equations. But few results so far can provide an effective way of designing optimal controllers for general nonlinear systems.

In the past, the design of controllers based on a linearized model of real control systems. In many cases a good response of complex and highly non-linear real process is difficult to obtain by applying conventional control techniques which often employ linear mathematical models of the process. One reason for this lack of a satisfactory performance is the fact that linearization of a non-linear system might be valid only as an approximation to the real system around a determined operating point.

However, fuzzy controllers are basically non-linear, and effective enough to provide the desired non-linear control actions by carefully adjusting their parameters.

In this chapter, we propose an effective method to nonlinear optimal control based on fuzzy control. The optimal fuzzy control methodology presented in this chapter is based on a quadratic performance index. The optimal fuzzy controller is designed by solving a minimization problem that minimizes a given quadratic performance function.

Both the controlled system and the fuzzy controller are represented by the affine T-S fuzzy model taking into consideration the effect of the constant term. Most of the research works analyzed the T-S model assuming that the non-linear system is linearized with respect to the origin in each IF-THEN rule, which means that the consequent part of each rule is a linear function with zero constant term. This will in turn reduce the accuracy of approximating non-linear systems. Moreover, in linear control theory, the independent term does not affect the dynamics of the system rather the input to it. In the case of fuzzy control, the blending of the independent term of each rule will no longer be a constant but a function of the variables of the system and thus affects the dynamics of the resultant system. A necessary condition has been added to deal with the independent term. The control is carried out based on the fuzzy model via the so-called parallel distributed compensation scheme. The idea is that for each local affine model, an affine linear feedback control is designed. The resulting overall controller, which is also a non-linear one, is again a blending of each individual affine linear controller.

LQR is used to determine best values for parameters in fuzzy control rules in which the robustness is inherent in the LQR thereby robustness in fuzzy control can be improved. With the aid of LQR, it provides an effective design method of fuzzy control to achieve rapid, robust and accurate tracking control of a class of nonlinear systems.

In this chapter, we will also show how the LQR, the structure of which is based on mathematical analysis, can be made more appropriate for actual implementation by introduction of fuzzy rules.

The results obtained show a robust and stable behaviour when the system is subjected to various initial conditions, moment of inertia and to disturbances.

The content of this chapter is organized as follows. In section 2, an overview of Kalman Filter's Estimation and Optimal Control Techniques for Fuzzy Systems are presented. Section 3 presents the identification of T-S model. Section 4 demonstrates the iterative parameters' identification using extended Kalman filter. In section 5, a design of a fuzzy optimal controller is developed. Section 6 entails the application of the proposed FC-LQR on nonlinear model to demonstrate the validity of the proposed approach. This example shows that the proposed approach gives a stable and well damped response in front of various initial conditions, moment of inertia and a robust behaviour in the presence of disturbances. The conclusion of the effectiveness and validity of the proposed approach is explained in section 7.

2. Overview of identification and estimation of fuzzy systems

Nonlinear control systems based on the T–S fuzzy model (Sugeno, M. & Tanaka, K. (1991).), (Sugeno, M. & Kang, G. (1988)) and (Takagi T. & Sugeno, M. (1985)) have attracted lots of attention during the last twenty years (e.g., see (Baranyi, P. (2003), (Tanaka, K.; Wang, H. O. (2001).), (Hou, Y.; Zurada, J. M.; Karwowski, W.; Marras, W. S. & Davis, K. (2007)), (Xian-Tu, P. (1990)), (Gang, F. (2006)), (Lian, K.-Y.; Su, C.-H. & Huang, C.-S. (2006)), (Hseng, T.; Li, S. & Tsai, S.-H. (2007)) and (Kim, J.-H.; Hyun, C.-H.; Kim, E. & Park, M. (2007).). It provides a powerful solution for development of function approximation, systematic techniques to stability analysis and controller design of fuzzy control systems in view of fruitful conventional control theory and techniques. They also allow relatively easy application of powerful learning techniques for their identification from data.

This model is formed by using a set of fuzzy rules to represent a nonlinear system as a set of local affine models which are connected by fuzzy membership functions (Cao, S. G.; Rees, N. W. & and Feng, G. (1996).).

This fuzzy modelling method presents an alternative technique to represent complex nonlinear systems (Fantuzzi, C. & Rovatti, R. (1996).), (Ying, H. (1998)) and (Zeng, K.; Zhang, N. Y. & Xu, W. L. (2000)) and reduces the number of rules in modelling higher order nonlinear systems (Takagi T. & Sugeno, M. (1985)) and (Gang, F. (2006)).

T–S fuzzy models are proved to be universal function approximators as they are able to approximate any smooth nonlinear functions to any degree of accuracy in any convex compact region (Fantuzzi, C. & Rovatti, R. (1996).), (Johansen, T. A.; Shorten, R. & Murray-Smith, R. (2000)), (Ying, H. (1998)) and (Zeng, K.; Zhang, N. Y. & Xu, W. L. (2000)). This result provides a theoretical foundation for applying T–S fuzzy models to represent complex nonlinear systems approximately.

Great attention has been paid to the identification of T–S fuzzy models and several results have been obtained (Cao, S. G.; Rees, N. W. & and Feng, G. (1997)), (Teixeira, M. C. M.; Assunção, E. & Avellar, R. G. (2003)) and (Yu, W. & Li, X. O. (2004). They are based upon two kinds of approaches, one is to linearize the original nonlinear system in various operating points when the model of the system is known, and the other is based on the input-output data collected from the original nonlinear system when its model is unknown. The authors in (Cao, S. G.; Rees, N. W. & and Feng, G. (1997) use a fuzzy clustering method to identify T–S fuzzy models, including identification of the number of fuzzy rules and parameters of fuzzy membership functions, and identification of parameters of local linear models by using a least squares method (Skrjanc, I.; Blazic, S. & Agamennoni, O. (2005)) and (Wang, L. X. & Mendel, J. M. (1992).). The goal is to minimize the error between T–S fuzzy models and the corresponding original nonlinear systems. In (Klawonn, F. & Kruse, R. (1997)), Klawonn *et al.* explained how fuzzy clustering techniques could be applied to design a fuzzy controller from the training data. In (Hong T. P. & Lee, C. Y. (1996)), Hong and Lee have analyzed that the disadvantages of most fuzzy systems are that the membership functions and fuzzy rules should be predefined to map numerical data into linguistic terms and to make fuzzy reasoning work. They suggested a method based on the fuzzy clustering technique and the decision tables to derive membership functions and fuzzy rules from numerical data. However, Hong and Lee's algorithm presented in (Hong T. P. & Lee, C. Y. (1996)) needs to predefine the membership functions of the input linguistic variables and it simplifies fuzzy rules by a series of merge operations. As the number of variables becomes larger, the decision table will grow tremendously and the process of the rule simplification based on the decision tables becomes more complicated.

In (Matía, F.; Jiménez, A. & Al-Hadithi, B. M. (2008)), the authors proposed to obtain the best features of Mamdani and Takagi-Sugeno models by using an affine global model with function approximation capabilities which maintains local interpretation. The suggested model is composed of variant coefficients which are independently governed by a zeroth order fuzzy inference system. This model may be interpreted as a generalization of T-S model in which dynamics coefficients have been decoupled. They have shown that Mamdani and Takagi-Sugeno models can be combined so that local and global interpretations are preserved.

The authors in (Johansen, T. A.; Shorten, R. & Murray-Smith, R. (2000)) suggest a method to identify T–S fuzzy models. Their method aims at improving the local and global approximation of T-S model. However, this complicates the approximation in order to obtain both targets. It has been shown that constrained and regularized identification methods may improve interpretability of constituent local models as local linearizations, and locally weighted least squares method may explicitly address the trade-off between the local and global accuracy of T–S fuzzy models.

In (Skrjanc, I.; Blazic, S. & Agamennoni, O. (2005)) a new method of interval fuzzy model identification was developed. The method combines a fuzzy identification methodology with some ideas from linear programming theory. The idea is then extended to modelling the optimal lower and upper bound functions that define the band which contains all the measurement values. This results in lower and upper fuzzy models or a fuzzy model with a set of lower and upper parameters. This approach can also be used to compress information in the case of large amount of data and in the case of robust system identification. The method can be efficiently used in the case of the approximation of the nonlinear functions family. The paper focuses on the development of an interval L_{∞}-norm function approximation methodology problem using the LP technique and the TS fuzzy logic approach. This results in lower and upper fuzzy models or a fuzzy model with lower and upper parameters.

In (Mencattini, A.; Salmeri M. & Salsano, A. (2005)) a constructive method to synthesize a MISO TS fuzzy logic system imposing the requested derivative constraints on the function representing its behaviour is presented. The values of that function and its partial derivatives on the grid points of the input space permit to define a suitable interpolator of the function itself.

In (Kim, J.; Suga, Y. & Won, S. (2006).), a new approach to fuzzy modelling using the relevance vector learning mechanism (RVM) based on a kernel-based Bayesian estimation is introduced. The main concern is to find the best structure of the T-S fuzzy model for modelling nonlinear dynamic systems with measurement error. The number of rules and the parameter values of membership functions can be found as optimizing the marginal likelihood of the RVM in the proposed FIS. Because the RVM is not necessary to satisfy Mercer's condition, selection of kernel function is beyond the limit of the positive definite continuous symmetric function of SVM. The relaxed condition of kernel function can satisfy various types of membership functions in fuzzy model. The RVM which was compared with support vector learning mechanism in examples had the small model capacity and described good generalization. Simulated results showed the effectiveness of the proposed FIS for modelling of nonlinear dynamic systems with noise.

In (Takagi T. & Sugeno, M. (1985)), the authors develop an interesting method to identify nonlinear systems using input-output data. They divide the identification process in three steps; premise variables, membership functions and consequent parameters. With respect to membership functions, they apply nonlinear programming technique using the complex method for the minimization of the performance index.

In 1991, Wang and Mendel developed a method for generating fuzzy rules by learning from examples (Wang, L. X. & Mendel, J. M. (1992).) and proved that a fuzzy inference system is a universal approximator by the Stone–Weierstrass theorem (Wang, L. (1994)).

In 1995, Wang proposed a new state-space analytical approach to fuzzy identification of nonlinear dynamical systems (Wang, L. X. & Mendel, J. M. (1995)). In 1996, Langari and Wang proposed achieving structure identification of a T-S fuzzy model by using a combination of fuzzy c-means clustering technique and a fuzzy discretization technique (Langari R. & Wang, L. (1996).

In (Nozaki, K.; Ishibuchi, H. & Tanaka, H. (1997), Nozaki *et al.* presented a heuristic method for generating T-S fuzzy rules from numerical data, and then converted the consequent parts of T-S fuzzy rules into linguistic representation.

In (Kumar et al., 2006), a study has outlined a new min–max approach to the fuzzy clustering, estimation, and identification with uncertain data. The proposed approach minimizes the worst-case effect of data uncertainties and modelling errors on estimation performance without making any statistical assumption and requiring a priori knowledge of uncertainties. Simulation studies have been provided to show the better performance of the proposed method in comparison to the standard techniques. The developed fuzzy estimation theory was applied to a real world application of physical fitness classification and modelling.

A new fuzzy system containing a dynamic rule base is proposed in (Chen, W. & Saif, M. (2005).). The characteristic of the proposed system is in the dynamic nature of its rule base which has a fixed number of rules and allows the fuzzy sets to dynamically change or move with the inputs. The number of the rules in the proposed system can be small, and chosen by the designer. The focus of article is mainly on the approximation capability of this fuzzy system. The proposed system is capable of approximating any continuous function on an arbitrarily large compact domain. Moreover, it can even approximate any uniformly continuous function on infinite domains. This paper addresses existence conditions, and as well provides constructive sufficient conditions so that the new fuzzy system can approximate any continuous function with bounded partial derivatives.

Fuzzy system optimization problem is studied in several works. Some articles focused on choosing proper rules in the inference engine (Cordon, O.; Herrera; Magdalena; F. L. & Villar P. (2001)) and (Xian-Tu, P. (1990)). Also tuning of the input and output scale factors are proposed (Cordon, O.; Herrera; Magdalena; F. L. & Villar P. (2001)), (Gudwin, R.; Gomide, F. & Pedrycz, W. (1998)) and (Pedrycz, W.; Gudwin, R. & Gomide, F. (1997)). Because of the importance of selecting proper MF's for fuzzy systems (Cordon, O.; Herrera. & Villar P. (2000)), several methods are used to deal with the problem of optimizing membership functions, which are either derivative-based or derivative-free methods. The derivative free approaches do not use the derivative of the performance of the system with respect to the MF's parameters, and they are desirable because they are more robust than derivative-based methods with respect to finding global minimum and with respect to a wide range of objective function and MFs types. The main drawback is that they converge more slowly than derivative-based techniques (Tao, C. & and Taur, J. (1999).

On the other hand, derivative-based methods have the advantage of fast convergence and fine tuning in finding the optimum functions, but they tend to converge to local minimums. In addition, due to their dependence on analytical derivatives, they are limited to specific objective functions and types of inference and MFs. The most common approaches are: gradient descent (Simon, D. (2000).), least squares (Skrjanc, I.; Blazic, S. & Agamennoni, O. (2005)), back propagation (Wang, L. & Mendel, J. (1992).) and Kalman filtering (Simon, D. (2002).), (Simon, 2002).

The use of Kalman filter training to optimize the MFs of a fuzzy system was introduced by Simon (Simon, D. (2002).) for motor winding current estimation. The used MFs were assumed as symmetric triangular forms. The Kalman filter training was extended to asymmetric triangles in (Simon, 2002), and a matrix was defined relating the parameters of the MFs together based on the sum-normality conditions, then projecting this matrix in each iteration of optimization to constrain the MFs to sum normal types.

Since the derivatives of the functions are used in Kalman filtering, it is limited to special type of MFs because of complicated and time consuming calculations. So far only triangular types are optimized for both inputs and outputs of a FLC Simon, D. (2002).), (Simon, 2002).

3. Identification of T-S model

An interesting method of identification is presented in (Takagi T. & Sugeno, M. (1985)). The idea is based on estimating the nonlinear system parameters minimizing a quadratic performance index. The method is based on the identification of functions of the following form:

$$\begin{aligned} &f:\Re^n \rightarrow \Re \\ &y = f(x_1, x_2, \ldots, x_n) \end{aligned} \tag{1}$$

Each IF-THEN rule $R^{i1\ldots in}$, for an nth order system can be rewritten as follows:

$$\begin{aligned} &S^{(i_1\ldots i_n)} : if\ x_1\ is\ M_1^{i_1}\ and\ x_2\ is\ M_2^{i_2}\ and \ldots x_n\ is\ M_n^{i_n}\ then \\ &\hat{y} = p_0^{(i_1\ldots i_n)} + p_1^{(i_1\ldots i_n)} x_1 + p_2^{(i_1\ldots i_n)} x_2 + \ldots + p_n^{(i_1\ldots i_n)} x_n \end{aligned} \tag{2}$$

Where the fuzzy estimation of the output is:

$$\hat{y} = \frac{\sum_{i_1=1}^{r_1} \cdots \sum_{i_n=1}^{r_n} w^{(i_1\ldots i_n)}(x) \left[p_0^{(i_1\ldots i_n)} + p_1^{(i_1\ldots i_n)} x_1 + \ldots + p_n^{(i_1\ldots i_n)} x_n \right]}{\sum_{i_1=1}^{r_1} \cdots \sum_{i_n=1}^{r_n} w^{(i_1\ldots i_n)}(x)} \tag{3}$$

Let m be a set of input/output system samples $\{x_{1k}, x_{2k}, \ldots, x_{nk}, y_k\}$. The parameters of the fuzzy system can be calculated as a result of minimizing a quadratic performance index:

$$J = \sum_{k=1}^{m} (y_k - \hat{y}_k)^2 = \|Y - XP\|^2 \tag{4}$$

where

$$\begin{aligned} Y &= \left[y_1 \; y_2 \cdots y_m \right]^t \\ P &= \left[p_0^{(1 \ldots 1)} \; p_1^{(1 \ldots 1)} \; p_2^{(1 \ldots 1)} \ldots p_n^{(1 \ldots 1)} \cdots p_0^{(r_1 \ldots r_n)} \ldots p_n^{(r_1 \ldots r_n)} \right]^t \end{aligned} \tag{5}$$

$$X = \begin{bmatrix} \beta_1^{(1..1)} & \beta_1^{(1..1)} x_{11} \ldots \beta_1^{(1..1)} x_{n1} \cdots \beta_1^{(r_1..r_n)} \ldots \beta_1^{(r_1..r_n)} x_{n1} \\ & \vdots \\ \beta_m^{(1..1)} & \beta_m^{(1..1)} x_{1m} \ldots \beta_m^{(1..1)} x_{nm} \cdots \beta_m^{(r_1..r_n)} \ldots \beta_m^{(r_1..r_n)} x_{nm} \end{bmatrix} \tag{6}$$

and

$$\beta_k^{(i_1 \ldots i_n)} = \frac{w^{(i_1 \ldots i_n)}(x_k)}{\sum_{i_1=1}^{r_1} \cdots \sum_{i_n=1}^{r_n} w^{(i_1 \ldots i_n)}(x_k)} \tag{7}$$

If X is a matrix of complete rank, the solution is obtained as follows:

$$\begin{aligned} J &= \|Y - XP\|^2 = (Y - XP)^t (Y - XP) \\ \nabla J &= X^t (Y - XP) = X^t Y - X^t XP = 0 \\ P &= (X^t X)^{-1} X^t Y \end{aligned} \tag{8}$$

4. Iterative parameters' identification

The inconvenient feature of the non iterative methods is the amplification of the matrix X throughout the time, so that they become inappropriate to be used in real time application as adaptive control for example (Jiménez, A.; Al-Hadithi, B. M. & Matía, F. (2008)). The solution is finding an iterative method so that the dimension of the calculation will not be augmented for each sample. In this work, we use an iterative method based on the extended Kalman.

4.1 Kalman filter

Kalman filter is widely used for state estimation. It was developed by Rudolph E. Kalman (Kalman, R. E. (1960). Kalman filter is known to be optimum for linear systems (Maybeck, P. S. (1979)) with white process and measurement noises. It is assumed that the system is described by the following sampled model:

$$\begin{aligned} & x(k+1) = \Phi x(k) + \Gamma u(k) + v(k) \\ & y(k) = C x(k) + e(k) \\ & x(k),\, x(k+1),\, v(k) \in \Re^n \quad u(k) \in \Re^m \quad y(k),\, e(k) \in \Re^p \end{aligned} \tag{9}$$

where $x(k)$ represents the state of the dynamic system, $u(k)$ is the input vector and $y(k)$ is the output vector. The vector $v(k)$ represents the Gaussian-white noise of the system and

$e(k)$ is Gaussian-white noise of the output measure. Both of them are independent from each other with zero mean. The objective of the Kalman filter is to obtain an optimum estimation $\hat{x}(k)$ of the state $x(k)$ from measurements of the input / output vectors. The covariance matrices are supposed to be known and are given as:

$$\begin{aligned} R_1 &= E\left(v(k)\cdot v^t(k)\right) \\ R_{12} &= E\left(v(k)\cdot e^t(k)\right) \\ R_2 &= E\left(e(k)\cdot e^t(k)\right) \end{aligned} \tag{10}$$

where E(.) is the expectation operator. It is also assumed that the initial condition $x(0)$ is Gaussian distributed with

$$\begin{aligned} m_0 &= E(x(0)) \\ R_0 &= E\left(\left(x(0)-m_0\right)\cdot\left(x(0)-m_0\right)^t\right) \end{aligned} \tag{11}$$

It is supposed that $\hat{x}(k/k-1), u(k)$ and $y(k)$ are known and the objective is to estimate $\hat{x}(k+1/k)$. The prediction problem can be improved by introducing the difference between the measured and estimated outputs, $\left(y(k)-C\hat{x}(k/k-1)\right)$ as a feedback gain:

$$\hat{x}(k+1/k) = \Phi\hat{x}(k/k-1) + \Gamma u(k) + K(k)\left(y(k)-C\hat{x}(k/k-1)\right) \tag{12}$$

The resultant prediction error is the difference between the state of the true system and the estimated one:

$$\varepsilon(k+1) = x(k+1) - \hat{x}(k+1/k) \tag{13}$$

It should be observed that as above mentioned Gaussian errors $v(k)$ and $e(k)$ are with zero mean, it can be verified that:

$$\overline{\varepsilon}(k+1) = \left(\Phi - K(k)C\right)\overline{\varepsilon}(k) \tag{14}$$

Thus,

$$\text{If } \ \overline{\varepsilon}(0)=0\ (\Rightarrow \hat{x}(0)=m_0) \Rightarrow \forall k>0\ \varepsilon(k)=0\ (\hat{x}(k)=m_k) \tag{15}$$

And if the dynamics of (3) is stable, then:

$$\forall x(0)\ \lim_{k\to\infty}\overline{e}(k)=0 \Rightarrow \lim_{k\to\infty}\hat{x}(k)=m_k \tag{16}$$

The secondary objective is to minimize the covariance matrix which denoted as $P(k)$,

$$P(k) = E((\varepsilon-\overline{\varepsilon})\cdot(\varepsilon-\overline{\varepsilon})^t) \tag{17}$$

in the sense that it approaches its minimum for:

$$\min(\alpha^t P(k)\alpha)\ \ \forall\alpha\in\Re^n \tag{18}$$

The algorithm of Kalman filter can be summarized by the following iterative process:

$$\begin{aligned} K(k) &= \left(\Phi P(k/k-1)C^t + R_{12}\right)\left(CP(k/k-1)C^t + R_2\right)^{-1} \\ \hat{x}(k+1/k) &= \Phi\hat{x}(k/k-1) + \Gamma u(k) + K(k)\left(y(k) - C\hat{x}(k/k-1)\right) \\ P(k+1/k) &= \Phi P(k/k-1)\Phi^t + R_1 - K(k)\left(CP(k/k-1)\Phi^t + R_{12}^t\right) \end{aligned} \tag{19}$$

This process is initialized with $\hat{x}(0) = m_0$ and $P(0) = R_0$ which have been initially estimated. The classic formulation of Kalman filter can be complemented with an additional useful filtering process for certain applications.

4.2 Extended Kalman filter

Kalman filter can also be used for state estimation of nonlinear systems. For nonlinear systems, e.g. fuzzy systems, the Kalman filter can not be applied directly; but if the nonlinearity of the system be sufficiently smooth, then we can linearize it about the current mean and covariance of the state estimation. This is called Extended Kalman Filter (EKF) with white process and measurement noises. Derivations of the extended Kalman filter are widely available in the literature (Gelb, A. (1974)). In this section, we briefly outline the algorithm and show how it can be applied to fuzzy system optimization.
Consider a nonlinear discrete time system of the form:

$$\begin{aligned} x(k+1) &= f\left(x(k), u(k)\right) + v(k) \\ y(k) &= g\left(x(k)\right) + e(k) \end{aligned} \tag{20}$$

In this case, Jacobian matrices are those which represent the nonlinear systems:

$$\begin{aligned} \Phi\left(x(k), u(k)\right) &= \left.\frac{\partial f}{\partial x}\right|_{x=x(k),\, u=u(k)} \\ \Gamma\left(x(k), u(k)\right) &= \left.\frac{\partial f}{\partial u}\right|_{x=x(k),\, u=u(k)} \\ C\left(x(k)\right) &= \left.\frac{\partial g}{\partial x}\right|_{x=x(k)} \end{aligned} \tag{21}$$

Moreover, the prediction formula for the nonlinear case is the following:

$$\hat{x}(k+1/k) = \Phi\hat{x}(k/k-1) + \Gamma u(k) + K(k)\left(y(k) - g\left(\hat{x}(k/k-1), u(k)\right)\right) \tag{22}$$

It must be noted that in this case, the system matrices in this depend on both the state and input of the system in each instant. Thus, it becomes necessary the calculation of these matrices in each iteration of the algorithm.

4.3 Kalman filter for parameters' identification

One of the applications of Kalman filter is the identification of parameters. Let us suppose that a function depends on q parameters $p_1, p_2, \ldots, p_q$

$$
\begin{aligned}
&f:\Re^n \to \Re^m \\
&y = f(x_1, x_2, \ldots, x_n, p_1, p_2, \ldots, p_q) = f(x,p)
\end{aligned}
\tag{23}
$$

The problem of identification of parameters can be explained as a problem of estimation of systems´ states.

$$
\begin{aligned}
&p(k+1) = p(k) \\
&y(k) = f(p(k)) + e(k)
\end{aligned}
\tag{24}
$$

Then, if we have a set of m samples $\{x_{1k}, x_{2k}, \ldots, x_{nk}, y_k\}$ of the function to be identified, Kalman filter can be used with the following particularities. The matrix Φ will be an identity matrix in this case. It is assumed a free system without an external input so the matrix Γ is null and the matrix C can be calculated as follows:

$$
C(p(k)) = \left.\frac{\partial f}{\partial p}\right|_{p=\hat{p}(k)}
\tag{25}
$$

The matrices R_1 y R_{12} become null, while R_2 is selected based on trial and error. If $y \in \Re$ and we suppose that $R_2 = I$, which would correspond to Gaussians error functions N(0,1), and the function is a linear one, the algorithm becomes equivalent to the recursive minimum square one.

The initial covariance state matrix is supposed to be $P(0) = cI$ where C is a number relatively large with respect to the data of the problem. The algorithm becomes:

$$
\begin{aligned}
&K(k) = \left(P(k/k-1)C^t\right)\left(CP(k/k-1)C^t + R_2\right)^{-1} \hat{p}(k+1/k) = \\
&\hat{p}(k/k-1) + \quad + K(k)\left(y_k - f(x_{1k}, x_{2k}, \ldots, x_{nk}, \hat{p}(k/k-1))\right) \\
&P(k+1/k) = P(k/k-1) - K(k)CP(k/k-1)
\end{aligned}
\tag{26}
$$

4.4 Application of Kalman filter for T-S fuzzy model

Motivated by the successful use of the Kalman filter for training neural networks (Puskorius, G. & Feldkamp, L. (1994).) and for defuzzfication strategies, we can apply a similar method to the training of fuzzy systems. In general, we can view the identification of fuzzy systems a weighted least-squares minimization problem, where the error vector is the difference between the fuzzy model outputs and the target values for those outputs. The proposed solution for its application is to combine it with a minimization of a weighting of the norm of the vector of parameters p. Let a function be represented as:

$$
\begin{aligned}
&f:\Re^n \to \Re \\
&y = f(x_1, x_2, \ldots, x_n)
\end{aligned}
\tag{27}
$$

The optimum approximation of the function is searched by describing the function as a fuzzy system represented in the following form:

$$
\begin{aligned}
&S^{(i_1 \ldots i_n)} : \mathit{if}\ x_1\ \mathit{is}\ M_1^{i_1}\ \mathit{and}\ x_2\ \mathit{is}\ M_2^{i_2}\ \mathit{and} \ldots x_n\ \mathit{is}\ M_n^{i_n} \\
&\qquad \mathit{then}\ \hat{y} = p_0^{(i_1 \ldots i_n)} + p_1^{(i_1 \ldots i_n)} x_1 + p_2^{(i_1 \ldots i_n)} x_2 + \ldots + p_n^{(i_1 \ldots i_n)} x_n
\end{aligned}
\tag{28}
$$

In order to cast the fuzzy system identification problem in a form suitable for Kalman filtering, we let the parameters of the rules constitute the state of a nonlinear system, and we consider the output of the fuzzy system as the output of the nonlinear system to which the Kalman filter is applied.

$$\begin{aligned} p(k+1) &= p(k) \\ y_k &= f(x_{1k}, x_{2k}, \ldots, x_{nk}, p(k)) + e(k) \end{aligned} \tag{29}$$

It should be noticed that the function f is a linear one with respect to the parameters and therefore it can be calculated in a direct form as follows:

$$\left.\frac{\partial f}{\partial p_0^{(i_1 \ldots i_n)}}\right|_{p=\hat{p}(k)} = \frac{w^{(i_1 \ldots i_n)}(x_k)}{\sum_{i_1=1}^{r_1} \ldots \sum_{i_n=1}^{r_n} w^{(i_1 \ldots i_n)}(x_k)} \tag{30}$$

and

$$\left.\frac{\partial f}{\partial p_j^{(i_1 \ldots i_n)}}\right|_{p=\hat{p}(k)} = \frac{w^{(i_1 \ldots i_n)}(x_k)}{\sum_{i_1=1}^{r_1} \ldots \sum_{i_n=1}^{r_n} w^{(i_1 \ldots i_n)}(x_k)} x_{jk} \quad \text{for } j = 1 \ldots n \tag{31}$$

Therefore, the Jacobian coincides with the row k of the matrix X defined in section II.

$$C(p(k)) = \left.\frac{\partial f}{\partial p}\right|_{p=\hat{p}(k)} = X_k = \left[\beta_k^{(1 \ldots 1)} \; \beta_k^{(1 \ldots 1)} x_{1k} \ldots \beta_k^{(1 \ldots 1)} x_{nk} \cdots \beta_k^{(r_1 \ldots r_n)} \ldots \beta_k^{(r_1 \ldots r_n)} x_{nk} \right] \tag{32}$$

And thus, the problem can be formulated as an estimation of the state of the linear system

$$\begin{aligned} p(k+1) &= p(k) \\ y_k &= C(\hat{p}(k)) \cdot p(k) + e(k) \end{aligned} \tag{33}$$

The prediction formula in this case becomes:

$$\hat{p}(k+1/k) = \hat{p}(k/k-1) + K(k)\big(y_k - C(p(k)) \cdot p(k)\big) \qquad (34$$

5. Design of optimal fuzzy controller

In order to show the effectiveness of the proposed estimation methods, a design of an optimal controller is carried out for a dynamic system whose model is of the following form:

$$x^{(n} = f(x, x', \ldots, x^{(n-1}, u) \tag{35}$$

Applying the proposed estimation method, the T-S model can be adjusted as follows:

$$\begin{aligned} &S^{(i_1 \ldots i_n)} : \textit{if } x \textit{ is } M_1^{i_1} \textit{ and } x' \textit{ is } M_2^{i_2} \textit{ and} \ldots x^{(n-1)} \textit{ is } M_n^{i_n} \textit{ then} \\ &x^{(n} = a_0^{(i_1 \ldots i_n)} + a_1^{(i_1 \ldots i_n)} x + a_2^{(i_1 \ldots i_n)} x' + \ldots + a_n^{(i_1 \ldots i_n)} x^{(n-1} + b^{(i_1 \ldots i_n)} u \end{aligned} \tag{36}$$

The controller fuzzy rule is represented in a similar form:

$$\begin{aligned} &C^{(i_1 \ldots i_n)} : if\ x\ is\ M_1^{i_1}\ and\ x'\ is\ M_2^{i_2}\ and \ldots x^{(n-1}\ is\ M_n^{i_n}\ then \\ &u = r - \left(k_0^{(i_1 \ldots i_n)} + k_1^{(i_1 \ldots i_n)} x + k_1^{(i_1 \ldots i_n)} x' + \ldots + k_1^{(i_1 \ldots i_n)} x^{(n-1} \right) \end{aligned} \tag{37}$$

5.1 Calculation of the affine term

The proposed methodology of design is based on the possibility of formulate the feedback system as shown previously

$$\begin{aligned} &SC^{(i_1 \ldots i_n)} : if\ x\ is\ M_1^{i_1}\ and\ x'\ is\ M_2^{i_2}\ and \ldots x^{(n-1)}\ is\ M_n^{i_n}\ then \\ &x^{(n} = a_0^{(i_1 \ldots i_n)} + a_1^{(i_1 \ldots i_n)} x + \ldots + a_n^{(i_1 \ldots i_n)} x^{(n-1} + b^{(i_1 \ldots i_n)} \left[r - \left(k_0^{(i_1 \ldots i_n)} + k_1^{(i_1 \ldots i_n)} x + \ldots + k_1^{(i_1 \ldots i_n)} x^{(n-1} \right) \right] \end{aligned} \tag{38}$$

Firstly, the affine term of the control action is used to eliminate the affine term of the system:

$$a_0^{(i_1 \ldots i_n)} + b^{(i_1 \ldots i_n)} k_0^{(i_1 \ldots i_n)} = 0 \Rightarrow \qquad k_0^{(i_1 \ldots i_n)} = -\frac{a_0^{(i_1 \ldots i_n)}}{b^{(i_1 \ldots i_n)}} \tag{39}$$

and the feedback system is rewritten as follows:

$$\begin{aligned} &SC^{(i_1 \ldots i_n)} : if\ x\ is\ M_1^{i_1}\ and\ x'\ is\ M_2^{i_2}\ and \ldots x^{(n-1)}\ is\ M_n^{i_n}\ then \\ &x^{(n} = a_1^{(i_1 \ldots i_n)} x + \ldots + a_n^{(i_1 \ldots i_n)} x^{(n-1} + b^{(i_1 \ldots i_n)} \left[r - \left(k_1^{(i_1 \ldots i_n)} x + \ldots + k_1^{(i_1 \ldots i_n)} x^{(n-1} \right) \right] \end{aligned} \tag{40}$$

5.2 State space feedback control based on the proposed estimation approach

Any control methodology by state feedback design can be applied to calculate the rest of control coefficients. Together with the proposed estimation method, the well known LQR method might be an appropriate choice (Aström, K. J.; Wittenmark, B1985). The system can be represented in state space form:

$$x' = Ax + Bu, \quad x \in \Re^n, u \in \Re^m, A \in \Re^{nxn}, B \in \Re^{nxm} \tag{41}$$

The objective is to find the control action u(t) to transfer the system from any initial state $x(t_0)$ to some final state $x(\infty) = 0$ in an infinite time interval, minimizing a quadratic performance index of the form:

$$J = \int_{t_0}^{\infty} \left(x^t Q x + u^t R u \right) dt \tag{42}$$

where $Q \in \Re^{nxn}$ is a symmetric matrix, at least positive a semidefinite one and $R \in \Re^{mxm}$ is also a symmetric positive definite matrix. The optimal control law is computed as follows:

$$u(t) = -Kx(t) = -R^{-1} B^t L x(t) \tag{43}$$

where the matrix $L \in \Re^{nxn}$ is a solution of the Riccati equation:

$$0 = -Q + LBR^{-1}B^{t}L - LA - A^{t}L \tag{44}$$

The design algorithm includes firstly the cancellation of the affine term in each subsystem of the form:

$$x^{(n} = a_0^{(i_1 \ldots i_n)} + a_1^{(i_1 \ldots i_n)} x + a_2^{(i_1 \ldots i_n)} x' + \ldots + a_n^{(i_1 \ldots i_n)} x^{(n\text{-}1)} + b^{(i_1 \ldots i_n)} u \tag{45}$$

The system is then represented in state space form as:

$$x = \begin{bmatrix} x & x' & \cdots & x^{(n-1)} \end{bmatrix}^{t} \tag{46}$$

$$A^{(i_1 \ldots i_n)} = \begin{bmatrix} 0 & 1 & 0 & \cdots & 0 \\ 0 & 0 & 1 & \cdots & 0 \\ \vdots & \vdots & \vdots & \ddots & \vdots \\ 0 & 0 & 0 & \cdots & 1 \\ a_1^{(i_1 \ldots i_n)} & a_2^{(i_1 \ldots i_n)} & a_3^{(i_1 \ldots i_n)} & \cdots & a_n^{(i_1 \ldots i_n)} \end{bmatrix}, \quad B^{(i_1 \ldots i_n)} = \begin{bmatrix} 0 \\ 0 \\ \vdots \\ 0 \\ b^{(i_1 \ldots i_n)} \end{bmatrix} \tag{47}$$

Secondly, the LQR methodology is applied for each subsystem using a common state weighting matrix Q and input matrix R for all the rules. Thus, Riccati equation is solved for each subsystem as follows:

$$0 = -Q + L^{(i_1 \ldots i_n)} B^{(i_1 \ldots i_n)} R^{-1} B^{(i_1 \ldots i_n)t} L^{(i_1 \ldots i_n)} - L^{(i_1 \ldots i_n)} A^{(i_1 \ldots i_n)} - A^{(i_1 \ldots i_n)t} L^{(i_1 \ldots i_n)} \tag{48}$$

Then the state feedback gain vector can be obtained as follows:

$$K^{(i_1 \ldots i_n)} = \begin{bmatrix} k_1^{(i_1 \ldots i_n)} & k_2^{(i_1 \ldots i_n)} & \ldots & k_n^{(i_1 \ldots i_n)} \end{bmatrix} = R^{-1} B^{(i_1 \ldots i_n)t} L^{(i_1 \ldots i_n)} \tag{49}$$

6. Example

In this section the proposed estimation method and its application to control design of FC-LQR is illustrated by an example of an inverted pendulum.

Consider the problem of stabilizing and balancing of swing up of an inverted pendulum (see figure 1). The control of this system is a widely used performance measure of a controller, since this system is unstable and highly nonlinear. The objective is to maintain the inverted pendulum upright with θ despite small disturbances due to wind or system noises. The inverted pendulum can be represented as follows:

$$\ddot{\varphi} = \frac{g \operatorname{sen}\varphi - \cos\varphi \left(\dfrac{u + ml\dot{\varphi}^2 \operatorname{sen}\varphi}{M+m} \right)}{l \left(\dfrac{4}{3} - \dfrac{m \cos^2 \varphi}{M+m} \right)} \tag{50}$$

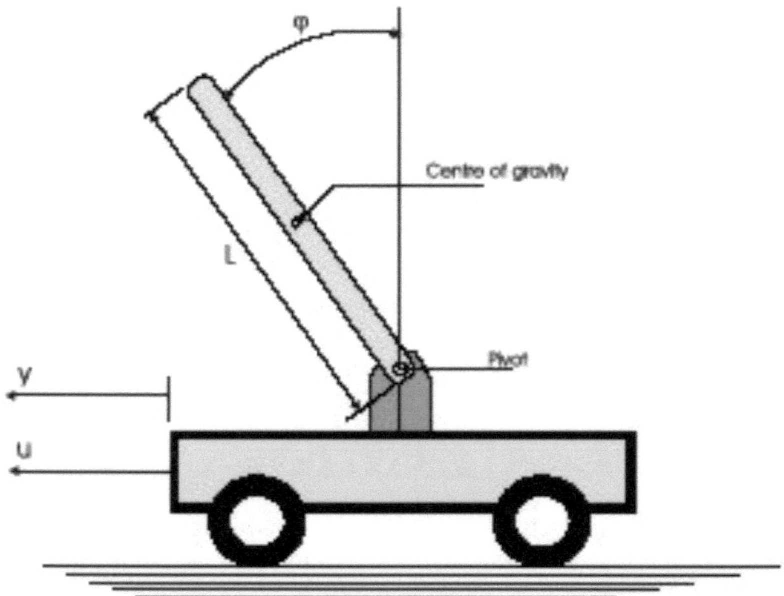

Fig. 1. Inverted pendulum

where θ denotes the angular position (in radians) deviated from the equilibrium position (vertical axis) of the pendulum and $\dot{\theta}$ is the angular velocity, g(gravity acceleration)=9.8 m/sec^2, M(mass) of the cart=1 kg, m(mass) of the pole=0.1 kg, l is the distance from the center of the mass (m) of the pole to the cart=0.5 m. Assuming that $x_1=\theta$ and $x_2=\dot{\theta}$, then the inverted pendulum model can be rewritten in state space form as follows:

$$
\begin{aligned}
x_1 &= \varphi \\
x_1' &= x_2 \\
x_2 &= \dot{\varphi} \\
x_2' &= \frac{g \operatorname{sen} x_1 - \cos x_1 \left(\dfrac{u + ml x_2{}^2 \operatorname{sen} x_1}{M+m} \right)}{l \left(\dfrac{4}{3} - \dfrac{m \cos^2 x_1}{M+m} \right)}
\end{aligned}
\tag{51}
$$

The aim is to move the pendulum to its instable equilibrium position, i.e., $x_1 = x_2 = u = 0$. The membership functions are as shown in figures 2 and 3:

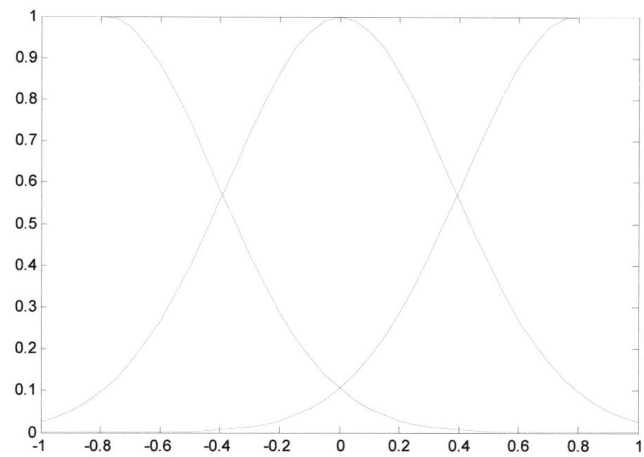

Fig. 2. Membership functions for the angle position

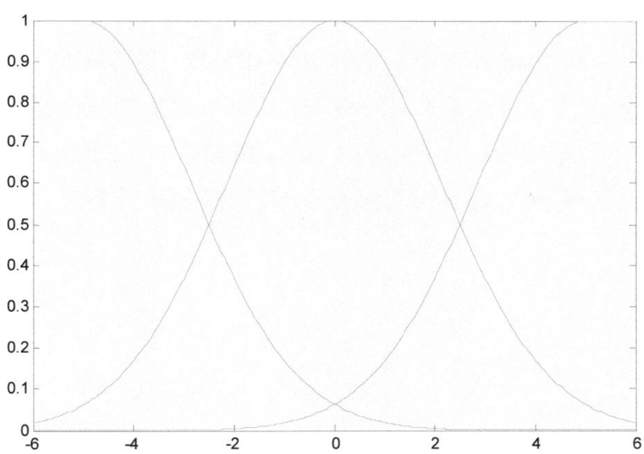

Fig. 3. Membership functions for the angular velocity

Using the iterative method mentioned above, the inverted pendulum fuzzy model can be represented as follows:

$$\begin{aligned}
&S^{11}: if\ x_1\ is\ M_1^1\ and\ x_2\ is\ M_2^1\ then\ x_2' = -2.9699 + 10.3602x_1 - 0.2535x_2 - 1.0001u \\
&S^{12}: if\ x_1\ is\ M_1^1\ and\ x_2\ is\ M_2^2\ then\ x_2' = -2.4941 + 10.4319x_1 - 0.0000x_2 - 1.0001u \\
&S^{13}: if\ x_1\ is\ M_1^1\ and\ x_2\ is\ M_2^3\ then\ x_2' = -2.9699 + 10.3602x_1 + 0.2535x_2 - 1.0001u \\
&S^{21}: if\ x_1\ is\ M_1^2\ and\ x_2\ is\ M_2^1\ then\ x_2' = -0.0066 + 12.7376x_1 - 0.0079x_2 - 1.5883u \\
&S^{22}: if\ x_1\ is\ M_1^2\ and\ x_2\ is\ M_2^2\ then\ x_2' = 13.9336x_1 - 0.0000x_2 - 1.5883u \\
&S^{23}: if\ x_1\ is\ M_1^2\ and\ x_2\ is\ M_2^3\ then\ x_2' = -0.0066 + 12.7376x_1 + 0.0079x_2 - 1.5883u \\
&S^{31}: if\ x_1\ is\ M_1^3\ and\ x_2\ is\ M_2^1\ then\ x_2' = 2.8833 + 10.7086x_1 + 0.2823x_2 - 1.0567u \\
&S^{32}: if\ x_1\ is\ M_1^3\ and\ x_2\ is\ M_2^2\ then\ x_2' = 2.1717 + 10.9258x_1 + 0.0000x_2 - 1.0567u \\
&S^{33}: if\ x_1\ is\ M_1^3\ and\ x_2\ is\ M_2^3\ then\ x_2' = 2.8833 + 10.7086x_1 - 0.2823x_2 - 1.0567u
\end{aligned} \tag{52}$$

The resultant mean square error from this approximation is 0.0014. For each one of these subsystems, a feedback state LQR controller has been designed with the affine term. Firstly, the affine term of the controller is used to eliminate the affine term of the system. The other terms are calculated by the LQR minimizing the following performance index:

$$J = \int_{t_0}^{\infty} \left(100x_1^2 + 10x_2^2 + u^2\right)dt \tag{53}$$

Thus, the resultant fuzzy optimal LQR is:

$$\begin{aligned}
&R^{11}: if\ x_1\ is\ M_1^1\ and\ x_2\ is\ M_2^1\ \ then\ \ u = -2.9695 + 24.7569x_1 + 7.4648x_2 \\
&R^{12}: if\ x_1\ is\ M_1^1\ and\ x_2\ is\ M_2^2\ \ then\ \ u = -2.4937 + 24.8803x_1 + 7.7301x_2 \\
&R^{13}: if\ x_1\ is\ M_1^1\ and\ x_2\ is\ M_2^3\ \ then\ \ u = -2.9695 + 24.7569x_1 + 7.9717x_2 \\
&R^{21}: if\ x_1\ is\ M_1^2\ and\ x_2\ is\ M_2^1\ \ then\ \ u = -0.0042 + 20.8385x_1 + 6.0150x_2 \\
&R^{22}: if\ x_1\ is\ M_1^2\ and\ x_2\ is\ M_2^2\ \ then\ \ u = 22.0756x_1 + 6.1480x_2 \\
&R^{23}: if\ x_1\ is\ M_1^2\ and\ x_2\ is\ M_2^3\ \ then\ \ u = -0.0042 + 20.8385x_1 + 6.0250x_2 \\
&R^{31}: if\ x_1\ is\ M_1^3\ and\ x_2\ is\ M_2^1\ \ then\ \ u = 2.7286 + 24.3712x_1 + 7.7638x_2 \\
&R^{32}: if\ x_1\ is\ M_1^3\ and\ x_2\ is\ M_2^2\ \ then\ \ u = 2.0551 + 24.7239x_1 + 7.5362x_2 \\
&R^{33}: if\ x_1\ is\ M_1^3\ and\ x_2\ is\ M_2^3\ \ then\ \ u = 2.7286 + 24.3712x_1 + 7.2294x_2
\end{aligned} \tag{54}$$

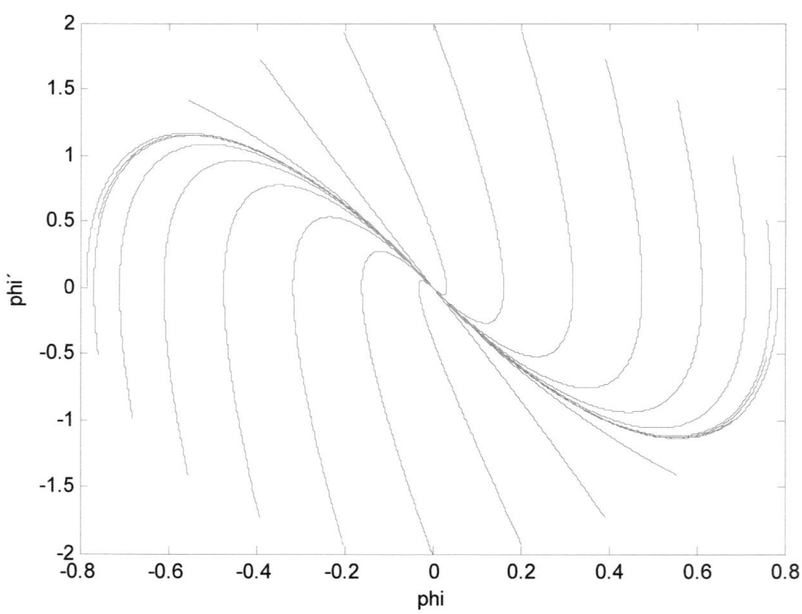

Fig. 4. Several trajectories in state space form of the system for several initial conditions

7. Conclusions

New efficient approach has been presented to improve the local and global estimation of T-S fuzzy model. The approach developed here can be considered as a generalized version of T-S method with optimized performance in approximating nonlinear functions. A simple and less computational method, based on the extended Kalman filter has been developed. A FC based LQR has been proposed in order to show the effectiveness of the estimation method developed here in control applications. An Illustrative example of an inverted pendulum has been chosen to evaluate the robustness and remarkable performance of the proposed method and the high accuracy obtained in approximating nonlinear and unstable systems locally and globally in comparison with the original T-S model. Simulation results have shown the potential, simplicity and generality of the algorithm.

8. References

Aström, K. J.; Wittenmark, B. (1997). Computer-Controlled Systems", Prentice Hall, USA.

Cordon, O.; Herrera; Magdalena; F. L. & Villar P. (2001). A Genetic Learning Process for the Scaling Factors, Granularity and Contexts of the Fuzzy Rule-Based System Data Base, Information Sciences, 136, 85- 107.

Cordon, O.; Herrera. & Villar P. (2000). "Analysis and Guidelines to Obtain a Good Uniform Fuzzy Partition Granularity for Fuzzy Rule-Based Systems Using Simulated Annealing, International Journal of Approximate Reasoning, 25, 187-216.

Gelb, A. (1974). Applied Optimal Estimation, MITPress, Cambridge, MA.

Hsiao, C. (1999). Modified gain fuzzy Kalman filtering algorithm, JSME Internat. J. Ser. C 42 363–368.

Jiménez, A.; Al-Hadithi, B. M. & Matía, F. (2008). "An Optimal T-S Model for the Estimation and Identification of Nonlinear Functions", WSEAS Transactions on Systems and Control, Vol. 3, Issue 10, pp. 897-906.

Kalman, R. E. (1960). "A New Approach to Linear Filtering and Prediction Problems," Transactions of the ASME-Journal of Basic Engineering, Vol. 82(series D), pp.35-45.

Kobayashi, K.; Cheok, K. & Watanabe, K.(1995). Estimation of the absolute vehicle speedusing fuzzy logic rule-based Kalman filter, American Control Conf., Seattle, pp. 3086–3090.

Maybeck, P. S. (1979). Stochastic models, estimation, and control, Vol. 1, Academic Press.

Puskorius, G. & Feldkamp, L. (1994). Neurocontrol of nonlinear dynamical systems with Kalman filter trained recurrent networks, IEEE Trans. Neural Networks 5, pp. 279–297.

Baranyi, P. (2003). SVD-based reduction to MISO TS models, *IEEE Trans. Ind. Electron.*, vol. 51, no. 1, pp. 232–242.

Cao, S. G.; Rees, N. W. & and Feng, G. (1996). Stability analysis of fuzzy control systems, *IEEE Trans. Syst., Man, Cybern., B, Cybern.*, vol. 26, no. 1, pp. 201–204.

Cao, S. G.; Rees, N. W. & and Feng, G. (1997). Analysis and design for a class of complex control systems— Part I: Fuzzy modeling and identification," *Automatica*, vol. 33, pp. 1017–1028.

Chen, W. & Saif, M. (2005). A Novel Fuzzy System With Dynamic Rule Base, IEEE Trans. Fuzzy Syst. 13(5), pp. 569-582.

Fantuzzi, C. & Rovatti, R. (1996). On the approximation capabilities of the homogeneousTakagi-Sugeno model, in *Proc. 5th IEEE Int. Conf. Fuzzy Systems*, New Orleans, LA, pp. 1067–1072.

Gang, F. (2006). A survey on analysis and design of model-based fuzzy control systems. IEEE Trans. Fuzzy Syst. 14(5), 676-697.

Gudwin, R.; Gomide, F. & Pedrycz, W. (1998). Context Adaptation in Fuzzy Processing and Genetic Algorithms, International Journal of Intelligent Systems, 13 , 929-948.

Hong T. P. & Lee, C. Y. (1996). Induction of fuzzy rules and membership functions from training examples, *Fuzzy Sets Syst.*, vol. 84, no. 1, pp. 33–47.

Hou, Y.; Zurada, J. M.; Karwowski, W.; Marras, W. S. & Davis, K. (2007). Identification of Key Variables Using Fuzzy Average With Fuzzy Cluster Distribution, IEEE Trans. Fuzzy Syst. 15(4), 673-685.

Hseng, T.; Li, S. & Tsai, S.-H. (2007). T–S Fuzzy Bilinear Model and Fuzzy Controller Design for a Class of Nonlinear Systems, *IEEE Trans. Fuzzy Syst.*, vol. 15, no. 3, pp. 494-506.

Jiménez, A.; Al-Hadithi, B. M. & Matía, F. (2008). An Optimal T-S Model for the Estimation and Identification of Nonlinear Functions", WSEAS Transactions on Systems and Control, Vol. 3, Issue 10, pp. 897-906.

Johansen, T. A.; Shorten, R. & Murray-Smith, R. (2000) On the interpretation and identification of dynamic Takagi–Sugeno models, *IEEE Trans. Fuzzy Syst.*, vol. 8, no. 3, pp. 297–313.

Kim, J.-H.; Hyun, C.-H.; Kim, E. & Park, M. (2007). New Adaptive Synchronization of Uncertain Chaotic Systems Based on T–S Fuzzy Model, *IEEE Trans. Fuzzy Syst.*, vol. 15, no. 3, pp. 359-369.

Kim, J.; Suga, Y. & Won, S. (2006). A New Approach to Fuzzy Modeling of Nonlinear Dynamic Systems With Noise: Relevance Vector Learning Mechanism", *IEEE Trans. Fuzzy Syst.*, vol. 14, no. 2, pp. 222-231.

Klawonn, F. & Kruse, R. (1997). Constructing a fuzzy controller from data, *Fuzzy Sets Syst.*, vol. 85, no. 2, pp. 177–193.

Mencattini, A.; Salmeri M. & Salsano, A. (2005). Sufficient Conditions to Impose Derivative Constraints on MISO Takagi–Sugeno Fuzzy Logic Systems", IEEE Trans. Fuzzy Syst., Vol. 13, No. 4.

Kumar, M.; Stoll, R. & Stoll, N. (2006). A Min–Max Approach to Fuzzy Clustering, Estimation, and Identification, *IEEE Trans. Fuzzy Syst.*, vol. 14, no. 2, pp. 248–262

Langari R. & Wang, L. (1996). Complex systems modeling via fuzzy logic," *IEEE Trans. Syst., Man, Cybern. B*, vol. 26, pp. 100–106.

Lian, K.-Y.; Su, C.-H. & Huang, C.-S. (2006). Performance Enhancement for T–S Fuzzy Control Using Neural Networks, *IEEE Trans. Fuzzy Syst.*, vol. 14, no. 5, pp. 619–627.

Matía, F.; Jiménez, A. & Al-Hadithi, B. M. (2008). An Affine model with Decoupled dynamics, Proceedings of IPMU'08, pp. 713-720, 22-27.

Mollov, S.; Babuska, R.; Abonyi, J. & Verbruggen, H. B. (2004). Effective optimization for fuzzy model predictive control, *IEEE Trans. Fuzzy Syst.*, vol. 12, no. 5, pp. 661–675.

Nozaki, K.; Ishibuchi, H. & Tanaka, H. (1997). A simple but powerful heuristic method for generating fuzzy rules from numerical data, *Fuzzy Sets Syst.*, vol. 86, no. 3, pp. 251–270.

Pedrycz, W.; Gudwin, R. & Gomide, F. (1997). Nonlinear Context Adaptation in the calibration of Fuzzy Sets, Fuzzy Sets and Systems, 88, pp. 91-97.

Ramaswamy, P.; Edwards, R. R. & Lee, K. (1993). Two approaches for automating the tuning process of fuzzy logic controllers, IEEE Conf. on Decision and Control, San Antonio, TX, pp.1753-1758.

Simon, D. (2000). Design and rule base reduction of a fuzzy filter for the estimation of motor currents, International Journal of Approximate Reasoning, 25, pp. 145-167.

Simon, D. (2002). Training Fuzzy Systems with the Extended Kalman Filter, Fuzzy Sets and Systems, Vol. 132, 189-199.

Simon, D. (2002). Sum normal optimization of fuzzy membership functions, International Journal of Uncertainty, Fuzziness and Knowledge-Based Systems, Vol. 10, No. 4, pp.363-384.

Sugeno, M. & Tanaka, K. (1991). Successive identification of a fuzzy model and its applications to prediction of a complex system, Fuzzy Sets and Systems 42, pp. 315–334.

Sugeno, M. & Kang, G. (1988). Structure identification of fuzzy model, *Fuzzy Sets Syst.*, vol. 28, pp.15–33.

Skrjanc, I.; Blazic, S. & Agamennoni, O. (2005). Interval Fuzzy Model identification Using l_∞-Norm, *IEEE Trans. Fuzzy Syst.*, vol.. 13, no. 5.

Takagi T. & Sugeno, M. (1985). Fuzzy identification of systems and its applications to modeling and control, *IEEE Trans. Syst., Man, Cybern.*, vol. SMC-15, no. 1, pp. 116–132.

Tanaka, K.; Wang, H. O. (2001). Fuzzy Control Systems Design and Analysis: A Linear Matrix Inequality Approach. New York: Wiley.

Tao, C. & and Taur, J. (1999). Design of Fuzzy Controllers with Adaptive Rule Insertion, IEEE Transactions on Systems, Man, and Cybernetics-Part B: Cybernetics, 29, pp. 389- 397.

Teixeira, M. C. M.; Assunção, E. & Avellar, R. G. (2003). On relaxed LMI based designs for fuzzy regulators and fuzzy observers, *IEEE Trans.Fuzzy Syst.*, vol. 11, no. 5, pp. 613–623.

Wang, L. & Mendel, J. (1992). Back-propagation of Fuzzy Systems as Nonlinear Dynamic System Identiers, IEEE International Conference on Fuzzy Systems, San Diego, California, pp. 1409-1418.

Wang, L. (1994). Adaptive Fuzzy Systems and Control: Design and Stability Analysis, Prentice-Hall, Englewood Cli6s, NJ, pp. 27-28.

Wang, L. X. & Mendel, J. M. (1995). Design and analysis of fuzzy identifiers of nonlinear dynamic systems," *IEEE Trans. Automat. Contr.*, vol. 40, pp. 11–23.

Wang, L. X. & Mendel, J. M. (1992). Generating fuzzy rules by learning from examples, *IEEE Trans. Syst., Man, Cybern.*, vol. 22, pp. 1414–1427.

Wang, L. & Yen, J. (1998). Extracting fuzzy rules for system modelling using a hybrid of genetic algorithms and Kalman filter, Fuzzy Sets and Systems 101, pp. 353–362.

Xian-Tu, P. (1990). Generating Rules for Fuzzy Logic Controllers by Functions," Fuzzy Sets and Systems 36, pp. 83-89.

Ying, H. (1998). General SISO Takagi–Sugeno fuzzy systems with linear rule consequent are universal approximators, *IEEE Trans. Fuzzy Syst.*, vol. 6, no. 4, pp. 582–587.

Yu, W. & Li, X. O. (2004). Fuzzy identification using fuzzy neural networks with stable learning algorithms, *IEEE Trans. Fuzzy Syst.*, vol. 12, no. 3, pp. 411–420.

Zeng, K.; Zhang, N. Y. & Xu, W. L. (2000). A comparative study on sufficient conditions for Takagi–Sugeno fuzzy systems as universal approximators, *IEEE Trans. Fuzzy Syst.*, vol. 8, no. 6, pp. 773–780.

5

Synthesis of a Robust $\mathcal{H}_\infty$ Fuzzy Controller for Uncertain Nonlinear Dynamical Systems

Wudhichai Assawinchaichote*
King Mongkut's University of Technology Thonburi
Thailand

1. Introduction

Over the past two decades, there has been rapidly growing interest in application of fuzzy logic to control problem. Researches have been focused on its application to industrial processes and a number of successful results have been reported in the literature. In spite of these successes, there are many basic issues remain to be addressed. One of them is how to achieve a systematic design that guarantees closed-loop stability and performance. Recently, a great amount of effort has been devoted to describing a nonlinear system using a Takagi-Sugeno fuzzy model (see [1-28]). The Takagi-sugeno fuzzy model represents a nonlinear system by a family of local linear models which smoothly blended together through fuzzy membership functions. Unlike conventional modelling techniques which uses a single model to describe the global behavior of a nonlinear system, fuzzy modelling is essentially a multi-model approach in which simple sub-models (typically linear models) are fuzzily combined to described the global behavior of a nonlinear system. Based on this fuzzy model, a number of systematic model-based fuzzy control design methodologies have been developed.
The aim of this paper is to study the problem of designing robust $\mathcal{H}_\infty$ fuzzy controller for a class of uncertain fuzzy systems. First, we approximate this class of uncertain nonlinear systems by a Takagi-Sugeno fuzzy model. Then based on an LMI approach, we develop a technique for designing robust $\mathcal{H}_\infty$ fuzzy state-feedback and output feedback controllers such that the $\mathcal{L}_2$-gain of the mapping from the exogenous input noise to the regulated output is less than a prescribed value.
This paper is organized as follows. In Section 2, system descriptions and definition are presented. In Section 3 and Section 4, based on an LMI approach, we respectively develop a technique for designing robust $\mathcal{H}_\infty$ fuzzy state-feedback and output-feedback controllers such that the $\mathcal{L}_2$-gain of the mapping from the exogenous input noise to the regulated output is less than a prescribed value for the system described in Section 2. The validity of this approach is demonstrated by an example from a literature in Section 5. Finally, conclusions are given in Section 6.

2. System descriptions and definitions

In this chapter, we generalize the TS fuzzy system to represent a TS fuzzy system with parametric uncertainties as follows:

*W. Assawinchaichote is with the Department of Electronic and Telecommnunication Engineering, King Mongkut's University of Technology Thonburi, 126 Prachautits Rd., Bangkok 10140, Thailand.

$$
\begin{aligned}
\dot{x}(t) &= \textstyle\sum_{i=1}^{r} \mu_i(\nu(t)) \Big[[A_i + \Delta A_i] x(t) + [B_{1_i} + \Delta B_{1_i}] w(t) \\
&\quad + [B_{2_i} + \Delta B_{2_i}] u(t) \Big], \quad x(0) = 0 \\
z(t) &= \textstyle\sum_{i=1}^{r} \mu_i(\nu(t)) \Big[[C_{1_i} + \Delta C_{1_i}] x(t) + [D_{12_i} + \Delta D_{12_i}] u(t) \Big] \\
y(t) &= \textstyle\sum_{i=1}^{r} \mu_i(\nu(t)) \Big[[C_{2_i} + \Delta C_{2_i}] x(t) + [D_{21_i} + \Delta D_{21_i}] w(t) \Big]
\end{aligned} \tag{1}
$$

where $\nu(t) = [\nu_1(t) \cdots \nu_\vartheta(t)]$ is the premise variable vector that may depend on states in many cases, $\mu_i(\nu(t))$ denotes the normalized time-varying fuzzy weighting functions for each rule (i.e., $\mu_i(\nu(t)) \geq 0$ and $\sum_{i=1}^{r} \mu_i(\nu(t)) = 1$), ϑ is the number of fuzzy sets, $x(t) \in \Re^n$ is the state vector, $u(t) \in \Re^m$ is the input, $w(t) \in \Re^p$ is the disturbance which belongs to $\mathcal{L}_2[0,\infty)$, $y(t) \in \Re^\ell$ is the measurement, $z(t) \in \Re^s$ is the controlled output, the matrices $A_i, B_{1_i}, B_{2_i}, C_{1_i}, C_{2_i}, D_{12_i}$ and D_{21_i} are of appropriate dimensions, and r is the number of IF-THEN rules. The matrices $\Delta A_i, \Delta B_{1_i}, \Delta B_{2_i}, \Delta C_{1_i}, \Delta C_{2_i}, \Delta D_{12_i}$ and ΔD_{21_i} represent the uncertainties in the system and satisfy the following assumption.

Assumption 1

$$
\begin{aligned}
\Delta A_i &= F(x(t),t) H_{1_i}, \\
\Delta B_{1_i} &= F(x(t),t) H_{2_i}, \ \Delta B_{2_i} = F(x(t),t) H_{3_i}, \\
\Delta C_{1_i} &= F(x(t),t) H_{4_i}, \ \Delta C_{2_i} = F(x(t),t) H_{5_i}, \\
\Delta D_{12_i} &= F(x(t),t) H_{6_i} \ \text{and} \ \Delta D_{21_i} = F(x(t),t) H_{7_i}
\end{aligned}
$$

where H_{j_i}, $j = 1,2,\cdots,7$ are known matrix functions which characterize the structure of the uncertainties. Furthermore, the following inequality holds:

$$
\|F(x(t),t)\| \leq \rho \tag{2}
$$

for any known positive constant ρ.

Next, let us recall the following definition.

Definition 1 *Suppose γ is a given positive number. A system (1) is said to have an $\mathcal{L}_2$-gain less than or equal to γ if*

$$
\int_0^{T_f} z^T(t) z(t) dt \leq \gamma^2 \left[\int_0^{T_f} w^T(t) w(t) dt \right], \ x(0) = 0 \tag{3}
$$

for all $T_f \geq 0$ and $w(t) \in \mathcal{L}_2[0, T_f]$.

Note that for the symmetric block matrices, we use $(*)$ as an ellipsis for terms that are induced by symmetry.

3. Robust $\mathcal{H}_\infty$ state-feedback control design

The aim of this section is to design a robust $\mathcal{H}_\infty$ fuzzy state-feedback controller of the form

$$
u(t) = \sum_{j=1}^{r} \mu_j K_j x(t) \tag{4}
$$

where K_j is the controller gain, such that the inequality (3) holds. The state space form of the fuzzy system model (1) with the controller (4) is given by

$$\begin{aligned} \dot{x}(t) &= \textstyle\sum_{i=1}^{r}\sum_{j=1}^{r}\mu_i\mu_j\Big[[(A_i + B_{2_i}K_j) \\ &\quad +(\Delta A_i + \Delta B_{2_i}K_j)]x(t) + [B_{1_i} + \Delta B_{1_i}]w(t)\Big], \quad x(0) = 0. \end{aligned} \tag{5}$$

The following theorem provides sufficient conditions for the existence of a robust $\mathcal{H}_\infty$ fuzzy state-feedback controller. These sufficient conditions can be derived by the Lyapunov approach.

Theorem 1 *Consider the system (1). Given a prescribed $\mathcal{H}_\infty$ performance $\gamma > 0$ and a positive constant δ, if there exist a matrix $P = P^T$ and matrices Y_j, $j = 1,2,\cdots,r$, satisfying the following linear matrix inequalities:*

$$P > 0 \tag{6}$$
$$\Omega_{ii} < 0, \quad i = 1,2,\cdots,r \tag{7}$$
$$\Omega_{ij} + \Omega_{ji} < 0, \quad i < j \le r \tag{8}$$

where

$$\Omega_{ij} = \begin{pmatrix} \begin{pmatrix} A_iP + PA_i^T \\ +B_{2_i}Y_j + Y_j^TB_{2_i}^T \end{pmatrix} & (*)^T & (*)^T \\ \tilde{B}_{1_i}^T & -\gamma I & (*)^T \\ \tilde{C}_{1_i}P + \tilde{D}_{12_i}Y_j & 0 & -\gamma I \end{pmatrix} \tag{9}$$

with

$$\tilde{B}_{1_i} = \begin{bmatrix} \delta I & I & \delta I & B_{1_i} \end{bmatrix},$$
$$\tilde{C}_{1_i} = \begin{bmatrix} \frac{\gamma\rho}{\delta}H_{1_i}^T & 0 & \sqrt{2}\lambda\rho H_{4_i}^T & \sqrt{2}\lambda C_{1_i}^T \end{bmatrix}^T,$$
$$\tilde{D}_{12_i} = \begin{bmatrix} 0 & \frac{\gamma\rho}{\delta}H_{3_i}^T & \sqrt{2}\lambda\rho H_{6_i}^T & \sqrt{2}\lambda D_{12_i}^T \end{bmatrix}^T,$$
$$\lambda = \left(1 + \rho^2\sum_{i=1}^{r}\sum_{j=1}^{r}\left[\|H_{2_i}^TH_{2_j}\|\right]\right)^{\frac{1}{2}},$$

then the inequality (3) holds. Furthermore, a suitable choice of the fuzzy controller is

$$u(t) = \sum_{j=1}^{r}\mu_jK_jx(t) \tag{10}$$

where

$$K_j = Y_jP^{-1}. \tag{11}$$

Proof: Using Assumption 1, the closed-loop fuzzy system (5) can be expressed as follows:

$$\dot{x}(t) = \textstyle\sum_{i=1}^{r}\sum_{j=1}^{r}\mu_i\mu_j\Big([A_i + B_{2_i}K_j]x(t) + \tilde{B}_{1_i}\tilde{w}(t)\Big) \tag{12}$$

where

$$\tilde{B}_{1_i} = \begin{bmatrix} \delta I & I & \delta I & B_{1_i} \end{bmatrix},$$

and the disturbance $\tilde{w}(t)$ is

$$\tilde{w}(t) = \begin{bmatrix} \frac{1}{\delta}F(x(t),t)H_{1_i}x(t) \\ F(x(t),t)H_{2_i}w(t) \\ \frac{1}{\delta}F(x(t),t)H_{3_i}K_jx(t) \\ w(t) \end{bmatrix}. \tag{13}$$

Let consider a Lyapunov function

$$V(x(t)) = \gamma x^T(t)Qx(t)$$

where $Q = P^{-1}$. Differentiate $V(x(t))$ along the closed-loop system (12) yields

$$\begin{aligned} \dot{V}(x(t)) &= \gamma\dot{x}^T(t)Qx(t) + \gamma x^T(t)Q\dot{x}(t) \\ &= \sum_{i=1}^{r}\sum_{j=1}^{r}\mu_i\mu_j\Big(\gamma x^T(t)(A_i + B_{2_i}K_j)^TQx(t) \\ &\quad +\gamma x^T(t)Q(A_i + B_{2_i}K_j)x(t) \\ &\quad +\gamma\tilde{w}^T(t)\tilde{B}_{1_i}^TQx(t) + \gamma x^T(t)Q\tilde{B}_{1_i}\tilde{w}(t)\Big). \end{aligned} \tag{14}$$

Adding and subtracting $-\tilde{z}^T(t)\tilde{z}(t) + \gamma^2\sum_{i=1}^{r}\sum_{j=1}^{r}\sum_{m=1}^{r}\sum_{n=1}^{r}\mu_i\mu_j\mu_m\mu_n[\tilde{w}^T(t)\tilde{w}(t)]$ to and from (14), we get

$$\begin{aligned} \dot{V}(x(t)) &= \gamma\sum_{i=1}^{r}\sum_{j=1}^{r}\sum_{m=1}^{r}\sum_{n=1}^{r}\mu_i\mu_j\mu_m\mu_n\Big(\begin{bmatrix} x^T(t) & \tilde{w}^T(t) \end{bmatrix} \times \\ &\quad \begin{pmatrix} \begin{pmatrix} (A_i + B_{2_i}K_j)^TQ \\ +Q(A_i + B_{2_i}K_j) \\ +\frac{(\tilde{C}_{1_i}+\tilde{D}_{12_i}K_j)^T(\tilde{C}_{1_m}+\tilde{D}_{12_m}K_n)}{\gamma} \end{pmatrix} & (*)^T \\ \tilde{B}_{1_i}^TQ & -\gamma I \end{pmatrix} \begin{bmatrix} x(t) \\ \tilde{w}(t) \end{bmatrix}\Big) \\ &\quad -\tilde{z}^T(t)\tilde{z}(t) + \gamma^2\sum_{i=1}^{r}\sum_{j=1}^{r}\sum_{m=1}^{r}\sum_{n=1}^{r}\mu_i\mu_j\mu_m\mu_n[\tilde{w}^T(t)\tilde{w}(t)] \end{aligned} \tag{15}$$

where

$$\tilde{z}(t) = \sum_{i=1}^{r}\sum_{j=1}^{r}\mu_i\mu_j[\tilde{C}_{1_i} + \tilde{D}_{12_i}K_j]x(t) \tag{16}$$

with

$$\tilde{C}_{1_i} = \begin{bmatrix} \frac{\gamma\rho}{\delta}H_{1_i}^T & 0 & \sqrt{2}\lambda\rho H_{4_i}^T & \sqrt{2}\lambda C_{1_i}^T \end{bmatrix}^T$$

and $\tilde{D}_{12_i} = \begin{bmatrix} 0 & \frac{\gamma\rho}{\delta}H_{3_i}^T & \sqrt{2}\lambda\rho H_{6_i}^T & \sqrt{2}\lambda D_{12_i}^T \end{bmatrix}^T.$

Pre and post multiply (7)-(8) by $\begin{pmatrix} Q & 0 & 0 \\ 0 & I & 0 \\ 0 & 0 & I \end{pmatrix}$ yields

$$\begin{pmatrix} \begin{pmatrix} (A_i + B_{2_i}K_i)^T Q \\ +Q(A_i + B_{2_i}K_i) \end{pmatrix} & (*)^T & (*)^T \\ \tilde{B}_{1_i}^T Q & -\gamma I & (*)^T \\ \tilde{C}_{1_i} + \tilde{D}_{12_i}K_i & 0 & -\gamma I \end{pmatrix} < 0, \tag{17}$$

$i = 1, 2, \cdots, r$, and

$$\left\{ \begin{pmatrix} \begin{pmatrix} (A_i + B_{2_i}K_j)^T Q \\ +Q(A_i + B_{2_i}K_j) \end{pmatrix} & (*)^T & (*)^T \\ \tilde{B}_{1_i}^T Q & -\gamma I & (*)^T \\ \tilde{C}_{1_i} + \tilde{D}_{12_i}K_j & 0 & -\gamma I \end{pmatrix} + \begin{pmatrix} \begin{pmatrix} (A_j + B_{2_j}K_i)^T Q \\ +Q(A_j + B_{2_j}K_i) \end{pmatrix} & (*)^T & (*)^T \\ \tilde{B}_{1_j}^T Q & -\gamma I & (*)^T \\ \tilde{C}_{1_j} + \tilde{D}_{12_j}K_i & 0 & -\gamma I \end{pmatrix} \right\} < 0, \tag{18}$$

$i < j \le r$, respectively. Applying the Schur complement on (17)-(18) and rearranging them, then we have

$$\begin{pmatrix} \begin{pmatrix} (A_i + B_{2_i}K_i)^T Q \\ +Q(A_i + B_{2_i}K_i) \\ + \frac{(\tilde{C}_{1_i} + \tilde{D}_{12_i}K_i)^T(\tilde{C}_{1_i} + \tilde{D}_{12_i}K_i)}{\gamma} \end{pmatrix} & (*)^T \\ \tilde{B}_{1_i}^T Q & -\gamma I \end{pmatrix} < 0, \tag{19}$$

$i = 1, 2, \cdots, r$, and

$$\left\{ \begin{pmatrix} \begin{pmatrix} (A_i + B_{2_i}K_j)^T Q \\ +Q(A_i + B_{2_i}K_j) \\ + \frac{(\tilde{C}_{1_i} + \tilde{D}_{12_i}K_j)^T(\tilde{C}_{1_i} + \tilde{D}_{12_i}K_j)}{\gamma} \end{pmatrix} & (*)^T \\ \tilde{B}_{1_i}^T Q & -\gamma I \end{pmatrix} + \begin{pmatrix} \begin{pmatrix} (A_j + B_{2_j}K_i)^T Q \\ +Q(A_j + B_{2_j}K_i) \\ + \frac{(\tilde{C}_{1_j} + \tilde{D}_{12_j}K_i)^T(\tilde{C}_{1_j} + \tilde{D}_{12_j}K_i)}{\gamma} \end{pmatrix} & (*)^T \\ \tilde{B}_{1_j}^T Q & -\gamma I \end{pmatrix} \right\} < 0, \tag{20}$$

$i < j \le r$, respectively. Using (19)-(20) and the fact that

$$\sum_{i=1}^{r} \sum_{j=1}^{r} \sum_{m=1}^{r} \sum_{n=1}^{r} \mu_i \mu_j \mu_m \mu_n M_{ij}^T N_{mn} \le \frac{1}{2} \sum_{i=1}^{r} \sum_{j=1}^{r} \mu_i \mu_j [M_{ij}^T M_{ij} + N_{ij} N_{ij}^T], \tag{21}$$

it is obvious that we have

$$\begin{pmatrix} \begin{pmatrix} (A_i + B_{2_i}K_j)^T Q \\ +Q(A_i + B_{2_i}K_j) \\ + \frac{(\tilde{C}_{1_i}+\tilde{D}_{12_i}K_j)^T(\tilde{C}_{1_i}+\tilde{D}_{12_i}K_j)}{\gamma} \end{pmatrix} & (*)^T \\ \tilde{B}_{1_i}^T Q & -\gamma I \end{pmatrix} < 0 \tag{22}$$

where $i, j = 1, 2, \cdots, r$. Since (22) is less than zero and the fact that $\mu_i \geq 0$ and $\sum_{i=1}^r \mu_i = 1$, then (15) becomes

$$\dot{V}(x(t)) \leq -\tilde{z}^T(t)\tilde{z}(t) + \gamma^2 \sum_{i=1}^r \sum_{j=1}^r \sum_{m=1}^r \sum_{n=1}^r \mu_i\mu_j\mu_m\mu_n[\tilde{w}^T(t)\tilde{w}(t)]. \tag{23}$$

Integrate both sides of (23) yields

$$\int_0^{T_f} \dot{V}(x(t))dt \leq \int_0^{T_f} \Big[-\tilde{z}^T(t)\tilde{z}(t) + \gamma^2 \sum_{i=1}^r \sum_{j=1}^r \sum_{m=1}^r \sum_{n=1}^r \mu_i\mu_j\mu_m\mu_n[\tilde{w}^T(t)\tilde{w}(t)] \Big] dt$$

$$V(x(T_f)) - V(x(0)) \leq \int_0^{T_f} \Big[-\tilde{z}^T(t)\tilde{z}(t) + \gamma^2 \sum_{i=1}^r \sum_{j=1}^r \sum_{m=1}^r \sum_{n=1}^r \mu_i\mu_j\mu_m\mu_n[\tilde{w}^T(t)\tilde{w}(t)] \Big] dt.$$

Using the fact that $x(0) = 0$ and $V(x(T_f)) \geq 0$ for all $T_f \neq 0$, we get

$$\int_0^{T_f} \tilde{z}^T(t)\tilde{z}(t)dt \leq \gamma^2 \left[\int_0^{T_f} \sum_{i=1}^r \sum_{j=1}^r \sum_{m=1}^r \sum_{n=1}^r \mu_i\mu_j\mu_m\mu_n[\tilde{w}^T(t)\tilde{w}(t)]dt \right]. \tag{24}$$

Putting $\tilde{z}(t)$ and $\tilde{w}(t)$ respectively given in (16) and (13) into (24) and using the fact that $\|F(x(t),t)\| \leq \rho$, $\lambda^2 = \left(1 + \rho^2 \sum_{i=1}^r \sum_{j=1}^r [\|H_{2_i}^T H_{2_j}\|]\right)$ and (21), we have

$$\begin{aligned} &\int_0^{T_f} \sum_{i=1}^r \sum_{j=1}^r \mu_i\mu_j \Big(2\lambda^2 x^T(t)[C_{1_i} + D_{12_i}K_j]^T[C_{1_i} + D_{12_i}K_j]x(t) \\ &+2\lambda^2\rho^2 x^T(t)[H_{4_i} + H_{6_i}K_j]^T[H_{4_i} + H_{6_i}K_j]x(t) \Big) dt \\ &\leq \gamma^2\lambda^2 \left[\int_0^{T_f} w^T(t)w(t)\, dt \right]. \end{aligned} \tag{25}$$

Adding and subtracting

$$\begin{aligned} \lambda^2 z^T(t)z(t) = {} & \lambda^2 \sum_{i=1}^r \sum_{j=1}^r \mu_i\mu_j \Big(x^T(t) \Big[C_{1_i} + F(x(t),t)H_{4_i} + D_{12_i}K_j + F(x(t),t)H_{6_i}K_j \Big]^T \\ & \Big[C_{1_i} + F(x(t),t)H_{4_i} + D_{12_i}K_j + F(x(t),t)H_{6_i}K_j \Big] x(t) \Big) \end{aligned}$$

to and from (25), one obtains

$$\int_0^{T_f} \Big\{\lambda^2 z^T(t)z(t) + \sum_{i=1}^{r}\sum_{j=1}^{r} \mu_i\mu_j \times$$
$$\Big(2\lambda^2 x^T(t)[C_{1_i} + D_{12_i}K_j]^T[C_{1_i} + D_{12_i}K_j]x(t)$$
$$+2\lambda^2\rho^2 x^T(t)[H_{4_i} + H_{6_i}K_j]^T[H_{4_i} + H_{6_i}K_j]x(t)$$
$$-\lambda^2 x^T(t)[C_{1_i} + F(x(t),t)H_{4_i} + D_{12_i}K_j + F(x(t),t)H_{6_i}K_j]^T$$
$$[C_{1_i} + F(x(t),t)H_{4_i} + D_{12_i}K_j + F(x(t),t)H_{6_i}K_j]x(t)\Big)\Big\}\, dt$$
$$\leq \gamma^2\lambda^2\left[\int_0^{T_f} w^T(t)w(t)\, dt\right]. \tag{26}$$

Using the triangular inequality and the fact that $\|F(x(t),t)\| \leq \rho$, we have

$$\lambda^2 \sum_{i=1}^{r}\sum_{j=1}^{r} \mu_i\mu_j\Big(x^T(t)\left[C_{1_i} + F(x(t),t)H_{4_i} + D_{12_i}K_j + F(x(t),t)H_{6_i}K_j\right]^T$$
$$\left[C_{1_i} + F(x(t),t)H_{4_i} + D_{12_i}K_j + F(x(t),t)H_{6_i}K_j\right]x(t)\Big)$$
$$\leq \sum_{i=1}^{r}\sum_{j=1}^{r} \mu_i\mu_j\Big(\Big\{2\lambda^2 x^T(t)\left[C_{1_i} + D_{12_i}K_j\right]^T\left[C_{1_i} + D_{12_i}K_j\right]x(t)\Big\}$$
$$+2\lambda^2\rho^2 x^T(t)\left[H_{4_i} + H_{6_i}K_j\right]^T\left[H_{4_i} + H_{6_i}K_j\right]x(t)\Big). \tag{27}$$

Using (27) on (26), we obtain

$$\int_0^{T_f} z^T(t)z(t) \leq \gamma^2 \int_0^{T_f} w^T(t)w(t)\, dt. \tag{28}$$

Hence, the inequality (3) holds. ■

4. Robust $\mathcal{H}_\infty$ output feedback control design

The nature of the information of the state available to the controller has a major effect on the complexity of the designing problem and of the resulting controller. The state-feedback control design problem is an easier problem in which all information are available. However, in most real physical systems, the state is not perfectly known, and so we must estimate it. The process of estimating the system state from the measurement output that are available is called the estimator design. By utilizing the state estimator, the output feedback problem is converted to the state-feedback problem for a new problem. This new problem employs the estimated state as its own state variable and the solution of the new state-feedback problem leads to the solution of the dynamic output feedback control problem. Basically, the dynamic output feedback is a coupling of control and estimation.

This section aims at designing a full order dynamic $\mathcal{H}_\infty$ fuzzy output feedback controller of the form

$$\begin{aligned} \dot{\hat{x}}(t) &= \textstyle\sum_{i=1}^{r}\sum_{j=1}^{r} \hat{\mu}_i\hat{\mu}_j\left[\hat{A}_{ij}\hat{x}(t) + \hat{B}_i y(t)\right] \\ u(t) &= \textstyle\sum_{i=1}^{r} \hat{\mu}_i\hat{C}_i\hat{x}(t) \end{aligned} \tag{29}$$

where $\hat{x}(t) \in \Re^n$ is the controller's state vector, $\hat{A}_{ij}$, $\hat{B}_i$ and $\hat{C}_i$ are parameters of the controller which are to be determined, and $\hat{\mu}_i$ denotes the normalized time-varying fuzzy weighting functions for each rule (i.e., $\hat{\mu}_i \geq 0$ and $\sum_{i=1}^{r} \hat{\mu}_i = 1$), such that the inequality (3) holds.
In this section, we consider the designing of the robust $\mathcal{H}_\infty$ output feedback control into two cases as follows. In Subsection A, we consider the case where the premise variable of the fuzzy model μ_i is measurable, while in Subsection B, the premise variable which is assumed to be unmeasurable is considered.

4.1 Case I–$\nu(t)$ is available for feedback

The premise variable of the fuzzy model $\nu(t)$ is available for feedback which implies that μ_i is available for feedback. Thus, we can select our controller that depends on μ_i as follows:

$$\begin{array}{rcl} \dot{\hat{x}}(t) & = & \sum_{i=1}^{r}\sum_{j=1}^{r} \mu_i\mu_j \left[\hat{A}_{ij}\hat{x}(t) + \hat{B}_i y(t)\right] \\ u(t) & = & \sum_{i=1}^{r} \mu_i \hat{C}_i \hat{x}(t). \end{array} \tag{30}$$

Before presenting our next results, the following lemma is recalled.

Lemma 1 *Consider the system (1). Given a prescribed $\mathcal{H}_\infty$ performance γ and a positive constant δ, if there exists a matrix $P = P^T$ satisfying the following linear matrix inequalities:*

$$P > 0 \tag{31}$$

$$\begin{pmatrix} \begin{pmatrix} A_{cl}^{ij}P \\ +P(A_{cl}^{ij})^T \end{pmatrix} & (*)^T & (*)^T \\ (B_{cl}^{ij})^T & -\gamma^2 I & (*)^T \\ C_{cl}^{ij}P & 0 & -I \end{pmatrix} < 0, \tag{32}$$

where $i,j = 1,2,\cdots,r$

$$A_{cl}^{ij} = \begin{bmatrix} A_i & B_{2_i}\hat{C}_j \\ \hat{B}_i C_{2_j} & \hat{A}_{ij} \end{bmatrix}, \quad B_{cl}^{ij} = \begin{bmatrix} \tilde{B}_{1_i} \\ \hat{B}_i \tilde{D}_{21_j} \end{bmatrix}$$

$$\text{and } C_{cl}^{ij} = [\tilde{C}_{1_i} \quad \tilde{D}_{12_i}\hat{C}_j]$$

with

$$\tilde{B}_{1_i} = \begin{bmatrix} \delta I & I & \delta I & 0 & B_{1_i} & 0 \end{bmatrix},$$

$$\tilde{C}_{1_i} = \begin{bmatrix} \frac{\gamma\rho}{\delta} H_{1_i}^T & 0 & \frac{\gamma\rho}{\delta} H_{5_i}^T & \sqrt{2}\lambda\rho H_{4_i}^T & \sqrt{2}\lambda C_{1_i}^T \end{bmatrix}^T,$$

$$\tilde{D}_{12_i} = \begin{bmatrix} 0 & \frac{\gamma\rho}{\delta} H_{3_i}^T & 0 & \sqrt{2}\lambda\rho H_{6_i}^T & \sqrt{2}\lambda D_{12_i}^T \end{bmatrix}^T,$$

$$\tilde{D}_{21_i} = \begin{bmatrix} 0 & 0 & 0 & \delta I & D_{21_i} & I \end{bmatrix}$$

$$\text{and } \lambda = \left(1 + \rho^2 \sum_{i=1}^{r}\sum_{j=1}^{r} \left[\|H_{2_i}^T H_{2_j}\| + \|H_{7_i}^T H_{7_j}\|\right]\right)^{\frac{1}{2}},$$

then the inequality (3) is guaranteed.

Proof: The state space form of the fuzzy system model (1) with the controller (30) is given by

$$\begin{aligned} \dot{\check{x}}(t) &= \sum_{i=1}^{r}\sum_{j=1}^{r}\mu_i\mu_j\left(A_{cl}^{ij}\check{x}(t)+B_{cl}^{ij}\tilde{w}(t)\right) \\ \check{z}(t) &= \sum_{i=1}^{r}\sum_{j=1}^{r}\mu_i\mu_j C_{cl}^{ij}\check{x}(t) \end{aligned} \tag{33}$$

where $\check{x}(t)=\left[x^T(t)\ \ \hat{x}^T(t)\right]^T$ and the matrix functions A_{cl}^{ij}, B_{cl}^{ij} and C_{cl}^{ij} are defined in Lemma 1 and the disturbance is

$$\tilde{w}(t)=\begin{bmatrix} \frac{1}{\delta}F(x(t),t)H_{1_i}x(t) \\ F(x(t),t)H_{2_i}w(t) \\ \frac{1}{\delta}F(x(t),t)H_{3_i}\hat{C}_j\hat{x}(t) \\ \frac{1}{\delta}F(x(t),t)H_{5_i}x(t) \\ w(t) \\ F(x(t),t)H_{7_i}w(t) \end{bmatrix}. \tag{34}$$

Let choose a Lyapunov function

$$V(\check{x}(t))=\check{x}^T(t)Q\check{x}(t), \tag{35}$$

where $Q=P^{-1}$. Differentiate $V(\check{x}(t))$ along the closed-loop system (33) yields

$$\begin{aligned} &\dot{V}(\check{x}(t))=\dot{\check{x}}^T(t)Q\check{x}(t)+\check{x}^T(t)Q\dot{\check{x}}(t) \\ &\sum_{i=1}^{r}\sum_{j=1}^{r}\mu_i\mu_j\Big(\check{x}^T(t)(A_{cl}^{ij})^TQ\check{x}(t)+\check{x}^T(t)QA_{cl}^{ij}\check{x}(t) \\ &+\tilde{w}^T(t)(B_{cl}^{ij})^TQ\check{x}(t)+\check{x}^T(t)QB_{cl}^{ij}\tilde{w}(t)\Big). \end{aligned} \tag{36}$$

Add and subtract $-\check{z}^T(t)\check{z}(t)+\gamma^2\sum_{i=1}^{r}\sum_{j=1}^{r}\sum_{m=1}^{r}\sum_{n=1}^{r}\mu_i\mu_j\mu_m\mu_n[\tilde{w}(t)^T\tilde{w}(t)]$ to and from (36) yields

$$\begin{aligned} \dot{V}(\check{x}(t)) = &\sum_{i=1}^{r}\sum_{j=1}^{r}\sum_{m=1}^{r}\sum_{n=1}^{r}\mu_i\mu_j\mu_m\mu_n\left[\ \check{x}^T(t)\quad \tilde{w}^T(t)\ \right] \\ &\left(\begin{array}{cc} \left(\begin{array}{c}(A_{cl}^{ij})^TQ+QA_{cl}^{ij} \\ +(C_{cl}^{ij})^TC_{cl}^{mn}\end{array}\right) & (*)^T \\ QB_{cl}^{ij} & -\gamma^2 I \end{array}\right)\left[\begin{array}{c}\check{x}(t) \\ \tilde{w}(t)\end{array}\right] \\ &-\check{z}^T(t)\check{z}(t)+\gamma^2\sum_{i=1}^{r}\sum_{j=1}^{r}\sum_{m=1}^{r}\sum_{n=1}^{r}\mu_i\mu_j\mu_m\mu_n[\tilde{w}^T(t)\tilde{w}(t)]. \end{aligned} \tag{37}$$

Now suppose there exits a matrix $P>0$ such that (32) holds, i.e.,

$$\begin{pmatrix} A_{cl}^{ij}P+P(A_{cl}^{ij})^T & (*)^T & (*)^T \\ (B_{cl}^{ij})^T & -\gamma^2 I & (*)^T \\ C_{cl}^{ij}P & 0 & -I \end{pmatrix}<0. \tag{38}$$

Pre and post multiply (38) by $\begin{pmatrix} Q & 0 & 0 \\ 0 & I & 0 \\ 0 & 0 & I \end{pmatrix}$ yields

$$\begin{pmatrix} (A_{cl}^{ij})^T Q + Q A_{cl}^{ij} & (*)^T & (*)^T \\ (B_{cl}^{ij})^T Q & -\gamma^2 I & (*)^T \\ C_{cl}^{ij} & 0 & -I \end{pmatrix} < 0. \tag{39}$$

The Schur complement of (39) is

$$\begin{pmatrix} (A_{cl}^{ij})^T Q + Q A_{cl}^{ij} + (C_{cl}^{ij})^T C_{cl}^{ij} & (*)^T \\ (B_{cl}^{ij})^T & -\gamma^2 I \end{pmatrix} < 0. \tag{40}$$

Using (40) and the fact in (21) together with the fact that $\mu_i \geq 0$ and $\sum_{i=1}^{r} \mu_i = 1$, then (37) becomes

$$\dot{V}(\breve{x}(t)) \leq -\breve{z}^T(t)\breve{z}(t) + \gamma^2 \sum_{i=1}^{r}\sum_{j=1}^{r}\sum_{m=1}^{r}\sum_{n=1}^{r} \mu_i\mu_j\mu_m\mu_n[\tilde{w}^T(t)\tilde{w}(t)]. \tag{41}$$

Integrate both sides of (41) yields

$$\begin{aligned} \int_0^{T_f} \dot{V}(\breve{x}(t))dt &\leq \int_0^{T_f} \Big(-\breve{z}^T(t)\breve{z}(t) + \gamma^2 \sum_{i=1}^{r}\sum_{j=1}^{r}\sum_{m=1}^{r}\sum_{n=1}^{r} \mu_i\mu_j\mu_m\mu_n[\tilde{w}^T(t)\tilde{w}(t)]\Big)dt \\ V(\breve{x}(T_f)) - V(\breve{x}(0)) &\leq \int_0^{T_f} \Big(-\breve{z}^T(t)\breve{z}(t) + \gamma^2 \sum_{i=1}^{r}\sum_{j=1}^{r}\sum_{m=1}^{r}\sum_{n=1}^{r} \mu_i\mu_j\mu_m\mu_n[\tilde{w}^T(t)\tilde{w}(t)]\Big)dt. \end{aligned}$$

Using the fact that $\breve{x}(0) = 0$ and $V(\breve{x}(T_f)) > 0$ for all $T_f \neq 0$, we have

$$\int_0^{T_f} \breve{z}^T(t)\breve{z}(t)dt \leq \gamma^2 \left[\int_0^{T_f} \sum_{i=1}^{r}\sum_{j=1}^{r}\sum_{m=1}^{r}\sum_{n=1}^{r} \mu_i\mu_j\mu_m\mu_n[\tilde{w}^T(t)\tilde{w}(t)] \right] dt. \tag{42}$$

Putting $\breve{z}(t)$ and $\tilde{w}(t)$ respectively given in (33) and (34) into (42) and using the fact that $\|F(x(t),t)\| \leq \rho$, $\lambda^2 = \left(1 + \rho^2 \sum_{i=1}^{r}\sum_{j=1}^{r} \left[\|H_{2_i}^T H_{2_j}\| + \|H_{7_i}^T H_{7_j}\| \right]\right)$ and (21), we have

$$\begin{aligned} &\int_0^{T_f} \sum_{i=1}^{r}\sum_{j=1}^{r} \mu_i\mu_j \Big(2\lambda^2 \breve{x}^T(t)[C_{1_i} \;\; D_{12_i}\hat{C}_j]^T [C_{1_i} \;\; D_{12_i}\hat{C}_j]\breve{x}(t) \\ &+ 2\lambda^2\rho^2 \breve{x}^T(t)[H_{4_i} \;\; H_{6_i}\hat{C}_j]^T [H_{4_i} \;\; H_{6_i}\hat{C}_j]\breve{x}(t) \Big) dt \\ &\leq \gamma^2\lambda^2 \left[\int_0^{T_f} w^T(t)w(t)\, dt \right]. \end{aligned} \tag{43}$$

Adding and subtracting

$$\begin{aligned} \lambda^2 z^T(t)z(t) &= \lambda^2 \sum_{i=1}^{r}\sum_{j=1}^{r} \mu_i\mu_j \Big(\breve{x}^T(t) \left[C_{1_i} + F(x(t),t)H_{4_i} \;\; D_{12_i}\hat{C}_j + F(x(t),t)H_{6_i}\hat{C}_j \right]^T \\ &\quad \left[C_{1_i} + F(x(t),t)H_{4_i} \;\; D_{12_i}\hat{C}_j + F(x(t),t)H_{6_i}\hat{C}_j \right] \breve{x}(t) \Big) \end{aligned}$$

to and from (43), one obtains

$$\int_0^{T_f} \Big\{ \lambda^2 z^T(t)z(t) + \sum_{i=1}^{r}\sum_{j=1}^{r} \mu_i\mu_j \times$$
$$\Big(2\lambda^2 \breve{x}^T(t)[C_{1_i}\ \ D_{12_i}\hat{C}_j]^T[C_{1_i}\ \ D_{12_i}\hat{C}_j]\breve{x}(t) + 2\lambda^2\rho^2\breve{x}^T(t) \times$$
$$[H_{4_i}\ \ H_{6_i}\hat{C}_j]^T[H_{4_i}\ \ H_{6_i}\hat{C}_j]\breve{x}(t)$$
$$-\lambda^2\breve{x}^T(t)[C_{1_i} + F(x(t),t)H_{4_i}\ \ D_{12_i}\hat{C}_j + F(x(t),t)H_{6_i}\hat{C}_j]^T$$
$$[C_{1_i} + F(x(t),t)H_{4_i}\ \ D_{12_i}\hat{C}_j + F(x(t),t)H_{6_i}\hat{C}_j]\breve{x}(t) \Big) \Big\}\, dt$$
$$\leq \gamma^2\lambda^2 \left[\int_0^{T_f} w^T(t)w(t)\, dt \right]. \tag{44}$$

Using the triangular inequality and the fact that $\|F(x(t),t)\| \leq \rho$, we have

$$\lambda^2 \sum_{i=1}^{r}\sum_{j=1}^{r} \mu_i\mu_j \Big(\breve{x}^T(t) \left[C_{1_i} + F(x(t),t)H_{4_i}\ \ D_{12_i}\hat{C}_j + F(x(t),t)H_{6_i}\hat{C}_j\right]^T$$
$$\left[C_{1_i} + F(x(t),t)H_{4_i}\ \ D_{12_i}\hat{C}_j + F(x(t),t)H_{6_i}\hat{C}_j\right]\breve{x}(t) \Big)$$
$$\leq \sum_{i=1}^{r}\sum_{j=1}^{r} \mu_i\mu_j \Big(2\lambda^2\breve{x}^T(t) \left[C_{1_i}\ \ D_{12_i}\hat{C}_j\right]^T \left[C_{1_i}\ \ D_{12_i}\hat{C}_j\right]\breve{x}(t)$$
$$+ 2\lambda^2\rho^2\breve{x}^T(t)\left[H_{4_i}\ \ H_{6_i}\hat{C}_j\right]^T\left[H_{4_i}\ \ H_{6_i}\hat{C}_j\right]\breve{x}(t) \Big). \tag{45}$$

Using (45) on (44), we obtain

$$\int_0^{T_f} z^T(t)z(t) \leq \gamma^2 \int_0^{T_f} w^T(t)w(t)\, dt. \tag{46}$$

Hence, the inequality (3) is guaranteed. ■

Knowing that the controller's premise variable is the same as the plant's premise variable, the left hand of (32) can be re-expressed as follows:

$$A_{cl}^{ij}P + P(A_{cl}^{ij})^T + \gamma^{-2}B_{cl}^{ij}(B_{cl}^{ij})^T + P(C_{cl}^{ij})^T C_{cl}^{ij}P. \tag{47}$$

Before providing LMI-based sufficient conditions for the system (1) to have an $\mathcal{H}_\infty$ performance, let us partition the matrix P as follows:

$$P = \begin{bmatrix} X & Y^{-1} - X \\ Y^{-1} - X & X - Y^{-1} \end{bmatrix} \tag{48}$$

where $X \in \Re^{n\times n}$ and $Y \in \Re^{n\times n}$. Utilizing the partition above, we define the new controller's input and output matrices as

$$\begin{aligned} \mathcal{B}_i &\triangleq [Y^{-1} - X]\hat{B}_i \\ \mathcal{C}_i &\triangleq \hat{C}_i Y. \end{aligned} \tag{49}$$

Using these changes of variable, we have the following theorem.

Theorem 2 *Consider the system (1). Given a prescribed* $\mathcal{H}_\infty$ *performance* $\gamma > 0$ *and a positive constant* δ*, if there exist matrices* $X = X^T$, $Y = Y^T$, $\mathcal{B}_i$ *and* $\mathcal{C}_i$, $i = 1, 2, \cdots, r$*, satisfying the following linear matrix inequalities:*

$$\begin{bmatrix} X & I \\ I & Y \end{bmatrix} > 0 \tag{50}$$

$$X > 0 \tag{51}$$

$$Y > 0 \tag{52}$$

$$\Psi_{11_{ii}} < 0, \quad i = 1, 2, \cdots, r \tag{53}$$

$$\Psi_{22_{ii}} < 0, \quad i = 1, 2, \cdots, r \tag{54}$$

$$\Psi_{11_{ij}} + \Psi_{11_{ji}} < 0, \quad i < j \leq r \tag{55}$$

$$\Psi_{22_{ij}} + \Psi_{22_{ji}} < 0, \quad i < j \leq r \tag{56}$$

where

$$\Psi_{11_{ij}} = \begin{pmatrix} \begin{pmatrix} A_i Y + Y A_j^T \\ +B_{2_i} \mathcal{C}_j + \mathcal{C}_i^T B_{2_j}^T \\ +\gamma^{-2} \tilde{B}_{1_i} \tilde{B}_{1_j}^T \end{pmatrix} & (*)^T \\ \left[Y \tilde{C}_{1_i}^T + \mathcal{C}_i^T \tilde{D}_{12_j}^T\right]^T & -I \end{pmatrix} \tag{57}$$

$$\Psi_{22_{ij}} = \begin{pmatrix} \begin{pmatrix} A_i^T X + X A_i \\ +\mathcal{B}_i C_{2_j} + C_{2_i}^T \mathcal{B}_j^T \\ +\tilde{C}_{1_i}^T \tilde{C}_{1_j} \end{pmatrix} & (*)^T \\ \left[X \tilde{B}_{1_i} + \mathcal{B}_i \tilde{D}_{21_j}\right]^T & -\gamma^2 I \end{pmatrix} \tag{58}$$

with

$$\tilde{B}_{1_i} = \begin{bmatrix} \delta I & I & \delta I & 0 & B_{1_i} & 0 \end{bmatrix},$$

$$\tilde{C}_{1_i} = \begin{bmatrix} \frac{\gamma\rho}{\delta} H_{1_i}^T & 0 & \frac{\gamma\rho}{\delta} H_{5_i}^T & \sqrt{2}\lambda\rho H_{4_i}^T & \sqrt{2}\lambda C_{1_i}^T \end{bmatrix}^T,$$

$$\tilde{D}_{12_i} = \begin{bmatrix} 0 & \frac{\gamma\rho}{\delta} H_{3_i}^T & 0 & \sqrt{2}\lambda\rho H_{6_i}^T & \sqrt{2}\lambda D_{12_i}^T \end{bmatrix}^T,$$

$$\tilde{D}_{21_i} = \begin{bmatrix} 0 & 0 & 0 & \delta I & D_{21_i} & I \end{bmatrix}$$

$$\text{and } \lambda = \left(1 + \rho^2 \sum_{i=1}^{r} \sum_{j=1}^{r} \left[\|H_{2_i}^T H_{2_j}\| + \|H_{7_i}^T H_{7_j}\|\right]\right)^{\frac{1}{2}},$$

then the prescribed $\mathcal{H}_\infty$ *performance* $\gamma > 0$ *is guaranteed. Furthermore, a suitable controller is of the form (30) with*

$$\begin{aligned} \hat{A}_{ij} &= \left[Y^{-1} - X\right]^{-1} \mathcal{M}_{ij} Y^{-1} \\ \hat{B}_i &= \left[Y^{-1} - X\right]^{-1} \mathcal{B}_i \\ \hat{C}_i &= \mathcal{C}_i Y^{-1} \end{aligned} \tag{59}$$

where

$$\begin{aligned} \mathcal{M}_{ij} = & -A_i^T - X A_i Y - X B_{2_i} \hat{C}_j Y \\ & -\left[Y^{-1} - X\right] \hat{B}_i C_{2_j} Y - \tilde{C}_{1_i}^T \left[\tilde{C}_{1_j} Y + \tilde{D}_{12_j} \hat{C}_j Y\right] \\ & -\gamma^{-2} \left\{X \tilde{B}_{1_i} + \left[Y^{-1} - X\right] \hat{B}_i \tilde{D}_{21_i}\right\} \tilde{B}_{1_j}^T. \end{aligned} \tag{60}$$

Proof: Suppose there exist X and Y such that the inequalities (50) and (51)-(52) hold. The inequality (50) implies that the matrix P defined in (47) is a positive definite matrix. Using the partition (48), the controller (49) and multiplying (47) to the left by $\begin{bmatrix} Y & I \\ Y & 0 \end{bmatrix}$ and to the right by $\begin{bmatrix} Y & Y \\ I & 0 \end{bmatrix}$, we have

$$\begin{bmatrix} \Phi_{11_{ij}} & 0 \\ 0 & \Phi_{22_{ij}} \end{bmatrix} \tag{61}$$

where

$$\begin{aligned} \Phi_{11_{ij}} &= A_iY + YA_i^T + B_{2_i}\mathcal{C}_j + \mathcal{C}_i^T B_{2_j}^T + \gamma^{-2}\tilde{B}_{1_i}\tilde{B}_{1_j}^T \\ &\quad + \left[Y\tilde{C}_{1_i}^T + \mathcal{C}_i^T\tilde{D}_{12_j}^T\right]\left[Y\tilde{C}_{1_i}^T + \mathcal{C}_i^T\tilde{D}_{12_j}^T\right]^T \end{aligned} \tag{62}$$

$$\begin{aligned} \Phi_{22_{ij}} &= A_i^TX + XA_i + \mathcal{B}_iC_{2_j} + C_{2_i}^T\mathcal{B}_j^T + \tilde{C}_{1_i}^T\tilde{C}_{1_j} \\ &\quad + \gamma^{-2}\left[X\tilde{B}_{1_i} + \mathcal{B}_i\tilde{D}_{21_j}\right]\left[X\tilde{B}_{1_i} + \mathcal{B}_i\tilde{D}_{21_j}\right]^T. \end{aligned} \tag{63}$$

Note that $\Phi_{11_{ij}}$ and $\Phi_{22_{ij}}$ are the Schur complements of $\Psi_{11_{ij}}$ and $\Psi_{22_{ij}}$, Using (53)-(56), we have (61) less than zero. Hence, by Theorem 2, we learn that the inequality (3) holds. ■

4.2 Case II–$\nu(t)$ is unavailable for feedback

The output feedback fuzzy controller is assumed to be the same as the premise variables of the fuzzy system model. This actually means that the premise variables of fuzzy system model are assumed to be measurable. However, in general, it is extremely difficult to derive an accurate fuzzy system model by imposing that all premise variables are measurable. In this subsection, we do not impose that condition, we choose the premise variables of the controller to be different from the premise variables of fuzzy system model of the plant. In here, the premise variables of the controller are selected to be the estimated premise variables of the plant. In the other words, the premise variable of the fuzzy model $\nu(t)$ is unavailable for feedback which implies μ_i is unavailable for feedback. Hence, we cannot select our controller which depends on μ_i. Thus, we select our controller as follows:

$$\begin{aligned} \dot{\hat{x}}(t) &= \sum_{i=1}^r\sum_{j=1}^r \hat{\mu}_i\hat{\mu}_j\left[\hat{A}_{ij}\hat{x}(t) + \hat{B}_iy(t)\right] \\ u(t) &= \sum_{i=1}^r \hat{\mu}_i\hat{C}_i\hat{x}(t). \end{aligned} \tag{64}$$

where $\hat{\mu}_i$ depends on the premise variable of the controller which is different from μ_i.
Let us re-express the system (1) in terms of $\hat{\mu}_i$, thus the plant's premise variable becomes the same as the controller's premise variable. By doing so, the result given in the previous case can then be applied here. First, let us rewrite (1) as follows:

$$\begin{aligned} \dot{x}(t) &= \sum_{i=1}^r \mu_i\Big[[A_i + \Delta A_i]x(t) + [B_{1_i} + \Delta B_{1_i}]w(t) + [B_{2_i} + \Delta B_{2_i}]u(t)\Big] \\ &\quad + \sum_{i=1}^r \hat{\mu}_i\Big[[A_i + \Delta A_i]x(t) + [B_{1_i} + \Delta B_{1_i}]w(t) + [B_{2_i} + \Delta B_{2_i}]u(t)\Big] \\ &\quad - \sum_{i=1}^r \hat{\mu}_i\Big[[A_i + \Delta A_i]x(t) + [B_{1_i} + \Delta B_{1_i}]w(t) + [B_{2_i} + \Delta B_{2_i}]u(t)\Big] \end{aligned}$$

$$
\begin{aligned}
z(t) &= \textstyle\sum_{i=1}^{r}\mu_i\Big[[C_{1_i}+\Delta C_{1_i}]x(t)+[D_{12_i}+\Delta D_{12_i}]u(t)\Big]\\
&\quad+\textstyle\sum_{i=1}^{r}\hat{\mu}_i\Big[[C_{1_i}+\Delta C_{1_i}]x(t)+[D_{12_i}+\Delta D_{12_i}]u(t)\Big]\\
&\quad-\textstyle\sum_{i=1}^{r}\hat{\mu}_i\Big[[C_{1_i}+\Delta C_{1_i}]x(t)+[D_{12_i}+\Delta D_{12_i}]u(t)\Big]\\
y(t) &= \textstyle\sum_{i=1}^{r}\mu_i\Big[[C_{2_i}+\Delta C_{2_i}]x(t)+[D_{21_i}+\Delta D_{21_i}]w(t)\Big]\\
&\quad+\textstyle\sum_{i=1}^{r}\hat{\mu}_i\Big[[C_{2_i}+\Delta C_{2_i}]x(t)+[D_{21_i}+\Delta D_{21_i}]w(t)\Big]\\
&\quad-\textstyle\sum_{i=1}^{r}\hat{\mu}_i\Big[[C_{2_i}+\Delta C_{2_i}]x(t)+[D_{21_i}+\Delta D_{21_i}]w(t)\Big].
\end{aligned}
\tag{65}
$$

Rearranging (65) together with employing Assumption 1, we obtain

$$
\begin{aligned}
&\dot{x}(t)=\textstyle\sum_{i=1}^{r}\hat{\mu}_i\Big([A_i+F(x(t),t)H_{1_i}+(\mu_1-\hat{\mu}_1)A_1+\cdots+(\mu_r-\hat{\mu}_r)A_r\\
&+F(x(t),t)(\mu_1-\hat{\mu}_1)H_{1_1}+\cdots+F(x(t),t)(\mu_r-\hat{\mu}_r)H_{1_r}]x(t)\\
&+[B_{1_i}+F(x(t),t)H_{2_i}+(\mu_1-\hat{\mu}_1)B_{1_1}+\cdots+(\mu_r-\hat{\mu}_r)B_{1_r}\\
&+F(x(t),t)(\mu_1-\hat{\mu}_1)H_{2_1}+\cdots+F(x(t),t)(\mu_r-\hat{\mu}_r)H_{2_r}]w(t)\\
&+[B_{2_i}+F(x(t),t)H_{3_i}+(\mu_1-\hat{\mu}_1)B_{2_1}+\cdots+(\mu_r-\hat{\mu}_r)B_{2_r}\\
&+F(x(t),t)(\mu_1-\hat{\mu}_1)H_{3_1}+\cdots+F(x(t),t)(\mu_r-\hat{\mu}_r)H_{3_r}]u(t)\Big)\\
&z(t)=\textstyle\sum_{i=1}^{r}\hat{\mu}_i\times\Big([C_{1_i}+F(x(t),t)H_{4_i}+(\mu_1-\hat{\mu}_1)C_{1_1}+\cdots+(\mu_r-\hat{\mu}_r)C_{1_r}\\
&+F(x(t),t)(\mu_1-\hat{\mu}_1)H_{4_1}+\cdots+F(x(t),t)(\mu_r-\hat{\mu}_r)H_{4_r}]x(t)\\
&+[D_{12_i}+F(x(t),t)H_{5_i}+(\mu_1-\hat{\mu}_1)D_{12_1}+\cdots+(\mu_r-\hat{\mu}_r)D_{12_r}\\
&+F(x(t),t)(\mu_1-\hat{\mu}_1)H_{5_1}+\cdots+F(x(t),t)(\mu_r-\hat{\mu}_r)H_{5_r}]u(t)\Big)\\
&y(t)=\textstyle\sum_{i=1}^{r}\hat{\mu}_i\Big([C_{2_i}+F(x(t),t)H_{6_i}+(\mu_1-\hat{\mu}_1)C_{2_1}+\cdots+(\mu_r-\hat{\mu}_r)C_{2_r}\\
&+F(x(t),t)(\mu_1-\hat{\mu}_1)H_{6_1}+\cdots+F(x(t),t)(\mu_r-\hat{\mu}_r)H_{6_r}]x(t)\\
&+[D_{21_i}+F(x(t),t)H_{7_i}+(\mu_1-\hat{\mu}_1)D_{21_1}+\cdots+(\mu_r-\hat{\mu}_r)D_{21_r}\\
&+F(x(t),t)(\mu_1-\hat{\mu}_1)H_{7_1}+\cdots+F(x(t),t)(\mu_r-\hat{\mu}_r)H_{7_r}]w(t)\Big)
\end{aligned}
\tag{66}
$$

Then, from (66), we get

$$
\begin{aligned}
\dot{x}(t) &= \textstyle\sum_{i=1}^{r}\hat{\mu}_i\Big[[A_i+\Delta\bar{A}_i]x(t)+[B_{1_i}+\Delta\bar{B}_{1_i}]w(t)\\
&\quad+[B_{2_i}+\Delta\bar{B}_{2_i}]u(t)\Big],\ x(0)=0\\
z(t) &= \textstyle\sum_{i=1}^{r}\hat{\mu}_i\Big[[C_{1_i}+\Delta\bar{C}_{1_i}]x(t)\\
&\quad+[D_{12_i}+\Delta\bar{D}_{12_i}]u(t)\Big]\\
y(t) &= \textstyle\sum_{i=1}^{r}\hat{\mu}_i\Big[[C_{2_i}+\Delta\bar{C}_{2_i}]x(t)\\
&\quad+[D_{21_i}+\Delta\bar{D}_{21_i}]w(t)\Big]
\end{aligned}
\tag{67}
$$

where

$$
\begin{gathered}
\Delta\bar{A}_i=\bar{F}(x(t),\hat{x}(t),t)\bar{H}_{1_i},\\
\Delta\bar{B}_{1_i}=\bar{F}(x(t),\hat{x}(t),t)\bar{H}_{2_i},\ \Delta\bar{B}_{2_i}=\bar{F}(x(t),\hat{x}(t),t)\bar{H}_{3_i},\\
\Delta\bar{C}_{1_i}=\bar{F}(x(t),\hat{x}(t),t)\bar{H}_{4_i},\ \Delta\bar{C}_{2_i}=\bar{F}(x(t),\hat{x}(t),t)\bar{H}_{5_i},\\
\Delta\bar{D}_{12_i}=\bar{F}(x(t),\hat{x}(t),t)\bar{H}_{6_i}\\
\text{and }\ \Delta\bar{D}_{21_i}=\bar{F}(x(t),\hat{x}(t),t)\bar{H}_{7_i}
\end{gathered}
$$

with

$$\bar{H}_{1_i} = \left[H_{1_i}^T \, A_1^T \cdots A_r^T \, H_{1_1}^T \cdots H_{1_r}^T\right]^T,$$

$$\bar{H}_{2_i} = \left[H_{2_i}^T \, B_{1_1}^T \cdots B_{1_r}^T \, H_{2_1}^T \cdots H_{2_r}^T\right]^T,$$

$$\bar{H}_{3_i} = \left[H_{3_i}^T \, B_{2_1}^T \cdots B_{2_r}^T \, H_{3_1}^T \cdots H_{3_r}^T\right]^T,$$

$$\bar{H}_{4_i} = \left[H_{4_i}^T \, C_{1_1}^T \cdots C_{1_r}^T \, H_{4_1}^T \cdots H_{4_r}^T\right]^T,$$

$$\bar{H}_{5_i} = \left[H_{5_i}^T \, C_{2_1}^T \cdots C_{2_r}^T \, H_{5_1}^T \cdots H_{5_r}^T\right]^T,$$

$$\bar{H}_{6_i} = \left[H_{6_i}^T \, D_{12_1}^T \cdots D_{12_r}^T \, H_{6_1}^T \cdots H_{6_r}^T\right]^T$$

$$\bar{H}_{7_i} = \left[H_{7_i}^T \, D_{21_1}^T \cdots \, D_{21_r}^T \, H_{7_1}^T \cdots H_{7_r}^T\right]^T$$

and $\bar{F}(x(t),\hat{x}(t),t) = \Big[F(x(t),t) \; (\mu_1 - \hat{\mu}_1) \; \cdots \; (\mu_r - \hat{\mu}_r) \; F(x(t),t)(\mu_1 - \hat{\mu}_1) \; \cdots \; F(x(t),t)(\mu_r - \hat{\mu}_r)\Big]$. Note that $\|\bar{F}(x(t),\hat{x}(t),t)\| \leq \bar{\rho}$ where $\bar{\rho} = \{3\rho^2 + 2\}^{\frac{1}{2}}$. $\bar{\rho}$ is derived by utilizing the concept of vector norm in basic system control theory and the fact that $\mu_i \geq 0, \hat{\mu}_i \geq 0, \sum_{i=1}^r \mu_i = 1$ and $\sum_{i=1}^r \hat{\mu}_i = 1$.
Note that the above technique is basically employed in order to obtain the plant's premise variable to be the same as the controller's premise variable; e.g. (22). Now, the premise variable of the system is the same as the premise variable of the controller, thus we can apply the result given in Case I.

Theorem 3 *Consider the system (1). Given a prescribed $\mathcal{H}_\infty$ performance $\gamma > 0$ and a positive constant δ, if there exist matrices X, Y, $\mathcal{B}_i$ and $\mathcal{C}_i$, $i = 1,2,\cdots,r$, satisfying the following linear matrix inequalities:*

$$\begin{bmatrix} X & I \\ I & Y \end{bmatrix} > 0 \quad (68)$$

$$X > 0 \quad (69)$$

$$Y > 0 \quad (70)$$

$$\Psi_{11_{ii}} < 0, \quad i = 1,2,\cdots,r \quad (71)$$

$$\Psi_{22_{ii}} < 0, \quad i = 1,2,\cdots,r \quad (72)$$

$$\Psi_{11_{ij}} + \Psi_{11_{ji}} < 0, \quad i < j \leq r \quad (73)$$

$$\Psi_{22_{ij}} + \Psi_{22_{ji}} < 0, \quad i < j \leq r \quad (74)$$

where

$$\Psi_{11_{ij}} = \begin{pmatrix} \begin{pmatrix} A_iY + YA_i^T \\ +B_{2_i}\mathcal{C}_j + \mathcal{C}_i^T B_{2_j}^T \\ +\gamma^{-2}\tilde{\bar{B}}_{1_i}\tilde{\bar{B}}_{1_j}^T \end{pmatrix} & (*)^T \\ [Y\tilde{\bar{C}}_{1_i}^T + \mathcal{C}_i^T \tilde{\bar{D}}_{12_j}^T]^T & -I \end{pmatrix} \quad (75)$$

$$\Psi_{22_{ij}} = \begin{pmatrix} \begin{pmatrix} A_i^T X + XA_i \\ +\mathcal{B}_i C_{2_j} + C_{2_i}^T \mathcal{B}_j^T \\ +\tilde{\bar{C}}_{1_i}^T \tilde{\bar{C}}_{1_j} \end{pmatrix} & (*)^T \\ [X\tilde{\bar{B}}_{1_i} + \mathcal{B}_i \tilde{\bar{D}}_{21_j}]^T & -\gamma^2 I \end{pmatrix} \tag{76}$$

with

$$\tilde{\bar{B}}_{1_i} = \begin{bmatrix} \delta I & I & \delta I & 0 & B_{1_i} & 0 \end{bmatrix},$$

$$\tilde{\bar{C}}_{1_i} = \begin{bmatrix} \frac{\gamma\bar{\rho}}{\delta}\bar{H}_{1_i}^T & 0 & \frac{\gamma\bar{\rho}}{\delta}\bar{H}_{5_i}^T & \sqrt{2}\bar{\lambda}\bar{\rho}\bar{H}_{4_i}^T & \sqrt{2}\bar{\lambda}C_{1_i}^T \end{bmatrix}^T,$$

$$\tilde{\bar{D}}_{12_i} = \begin{bmatrix} 0 & \frac{\gamma\bar{\rho}}{\delta}\bar{H}_{3_i}^T & 0 & \sqrt{2}\bar{\lambda}\bar{\rho}\bar{H}_{6_i}^T & \sqrt{2}\bar{\lambda}D_{12_i}^T \end{bmatrix}^T,$$

$$\tilde{\bar{D}}_{21_i} = \begin{bmatrix} 0 & 0 & 0 & \delta I & D_{21_i} & I \end{bmatrix}$$

$$\text{and } \bar{\lambda} = \left(1 + \bar{\rho}^2 \sum_{i=1}^{r}\sum_{j=1}^{r} \left[\|\bar{H}_{2_i}^T \bar{H}_{2_j}\| + \|\bar{H}_{7_i}^T \bar{H}_{7_j}\| \right] \right)^{\frac{1}{2}},$$

then the prescribed $\mathcal{H}_\infty$ performance $\gamma > 0$ is guaranteed. Furthermore, a suitable controller is of the form (64) with

$$\begin{aligned} \hat{A}_{ij} &= \left[Y^{-1} - X\right]^{-1} \mathcal{M}_{ij} Y^{-1} \\ \hat{B}_i &= \left[Y^{-1} - X\right]^{-1} \mathcal{B}_i \\ \hat{C}_i &= \mathcal{C}_i Y^{-1} \end{aligned} \tag{77}$$

where

$$\begin{aligned} \mathcal{M}_{ij} = & -A_i^T - XA_iY - XB_{2_i}\hat{C}_jY \\ & -\left[Y^{-1} - X\right]\hat{B}_i C_{2_j} Y - \tilde{\bar{C}}_{1_i}^T \left[\tilde{\bar{C}}_{1_j} Y + \tilde{\bar{D}}_{12_j}\hat{C}_j Y\right] \\ & -\gamma^{-2}\left\{X\tilde{\bar{B}}_{1_i} + \left[Y^{-1} - X\right]\hat{B}_i \tilde{\bar{D}}_{21_i}\right\}\tilde{\bar{B}}_{1_j}^T. \end{aligned} \tag{78}$$

Proof: Since (67) is of the form of (1), it can be shown by employing the proof for Theorem 2. ■

5. Example

Consider the following problem of the chaotic Lorenz system which is described by the following equations (see [29]).

$$\begin{aligned} \dot{x}_1(t) &= -\sigma x_1(t) + \sigma x_2(t) + u(t) + 0.1w_1(t) \\ \dot{x}_2(t) &= r x_1(t) - x_2(t) - x_1(t)x_3(t) + 0.1w_2(t) \\ \dot{x}_3(t) &= x_1(t)x_2(t) - b x_3(t) + 0.1w_3(t) \\ z(t) &= \begin{bmatrix} x_1^T(t) & x_2^T(t) & x_3^T(t) \end{bmatrix}^T \\ y(t) &= Jx(t) + 0.1w_1(t) \end{aligned} \tag{79}$$

where $x_1(t)$, $x_2(t)$, $x_3(t)$ denote the state vectors, $u(t)$ is the control input, $w_1(t)$, $w_2(t)$, $w_3(t)$ are the disturbance noise inputs, $y(t)$ is the measurement output, $z(t)$ is the controlled output, J is the sensor matrix and the bounded uncertain parameters σ, r and b are given by $10 \pm 30\%$, $28 \pm 30\%$ and $8/3 \pm 30\%$, respectively. Note that the variables $x_1(t)$, $x_2(t)$ and $x_3(t)$ are treated as the deviation variables (variables deviate from the desired trajectories).

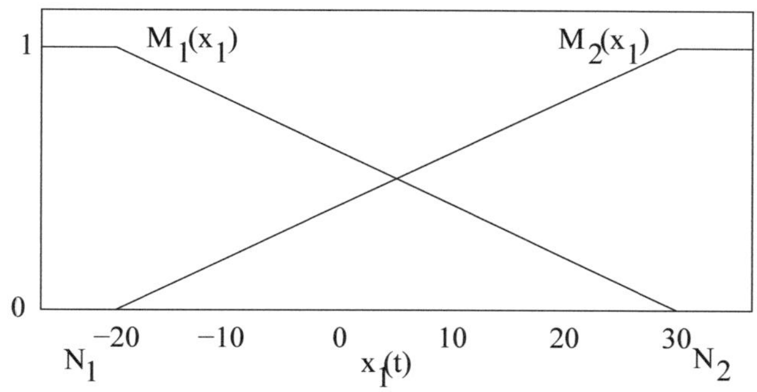

Fig. 1. Membership functions for the two fuzzy set.

Since the nonlinear terms in (79) can be viewed as a function of $x_1(t)$, we can re-expressed (79) as

$$\begin{aligned} \dot{x}_1(t) &= -\sigma x_1(t) + \sigma x_2(t) + u(t) + 0.1w_1(t) \\ \dot{x}_2(t) &= rx_1(t) - x_2(t) - (x_1(t)) \cdot x_3(t) + 0.1w_2(t) \\ \dot{x}_3(t) &= (x_1(t)) \cdot x_2(t) - bx_3(t) + 0.1w_3(t) \\ z(t) &= \begin{bmatrix} x_1^T(t) & x_2^T(t) & x_3^T(t) \end{bmatrix}^T \\ y(t) &= Jx(t) + 0.1w_1(t). \end{aligned} \tag{80}$$

The control objective is to control the state variable $x_1(t)$ for the range $x_1(t) \in [N_1\ N_2]$. For the sake of simplicity, we will use as few rules as possible. Note that Figure 1 shows the plot of the membership functions represented by

$$M_1(x_1(t)) = \frac{-x_1(t) + N_2}{N_2 - N_1} \text{ and } M_2(x_1(t)) = \frac{x_1(t) - N_1}{N_2 - N_1}.$$

Knowing that $x_1(t) \in [N_1\ N_2]$, the nonlinear system (80) can be approximated by the following two rules TS model:

Plant Rule 1: IF $x_1(t)$ is $M_1(x_1(t))$ THEN

$$\begin{aligned} \dot{x}(t) &= [A_1 + \Delta A_1]x(t) + B_{1_1}w(t) + B_{2_1}u(t),\ x(0) = 0, \\ z(t) &= C_{1_1}x(t), \\ y(t) &= C_{2_1}x(t) + D_{21_1}w(t). \end{aligned}$$

Plant Rule 2: IF $x_1(t)$ is $M_2(x_1(t))$ THEN

$$\begin{aligned} \dot{x}(t) &= [A_2 + \Delta A_2]x(t) + B_{1_2}w(t) + B_{2_2}u(t),\ x(0) = 0, \\ z(t) &= C_{1_2}x(t), \\ y(t) &= C_{2_2}x(t) + D_{21_2}w(t) \end{aligned}$$

where

$$A_1 = \begin{bmatrix} -10 & 10 & 0 \\ 28 & -1 & -N_1 \\ 0 & N_1 & -8/3 \end{bmatrix},\ A_2 = \begin{bmatrix} -10 & 10 & 0 \\ 28 & -1 & -N_2 \\ 0 & N_2 & -8/3 \end{bmatrix},$$

$$B_{1_1} = B_{1_2} = \begin{bmatrix} 0.1 & 0 & 0 \\ 0 & 0.1 & 0 \\ 0 & 0 & 0.1 \end{bmatrix}, \; B_{2_1} = B_{2_2} \begin{bmatrix} 1 \\ 0 \\ 0 \end{bmatrix},$$

$$C_{1_1} = C_{1_2} \begin{bmatrix} 1 & 0 & 0 \\ 0 & 1 & 0 \\ 0 & 0 & 1 \end{bmatrix}, \; C_{2_1} = C_{2_2} = J,$$

$$D_{21_1} = D_{21_2} = \begin{bmatrix} 0.1 & 0 & 0 \end{bmatrix}, \; \Delta A_1 = F(x(t),t)H_{1_1}, \; \Delta A_2 = F(x(t),t)H_{1_2},$$

$$x(t) = [x_1^T(t)\; x_2^T(t)\; x_3^T(t)]^T \text{ and } w(t) = [w_1^T(t)\; w_2^T(t)\; w_3^T(t)]^T.$$

Let us choose the value of $[N_1 \; N_2]$ in the membership function as $[-20 \; 30]$. Now, by assuming that in (2), $\|F(x(t),t)\| \leq \rho = 1$ and since the values of σ, r, b are uncertain but bounded within 30% of their nominal values given in (79), we have

$$H_{1_1} = H_{1_2} = \begin{bmatrix} -0.3\sigma & 0.3\sigma & 0 \\ 0.3r & 0 & 0 \\ 0 & 0 & -0.3b \end{bmatrix}.$$

State-feedback controller design

Using the LMI optimization algorithm and Theorem 1 with $\gamma = 1$ and $\delta = 1$, we obtain

$$P = \begin{bmatrix} 104.7498 & -8.1629 & -1.1823 \\ -8.1629 & 5.1783 & 0.9345 \\ -1.1823 & 0.9345 & 6.7383 \end{bmatrix},$$

$$K_1 = \begin{bmatrix} -38.8875 & -816.1115 & -3.9273 \end{bmatrix}, \quad K_2 = \begin{bmatrix} -37.4290 & -815.5695 & 4.1287 \end{bmatrix}.$$

The resulting fuzzy controller is

$$u(t) = \sum_{j=1}^{2} \mu_j K_j x(t)$$

where

$$\mu_1 = M_1(x_1(t)) \text{ and } \mu_2 = M_2(x_1(t)).$$

Output feedback controller design

Case I: $v(t)$ are available for feedback

In this case, $x_1(t) = v(t)$ is assumed to be available for feedback; for instance, $J = [1 \; 0 \; 0]$. This implies that μ_i is available for feedback. Using the LMI optimization algorithm and Theorem 2 with $\gamma = 1$ and $\delta = 1$, we obtain the following results:

$$X = \begin{bmatrix} 40.9617 & -0.3001 & 0.0003 \\ -0.3001 & 0.0326 & -0.0020 \\ 0.0003 & -0.0020 & 0.0529 \end{bmatrix}, \quad Y = \begin{bmatrix} 64.0418 & -6.6279 & -0.0180 \\ -6.6279 & 0.7784 & 0.0345 \\ -0.0180 & 0.0345 & 0.8385 \end{bmatrix},$$

$$\hat{A}_{11} = \begin{bmatrix} -52.6459 & 913.0329 & 11.1683 \\ 0.4211 & -93.8119 & -1.1292 \\ 2.3239 & -0.4233 & 0.0865 \end{bmatrix}, \; \hat{A}_{12} = \begin{bmatrix} -52.9740 & 909.6351 & 0.8313 \\ 0.5070 & -93.0535 & -0.2157 \\ 2.3414 & -0.2540 & 0.1024 \end{bmatrix},$$

$$\hat{A}_{21} = \begin{bmatrix} -54.8390 & 912.4579 & -6.7553 \\ 1.4467 & -93.6196 & 0.6829 \\ -3.5367 & -0.1599 & 0.2080 \end{bmatrix}, \ \hat{A}_{22} = \begin{bmatrix} -54.7676 & 913.4610 & -17.1638 \\ 1.3897 & -94.0748 & 1.5985 \\ -3.5229 & -0.0374 & 0.1865 \end{bmatrix},$$

$$\hat{B}_1 = \begin{bmatrix} -110.4306 \\ 4.8589 \\ 2.9909 \end{bmatrix}, \qquad \hat{B}_2 = \begin{bmatrix} 113.2188 \\ 6.1387 \\ -4.5464 \end{bmatrix},$$

$$\hat{C}_1 = \begin{bmatrix} -36.1488 & -710.9845 & -3.2817 \end{bmatrix}, \ \hat{C}_2 = \begin{bmatrix} -35.9847 & -709.7215 & 5.1803 \end{bmatrix}.$$

The resulting fuzzy controller is

$$\begin{aligned} \dot{\hat{x}}(t) &= \sum_{i=1}^{2}\sum_{j=1}^{2} \mu_i\mu_j\hat{A}_{ij}\hat{x}(t) + \sum_{i=1}^{2}\mu_i\hat{B}_i y(t) \\ u(t) &= \sum_{i=1}^{2}\mu_i\hat{C}_i\hat{x}(t) \end{aligned}$$

where

$$\mu_1 = M_1(x_1(t)) \text{ and } \mu_2 = M_2(x_1(t)).$$

Case II: $\nu(t)$ are unavailable for feedback

In this case, $x_1(t) = \nu(t)$ is assumed to be unavailable for feedback; for instance, $J = [0\ 0\ 1]$. This implies that μ_i is unavailable for feedback. Using the LMI optimization algorithm and Theorem 3 with $\gamma = 1$ and $\delta = 1$, we obtain the following results:

$$X = \begin{bmatrix} 15.3866 & -0.0454 & 0.0001 \\ -0.0454 & 0.0086 & -0.0005 \\ 0.0001 & -0.0005 & 0.0121 \end{bmatrix}, \qquad Y = \begin{bmatrix} 195.0825 & -19.8577 & -0.0836 \\ -19.8577 & 2.3203 & 0.1018 \\ -0.0836 & 0.1018 & 2.5038 \end{bmatrix},$$

$$\hat{A}_{11} = \begin{bmatrix} -72.5111 & 1594.5334 & 6.34563 \\ 5.0232 & -162.6656 & -0.6001 \\ 1.2000 & -0.7556 & 0.1000 \end{bmatrix}, \hat{A}_{12} = \begin{bmatrix} -72.9233 & 1603.7455 & -9.7233 \\ 5.1345 & -162.8555 & 0.9974 \\ 1.2000 & -0.5689 & 0.1000 \end{bmatrix},$$

$$\hat{A}_{21} = \begin{bmatrix} -74.5456 & 1595.2543 & -5.6743 \\ 5.5411 & -162.1785 & 0.5609 \\ -1.7009 & -0.9421 & 0.2000 \end{bmatrix}, \hat{A}_{22} = \begin{bmatrix} -74.5290 & 1595.2231 & -5.6744 \\ 5.5411 & -162.1323 & 0.5966 \\ -1.7008 & -0.9432 & 0.2000 \end{bmatrix},$$

$$\hat{B}_1 = \begin{bmatrix} -166.7783 \\ 7.4682 \\ 4.5048 \end{bmatrix}, \qquad \hat{B}_2 = \begin{bmatrix} -173.8473 \\ 9.1193 \\ -6.8346 \end{bmatrix},$$

$$\hat{C}_1 = \begin{bmatrix} 14.1938 & -410.5257 & -0.3593 \end{bmatrix}, \quad \hat{C}_2 = \begin{bmatrix} 14.2366 & -412.9750 & 3.8984 \end{bmatrix}.$$

The resulting fuzzy controller is

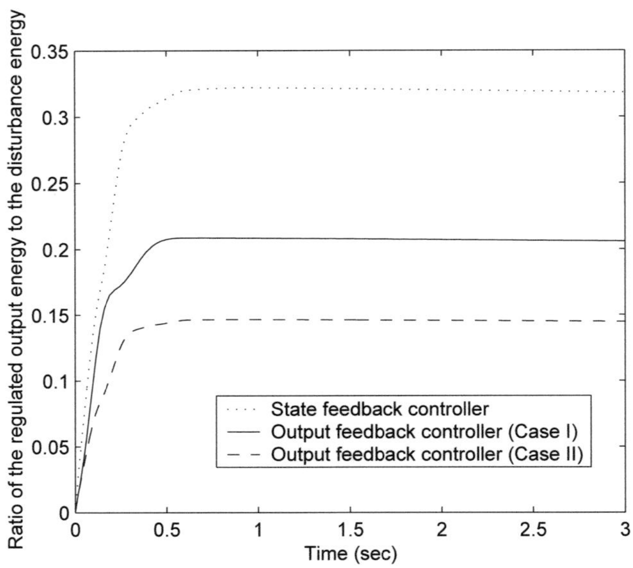

Fig. 2. The ratio of the regulated output energy to the disturbance noise energy: $\left(\frac{\int_0^{T_f} z^T(t)z(t)dt}{\int_0^{T_f} w^T(t)w(t)dt}\right)$.

$$
\begin{aligned}
\dot{\hat{x}}(t) &= \sum_{i=1}^{2}\sum_{j=1}^{2}\hat{\mu}_i\hat{\mu}_j\hat{A}_{ij}\hat{x}(t) + \sum_{i=1}^{2}\hat{\mu}_i\hat{B}_i y(t) \\
u(t) &= \sum_{i=1}^{2}\hat{\mu}_i\hat{C}_i\hat{x}(t)
\end{aligned}
$$

where

$$\hat{\mu}_1 = M_1(\hat{x}_1(t)) \text{ and } \hat{\mu}_2 = M_2(\hat{x}_1(t)).$$

Remark 1 *Both robust fuzzy state and output controllers guarantee that the $\mathcal{L}_2$-gain, γ, is less than the prescribed value. The ratio of the regulated output energy to the disturbance input noise energy which is obtained by using the $\mathcal{H}_\infty$ fuzzy controllers is depicted in Figure 2. The disturbance input signals, $w_1(t)$, $w_2(t)$ and $w_3(t)$, which were used during the simulation is given in Figure 3. After 3 seconds, the ratio of the regulated output energy to the disturbance input noise energy tends to a constant value which is about 0.32 for the state-feedback controller, and 0.21 for the output feedback controller in Case I and 0.14 in Case II. Thus, for the state-feedback controller where $\gamma = \sqrt{0.32} = 0.566$, for output feedback controller in Case I where $\gamma = \sqrt{0.21} = 0.458$ and in Case II where $\gamma = \sqrt{0.14} = 0.374$, all are less than the prescribed value 1.* □

6. Conclusion

This chapter has investigated the problem of designing a robust fuzzy controller for a TS fuzzy system with parametric uncertainties that guarantees the $\mathcal{L}_2$-gain from an exogenous input to a regulated output being less than or equal to the prescribed value. An LMI-based approach has been employed to derive sufficient conditions for the existence of a robust $\mathcal{H}_\infty$ fuzzy controller in terms of a family of LMIs. Finally, a numerical simulation example has been presented to illustrate the effectiveness of the designs.

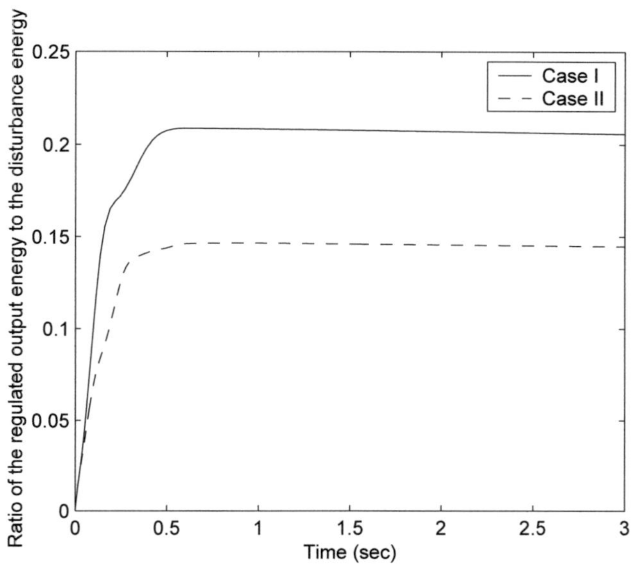

Fig. 3. The disturbance input signals, $w_1(t)$, $w_2(t)$ and $w_3(t)$.

7. References

[1] L. A. Zadeh (1965). "Fuzzy set," *Information and Contr.*, vol. 8, pp. 338–353.

[2] L. A. Zadeh (1973). "Outline of a new approach to the analysis of complex systems and decision processes," *IEEE Trans. Syst. Man, Cybern.*, vol. 3, pp. 28–44.

[3] E. H. Mamdani and S. Assilian (1975). "An experiment in linquistic synthesis with a fuzzy logic controller," *Int. J. Man-Machine-Studies.*, vol. 7, pp. 1–13.

[4] L. X. Wang (1997). *A course in fuzzy systems and control.* Englewood Cliffs, NJ: Prentice-Hall, Inc.

[5] J. Yoneyama, M. Nishikawa, H. Katayama, and A. Ichikawa (2000). "Output stabilization of Takagi-Sugeno fuzzy system," *Fuzzy Sets Systs.*, vol. 111, pp. 253–266.

[6] K. Tanaka and M. Sugeno (1992). "Stability analysis and design of fuzzy control systems", *Fuzzy Sets Systs.*, vol. 45, pp. 135–156.

[7] K. Tanaka (1995). "Stability and stabiliability of fuzzy neural linear control systems", *IEEE Trans. Fuzzy Syst.*, vol. 3, pp. 438–447.

[8] K. Tanaka, T. Ikeda, and H. O. Wang (1996). "Robust stabilization of a class of uncertain nonlinear systems via fuzzy control: Quadratic stabilizability, H_∞ control theory, and linear matrix inequality", *IEEE Trans. Fuzzy Syst.*, vol. 4, pp. 1–13.

[9] H. O. Wang, K. Tanaka, and M. F. Griffin (1996). "An approach to fuzzy control of nonlinear systems: Stability and design issues", *IEEE Trans. Fuzzy Syst.*, vol. 4, pp. 14-23.

[10] S. G. Cao, N. W. Ree, and G. Feng (1996). "Quadratic stability analysis and design of

continuous-time fuzzy control systems", *Int. J. Syst. Sci.*, vol. 27, pp. 193–203.
[11] W. Assawinchaichote and S.K. Nguang (2002). "Fuzzy observer-based controller design for singularly perturbed nonlinear systems: An LMI approach", *IEEE Conf. on Decision and Contr.*, pp. 2165–2170.
[12] T. Takagi and M. Sugeno (1985). "Fuzzy identification of systems and its applications to modelling and control", *IEEE Trans. Syst. Man. Cybern.*, vol. 15, pp. 116–132.
[13] C. L. Chen, P. C. Chen, and C. K. Chen (1995). "Analysis and design of fuzzy control system", *Fuzzy Sets Systs.*, vol. 57, pp. 125–140.
[14] X. J. Ma, Z. Q Sun, and Y. Y He (1998). "Analysis and design of fuzzy controller and fuzzy observer", *IEEE Trans. Fuzzy Syst.*, vol. 6, pp. 41–51.
[15] B. S. Chen, C. S. Tseng, and H. J. Uang (2000). "Mixed $\mathcal{H}_2/\mathcal{H}_\infty$ fuzzy output feedback control design for nonlinear dynamic systems: An LMI approach", *IEEE Trans. Fuzzy Syst.*, vol. 8, pp. 249–265.
[16] S.K. Nguang and P. Shi (2000). "Stabilisation of a class of nonlinear time-delay systems using fuzzy models", *Proc. 39th IEEE Conf. on Decision and Contr.*, pp. 4415–4419.
[17] S. K. Nguang and P. Shi (2001). "$\mathcal{H}_\infty$ fuzzy output feedback control design for nonlinear systems: An LMI approach", *40th IEEE Conf. on Decision and Contr.*, pp. 2501–2506.
[18] S. K. Nguang and P. Shi (2001). "Fuzzy $\mathcal{H}_\infty$ output feedback control of nonlinear systems under sampled measurements", *40th IEEE IEEE Conf. on Decision and Contr.*, pp. 120–126.
[19] M. Teixeira and S. H. Zak (1999). "Stabilizing controller design for uncertain nonlinear systems using fuzzy models", *IEEE Trans. Fuzzy Syst.*, vol. 7, pp. 133–142.
[20] S. H. Zak (1999). "Stabilizing fuzzy system models using linear controllers", *IEEE Trans. Fuzzy Syst.*, vol. 7, pp. 236–240.
[21] L. X. Wang (1997). *A course in fuzzy systems and control.* Englewood Cliffs, NJ: Prentice-Hall.
[22] S. K. Nguang and P. Shi (2003). "$\mathcal{H}^\infty$ fuzzy output feedback control design for nonlinear systems: An LMI approach ," *IEEE Trans. Fuzzy Syst.*, vol. 11, pp. 331–340.
[23] S. K. Nguang and W. Assawinchaichote (2003). "$\mathcal{H}_\infty$ filtering for fuzzy dynamic systems with pole placement," *IEEE Trans. Circuits Systs. I*, vol. 50, pp. 1503-1508.
[24] W.Assawinchaichote and S. K. Nguang (2004). "$\mathcal{H}^\infty$ filtering for nonlinear singularly perturbed systems with pole placement constraints: An LMI approach", *IEEE Trans. Signal Processing*, vol. 52, pp. 579–588.
[25] L. X. Wang (1995). "Design and analysis of fuzzy identifiers of nonlinear dynamic systems," *IEEE Trans. Automat. Contr.*, vol. 40, pp. 11–23.
[26] Z. X. Han and G. Feng (1998). "State-feedback $\mathcal{H}_\infty$ controllers design for fuzzy dynamic system using LMI technique," in *Proc. Fuzzy-IEEE Conf.*, pp. 538–544.
[27] Z. X. Han, G. Feng, B. L. Walcott, and Y. M. Zhang (2000). "$\mathcal{H}_\infty$ controller design of fuzzy dynamic systems with pole placement constraints," in *Proc. Amer. Contr. Conf.*, pp. 1939–1943.
[28] S. K. Nguang and P. Shi, "Fuzzy $\mathcal{H}_\infty$ output feedback control of nonlinear systems under sampled measurements (2001). " in *Proc. IEEE Conf. on Decision and Contr.*, (Orlando), pp. 120–126.
[29] H. J. Lee, J. B. Park, and G. Chen (2001). "Robust fuzzy control of nonlinear system with parametric uncertainties," *IEEE. Trans. Fuzzy Syst.*, vol. 9, pp. 369–379.

6

Affine-TS-Based Fuzzy Tracking Design

Shinq-Jen Wu
Department of Electrical Engineering, Da-Yeh University, Chang-Hwa
Taiwan, R.O.C.

1. Introduction

Research in fuzzy modelling and fuzzy control have come of age (1), (2), (3), (4). There are two model-based approaches to theoretically construct the T-S fuzzy system of a nonlinear system. One is from local linear approximation, which generates linear singleton-included rule-consequences (*affine* T-S fuzzy system). The other is via the sector nonlinearity concept (5), (6), (7), which generates linear singleton-free rule-consequences (*linear* T-S fuzzy system). Both are demonstrated to be universal approximations to any smooth nonlinear systems (8), (9), (10). The *linear* type T-S system is popular due to its further intrinsic analysis. A linear matrix inequality (LMI)-based fuzzy controller was used to minimize the upper bound of a performance index (9). Structure-oriented and switching fuzzy controllers were developed for more complicated systems (7), (11), (12). Optimal fuzzy control techniques were proposed to minimize a performance index from local-concept and global-concept approach, respectively (13), (14), (15). Yang and coworkers used an input-free T-S fuzzy system to approximate a uncertain nonlinear state function, and adopted hybrid sliding-mode, adaptive and back-stepping control techniques to control a strick-feedback uncertainty-included nonlinear system (16). Via a fuzzy-static-output-feedback technique, Lo and Lin transformed a robust H_∞ quadratic tracking problem into a bilinear-matrix inequality (17).

Target tracking is common in the real world. However, it is tough work to construct a system to achieve perfect tracking. We derived local-concept-based tracking technologies for various tracking problems (18). Cuevas and Toledo solved a chaotic-synchronization problem, and found out two Lorenz' attractors (19). Uang and Hung focused on a model-following tracking problem (20). Chen and coauthors reformulated a H_∞ tracking problem into a LMI problem (21). They also adopted this technique to derive a reference-tracking-control design for an interconnected system (22). Recently, they used a T-S fuzzy model to describe a fuzzy stochastic moving-average system, and derived a minimum-variance (23).

However, it is impractical to *theoretically* convert a mathematical model into a T-S fuzzy model if a nonlinear system is too complex to describe. More and more researchers attempt to identify fuzzy models from input-output data (24), (25). The approach of model-free nonlinear systems to guarantee the proposed fuzzy model under limited modelling error and the corresponding fuzzy control with desirable implementation is still in development. For this model-free approach, an *affine* type fuzzy model will be more preferred than *linear* type on providing one more adjustable parameter during computation-intelligent (neural-fuzzy-evolution) learning process (26). However, no affine-type tracking-controller and few affine-type regulating-controllers were proposed. Hsiao and coworkers proposed

a hybrid-compensation controller (27). E. Kim and coworkers used convex optimization technique to construct a LMI-based affine-type fuzzy controller (28), (29). They recently specialized in an affine T-S fuzzy system with *constant input-matrix* and transformed a regulating problem into a bilinear-matrix inequality (30). P. Bergsten and coworkers tried to derive an affine-type observer by regarding the singleton of an affine rule-consequence as a trivial term. Therefore, the result was, in fact, belong to a typical *linear*-type case (31).
Here, we realize a tracking system as an affine T-S fuzzy systems, and formulate a tracking problem as a fuzzy quadratic-tracking problem. The tracking-control deign schemes for an affine TS-based nonlinear system to trace two kinds of targets (moving target and model-following target) are derived in Sections 2 and 3. These two sections describe fuzzy quadratic tracking problems, the derived optimal fuzzy tracking-controllers, and the Lyapunov-based stability analysis. The performance of the proposed affine-based trackers for these two targets is examined in Section 4. Section 5 summarizes the results of our research and suggests areas for further research.

2. Moving-target tracking problem

By local-linear approximation or neural fuzzy inference networks, a nonlinear system can be realized as an *affine* T-S fuzzy system,

$$\begin{aligned} R^i\ :\ \text{If } x_1 \text{ is } T_{1i},\ \ldots,\ x_n \text{ is } T_{ni}, \text{ then } \dot{X}(t) &= A_iX(t)+B_iu(t)+D_i,\ i=1,\ \ldots,r, \\ Y(t) &= CX(t), \end{aligned} \tag{1}$$

where R^i denotes the ith rule of the fuzzy model; $x_1, \ldots, x_n$ are system states; $T_{1i}, \ldots, T_{ni}$ are input fuzzy terms in the ith rule; $X(t)=[x_1,\ldots,x_n]^t \in \Re^n$ is state vector, $Y(t)=[y_1,\ldots,y_{n'}]^t \in \Re^{n'}$ is system output vector, $u(t)\in\Re^m$ is system input; and A_i, B_i, C_i and D_i are $n\times n$, $n\times m$, $n'\times n$ and $n\times 1$ matrices, respectively. We note that the entire T-S fuzzy system in Eq. (1) can be expressed as

$$\dot{X}(t)=\sum_{i=1}^{r} h_i(X(t))(A_iX(t)+B_iu(t)+D_i) \tag{2}$$

with $X(0)=X_0\in\Re^n$; $h_i(X(t))$ denotes the normalized firing-strength of the i th rule of the fuzzy system, $h_i(X(t))=\alpha_i/\sum_{i=1}^{r}\alpha_i$ with $\alpha_i=\Pi_{j=1}^{n}\mu_{T_{ji}}(X(t))$, where $\mu_{T_{ji}}(X(t))$ is the membership function of fuzzy term T_{ji}.
The problem of minimal energy consumption for the moving-target tracking control of a nonlinear system is to control the system such that its output $Y(t)$ *keeps close* to the moving-target $Y^d(t)$ under a minimal energy condition. Therefore, we can formulate it as a fuzzy quadratic tracking problem.
PROBLEM 1. Given a rule-based fuzzy tracking system in Eq. (1) with $X(t_0)=X_0\in\Re^n$ and a rule-based fuzzy tracking-controller,

$$R^i\ :\ \text{If } y_1 \text{ is } S_{1i},\ \ldots,\ y_{n'} \text{ is } S_{n'i}, \text{ then } u(t)=r_i(t),\ i=1,\ \ldots,\delta, \tag{3}$$

find the individual tracking-law, $r_i^*(\cdot), i=1,\ldots,\delta$, such that the composed tracking controller, $u^*(\cdot)$, can minimize a quadratic cost function,

$$J(u(\cdot))=\int_{t_0}^{\infty}[u^t(t)Su(t)+X^t(t)L_1X(t)+(Y(t)-Y^d(t))^tL_2(Y(t)-Y^d(t))]dt, \tag{4}$$

where $L_1 = [I_n - C^t(CC^t)^{-1}C]^t L_3 [I_n - C^t(CC^t)^{-1}C]$; S, L_2 and L_3 are, respectively, $m \times m$, $n' \times n'$ and $n \times n$ positive symmetric matrices; $X^t(t)L_1X(t)$ is the state-trajectory penalty to produce smooth response, $u^t(t)Su(t)$ denotes fuel consumption, and the last term in $J(u(\cdot))$ relates to error cost. Let $L = L_1 + C^t L_2 C$. And, we define an *artificial desired-trajectory* ($X^d(t) = C^t[CC^t]^{-1}Y^d(t)$) to simplify the cost function as

$$J(u(\cdot)) = \int_{t_0}^{\infty} [u^t(t)Su(t) + (X(t) - X^d(t))^t L(X(t) - X^d(t))]dt. \tag{5}$$

According to a dynamic-programming formalism, this quadratic optimal problem can be regarded as a successively on-going dynamic problem with regard to the state from the previous decision. At any time-instant, the energy of the entire fuzzy system is the "fuzzy summation" of the energy of each fuzzy subsystem. Therefore, solving a quadratic optimal tracking-control problem is to find *only one corresponding optimal* solution of the fuzzy tracking-controller for *each* rule of the *affine* fuzzy model. We further introduce an *augmented target* to re-formulate the *affine-type* local quadratic problem into a *linear-type* problem. And then, we can obtain our tracking-control design scheme as follows.

Theorem 1 (moving-target) *For affine T-S fuzzy system in Eq. (1) and fuzzy tracking-controller in Eq. (3), if A_i is nonsingular, $\bar{\pi}_i^{-1}(L + A_i^t\bar{\pi}_i) > 0$, (A_i, B_i) is completely controllable (c.c.), and (A_i, C) is completely observable (c.o.) for $i = 1, \ldots, r$, then* **(1)** *the local fuzzy tracking-law is*

$$r_i^*(t) = -S^{-1}B_i^t\bar{\pi}_i X^*(t) + \bar{r}_i^s + \bar{r}_i^{ext}(t),\ i = 1, \ldots, r; \tag{6}$$

their "blending" global fuzzy tracking-controller ($u^*(t) = \sum_{i=1}^r h_i(X^*(t))r_i^*(t)$) minimizes $J(u(\cdot))$ in (4), where $\bar{r}_i^s = -S^{-1}B_i^t(\bar{\pi}_i\bar{X}_i^s + \bar{b}_i^s)$, $\bar{r}_i^{ext}(t) = -S^{-1}B_i^t\bar{b}_i(t)$, $\bar{X}_i^s = A_i^{-1}D_i$, $\bar{b}_i(t)$ is the target-dependent variable for adapting to the target-variation, $\bar{b}_i^s$ is a fuzzy singleton-related constant,

$$\dot{b}_i(t) = -(A_i - B_iS^{-1}B_i^t\bar{\pi}_i)^t b_i(t) + LX^d(t),\ b_i(\infty) = \mathbf{0}_{n\times 1}, \tag{7}$$

$$\bar{b}_i^s = -\int_0^{\infty} e^{[A_i - B_iS^{-1}B_i^t\bar{\pi}_i]^t\tau}d\tau \cdot L\bar{X}_i^s, \tag{8}$$

and $\bar{\pi}_i$ is a unique symmetric positive-definite solution of a Riccati equation,

$$K_iA_i + A_i^tK_i - K_iB_iS^{-1}B_i^tK_i + L = \mathbf{0}; \tag{9}$$

(2) *the entire feedback fuzzy tracking system is stable,*

$$\dot{X}^*(t) = \sum_{i=1}^{r} h_i(X^*(t))[(A_i - B_iS^{-1}B_i^t\bar{\pi}_i)X^*(t) + B_i(\bar{r}_i^s + \bar{r}_i^{ext}(t)) + D_i]. \tag{10}$$

Proof. See the Appendix.

3. Model-following tracking problem

In this section, we consider another fuzzy tracking problem, whose target comes from the response of a reference model. We shall derive a tracking design scheme to control a nonlinear system such that system-output $Y(t)$ keeps following the model-response-target $Y^d(t)$ with minimal energy consumption.

PROBLEM 2. Given an affine T-S fuzzy tracking system in Eq. (1) and a fuzzy tracking-controller in Eq. (3) with $X(t_0) = X_0 \in \Re^n$, find the individual tracking-law, $r_i^*(\cdot)$, $i = 1,\ldots,\delta$, such that the composed tracking-controller, $u^*(\cdot)$, can minimize $J(u(\cdot))$ in Eq. (4) and follow the target $Y^d(t)$, which is the response of a linear model,

$$\begin{aligned} \dot{z_1}(t) &= F_1 z_1(t) + J_1 v(t), \\ Y^d(t) &= E_1 z_1(t) \end{aligned} \tag{11}$$

with $z_1(t_0) = z_{10}$; and input-command $v(t) \in \Re^{m'}$ is the zero-input response of the system: $\dot{z_2}(t) = F_2 z_2(t)$ and $v(t) = E_2 z_2(t)$ with $z_2(t_0) = z_{20}$, where $z_1(t) \in \Re^h$ and $z_2(t) \in \Re^{h'}$ are system states; F_1, J_1, E_1, F_2 and E_2 are respectively $h \times h$, $h \times m'$, $n' \times h$, $h' \times h'$ and $m' \times h'$ matrices.
By defining $Z(t) = [z_1^t(t)\ \ z_2^t(t)]^t$, we can rewrite the desired tracked system as

$$\begin{aligned} \dot{Z}(t) &= \begin{bmatrix} F_1 & J_1 E_2 \\ \mathbf{0}_{h' \times h} & F_2 \end{bmatrix} Z(t) = F Z(t), \\ Y^d(t) &= [E_1\ \ \mathbf{0}_{n' \times h'}] Z(t) = E Z(t). \end{aligned} \tag{12}$$

We further define $\tilde{X}(t) = [X^t(t)\ \ Z^t(t)]^t$ to simply Problem 2 into the following *augmented regulating* problem.
PROBLEM 2.1. Given an *augmented* affine T-S fuzzy *regulating* system,

$$\dot{\tilde{X}}(t) = \sum_{i=1}^{r} h_i(\tilde{X}(t))[\tilde{A}_i \tilde{X}(t) + \tilde{B}_i u(t) + \tilde{D}_i] \tag{13}$$

with $\tilde{X}(t_0) = \tilde{X}_0 \in \Re^{n+h+h'}$, $h_i(\tilde{X}(t)) = h_i(X(t))$, and rule-based fuzzy controller in Eq. (3), find the individual regulating law, $r_i^*(\cdot)$, $i = 1,\ldots,\delta$, to minimize

$$J(r_i(\cdot)) = \int_{t_0}^{\infty} [\tilde{X}^t(t) \tilde{L} \tilde{X}(t) + u^t(t)(t) S u(t)] dt, \tag{14}$$

where parameters
$\tilde{B}_i = \begin{bmatrix} B_i \\ \mathbf{0}_{(h+h') \times m} \end{bmatrix}$, $\tilde{D}_i = \begin{bmatrix} D_i \\ \mathbf{0}_{(h+h') \times 1} \end{bmatrix}$, $\tilde{A}_i = \begin{bmatrix} A_i & \mathbf{0}_{n \times (h+h')} \\ \mathbf{0}_{(h+h') \times n} & F \end{bmatrix}$,
and
$\tilde{L} = \begin{bmatrix} L & -LC^t[CC^t]^{-1}E \\ -E^t[CC^t]^{-1}CL & E^t[CC^t]^{-1}CLC^t[CC^t]^{-1}E \end{bmatrix}$.
To solve this issue, we first regards Problem 2.1 as Problem 1 in case of $Y^d(t) = 0_{n' \times 1}$. Then, we introduce two parameters, $\tilde{K}_i(t) = \begin{bmatrix} K_i(t) & K_i^{21^t}(t) \\ K_i^{21}(t) & K_i^{22}(t) \end{bmatrix}$ and $\tilde{b}_i(t) = \begin{bmatrix} b_i^s(t) \\ b_{2i}(t) \end{bmatrix}$. After a series of complicated matrix-manipulations, we derive the following theorem.

Theorem 2 (model-following) *For affine T-S fuzzy system in Eq. (1) and fuzzy tracking-controller in Eq. (3), let an artificial desired trajectory* $X^d(t)$ *be defined as* $Y^d(t) = CX^d(t)$*, where* $Y^d(t)$ *is the output of a tracked model in Eq. (11), and*
$Z(t) = \begin{bmatrix} z_1(t) \\ z_2(t) \end{bmatrix}$, $F = \begin{bmatrix} F_1 & J_1 E_2 \\ \mathbf{0}_{h' \times h} & F_2 \end{bmatrix}$,

$E = [E_1 \quad \mathbf{0}_{n' \times h'}]$. *If* A_i *is nonsingular,* $\bar{\pi}_i^{-1}(L + A_i^t \bar{\pi}_i) > 0$, (A_i, B_i) *is c.c. and* (A_i, C) *is c.o. for* $i = 1, \ldots, r$, *then*
$(\mathbf{1})$ *the local fuzzy tracking-law is*

$$r_i^*(t) = -S^{-1}B_i^t[\bar{\pi}_i X^* + \bar{\pi}_i^{21^t} Z(t)] + \bar{r}_i^s,\ i = 1, \ldots, r; \tag{15}$$

their "blending" global fuzzy tracking-controller ($u^*(t) = \sum_{i=1}^r h_i(X^*(t)) r_i^*(t)$) *minimizes* $J(u(\cdot))$ *in (4), where* $\bar{r}_i^s = -S^{-1}B_i^t(\bar{\pi}_i \bar{X}_i^s + \bar{b}_i^s)$, $\bar{X}_i^s = A_i^{-1} D_i$, $\bar{b}_i^s$ *satisfies Eq. (8),* $\bar{\pi}_i$ *is the unique solution of the Riccati equation in Eq. (9), and*

$$\bar{\pi}_i^{21} = -\int_0^{\infty} e^{F^t \tau} \cdot E^t (CC^t)^{-1} CL \cdot e^{(A_i - B_i S^{-1} B_i^t \bar{\pi}_i)\tau} \cdot d\tau; \tag{16}$$

$(\mathbf{2})$ *the entire feedback fuzzy tracking system is stable,*

$$\dot{X}^*(t) = \sum_{i=1}^{r} h_i(X^*(t))[(A_i - B_i S^{-1} B_i^t \bar{\pi}_i) X^*(t) - B_i S^{-1} B_i^t \bar{\pi}_i^{21^t} Z(t) + B_i \bar{r}_i^s + D_i]. \tag{17}$$

Proof. See the Appendix.

4. Numerical simulation

In this section, we use an affine TS-based nonlinear system to examine the performance of our fuzzy tracking-controllers. As we know, via analytical or hybrid-soft-computing technique any nonlinear system can be approximated by an affine T-S fuzzy system. Therefore, we can choose any affine-TS-based nonlinear system as our tracking system. We shall examine the tracking performance for moving-target first, and then for model-following-target. We consider our system as

$$\begin{aligned}
R^1: &\quad \text{If } x(t) \text{ is } F_1^1 \text{ and } \dot{x}(t) \text{ is } F_2^1, \text{ then } \dot{X}(t) = A_1 X(t) + B_1 u(t) + D_1, \\
R^2: &\quad \text{If } x(t) \text{ is } F_1^1 \text{ and } \dot{x}(t) \text{ is } F_2^2, \text{ then } \dot{X}(t) = A_2 X(t) + B_2 u(t) + D_2, \\
R^3: &\quad \text{If } x(t) \text{ is } F_1^2 \text{ and } \dot{x}(t) \text{ is } F_2^1, \text{ then } \dot{X}(t) = A_3 X(t) + B_3 u(t) + D_3, \\
R^4: &\quad \text{If } x(t) \text{ is } F_1^2 \text{ and } \dot{x}(t) \text{ is } F_2^2, \text{ then } \dot{X}(t) = A_4 X(t) + B_4 u(t) + D_4
\end{aligned} \tag{18}$$

with system-output $Y(t) = CX(t)$, where for each rule $C = [0\ 1]$ and

$$X(t) = \begin{bmatrix} \dot{x}(t) \\ x(t) \end{bmatrix}; D_1 = \begin{bmatrix} 1 \\ 1 \end{bmatrix}, D_2 = \begin{bmatrix} 1 \\ 0.5 \end{bmatrix}, D_3 = \begin{bmatrix} 1 \\ 0 \end{bmatrix}, D_4 = \begin{bmatrix} 0.3 \\ 1 \end{bmatrix};$$

$$A_1 = \begin{bmatrix} 0 & -0.02 \\ 1 & 0 \end{bmatrix}, A_2 = \begin{bmatrix} -0.225 & -0.02 \\ 1 & 0 \end{bmatrix}, A_3 = \begin{bmatrix} 0 & -1.5275 \\ 1 & 0 \end{bmatrix},$$

$$A_4 = \begin{bmatrix} -0.225 & -1.5275 \\ 1 & 0 \end{bmatrix}; B_i = \begin{bmatrix} 1 \\ 0 \end{bmatrix}, i = 1, \ldots, 4.$$

The membership functions are chosen as $\mu_{F_1^1}(x(t)) = 1 - \frac{x^2(t)}{2.25}$, $\mu_{F_1^2}(x(t)) = \frac{x^2(t)}{2.25}$, $\mu_{F_2^1}(\dot{x}(t)) = 1 - \frac{\dot{x}^2(t)}{2.25}$, and $\mu_{F_2^2}(\dot{x}(t)) = \frac{\dot{x}^2(t)}{2.25}$. We shall design a fuzzy-rule-based tracking-controller,

$$R^1: \quad \text{If } x(t) \text{ is } F_1^1 \text{ and } \dot{x}(t) \text{ is } F_2^1, \text{ then } u(t) = r_1(t),$$
$$R^2: \quad \text{If } x(t) \text{ is } F_1^1 \text{ and } \dot{x}(t) \text{ is } F_2^2, \text{ then } u(t) = r_2(t) \tag{19}$$
$$R^3: \quad \text{If } x(t) \text{ is } F_1^2 \text{ and } \dot{x}(t) \text{ is } F_2^1, \text{ then } u(t) = r_3(t),$$
$$R^4: \quad \text{If } x(t) \text{ is } F_1^2 \text{ and } \dot{x}(t) \text{ is } F_2^2, \text{ then } u(t) = r_4(t), \tag{20}$$

such that the designed affine-type closed-loop fuzzy system can keep tracing the moving-target with minimal cost consumption,

$$J(u(\cdot)) = \int_0^\infty [u^t(t)Su(t) + X^t(t)L_1(t)X(t) + e_y(t)^t L_2 e_y(t)]dt \tag{21}$$

with $e_y(t) = Y(t) - Y^d(t)$ and $L_1 = [I_2 - C^t(CC^t)^{-1}C]^t L_3 [I_2 - C^t(CC^t)^{-1}C]$. We now set penalty-parameters as $S = 0.001$, $L_3 = I_2$, and $L_2 = I_1$. (These parameters can be regarded as weighting factors for cost, trajectory-smoothness and output-error. Therefore, they can be chosen optionally.) Since each fuzzy subsystem is well-behaved (rank$[A_i \;\; A_iB_i] = 2$ and rank$[C^t \;\; A_i^tC^t]^t = 2$ for $i = 1, \ldots, 4$), we have the unique symmetric positive-definite solution of the algebraic Riccati equation,

$\bar{\pi}_1 = \begin{bmatrix} 0.0326 & 0.0316 \\ 0.0316 & 1.0311 \end{bmatrix}$,

$\bar{\pi}_2 = \begin{bmatrix} 0.0324 & 0.0316 \\ 0.0316 & 1.0311 \end{bmatrix}$,

$\bar{\pi}_3 = \begin{bmatrix} 0.0326 & 0.0301 \\ 0.0301 & 1.0309 \end{bmatrix}$, $\bar{\pi}_4 = \begin{bmatrix} 0.0323 & 0.0301 \\ 0.0301 & 1.0306 \end{bmatrix}$. And, we have $\bar{\pi}_i^{-1}(L + A_i^t\bar{\pi}_i) > 0$ for each rule.

So, the tracking-controller is $u^*(t) = \sum_{i=1}^r h_i(X^*(t))[-S^{-1}B_i^t\bar{\pi}_iX^*(t) + \bar{r}_i^s + \bar{r}_i^{ext}(t)]$, where $\bar{r}_i^s = -S^{-1}B_i^t(\bar{\pi}_i\bar{X}_i^s + \bar{b}_i^s)$, $\bar{r}_i^{ext}(t) = -S^{-1}B_i^t\bar{b}_i(t)$, $\bar{X}_i^s = A_i^{-1}D_i$. Figure 1 shows the tracking trajectories for various moving targets (Y^d is a step'wise function, $Y^d(t) = 3 + 2\sin 0.2t$, $Y^d(t) = 3 + 4e^{-0.3t}$, and $Y^d(t) = 0.5 + 2\log(3 + t)$).

This affine TS fuzzy system is also used for model-following-target tracking. Our tracked target is from a model-response $Y^d(t)$ in Eq. (11) with initial-condition $z_{10} = 10$, where parameters are set at $(F_1, J_1, E_1) = (-1, 1, 1)$; and input-command v is from a zero-input linear system with initial-condition $z_{20} = 10$ and parameters $E_2 = 1$, $F_2 = -0.2$. That is, our augmented tracked system $Z(t)$ is in Eq. (12) with initial condition,

$Z(0) = \begin{bmatrix} z_{10} \\ z_{20} \end{bmatrix} = \begin{bmatrix} 10 \\ 10 \end{bmatrix}$,

and parameters,

$F = \begin{bmatrix} F_1 & J_1E_2 \\ \mathbf{0} & F_2 \end{bmatrix} = \begin{bmatrix} -1 & 1 \\ 0 & -0.2 \end{bmatrix}$,

$E = [E_1 \;\; \mathbf{0}] = [1\; 0]$. Based on Theorem 2, we have the model-following controller, $u^*(t) = \sum_{i=1}^r h_i(X^*(t))[-S^{-1}B_i^t(\bar{\pi}_iX^* + \bar{\pi}_i^{21^t}Z(t)) + \bar{r}_i^s]$, where $\bar{\pi}_i^{21} = -\int_0^\infty e^{F^t\tau} \cdot E^t(CC^t)^{-1}CL \cdot e^{(A_i - B_iS^{-1}B_i^t\bar{\pi}_i)\tau} \cdot d\tau$. Figure 2 shows the tracking-performance also for $(F_1, F_2) = (-0.2, -1)$, $(-5, -\frac{1}{30})$ and $(-\frac{1}{30}, -5)$. Simulation results show that the designed affine-type optimal fuzzy tracking-controllers can efficiently push the tracking system to trace various moving-targets (Fig. 1) and to follow various parameter-variation tracked model (Fig. 2) in a short time.

5. Conclusions

Although a *linear* type T-S fuzzy system is very popular, and has been successfully applied to various fields, the *affine* type system is more preferred for computation-intelligent (neural-fuzzy-evolution) modelling as a system is too complex to be described. In this paper, we derive an affine-type fuzzy tracking-controller for tracking various moving-targets and another for keeping following a linear system whose input-command is generated from another zero-input system. Both designed closed-loop tracking systems are demonstrated to be globally stable. We use an affine-based nonlinear system to demonstrate that the proposed tracking-controllers can quickly reach a perfect tracking-effect. In the future, we shall discuss the robustness of the designed systems.

6. Appendix

Proof of Theorem 1.

(**1**) From the essence of the dynamic programming formalism, the operation of minimizing $J(u(\cdot))$ in Eq. (**??**) can be decomposed as follows:

$$\min_{u_{[t_0,\infty]}} J(u(\cdot)) = \min_{u_{[t,\infty]}}\{\int_t^{\infty}(e_{x_l}^t L e_{x_l} + u_l^t S u_l)dl + \min_{u_{[t_0,t]}}\int_{t_0}^{t}(e_{x_l}^t L e_{x_l} + u_l^t S u_l)dl\}, \tag{22}$$

where state-error $e_{x_l} = X_l - X_l^d$ and the lower index is used to denote time-dependence for notation-simplification (X_l for $X(l)$). Therefore, the quadratic optimization problem is, in fact, a successively on-going dynamic problem with regard to the system-state resulting from the previous decision, i.e., the initial system-state at time t is $X_{0_t} = X_t^*$. So, the objective of Problem 1 is to successively find the *optimal global decision (global optimal fuzzy controller)* u_t^* for minimizing the cost function,

$$J_t(u_t) = \int_t^{\infty}(e_{x_l}^t L e_{x_l} + u_l^t u_l)dl,\ t \in [t_0,\infty], \tag{23}$$

and for estimating $X_{t^+}^*$ with regard to initial-state X_t^*, where t^+ denotes the time-instant slightly later than time t; and then, with the new initial-state, $X_{t^+}^*$, resolving $u_{t^+}^*$ to minimize $J_{t^+}(u_{t^+})$. *At any time-instant t*, the *optimal local decision (local optimal fuzzy tracking-law)* derives from minimizing $J_t(u_t)$ in Eq. (23) with regard to the *fuzzy subsystem,*

$$\dot{X}_l = A_i X_l + B_i u_l + D_i,\ l \in [t,\infty],\ i = 1,\ldots,r; \tag{24}$$

and the *optimal global decision* derives from minimizing $J_t(u_t)$ with regard to the *entire fuzzy system,*

$$\dot{X}_l = \sum_{i=1}^{r} h_i(X_l)(A_i X_l + B_i u_l + D_i),\ l \in [t,\infty]. \tag{25}$$

Since u_t^* is just a variable to be solved either for the aforementioned local optimization problem or for the global optimization issue, we can use $r_{i_t}^*$ to denote the optimal local decision of the i-th fuzzy subsystem.

(**2**) We shall further demonstrated that the global optimal decision in Problem 1 can be obtained by fuzzily blending those optimal local decisions. Now, let $\zeta_l(X_l,u_l)$ and $\zeta_{i_l}(X_l,r_{i_l})$, $i = 1,\ldots,r$, denote, respectively, the entire energy and local energy at any time-instant l, $l \in [t,\infty]$. Then, $J_t(u_t) = \int_t^{\infty}\zeta_l(X_l,u_l)dl$ and $J_t(r_{i_t}) = \int_t^{\infty}\zeta_{i_l}(X_l,r_{i_l})dl$. At any time-instant, the energy of the entire fuzzy system is *some kinds of nonlinear combination* (fuzzy summation) of the energy of fuzzy subsystems. In other words, the global energy can be expressed in terms of rule-based local energy. We note that this combination is only state-dependent, which is nothing to do with system-input. Therefore, no matter that system behavior is nonlinear with regard to input or not, the input-term cannot be included into fuzzy-precondition for physical realizable consideration, even it is reasonable in mathematical concept. And, this nonlinear combination is not necessary to be the same type as that for blending fuzzy subsystems into an entire system. Therefore, we use $h'(X(t))$ to denote that (a) nonlinear summation is only state dependent; (b) the energy-relationship between entire system and subsystems could be totally different from the behavior-relationship, which is denoted by normalized membership function $h(X(t))$. Therefore, we write $\zeta_l(X_l,u_l) = \sum_{i=1}^{r} h'_i(X_l)\zeta_{i_l}(X_l,r_{i_l})$. At time-instant t with initial-condition X_t^*, let $r_{i_t}^*$ denote the optimal local decision to minimize $J_t(r_{i_t})$ for all $i = 1\ldots,r$, i.e.,

$$\frac{\partial J_t(r_{i_t})}{\partial r_{i_t}}\, |_{r_{i_t}^*} = \frac{\partial}{\partial r_{i_t}} \int_t^\infty \zeta_{i_l}(X_l,r_{i_l})dl\, |_{r_{i_t}^*} = \frac{\partial \zeta_{i_t}(X_t^*,r_{i_t})}{\partial r_{i_t}}\, |_{r_{i_t}^*} = 0,$$

$$\frac{\partial^2 J_t(r_{i_t})}{\partial r_{i_t}^2}\, |_{r_{i_t}^*} = \frac{\partial^2 \zeta_{i_t}(X_t^*,r_{i_t})}{\partial r_{i_t}^2}\, |_{r_{i_t}^*} > 0$$

.

Their corresponding global decision $\breve{u}_t = \sum_{i=1}^{r} h_i(X_t^*) r_{i_t}|_{r_{i_t}^*}$ can satisfy

$$\begin{aligned}
\frac{\partial J_t(u_t)}{\partial u_t}\, |_{\breve{u}_t} &= \frac{\partial}{\partial u_t}\int_t^\infty \zeta_l(X_l,u_l)dl\, |_{\breve{u}_t} \\
&= \frac{\partial}{\partial u_t}\int_t^\infty \sum_{i=1}^{r} h'_i(X_l)\zeta_{i_l}(X_l,r_{i_l})dl\, |_{\breve{u}_t} \\
&= \sum_{i=1}^{r} h'_i(X_t^*)\frac{\partial \zeta_{i_t}(X_t^*,r_{i_t})}{\partial u_t}\, |_{\breve{u}_t} \\
&= \sum_{i=1}^{r} h'_i(X_t^*)\frac{\partial \zeta_{i_t}(X_t^*,r_{i_t})}{\partial r_{i_t}} \cdot \frac{\partial r_{i_t}}{\partial u_t}\, |_{\breve{u}_t} = 0, \\
\frac{\partial^2 J_t(u_t)}{\partial u_t^2}\, |_{\breve{u}_t} &= \sum_{i=1}^{r} h'_i(X_t^*)\frac{\partial^2 \zeta_{i_t}(X_t^*,r_{i_t})}{\partial r_{i_t}^2} \cdot (\frac{\partial r_{i_t}}{\partial u_t})^2\, |_{\breve{u}_t} \\
&\quad + \sum_{i=1}^{r} h'_i(X_t^*)\frac{\partial \zeta_{i_t}(X_t^*,r_{i_t})}{\partial r_{i_t}} \cdot \frac{\partial^2 r_{i_t}}{\partial u_t^2}\, |_{\breve{u}_t} > 0,
\end{aligned}$$

i.e., $\breve{u}_t = u_t^*$. Therefore, at any time instant t if we can find $r_{i_t}^*$ to minimize $J_t(r_{i_t})$, then it follows that their composed global decision u_t^* can be the global minimizer of the total cost $J_t(u_t)$.

(**3**) *We assume A_i to be nonsingular for $i = 1,\ldots,r$, and let $\hat{X}(t) = X(t) + \bar{X}_i^s$, where $\bar{X}_i^s = A_i^{-1}D_i$.* An *affine*-type local tracking problem can be rewritten as a *linear*-type tracking issue with *augmented target $\hat{X}_i^d(t) = \bar{X}_i^s + X^d(t)$*. In other words, our problem is reformulated as: Given a fuzzy subsystem, $\dot{\hat{X}}_l = A_i\hat{X}_l + B_i r_{i_l}, l \in [t,\infty], i = 1,\ldots,r$ with $\hat{X}_{0_t} = \hat{X}_t^*$, find the local decision at time-instant t, $r_{i_t}^*$, for minimizing a cost function,
$J_t(r_{i_t}) = \int_t^\infty ((\hat{X}_l - \hat{X}_i^d(t))^t L(\hat{X}_l - \hat{X}_i^d(t)) + r_{i_l}^t S r_{i_l})dl$. Then, we obtain the tracking law (18), $r_i^*(t) = -S^{-1}B_i^t[\bar{\pi}_i\hat{X}^*(t) + \hat{b}_i(t)]$, the fuzzy subsystem,

$\dot{X}^*(t) = (A_i - B_iS^{-1}B_i^t\bar{\pi}_i)\hat{X}^*(t) - B_iS^{-1}B_i^t\hat{b}_i(t)$, where $\bar{\pi}_i$ satisfies Eq. (9) and $\hat{b}_i(t)$ satisfies

$$\dot{\hat{b}}_i(t) = -(A_i - B_iS^{-1}B_i^t\bar{\pi}_i)^t\hat{b}_i(t) + L\hat{X}_i^d(t),\ \hat{b}_i(\infty) = \mathbf{0}_{n\times 1}. \tag{26}$$

According to the linearity property, we have $\hat{b}_i(t) = b_i^s(t) + b_i(t)$, where $b_i(t) = \bar{b}_i(t)$ in Eq. (7) is to adaptively trace the target and

$$\dot{b}_i^s(t) = -(A_i - B_iS^{-1}B_i^t\bar{\pi}_i)^t b_i^s(t) + L\bar{X}_i^s,\ b_i^s(\infty) = \mathbf{0}_{n\times 1}. \tag{27}$$

Further, (A_i, B_i) is c.c. and (A_i, C) is c.o. So, we have $b_i^s(t) = \bar{b}_i^s$ in Eq. (8) to response to fuzzy consequence-singleton D_i. By using $\bar{r}_i^s = -S^{-1}B_i^t(\bar{\pi}_i\bar{X}_i^s + \bar{b}_i^s)$ to denote the local singleton-related law, and $\bar{r}_i^{ext}(t) = -S^{-1}B_i^t\bar{b}_i(t)$ to denote local target-related law, we obtain the tracking law $r_i^*(t)$ in Eq. (6) and the fuzzy system $X_i^*(t)$ in Eq. (10).

(**4**) Stability analysis: We use $\bar{U}_i^{aug}$ to denote an augmented-target-associated input, $\bar{U}_i^{aug} = B_i(\bar{r}_i^s + \bar{r}_i^{ext}) + D_i$. Then, the designed feedback system in Eq. (10) can be rewritten as Eq. (28). Its stability concurs with the zero-input system in Eq. (29).

$$\dot{X}^*(t) = \sum_{i=1}^{r} h_i(X^*(t))[A_i - B_iS^{-1}B_i^t\bar{\pi}_i]X^*(t) + \bar{U}_i^{aug}, \tag{28}$$

$$\dot{X}^*(t) = \sum_{i=1}^{r} h_i(X^*(t))[A_i - B_iS^{-1}B_i^t\bar{\pi}_i]X^*(t). \tag{29}$$

We define a Lyapunov function $V(X) = X^tPX$, where P is a symmetric positive-definite matrix. According to Eq. (9), we obtain
$A_i - B_iS^{-1}B_i^t\bar{\pi}_i = -\bar{\pi}_i^{-1}(L + A_i^t\bar{\pi}_i)$,
and

$$\begin{aligned}
\dot{V}(X) = \quad & \dot{X}^tPX + X^tP\dot{X} \\
= \quad & [\sum_{i=1}^{r} h_i(X(t))X^t(A_i - B_iS^{-1}B_i^t\bar{\pi}_i)^t]PX \\
& +X^tP[\sum_{i=1}^{r} h_i(X(t))(A_i - B_iS^{-1}B_i^t\bar{\pi}_i)X] \\
= \quad & -\sum_{i=1}^{r} h_i(X(t))\{X^t[(L + A_i^t\bar{\pi}_i)^t\bar{\pi}_i^{-1}P \\
& +P\bar{\pi}_i^{-1}(L + A_i^t\bar{\pi}_i)]X\} \\
= \quad & -2\sum_{i=1}^{r} h_i(X(t))[X^tP\bar{\pi}_i^{-1}(L + A_i^t\bar{\pi}_i)X] \\
= \quad & -2\sum_{i=1}^{r} h_i(X(t))[X^t\bar{\pi}_i^{-1}(L + A_i^t\bar{\pi}_i)X] < 0
\end{aligned}$$

for $P = I$ and $\bar{\pi}_i^{-1}(L + A_i^t\bar{\pi}_i) > 0$ since $h_i(X(t))$ is a positive number always.

Proof of Theorem 2.

(1) An affine-type fuzzy regulating issue in Problem 2.1 is equivalent to Problem 1 in the case of $Y^d(t) = \mathbf{0}_{n'\times 1}$. Therefore, based on Theorem 1 and its proof, we have

$$
\begin{aligned}
r_i^*(t) &= -S^{-1}\tilde{B}_i{}^t\tilde{\pi}_i(t,t_1)\tilde{X}^*(t)+\tilde{r}_i^s(t),\\
\dot{\tilde{X}}^*(t) &= [\tilde{A}_i-\tilde{B}_iS^{-1}\tilde{B}_i{}^t\tilde{\pi}_i(t,t_1)]\tilde{X}^*(t)+\tilde{B}_i\tilde{r}_i^s(t)+\tilde{D}_i,\\
\dot{\tilde{b}}_i^s(t) &= -[\tilde{A}_i-\tilde{B}_iS^{-1}\tilde{B}_i{}^t\tilde{\pi}_i(t,t_1)]^t\tilde{b}_i^s(t)+\tilde{L}\tilde{\bar{X}}_i^s,\ \tilde{b}_i^s(t_1)=\mathbf{0}_{(n+h+h')\times 1},
\end{aligned}
$$

where
$\tilde{r}_i^s(t)=-S^{-1}\tilde{B}_i{}^t(\tilde{\pi}_i(t,t_1)\tilde{\bar{X}}_i^s+\tilde{b}_i^s(t))$, $\tilde{\bar{X}}_i^s=\tilde{A}_i{}^{-1}\tilde{D}_i=\begin{bmatrix}\bar{X}_i^s\\ \mathbf{0}_{h\times 1}\end{bmatrix}$, and $\tilde{\pi}_i(t,t_1)$ is the symmetric positive-definite solution of a Riccati equation,

$$-\dot{\tilde{K}}_i(t)=\tilde{K}_i(t)\tilde{A}_i+\tilde{A}_i{}^t\tilde{K}_i(t)-\tilde{K}_i(t)\tilde{B}_iS^{-1}\tilde{B}_i{}^t\tilde{K}_i(t)+\tilde{L},\ \tilde{K}_i(t_1)=\mathbf{0}_{(n+h)\times(n+h)}.$$

We here replace $\tilde{b}_i^s(\infty)$ *and* $\tilde{\bar{\pi}}_i$ *by* $\tilde{b}_i^s(t_1)$ *and* $\tilde{\pi}(t,t_1)$ *for further derivation;* in fact, $\tilde{\bar{\pi}}_i=\lim_{t_1\to\infty}\tilde{\pi}(t,t_1)$.
Now, let
$\tilde{K}_i(t)=\begin{bmatrix}K_i(t) & K_i^{21^t(t)}\\ K_i^{21}(t) & K_i^{22}(t)\end{bmatrix}$,
$\tilde{b}_i(t)=\begin{bmatrix}b_i^s(t)\\ b_{2i}(t)\end{bmatrix}$,
and
$\tilde{X}(t)=\begin{bmatrix}X(t)\\ Z(t)\end{bmatrix}$.
For infinite-horizon case ($t_1=\infty$), after a series of complicated matrix-manipulations we obtain $r_i^*(t)$ in Eq. (15) and $X^*(t)$ in Eq. (17), where $\bar{r}_i^s=-S^{-1}B_i^t(\bar{\pi}_i\bar{X}_i^s+\bar{b}_i^s)$; $\bar{b}_i^s$ is in Eq. (8) as (A_i,B_i) is c.c. and (A_i,C) is c.o.; $\bar{\pi}_i=\lim_{t_1\to\infty}\pi(t,t_1)$ is the unique solution of the Riccati equation in Eq. (9); $b_{2i}(t)$, K_i^{21} and $K_i^{22}(t)$ satisfy

$$\dot{b}_{2i}(t)=K_{21}(t)B_iS^{-1}B_i^tb_i^s(t)+F^tb_i(t)-E^t(CC^t)^{-1}CL\bar{X}_i^s, \tag{30}$$

$$-\dot{K}_{21}(t)=F^tK_{21}(t)+K_{21}(t)A_i-K_{21}(t)B_iS^{-1}B_i^t\bar{\pi}_i-E^t(CC^t)^{-1}CL, \tag{31}$$

$$-\dot{K}_{22}(t)=E^t(CC^t)^{-1}CLC^t(CC^t)^{-1}E+F^tK_{22}(t)-K_{21}(t)B_iS^{-1}B_i^tK_{21}^t(t)+K_{22}(t)F \tag{32}$$

with $b_{2i}(\infty)=\mathbf{0}_{h\times 1}$, $K_{21}(\infty)=\mathbf{0}_{h\times n}$, and $K_{22}(\infty)=\mathbf{0}_{h\times h}$.
(2) We will derive the solution of Eq. (31) is $\bar{\pi}_i^{21}$ in Eq. (16). Now, we rewrite Eq. (31) as

$$-\dot{K}_{21}(t)=F^tK_{21}(t)+K_{21}(t)A_{ci}-L_{21}, \tag{33}$$

where $A_{ci}=A_i-B_iS^{-1}B_i^t\bar{\pi}_i$ and $L_{21}=E^t(CC^t)^{-1}CL$. We then obtain

$$K_{21}(t)=\phi_1(t,t_0)K_{21}(t_0)\phi_2^t(t,t_0)+\int_{t_0}^{t}\phi_1(t,\tau)L_{21}\phi_2^t(t,\tau)d\tau, \tag{34}$$

where $\phi_1(t,t_0)$ and $\phi_2(t,t_0)$ are state-transition matrices of $\dot{X}(t)=-F^tX(t)$ and $\dot{X}(t)=-A_{ci}^tX(t)$, respectively. Therefore, we have

$$
\begin{aligned}
K_{21}(t_1) &= \phi_1(t_1,t_0)K_{21}(t_0)\phi_2^t(t_1,t_0)+\int_{t_0}^{t_1}\phi_1(t_1,\tau)L_{21}\phi_2^t(t_1,\tau)d\tau,\\
K_{21}(t_0) &= \phi_1(t_0,t_1)K_{21}(t_1)\phi_2^t(t_0,t_1)-\int_{t_0}^{t_1}\phi_1(t_0,\tau)L_{21}\phi_2^t(t_0,\tau)d\tau.
\end{aligned}
$$

Substituting $K_{21}(t_0)$ into Eq. (34), we obtain

$$K_{21}(t) = \phi_1(t,t_1)K_{21}(t_1)\phi_2^t(t,t_1) - \int_t^{t_1} \phi_1(t,\tau)L_{21}\phi_2^t(t,\tau)d\tau.$$

Since $\lim_{t_1\to\infty} K_{21}(t_1) = \mathbf{0}_{h\times n}$, we have the solution of $\bar{K}_{21}(t)$ in Eq. (31),

$$\bar{K}_{21}(t) = -\int_t^{\infty} e^{-F^t(t-\tau)} \cdot L_{21} \cdot e^{-A_{ci}^t(t-\tau)}d\tau = -\int_0^{\infty} e^{F^t\tau} \cdot L_{21} \cdot e^{A_{ci}^t\tau}d\tau. \tag{35}$$

Therefore, we have $\bar{\pi}_i^{21}$ in Eq. (16) satisfies Eq. (35) and also Eq. (31).

(3) Stability analysis: $S^{-1}B_i^t\bar{\pi}_i^{21^t}Z(t)$ in Eq. (17) is associated only with the target. $B_i\bar{r}_i^s + D_i$ in Eq. (17) relates to the fuzzy-singleton. So, we lump these two together into an augmented artificial-target, $\bar{U}_i^{art}$. Then, we can rewrite the proposed closed-loop tracking-control system in Eq. (17) as

$$\dot{X}^*(t) = \sum_{i=1}^{r} h_i(X^*(t))[(A_i - B_iS^{-1}B_i^t\bar{\pi}_i)X^*(t) + \bar{U}_i^{art}], \tag{36}$$

where $\bar{U}_i^{art} = S^{-1}B_i^t\bar{\pi}_i^{21^t}Z(t) + B_i\bar{r}_i^s + D_i$. As we know, the stability of nonlinear tracking fuzzy system in Eq. (36) is coincident with that of zero-input fuzzy system in Eq. (29). In Proof of Theorem 1, we have demonstrated that the system in Eq. (29) is globally stable if each fuzzy subsystem satisfies (A_i, B_i) c.c. and (A_i, C) c.o. and $\bar{\pi}_i^{-1}(L + A_i^t\bar{\pi}_i) > 0$.

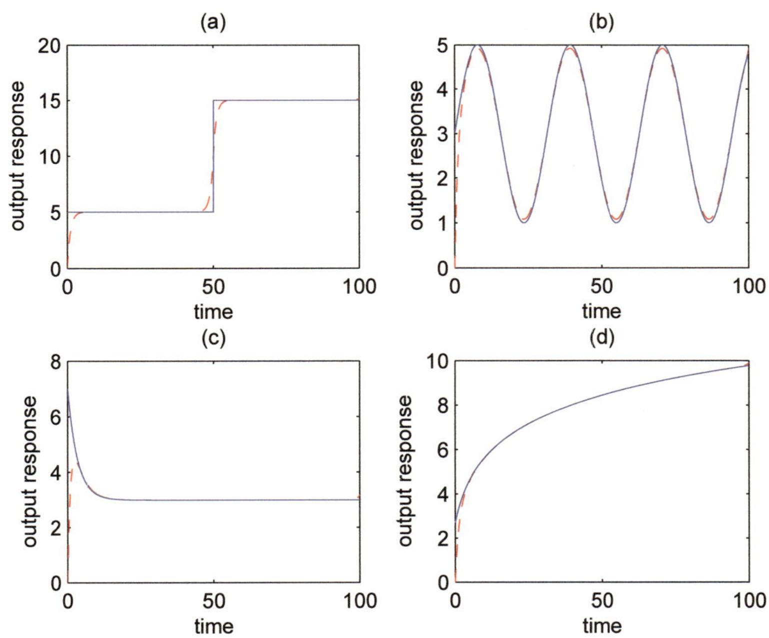

Fig. 1. Output responses (denoted by dashed line) of the affine T-S fuzzy tracking system with the designed affine-type fuzzy *moving-target* tracking controllers in Section 2 for various moving targets (denoted by solid line), where (a) $Y^d(t)$ being a step'wise target, (b) $Y^d(t) = 3 + 2\sin 0.2t$, (c) $Y^d(t) = 3 + 4e^{-0.3t}$ and (d) $Y^d(t) = 0.5 + 2\log(3+t)$.

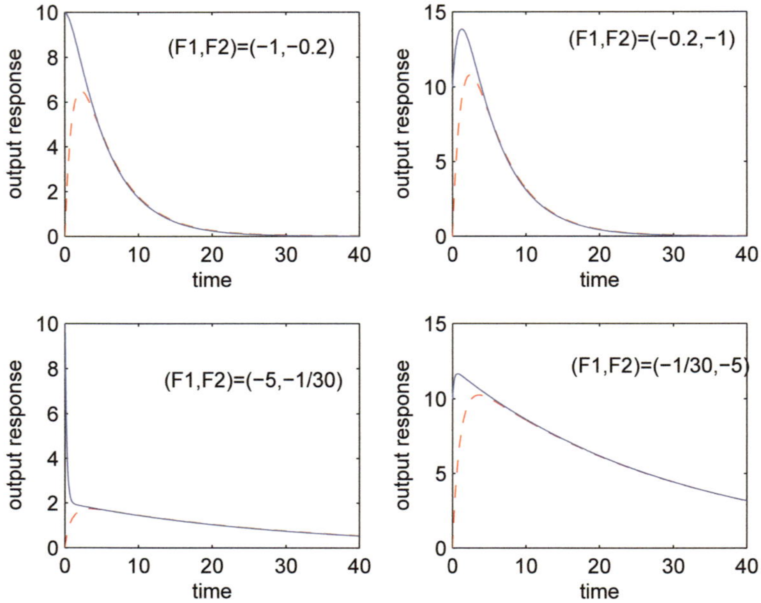

Fig. 2. Output responses (denoted by dashed line) of the affine T-S fuzzy tracking system with the designed affine-type fuzzy *model-following* tracking controllers in Section 3 for the targets (denoted by solid line) from the *tracked model* in Eq. (11) with $E_1 = 1$, $E_2 = 1$ and four different sets of parameters $(F_1, F_2) = (-1, -0.2)$, $(-0.2, -1)$, $(-5, -1/30)$ and $(-1/30, -5)$.

7. References

[1] Cao, S. G., Rees, N. W., and Feng, G.: 'Analysis and design for a class of complex control systems', *Automatica*, 1997, 33, (6), pp. 1017-1039.

[2] Tanaka, K., Ikeda, T., and Wang, H. O.: 'Robust stabilization of a class of uncertain nonlinear systems via fuzzy control: quadratic stabilizability, H^∞ control theory and linear matrix inequalities', *IEEE Trans. Fuzzy Systems*, 1996, 4, (1), pp. 1-13.

[3] Korba, P., Babuska, R., Verbruggen, H. B., and Frank,P. M.: 'Fuzzy gain scheduling: Controller and observer design based on lyapunov method and convex optimization', *IEEE Trans. Fuzzy Systems*, 2003, 11, pp. 285-298.

[4] Taniguchi, T., Tanaka, K., Ohtake, H., and Wang, H. O.: "Model construction, rule reduction and robust compensation for generalized form of Takagi-Sugeno fuzzy sytem', *IEEE Trans. Fuzzy Systems*, 2001, 9, (4), pp. 525-538, 2001.

[5] Tanaka, K., Taniguchi, T., and Wang, H. O.: 'Generalized Takagi-Sugeno fuzzy systems: rule reduction and robust control', *Proc. IEEE Int. Conf. Fuzzy Systems*, San Antonio, 2000, pp. 688-693.

[6] Ohtake, H., Tanaka, K., and Wang, H. O.: 'Fuzzy Modelling via Sector Nonlinearity Concept', *Proc. Int. Conf. IFSA/NAFIPS*, Canada, 2001, pp. 127-132.

[7] Tanaka, K., Taniguchi, T., Hori, S., and Wang, H. O.: 'Structure-oriented design for a class of nonlinear systems', *Proc. IEEE Int. Conf. Fuzzy Systems*, Australia, 2001, pp. 696-699.

[8] Wang, H. O., Li, J., Niemann, D., and Tanaka, K.: 'T-S fuzzy model with linear rule

consequence and PDC controller: a universal framework for nonlinear control system', *Proc. IEEE Int. Conf. Fuzzy Systems*, 2000, pp. 549-554.

[9] Tanaka, K., and Wang, H. O.: 'Fuzzy control systems design and analysis' (Wiley Press, 2001).

[10] Zeng, X. J., and Singh, M. G.: 'Approximation Theory of Fuzzy Systems-MIMO Case', *IEEE Trans. Fuzzy Systems*, 1995, 3, (2), pp. 219-235.

[11] Tanaka, K., Iwazaki, M., and Wang, H. O.: 'Switching Control of an R/C Hovercraft: Stabilization and Smooth Switching', *IEEE Trans. Fuzzy Systems*, 2001, 31, pp. 853-863.

[12] Ohtake, H., and Tanaka, K.: 'A construction method of switching Lyapunov function for nonlinear systems', *Proc. IEEE Int. Conf. Fuzzy Systems*, Hawaii, 2002, pp. 221-226.

[13] Wu, S. J., and Lin, C. T.: 'Optimal fuzzy controller design: local concept approach', *IEEE Trans. on Fuzzy Systems*, 2000, 8, (2), pp. 171-185.

[14] Wu, S. J., and Lin, C. T.: 'Optimal Fuzzy Controller Design in Continuous Fuzzy System: Global Concept Approach', *IEEE Trans. Fuzzy Systems*, 2000, 8, (6), pp. 713-729.

[15] Wu, S. J., and Lin, C. T.: 'Discrete-time Optimal Fuzzy Controller Design: Global Concept Approach', *IEEE Trans. Fuzzy Systems*, 2002, 10, (1), pp.21-38.

[16] Yang, Y., Feng, G., and Ren, J.: 'A Combined Backstepping and Small-Gain Approach to Robust Adaptive Fuzzy Control for Strict-Feedback Nonlinear Systems', *IEEE Trans. Systems, Man and Cybernetics-PART A*, 2004, 34, (3), pp. 406-420.

[17] Lo, J. C., and Lin, M. L.: 'Robust H_∞ Nonlinear Control via Fuzzy Static Output Feedback', *IEEE Trans. Circuits and Systems-PART I*, 2003, 50, (11), pp. 1494-1502.

[18] Wu, S. J., and Lin, C. T.: 'Global Optimal Fuzzy Tracker Design Based on Local Concept Approach', *IEEE Trans. Fuzzy Systems*, 2002, 10, (2), pp. 128-43.

[19] Cuevas, J. J., and Toledo, B. C.: 'Fuzzy Tracking Control for a Class of Chaotic Systems', *Proc. IEEE Int. Sym. Intelligent Control*, Cyprus, 2005.

[20] Uang, H. J., and Huang, G. S.: 'A Robust Fuzzy Model Following Observer-Based Control Design for Nonlinear System', *Proc. IEEE Int. Conf. Control Application*, Taiwan, 2004.

[21] Tseng, C. S., Chen, B. S., and Uang, H. J.: 'Fuzzy Tracking Control Design for Nonlinear Dynamic Systems via T-S Fuzzy Model," *IEEE Trans. Fuzzy Systems*, 2001, 9, (3), pp. 381-392.

[22] Tseng, C. S., and Chen, B. S.: 'H_∞ Decentralized Fuzzy Model Reference Tracking Control Design for Nonlinear Interconnected Systems', *IEEE Trans. Fuzzy Systems*, 2001, 9, (6), pp. 795-809.

[23] Chen, B. S., Lee, B. K., and Guo, L. B.: 'Optimal Tracking Design for Stochastic Fuzzy Systems', *IEEE Trans. Fuzzy Systems*, 2003, 11, (6), pp. 796-813.

[24] Yen, J., Wang, L., and Gillespie, C. W.: 'Improving the interpretability of TSK fuzzy models by combining global learning and local learning', *IEEE Trans. Fuzzy Systems*, 1998, 6, pp. 530-537.

[25] Chuang,C. C., Su, S. F., and Chen, S. S.: 'Robust TSK fuzzy modeling for function approximation with outliers', *IEEE Trans. Fuzzy Systems*, 2001, 9, pp. 810-821.

[26] Wu, S. J., Chiang, H. H., Lin H. H., and Lee, T. T.: 'Neural-Network-Based Optimal Fuzzy Controller Design for Nonlinear Systems', *Fuzzy Set Systems*, 2005, 154, pp. 182-207.

[27] Hsiao, C. C., Su, S. F., Lee, T. T., and Chuang, C. C.: 'Hybrid Compensation Control for Affine TSK Fuzzy Control Systems', *IEEE Trans. Systems, Man and Cybernetics-PART B*, 2004, 34, (4), pp. 1865-1873.

[28] Kim, E., and Kim, D.: 'Stability Analysis and Synthesis for an Affine Fuzzy System via

LMI and ILMI: Discrete Case', *IEEE Trans. Systems, Man and Cybernetics-PART B*, 2001, 31, (1), pp. 132-140.

[29] Kim, E., and Kim, S.: 'Stability Analysis and Synthesis for an Affine Fuzzy System via LMI and ILLMI: Continuous Case', *IEEE Tran. Fuzzy Systems*, 2002, 10, (3), pp. 391-400.

[30] Kim, E., Lee, C. H., and Cho, Y. W.: 'Analysis and Design of an Affine Fuzzy System via Bilinear Matrix Inequality', *IEEE Trans. Fuzzy Systems*, 2005, 13, (1), pp. 115-123.

[31] Bergsten, P., Palm, R., and Driankov, D.:"Observers for Takagi-Sugeno Fuzzy Systems", *IEEE Tran. Systems, Man and Cybernetics-PART B*, 2002, 32, (1), pp. 114-121.

[32] Callier, F. M., and Desoer, C. A.:*Linear System Theory*, Springer–Verlag Press, 1991.

7

Building an Intelligent Controller using Simple Genetic Type-2 Fuzzy Logic System

Ibrahim A. Hameed, Claus G. Sorensen and Ole Green
Aarhus University, Foulum Research Centre
Blichers Allé 20, DK-8830, Tjele,
Denmark

1. Introduction

Despite the advantages offered by type-2 fuzzy systems (T2FS) in handling uncertainties in control applications, one major problem that hinders its wide-spread implementation in real-time applications is its high computational cost (Hameed, 2010). In order to reduce the computational burden of T2FS, a simplified T2FS based on a hybrid structure of four type-1 fuzzy systems (T1FS) and a genetic algorithm (GA) is introduced (Hameed, 2009). In addition to its rule in providing the system with adaptability to cope with changing conditions, a GA provides the system with a tool to detect and illustrate the amount of uncertainty incorporated in the system. In order to show the robustness and reliability of the new implementation, the developed approach is applied to: (a) control a nonlinear multi-input multi-output (MIMO) system equipped with various types of uncertainties as an example of using T2FS in industrial applications, and (b) evaluate students' learning achievement as an example of using T2FS in decision support systems. The new implementation of T2FS showed a superior response compared to the very complex and computational costly type-reduction approach. In addition, the ease of using the new implementation, which does not require more than the basic knowledge of T1FS and GA, is expected to help advancing the application of T2FS in multiple different areas of applications.

FLS constructed based on type-1 fuzzy systems (T1FS), referred to as T1FLS, have demonstrated their ability in many applications, especially for the control of complex nonlinear systems that are difficult to model analytically (Zadeh, 1973; King & Mamdani, 1997). However, researchers have shown that T1FLS have difficulty in modeling and minimizing the effect of uncertainties (Mendel, 2001). A reason being that, T1FS are certain in the sense that for each input there is a crisp membership grade. T2FS, characterized by membership grades that are themselves fuzzy, were first introduced by Zadeh in 1975 to account for this problem (Zadeh, 1975a). As it is illustrated in Fig. 1, the MF of a T2FS has a footprint of uncertainty (FOU), which represents the uncertainties in the shape and position of T1FS (Wu & Tan, 2004). The FOU is bounded up by an upper MF (UMF) and lower by a lower MF (LMF), both of which are T1MF. Since the FOU of T2FS provides an extra mathematical dimension, they are very useful in circumstances where it is difficult to determine an exact membership grade for FS. Therefore, the amount of uncertainty in a system could be reduced by using T2FLS since it offers better capabilities to handle linguistic uncertainties by modeling vagueness and unreliability of information and hence have the potential to outperform its T1 counterpart (Karnik & Mendel, 2001; Sepulveda et al., 2007a).

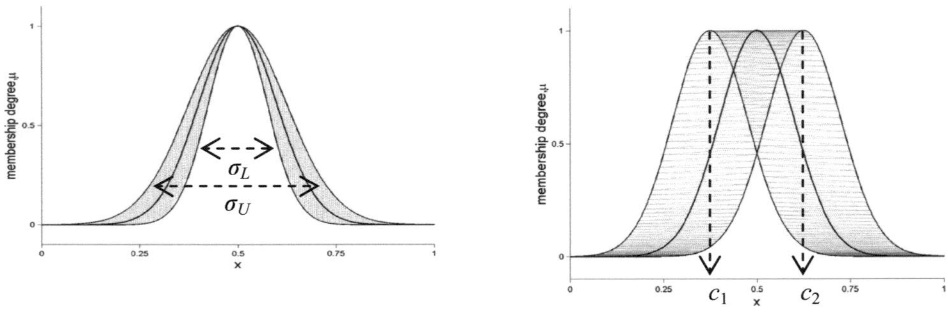

(a) (b)

Fig. 1. Gaussian type-2 FS: (a) blurring the width of type-1 FS where σ_L and σ_U are the minimum and maximum resultant widths respectively, (b) blurring the center of type-1 FS where c_1 and c_2 are minimum and maximum resultant centers respectively.

The ability of T2FLS to eliminate persistent oscillations surpasses that of its T1 counterpart. One reason is that the control surface of a T2FLS is smoother than that of T1FLS, especially around the origin (Tan & Pall, 2003). As a result, small disturbances around steady state will not result in significant control signal changes and thus minimizing the amount of oscillation. The additional degree of freedom provided by the FOU allows T2FLS to handle modeling uncertainties better than conventional T1FLS can do. This advantage is practically useful because many fuzzy controllers are designed offline using genetic algorithms (GA) and a model of the controlled process. As it is impossible for a model to capture all the characteristics of the actual plant, the performance of a controller designed using a model will inevitably deteriorate when it is applied to the actual plant, therefore a controller that is equipped with the ability to handle modeling uncertainties would be valuable.

Despite the advantages offered by T2FLS, one major problem that may hinder its use in real-time applications is its high computational cost. Type-reduction, which is used to convert T2FS into T1FS so that they can be processed by the defuzzifier to give a crisp output, is very computationally intensive, especially when there are many MFs and the rule base is large (Karnik & Mendel, 1998, 1999). To reduce the computational burden while preserving the advantages of T2FLS, two approaches may be considered: 1) faster type-reduction methods, such as the uncertainty bound method (Wu & Mendel, 2002); and 2) a simpler architecture, such as using only one T2FS in each input domain (Wu & Tan, 2004). In this chapter, a simplified implementation of T2FLS is proposed. The proposed approach only requires the basic knowledge of T1FLS and GA. Fuzzy Logic Toolbox™ and Optimization Toolbox™ from MathWorks™ are used for carrying out this purpose.

The rest of the chapter is organized as follows: Section 2 introduces the proposed simplified implementation of T2FLS using four embedded T1FSs. How GA is used to adjust the controller parameters is described in Section 3. The greenhouse climate control (GCC) problem and a simulation study to assess the ability of the proposed implementation to handle uncertainties are presented in Section 4. Finally, conclusions are drawn in Section 5.

2. A simplified implementation of T2FS

As illustrated in Fig. 1, a T2FS could be obtained by blurring a T1FS. A Gaussian T1FS is often used to represent vague linguistic terms and it is given by:

$$\mu_{A^i}(x) = \exp\left(-\left(c_i - x\right)^2 / 2\sigma_i^2\right), \tag{1}$$

where ci and σi are the center and width of the ith fuzzy set Ai, respectively, i = 1, 2, …, n, and n is the total number of MFs used to represent a universe of discourse. A Gaussian MF (GMF) with uncertain width (i.e., variance) is obtained by blurring its width and keeping its mean (i.e., center) fixed, as shown in Fig. 1(a). On the other hand, a GMF with an uncertain center is obtained by blurring its center and keeping its width fixed, as shown in Fig. 1(b). In this paper and for the sake of simplicity, GMF with uncertain width has been adopted. The upper and lower bounds of a Gaussian T2FS with uncertain width could be represented by:

$$\mu_{A_U^i}(x) = \exp\left(-\left(c_i - x\right)^2 / 2\sigma_{Ui}^2\right), \tag{2}$$

$$\mu_{A_L^i}(x) = \exp\left(-\left(c_i - x\right)^2 / 2\sigma_{Li}^2\right), \tag{3}$$

where $\sigma_{Ui} \geq \sigma_{Li}$, shown in Fig. 1 (a). The upper and lower bounds of each GMF can be further decomposed into the left and the right side MF and represented in the form:

$$\mu_{A_{UL}^i}(x) = \exp\left(-\left(c_i - x\right)^2 / 2\sigma_{Ui}^2\right),\ x < c_i, \tag{4}$$

$$\mu_{A_{UR}^i}(x) = \exp\left(-\left(c_i - x\right)^2 / 2\sigma_{Ui}^2\right),\ x \geq c_i, \tag{5}$$

$$\mu_{A_{LL}^i}(x) = \exp\left(-\left(c_i - x\right)^2 / 2\sigma_{Li}^2\right),\ x < c_i, \tag{6}$$

$$\mu_{A_{LR}^i}(x) = \exp\left(-\left(c_i - x\right)^2 / 2\sigma_{Li}^2\right),\ x \geq c_i, \tag{7}$$

A T2FS can be thought of as a set of an infinite number of T1FSs, and correspondingly, the defuzzified output of T2FLS could be obtained by aggregating the centroids of an infinite number of embedded T1FLSs. When the antecedent and consequent membership grades in T2FLS have a continuous domain, the number of embedded T1FLSs becomes uncountable. For the sake of simplicity and without loss of generality, each T2MF will be represented by its upper (U) and lower (L) bounds which are T1MFs, as shown in Fig. 2. Therefore, each two neighbor T2MFs will intersect in four points instead of one point as is the case of the traditional T1MFs. The four intersection points are referred to by upper point, right point, lower point and left point, as shown in Fig. 2. MFs, constitute the upper intersection points, are the combination of the right side of the upper bound of each T2MF with the left side of the upper bound of its neighbor. MFs, constitute the right intersection points, are the combination of the right side of the upper bound of each T2MF with the left side of the lower bound of its neighbor. MFs, constitute the lower intersection points, are the combination of the right side of the lower bound of each T2MF with the left side of the upper bound of its neighbor. Each intersection point occurs equally likely to each of the other intersection points. The corresponding TIMFs, shown in Fig. 3, could be summarized as follows:

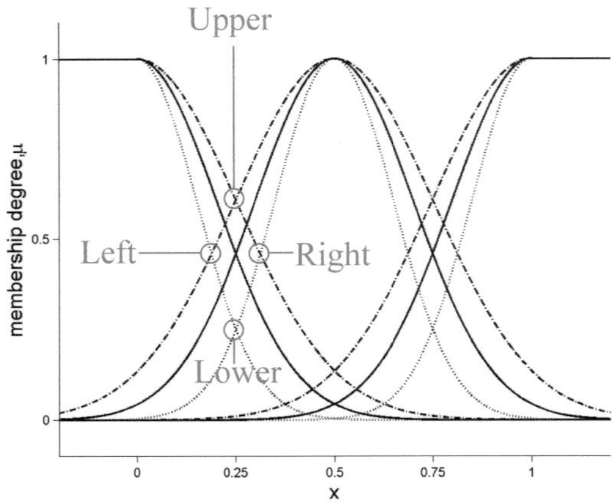

Fig. 2. Illustration of decomposing T2MFs into 4 T1MFs.

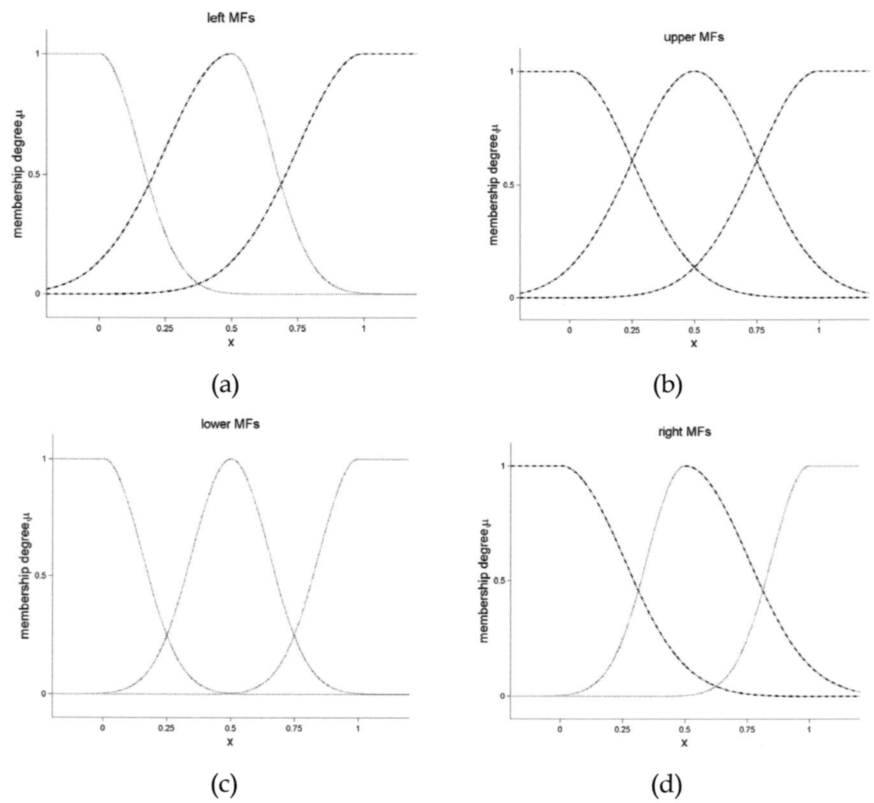

Fig. 3. (a) Membership functions of left intersection points. (b) Membership functions of upper intersection points. (c) Membership functions of lower intersection points, and (d) Membership functions of right intersection points.

i. $MF_{upper} = \{(A^{i}_{UR}, A^{i+1}_{UL}): i = 1, 2, \ldots, n\text{-}1\}$ is used to construct the input/output MFs of the so called upper FLS (UFLS),
ii. $MF_{right} = \{(A^{i}_{UR}, A^{i+1}_{LL}): i = 1, 2, \ldots, n\text{-}1\}$ is used to construct the input/output MFs of the so called right FLS (RFLS),
iii. $MF_{lower} = \{(A^{i}_{LR}, A^{i+1}_{LL}): i = 1, 2, \ldots, n\text{-}1\}$ is used to construct the input/output MFs of the so called lower FLS (LWFLS), and
iv. $MF_{left} = \{(A^{i}_{LR}, A^{i+1}_{UL}): i = 1, 2, \ldots, n\text{-}1\}$ is used to construct the input/output MFs of the so called left FLS (LFLS).

MFs constitute the upper, right, lower and left intersection points will be used as the input/output MFs of the upper, right, lower and left T1FLSs respectively. The defuzzified output of the T2FLS is then obtained by averaging the defuzzified outputs of the resultant four embedded T1FLSs, as shown in Fig. 4. When uncertainty equals zero, the four intersection points become one and T2MF degrades to T1MF. Therefore, the proposed structure will vary between T1 and T2 according to the level of uncertainty detected in the system. The proposed method has more degrees of freedom compared to the method represented by Sepulveda and his colleagues in which type-2 MF is decomposed into only UMF and LMF (Sepulveda et al., 2007a; Sepulveda et al., 2007b).

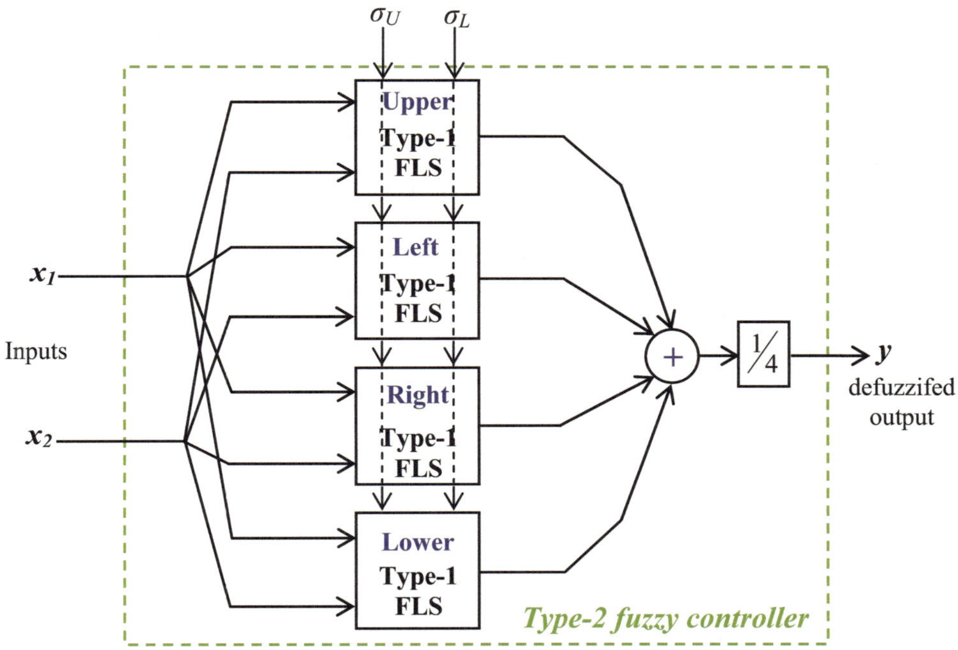

Fig. 4. Simplified type-2 fuzzy logic system: controller output is the average of the four outputs of the embedded upper, left, right, and lower type-1 fuzzy logic systems, x_1 and x_2 are the controller inputs and y is the controller output.

3. Genetic Algorithm (GA)

A genetic algorithm (GA) is a search technique used in computing to find exact or approximate solutions to optimization and search problems. GAs was first introduced by John

Holland in 1975 (Holland, 1975; Goldberg, 1988). In this chapter, a GA will be used to evolve the parameters of the proposed implementation of T2FLS to test the hypothesis that the simplified architecture retains the ability to handle measurement and modeling uncertainties. It is not mandatory to use a GA to adjust the controller parameters and instead the controller parameters could be set manually. GA will not only be used as an optimization algorithm but rather it will be used as an uncertainty sensor to detect the level of uncertainty which exist in the controlled system. In other applications such as students\s evaluation, GA can not be used and a proper thickness of T2FS would be manually selected. The thickness of a T2FS will increase as the amount of uncertainty detected in the systems is increased and vice versa. When the uncertainty level is very low or zero, the thickness of a T2FS will equal to zero and the controller will simply behave like a T1FLS. In this chapter, seven MFs are used. The centers of the MFs are set constant, -1 for negative big (NB), -2/3 for negative medium (NM), -1/3 for negative small (NS), 0 for zero (Z), 1/3 for positive small (PS), 2/3 for positive medium (PM) and 1 positive big (PB) and their optimum widths are obtained using a real-valued GA. Each T2GMF has two widths, σ_U and σ_L where $\sigma_U \geq \sigma_L$ while T1GMF has only one width value, σ. Since each controller input and output variables are set to the same range of universe of discourse, [-1, 1], three additional parameters, called scale factors (SFs), could be tuned. SFs are real constants which multiply the values of the variables (input or output variables), modifying the limits of their variation range, and therefore have a significant impact on the performance of the resulting fuzzy control system, and hence they are often a convenient parameter for tuning. The modification of the input scale factors has a general effect on the behaviour of the system: increasing input gains implies reducing their universes of discourse, having a direct consequence on control: the response is faster and more oscillatory, reducing the stationary error. It thus improves the transient response by reducing rise time and set-up time, but it does increase the risk of instability with the overshoot increment. On the other side, reducing input gains produces the opposite effects; the wider the membership functions the rougher control can be achieved, which produces a slower response with less overshoot. However, the variation of the output gain has a complex relation with the behaviour of the controller and has not been analysed in depth (Rojas et al., 2006). For the sake of simplicity, it is assumed that all MFs have equal widths. For T2FLS, five parameters namely, σ_U, σ_L, SF_1, SF_2, and SF_3 and for T1FLS, four parameters, namely, σ, SF_1, SF_2, and SF_3 have to be tuned.
For the proposed T2FLS, up to $4(2n+3)$ parameters could be optimized, where 4 stands for 4 embedded T1FLSs, 2 stands for the center and the width of the GMF, n stands for the number of MFs used in universe of discourse, and 3 stands for 3 SFs of the input and output parameters of each embedded T1FLS, which could result in better results but also requires greater computational costs. The fitness function used to quantify the optimality of a solution (i.e., chromosome) is the reciprocal of the Integral of Square Error (ISE), given in Eq. (8) where the error e is the difference between the desired set point and the actual system output (Sepulveda et al., 2007b). Chromosomes in a population are ranked according to their fitness value. Optimal or near optimal chromosomes (i.e., solutions) are allowed to reproduce through new generations that will (hopefully) be even better. In this paper, the maximum number of generations is set to 30. The number of chromosomes or solutions in a population is set to 20. The mutation and crossover probability are set to 0.2 and 0.25 respectively. The roulette wheel selection method is used to select the fittest chromosomes, the generational process is repeated until a termination condition has been reached; a solution is found that satisfies minimum criteria or a fixed number of generations reached.

$$\text{ISE}=\int_0^{\infty}\left(e(t)\right)^2 dt \,. \tag{8}$$

4. Simulation experiments

In this section, the developed implementation of T2FS will applied to Greenhouse climate control (GCC) problem as an example of an industrial application. It will also applied to the problem of students' evaluation as an example of using T2FS as a decision support system. GCC has received considerable attention in agricultural engineering research (Albright et al., 2001; Koutb et al., 2004; Van Henten & Bontsema, 2009). Controlling the climate inside a greenhouse is a challenging task because of the many sources of uncertainty. Such uncertainty could arise from using none or near accurate models, greenhouse orientation, age and type of crop inside the greenhouse, sensor measurements, actuators and outdoor climate conditions. In this chapter, a simple greenhouse heating-cooling ventilating (HCV) model will be used to control temperature and humidity ratio inside a greenhouse by means of heating, ventilating, and humidifying the air inside the greenhouse.). In this chapter, two types of uncertainty will be introduced to the system to evaluate the performance of the proposed controller; 1) measurement uncertainty which is introduced to the system by adding random noise to sensory measurements, and 2) modeling uncertainty which is introduced to the system by changing the model parameters by ±10%.

A first simulation experiment has been conducted to demonstrate the ability of control scheme to provide non-interacting control and smooth closed-loop response to set-point step change. Measurement uncertainty has been introduced by adding a 10% multiplicative error to all the measured signals. The responses for set-point step changes in temperature and humidity ratio for T1 and T2 controllers are shown in Fig. 5. Fig. 6 illustrates the controller outputs. A simulation of the outside weather conditions of a normal hot day are shown in Fig. 7. The T1MFs and T2MFs for both temperature and humidity loops are shown in Fig. 8, respectively. Fig. 9 illustrates the control surface for both T1 and T2 controllers, respectively.

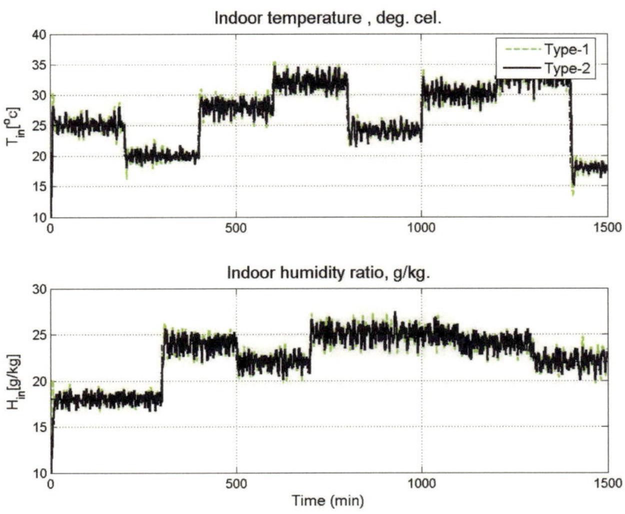

Fig. 5. Greenhouse outputs: indoor air temperature (upper) and indoor air humidity ratio (bottom).

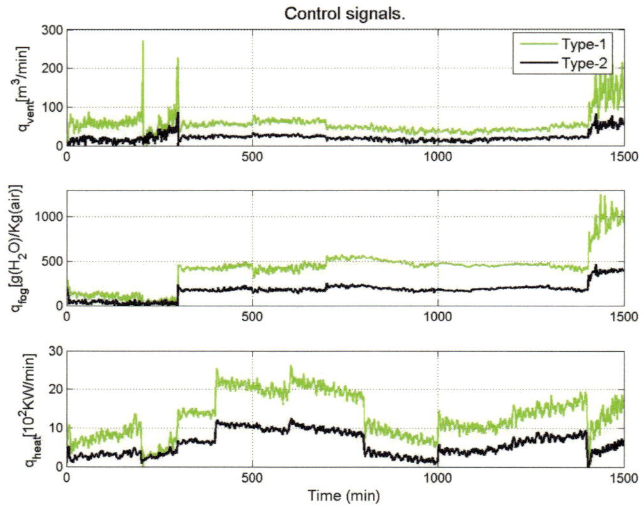

Fig. 6. Control outputs: ventilation rate (upper), humification rate (middle) and heating rate (bottom).

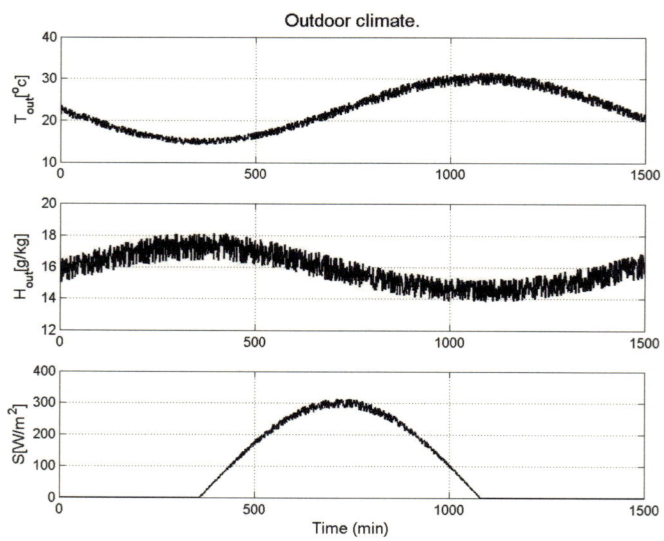

Fig. 7. Climate variables: outdoor air temperature (upper), outdoor humidity ratio (middle) and outdoor solar radiation (bottom).

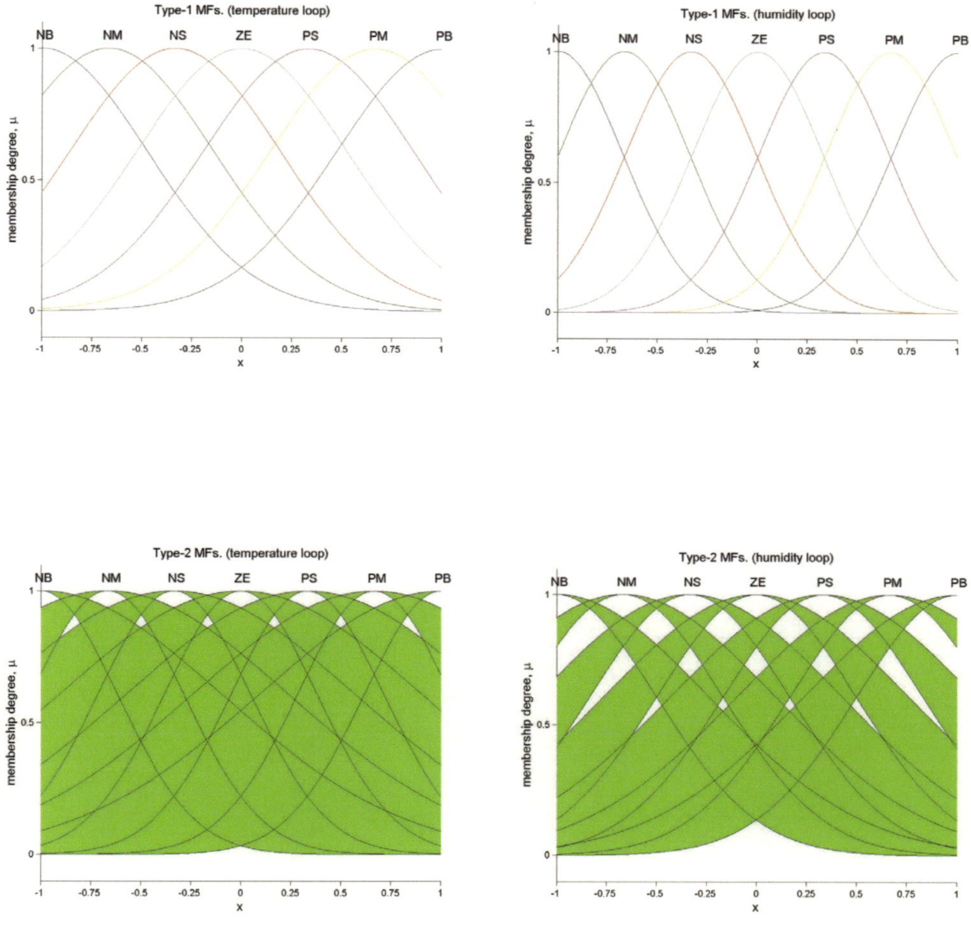

Fig. 8. MF's: type-1 fuzzy logic controller of temperature loop (left upper), type-1 fuzzy logic controller of humidity ratio loop (right upper), type-2 fuzzy logic controller of temperature loop (left bottom) and type-2 fuzzy logic controller of humidity ratio loop (right bottom).

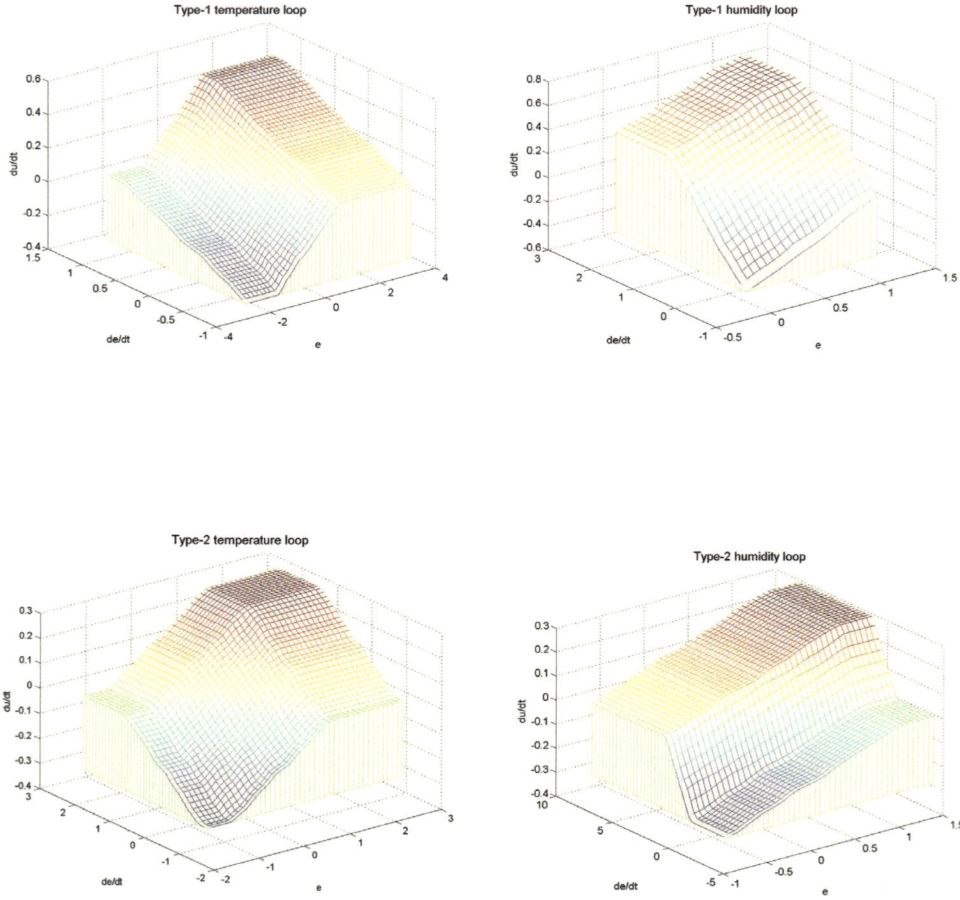

Fig. 9. Control surface: type-1 fuzzy logic controller of temperature loop (left upper), type-1 fuzzy logic controller of humidity ratio loop (right upper), type-2 fuzzy logic controller of temperature loop (left bottom) and type-2 fuzzy logic controller of hu humidity ratio loop (right bottom).

In the second simulation experiment, measurement uncertainty has been removed and model parameters are multiplied by values in the range [0.9, 1.1] to demonstrate the ability of the controller to overcome the modeling uncertainties. The system responses and the controller outputs are shown in Figs. 10-11. T1MFs and T2MFs and their respective control surface plot are given Figs 14-15, respectively.

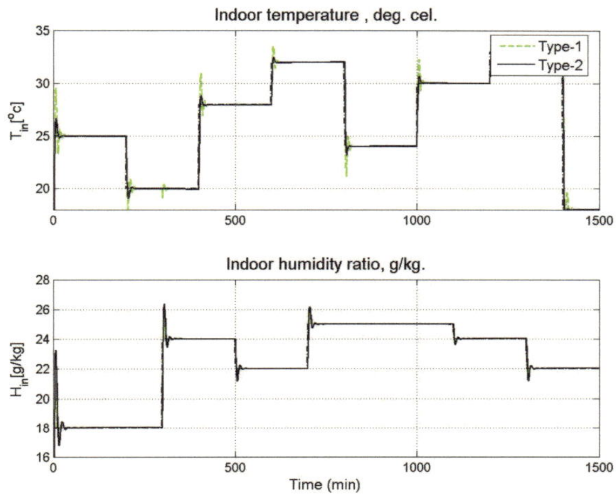

Fig. 10. Greenhouse outputs: indoor air temperature (upper) and indoor air humidity ratio (bottom).

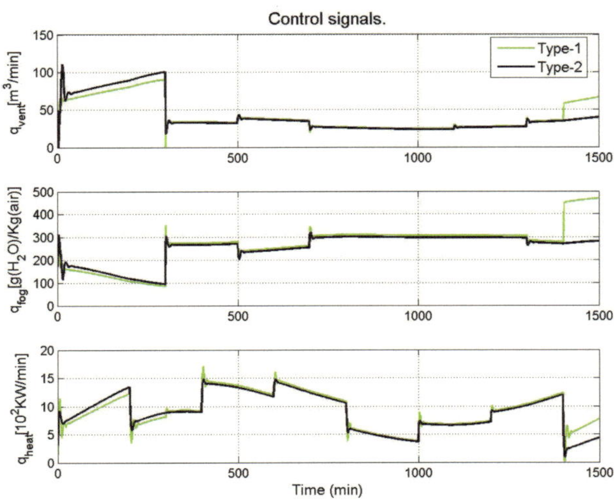

Fig. 11. Control outputs: ventilation rate (upper), humification rate (middle) and heating rate (bottom).

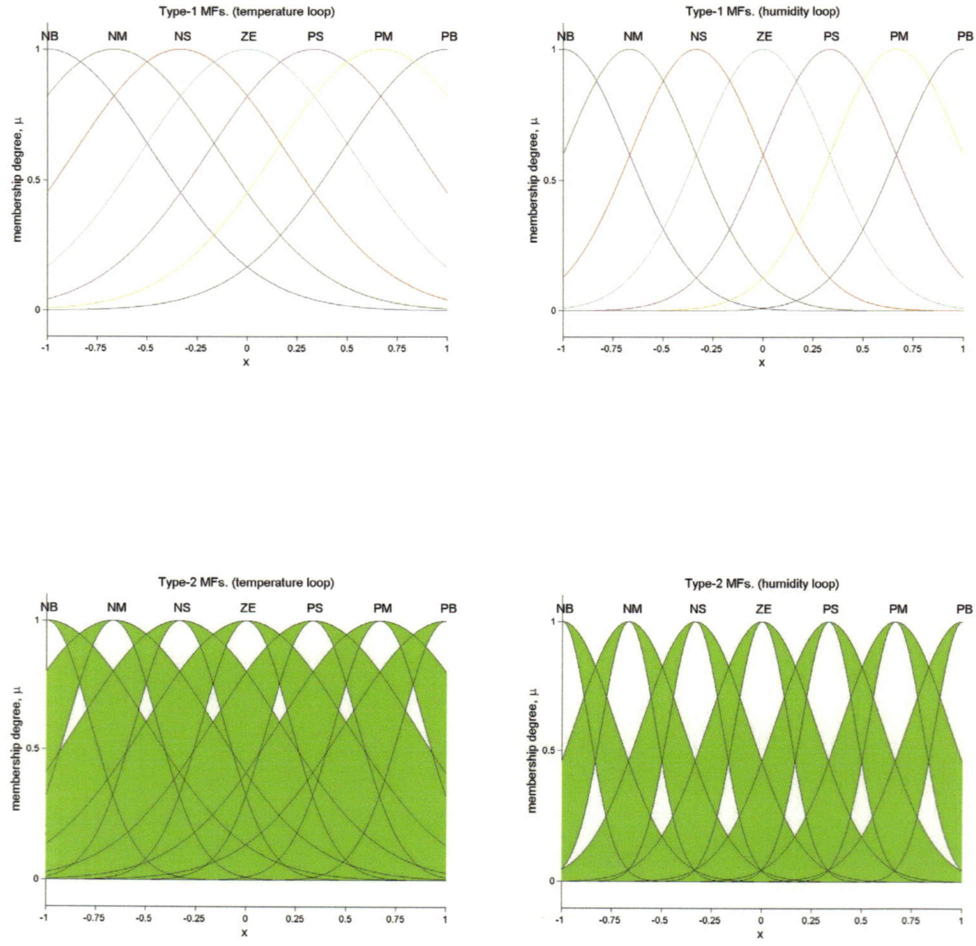

Fig. 12. MF's: type-1 fuzzy logic controller of temperature loop (left upper), type-1 fuzzy logic controller of humidity ratio loop (right upper), type-2 fuzzy logic controller of temperature loop (left bottom) and type-2 fuzzy logic controller of humidity ratio loop (right bottom).

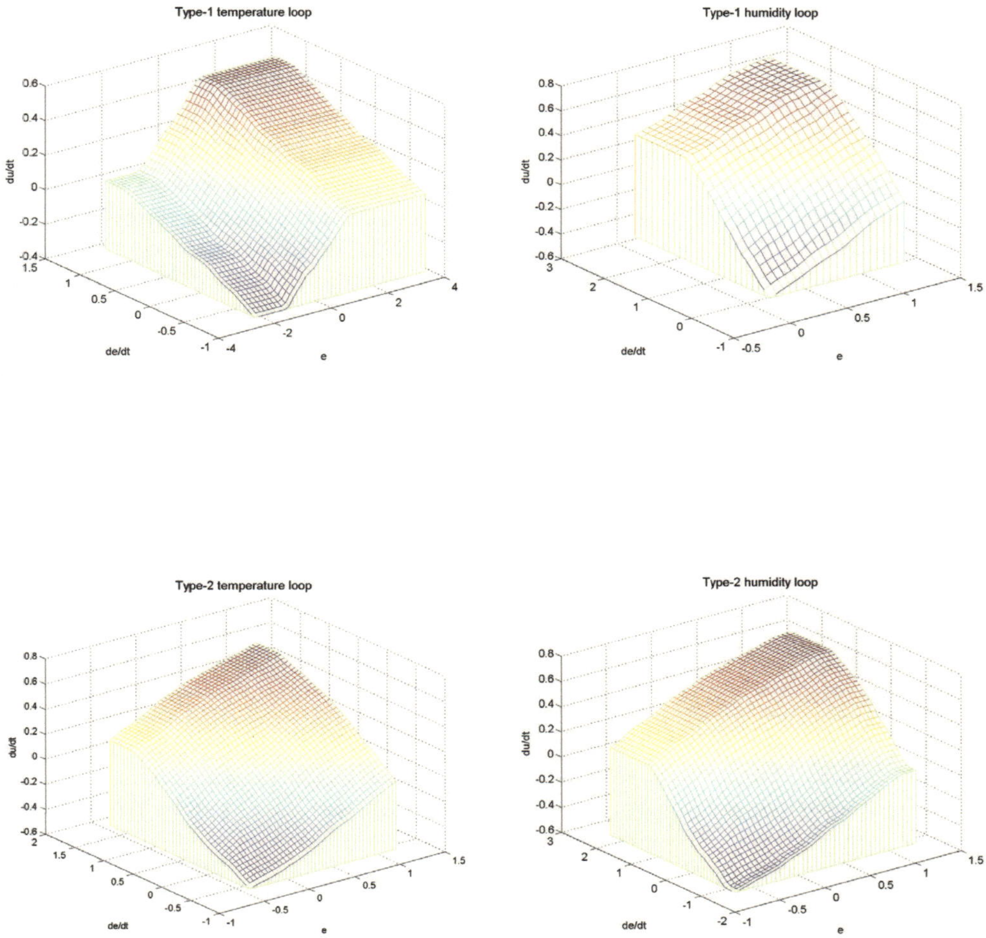

Fig. 13. Control surface: type-1 fuzzy logic controller of temperature loop (left upper), type-1 fuzzy logic controller of humidity ratio loop (right upper), type-2 fuzzy logic controller of temperature loop (left bottom) and type-2 fuzzy logic controller of humidity ratio loop (right bottom).

Exp.		Temperature control-loop					Humidity control-loop				
		σ_L	σ_U	SF_e	$SF_{\Delta e}$	$SF_{\Delta u}$	σ_L	σ_U	SF_e	$SF_{\Delta e}$	$SF_{\Delta u}$
1	T1	0.5297	-	0.1501	0.0538	12.6897	0.3282	-	0.0594	0.1290	9.4390
	T2	0.3835	0.9103	0.1072	0.0910	13.7273	0.5007	0.7665	0.0587	0.3083	12.7123
2	T1	0.5297	-	0.1501	0.0538	14.1524	0.3282	-	0.0594	0.1290	9.4390
	T2	0.2223	0.5009	0.0404	0.0601	14.9196	0.1336	0.2683	0.0500	0.0893	5.4417

Table 1. Parameters of type-1 (T1) and type-2 (T2) fuzzy logic controllers obtained by GA where measurement uncertainty is introduced in experiment 1 and modeling uncertainty is introduced in experiment 2. SF_e, $SF_{\Delta e}$, and $SF_{\Delta u}$ are the scale factors of error, change of error and change of control signal respectively.

The parameters of T1 and T2 controllers are shown in Table 1. From the table, the difference between σ_L and σ_U increases as the level of uncertainty detected in the system increases. For the sake of comparison, Mean Squared Error (MSE) and Signal-to-Noise Ration (SNR) for temperature and humidity loops are computed for T1, T2 (the proposed structure), T2 structure proposed by Sepulveda and his colleagues (Sepulveda et al., 2007b) and T2 using type-reduction method (Mendel, 1998), as shown in Table 2. Although the performance of the proposed structure of T2FLS using four embedded T1FLSs is similar to the performance of T2 using type-reduction (T2TR) but implementing T2TR requires acquiring new knowledge and writing new codes but in the case of the proposed T2 structure using four embedded T1FLSs, only the basic knowledge of T1 fuzzy sets is required and take the advantage of using MATLAB® Fuzzy Logic Toolbox™ and Optimization Toolbox™ from MathWorks™ for ease of implementation.

Exp.	Controller type	MSE	SNRT	SNRH
1	Type-1 fuzzy controller	4.0674	0.0154	0.0163
	Type-2 fuzzy controller using Sepulveda's method	4.0425	0.0235	0.0342
	Type-2 fuzzy controller using four embedded type-1 fuzzy controllers (proposed)	3.9608	0.0256	0.0486
	Type-2 fuzzy controller using type- reduction method	3.9727	0.0259	0.0441
2	type-1 fuzzy controller	1.8855	0.0232	0.0348
	Type-2 fuzzy controller using Sepulveda's method	1.7942	0.0249	0.0297
	Type-2 fuzzy controller using four embedded type-1 fuzzy controllers (proposed)	1.7452	0.0248	0.0243
	Type-2 fuzzy controller using type- reduction method	1.7439	0.0294	0.0309

Table 2. Mean squared error (MSE) and signal-to-noise ratio of temperature (SNRT) and humidity ratio (SNRH) of different types of controllers when measurement uncertainty is introduced in experiment 1 and modeling uncertainty is introduced in experiment 2

Saleh and Kim (2009) proposed a three nodes fuzzy system to evaluate students' learning achievement. The transparency and objective nature of the fuzzy system makes their method easy to understand and enables teachers to explain the results of the evaluation to sceptic students. The method involved conventional triangular MFs of fixed parameters which could result in different results when changed. In order to improve the reliability and robustness of the system, Gaussian membership functions (GMFs) are proposed as an alternative to the traditional triangular MFs (Hameed & Sorensen, 2010). When the three nodes system based on Gaussian membership of width of 4.0 is applied to all students, the resultant new total scores of students rounded to two digits are equal to that of the classical scores but with new ranking orders. The same result is obtained when the T2FS for σ_L and σ_U of 0.2 and 0.4, respectively, are applied.

5. Conclusions

The proposed architecture of Type-2 FLS using four embedded Type-1 FLSs provides a smoother control surface and a greater ability to detect and treat the measurement and modeling uncertainties in the controlled system with the aid of a GA. It also achieved a dramatic reduction in computational complexity without sacrificing performance compared to its equivalent type-2 FLS with type-reduction method. The proposed T2FLS is easy to implement using MATLAB® Fuzzy Logic Toolbox™ from MathWorks™ and it does not require more than the basic knowledge of T1FLS.

6. References

Albright, L. D., Gates, R. S., Arvanities, K. G., and Drysdale, A. E. (2001). Environmental control for plants on earth and in space. *IEEE Control System Magazine*, 2001, 21(5), 28–47.

Goldberg, D. E. (1989). *Genetic algorithms in search, optimization and machine learning*. 1989 (Addison-Wesley, Massachusetts, USA).

Hameed, I. A. (2009). Simplified architecture of a type-2 fuzzy controller using four embedded type-1 fuzzy controllers and its application to a greenhouse climate control system. *Proc. IMechE Part I: Journal of Systems and Control Engineering*, 223, 5, pp. 619-631

Hameed, I. A. (2010). *New applications and developments of fuzzy systems*. PhD thesis, Seoul, Korea, pp. 48-68.

Hameed, I. A. and Sorensen, C. G. (2010). Fuzzy Systems in Education: A More Reliable System for Student Evaluation. *Fuzzy Systems*, Ahmad Taher Azar (Ed.), ISBN: 978-953-7619-92-3, INTECH, Croatia.

Holland, J. H. (1975). *Adaptation in natural and artificial systems*. University of Michigan Press, Ann Arbor.

Karnik, N. N. and Mendel, J. M. (1998). Type-2 fuzzy logic systems: type-reduction. *In Proceedings of the IEEE Conference on Systems, Man, and Cybernetics*, San Diego, California, USA, 1998, pp. 2046–2051.

Karnik, N. N. and Mendel, J. M. (1999). Type-2 fuzzy logic systems. IEEE Transaction of Fuzzy Systems, 1999, 7(6), pp. 643–658.

Karnik, N. N. and Mendel, J. M. (2001).Operations on type-2 fuzzy sets. *International Journal of Fuzzy Sets and Systems*, 2001, 122(2), pp. 327–348.

King, P. and Mamdani, E. (1997).The application of fuzzy control to industrial processes. *Automatica*, 1997, 13, pp. 235–242.

Koutb, M., El-Rabaie, N., Awad, H., and Abd-El-Hameedid, I. A. (2004)S. Environmental control for plants using intelligent control systems. *In Proceedings of AIA'04*, IFAC, Cairo, Egypt, 2004, pp. 101–106.

Mendel, J. M. (2001). *Rule-based fuzzy logic systems: introduction and new directions*, 2001 (Prentice Hall, Upper Saddle River, New Jersey).

Rojas, I., Pomares, H., Gonzalez, J., Herrera, L. J., Guillen, A., Rojas, F., and Valenzuela, O. (2006). Adaptive fuzzy controller: application to the control of the temperature of a dynamic room in real time. *Fuzzy Sets and Systems*, 2006, 157, pp. 2241–2258.

Saleh, I. ; Kim, S.-I. (2009). A fuzzy system for evaluating students' learning achievement. *Expert Systems with Applications*, 36, 3, pp. 6236-6243.

Sepulveda, R., Castillo, O., Melin, P., Rodriguez-Diaz, A., and Montiel, O. (2007a). Experimental study of intelligent controllers under uncertainty using type-1 and type-2 fuzzy logic. *Information Sciences*, 2007, 177, 2023–2048.

Sepulveda, R., Castillo, O., Melin, P., Rodriguez-Diaz, A., and Montiel, O. (2007b). An efficient computational method to implement type-2 fuzzy logic in control applications. *In Analysis and design of intelligent systems using soft computing techniques* (Eds P. Melin, O. Castillo, E. G. Ramı´rez, J. Kacprzyk, and W. Pedrycz). Series Advances in intelligent and soft computing, 2007 vol. ,41, pp. 45–52 (Springer-Verlag, Berlin).

Tan, W. W. and Pall, S.N.. (2003). Performance study of type-2 fuzzy controllers. *In Proceedings of 2nd International Conference on Computational intelligence, robot, and autonomous systems*, Singapore, 2003, PS01-4-07.

Van Henten, E. J. and Bontsema, J. (2009). Time-scale decomposition of an optimal control problem in greenhouse climate management. *Control Engineering Practice*, 2009, 17(1), pp. 88–96.

Wu, D. and Tan, W. W. (2004). A simplified architecture for type-2 FLSs and its application to nonlinear control. *In Proceedings of the 2004 IEEE Conference on Cybernetics and intelligent systems*, Singapore, 2004, pp. 485–490.

Wu, H. and Mendel, J. M. (2002). Uncertainty bounds and their use in the design of interval type-2 fuzzy logic systems. *IEEE Transaction of Fuzzy Systems*, 2002, 10(5), 622–639.

Zadeh, L. A. (1973). Outline of a new approach to the analysis of complex systems and decision processes. *IEEE Transaction of Systems, Man, and Cybernetics*, 1973, 3(1), pp. 28–44.

Zadeh, L. A. (1975a). The concept of a linguistic variable and its application to approximate reasoning, Part I. *Information Sciences*, 1975, 8(3), pp. 199–249.

Zadeh, L. A. (1975b).The concept of a linguistic variable and its application to approximate reasoning, Part II. *Information Sciences*, 1975, 8(4), pp. 301–357.

Zadeh, L. A. (2005). Towards a generalized theory of uncertainty (GTU) - an outline. *Information Sciences*, 2005, 172, pp. 1–40.

8

Molten Steel Level Control of Strip Casting Process Monitoring by Using Self-Learning Fuzzy Controller

Hung-Yi Chen[1] and Shiuh-Jer Huang[2]
[1]*Ming Chi University of Technology,*
[2]*National Taiwan University of Science and Technology*
Taiwan, R.O.C.

1. Introduction

The twin-roll strip casting process is a typical steel-strip production method which combines continuous casting and hot rolling process. The production line from molten liquid steel to the final steel-strip is shortened and the production cost is reduced significantly compared to the conventional continuous casting. The twin-roll strip casting process can produce 1-5 mm thin steel strip directly from the molten steel. Furthermore, since the strip casting process has high cooling rate, it can improve the mechanical properties of steel (Liang et al. 1997; Cook et al. 1995). Usually, the molten steel level is controlled at a preset desired level to monitor the normal strip casting operation. During the roll casting process, once the molten metal contacts with the rotating rolls, a thin solidification shell is formed on the surface of each roll. The shell thickness gradually grows from each roll surface, finally contacts with each other and weld together at a position around the roll exit, called the solidification final point. If the molten metal level is higher than the specified value, the solidification final point will occur at a point above the roll exit. That will result in heat cracking and damage to the cooling roll surface in addition to material structural abnormalities of the steel strip. If the molten metal level is lower than the desirable value, the solidification final point will occur at a point below the roll exit. The steel strip surface will have inferior quality due to the breakout and oxidation. Hence, the molten metal level is an important process control parameter to guarantee the solidification final point and rolling strip quality. The molten steel level must maintain within a specific range during the full casting process except the initial startup operating mode by filling the molten steel into the twin roll cylinders from the tundish.

Since the strip casting process has nonlinear dynamics uncertainty and coupled behaviors, accurate molten steel level control problem is still an important research topic to guarantee the steel strip quality. Graebe et al. (1995) verified the dynamic model and various nonlinearities appearing in the continuous casting process and proposed different issues that had to be solved in controller design. Hesketh et al. (1993) applied an adaptive control strategy for the mold level control of a continuous steel slab casting. Hong et al. (2001) investigated the modeling and control problem of a twin-roll strip caster. They analyzed different critical dynamics, including molten steel pool leveling, and developed a two-level control strategy to achieve a constant strip thickness and maintain a constant roll separating force.

Since the dynamic characteristic of this strip casting process is very complicated, it is difficult to establish an appropriate dynamic model for a model-based controller design. Hence, a model-free fuzzy control strategy is considered to solve this problem (Dussud et al. 1998; Joo et al. 2002; Park and Cho 2005). However, the design of a traditional fuzzy controller fully depends on an expert, or the experience of an operator, to establish the fuzzy rule bank. Generally, this knowledge is difficult to obtain. A time consuming adjusting process is required to achieve the specified control performance. These factors hinder its application and implementation.

Herein, a self-learning fuzzy controller with learning ability is utilized without the process dynamic model requirement to control the molten steel level of strip casting process. This control strategy can establish the fuzzy control rule tables automatically from zero initial rules and adjust on line to tackle the system variation and disturbance for reducing the effort of trial-and-error process. Here, the self-learning fuzzy controller is designed for regulating the height of the stopper controlled by an electric servomotor to achieve the desired molten steel level during the strip casting process. The control performance of the designed controller is evaluated based on numerical simulation results. For approaching a real case implementation, the simulation cases are selected based on the semi-experimental system dynamic model and parameters (Joo et al. 2002). In addition, the performance of this intelligent controller is compared with that of a traditional PID technique to show the performance improvement.

This article is organized as follows: Section 2 describes the twin-roll strip casting process dynamics and system model for simulation purpose. Section 3 presents the model-free self-learning fuzzy control strategy. Section 4 describes the numerical results of this intelligent controller. Final conclusions are presented in Section 5.

2. Process dynamics and system model for simulation purposes

A process mathematical model, which describes the relationship between the command inputs and the measured outputs, is required for the numerical simulation to evaluate the dynamic performance of a model-free controller. The mathematical model for the molten steel leveling dynamics developed in (Joo et al. 2002) is adopted and described in this section. Fig. 1 shows a schematic drawing of a twin-roll strip casting process. For developing the mathematical model, it is assumed that the molten steel is incompressible and two rolls are identical. The continuity equation of the liquid steel can be described as:

$$\frac{dV}{dt} = Q_{in} - Q_{out} \tag{1}$$

where V is the volume of the molten steel stored between the twin-roll cylinders, Q_{in} is the input flow rate into the space between roll cylinders and Q_{out} is the output flow rate from the roll cylinders. The volume V can be calculated as:

$$V = AL_r \tag{2}$$

where L_r is the length of the roll cylinders and A is the oblique area shown in Fig. 1.

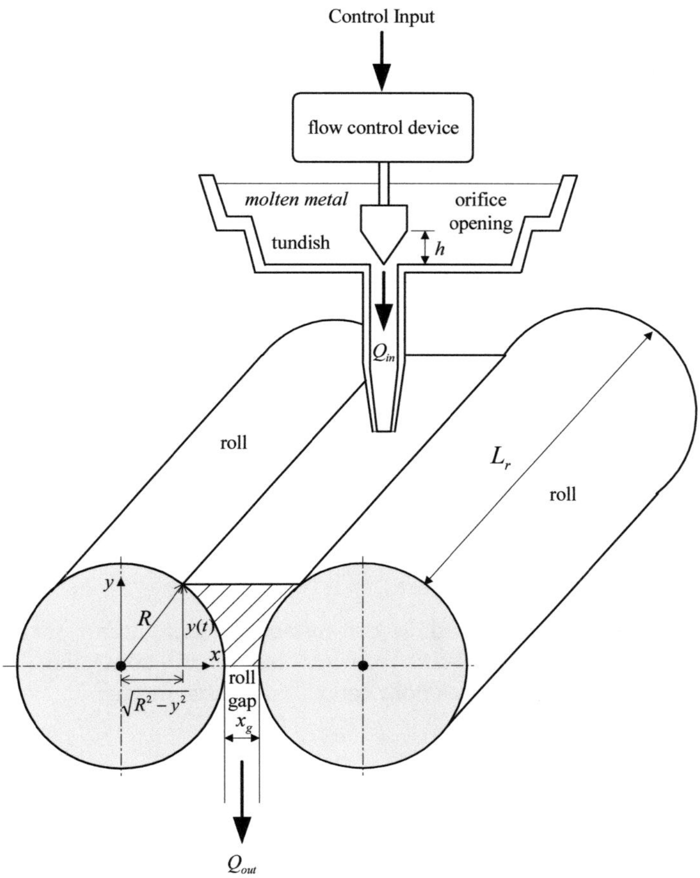

Fig. 1. Schematic diagram of the twin-roll strip casting process

$$A = 2\int_0^y \left[\frac{x_g(t)}{2} + R - \sqrt{R^2 - y^2}\right] dy \tag{3}$$

where $x_g(t)$ is the roll gap, R is the radius of the roll cylinder and $y(t)$ is the height of molten metal above the axis of rollers. By substituting equations (2) and (3) into equation (1), obtain:

$$\frac{dV}{dt} = L_r \frac{dA}{dt} = L_r \left[y\frac{dx_g}{dt} + \left(x_g + 2R - 2\sqrt{R^2 - y^2}\right)\frac{dy}{dt}\right] \tag{4}$$

If $\left(x_g + 2R - 2\sqrt{R^2 - y^2}\right)$ is defined as $B_r(x_g, y)$, the following form can be derived from equation (1).

$$\frac{dy}{dt} = \frac{1}{B_r(x_g, y)L_r}\left(Q_{in} - Q_{out} - L_r y\frac{dx_g}{dt}\right) \tag{5}$$

Here, the input flow rate Q_{in} can be derived from the stopper opening height $h(t)$ and a nonlinear time varying input flow rate parameters $a(t)$ depends on the shape of the nozzle and the stopper, clogging/unclogging dynamics and the height and the viscosity of the molten metal in the tundish.

$$Q_{in} = a(t) \cdot h(t) \tag{6}$$

where the orifice opening, $h(t)$, equal to the height of the stopper is controlled by an electric servomotor. Due to fast response of the electric servomotor, the stopper motion dynamics is assumed to be negligible. In addition, if the response of the stopper actuator is fast enough, the orifice opening can be derived as:

$$h(t) = ku(t) \tag{7}$$

where $u(t)$ denotes the control input and k is the servo gain.
The output flow rate Q_{out} can be derived from the product of roll surface tangential velocity v_r, roll gap x_g and the length of the roll cylinder L_r.

$$Q_{out} = L_r x_g v_r \tag{8}$$

The dynamic model will only be used in the numerical simulations for evaluating the dynamic performance of the model-free self-learning fuzzy controller. The designing process of this intelligent controller does not need this dynamic model.

3. Self-learning fuzzy control strategy

Generally, for a non-linear dynamic system with uncertainties, it is very difficult to establish an accurate mathematical model for designing the control laws. Although the linearized model or simplified model can be employed to design the controller, the control performance of these model-based controllers still depends on many factors, such as the working position and operating conditions. Hence, model-free fuzzy control strategy was proposed to solve this kind of problem. It does not need a mathematical model for designing a fuzzy logic control law. In addition, a fuzzy logic controller can compensate the environmental variation during operation processes. However, to establish the fuzzy rule tables of a traditional fuzzy controller still depends on an expert or the experience of an operator. Generally, this knowledge is not easy to obtain and a time-consuming adjusting process is required to achieve the specified control performance.
A self-learning fuzzy controller with learning ability was utilized to establish the fuzzy rule tables on-line automatically for reducing the effort of trial-and-error process (Chen and Huang 2004). It facilitates the design process of a fuzzy controller and makes the implementation of a fuzzy controller easier. Usually, the output response error and the change of error are selected as the fuzzy input variables. Both of them stimulate two fuzzy subsets (E and CE) for each sampling instant. Then, maximum four fuzzy rules in the fuzzy rule table are fired instead of the entire rule table and only these four rules are modified in each sampling time. This method can significantly reduce the computing time, therefore increasing the sampling frequency. Since this approach has learning ability to establish and regulate the fuzzy rule tables continuously, its control implementation can begin with zero

initial fuzzy rules. The fuzzy rules were adjusted on-line by means of a simple modification equation for each rule instead of a performance decision table.

Fig. 2 shows that the self-learning part is added into a traditional fuzzy controller to form a self-learning fuzzy controller. Among them, the traditional fuzzy controller carries out the mission of control and the self-learning part is responsible for real-time recognition of the system variation. The self-learning part contains three steps: performance measure, model estimation and rule modification. The system performance measure is to calculate the deviation between the system output and the specified values. The purpose of system performance measure is to establish a successful correcting basis for a learning controller. Usually, two physical features including system output error and the change of error are chosen as performance indices to establish a performance decision table, which is similar to establish a fuzzy rule table.

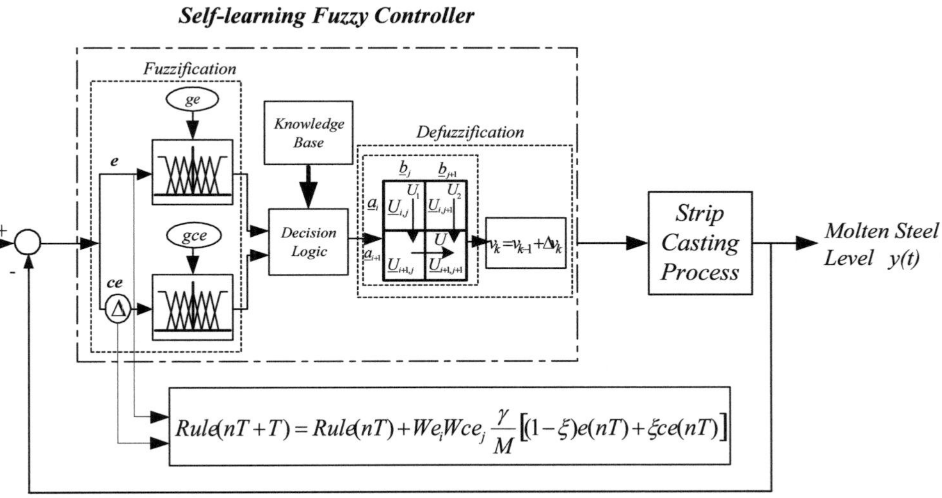

Fig. 2. The self-learning fuzzy control block diagram

The purpose of model estimation is to find the relationship between the system output performance and the control input. Based on the estimation model, the performance measure can be used to calculate the correction value of each fuzzy rule. However, it's difficult to establish an appropriate performance decision table for each control system. A real-time linguistic self-learning fuzzy control strategy with a modification equation is used instead of the performance decision table to eliminate this difficulty. During the rule modification period, the size of rule table is limited to that of the original fuzzy rule table, and the correction value of each fuzzy rule is introduced into the original fuzzy rules as a new control rule. This approach can both improve the database expansion shortcoming of the Procky scheme (Procky and Mamdani 1979) and increase the computing speed. In addition, the system output characteristic can be monitored by definite design parameters. An auto-regression and moving average (ARMA) model can be used to represent the system dynamic response feature:

$$X(nT) = A(z^{-1})X(nT - T) + Mu(nT - mT) + B(z^{-1})u(nT - mT - T)$$

$$A(z^{-1}) = a_0 + a_1 z^{-1} + \cdots + a_{r-1} z^{-(r-1)} \quad (9)$$

$$B(z^{-1}) = b_0 + b_1 z^{-1} + \cdots + b_{s-m-1} z^{-(s-m-1)}$$

where mT is the time delay of the system and M is the system direct forward gain of the control system. The values of r, s and m depend on the dynamic characteristics of the control system. They are difficult to estimate for the given system due to the non-linearity and uncertainty. Fortunately, fuzzy control has model-free feature and it does not require a definite mathematical model and system parameters. If the system is excited with a different control input $u'(nT - mT)$ at time step $nT - mT$, there will be a new output value $X'(nT)$ at time step nT. Substituting $u'(nT - mT)$ into Equation (9) will generate:

$$X'(nT) = A(z^{-1})X(nT - T) + Mu'(nT - mT) + B(z^{-1})u(nT - mT - T) \quad (10)$$

Then, the output difference between Equation (9) and (10) can be obtained:

$$\Delta X \equiv X'(nT) - X(nT)$$

$$\Delta u \equiv u'(nT - mT) - u(nT - mT) \quad (11)$$

The relationship between control input difference and corresponding output deviations are established.

$$X'(nT) - X(nT) = M[u'(nT - mT) - u(nT - mT)] \quad (12)$$

$$\Delta X = M\Delta u \quad \text{or} \quad \frac{\Delta X}{\Delta u} = M \quad (13)$$

If a system at time step nT has an output error ΔX and an error change $\Delta\dot{X}$ needed be compensated, the theoretical correction values of the corresponding control input are Δu_e and Δu_{ce}, respectively. Then

$$\Delta u_e = \frac{\Delta X}{M} \quad \text{and} \quad \Delta u_{ce} = \frac{T\Delta\dot{X}}{M} \quad (14)$$

Since the system has one control input *u* only, the above two terms must be combined together appropriately into the control input correction. Generally, the following equation can be chosen:

$$\Delta u = (1 - \xi)\Delta u_e + \xi\Delta u_{ce}, \quad 0 \le \xi < 1 \quad (15)$$

where ξ is a design parameter representing the weighting distribution between Δu_e and Δu_{ce}. If there is a large deviation between the system output $X(nT)$ and the desired value X_d, the suitable $X'(nT)$ value is chosen between $X(nT)$ and X_d with a weighting parameter γ. Then the system output response X can approach X_d gradually.

$$X'(nT) = (1-\gamma)X(nT) + \gamma X_d, \quad 0 < \gamma < 1 \tag{16}$$

Then the output and output change rate deviations become

$$\Delta X(nT) = \gamma[X_d - X(nT)] = \gamma e(nT) \tag{17}$$

$$\Delta\dot{X}(nT) = \gamma\dot{e}(nT) = \frac{\gamma}{T}ce(nT) \tag{18}$$

From Equations (13) and (17), the correction value of the control input can be represented as:

$$\Delta u = \frac{\gamma}{M}[(1-\xi)e(nT) + \xi ce(nT)] \tag{19}$$

In this study, the output error E and the change of error CE are normalized and divided into eleven equal span fuzzy subsets within [-1, +1]. The fuzzy input variables, i.e. the system output error and the change of error will stimulate two fuzzy subsets of the E and CE universe of discourse, respectively for each control step. Since the control input u is derived from the inference of fuzzy rules, four fuzzy rules will be influenced by the rule modification for each control step. The correction value of each fuzzy rule is proportional to its excitation strength w, which is designed as a triangular membership function and calculated with a linear interpolation algorithm. Then the control input correction equation of the *i*th rule is:

$$u_i(nT+T) = u_i(nT) + \Delta u_i$$

$$= u_i(nT) + w_{ei}w_{cei}\frac{\gamma}{M} \times [(1-\xi)e(nT) + \xi ce(nT)] \tag{20}$$

The term γ / M in the above equation can be considered as a designing learning factor. Besides this intelligent has a rule modification equation as the above equation, its operating processes are the same as the fuzzy logic controller. The general form of a self-learning fuzzy control rule can be expressed as:

$$\text{Rule}_i: \text{IF } \Delta X \text{ is } A \text{ AND } \Delta\dot{X} \text{ is } B, \text{THEN } U \text{ is } C \tag{21}$$

where Rule_i is the *i*th rule, ΔX and $\Delta\dot{X}$ are the states of the system output to be controlled, *U* is the control input and *A*, *B* and *C* are the corresponding fuzzy subsets of the input and output universe of discourse, respectively. The output importance of each rule is dependent on the membership functions of the linguistic input and output variables. An equal-span triangular membership function shown in Fig. 3 is employed in this article for fuzzifying the input and output variables. The membership function used in the present article for fuzzification is of a triangular type. The function can be expressed as:

$$\mu(x) = \frac{1}{W}(-|x-\delta| + W) \tag{22}$$

where W is the distribution span of the membership function, x is the fuzzy input variable and δ is the parameter defining the value 1 of the membership function. The height method is employed to defuzzify the fuzzy variable in order to obtain the control input for each control step. The equation can be described as:

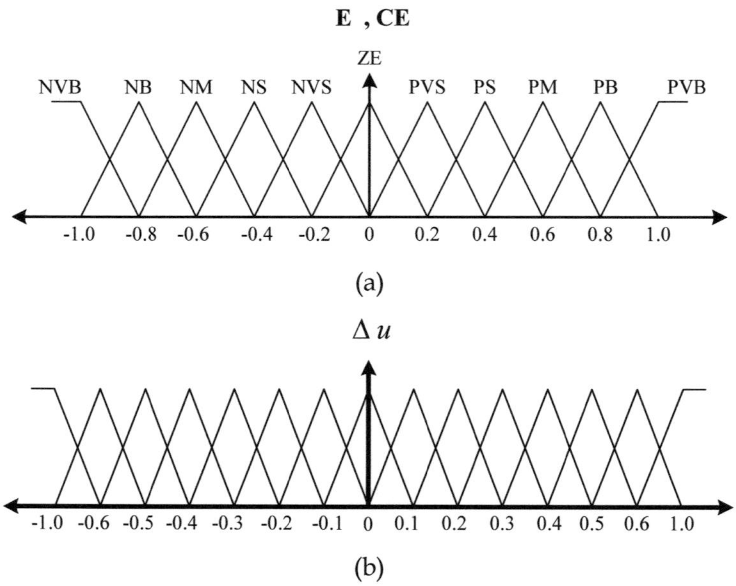

Fig. 3. The fuzzy membership functions for (a) the inputs control variables errors; (b) the control input

$$y^0 = \frac{\sum w_i y_i}{\sum w_i}, \qquad w_i = \prod_j \mu_{A_{ij}}(x_j^0) \tag{23}$$

where $\mu_{A_{ij}}(x_j^0)$ is the linguistic value of the fuzzy set variable, w_i is the weight of the corresponding rules that have been activated, y_i is the resulting fuzzy control value of the ith fuzzy rule and y^0 is the net fuzzy control action. The two dimensional linear interpolation algorithm also can be used to calculate the inference of four fired fuzzy rules for obtaining the control value of each control step.

4. Numerical results

In order to verify the effectiveness of this intelligent controller, the following numerical simulations are performed in this study. The system parameters used in the simulation study are selected as: $R = 650$ (mm), $L_r = 1350$ (mm). These values are chosen from the previous researches (Joo et al. 2002, Park and Cho 2005). The variation of the input flow rate, $a(t)$, to describe the slow nozzle clogging and sudden unclogging is shown in Fig. 4 from reference (Joo et al. 2002). The input flow rate is dependent upon the viscosity of the molten steel, the molten steel level in the tundish, clogging and unclogging. The initial molten steel level and desired molten steel level were set to be 200 and 250 mm, respectively. The sampling frequency was selected as 100 Hz. The fuzzy control parameters ge and gce are chosen as 35 and 150. The weighting parameter ξ and the learning factor γ / M in Equation

(20) were chosen as 0.5 and 1/1.9, respectively. An equal-span triangular membership function shown in Fig. 3 is employed for fuzzifying the input and output variables.

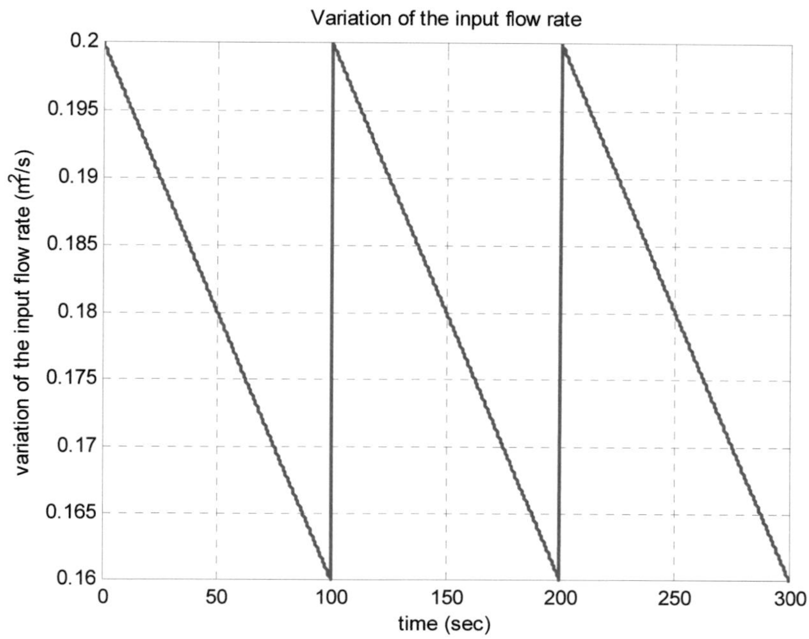

Fig. 4. Variation of the input flow rate

Case A: The parameters x_g and v_r are constants:

The system parameters roll gap x_g and roll speed v_r used in this simulation are set as constants, $v_r = 13$ (mpm) and $x_g = 2$ (mm). In practice, they are important to reach the desired molten steel level y_d in short period of time without overshooting, and to guarantee the molten steel level within a bounded endurable region during the casting process. The dynamic responses of the controller based on numerical results are shown in Fig. 5 (transient response) and Fig. 6 (steady-state response). The variations of orifice opening is shown in Fig. 7. The dynamic responses and the variations of orifice opening of the traditional PID controller ($k_p = 25$, $k_i = 0.15$, $k_d = 1$) is shown in Figs. 8 and 9, respectively. Since the variation of the input flow rate has a sudden change from 0.16 to 0.2 m^2/s at the moment of 100, 200 and 300 sec. The small change in times 100 and 200 sec in Fig. 6 is due to the sudden variation of the input flow. It takes about 10 steps (0.1 sec) for the height of molten steel, y, converges to the desired molten steel level, y_d by using this intelligent controller. The converging time of the molten steel level is faster than the result, 0.15 sec of the PID controller. It can be observed that the steady-state error can be kept within 0.02 mm to the end of the control process even at the instants with the input flow rate variations due to the sudden unclogging shown in Fig. 4. The steady-state error is smaller than the result, 0.5 mm of the PID controller.

Case B: The parameters x_g and v_r are not constants:

Since the system roll gap x_g and roll speed v_r parameters may have some perturbations in the real strip casting process, the values of x_g and v_r with certain variation instead of constants are chosen in this simulation. These parameter perturbations are set as random variations with the maximum amplitude of 25% system nominal parameter values. The disturbances are added for the entire control process to represent the parameter perturbations. The dynamic responses of this intelligent controller based on numerical results are shown in Fig. 10 (transient response) and Fig. 11 (steady-state response). The variations of orifice opening is shown in Fig. 12. The dynamic responses and the variations of orifice opening of the traditional PID controller ($k_p = 25$, $k_i = 0.15$, $k_d = 1$) is shown in Figs. 13 and 14, respectively. It takes about 10 steps (0.1 sec) for the height of molten steel, y, to converge to the desired molten steel level, y_d, with ± 0.3 mm steady-state error by using this intelligent controller. The converging time of the molten steel level is faster than the result, 015 sec of the PID controller and the steady-state error is smaller than the result, ± 1 mm of the PID controller even at the instants with the input flow rate variations due to the sudden unclogging.

Based on the simulation results, it can be observed that the self-learning fuzzy controller can regulate the molten steel level at the preset desired level without overshooting effectively.

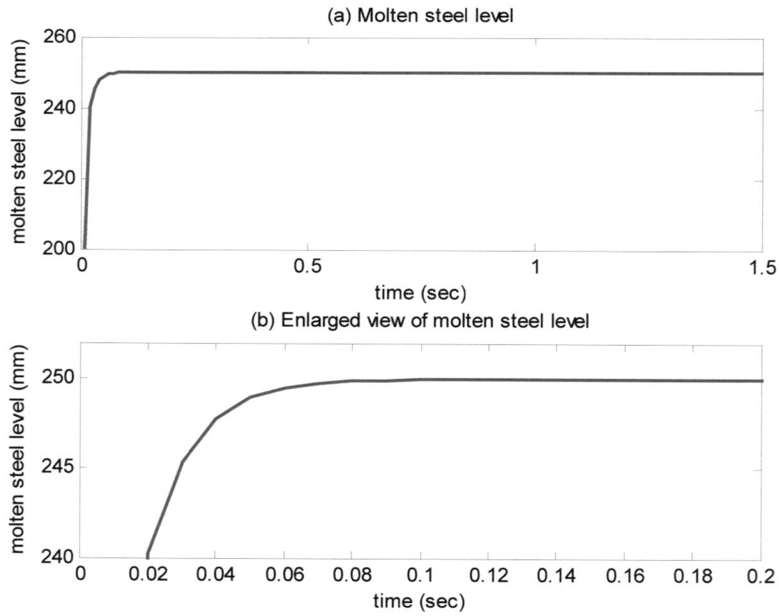

Fig. 5. Case A: Molten steel level (transient response)

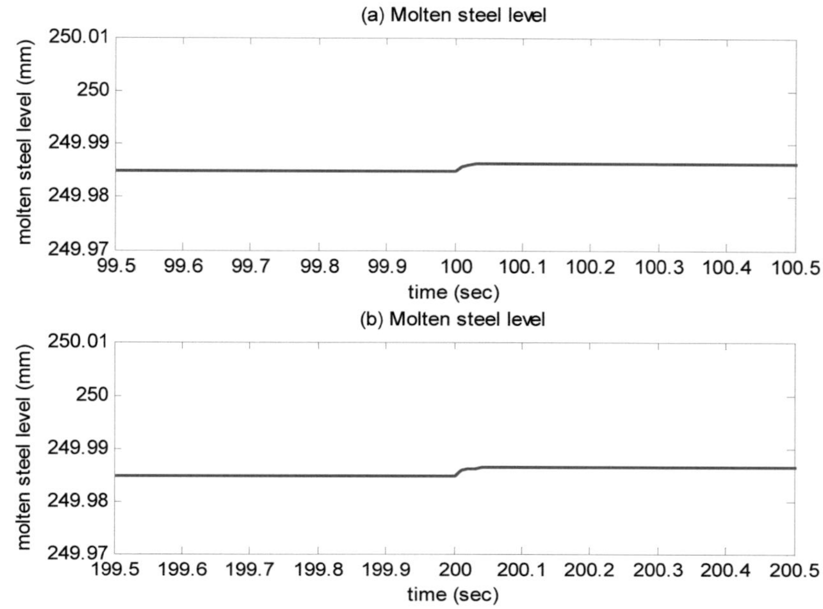

Fig. 6. Case A: Molten steel level (steady-state response)

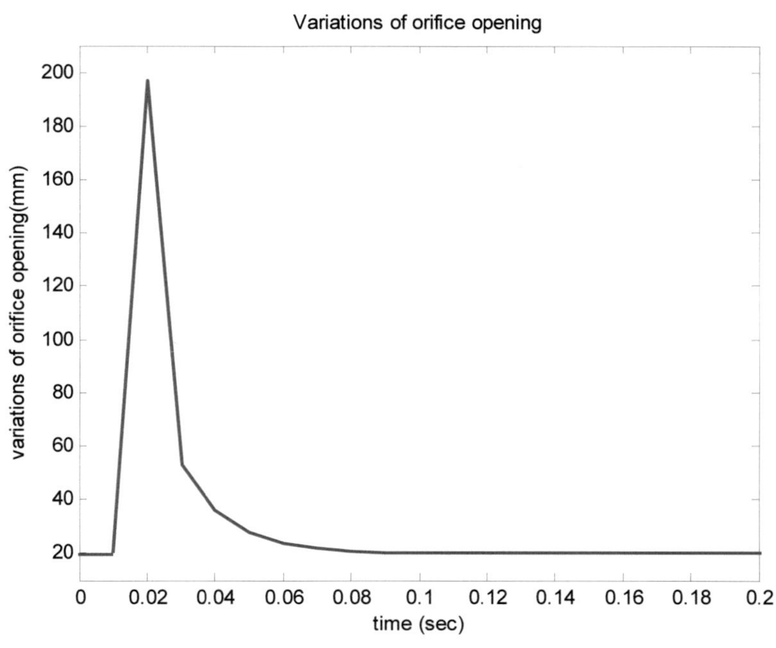

Fig. 7. Case A: Variations of orifice opening

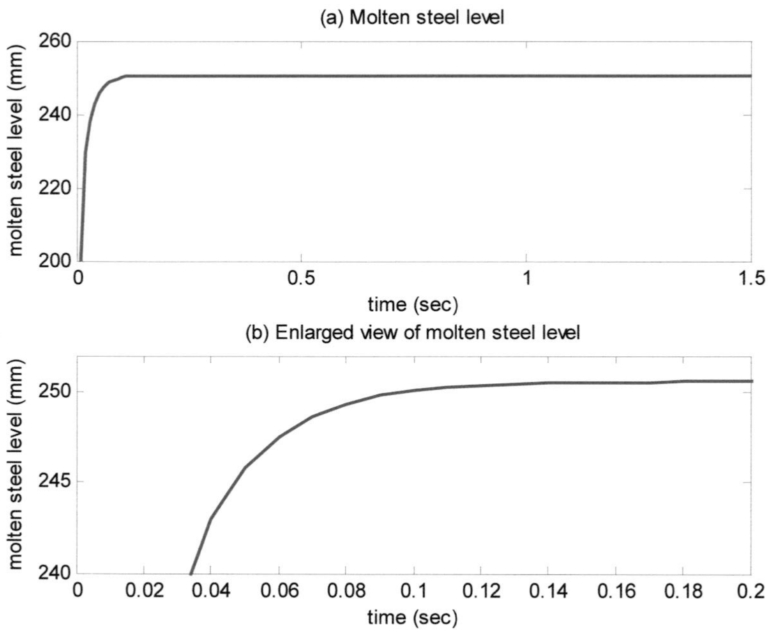

Fig. 8. Case A: Molten steel level (PID controller: $k_p = 25$, $k_i = 0.15$, $k_d = 1$)

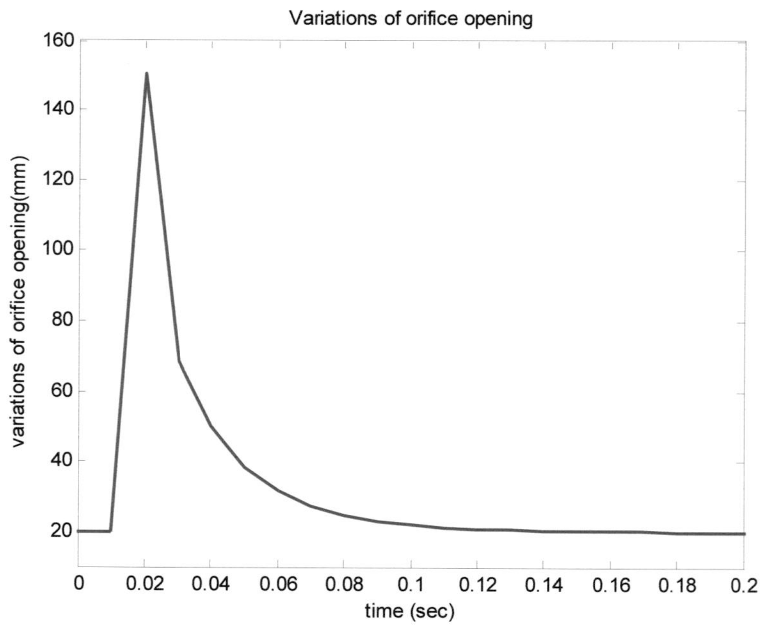

Fig. 9. Case A: Variations of orifice opening (PID controller: $k_p = 25$, $k_i = 0.15$, $k_d = 1$)

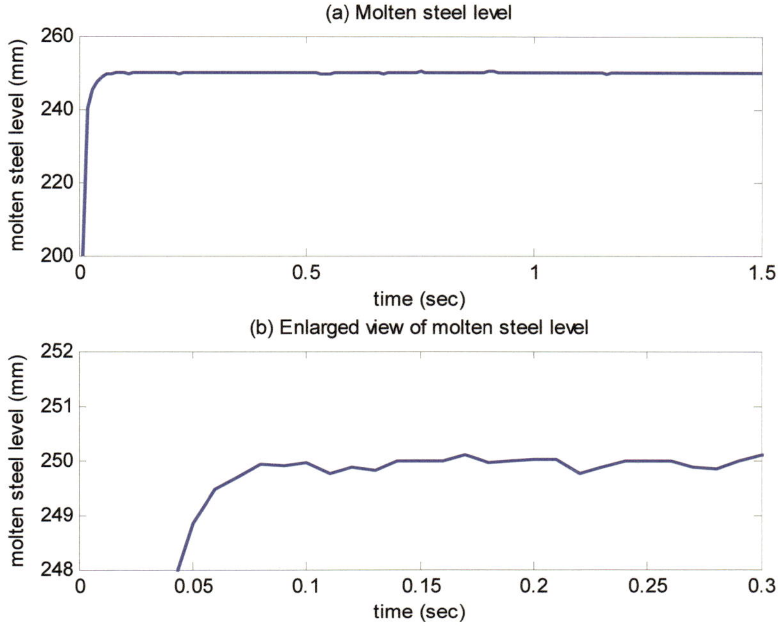

Fig. 10. Case B: Molten steel level (transient response)

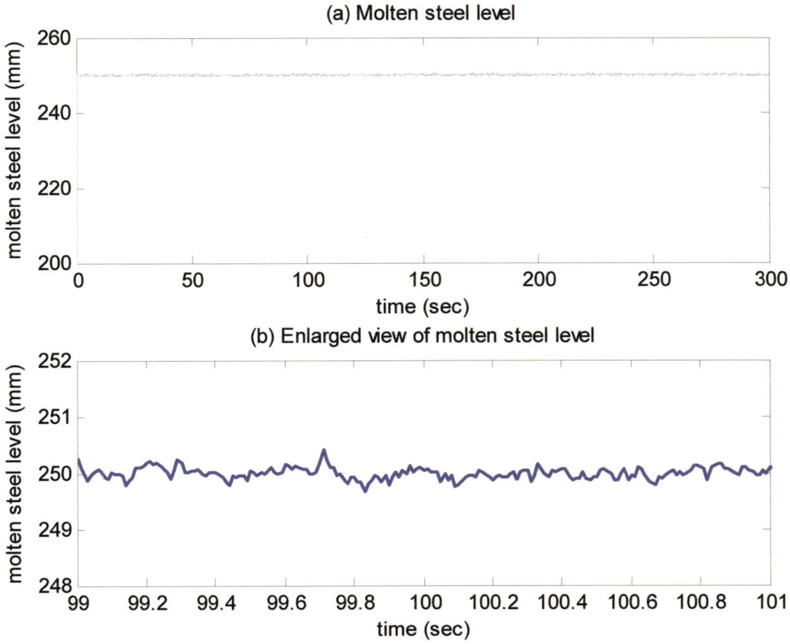

Fig. 11. Case B: Molten steel level (steady-state response)

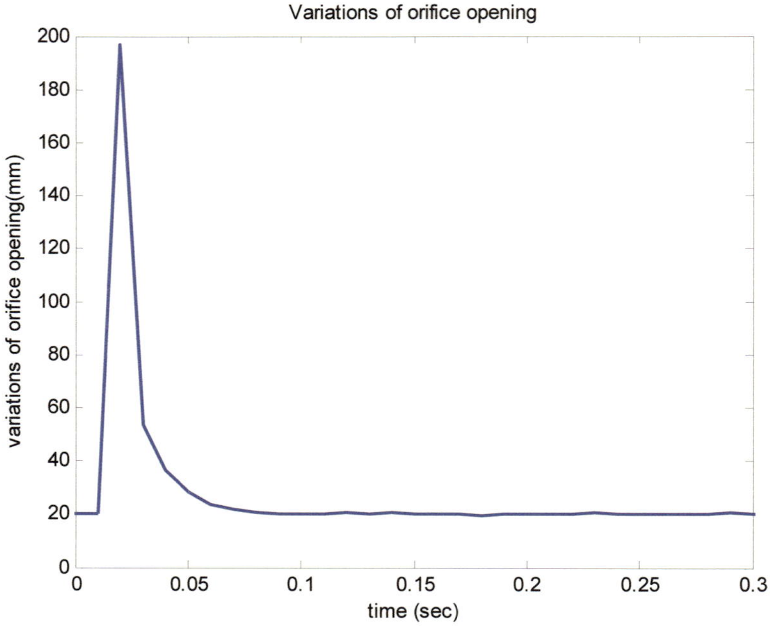

Fig. 12. Case B: Variations of orifice opening

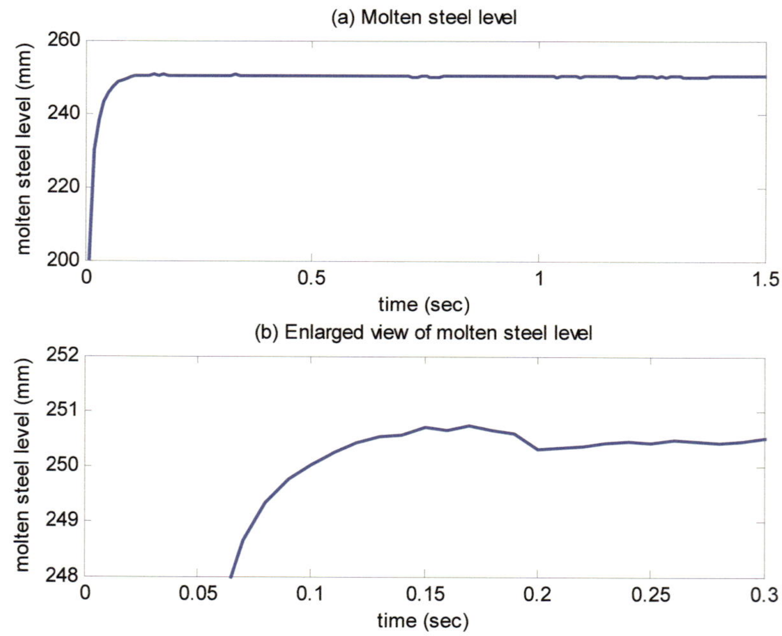

Fig. 13. Case B: Molten steel level (PID controller: $k_p = 25$, $k_i = 0.15$, $k_d = 1$)

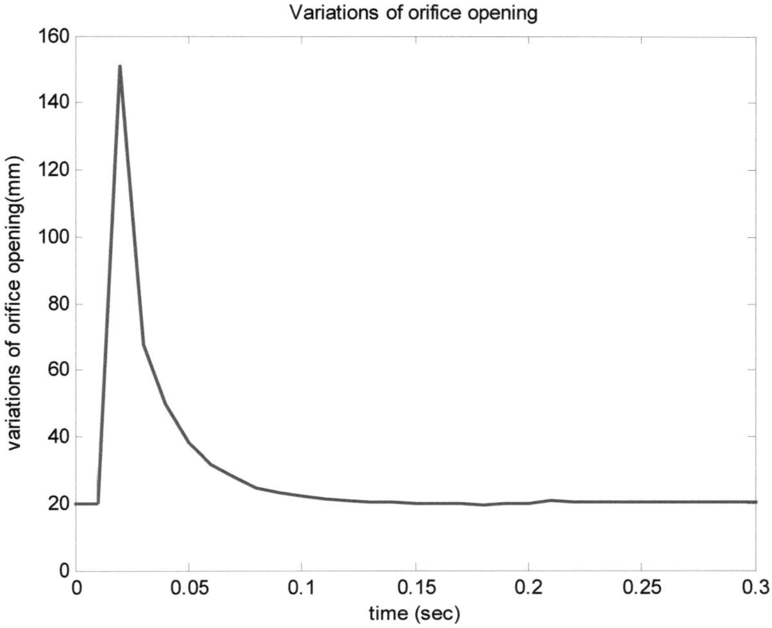

Fig. 14. Case B: Variations of orifice opening (PID controller: $k_p = 25$, $k_i = 0.15$, $k_d = 1$)

5. Conclusion

The twin-roll strip casting process dynamics has the properties of nonlinear uncertainty and time-varying characteristics. It is difficult to establish an accurate process model for designing a model-based controller to monitor the strip quality. A model-free self-learning fuzzy controller is employed to control the molten steel level of the strip casting process. This intelligent control strategy has online learning ability for responding to the system's nonlinear and time-varying behaviors during the molten steel level control. From the simulation results, it can be observed that the converging time of the molten steel level is less than 0.1 sec and the steady-state error is less than 0.3 mm for both simulation cases. In addition, this control strategy can monitor the molten steel at the preset desired level without overshooting effectively to guarantee the steel strip casting quality. Furthermore, from the control results, it can be concluded that the performance of this self-learning fuzzy controller is better than that of a traditional PID controller. This has reduced significantly the trial-and-error efforts of implementing a PID control strategies.

6. References

Chen, H.Y. & Huang, S.J. (2004). Ti6Al4V laser alloying process control by using a self-organizing fuzzy controller. *International Journal of Machine Tools & Manufacture*, Vol. 44, pp. 1653-1665.

Cook, R., Grocock, P.G., Thomas, P.M., Edmonds, D.V. & Hunt, J.D. (1995). Development of the twin-roll casting process. *Journal of Materials Processing Technology*, Vol. 55, pp. 76-84.

Dussud, M., Galichet, S. & Foulloy, L.P. (1998). Application of fuzzy logic control for continuous casting mold level control. *IEEE Transactions on Control System Technology*, Vol. 6, pp. 246-256.

Graebe, S.F., Goodwin, G.C. & Elsley, G. (1995). Control design and implementation in continuous steel casting. *IEEE Control Systems Magazine*, Vol. 15, pp. 64-71.

Hesketh, T., Clements, D.J. & Williams, R. (1993). Adaptive mould level control for continuous steel slab casting. *Automatica*, Vol. 29, pp. 851-864.

Hong, K.S., Kim, J.G. & Tomizuka, M. (2001). Control of strip casting process: decentralization and optimal roll force control. *Control Engineering Practice*, Vol. 9, pp. 933-945.

Joo, M.G., Kim, Y.H. & Kang, T. (2002). Stable adaptive fuzzy control of the molten steel level in the strip casting process. *IEE Proceedings on Control Theory Applications*, Vol. 149, pp. 357-364.

Liang, X., Pan, F., Zhou, S., Ding, P. & Xu, X. (1997). Edge containment of a twin-roll caster for near-net-shape strip casting. *Journal of Materials Processing Technology*, Vol. 63, pp. 788-791.

Park, Y. & Cho, H. (2005). A fuzzy logic controller for the molten steel level control of strip casting process. *Control Engineering Practice*, Vol. 13, pp. 821-834.

Procky, T.J. & Mamdani, E.H. (1979). A linguistic self-organizing process controller. *Automatica*, Vol. 15, pp. 15-30.

9

Fuzzy Maximum Power Point Tracking Techniques Applied to a Grid-Connected Photovoltaic System

Neson Diaz, Johann Hernández, Oscar Duarte
Universidad Nacional, División de Investigación Bogotá, LIFAE, Universidad Distrital F.J.C.
Colombia

1. Introduction

Issues such as the increasing worried about global warming caused by the use of energy resources based on fossil fuel such as oil, gas and coal, have pointed the target toward sustainable energy resources free of greenhouse gas emissions. The PhotoVoltaic (PV) energy plays an important role into the called green energies sources, reason why its use has been rapidly invigorated A. Yafaoui (2009). However of this, a PV generator has two significant problems; the mismatch between the load and the conductance of the PV generator . Since, the load must match PV conductance of the PV generator to ensure the maximum power transfer A. Yafaoui (2009), Hohm & Ropp (2000). The other point, is that the PV generation depends of the weather conditions, such as solar irradiance and temperature Mutoh et al. (2006).
To ensure the maximum power transfer the load seen from the PV generator must be continuously adjusted. Therefore, a Maximum Power Point Tracking (MPPT) algorithm must be implemented to achieve the match between the PV generator (PVG) and the load in real time, taking into account that the maximum power point is not known a priori it is not an easy task to track the maximum power point Mutoh et al. (2006) Kim et al. (2006), Zeng & Liu (2009). Additionally, regarding the low efficiency of a PVG it would be desirable to obtain the maximum power under any weather condition Mutoh et al. (2006), Roman et al. (2006).
Many MPPT algorithm methods have been proposed to deal with the problem of the power generation variations due to changes at the solar irradiance and at PV cell temperature. They range from simple algorithm based on perturbation and observation to more complex based on neural network, and fuzzy logic control A. Yafaoui (2009), Hohm & Ropp (2000), Zeng & Liu (2009).
A PV system can be implemented as a stand-alone system or as a grid connected generator. A stand-alone system requires a battery bank to store the energy obtained from the PV generator. That kind of system is frequently used in low power system to support a local energy requirement. On the other hand, a grid-connected PV system (GCPVS) usually does not require the battery bank and has become the primary method for high-power applications Kim et al. (2006). A GCPVS takes an important part into distributed power generation systems such as low-voltage distribution grids Alonso-Martinez et al. (2009), Vandoorn et al. (2009), Xue et al. (2004). Where, the energy generated by the GCPVS is sent to the power grid and consumed by the nearest customers. This is accomplished through an efficient DC/AC conversion by means of a solid-state Inverter. The inverter becomes the interface between the

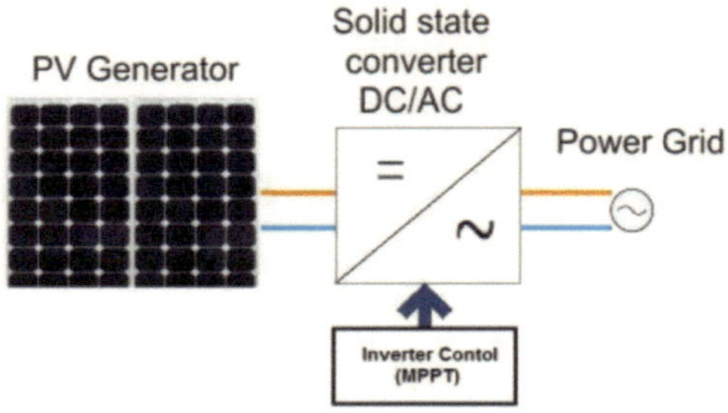

Fig. 1. Grid-Connected Photovoltaic System schematic.

AC grid load and the PVG, it has to match the PVG output resistance to ensure the MPPT (active power flow control).
In this chapter, a controller for a solid state inverter in a single phase GCPVS is proposed looking for MPPT. First the components of the GCPVS are explorer and the nonlinear current-Power relationship of a PVG is analyzed. Second a MPPT algorithm based on fuzzy logic is proposed and improved by means a short circuit current estimator based on a TakagiSugeno (TS) fuzzy model BABUSKA (2009). Third simpler linear controllers are used to achieve the maximum power point where the reference is imposed by the short circuit current estimator. The controllers were verified in simulation under various weather conditions.

2. Proposed grid connected photovoltaic system

A typical GCPVS as shown in figure 1 is composed by the PV modules, a Solid-state DC/AC conversion stage which is the interface between the variable DC generator and the power grid. For instance, at this case of study, the system will supply power to a single power grid $V_s = 120V \stackrel{to}{\rightarrow} 60Hz$. The conversion stage can be composed by a single o dual power processing stage Xue et al. (2004), Kjaer et al. (2005). Moreover, the conversion stage must also include a MPPT algorithm in order to obtain the maximum power generated from the PVG Kjaer et al. (2002). Next follows a brief analysis and description for each CGPVS component.

2.1 PV generator

By means of a p-n semiconductor junction it is possible to convert the solar radiation into DC currents using the photovoltaic effect. A PV panel is composed by an array of PV cells grouped together in series to increase the output voltage (usually 12 or 24 V), or in parallel to increase the electrical current that the PV module can provide to the load Kim et al. (2006), Molina & Mercado (2008). The traditional equivalent circuit of a solar cell is build by a photocurrent source I_{ph}, a diode parallel to the source, a series resistor R_s, and a shunt resistor R_{sh} as shown in figure 2 Kim et al. (2006), Xiao et al. (2006). A PV panel is composed by an array of cells, then an equivalent circuit for the PV module has the same configuration. Hence, the model of a single cell can be extrapolated to a PV panel model and consequently to a PV panels array interconnected in serial or parallel configuration. The equivalent circuit shown in figure 2, is useful to obtain a model of the PVG to simulate the system under different weather conditions Mutoh et al. (2006), Kim et al. (2006).
From the circuit in figure 2 the output current I is expressed by Mutoh et al. (2006):

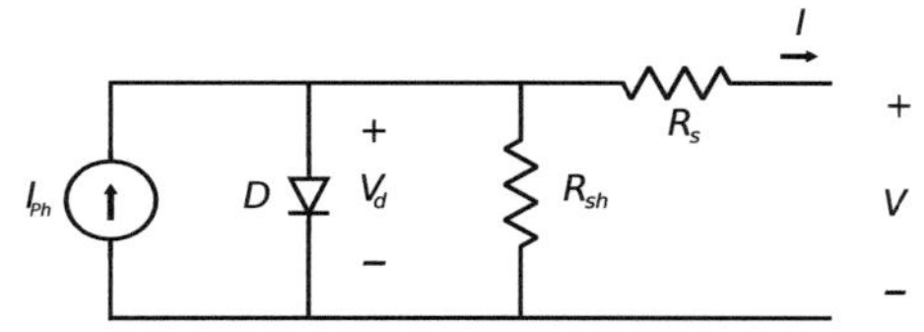

Fig. 2. Equivalent circuit of a PV generator.

$$I = I_{ph} - I_0 \left[exp^{\left(\frac{V+IR_s}{V_t}\right)} - 1 \right] - (V + IR_s) / R_{sh} \tag{1}$$

Where:

- $V_t = \frac{nKT}{q}$;
- n is the diode factor (ideality factor $(= 1)$ maximum value 2) Mutoh et al. (2006),Kim et al. (2006);
- I_O cell reverse saturation current;
- K Boltzmanns constant $(= 1.38x10^{-23} Nm/K)$;
- T cell temperature (in kelvin);
- q electronic charge$(= 1.6x10^{-19}C)$;
- I Output current (A).
- V Output voltage (V).

The two internal resistances R_s and R_{sh} are usually neglected in order to simplify the model Mutoh et al. (2006), Kjaer et al. (2005). Hence, (1) is simplified to:

$$I = I_{ph} - I_0 \left[exp^{\left(\frac{V}{V_t}\right)} - 1 \right] \tag{2}$$

However, it is not an easy task for the users to obtain further information about n and I_0. Generally Those parameters are not listed in data sheets. Instead of those parameters in data sheets are listed the short-circuit current I_{sc} and the open circuit voltage V_{oc} under standard irradiance conditions ($1000W/m^2$ at 25^oC in a cell) Mutoh et al. (2006). Furthermore, the following expression can be used.

$$I_{sc} = I_{ph}\ (V = 0,\ I = I_{sc}) \tag{3}$$

$$I_0 = I_{sc} exp^{\left(-\frac{V_{oc}}{V_t}\right)}; (I = 0,\ V = V_{oc}) \tag{4}$$

The maximum power generated by the PV panel is also specified in the data sheet. That power is written in terms of the Current I_{pm} and Voltage V_{pm} at maximum-power point. Those parameters have been measured under standard condition. From (2) to (4) regarding that $exp^{\left(\frac{V+IR_s}{V_t}\right)} > 1$ under normal operation of the diode, the following expressions can be approximated as Mutoh et al. (2006):

$$I_{pm} = I_{sc}\left[1 - exp^{\left(\frac{V_{pm}-V_{oc}}{V_t}\right)}\right] \tag{5}$$

$$\frac{1}{V_t} = \frac{1}{(V_{pm} - V_{oc})}\log\left(1 - \frac{I_{pm}}{I_{sc}}\right) \tag{6}$$

Thus V_t and hence n can be obtained from (6). The output voltage of the PV generator can be expressed as a function of the output current, using parameters such as V_{oc}, I_{sc}.

$$V = V_{oc}\left\{1 + V_t\log\left(1 - \frac{I}{I_{sc}}\right)\right\} \tag{7}$$

(7) can be used as the model of the PVG. The power generated from the PV array is:

$$P = I * V = I * V_{oc}\left\{1 + V_t\log\left(1 - \frac{I}{I_{sc}}\right)\right\} \tag{8}$$

Other important parameters provided by the manufacturer are the Cell temperature coefficients, those parameters provide information about how the electrical parameters could vary under temperature change. In the table 1 are summarized the main electrical data provided by the manufacturer under standard condition. In this case for the study as PVG are used two panels ASE-300-DGF/17, with a nominal power of 300W each one. The two panels are connected in series hence the PV generator can provide a nominal power of 600W. The Open-circuit voltage temperature coefficient $T_K(V_{oc})$, and the value of n obtained from (6) are also summarized at the table 1.
The data reported in table 1 are used in the expression (7) to obtain the I-V curve under SIC; however, it would be desirable to obtain the I-V curve under different weather conditions. Taking into account the expression (3), there is also a proportional relationship between the short-circuit current I_{sc} and the solar irradiance Mutoh et al. (2006). Hence, by assuming that the I_{sc} change in the same proportion than the solar irradiance, it is possible to obtain the I-V curve under different weather conditions as is shown in fig 3. Figure 4 shows P-I curves under different weather conditions obtained from (8).

	PV panel	PV generator
P_{max} (Watts)	300 W	600 W
V_{pm}	17.2 V	34.4 V
I_{pm}	17.4 A	17.4 A
V_{oc}	20 V	40 V
I_{sc}	19.1 A	19.1 A
$T_K(V_{oc})$	$-0.38\%/C$	$-0.38\%/C$
n	1.6311	1.6311

Table 1. Data PV panel and PV generator

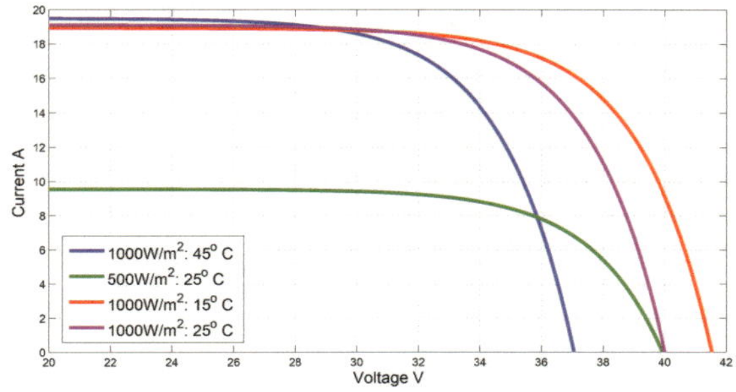

Fig. 3. I-V Curve under different environmental conditions.

2.2 Inverter

The main function of an inverter is to convert the DC voltage obtained from the PV generator into an AC current. Besides, it is the interface between the variable DC generator and the power grid. The inverter involves three major tasks; Inject sinusoidal current into the power grid; provide compensation against harmonic and reactive power; and finally the inverter must ensure maximum power tracking (MPPT) Kjaer et al. (2005), Patel & Agarwal (2006).
A dual-stage inverter have been selected for the GCPVS like the shown in figure 5, it offers an additional degree of freedom in the operation of the system than the one-stage configuration Xue et al. (2004), Kjaer et al. (2005). Instead of the degree of freedom, it is decreased global efficiency of the inverter because of the connection of two converters.
The first stage is a DC- DC boost converter that boosts and regulates the voltage V_{dc}, advisable for a normal operation of the inverters since it requires that $V_{dc} > V_s$ in spite of disturbances (the PV voltage vary in a wide range) Zhang & Xu (2001). The output voltage is a function of the input voltage, the duty cycle D (period of time in witch the MOSFET Q_1 in figure 5 is active), the load current as well as the values of converter components. Neglecting losses the output voltage of the boost converter is given by the equation (9) Erickson & Maksimovic (2000).

$$V_{dc} = \frac{V}{(1-D)} \tag{9}$$

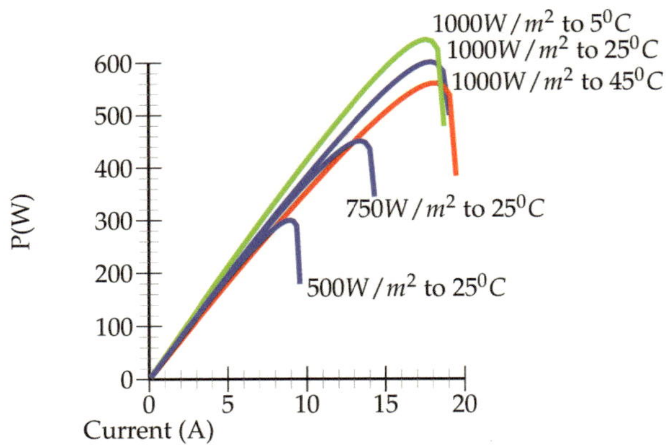

Fig. 4. P-I curves.

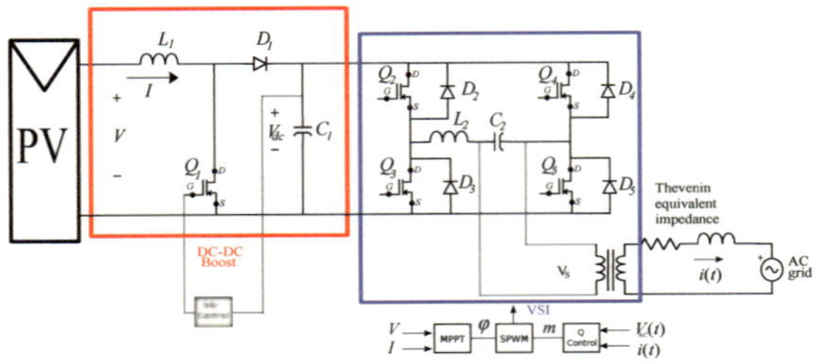

Fig. 5. Two-stage boost inverter Xue et al. (2004).

At this case the boost converter has been dimensioned for an output voltage $Vdc = 70V$. Hence, a compensator has been designed regarding the worst phase margin obtained from load variations and input voltage variations, to attain adequate phase margin and good rejection of expected disturbances. The compensator design was developed by frequency domain response. In figure 6 is shown the frequency response of the compensated loop gain $T(S)$ and the sensitivity function $1/(1+T(S))$ Erickson & Maksimovic (2000). The compensator design will not be explored in deep at this chapter, because of, it is out of the scope of this Chapter.
The second stage, a voltage-source inverter (VSI), converts the regulate DC voltage V_{dc} into an AC current. The inverter becomes the load seen from the first stage. Hence, the VSI operation point is adjusted to perform the MPPT. A sinusoidal AC voltage $v_c(t)$ as shown in (10) can be virtually generated at any angle and amplitude using Sinusoidal Pulse Wide Modulation (SPWM) techniques at forced commutation and subsequent filtering of high frequency components. The active and reactive power flow can be independently controlled manipulating the phase and amplitude of the AC wave voltage generated by the converter Sood (2004), Diaz et al. (2007), Zhang & Xu (2001), Gengyin et al. (2004), Padiyar & Prabhu (2004). This assumption is based on the fact that the VSI connected to an active AC grid behaves like the stator of a synchronous machine (figure 7), regarding only the fundamental frequency component. The active and reactive power flow neglecting the losses are given by (11) and (12), Diaz et al. (2007), Ruihua et al. (2005), Li et al. (2006). In (11) and (12) V_c is the fundamental component of the converter voltage, V_s is the fundamental component of the AC grid voltage, X is the reactance of the reactor that connects the two voltage sources, φ is the phase shift between V_c and V_s. At figure 7, r represents the losses at the conversion stage. In order to simplify the analysis r is neglected; this assumption can be done taking into account that typically the VSI losses are usually less than 5% of the rated capacity Diaz et al. (2007),

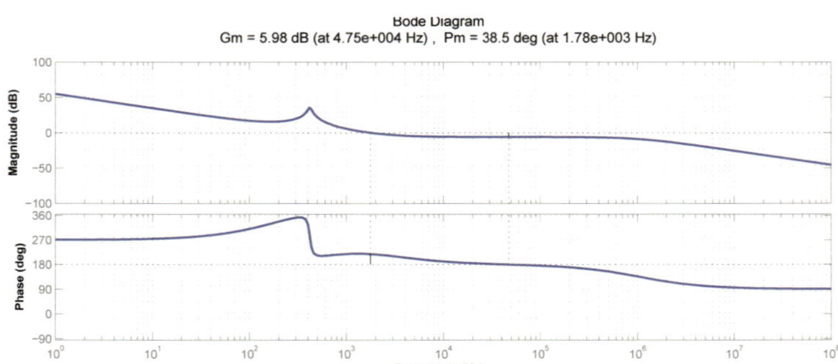

Fig. 6. Frequency response of the compensated loop Erickson & Maksimovic (2000).

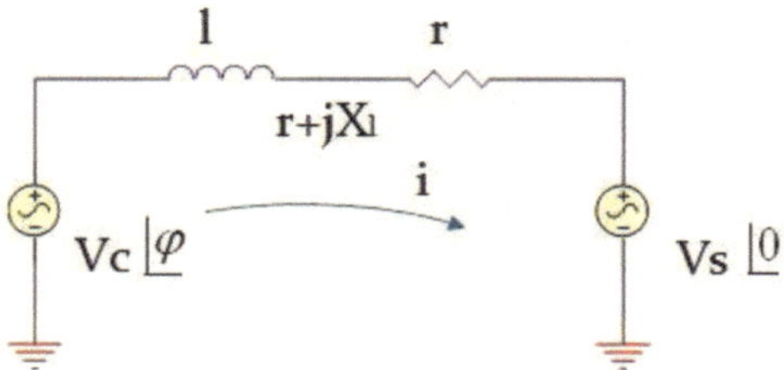

Fig. 7. Equivalent circuit of a VSI interconnected to the AC grid.

Zhang & Xu (2001).

$$v_c(t) = mV_{dc}\sin(\omega t + \varphi) \tag{10}$$

$$P = \frac{V_c V_s}{X}\sin(\varphi) \tag{11}$$

$$Q = \frac{V_s(V_s - V_c\cos(\varphi))}{X} \tag{12}$$

(11) and (12) show that P depends mainly of the angle φ and Q depends mainly of V_c amplitude, which is controlled by the modulation ratio m that is the relationship between the peak AC output voltage and the DC voltage $m = V_{c(peak)}/V_{dc}$ Zhang & Xu (2001), Li et al. (2006). In that sense it is possible to control independently the active and reactive power, adjusting the values of φ and V_c respectively Diaz et al. (2007). However, the VSI is a nonlinear double input double output coupled control system Zhang & Xu (2001). So the system cannot be easily controlled through conventional feedback controllers with fixed-gain. In addition, the power converter has important variations on its principal parameters, so, classical feedback controllers cannot compensate variations in the parameters of the system, and cannot be adapted to changes in the environment easily Gounden et al. (2009). Therefore, nonlinear controller appears as a possibility to control reactive and active power. A nonlinear fuzzy controller can work easily and directly with nonlinear systems and system that does not have constant parameters at the whole range of operating points, like the solid state converters. The fuzzy controllers do not use the parameters of the plant for their design Diaz et al. (2007), BABUSKA (2009). Then, fuzzy controllers may be used to control the active and reactive power flow and assure the MPPT by matching the impedance seen from the DC-DC converter under environmental changes.
The conversion stage is also composed by a step-up line-frequency coupling transformer and a low pass sine wave filter, designed to reduce the perturbation on the distribution system due to high-frequency switching harmonics generated by PWM control Xue et al. (2004), Kjaer et al. (2005), Molina & Mercado (2008).

3. MPPT algorithm

The slope of P-I curve (dP/dI) shown in figure 4 is positive on the left side of the maximum power point (MPP), negative on the right side of MPP and zero at MPP ($dP/dI = 0$). Based on that characteristic, the MPPT algorithm can be indicated as:

$$if\ dP/dI > 0;\ left\ of\ MPP,\ Then\ I\ must\ be\ increased.$$
$$if\ dP/dI = 0;\ at\ MPP,\ Then\ I\ must\ remain\ constant. \tag{13}$$
$$if\ dP/dI < 0;\ rigth\ of\ MPP,\ Then\ I\ must\ be\ decreased.$$

Adjusting the current at the PVG it is possible to track the maximum power point (MPP). The current at the DC side I_{dc} of the inverter is related to the ac current $i_{ac}(t)$ by the equation (14).

$$I_{dc} = Si_{ac}(t) \tag{14}$$

$$S = m \sin(\omega t + \varphi) \tag{15}$$

S is the rectangle switching function whose AC fundamental component is expressed in (15) Li et al. (2006). Besides the PV current I is related to DC current I_{dc} by (16) Erickson & Maksimovic (2000).

$$I = \frac{I_{dc}}{(1-D)} \tag{16}$$

$$I = \frac{m}{(1-D)} \frac{V_c}{X} \frac{\sin(2\varphi)}{2} \tag{17}$$

The PV current I depends of the duty cycle D at the first conversion stage, the modulation index m and the phase shift φ as can be seen in (17). Regarding a regulated DC voltage I depends mainly of the angle φ like the active power. So, the MPP can be obtained by adjusting the angle φ taking into account that m and D are imposed by the V_{dc} control and reactive power control respectively.
Taking into account that the power generated depends on solar irradiance and temperature as is shown in figure 4. It is desirable that if the system is close to the MPP the angle φ change a few. But if the system is far from the MPP the angle must change a lot.

4. Fuzzy MPPT algorithm

A fuzzy logic controller can easily incorporate all the qualitative knowledge above mentioned and summarized in (13) about the behavior of the system required to perform the MPPT. The fuzzy control also has the advantage to be robust and relatively simple to design, since it does not require the knowledge of the exact model Zeng & Liu (2009), Gounden et al. (2009), Larbes et al. (2009). A Mamdani fuzzy logic controller has been proposed to perform the MPPT, this kind of controller are usually used in feedback control mode, because they are computationally simple, present low sensibility to noise in the input (what is important in power system), and can easily represent the knowledge about the control action BABUSKA (2009). The knowledge is represented by means of rules in the form if-then and synthesized in form of an input-output mapping between the antecedent and the consequent variables BABUSKA (2009).

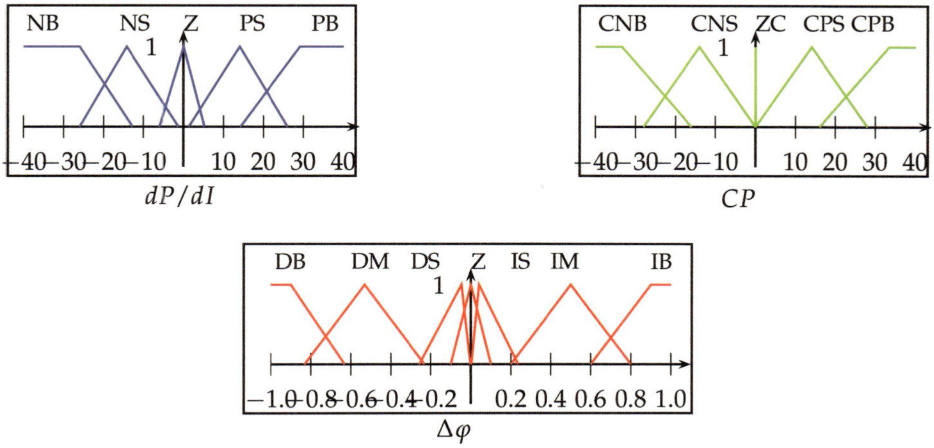

Fig. 8. FLC membership function for dP/dI, CP and $\Delta\varphi$.

A PD fuzzy logic controller (FLC) has been proposed in order to synthesize the MPPT algorithm. The inputs are the slope of the curve P-I (dP/dI) which shows the actual operation point, and the change of the power CP which expresses the moving direction of this point. In samples time $k = 1.4ms$. the inputs variables are defines as follow:

$$\frac{dP}{dI} = \frac{\Delta P}{\Delta I} = \frac{P(k) - P(k-1)}{I(k) - I(k-1)} \tag{18}$$

$$CP = \Delta P = P(k) - P(k-1) \tag{19}$$

The control rules are indicated in Table 2. Where (dP/dI) and CP are the inputs and the change in the phase shift $\Delta\varphi$ is the output. The membership function of the two input variables and the control action $\Delta\varphi$ are triangular and trapezoidal membership functions because of they are computationally simpler in figure 8 BABUSKA (2009). The membership functions were tuned searching the minimum error in steady state and the minimum oscillation in transitory state by trial and error method using the toolbox FIS of MATLAB. The input and output membership function are shown in figure 8 BABUSKA (2009).

4.1 Improvement of the MPPT by means of a fuzzy I_{sc} estimator

To avoid small current increments at high solar irradiance level and slow response of the MPPT, or high increments of the current at low irradiance level, that may cause high oscillations around the MPP, it is desirable a smaller step size of $\Delta\varphi$ under low irradiance,

CP dP/dI	CNB	CNS	ZC	CPS	CPV
NB	IB	IB	IB	IB	IM
NS	IM	IP	IP	Z	Z
Z	IP	Z	Z	Z	DP
PS	IM	IP	IP	Z	Z
PB	DN	DB	DB	DB	DB

Table 2. Rule Base FLC

and a higher step size of $\Delta\varphi$ under high irradiance. The step size of $\Delta\varphi$ might be weighted by the I_{sc} under different solar irradiance conditions. However, it is difficult to know in advance I_{sc} for all solar irradiance range and temperatures to weight the step size. To obtain the I_{sc} the PV generator should be disconnected from the system and by a short circuit in the generator the I_{sc} can be measured. A problem with this procedure is that available energy is wasted when the generator is disconnected from the system.

Figure 4, shows that the slope (dP/dI) for different levels of irradiance are similar in relation with the gap between the operating point and MPP location, where the gap depends on I_{sc}. Figure 9 shows different surfaces obtained by plotting the dP/dI values (under irradiance levels of $1000W/m^2$, $750W/m^2$ and $500W/m^2$) versus the normalized PV current I/I_{sc} and temperature. The figures are similar and they cannot be distinguished. Therefore, the curves under different weather conditions could be represented by an unique nonlinear model.

The nonlinear curves in figure 9 can be approximated by using a Takagi-Sugeno (TS) fuzzy model BABUSKA (2009). A TS fuzzy model can represent the nonlinear function as a smoothed piece-wise linear approximation as shown in figure 10. TS fuzzy model uses crisp functions of the antecedent variable at the consequents rather than fuzzy preposition like in FLC BABUSKA (2009). Hence, the model can be seen as a combination of linguistic and mathematical regression modeling in the sense that the antecedents describe fuzzy regions in the input space in which the consequent functions are valid BABUSKA (2009).

The TS model is obtained by means of fuzzy clustering algorithms that are used to partition an input-output data base into groups of similar objects. The term "similarity" should be understood as mathematical similarity, it is often defined by means of a distance norm from a data vector to some prototypical object or center of cluster. The centers of clusters are usually unknown a priori, they are obtained by the clustering algorithms simultaneously with the partitioning of the data. The concept of graded membership is used to represent the degree at which a given data is similar to some center of cluster. Based on the similarity, the data can be clustered such that the data within a cluster are as similar as possible, then a cluster is a group of objects that are more similar to one another than to members of other clusters. The prototypes may be vectors of the same dimension as the data objects, but they can also be defined as "higher-level" geometrical objects, such as linear or nonlinear subspaces or functions. Fuzzy clustering methods, allow the objects to belong to several clusters simultaneously, with different degrees of membership between 0 and 1 indicating their partial membership. That provides interpolation between clusters, what allow to approximate the nonlinear function BABUSKA (2009).

A clustering algorithm was used for the automatic generation of fuzzy models. The algorithm

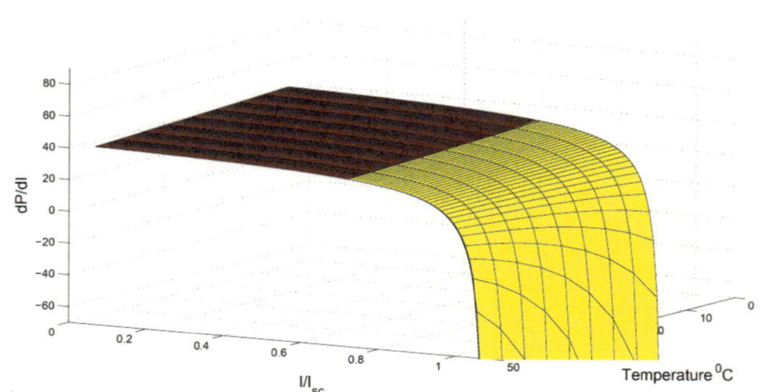

Fig. 9. dP/dI Surfaces.

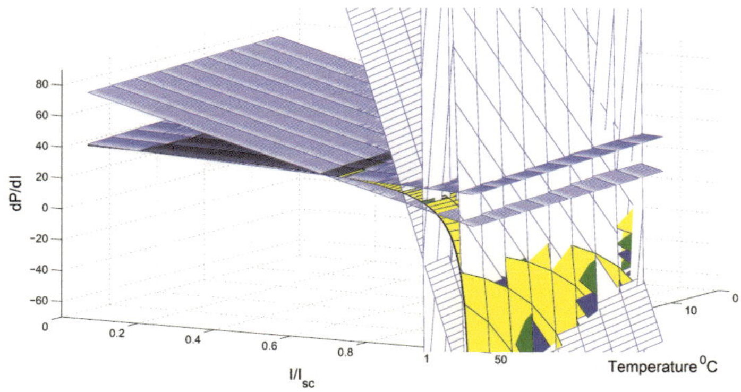

Fig. 10. Piece-wise linear approximation.

is based on optimization of the basic c-means objective function as exposed in BABUSKA (2009). The data base used to perform the algorithm is composed by the inputs dP/dI and temperature $Temp$, and the output of the model which is the normalized current I/I_{sc}. The data base is obtained from the PV generator model exposed before under variations of iradiance and temperature. Each obtained cluster is represented by one rule in the Takagi-Sugeno model.

The data base were partitioned into five clusters. Figure 10 shows the five local linear models obtained through clustering. Figure 11 shows the corresponding fuzzy partition of the consequents dP/dI and T. The parameters of the local linear models of each rule were obtained by least-squares estimation BABUSKA (2009). The TS rule base obtained is summarized as follow:

1. **If** dP/dI is A_{11} **and** $Temp$ is A_{12} **then**
   $I/I_{sc}(k) = 1.73 \cdot 10^{-3}u_1 - 4.21 \cdot 10^{-3}u_2 + 9.16 \cdot 10^{-1}$

2. **If** dP/dI is A_{21} **and** $Temp$ is A_{22} **then**
   $I/I_{sc}(k) = 2.50 \cdot 10^{-4}u_1 - 6.49 \cdot 10^{-4}u_2 + 9.97 \cdot 10^{-1}$

3. **If** dP/dI is A_{31} **and** $Temp$ is A_{32} **then**
   $I/I_{sc}(k) = -3.97 \cdot 10^{-3}u_1 + 2.97 \cdot 10^{-4}u_2 + 9.29 \cdot 10^{-1}$

4. **If** dP/dI is A_{41} **and** $Temp$ is A_{42} **then**
   $I/I_{sc}(k) = -3.52 \cdot 10^{-2}u_1 - 3.58 \cdot 10^{-3}u_2 + 1.90 \cdot 10^{0}$

5. **If** dP/dI is A_{51} **and** $Temp$ is A_{52} **then**
   $I/I_{sc}(k) = -1.20 \cdot 10^{-1}u_1 - 1.88 \cdot 10^{-2}u_2 + 5.31 \cdot 10^{0}$

Since, the PV current can be measured, it is possible to estimate the short-circuit current I_{sce} without disconnecting the PVG and measuring the short-circuit current. Figure 12 shows a comparison between the estimated short circuit current I_{sce} and the expected short circuit current I_{sc}. The percentile variance accounted for (VAF) between the I_{sc} and I_{sce} (formula 20) was used as a performance index of the TS fuzzy model where $VAF = 96.13\%$.

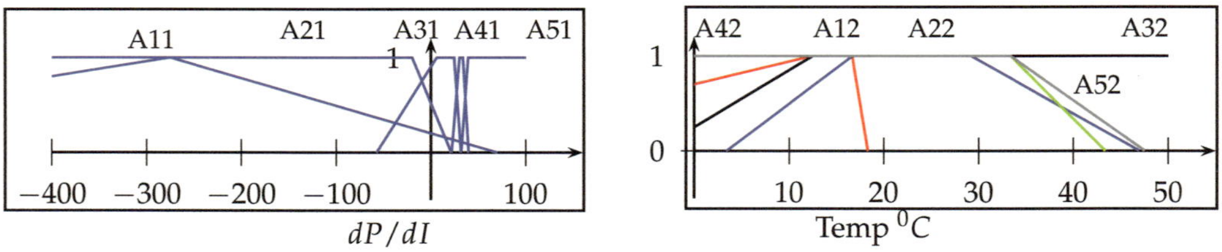

Fig. 11. TS fuzzy model input membership functions

$$VAF = 100\% \left[1 - \frac{var(I_{sc} - I_{sce})}{var\,(I_{sc})}\right] \tag{20}$$

The estimated I_{sce} weights the output of the (FLC) which allows adjust the step-size under different solar irradiance and then assure a step-size $\Delta\varphi$ proportional to the irradiance level. Another problem to solve is the operation of the system under solar irradiance decrements. When the solar irradiance deceases drastically the system operates in the right side of the MPP and hence the voltage on the PVG and the voltage V_{dc} become zero due to the relation given by (9). That may cause instability in the system since the condition for a normal operation of the system ($Vdc > Vs$) is not satisfied. Hence, the load should be decreased and the inverter should be turned off. To do that an additional crisp function has been added to the MPPT algorithm, it has the main function of reduce the angle φ to a half of its value when the PVG voltage decreases below 20V.

The fuzzy controllers are also composed of dynamic pre and post-filters the pre-filter used is an approximation of the derivative effect in the domain of discrete time, this approximation is often used and well accepted for computational implementation, the propose of the derivative effect is obtain a fast response to perturbations. To improve the precision in steady state was used an integrator as dynamic pos-filter in the output of the fuzzy controller Diaz et al. (2007), BABUSKA (2009).

4.2 Reactive power control

Since the inverter would be connected to power grid, the standards given by the utility companies must be obeyed (The power converter in a GCPV must have high conversion efficiency and a power factor exceeding 90% for wide operating range, while maintaining current harmonics THD less than 5%) Kjaer et al. (2005), Eltawil & Zhao (2010). The reactive power flow can be regulated by adjusting the AC voltage generated by the converter V_c as

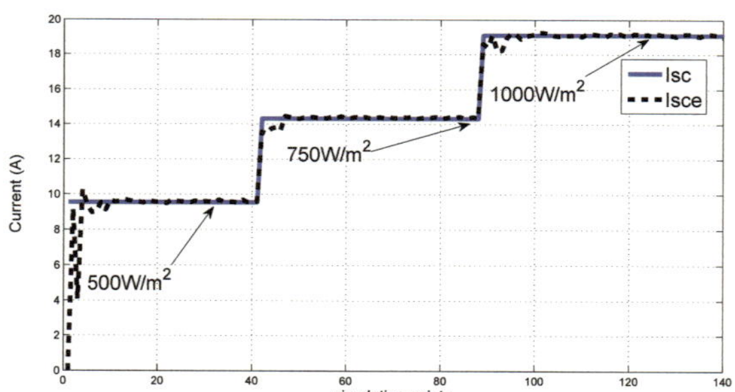

Fig. 12. Comparison between I_{sce} and I_{sc}.

ΔeQ / eQ	CNB	CNS	ZC	CPS	CPV
PB	Z	IS	IS	IM	IG
PS	DS	Z	IS	IS	IM
Z	DS	Z	Z	Z	IS
NS	DM	DS	DS	Z	IS
NB	DB	DM	DS	DS	Z

Table 3. Rule Base FCQ

is shown in (12). The V_c amplitude is regulate mainly by the modulation index m which is controlled by the SPWM signal. A Mamdani fuzzy controller has been designed to regulate the reactive power flow close to zero and deal with the nonlinear behavior.
The proposed controller is a kind of Fuzzy PD controller in counterpart of linear Proportional Derivative controllers BABUSKA (2009). The rule base of the the FCQ (Fuzzy Control of Q) has two inputs as antecedents; the error (eQ), and the error change (ΔeQ), In order to obtain a derivative effect. The output of the fuzzy inference system is the incremental variable (Δm). The rule base of FCQ is summarized in table 3. The FCQ was tuned in MATLAB using the fuzzy inference system toolbox. Dynamic pre and post-filters were also used on this controller.

5. Simulation results

The GCPVS was tested by simulation in the SimPowerSystem toolbox of MATLAB. The system is schematized in figure 5.
The simulation results in figure 13 show that the MPPT is achieved under different solar irradiance at 25^0C in the cell. The converter has a efficiency of 97%, and a settling time around $150ms$. The reactive power is also compensated by remaining it close to zero, then the power factor is close to one in steady state as shown in figure 14.
The TS fuzzy system became an efficient tool to estimate the short circuit current without disconnect the system. The estimator can be used in simpler MPPT methods like the short circuit current method, without having to shutdown the system in order to measure the short circuit current.

6. Short circuit current method

The P-I curves of the PV generator suggest a linear relation between the open short-circuit current (I_{sc}) and the maximum power point current (I_{MPP}) at different irradiance and temperature conditions A. Yafaoui (2009), Mutoh et al. (2006). This relation can be described by:

$$I_{MPP} = kI_{sc} \quad k < 1 \tag{21}$$

The value of the constant K depends on characteristics of the PV generator, but a commonly used value is 90% Mutoh et al. (2006). The short circuit current method is a very simple MPPT method, the PV current is compared with a constant reference current that corresponds to the I_{MPP}. The error signal can be used in simple controllers with integral action to eliminate the error in steady state Tariq & Asghar (2005).
One of the main drawback of this method is that available energy is wasted when the load is disconnected from the PV generator to measure the (I_{sc}). The measurement of the (I_{sc})

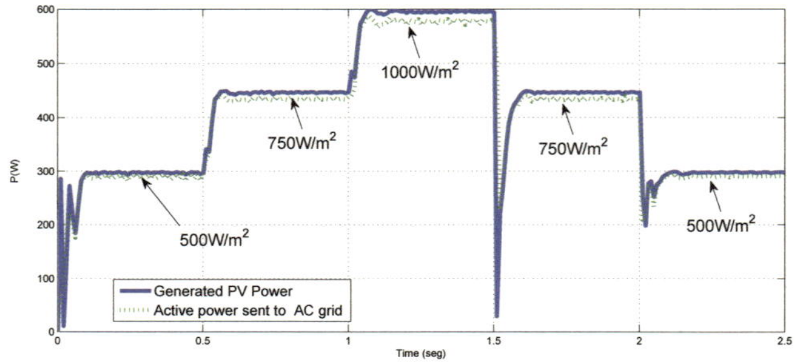

Fig. 13. Simulation results depicting the change of Power vs time.

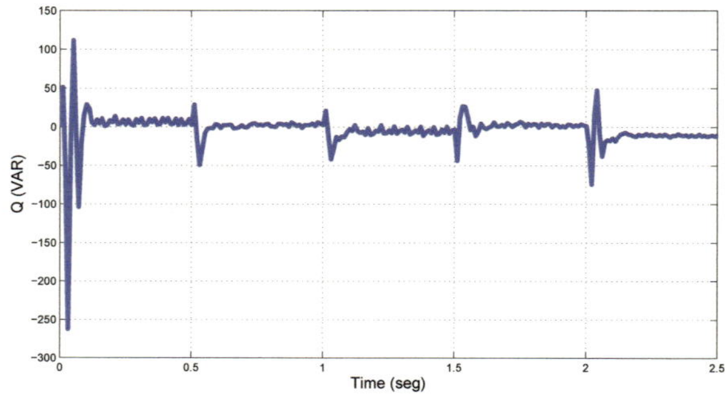

Fig. 14. Simulation results depicting the Reactive Power vs time.

during the operation of the system also increases the complexity of the circuit (I_{sc}). Moreover, the ambient conditions may change between the different measurements intervals and the PV generator conditions may vary A. Yafaoui (2009), Mutoh et al. (2006), Tariq & Asghar (2005). Those problems make this method less popular despite of its simplicity.
However, with the fuzzy short circuit estimator proposed before, the (I_{sc}) can be estimate without additional power power losses. The estimated short circuit current I_{sce} can be multiplied by the factor k in order to estimate the maximum power point current $(I_{MPPe}) = kI_{sce}$.
In order to verify this method a simple proportion integral (PI) controller has been designed. The reference of the controller is the I_{sce} multiplied by a factor $k = 0.88$. The simulation results in figure 15 show that the MPPT is achieved under different solar irradiance at 25^{0}C in the cell.

7. Conclusion

The MPPT algorithm can be easily synthesize by means of a fuzzy logic controller. The shape of the membership function of the fuzzy controllers can be adjusted in order to make the control action proportional to the gap between the operation point and the maximum power point. The increment of the conductance must be proportional to the solar irradiance to avoid high steps size under low irradiance or low step size under high irradiance, which may cause high oscillation around the maximum power point or high settling time under high solar irradiance. A good commitment has been achieved by weighting the step size of the MPPT algorithm by the short-circuit current.

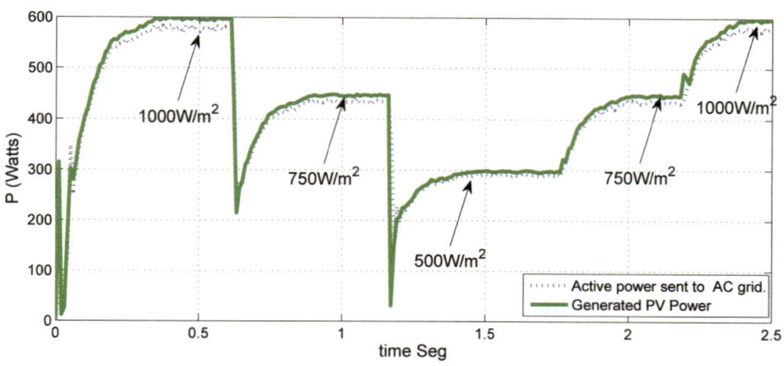

Fig. 15. Simulation results depicting the change of Power vs time with short circuit current method.

TS fuzzy system became an efficient tool to estimate the short circuit current without disconnecting the system. The estimator can be used in simpler MPPT methods like the short circuit current method, without having to shutdown the system in order to measure the short circuit current and then, overpass the main problem of this method. A similar strategy could be used to estimate the open circuit voltage improving the efficiency of this method since it will not be necessary to disconnect the panel from the PV system.

8. References

A. Yafaoui, B. Wu, R. C. (2009). Photovoltaic energy system part 2: System control technology, IEEE Canadian Review(61): 14–17.

Alonso-Martinez, J., Eloy-Garcia, J. & Arnaltes, S. (2009). Control of a three-phase grid-connected inverter for photovoltaic applications with a fuzzy mppt under unbalanced conditions, pp. 1 –7.

BABUSKA, R. (2009). *FUZZY AND NEURAL CONTROL DISC Course Lecture Notes*, Delft University of Technology.

Diaz, N., Barbosa, F. & Trujillo, C. (2007). Analysis and design of a nonlinear fuzzy controller applied to a vsc to control the active and reactive power flow, pp. 417 –422.

Eltawil, M. A. & Zhao, Z. (2010). Grid-connected photovoltaic power systems: Technical and potential problems–a review, *Renewable and Sustainable Energy Reviews* 14(1): 112 – 129.
URL: *http://www.sciencedirect.com/ science/ article/B6VMY -4WXB2C1- 2/2/ 409f2328d21fe83ec94cdc9198c79b76*

Erickson, R. W. & Maksimovic, D. (2000). Fundamentals of power electronics, second edition.

Gengyin, L., Ming, Z., Jie, H., Guangkai, L. & Haifeng, L. (2004). Power flow calculation of power systems incorporating vsc-hvdc, Vol. 2, pp. 1562 – 1566 Vol.2.

Gounden, N. A., Peter, S. A., Nallandula, H. & Krithiga, S. (2009). Fuzzy logic controller with mppt using line-commutated inverter for three-phase grid-connected photovoltaic systems, *Renewable Energy* 34(3): 909 – 915.
URL: *http://www.sciencedirect.com/ science/ article/ B6V4S -4SYKKV4- 3/2/ e53631c13f46e2efa5b430390e206d7a*

Hohm, D. & Ropp, M. (2000). Comparative study of maximum power point tracking algorithms using an experimental, programmable, maximum power point tracking test bed, pp. 1699 –1702.

Kim, I.-S., Kim, M.-B. & Youn, M.-J. (2006). New maximum power point tracker using sliding-mode observer for estimation of solar array current in the grid-connected photovoltaic system, *Industrial Electronics, IEEE Transactions on* 53(4): 1027 –1035.

Kjaer, S., Pedersen, J. & Blaabjerg, F. (2002). Power inverter topologies for photovoltaic modules-a review, Vol. 2, pp. 782 – 788 vol.2.

Kjaer, S., Pedersen, J. & Blaabjerg, F. (2005). A review of single-phase grid-connected inverters for photovoltaic modules, *Industry Applications, IEEE Transactions on* 41(5): 1292 – 1306.

Larbes, C., Cheikh, S. A., Obeidi, T. & Zerguerras, A. (2009). Genetic algorithms optimized fuzzy logic control for the maximum power point tracking in photovoltaic system, *Renewable Energy* 34(10): 2093 – 2100.
URL: *http://www.sciencedirect.com/ science/ article/ B6V4S -4VNCBXY- 1/2/ 48067b857bf072d0f7cc7c5fcd983d70*

Li, G., Li, G., Liang, H., Zhao, C. & Yin, M. (2006). Research on dynamic characteristics of vsc-hvdc system, p. 5 pp.

Molina, M. & Mercado, P. (2008). Modeling and control of grid-connected photovoltaic energy conversion system used as a dispersed generator, pp. 1 –8.

Mutoh, N., Ohno, M. & Inoue, T. (2006). A method for mppt control while searching for parameters corresponding to weather conditions for pv generation systems, *Industrial Electronics, IEEE Transactions on* 53(4): 1055 –1065.

Padiyar, K. & Prabhu, N. (2004). Modelling, control design and analysis of vsc based hvdc transmission systems, Vol. 1, pp. 774 – 779 Vol.1.

Patel, H. & Agarwal, V. (2006). Pv based distributed generation with compensation feature under unbalanced and non-linear load conditions for a 3- 003d5;, 4 wire system, pp. 322 –327.

Roman, E., Alonso, R., Ibanez, P., Elorduizapatarietxe, S. & Goitia, D. (2006). Intelligent pv module for grid-connected pv systems, *Industrial Electronics, IEEE Transactions on* 53(4): 1066 –1073.

Ruihua, S., Chao, Z., Ruomei, L. & Xiaoxin, Z. (2005). Vscs based hvdc and its control strategy, pp. 1 –6.

Sood, V. K. (2004). *HVDC and FACTS Controllers: Applications of Static Converters in Power Systems*, 1 edn, Springer.

Tariq, A. & Asghar, J. (2005). Development of an analog maximum power point tracker for photovoltaic panel, Vol. 1, pp. 251 –255.

Vandoorn, T., Renders, B., Belie, F. D., Meersman, B. & Vandevelde, L. (2009). A voltage-source inverter for microgrid applications with an inner current control loop and an outer voltage control loop.

Xiao, W., Lind, M., Dunford, W. & Capel, A. (2006). Real-time identification of optimal operating points in photovoltaic power systems, *Industrial Electronics, IEEE Transactions on* 53(4): 1017 –1026.

Xue, Y., Chang, L., Kjaer, S. B., Bordonau, J. & Shimizu, T. (2004). Topologies of single-phase inverters for small distributed power generators: an overview, *Power Electronics, IEEE Transactions on* 19(5): 1305 – 1314.

Zeng, G. & Liu, Q. (2009). An intelligent fuzzy method for mppt of photovoltaic arrays, Vol. 2, pp. 356 –359.

Zhang, G. & Xu, Z. (2001). Steady-state model for vsc based hvdc and its controller design, Vol. 3, pp. 1085 –1090 vol.3.

10

Optimal Tuning of PI-like Fuzzy Controller Using Variable Membership Function's Slope

Sun Lim[1] and Byungwoon Jang[2]
[1]*Korea Electronics Technology Institute(KETI)*
[2]*Yonsei Univ*
Korea

1. Introduction

As the speed controlled BLDC motor drive systems are increasingly employed in the industrial drive systems, the various requirements for the performance of such systems become severe. In this investigation, we employ a simple and natural method to design a controller to control the BLDC motor drive system, which is so-called Takagi-Sugeno fuzzy model [1].

Recently, there have been a lot of researches in the Takagi-Sugeno fuzzy model [2], [3], [4]. They offer a systematic procedure to design controllers of BLDC motor drive systems. Servo motor position controller using the fuzzy control algorithm has been developed by Li and Lau [15], and they discuss the steady-state error, settling time, and response time. According to their paper, the performance of the fuzzy controller is better than that of the conventional PI controller and as good as that of the Model Reference Adaptive Control. We do not think a general method can be found to obtain optimum values for fuzzy controllers, because any optimum values always depend on specific models of the process and the control objectives. So, tuning fuzzy controllers must done based on experts' knowledge of the controlled plant, not by computation.

In this paper, our objective is to prescribe a methodology for tuning fuzzy controllers, and this paper presents a scheme for obtaining optimum values of fuzzy membership function's slope. In other words, an optimal slope is sought by evaluating various fuzzy membership function 's slope values. With this imformation, you can tune your fuzzy control systems easier and faster, also of course based on your knowledge of the controlled plant.

This paper is organized as follow. A brief description of the used fuzzy system are presented in Section 2. Section 3 present fuzzy membership functions. Simulation results are presented in Section 4 with setup of the BLDC motor drive system. Section 5 concludes this paper.

2. Used fuzzy systems

The used fuzzy logic system is a zero-order Takagi-Sugeno fuzzy system which performs a mapping from an input vector $z = [z_1 \quad \cdots \quad z_m] \in \Omega_z \subset \mathbb{R}^m$ to a scalar output variable $y_f \in \mathbb{R}$, where $\Omega_z = \Omega_{z_1} \times \cdots \times \Omega_{z_m}$ and $\Omega_{z_i} \subset \mathbb{R}$. If we define M_i fuzzy sets F_i^j, $j = 1, \ldots, M_i$, for each input z_i, then the fuzzy system will be characterized by a set of if-then rules of the form[5,14]

$$R^k : \text{If } z_1 \text{ is } G_1^k \text{ and...and } z_m \text{ is } G_m^k$$

$$\text{Then } u \text{ is } u^k \ (k = 1,\ldots,N) \tag{1}$$

where $G_i^k \in \left\{F_i^1,\ldots,F_i^{M_i}\right\}$, $i = 1,\ldots,n$, y^k is the crisp output of the k-th rule, and N is the total number of rules.

The FLC can operate either on the actual universes of discourse or on the normalized universes of discourse of the variables. In case of operating on the actual universe of discourse, the FLC has three main stages, as shown in Fig. 7, which are:

1. *Fuzzification*, a process of producing a fuzzy input on the base of a crisp one.
2. *Inference engine and rule-base*, a process of tranforming fuzzy input into a fuzzy output by dealing with fuzzy rules and as a result the response corresponding to the inputs is produced.
3. *Defuzzification*, a process of producing a crisp output on the base of a fuzzy one.

However, in case of operating on the normalized universe of discourse, we add two more stages - one before fuzzification and one after defuzzification -, which are:

1. *Normalization*, a process of mapping the actual value of the input variable to the normalized space of the same variable.
2. *Denormailization*, a process of mapping the normalized value of the output control signal to the actual space of the same output control signal.

By using the singleton fuzzifier, product inference engine, and center-average defuzzifier, the final output of the fuzzy system is given as follows [5]:

$$u_l(z) = \frac{\sum_{k=1}^{N} \mu_k(z) y^k}{\sum_{k=1}^{N} \mu_k(z)} \tag{2}$$

where

$$\mu_k(z) = \prod_{i=1}^{m} \mu_{G_i^k}(z_i) \text{ with } \mu_{G_i^z} \in \left\{\mu_{F_i^1},\ldots,\mu_{F_i^{M_i}}\right\}$$

where $\mu_{F_i^j}(x_i)$ is the membership function of the fuzzy set F_i^j.

By introducing the concept of fuzzy basis function [5], the output given by Eq. (2) can be rewritten in the following compact form:

$$u(z) = w^T(z)\theta \tag{3}$$

where $\theta = \left[w^1,\ldots,w^N\right]^T$ is a vector grouping all consequent parameters, and $w(z) = \left[w_1(z),\ldots,w_N(z)\right]^T$ is a set of fuzzy basis functions defined as

$$w_k(z) = \frac{\mu_k(z)}{\sum_{i=1}^{N} \mu_j(z)}, \ k = 1,\ldots N$$

The fuzzy system (3) is assumed to be well defined so that $\sum_{i=1}^{N} \mu_j(z) \neq 0$ for all $z \in \Omega_z$.

The fuzzy system (3) is a universal approximator of continuous functions over a compact set if its parameters are suitably selected [5].

4. Membership function and slope

In practical control applications, the triangular membership function is generally selected for representing fuzzy sets. Because, in term of real-time requirements by the inference engine, their parametric, functional description of membership function can be easily obtained, stored with minimal use of memory, and manipulated efficiently [11].

A triangular membership function is described by three parameters a, b and c and given by the expression

$$f(x,a,b,c) = \max\left\{\min\left(\frac{x-a}{b-a},\frac{c-x}{c-b}\right),0\right\} \tag{4}$$

where the parameters a and c locate the "feet" of the triangle and the parameter b locates the peak, as shown in Fig. 1

We confine our discussion to a PI like fuzzy controller with triangle membership functions. PI-like fuzzy controllers are so named because their inputs and outputs are equivalent to traditional PI controllers. In a PI-like fuzzy controller, the following parameters can be tuned.

SCALING FACTORS of IF-part/THEN-part fuzzy variables. We define a scaling factor as the maximum peak value, which defines the universe of discourse of the fuzzy variable (Fig. 2).

PEAK VALUE : the value at which the membership function is 1.0 (Fig. 2).

WIDTH VALUE : the interval from the peak value to the point at which membership becomes 0.0 (Fig. 2).

We define the membership functions with equal-interval peak values shown in Fig. 2 as standard membership functions. When the standard membership functions are used on a PI-like fuzzy controller, the relationship between output μ (membership value) and input x (crisp value) can be expressed approximately as follows: (d = width value)

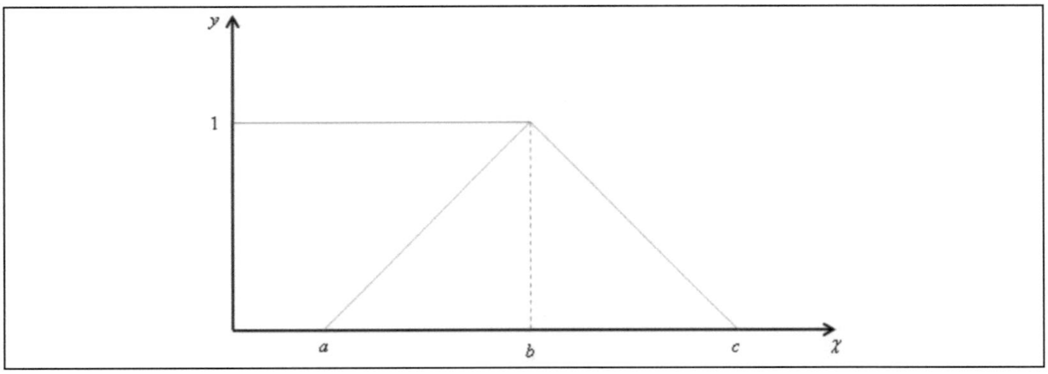

Fig. 1. Triangular Membership Function

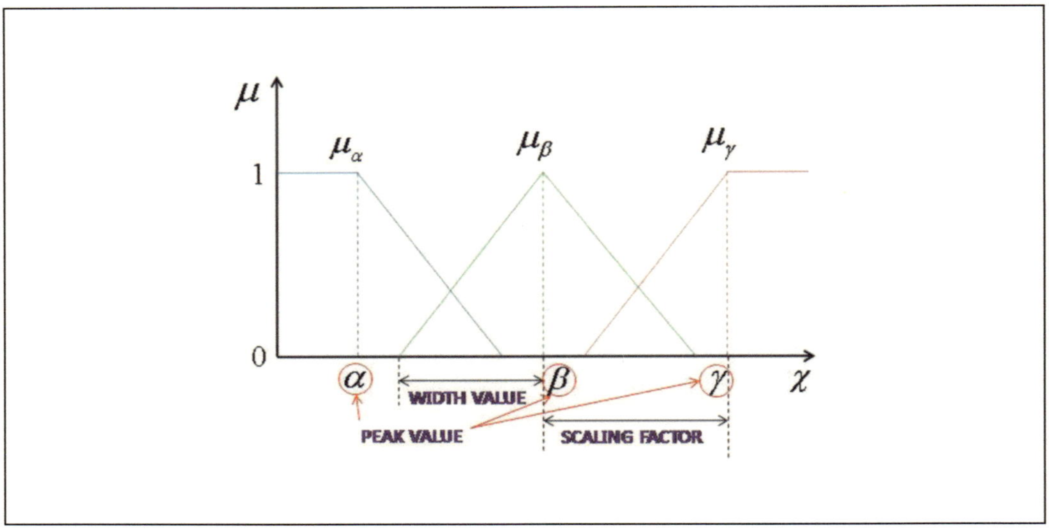

Fig. 2. Scaling Factor of a Membership Function

$$\text{if } x \le a \text{ then} \begin{cases} \mu_\alpha = 1 \\ \mu_\beta \Rightarrow \begin{cases} \text{if } \dfrac{1}{d} \le \beta - x \text{ then } 0 \\ \text{if } \dfrac{1}{d} > \beta - x \text{ then } 1-(\beta - x)d \end{cases} \\ \mu_\gamma \Rightarrow \begin{cases} \text{if } \dfrac{1}{d} \le \gamma - x \text{ then } 0 \\ \text{if } \dfrac{1}{d} > \gamma - x \text{ then } 1-(\gamma - x)d \end{cases} \end{cases} \tag{5}$$

$$\text{if } \alpha < x \le \beta \text{ then} \begin{cases} \mu_\alpha = \begin{cases} \text{if } \dfrac{1}{d} \le x - \alpha \text{ then } 0 \\ \text{if } \dfrac{1}{d} > x - \alpha \text{ then } 1\text{-}(x - \alpha)d \end{cases} \\ \mu_\beta = \begin{cases} \text{if } \dfrac{1}{d} \le \beta - x \text{ then } 0 \\ \text{if } \dfrac{1}{d} > \beta - x \text{ then } 1\text{-}(\beta - x)d \end{cases} \\ \mu_\gamma = \begin{cases} \text{if } \dfrac{1}{d} \le \gamma - x \text{ then } 0 \\ \text{if } \dfrac{1}{d} > \gamma - x \text{ then } 1\text{-}(\gamma - x)d \end{cases} \end{cases} \tag{6}$$

$$\text{if } \beta < x \le \gamma \text{ then } \begin{cases} \mu_\alpha = \begin{cases} \text{if } \dfrac{1}{d} \le x - \alpha \text{ then } 0 \\ \text{if } \dfrac{1}{d} > x - \alpha \text{ then } 1\text{-}(x-\alpha)d \end{cases} \\ \mu_\beta = \begin{cases} \text{if } \dfrac{1}{d} \le x - \beta \text{ then } 0 \\ \text{if } \dfrac{1}{d} > x - \beta \text{ then } 1\text{-}(\beta - x)d \end{cases} \\ \mu_\gamma = \begin{cases} \text{if } \dfrac{1}{d} \le \gamma - x \text{ then } 0 \\ \text{if } \dfrac{1}{d} > \gamma - x \text{ then } 1\text{-}(\gamma - x)d \end{cases} \end{cases} \tag{7}$$

$$\text{if } \gamma < x \text{ then } \begin{cases} \mu_\alpha = \begin{cases} \text{if } \dfrac{1}{d} \le x - \alpha \text{ then } 0 \\ \text{if } \dfrac{1}{d} > x - \alpha \text{ then } 1\text{-}(x-\alpha)d \end{cases} \\ \mu_\beta = \begin{cases} \text{if } \dfrac{1}{d} \le x - \beta \text{ then } 0 \\ \text{if } \dfrac{1}{d} > x - \beta \text{ then } 1\text{-}(\beta - x)d \end{cases} \\ \mu_\gamma = 1 \end{cases} \tag{8}$$

where d is membership function's slope

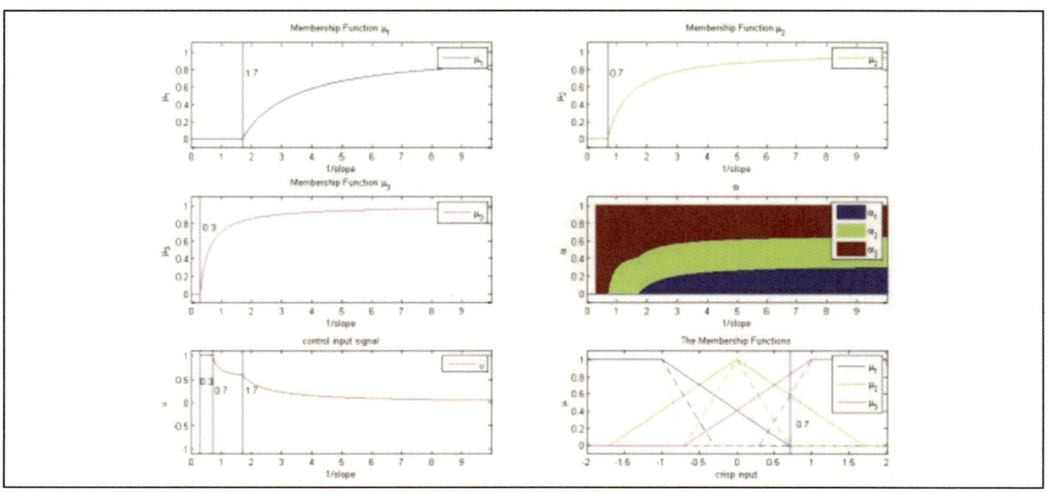

Fig. 3. Different Slopes

$$w_a = \frac{\mu_\alpha}{\mu_\alpha + \mu_\beta + \mu_\gamma}, \; w_\beta = \frac{\mu_\beta}{\mu_\alpha + \mu_\beta + \mu_\gamma}, \; w_\gamma = \frac{\mu_\gamma}{\mu_\alpha + \mu_\beta + \mu_\gamma} \tag{9}$$

$$u = \frac{\mu_\alpha \alpha + \mu_\beta \beta + \mu_\gamma \gamma}{\mu_\alpha + \mu_\beta + \mu_\gamma} = w_\alpha \alpha + w_\beta \beta + w_\gamma \gamma \tag{10}$$

5. Simulation results

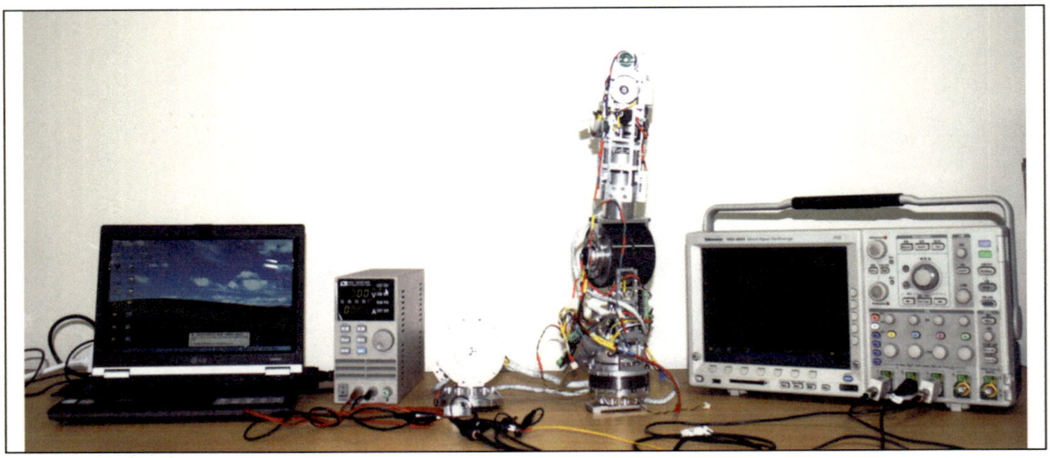

Fig. 4. BLDC Test Platform

3.1 Control system setup

We will assume the following values for the physical parameters. These values were derived by Maxon Motor Catalog.

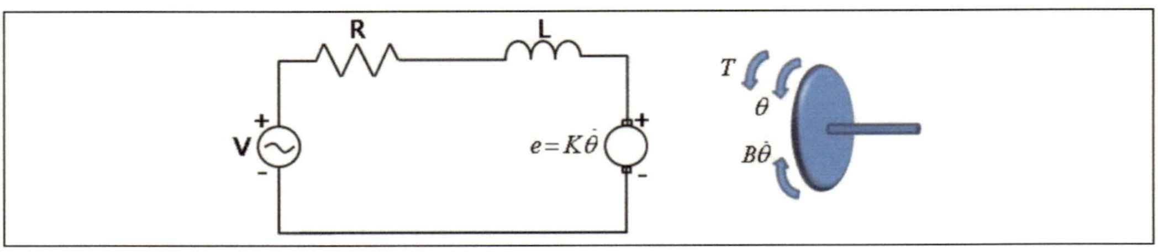

Fig. 5. The electric circuit of the armature and the free body diagram of the rotor.

The motor torque, $T(t)$, is related to the armature current, i, by a constant factor K_T. $T_L(t)$ is load torque. The back emf, e, is related to the rotational velocity by the following equations:

$$T(t) = K_T i \tag{11}$$

$$e = K_e \dot{\theta}$$

In SI units (which we will use), K_T (armature constant) is equal to K_e (motor constant).

From the figure above we can write the following equations based on Newton's law combined with
Kirchhoff's law:

$$J\ddot{\theta} - B\dot{\theta} = K_T i$$

$$L\frac{di}{dt} + Ri = V - K_e\dot{\theta} \qquad (12)$$

Using Laplace Transforms, the above modeling equations can be expressed in terms of s

$$s(Js + B)\theta(s) = K_T I(s)$$

$$(Ls + R)I(s) = V - Ks\theta(s)$$

By eliminating $I(s)$ we can get the following open-loop transfer function, where the rotational speed is the output and the voltage is the input.

$$\frac{\dot{\theta}}{V} = \frac{K}{(Js + B)(Ls + R) + K^2} \qquad (13)$$

In the state-space form, the equations above can be expressed by choosing the rotational speed and electric current as the state variables and the voltage as an input. The output is chosen to be
the rotational speed.

$$\frac{d}{dt}\begin{bmatrix}\dot{\theta} \\ i\end{bmatrix} = \begin{bmatrix} -\frac{B}{J} & \frac{K}{J} \\ -\frac{K}{L} & -\frac{R}{L}\end{bmatrix}\begin{bmatrix}\dot{\theta} \\ i\end{bmatrix} + \begin{bmatrix}0 \\ \frac{1}{L}\end{bmatrix}V \qquad (14)$$

$$\dot{\theta} = \begin{bmatrix}1 & 0\end{bmatrix}\begin{bmatrix}\dot{\theta} \\ i\end{bmatrix}$$

And, the block diagram of BLDC motor drive system is shown in Fig.6.

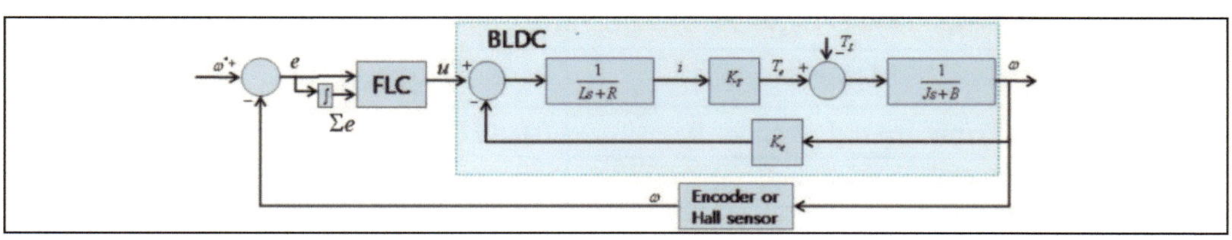

Fig. 6. The block diagram of BLDC motors drive system.

Figure 7 shows the general structure of a FLC which accepts the input variables, process state variables, as crisp values and produce an output control signal, process input, also as crisp values [18]. The input variables are selected among:

1. *Error signal, denoted by* e *;*
2. *Sum of errors or error integral, denoted by* $\sum e$ *;*

The output control signals are selected among:

3. *Control output, denoted by* u *.*

This controller describes with the aid of fuzzy if-then rules the relationship between the control output $u(k)$ on the one hand, and the error $e(k)$ and its sum $\sum e(k)$ on the other hand as shown in Fig. 7.

$$u(k) = f\left[e(k), \sum e(k)\right]$$

This can be seen as a mapping of the pair $e(k)$ and $\sum e(k)$ to the corresponding control output $u(k)$. This is similar to the well-known conventional PI controller described by the equation:

$$u(k) = K_P e(t) + K_I \int_0^t e(t)dt$$

In the case of conventional PI controller, the relationship is linear, while in PI-like FLC it is nonlinear in general[18].

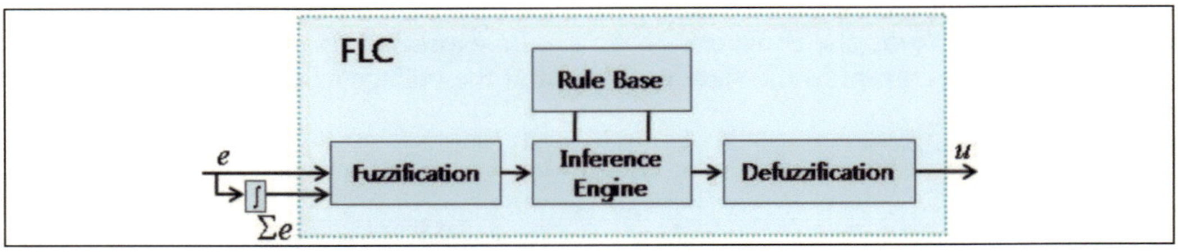

Fig. 7. The block diagram of a basic Fuzzy control system.

Specifications	Units
Number of poles	1
Moment of inertia, J	0.00000512 $kg\,m^2/s^2$
Viscous damping constant, B	0.00057875 Nms
Torque constant, K_T	0.028 Nm/Amp
Back-EMF constant, K_e	0.028 Nm/Amp
Armature inductance, L	0.000186 H
Terminal resistance, R	1.35 Ω
Rated speed	6540 rpm
Rated torque	0.088 Nm
Rated current	3.39A

Table 1. MOTOR RATINGS

3.2 B. Simulation results

μ_{α_1}, μ_{α_2} 's slope	μ_{β_1}, μ_{β_2} 's slope	μ_{γ_1}, μ_{γ_2} 's slope		
		0.5	1	2
0.5	0.5	0.312	0.731	0.422
	1	0.296	0.1	0.116
	2	0.279	0.128	0.155
1	0.5	0.758	0.192	0.067
	1	0.103	0.065	0.066
	2	0.132	0.181	0.065
2	0.5	0.448	0.036	0.066
	1	0.114	0.036	0.066
	2	0.118	0.035	0.065

Table II. Settling time Unit : second

	Sum of Error			
Error	$\sum e$ / e	μ_α	μ_β	μ_γ
	μ_α	0	0.3	0.6
	μ_β	0.7	1	1.3
	μ_γ	1.4	1.7	2

Table III. Rule Table

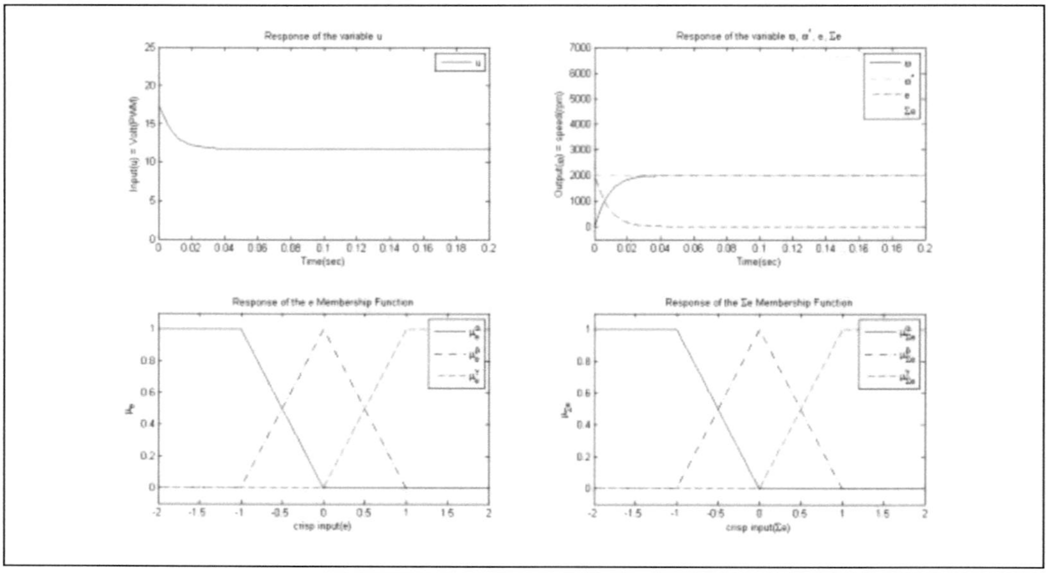

Fig. 8. μ_e^{α} , $\mu_{\sum e}^{\alpha}$, μ_e^{β} , $\mu_{\sum e}^{\beta}$, μ_e^{γ} , $\mu_{\sum e}^{\gamma}$'s slope = [1, 1, 1, 1, 1, 1]

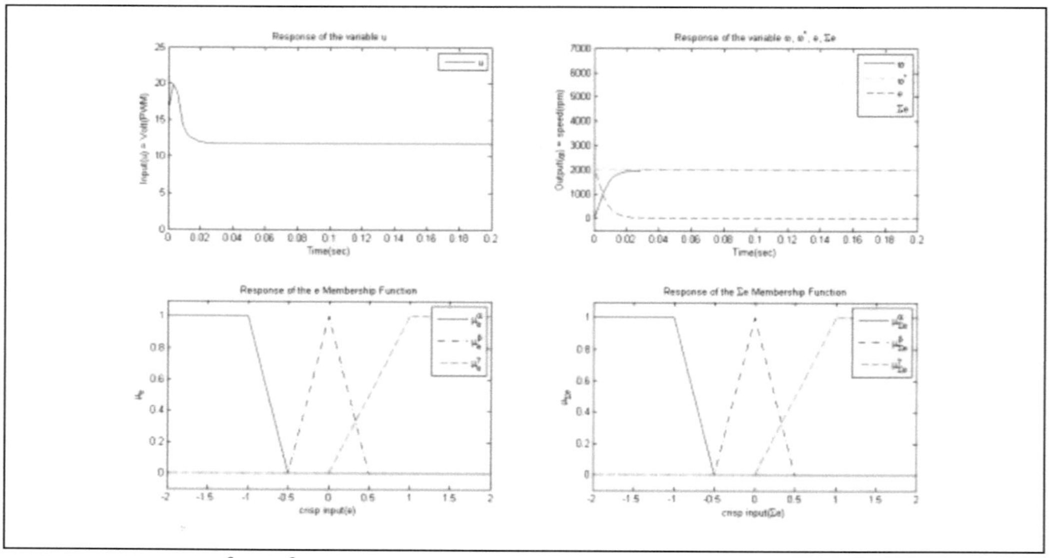

Fig. 9. μ_e^{α} , $\mu_{\sum e}^{\alpha}$, μ_e^{β} , $\mu_{\sum e}^{\beta}$, μ_e^{γ} , $\mu_{\sum e}^{\gamma}$'s slope = [2, 2, 2, 2, 1, 1]

6. Conclusions

This paper has focused on the effect of fuzzy membership function's slope for PI-like fuzzy control system. We use three membership functions to construct a fuzzy system. It was also proven that the fuzzy system guarantees that the output converged to the desired value. We confirmed that increasing the slopes of the triangular membership functions (left and center) for fuzzifying the error and the sum of error can improve the starting and steady state performance of the BLDC motor drive system. It is also observed that changing of the slope of the membership functions (right) for fuzzifying the error and the sum of the error has a detrimental effect on the performance.

7. References

H. 0. Wang; K. Tanaka & M. Griffin (1996). *An Approach to Fuzzy Control of Nonlinear Systems: Stability and Design Issues*, IEEE Transaction on Fuzzy Systems, Vol.4, No.1,

J. P. Su; C. Y. Liang & H. M. Chen (2002) *Robust Cotrol of a Class of Nonlinear Systems and Its Application to a Twin Rotor MIMO System*, Proceedings of the 2002 IEEE International Conference on Industrial Technology

K. Tanaka & M. Sano (1994) *A Robust stabilization problem of fuzzy control systems and its application to backing up control of a truck-trailer*, IEEE Trans. Fuzzy Systems, Vol.2, No.2, pp.1 19-134

H. N. Wu (2004) *Reliable LQ Fuzzy Control for Continuous-Time Nonlinear Systems With Actuator Faults*, IEEE Transactions on Systems, Man, and Cybernetics-Part B. Cybernetic, Vol.34, No.4

L . X . Wang (1994) *Adaptive Fuzzy Systems and Control: Design and Stability Analysis*, Prentice-Hall, Englewood Cliffs, NJ,

C.T. Lin; C.W. Hung & C.W. Liu. (2007) *Fuzzy PI Controller for BLDC motors Considering Variable Sampling Effect* , IECON, pp. 1180 - 1185

L. A. Zadeh. (1965) *Fuzzy Sets*, Information an Control, Vol. 8, pages 338-353

E. H. Mamdani & S. Assililan. (1975) *An Experiment in Linguistic Systhesis with Fuzzy Logic Controller*, Int. Jour. Man Mach. Studies, VO1.7, pp. 1-13

Sugeno. M. & M. Nishida (1985) *Fuzzy control of model car*, Fuzzy Sets and Systems, pp. 103-113

Shi. Y & Scn. P.C (2000) *Effects of Different Slopes of Membership Functions on the Fuzzy Control of DC-DC Converters*, IPEMC, pp.1160 - 1165 vol.3

D. Driankov; H. Hellendoom & M. Reinfrank. (1996) *An Introduction to Fuzzy Control*, Second Edition, Springer Publication, pp. 115-126

C. C. Lee (1990) *Fuzzy Logic in Control Systems: Fuzzy Logic Controller- Part I and 11*, IEEE Trans. Sys. Man Cybem., v01.20 N0.2, pp.404-435

L.X.Wang (1997) *A Course in Fuzzy Systems and Control*, Prentice-Hall, Upper Saddle River, NJ

S. Labiod & M.S. Boucherit (2003) *Direct stable fuzzy adaptive control of a class of SISO nonlinear systems*, Arch. Control Sci. 13 (1) 95 - .110

Y.F. Li & C.C. Lau (1989) *Development of fuzzy algorithms for servo system*, IEEE Control Systems Magazine 9 3, pp. 65 - 72

T.Takagi & M.Sugeno (1985) *Fuzzy identification of systems and its applications to modeling and control*, IEEE Trans. Syst, Man Cybern., vol.SMC-15, no.1, pp.116-132

Chowdhuri. S ; Biswas. S.K & Mukherjee. A (2006) *Performance Studies of Fuzzy Logic Based PI-like Controller Designed for Speed Control of Switched Reluctance Motor*, Industrial Electronics and Applications, 1ST IEEE Conference, pp.1-5

R.R. Yager & D. P. Filev (1994) *Essentials of Fuzzy Modeling and Control*, John Wiley & Sons, New York

11

Control of Atomic Force Microscope Based on the Fuzzy Theory

Amir Farrokh Payam[1], Eihab M. Abdel Rahman[2] and Morteza Fathipour[1]
[1]*Nanoelectronics Center of Exellence, Department of Electrical and Computer Engineering, University of Tehran, Tehran*
[2]*Department of Systems Design Engineering, University of Waterloo, Waterloo, ON*
[1]*Iran*
[2]*Canada*

1. Introduction

The atomic force microscope (Binnig *et al.*, 1986) utilizes a sharp tip moving over the surface of a sample in a raster scan mode to measure the topography and material properties of the surface. The tip is located at the free end of a cantilever microbeam (probe) which bends in response to the interaction forces between the tip and the sample. An estimate of the microbeam stiffness is used to determine the interaction forces from measurements of these deflections.

A precision positioning device, usually made of a piezoelectric tube, is used to move the tip or the sample. AFMs can be operated in one of two principal modes: (i) with feedback control or (ii) without feedback control. Though widely practiced, open-loop operation has the potential for chaotic probe tip response, thus rendering erroneous topographical information. Therefore, in a typical imaging operation the cantilever deflection is maintained at a set point by means of a feedback controller, while scanning the sample surface. The control effort is used as a measure of the sample surface profile. Actuator creep, hysteresis, probe vibrations, modeling errors, and nonlinearities are major sources of error in AFM measurements (Barret & Quate, 1991; Devasia et al., 2007; Jung 7 Gwon, 2000).

In addition to analytical methodologies for compensation of the above mentioned errors, feedback control strategies have been developed in order to improve AFM region of operation. Conventional PD, PI, and PID feedback controllers of the AFM probe were presented in (Ashhab *et al.*, 1999) and (Sinha, 2005). Two nonlinear control techniques using a learning-based algorithm were presented in (Fang *et al.*, 2005). H_∞ and Glover-McFarlane controllers (Sebastian *et al.*, 2003), (Salapaka *et al.*, 2005) were also designed to achieve high bandwidth and robustness during AFM scanning. Other controllers based on inverse model control and combinations of feedforward and feedback and L_1 and H_∞ controllers were proposed to increase the scanning speed and overcome nonlinear effects in piezoelectric actuation (Jalili *et al.*, 2004; Leang & Devasia, 2007; Pao *et al.*, 2007; Rafai & Toumi, 2004; Salapaka *et al.*, 2002; Schitter *et al.*, 2004; Schitter *et al.*, 2004; Sebastian *et al.*, 2007).

Although these methods can overcome modeling errors and have the robustness to overcome some parameter variations, they provide limited vibration compensation. In addition, in most of these methods, design complexity is combined with the use of linear

system models extracted from experimentally-measured frequency-response curves. For this reason, they neglect the nonlinear dynamics of the system and the control system is only locally stable.
The design of fuzzy controllers is simpler and faster than conventional controllers, especially in the presence of nonlinear dynamics or uncertainties where the system is not a well-posed linear system. Fuzzy control handles the nonlinearities and uncertainties of the system using rules, membership functions, and the inference process. In addition, when uncertainties or complex dynamics, which can not be modeled easily, are present in the system, the use of a fuzzy system to model the system and design the controller gives the designer the ability to implement the controller on a simple system model and extend it later to more complex or more practical systems. Moreover, fuzzy controller has an improved performance, a simpler implementation, and a reduced design and implementation cost.
In this chapter, we present an efficient PD-fuzzy controller that improves the operating characteristics of AFMs by increasing the bandwidth of the feedback controller, thereby allowing for faster scan rates and higher resolutions. We present the AFM system model in section 2, a basic fuzzy controller in section 3, our hybrid PD-fuzzy controller in section 4, and a comparative study for the performance of the two controllers and a high-gain PD controller proposed in (Leang & Devasia, 2007) in section 5. Finally, in section 6 we provide concluding remarks.

2. System model

The dynamics of the probe-sample system in an AFM can be modeled by the following lumped-mass system (Sinha, 2005):

$$m\ddot{x} + b\dot{x} + kx + F(x) = u \tag{1}$$

where x denotes the tip displacement, m, b, and k denote the probe mass, damping coefficient, and stiffness, respectively, u(t) represents the controller force input, and F(x) denotes the interaction forces between the tip and surface defined by (Ashhab *et al.*, 1999):

$$F(x) = \frac{Dk}{(z_0 + x)^2} - \frac{\sigma^6 Dk}{30(z_0 + x)^8} \tag{2}$$

z_o is the cantilever tip equilibrium position, σ denotes the molecular diameter, D is defined as:

$$D = \frac{A_H R}{6k} \tag{3}$$

A_H is the Hamaker constant, and R is the tip radius. A schematic of the probe and sample system is shown in Figure 1.
The tip displacement $x(t)$ is measured with respect to the equilibrium position zo. To prevent contact between the tip and the surface, it is constrained by following inequality [5]:

$$(z_0 + x) \geq R \tag{4}$$

A block diagram of the AFM feedback control system is shown in Figure 2.

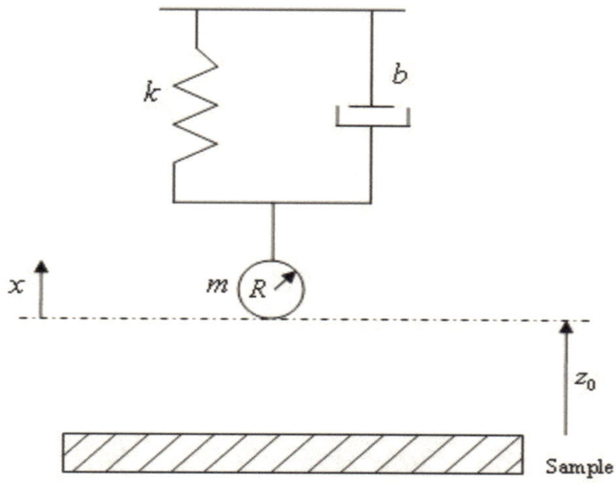

Fig. 1. A schematic of the AFM as a 1-DOF harmonic oscillator.

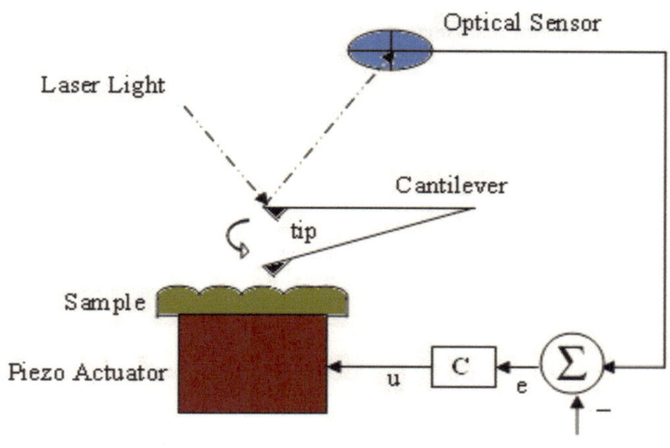

Fig. 2. A schematic of the AFM feedback control system.

3. Design of the basic fuzzy controller

The first step in the design of the fuzzy controller is to determine the inputs and outputs of the fuzzy system. The error between the reference and actual tip position e(t) and its time derivative $\dot{e}(t)$ are taken as the system inputs and the controller input force u(t) is taken as the fuzzy system output. The linguistic variables listed in table 1 are chosen to represent the size of the inputs and output. The shape of membership functions of these rules has a key role in the controller design.Although trapezoidal and bell-curve functions are used in fuzzy control systems, the triangular function is computationally simpler. Other important factors in the design membership functions are the number of curves and their position. The membership functions for each linguistic variable are shown in Figures 3-5. The inputs/output is normalized to vary between -1 and 1 using the scaling boxes Gain(i) and G(i) in the Simulink diagrams, Figures 6 and 7, respectively. The membership functions for the linguistic variables "PS" and "NS" strongly influence the steady state error of the system, whereas the membership functions for the linguistic variables "NB" and "PB" strongly influence the initial undershoot and overshoot, respectively, following a disturbance. The control surface, Figure 3, shows the operation of the fuzzy controller schematically. The magnitude of the controller input force is strongly influenced by both the error and the derivative error.

The rules commanding the fuzzy system response (output) are given in table 2. For example, when the error between the reference and actual tip position and its derivative are "small negative" and "small positive", respectively, the output of the fuzzy controller is a "negative small" force. We selected Mamdani method to design the fuzzy inference engine using "min-function" for "and-method", "max-function" for "or-method", and aggregation. The "bisector-method" was used for defuzzification; that is to transform the fuzzy output to a crisp output.

NB	Negative Big
NS	Negative Small
PS	Positive Small
PB	Positive Big

Table 1. Linguistic Variables for Input/Output.

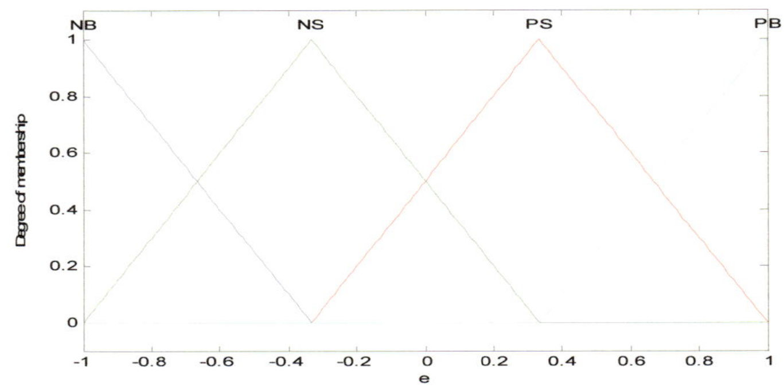

Fig. 3. Error e(t) and input force u(t) membership functions.

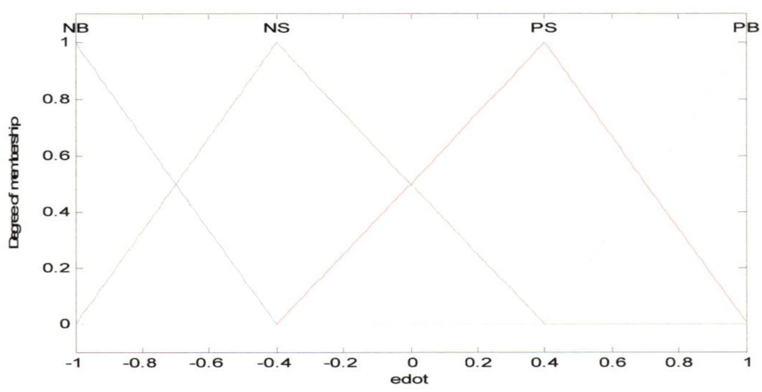

Fig. 4. Error derivative $\dot{e}(t)$ membership function.

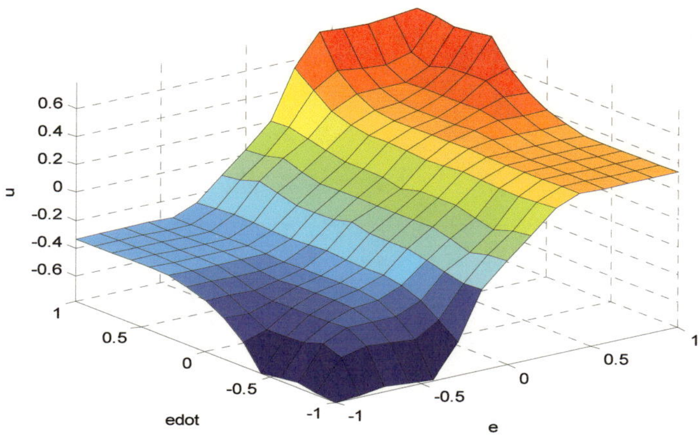

Fig. 5. Control surface of the fuzzy controller.

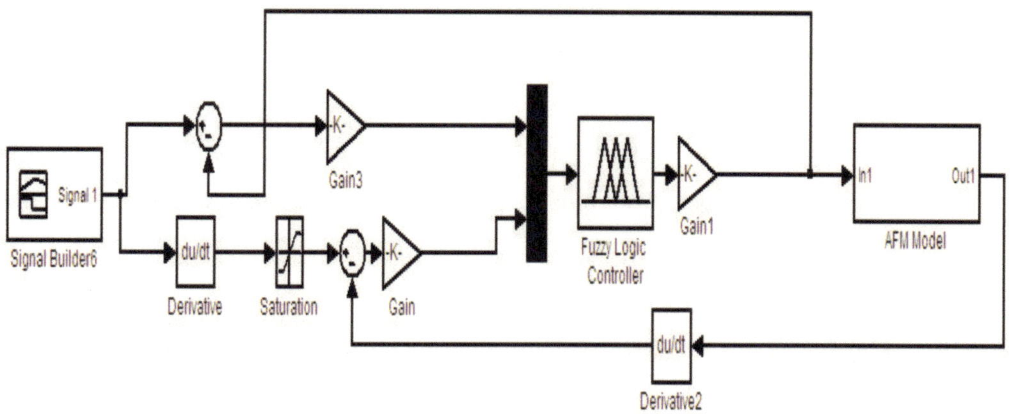

Fig. 6. Simulink block diagram of the system and the fuzzy controller.

$e \backslash \dot{e}$	**NB**	**NS**	**PS**	**PB**
NB	NB	NB	NS	NS
NS	NB	NS	NS	NS
PS	PS	PS	PS	PB
PB	PS	PS	PB	PB

Table 2. Tabulated Fuzzy Rules.

4. Design of the PD-fuzzy controller

To improve the performance of the PD controller proposed in (Leang & Devasia, 2007) against external disturbances and increase the operation bandwidth of the control system, we used Mamdani fuzzy control to design a PD-fuzzy controller that will automatically tune the gains. Figure 7 shows the block diagram of the controller.

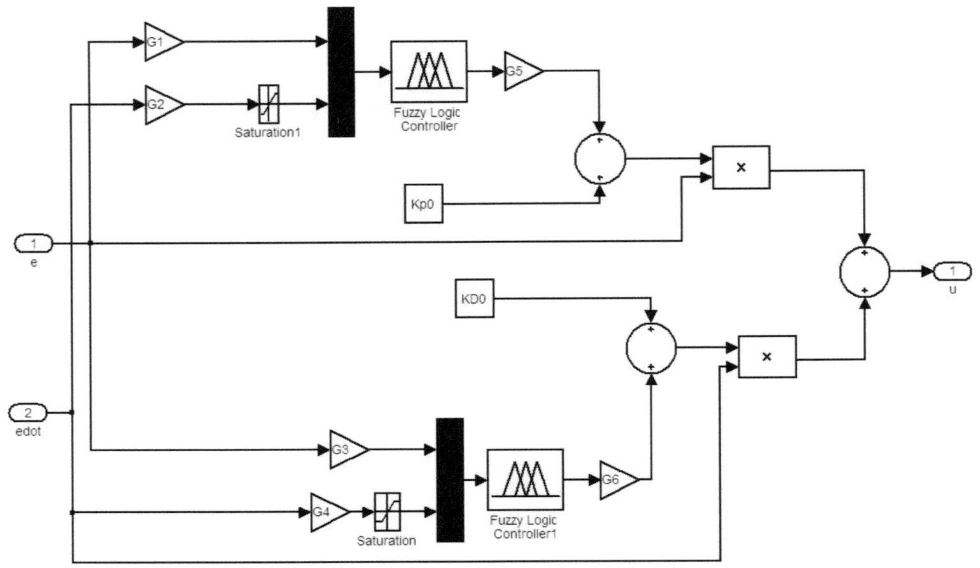

Fig. 7. Block diagram of the PD- fuzzy controller.

In this controller, the standard PD control law:

$$u = u_1 + u_2 \tag{5}$$

where u_1 is the proportional control input and u_2 is the derivative control input, is replaced with:

$$u(t) = (k_{p0} + Fk_p)e(t) + (k_{D0} + Fk_D)\dot{e}(t) \tag{6}$$

where k_{po} = 5000 and k_{Do} = 10 are fixed gains acting as the nominal values of the PD controller. The value of Fk_P and Fk_D are to be determined by fuzzy logic based on the system inputs and added to the nominal gains. Figure 7 shows the manner of adding fuzzy parts of proportional and derivative parts of the PD-Fuzzy control input. After that Fk_P and Fk_D are constructed by fuzzy logic section they are added to fixed proportional and derivative gains. The fuzzy logic part of the system is designed to improve the robustness of the PD control system against parameter uncertainties and external disturbances. Table 3 lists the scaling factors which are shown in Figure 7 and used in the PD-Fuzzy control system. Figures 8-10 show the membership functions of the inputs and output of the hybrid PD-Fuzzy controller. Figure 11 shows the control surface of the controller. The error input dominates the output of the fuzzy control indicating that the fuzzy-side of the controller has to compensate particularly for deficiencies in proportional gain.

G_1=4e7	G_2=1250	G_3=8e6
G_4=250	G_5=10000	G_6=100

Table 3. Scaling Factors.

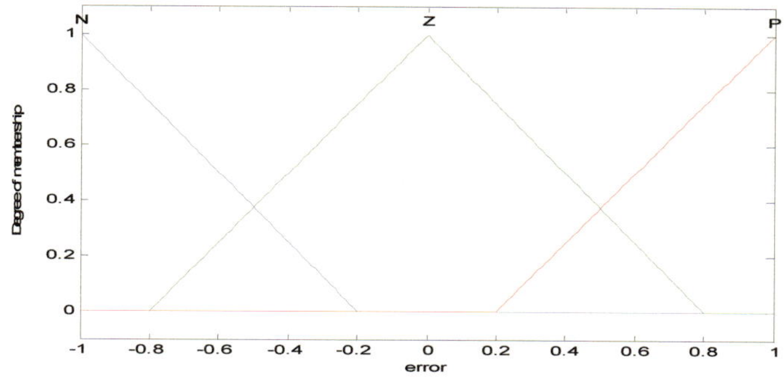

Fig. 8. Error membership functions for the PD-Fuzzy controller.

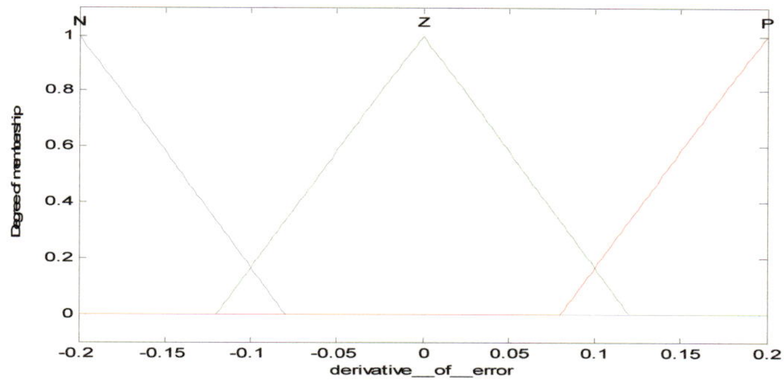

Fig. 9. Error derivative membership functions for the PD-Fuzzy controller.

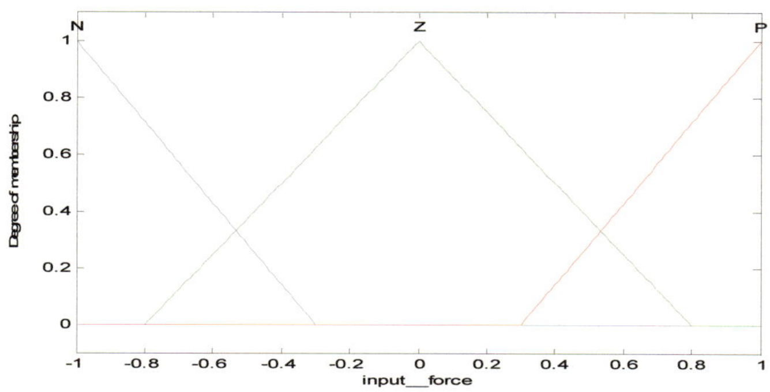

Fig. 10. Output membership functions for the PD-Fuzzy controller.

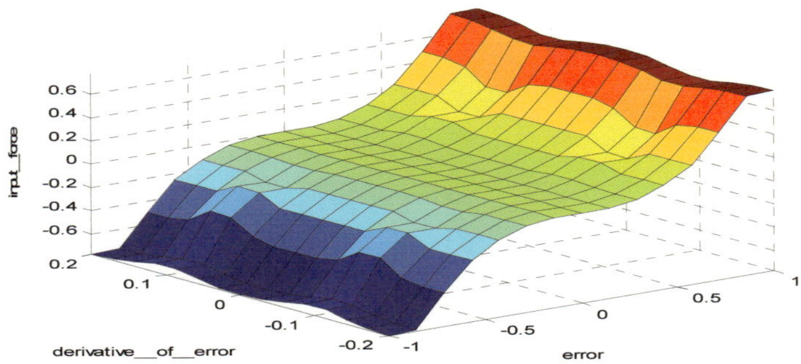

Fig. 11. Control surface of the PD-Fuzzy controller.

5. Results

A set of simulated tests was designed to compare the efficiency of the proposed controllers against that of the controller proposed in (Leang & Devasia, 2007). The tests were conducted on an AFM probe [19] with the following specifications: Length=225 μm, Width=45 μm, Thickness=2.5 μm, and tip radius R = 5 nm. Also, $\rho = 2330\ kg / m^3$ and $E^* = 1.69 \times 10^{11}\ N / m^2$. According to these dimensions and parameters, the lumped stiffness was found by:

$$k = \frac{3E^* I}{L^3} \tag{7}$$

$$m = \rho L A \tag{8}$$

So, m=5.89e-11 Kg and k = 2.6 N/m and f=33.5 KHz. We conducted three sets of tests imposing progressively more stringent demands on the controllers' performance.

5.1 Test one

The controller performance was investigated for a sinusoidal terrain and sinusoidal tip displacement trajectory for a range of scan rates from 0.3 μm/s to 15 μm/s. The AFM is traversing in the sinusoidally varying grating with a pitch of 10 nm, resulting in frequencies of encounter varying from 30 Hz to 1500Hz. Figures 12-15 show the tracking-error using the high gain PD controller, the PD-fuzzy, and the fuzzy controllers for 30 Hz, 200 Hz, 500 Hz and 1500Hz, respectively. We found that the tracking-errors of the fuzzy and PD-fuzzy controllers were consistently better than that of the PD controller. In comparison between the fuzzy controller and PD-fuzzy controller, we found that the fuzzy controller had consistently smaller tracking-errors. On the other hand, the fuzzy controller assumes that the plant can supply infinite power, while the PD-fuzzy sets the gains at practically attainable power levels.

However, Figure 13(b) shows that the abrupt gain changes in the PD-fuzzy controller can induce oscillations in the tip position. With this drawback in mind and considering the results obtained in (Salapaka et al., 2005) and (Leang & Devasia, 2007), it is concluded that the PD-fuzzy controller has a very good response that balances error minimization against limiting demands on the plant.

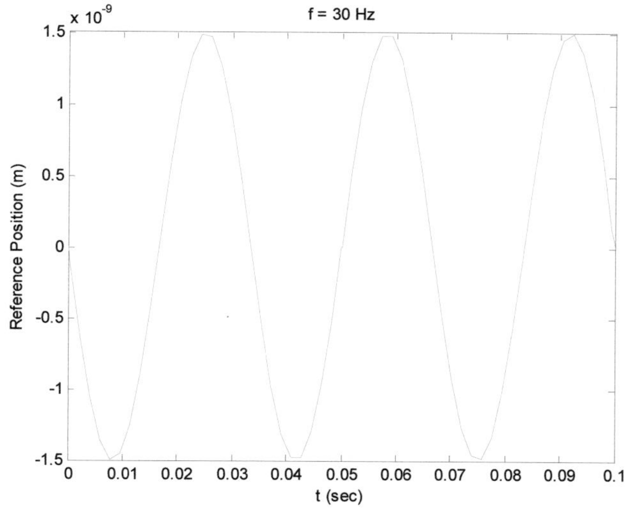

a) Reference signal

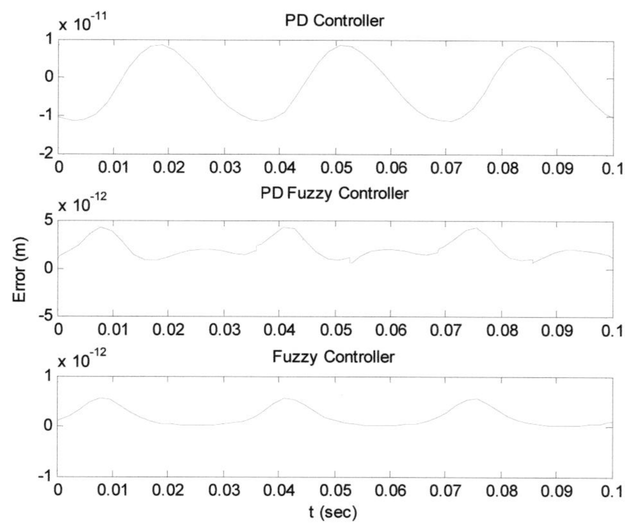

b) Error signals

Fig. 12. Tip tracking-error using PD, PD-Fuzzy, and Fuzzy controllers at an encounter frequency of 30 Hz.

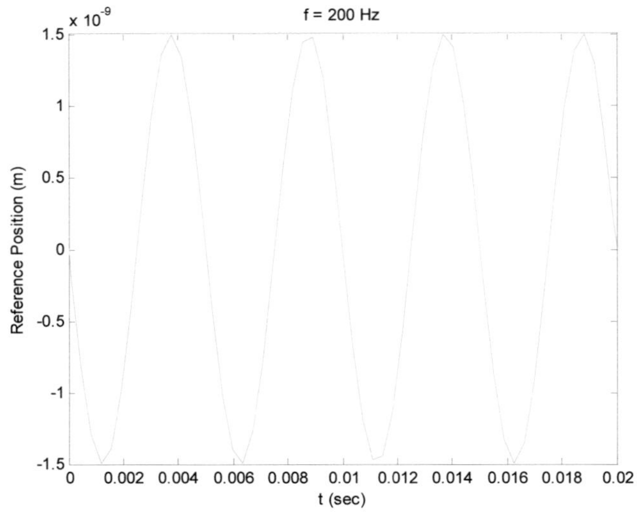

a) Reference signal

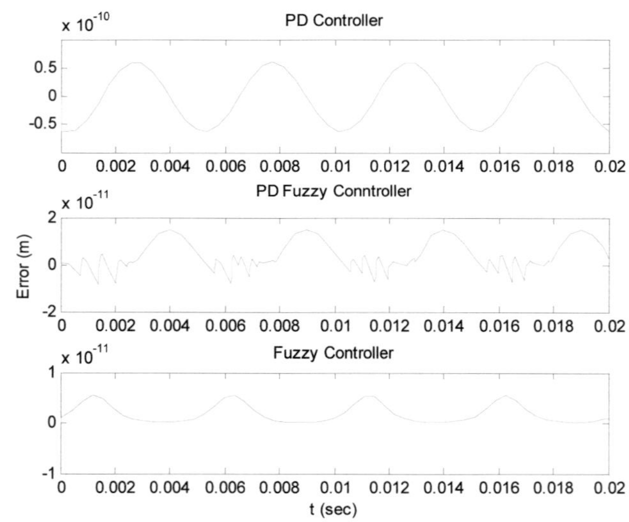

b) Error signals

Fig. 13. Tip tracking-error using PD, PD-Fuzzy, and Fuzzy controllers at an encounter frequency of 200 Hz.

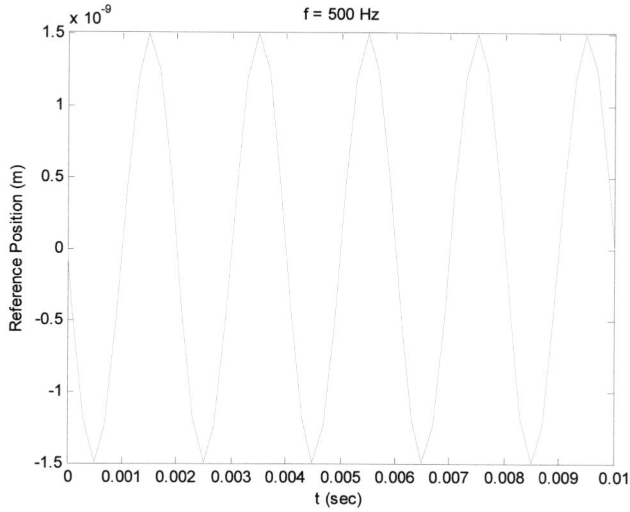

a) Reference signal

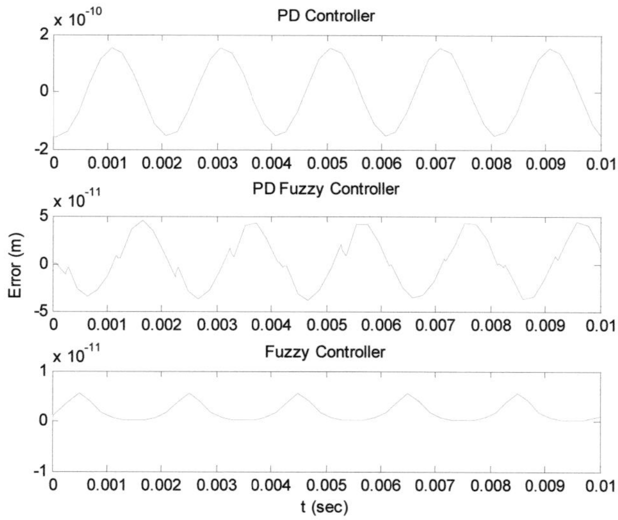

b) Error signals

Fig. 14. Tip tracking-error using PD, PD-Fuzzy, and Fuzzy controllers at an encounter frequency of 500 Hz.

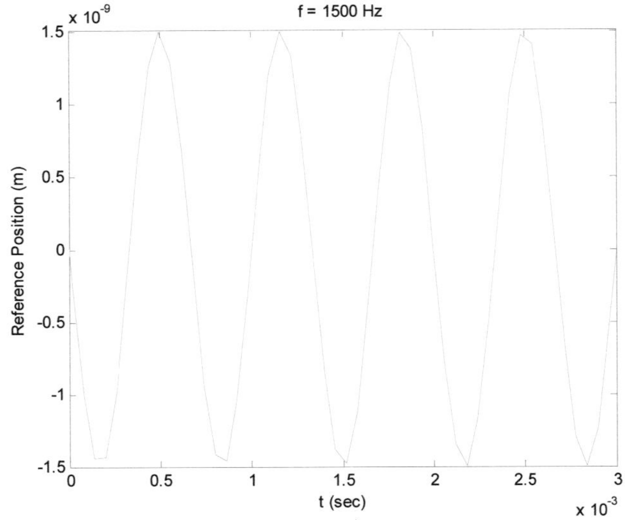

a) Reference signal

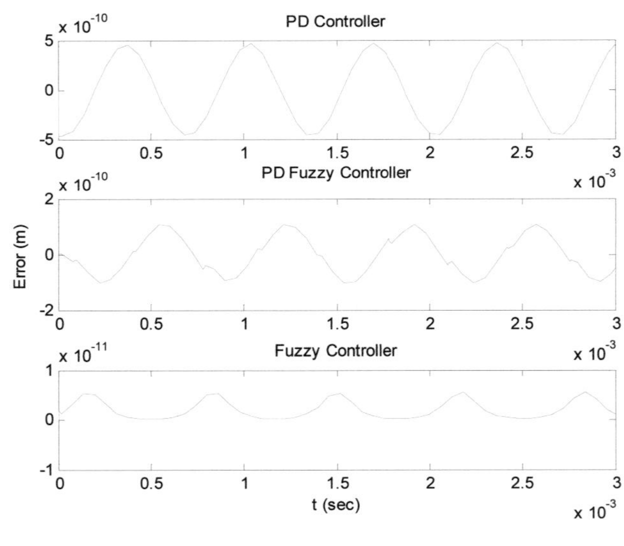

b) Error signals

Fig. 15. Tip tracking-error using PD, PD-Fuzzy, and Fuzzy controllers at an encounter frequency of 1500 Hz.

We use the root-mean-square of the error (erms) (Leang & Devasia, 2007):

$$e_{rms}(\%) = \left(\frac{\sqrt{\frac{1}{T}\int_0^T e^2(t)dt}}{\max(x_{ref}) - \min(x_{ref})} \right) \times 100\% \qquad (7)$$

As a figure-of-merit to quantify the performance of each of the controllers. Tab.4 lists the tracking root-mean-square error for each controller in each of the test cases above as a percentage of the total output range (3 nm). We find that the performance of the fuzzy and fuzz-PD controllers are consistently, at least, one-order of magnitude, better than that of the PD controller.

Frequency (Hz) \ Controller	PD	PD-Fuzzy	Fuzzy
30	.3	.0638	0.044
200	1.53	.14	0.069
500	3.67	.58	0.084
1500	10.12	1.62	0.1

Table 4. Tracking-error performance for sinusoidal trajectories $e_{rms}(\%)$.

5.2 Test two

This simulation examines the tip response to a triangular terrain resulting in the tip displacement trajectories shown in Figures 16(a) and 17(a). The figures show the tracking-error for scan rates of 0.5 μm/s and 2 μm/s, respectively, resulting in encounter frequencies of 50 Hz and 200 Hz. We find that the abrupt position changes in the trajectory result in similar error levels for the PD and the PD-fuzzy controllers that are twice as large as those seen in the fuzzy controller. However, away from these sharp position changes the PD-fuzzy controller performs better than the PD controller. When we compare the results obtained as well as those in (Salapaka *et al.*, 2005) and (Leang & Devasia, 2007), we conclude that both fuzzy and PD-fuzzy controller offer enhanced AFM tip tracking performances.

Tab.5 shows the tracking root-mean-square error for each controller in the two test cases. While the PD-fuzzy controller has smaller errors than that of the PD controller, they are of the same order, whereas the error of the fuzzy controller is one order of magnitude smaller than both of them.

Frequency (Hz)\Controller	PD	PD-Fuzzy	Fuzzy
50	.35	.11	.07
200	1.31	.42	.075

Table 5. Tracking-error performance for triangular trajectories $e_{rms}(\%)$.

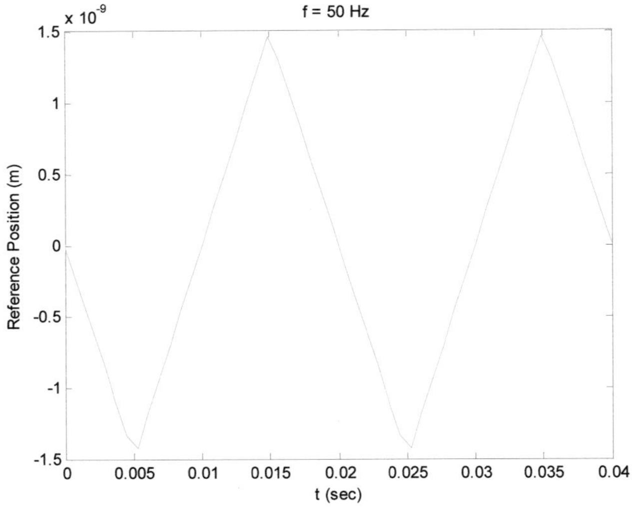

a) Reference signal

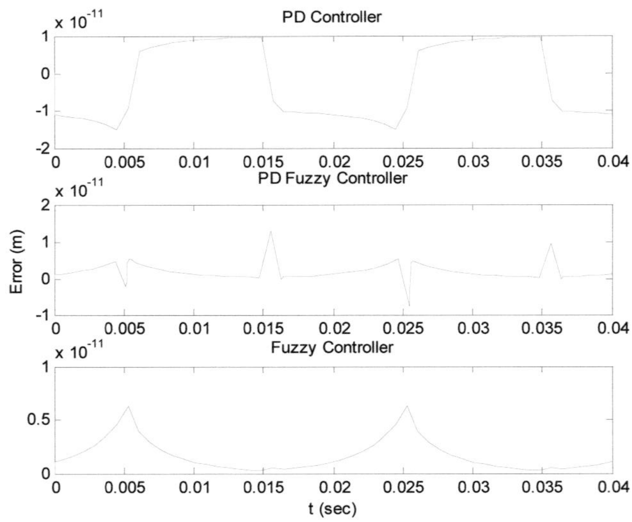

b) Error signals

Fig. 16. AFM response with 50 Hz.

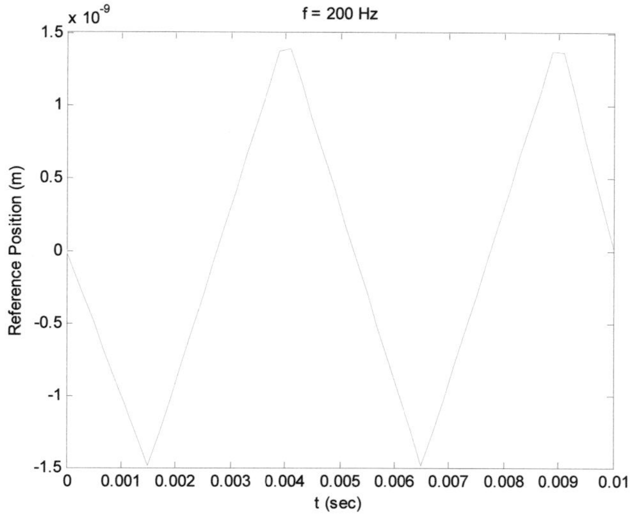

a) Reference signal

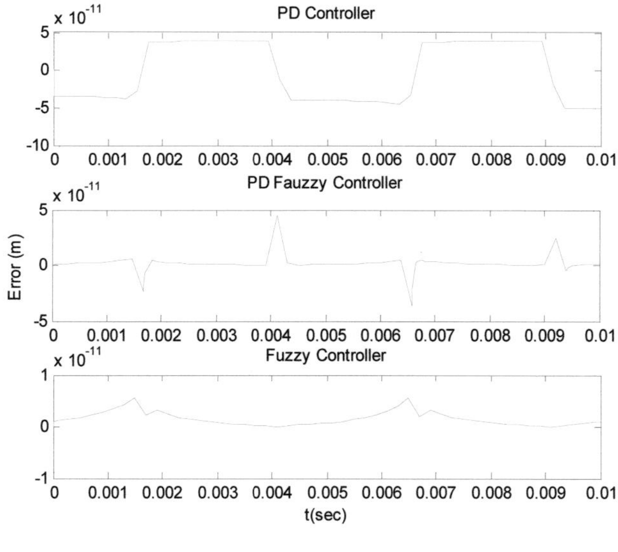

b) Error signals

Fig. 17. AFM response with 200 Hz.

5.3 Test three

We investigate the response of the controllers to a train of sharp terrain changes resulting in a tip trajectory similar to that shown in Figure 18(a), while the AFM is scanning at a rate of 1 μm/s. This condition represents a more general specimen surface with irregular and sharp height changes representing the asperities of the surface. The error in the fuzzy controller is one-order of magnitude smaller than those of the PD and PD-fuzzy controllers. The PD-Fuzzy controller tracking-error is smaller both in absolute and average senses than that of the PD controller as shown in Figure 18(b) and Tab.6, respectively.

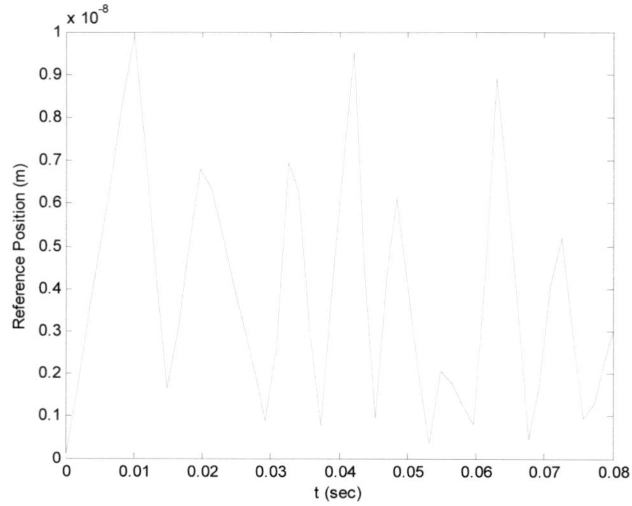

a) Reference signal

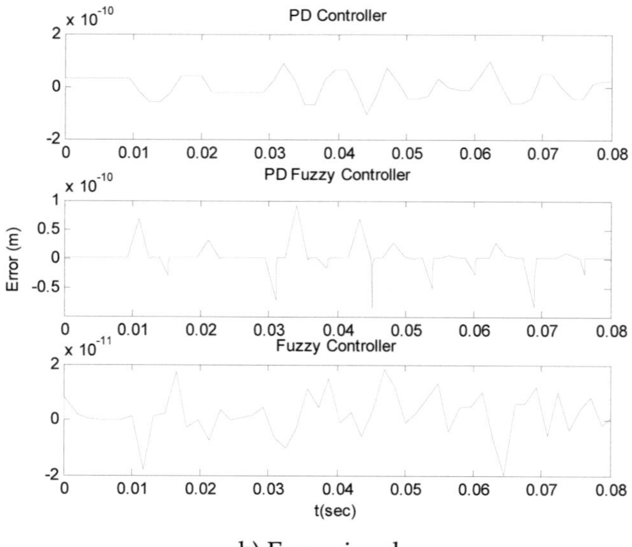

b) Error signals

Fig. 18. AFM response in random reference.

PD	PD-Fuzzy	Fuzzy
.46	.15	.08

Table 6. Tracking-error performance for the random trajectory $e_{rms}(\%)$.

6. Conclusion

In this paper we used fuzzy control theory to design two controllers for closed-loop feedback control of an AFM probe. These controllers are designed based on conventional fuzzy Mamdani control theory and the introduction of a fuzzy controller to a PD controller to tune online the PD gains resulting in a hybrid PD-fuzzy controller. Comparing the results of these controllers and a baseline a high-gain PD controller, we found that the fuzzy controller had the best position-tracking performance. However since it imposes unrealistic power demands on the AFM plant, it was concluded that the PD-fuzzy controller represents the best balance between minimization of the tracking-error and realistic power demands on the plant.

Since the PD-fuzzy controller had smaller tracking-error than other controllers reviewed in this chapter , it allows the AFM to operate at faster scanning rates, resulting in wider bandwidth of encounter frequencies, for the same error tolerance levels. Finally, it was found that the PD-fuzzy controller can induce oscillations in the position of the probe tip. Therefore, we recommend enhancing the PD-fuzzy controller to mitigate this negative effect of abrupt changes in the PD controller gains.

7. References

Ashhab, M.; Salapaka, M.V.; Dahleh, M. & Mezic, I. (1999). Melnikov-Based Dynamical Analysis of Microcantilevers in Scanning Probe Microscopy, *Nonlinear Dynamics*, Vol. 20, PP. 197-220.

Barrett, R. C. & and Quate, C. F. (1991). Optical scan-correction system applied to atomic force microscopy, *Rev. Sci. Instrum.*, Vol. 62, PP. 1393–1399.

Binnig, G.; Gerber, C. & Quate, C. (1986). Atomic force microscope, *Phys. Rev. Lett.*, Vol. 56, PP. 930-933.

Devasia, S.; Eleftheriou, E. & Moheimani, S. O. R. 92007). A Survey of Control Issues in Nanopositioning, *IEEE Trans. Ctrl. Sys. Tech.*, Vol. 15, PP. 802-823.

Fang, Y.; Feemster, M.; Dawson, D. & Jalili, N.M. (2005). Nonlinear control techniques for an atomic force microscope system, *Control Theory & Applications Journal*, Vol. 3, PP. 85-92.

Jalili, N.; Dadfarnia, M. & Dawson, D. M. (2004). A Fresh Insight Into the Microcantilever Sample Interaction Problem in Non-Contact Atomic Force Microscopy, *Journal of Dynamic Systems, Measurement, and Control,* Vol. 126, PP. 327-335.

Jung, H. & Gweon, D. G. (2000). Creep characteristics of piezoelectric actuators, *Rev. Sci. Instrum.*, Vol. 71, PP. 1896–1900.

Leang, K. K. & Devasia, S. (2007). Feedback-Linearized Inverse Feedforward for Creep, Hysteresis, and Vibration Compensation in AFM Piezoactuators, *IEEE Trans. Ctrl. Sys. Tech.*, Vol. 15, PP. 927-935.

Pao, L. Y.; Butterworth, J. A. & Abramovitch, D. Y. (2007). Combined Feedforward/Feedback Control of Atomic Force Microscopes, *Proceedings of the 2007 American Control Conference* , USA, July 2007, New York.

Rifai, O. M. EI. & Toumi, K. Y. (2004). On Automating Atomic Force Microscopes: An Adaptive Control Approach, 43rd *IEEE Conference on Decision and Control,* December 2004 Atlantis, Paradise Island, Bahamas.

Salapaka, S. M.; De, T. & Sebastian, A. (2005). A Robust Control Based Solution to the Sample-Profile Estimation Problem in Fast Atomic Force Microscopy, *Int. J. Robust Nonlinear Control*, Vol. 15, PP. 821–837.

Salapaka, S.M.; Sebastian, A.; Cleveland, J. P. & Salapaka, M. V. (2002). High Bandwidth Nano-Positioner: A Robust Control Approach, *Rev. Sci. Instr.*, 2002.

Schitter, G.; Stark, R. W. & Stemmer, A. (2004). Fast Contact-Mode Atomic Force Microscopy on Biological Specimen by Model-Based Control, *Ultramicroscopy*, Vol. 100, PP. 253-257.

Schitter, G.; Stark, R. W. & Stemmer, A. (2004). Identification and Open- Loop Tracking Control of a Piezoelectric Tube Scanner for High- Speed Scanning-Probe Microscopy, *IEEE Trans. Ctrl. Sys. Tech.*

Schitter, G.; Menold, P. H.; Knapp, H. F.; Allgöwer, F. & Stemmer, A. (2001). High Performance Feedback for Fast Scanning Atomic Force Microscopes, *Rev. Sci. Instr.*, Vol. 72.

Sebastian, A.; Gannepalli, A. & Salapaka, M. V. (2007). A Review of the Systems Approach to the Analysis of Dynamic-Mode Atomic Force Microscopy, *IEEE Trans. Ctrl. Sys. Tech.*, Vol. 15, PP. 952-959.

Sebastian, A.; Salapaka, M.V. & Cleveland, J. P. (2003). Robust Control Approach to Atomic Force Microscopy, *Proceedings of the 42nd IEEE Conference on Decision and Control*, USA, December 2003, Maui, Hawaii.

Sinha, A. (2005). Nonlinear dynamics of atomic force microscope with PI feedback, *Journal of Sound and Vibration*, Vol. 288, PP. 387–394.

12

An Application of Fuzzy Controllers: Autonomic Computing Systems

Harish S. V., Reader, Dept. of CS&E,[1] and
Chandra Sekaran K., Professor, Dept. of CS&E,[2]
[1]Manipal Institute of Technology, Manipal - 576 104,
[2]National Institute of Technology – Karnataka, Surathkal, Mangalore – 575 025, India

1. Introduction

The difficulty of managing today's computing systems goes well beyond the administration of individual software environments. The need to integrate several heterogeneous environments into corporate-wide computing systems, and to extend that beyond company boundaries into the Internet, introduces new levels of complexity. Relying solely on further innovations in programming methods will not get us through the present complexity crisis. The only option remaining is Autonomic Computing - computing systems that can manage themselves given high level objectives from administrators.

An autonomic system has four major characteristics: self-configure, self-heal, self-optimize and self-protect (Salehie & Tahvildari, 2005).

Self-configuring is the capability of adapting automatically and dynamically to environmental changes. This characteristic has two aspects

1. installing, (re-)configuring and integrating large, complex network intensive systems
2. adaptability in architecture or component level to re-configure the system for achieving the desired quality factors.

Self-healing is the capability of discovery, diagnosing and reacting to disruptions. Such a system must be able to recover by detecting a failed component, taking it off-line to be fixed, and replacing the fixed component into the system without any apparent disruption.

Self-optimizing is the capability to efficiently maximize resource allocation and utilization for satisfying requirements of different users. While, in a short term, self-optimizing can address the complexity of managing system performance, in a long run its components will automatically and proactively seek ways to tune their operations and make themselves more cost efficient.

Self-protecting is the capability of reliably establishing trust, and anticipating, detecting and recovering from the effects of attacks with two aspects

1. defending the system against correlated problems arising from malicious attacks or cascading failures that remain uncorrected by self-healing measures
2. anticipating problems based on early reports from sensors and taking steps to avoid or mitigate them.

The autonomic computing architecture (explained later) provides a blue print for developing feedback control loops for self-managing systems. This observation suggests that control theory might provide guidance as to the structure of and requirements for autonomic managers.

Intelligent control emerged as a viable alternative to conventional model-based control schemes because issues such as uncertainty or unknown variations in plant parameters and structure can be dealt with more effectively. This improves the robustness of the control system. One of the ways of developing an intelligent control system is through Fuzzy control. Fuzzy logic offers the important concept of fuzzy set theory, fuzzy if-then rules and approximate reasoning which deals with imprecision and information granularity.

E-commerce is an area where an Autonomic Computing system could be very effectively deployed. E-commerce has created demand for high quality information technology (IT) services and businesses seek ways to improve the quality of service (QoS) in a cost-effective way. Properly adjusting tuning parameters for best values is time-consuming and skills-intensive.

The objectives of this chapter are to minimize response time by maximizing system utilization and also to maximize the profit of an e-commerce system by maximizing system utilization. The outline of the chapter is as follows. Initially the basic concepts of Autonomic Computing, Fuzzy Control and applications of Fuzzy Control to e-commerce system are explained. Then the contributions made in these areas are clearly explained focussing on the methods used.

1.1 Concepts of autonomic computing system

Figure 1.1 depicts the components and key interactions for a single autonomic manager and a single resource. The resource, sometimes called a managed element, is what is being made more self-managing. This could be a single system (or even an application within a system), or it may be a collection of many logically related systems. Sensors provide a way to obtain measurement data from resources, and effectors provide a means to change the behavior of the resource. Autonomic managers read sensor data and manipulate effectors to make resources more self-managing. The autonomic manager contains components for monitoring, analysis, planning, and execution. Common to all of these is knowledge of the computing environment, service level agreements, and other related considerations. The monitoring component filters and correlates sensor data. The analysis component processes these refined data to do forecasting and problem determination, among other activities. Planning constructs workflows that specify a partial order of actions to accomplish a goal specified by the analysis component. The execute component controls the execution of such workflows and provides coordination if there are multiple concurrent workflows. (The term "execute" may be broadened to "enactment" to include manual actions as well.) Scaling is achieved by having a single autonomic manager control multiple resources and by applying the architecture recursively so that lower level managers are treated as resources by higher level managers. In essence, the autonomic computing architecture provides a blue print for developing feedback control loops for self-managing systems. This observation suggests that control theory might provide guidance as to the structure of and requirements for autonomic managers.

1.2 Fuzzy logic concepts

Fuzzy logic refers to a logical system that generalizes classical two valued logic for reasoning under uncertainty. In a broad sense fuzzy logic refers to all the theories that employ fuzzy sets which are classes with boundaries that are not sharply defined.

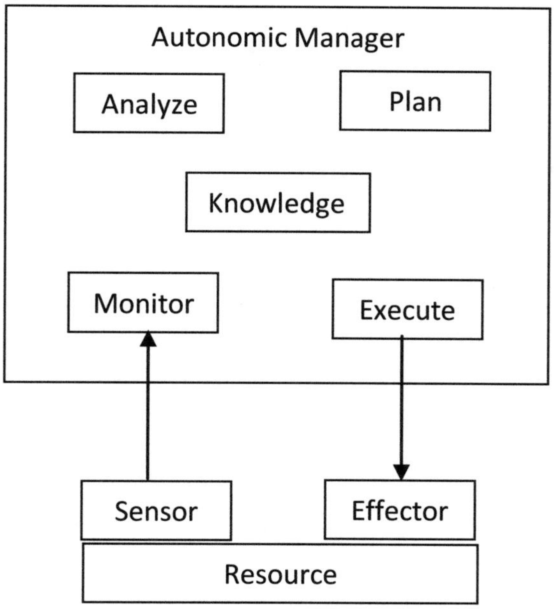

Fig. 1.1. Autonomic Computing architecture

Fuzzy logic is a technology for developing intelligent control. It achieves machine intelligence by offering a way for representing and reasoning about human knowledge that is imprecise by nature. Even though fuzzy logic is not the only technique for developing AI systems, it is unique in its approach for explicit representation of the impreciseness in human knowledge and problem solving techniques. Fuzzy logic offers a practical way for designing nonlinear control systems. It achieves nonlinearity through piece wise linear approximation. The basic building block of a fuzzy logic control system is a set of fuzzy if then rules that approximates a functional mapping.

Fuzzy logic can be used for controlling a process that is too nonlinear or too ill understood to use conventional control designs. It also enables control engineers to easily implement control strategies used by human operators. Briefly fuzzy logic is mainly to deal with complex systems and also for the ease of describing human knowledge.

Fuzzy logic has emerged as a viable alternative to conventional model-based control schemes because issues such as uncertainty or unknown variations in plant parameters and structure can be dealt with more effectively. This improves the robustness of the control system. Fuzzy logic offers the important concept of fuzzy set theory, fuzzy if-then rules and approximate reasoning which deals with imprecision and information granularity.

The three main steps that are part of any fuzzy control system (Yen & Langari, 2005) -

i) Fuzzification ii) Inference mechanism iii) Defuzzification

The heart of the fuzzy controller involves a set of IF-THEN rules stored in a rule base. The rules are expressed using linguistic variables and linguistic values. For example, "IF *temperature* IS *high* THEN *speed* IS *high*". This means, increase the speed of the fan if temperature is high. The terms *temperature* and *speed* are linguistic variables, while *high* is a linguistic value. Linguistic variables exist in one-to-one correspondence with numeric variables. Linguistic variables take on linguistic values that correspond to the values of the corresponding numeric variables. For example, *temperature* can take on values high, medium or low corresponding to the numeric variable for temperature. Converting the input numeric variables into linguistic values of linguistic variables is known as fuzzification. Membership functions are used for the conversion. Next the inference mechanism invokes each appropriate rule, generates a result for each, then combines the results of all the rules. Defuzzification involves converting the combined result back into a specific numeric output value.

1.3 Application of fuzzy control to e-commerce – an overview

E-commerce is one area where an Autonomic Computing system could be very effectively deployed. E-commerce has created demand for high quality information technology (IT) services. For example, a "buy" transaction that takes more than a few seconds may cause the customer to abandon the purchase. As a result, businesses are seeking quality of service (QoS) guarantees from their service providers. (Diao et al., 2002a). These guarantees are expressed as part of service level agreements (SLAs). SLA is a part of a service contract where the level of service is formally defined. It is a contract that exists between customers and their SP, client or between SPs. Many SLAs include specifications (Diao et al., 2001) of:

- revenue that is accrued to the SP for services delivered and
- costs that are incurred by the SP in the form of rebates to customers if previously agreed constraints are violated or the service is unavailable.

An SLA is characterized by a profit model. Consider a profit model described by 3 parameters

1. r, the revenue received for each completed transaction;
2. W, the response time constraint; and
3. c, the cost incurred if a transaction's response time exceeds W (offending transaction)

Thus, Profit = Revenue – Cost, where
Revenue = r * (number of completed transactions)
Cost = c * (number of offending transactions)

Since demand for services is often unpredictable, providers must sometimes make tradeoffs between losing revenue and incurring penalties. Making such choices is skill intensive and time consuming, and the decisions must be made in real time.

An ecommerce system is basically a client server system. The server being the most important part, it is very advantageous if autonomic computing concepts are incorporated into the server. The system studied here is the Apache web server. In Apache version 2.2 (configured to use Multi-Processing Module prefork), there are a number of worker processes monitored and controlled by a master process. The worker processes are responsible for handling the communications with the web clients, including the work required to generate the responses. A worker process handles at most one connection at a time, and it continues to handle only that connection until the connection is terminated. Thus, the worker is idle between consecutive requests from its connected client.

A parameter termed MaxClients limits the size of this worker pool, thereby providing a kind of admission control in which pending requests are kept in the queue. MaxClients should be large enough so that more clients can be served simultaneously, but not so large that resource contention occurs. The optimal value depends on server capacity and the nature of the workload. If MaxClients is too small, there is a long delay due to waits in the queue. If it is too large resources become over utilized which degrades performance as well. The combined effect is that the response time is a concave upward function of MaxClients (Diao et al., 2002a).

The setting of MaxClients can also be carried out by looking at the profits (Diao et al., 2002b). Consider an e-commerce system, in which revenues accrue if the admitted requests are processed within the specified deadline and costs are incurred otherwise. If MaxClients is too small, the number of requests that can be processed in a given interval is small. Though the number of violations and hence, costs will be small (mostly zero), profits will be less because of decreased revenue. As MaxClients increases, revenue increases proportionately till the point where the server gets saturated. Thereafter there will be no further increase in revenue but there will be an increase in costs because of increased violations. The combined effect is that profits are concave downwards in the parameter, MaxClients.

2. Minimizing response time

2.1 Simulation using M/M/1 queue and processes

Here the client server architecture is simulated using an M/M/1 queue and processes. Parameter MaxClients is simulated by max-requests. The response time is minimum for an optimum value of max-requests. In the next subsection, the simulation environment used is described. Later, the design and implementation of a fuzzy controller for optimizing the value of max-requests is presented. This ensures that the response time is minimized.

2.1.1 Simulation environment

A workload generator is used to simulate the generation of requests from many clients. The workload generator generates requests such that the time between generations of consecutive requests is exponentially distributed. The processing of these requests by the server is simulated by a program, in which the parent process creates a child process every time a request is received. Each child process sleeps for a time which is exponentially distributed before exiting. Thus, the client server architecture is simulated here as an M/M/1 queue.

2.1.2 Design and Implementation of Fuzzy Controller

The block diagram of the fuzzy control system is shown in **Figure 2.1**. The fuzzy controller has two inputs: change-in-response-time (dr) and change-in-max-requests (dm) between

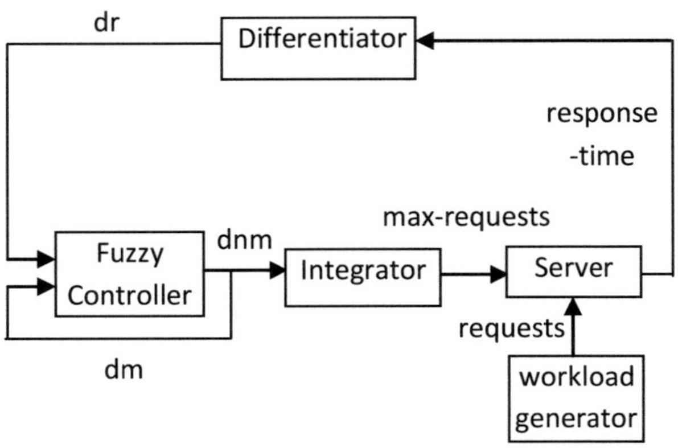

Fig. 2.1. Fuzzy control system – minimizing response time

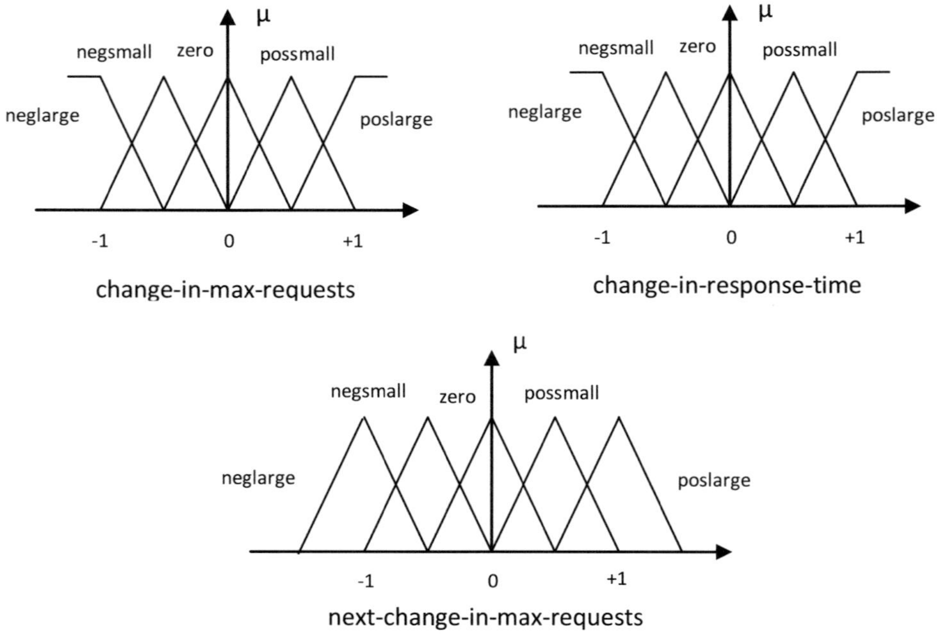

Fig. 2.2. Membership functions – minimizing response time

intervals. The controller's output is next-change-in-max-requests (dnm). An integrator converts this value into max-requests. Next-change-in-max-requests of this interval is taken as change-in-max-requests for the next interval. The value of change-in-response-time is obtained from the differentiator.

The triangular membership functions used for the fuzzification of the inputs and defuzzification of the output are shown in **Figure 2.2**. In each case, the parameter is divided into 5 intervals called neglarge, negsmall, zero, possmall and poslarge. The measured numeric values are multiplied by normalized gains. This is the reason why the x-axis shows -1 and 1 for all the membership functions. Inputs change-in-response-time (dr) and change-in-max-requests (dm) are multiplied by ng-dr and ng-dm respectively. Output is denormalized by multiplying by ng-dnm to obtain next-change-in-max-requests (dnm). Response time is a concave upward function of max-requests. Hence, a gradient descent procedure is used to minimize response times. This is described using fuzzy rules shown in **Table 2.1**.

Since the value of max-requests that minimizes the response-time is not known, these rules are described in terms of changes to max-requests and reponse-times. As an example, consider rule 5. It means that max-requests has been increased by a large amount (in the beginning of the current measurement interval) and it is observed that the response-time has decreased by a large amount by the end of the interval. This means the change to max-requests is in the correct direction. Hence, it is continued to be changed in the same direction. That is, for the next interval, max-requests is increased further. Thus, rules 1 through 10 take care of the correct situations where as rules 16 through 25 handle the incorrect situations. In rules 16 through 25 the previous action caused the response-time to increase, so the direction has to be "reversed". Later the consequents from all the activated rules are weighted using the centre of gravity method to obtain the (normalized) output value.

Rule	IF			THEN
	change-in-max-requests	AND	change-in-response-time	next-change-in-max-requests
1	neglarge	AND	neglarge	neglarge
2	negsmall	AND	neglarge	negsmall
3	zero	AND	neglarge	possmall
4	possmall	AND	neglarge	possmall
5	poslarge	AND	neglarge	poslarge
6	neglarge	AND	negsmall	neglarge
7	negsmall	AND	negsmall	negsmall
8	zero	AND	negsmall	zero
9	possmall	AND	negsmall	possmall
10	poslarge	AND	negsmall	poslarge
11	neglarge	AND	zero	negsmall
12	negsmall	AND	zero	zero
13	zero	AND	zero	zero
14	possmall	AND	zero	zero
15	poslarge	AND	zero	possmall
16	neglarge	AND	possmall	poslarge
17	negsmall	AND	possmall	possmall
18	zero	AND	possmall	zero
19	possmall	AND	possmall	negsmall
20	poslarge	AND	possmall	neglarge
21	neglarge	AND	poslarge	poslarge
22	negsmall	AND	poslarge	possmall
23	zero	AND	poslarge	negsmall
24	possmall	AND	poslarge	negsmall
25	poslarge	AND	poslarge	neglarge

Table 2.1. Fuzzy rules – minimizing response time

Normally, when one or both inputs are zero, the output is set to zero. But in the rules 3, 11, 15, and 23, the output is set to a small value. This helps the controller to converge faster. As an example, let us consider rule 23. Without any change in max-requests, there is a large increase in response-time. This means that the incoming requests need larger service times and the number of requests admitted should be decreased. Hence, max-requests is decreased by a small value.

The set-up for the simulation consists of

- a workload generator program to generate requests,
- a server program to service the requests,
- a differentiator routine,
- a fuzzy controller program and
- an integrator routine.

The incoming request from the workload generator is first put into a queue in the server. When the server becomes free, the first request in the queue is dequeued. Workload generator is set to generate requests such that the time between arrivals of consecutive requests on an average (mean inter-arrival) is 0.2 second. That is 300 requests per minute on an average. Mean service time is set to 60 seconds.

Simulation readings are recorded after every measurement interval. At the end of every measurement interval, response time of that interval is sent to the differentiator whose output is the change-in-response-time (dr) between current and previous intervals. The number of requests accepted by the server, is limited by the parameter max-requests, which is updated by the integrator at the beginning of every measurement interval. The parameter max-requests correspond to MaxClients in an Apache web server.

A measurement interval of 3 minutes is used. To ensure that transients do not affect the readings, readings are taken for the last 1 minute of the 3 minute interval. Response time values of the requests which entered service in the last 1 minute are noted and the average is calculated. For the normalizing gains, large values increase the speed of the controller, but too large values will cause the system to oscillate. After experimenting with a few values, the values selected were ng-dr = ng-dm = 1/10 and ng-dnm = 10. This means a change of 10 in response-time or in max-requests is considered to be large.

2.2 Results

Here to minimize the response time the client server architecture is simulated as an M/M/1 queue and processes. That is, the time between generations of consecutive requests is exponentially distributed. Also processing of each request is simulated by a process which runs for a time which is exponentially distributed. Parameter MaxClients is simulated by max-requests. The response time is minimum for an optimum value of max-requests. The controller minimizes the response time by finding an optimum value for max-requests.

The variation of response time with respect to max-requests is plotted in **Figures 2.3, 2.4 and 2.5.** The mean of the distribution of the inter-arrival times between consecutive requests is kept constant at 0.2 second. This facilitates easy comparison among the three sets of results.

Figure 2.3 shows the result for the case where mean of the service time distribution is 40 seconds. One can see that there is some oscillation. Parameter max-requests increases to 100, before settling to a value around 80. The minimum response time obtained is about 49 seconds. Initially change-in-max-requests is positive, while change-in-response-time is negative. This means the value of max-requests is increasing towards the optimum value. However there is an overshoot and so the controller decreases max-requests towards the optimum.

Figure 2.4 shows the result for the case where mean of the service time distribution is 30 seconds. Once again there is some oscillation, but it is reduced. Parameter max-requests increases to about 104, before settling to a value around 98. The minimum response time obtained is about 30 seconds. The response time is smaller because of the reduced service time. As before, there is an overshoot before the controller decreases max-requests towards the optimum.

Figure 2.5 shows the result for the case where mean of the service time distribution is 20 seconds. There is almost no oscillation. Parameter max-requests settles to a value of about 103. Since the service time is smaller than the previous two cases, the response time obtained of around 20 seconds is also lesser than that obtained previously.

Thus, it is seen that the controller always adjusts the value of max-requests for minimizing response-time.

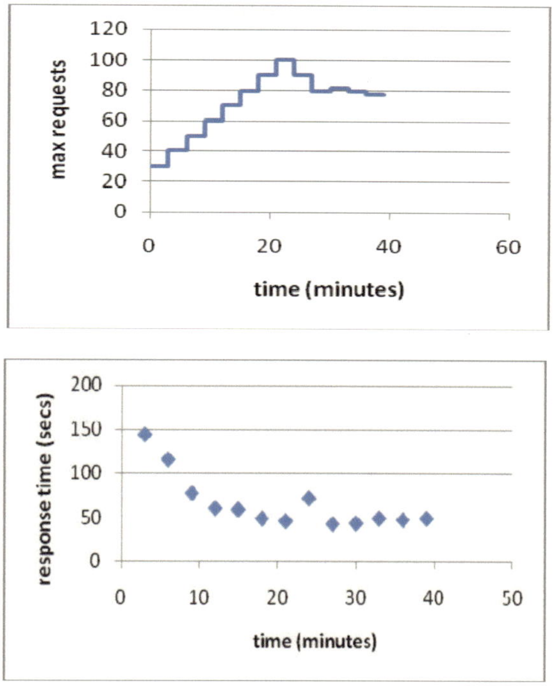

Fig. 2.3. With mean of the service time distribution = 40 secs

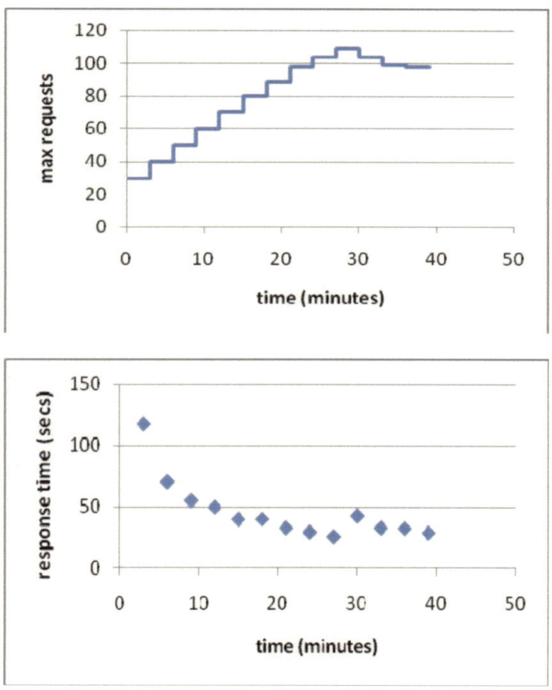

Fig. 2.4. With mean of the service time distribution = 30 secs

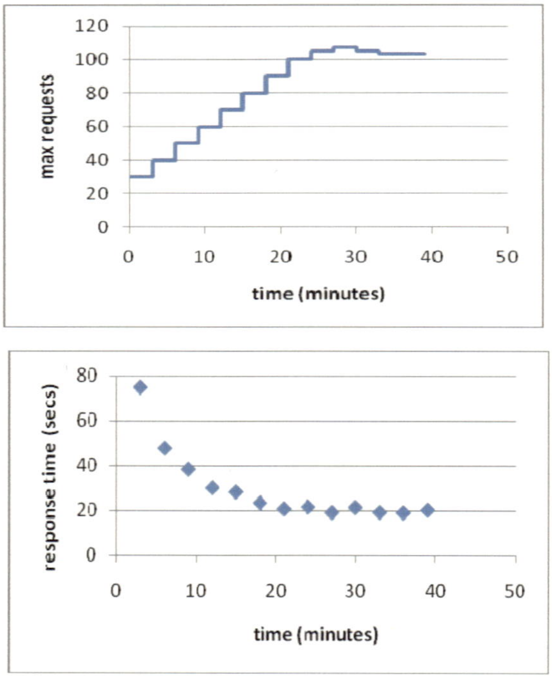

Fig. 2.5. With mean of the service time distribution = 20 secs

3. Maximizing profit of an e-commerce system

3.1 Simulation using M/M/1 queue and processes

Here also the client server architecture is simulated using an M/M/1 queue and processes. As before, parameter MaxClients is simulated by max-requests. The profit is maximum for an optimum value of max-requests. In the next subsection, the simulation environment used is described. This is followed by the design and implementation of a fuzzy controller for optimizing the value of max-requests. This ensures that the profit is maximized.

3.1.1 Simulation environment

A workload generator is used to simulate the generation of requests from many clients. The workload generator generates requests such that the time between generations of consecutive requests is exponentially distributed. The processing of these requests by the server is simulated by a program, in which the parent process creates a child process every time a request is received. Each child process sleeps for a time which is exponentially distributed before exiting. Thus, the client server architecture is simulated here as an M/M/1 queue.

3.1.2 Design and Implementation of Controller

The block diagram of the fuzzy control system is shown in **Figure 3.1**. The client server architecture is simulated here as an M/M/1 queue. The number of requests accepted by the server is limited by the parameter max-requests, which is updated by the integrator at the beginning of every measurement interval. The parameter max-requests corresponds to

MaxClients in an Apache web server. The number of child processes which are able to run to completion are called completed transactions, while those which are unable to run to completion are called violating transactions. These two values are sent to the profit module for calculating profit. This value of profit is input to a differentiator whose output is the change-in-profit (dft) between current and previous intervals. The fuzzy controller has two inputs: change-in-profit (dft) and change-in-max-requests (dm) between intervals. The controller's output is next-change-in-max-requests (dnm), whose value is taken as the change-in-max-requests for the next interval. An integrator converts this value into max-requests.

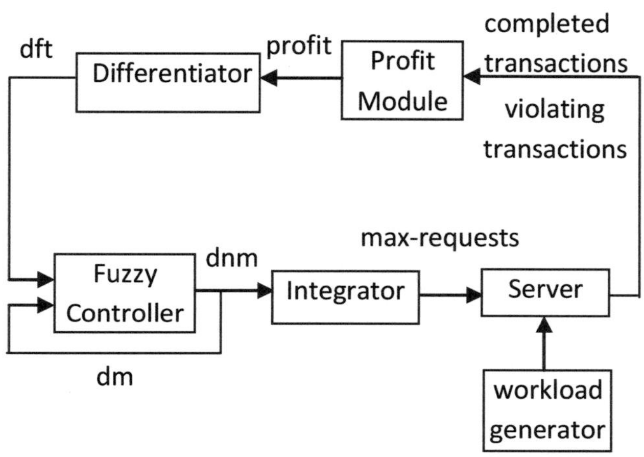

Fig. 3.1. Fuzzy control system - maximizing profit

The triangular membership functions used for the fuzzification of the inputs and defuzzification of the output are shown in **Figure 3.2**. In each case, the parameter is divided into 5 intervals called neglarge, negsmall, zero, possmall and poslarge. The measured numeric values are multiplied by the normalized gains. Value change-in-profit (dft) is multiplied by ng-dft, while change-in-max-requests (dm) is multiplied by ng-dm. The output value next-change-in-max-requests (dnm) is denormalized by multiplying by the normalized gain, ng-dnm, to obtain the actual output value. It is previously noted that profit is a concave downward function of max-requests. Hence, a hill climbing procedure is used to maximize profit. This is described using fuzzy rules shown in **Table 3.1.**

Since the value of max-requests that maximizes the profit is not known, these rules are described in terms of changes to max-requests and profit. As an example, consider rule 25. It means that max-requests has been increased by a large amount (in the beginning of the current measurement interval) and it is observed that the profit has increased by a large amount by the end of the interval. This means the change to max-requests is in the correct direction. Hence, it is continued to be changed in the same direction. That is, for the next interval, max-requests is increased further. Thus, rules 16 through 25 take care of the correct situations where as rules 1 through 10 handle the incorrect situations. In rules 1 through 10 the previous action caused the profit to decrease, so the direction has to be "reversed". Later the consequents from all the activated rules are weighted using the centre of gravity method to obtain the (normalized) output value.

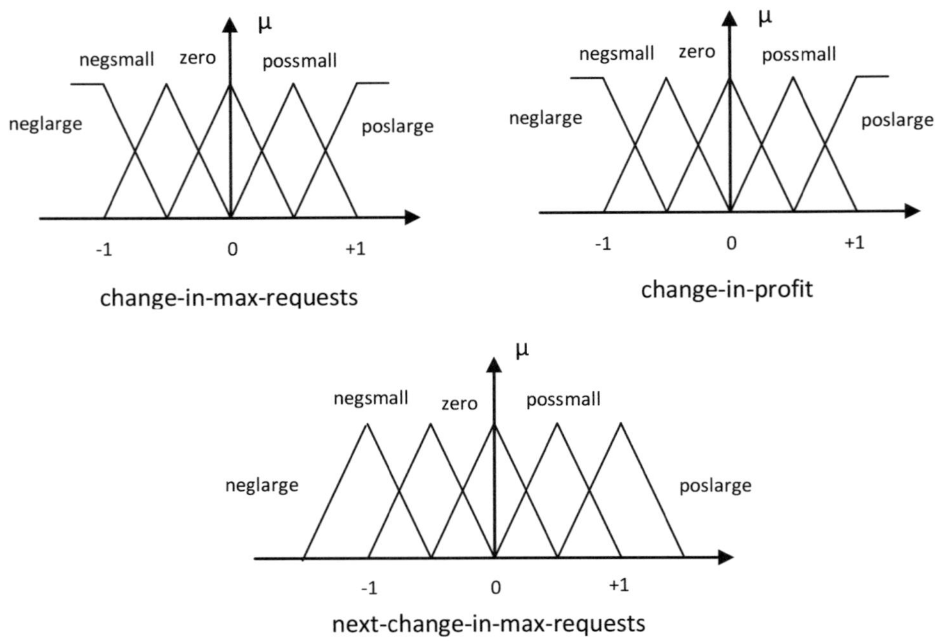

Fig. 3.2. Membership functions - maximizing profit

Normally, when one or both inputs are zero, the output is set to zero. But in the rules 3, 11, 15, and 23, the output is set to a small value. This helps the controller to converge faster. As an example, let us consider rule 23. Without any change in max-requests, there is a large increase in profit. This means that the incoming requests need smaller service times and and more such requests can be admitted. Hence, max-requests is increased by a small value.

The simulation environment consists of

- a workload generator program to generate requests,
- a server program to service the requests,
- a profit module for calculating profit values,
- a differentiator routine,
- a fuzzy controller program and
- an integrator routine.

Simulation readings are recorded after every measurement interval. A measurement interval of 60 seconds was used.

The profit module contains the profit model which is characterized by r, the revenue per completed transaction and c, the cost per violating transaction. Three profit models are defined. P1: r = c, that is, equal weight is assigned to completed and violating transactions; P2: r = k*c, more weight is assigned to completed transactions; P3: r = c/k, more weight is assigned to offending transactions. The constant k should be specified in the SLA. In this work, value for k is taken as 5.

Too large normalizing gains result in the controller oscillating, while too small ones result in a slow performance. For better performance, different values of normalizing gains were selected for different profit models. For profit model P1, ng-dft = ng-dm = 1/5 and ng-dnm = 5. For P2, ng-dft = 1/25, ng-dm = 1/5 and ng-dnm = 5. For P3, ng-dft = 1/10, ng-dm = 1/5 and ng-dnm = 5.

Rule	IF			THEN
	change-in-max-requests	AND	change-in-profit	next-change-in-max-requests
1	neglarge	AND	neglarge	poslarge
2	negsmall	AND	neglarge	possmall
3	zero	AND	neglarge	negsmall
4	possmall	AND	neglarge	negsmall
5	poslarge	AND	neglarge	neglarge
6	neglarge	AND	negsmall	poslarge
7	negsmall	AND	negsmall	possmall
8	zero	AND	negsmall	zero
9	possmall	AND	negsmall	negsmall
10	poslarge	AND	negsmall	neglarge
11	neglarge	AND	zero	negsmall
12	negsmall	AND	zero	zero
13	zero	AND	zero	zero
14	possmall	AND	zero	zero
15	poslarge	AND	zero	possmall
16	neglarge	AND	possmall	neglarge
17	negsmall	AND	possmall	negsmall
18	zero	AND	possmall	zero
19	possmall	AND	possmall	possmall
20	poslarge	AND	possmall	poslarge
21	neglarge	AND	poslarge	neglarge
22	negsmall	AND	poslarge	negsmall
23	zero	AND	poslarge	possmall
24	possmall	AND	poslarge	possmall
25	poslarge	AND	poslarge	poslarge

Table 3.1. Fuzzy rules - maximizing profit

3.2 Results

Here to maximize the profit, the client server architecture is simulated as an M/M/1 queue and processes. That is, the time between generations of consecutive requests is exponentially distributed. Also processing of each request is simulated by a process which runs for a time which is exponentially distributed. Parameter MaxClients is simulated by max-requests. Parameter max-requests is the upper limit of the number of requests accepted by the server in the given interval. The number of requests which are able to run to completion are called processed-requests. These contribute to the revenue, while those which are not able to run to completion, called, violating-requests contribute to the cost. The contributions of processed-requests and violating-requests towards the profit are decided by the profit model.

Let 'r' be the revenue per processed-requests, 'c' the cost per violating-requests and 'k' be a constant. For profit model P1, r = c, that is, equal weight is assigned to processed-requests and violating-requests. For profit model P2, r = c * k, that is, more weight is assigned to processed-requests. For profit model P3, r = c / k, that is, more weight is assigned to violating-requests. Irrespective of the profit model, profit is maximum for an optimum value

of max-requests. The controller maximizes the profit by finding an optimum value for max-requests.
The variation of profit with respect to max-requests for various profit models are plotted in **Figures 3.3, 3.4 and 3.5**. In this simulation, values selected are r = 1, c = 1 and k = 5.
The results for profit model P1 are shown in **Figure 3.3**. As mentioned before, equal weight is assigned to processed-requests as well as violating-requests. It can be seen that the controller sets max-requests to moderate values. The profit is also moderate.
The results obtained for profit model P3 are shown in **Figure 3.4**. In this case, more weight is assigned to the violating-requests. In an attempt to reduce the number of violating-requests, the controller tries to be more conservative and sets max-requests to comparatively smaller values. The profit is smaller, but it will reduce further if the controller increases the value of max-requests. Thus the controller has maximized the profit, even in the presence of constraints.
The results obtained for profit model P2 are shown in **Figure 3.5**. Since more weight is assigned to processed-requests, the controller is more aggressive and sets max-requests to comparatively larger values. This can be seen when these results are compared with that of **Figure 3.3**. Larger values of max-requests combined with a more favorable profit model leads to a high value of profit.

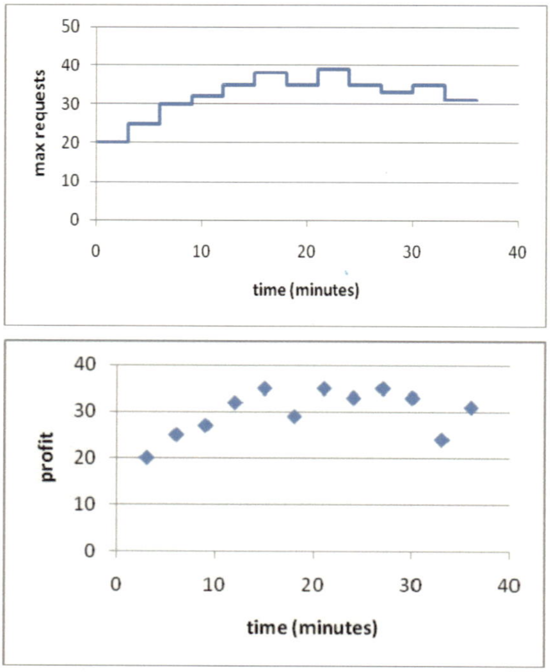

Fig. 3.3. For profit model P1

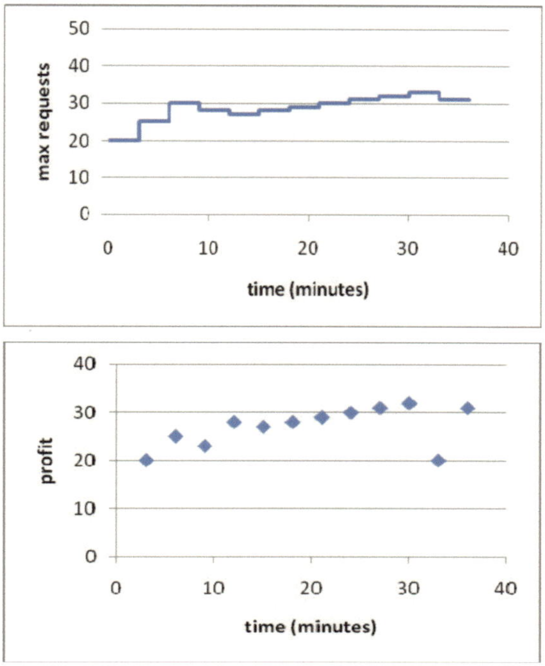

Fig. 3.4. For profit model P3

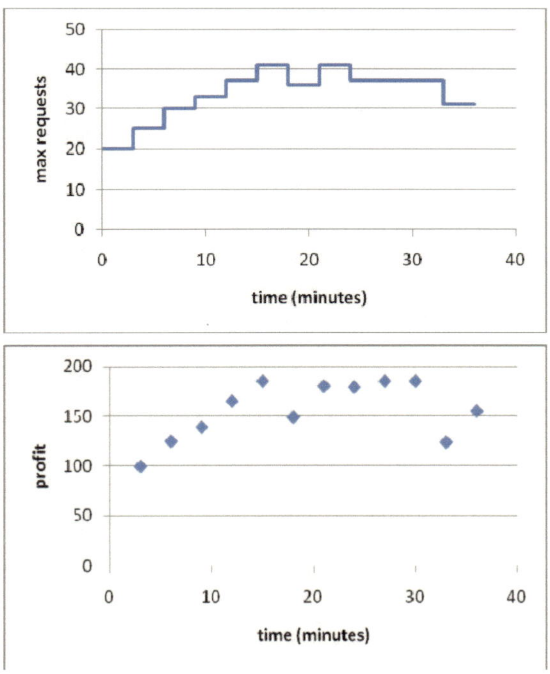

Fig. 3.5. For profit model P2

4. Conclusions

This chapter focuses on two objectives: i) Minimize the response time, and ii) Maximize the profit of an e-commerce system. The client server architecture is simulated using an M/M/1 queue and processes. In case the server is busy, the incoming requests wait in a queue. The average time spent by requests in the queue is the response-time. Here, MaxClients is simulated by max-requests. A fuzzy controller is designed and implemented for minimizing the response-time by optimizing the value of max-requests. The results obtained are also presented. It is seen that the fuzzy controller was successful in minimizing response-time.
To meet the second objective, the client server architecture is again simulated using an M/M/1 queue. Here also, MaxClients is simulated by max-requests. A fuzzy controller is designed and implemented for maximizing the profit by optimizing the value of max-requests. For these simulations, it is seen that the fuzzy controller is able to maximize profit. Thus it can be concluded that fuzzy controllers play a vital role in the area of autonomic computing systems.

5. References

Diao, Y., Hellerstein, J. L. and Parekh, S. (2001). "A Business-Oriented approach to the Design of Feedback Loops for Performance Management," *Proceedings of the 12th IEEE International Workshop on Distributed Systems: Operations and Management.*

Diao, Y., Hellerstein, J. L. and Parekh, S. (2002a). "Optimizing Quality of Service using fuzzy control," *Proceedings of Distributed Systems Operations and Management,* Vol: 2506 Springer, 42-53.

Diao, Y., Hellerstein, J. L. and Parekh, S. (2002b). "Using fuzzy control to maximize profits in service level management," *IBM Systems Journal,* Vol. 41, No. 3, 403-420.

Harish S. V., and Chandra Sekaran, K. (2009). "Maximizing Profit in an Autonomic Computing System: A Fuzzy Control approach," *International Journal of Recent Trends in Engineering,* Vol. 2, No. 1, Association of Computer, Electronics and Electrical Engineers and Academy Publishers, Finland.

Harish S. V., and Chandra Sekaran, K. (2010). "Minimizing Response Time in an Autonomic Computing System: A Fuzzy Control approach," *International Journal of Computer Science and Systems,* Vol. 1, No. 3, Universal Society of Applied Research (USAR), Prague, Czech Republic.

Kephart, J. O., Chess, D. M. (2003). "The vision of Autonomic Computing," *IEEE Computer Society,* 41-50.

Liu, X., Sha, L., Diao, Y., Froehlich, S., Hellerstein, J. L. and Parekh, S. (2003). "Online Response Time Optimization of Apache Web Server," *Springer-Verlag, Berlin,* 461-478.

Salehie, M. & Tahvildari, L. (2005). Autonomic Computing: Emerging Trends and Open Problems, *Proceedings of the Workshop on the Design and Evolution of Autonomic Application Software,* 2005.

Yen, J. and Langari, R. (2005). *Fuzzy Logic: Intelligence, Control and Information,* Pearson Education, India.

Part 2

Fuzzy Controllers: Theoretical Design and Experimental Validation

13

Type-2 Fuzzy Control of an Automatic Guided Vehicle for Wall-Following

Leehter Yao and Yuan-Shiu Chen
National Taipei University of Technology
Taiwan

1. Introduction

Fuzzy logic inference system (FIS) has been widely applied to the controller design for automatic guided vehicles (AGV) because FIS allows easier controller design under uncertainty and nonlinearity (Hwang et al., 2007; Godjevac & Steele, 1999; Baturone et al., 2008; Er &Deng, 2004; Ng & Trivedi, 1998). Wall following is a commonly adopted scheme for an AGV to navigate in the indoor or outdoor environments. Sonar system is usually the most popular hardware system installed on the AGV for wall following due to its cost-effective functionality and computational efficiency. There has been some research applying FIS to the sonar-based wall following task (Tsui et al., 2008; Li et al., 2003; Juang & Hsu, 2009). The sonar constantly transmits ultra-sound signals during the wall following process. The ultra-sound signals cannot go through most of the objects, walls or structures in the environment, and thus are reflected back to the sonar. By calculating the difference between the time when the ultra-sound signals are transmitted and are received, the AGV is able to constantly detect the distance between the AGV and the object the ultra-sound signals are reflected from. For the wall following, the AGV is controlled to navigate along the wall while maintaining a fixed distance based on the received ultra-sound signals. If the surface or texture of the wall varies as AGV navigates in the environment, the ultra-sound signals might not be directly reflected back to the receiver or the intensity of received signals might not be constant all the time. The time difference of the transmitted and received ultra-sound signals is determined by calculating the time when the transmitted signal is above a threshold and the time when the received signal is above another threshold. The deflection of the ultra-sound signals due to the variation of object surface and the reduction of reflected signals due to the surface texture and material characteristic will cause the uncertainty of distance detection based on reflected ultra-sound signals. In other words, the calculated distance is corrupted by inevitable noise and disturbance contained in the received ultra-sound signals.
Although fuzzy controllers are credited with a high degree of reliability for controlling such a complicated system as AGV, the type-1 fuzzy controller sometimes is not robust enough to cope with the uncertainty existed in the noise-corrupted sonar signals. In this paper, a type-2 fuzzy controller (Mendel, 2001; Mendel & John, 2002) is proposed to control both the left and right drive wheel of an nonholonomic AGV for the wall following. It will be shown in this paper that the proposed type-2 fuzzy controller resolves the inevitable noise problem due to its flexibility of processing controller's input and output signals with uncertainty and

its robustness held in the type-2 fuzzy control system. AGV usually works in uncertain environments with noisy sensing data and has nonlinear interactions with the changing environments. In some situations or applications, the type-2 FIS is more suitable to being applied to the design of AGV controllers. Recently, some research has applied the type-2 FIS to the control of AGV. In (Hagras, 2004), a hierarchical type-2 fuzzy controller was design for a mobile robot navigating in new environments. In (Zhang & Wang, 2007), a type-2 fuzzy controller was successfully designed to control the periodic walking motion for a biped robot. The type-2 FIS was also integrated with a neural network. A type-2 fuzzy-neural network was designed for the environment recognition as part of the navigation control of a mobile robot (Nurmaini et al., 2009). To reduce the heavy computational efforts in type-reduction process of a type-2 FIS, several efficient type-reduction schemes have been proposed to simplify the computation for defuzzification (Karnik & Mendel, 2001; Wu & Tan, 2005; Wu & Mendel, 2002).

2. Problem statement and interval type-2 fuzzy controller

Given that an AGV is to navigate within an environment by following walls or structures in the environment. For the convenience and simplicity of description, the wall or structure for the AGV to follow is called the wall in the rest of this paper. The AGV is controlled to maintain constant distance between the AGV and the wall despite that the texture and the surface of the wall may vary to some extent during the wall following process. Assume that the sonar system is utilized on AGV to detect the distance between the wall and the AGV. As shown in Fig. 1, the AGV used in this paper is equipped with 12 sonar transceivers around the vehicle body.

In this paper, a fuzzy controller is designed to control the steering of both AGV's drive wheels for wall following despite the noise and disturbance that might cause miscalculation of distance between the AGV and the wall. A type-2 FIS is adopted in the proposed fuzzy controller due to the flexibility to describe controller's input and output signals and the robustness held in the type-2 fuzzy control system. It is known from Fig. 1 that both front and rear sonar transceivers numbered 1 and 9 are used for following the right wall while two sonar transceivers numbered 6 and 14 are used for following the left wall. Denote D as the distance the AGV is controlled to keep away from the wall during the wall following process. Let T be the sampling interval, $d_1(kT)$ and $d_2(kT)$ be the measured distance based on the ultra-sound signals received by the front and rear sonar transceivers, respectively, at k-th sampling interval. For the convenience of notation, the sampling interval T is omitted for the following signal notations. If $e_1(k) = D - d_1(k)$ and $e_2(k) = D - d_2(k)$, the type-2 fuzzy controller for the wall following is to control the AGV's increment of rotation angle, $b(k) \equiv \Delta\theta(k)$ as following:

$$if\ e_1(k)\ is\ \tilde{A}_1^{(i_1)}\ and\ e_2(k)\ is\ \tilde{A}_2^{(i_2)}\ then\ b(k)\ is\ \tilde{B}^{(i_1 i_2)} \tag{1}$$

where $\tilde{A}_1^{(i_1)}$, $\tilde{A}_2^{(i_2)}$ are the i_1-th and i_2-th type-2 fuzzy sets for controller inputs e_1, e_2, while $\tilde{B}^{(i_1 i_2)}$ is the corresponding output $i_1 = 1 \dots N_1$, $i_2 = 1 \dots N_2$, and $i_3 = 1 \dots N_3$. Assume that N_1, N_2 and N_3 type-2 fuzzy sets are defined to describe the fuzzy inputs e_1, e_2 and output y, respectively. M fuzzy rules are assigned in the fuzzy controller. As the rotational increment $b(k)$ is determined by the fuzzy controller at every k-th sampling interval, AGV's rotation angle at $(k+1)$-th sampling interval is defined as:

$$\theta(k+1) = \theta(k) + b(k) = \theta(k) + \Delta\theta(k) \tag{2}$$

To increase the computational efficiency of the fuzzy controller, the input type-2 fuzzy sets are defined as interval type-2 fuzzy sets, i.e.,

$$\tilde{A}_h = \sum_{e_h \in E_h} \mu_{\tilde{A}_h}(e_h)/e_h = \sum_{e_h \in E_h} \Big(\sum_{q_h \in \left[\underline{\mu}_{\tilde{A}_h}, \overline{\mu}_{\tilde{A}_h}\right]} 1/q_h \Big) \Big/ e_h \,, \; h = 1 \ldots 2. \tag{3}$$

where $\mu_{\tilde{A}_h}(e_h)$ is the secondary membership of the type-2 fuzzy set $\tilde{A}_h$ for the *h-th* input signal e_h, and E_h is universe of discourse of e_h. The primary membership values are set to be 1 for primary variable $q_h \in [\underline{\mu}_{\tilde{A}_h}, \overline{\mu}_{\tilde{A}_h}]$.

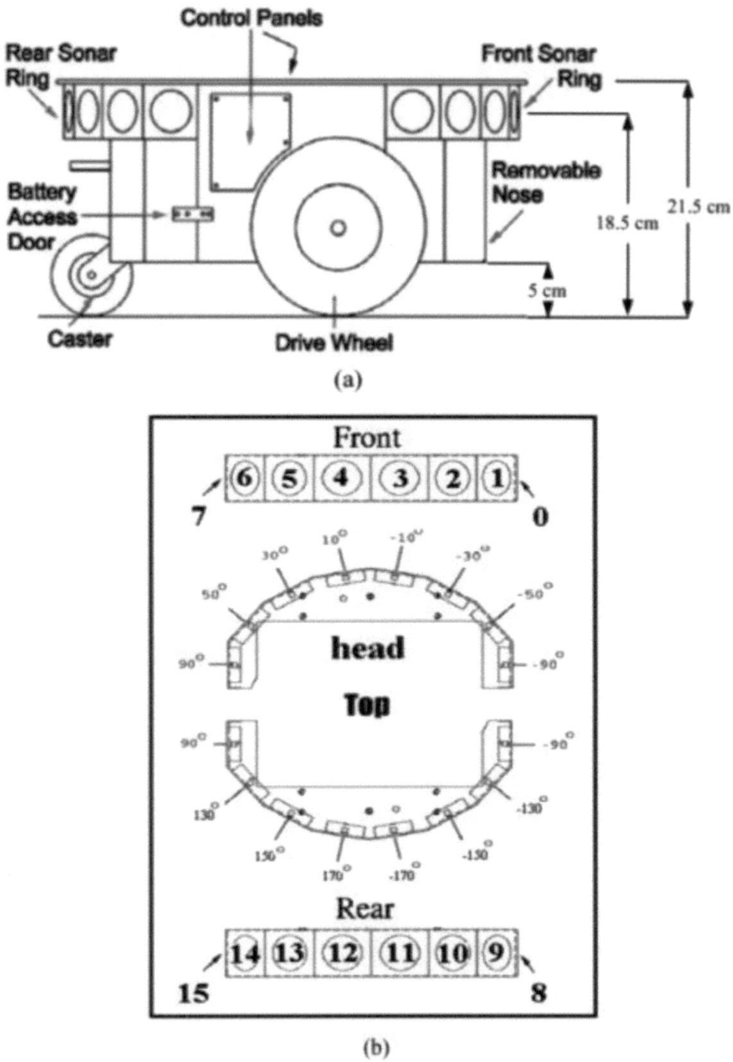

Fig. 1. (a) Side view of an AGV. (b) Sonar transceivers around the AGV.

3. Calculation of AGV's rotational increment

The measured signals $e_1(\cdot)$ and $e_2(\cdot)$ are transformed to be type-2 fuzzy singletons. At every *k-th* sampling interval, assume that the $e_1(k) = e_1^{'}$ and $e_2(k) = e_2^{'}$. The degree of firing (DOF) of every fuzzy rule in the fuzzy rule base $\Gamma^{(i_1i_2)}(e_1^{'},e_2^{'}) = [\underline{\gamma}^{(i_1i_2)}(e_1^{'},e_2^{'}),\overline{\gamma}^{(i_1i_2)}(e_1^{'},e_2^{'})]$,where

$$\underline{\gamma}^{(i_1i_2)} = \underline{\mu}_{\tilde{A}_1^{(i_1)}}(e_1^{'})\underline{\mu}_{\tilde{A}_2^{(i_2)}}(e_2^{'}) \tag{4}$$

$$\overline{\gamma}^{(i_1i_2)} = \overline{\mu}_{\tilde{A}_1^{(i_1)}}(e_1^{'})\overline{\mu}_{\tilde{A}_2^{(i_2)}}(e_2^{'}) \tag{5}$$

The center-of-sets type reduction scheme (Mendel, 2001;Mendel & John, 2002) is to be used along with the defuzzification approach. The centroid of the type-2 output fuzzy set $\tilde{B}^{(i_1i_2)}$ in (1) is represented by $C_{\tilde{B}^{(i_1i_2)}}$, which is a type-1 interval fuzzy set $[c_l^{(i_1i_2)}, c_r^{(i_1i_2)}]$, i.e.,

$$C_{\tilde{B}^{(i_1i_2)}} = \sum_{c\in[c_l^{(i_1i_2)},\ c_r^{(i_1i_2)}]} 1/c = [c_l^{(i_1i_2)}, c_r^{(i_1i_2)}]\,. \tag{6}$$

The type-reduced fuzzy output, denoted as b_{cos}, generated from the fuzzy controller in (1) is also an interval fuzzy set. Let $b_{cos} = [b_l, b_r]$. In order to calculate both b_l and b_r, assume that the DOF associated with $c_l^{(i_1i_2)}$ is denoted as $\gamma_l^{(i_1i_2)}$ and the DOF associated with $c_r^{(i_1i_2)}$ is denoted as $\gamma_r^{(i_1i_2)}$. Then,

$$b_l = \left(\sum_{i_1=1}^{N_1}\sum_{i_2=1}^{N_2}\gamma_l^{(i_1i_2)}c_l^{(i_1i_2)}\right) / \left(\sum_{i_1=1}^{N_1}\sum_{i_2=1}^{N_2}\gamma_l^{(i_1i_2)}\right), \tag{7}$$

and

$$b_r = \left(\sum_{i_1=1}^{N_1}\sum_{i_2=1}^{N_2}\gamma_r^{(i_1i_2)}c_r^{(i_1i_2)}\right) / \left(\sum_{i_1=1}^{N_1}\sum_{i_2=1}^{N_2}\gamma_r^{(i_1i_2)}\right). \tag{8}$$

Note that the DOF $\gamma_l^{(i_1i_2)}$ and $\gamma_r^{(i_1i_2)}$ in (7) and (8) are set as either $\underline{\gamma}^{(i_1i_2)}$ or $\overline{\gamma}^{(i_1i_2)}$ depending on the calculated values of b_l, b_r, and $c_l^{(i_1i_2)}$ and $c_r^{(i_1i_2)}$ in the following iterative computation process for b_l or b_r. The computation process for b_l is described as following.

1. Compute b_l in (7) by initially setting $\gamma_l^{(i_1i_2)} = (\overline{\gamma}^{(i_1i_2)} + \underline{\gamma}^{(i_1i_2)})/2$, $i_1 = 1\ldots N_1$, $i_2 = 1\ldots N_2$. Let $b_l^{'} = b_l$.
2. Update b_l in (7) with $\gamma_l^{(i_1i_2)} = \overline{\gamma}^{(i_1i_2)}$ if $c_l^{(i_1i_2)} \le b_l^{'}$ and $\gamma_l^{(i_1i_2)} = \underline{\gamma}^{(i_1i_2)}$ if $c_l^{(i_1i_2)} > b_l^{'}$, $i_1 = 1\ldots N_1$, $i_2 = 1\ldots N_2$. Let $b_l^{''} = b_l$.
3. If $b_l^{''} \ne b_l^{'}$, go to step 4; otherwise stop and set $b_l = b_l^{''}$.
4. Set $b_l^{'} = b_l^{''}$ and return to step 2.

The value of b_r can be obtained by the process similar to the above except that both $\gamma_l^{(i_1i_2)}$ and $c_l^{(i_1i_2)}$ in the above computation process are replaced with $\gamma_r^{(i_1i_2)}$ and $c_r^{(i_1i_2)}$, respectively. In step 2 of the computation process for b_r, $\gamma_r^{(i_1i_2)} = \underline{\gamma}^{(i_1i_2)}$ if $c_r^{(i_1i_2)} \le b_r^{'}$ and $\gamma_r^{(i_1i_2)} = \overline{\gamma}^{(i_1i_2)}$ if $c_r^{(i_1i_2)} > b_r^{'}$, i_1 =

$1 \ldots N_1$, $i_2 = 1 \ldots N_2$. Different from the type reduction process proposed in (Mendel, 2001;Mendel & John, 2002), the values of $c_l^{(i_1 i_2)}$, $i_1 = 1 \ldots N_1$, $i_2 = 1 \ldots N_2$, need not be pre-arranged in an ascending order. The type-reduction scheme proposed in this paper directly uses $c_l^{(i_1 i_2)}$ to calculate $\gamma_l^{(i_1 i_2)}$ for every indices pair (i_1 i_2) rather than locating the order of $b_l^{'}$ in the ascending values of all $c_l^{(i_1 i_2)}$ before determining the value of $\gamma_l^{(i_1 i_2)}$. Therefore, the proposed modification of type-reduction scheme saves the computation effort compared to the one in (Mendel, 2001; Mendel & John, 2002).

After calculating both b_l and b_r in the type-reduced output b_{cos} of an interval singleton type-2 fuzzy controller based on (4)-(8) with $e_1(k) = e_1^{'}$ and $e_2(k) = e_2^{'}$, the defuzzified output

$$b(\mathrm{k}) \equiv \Delta\theta(k) = (b_l + b_r)/2. \tag{9}$$

4. Implementation of AGV's wall following control

It is shown in the above discussion that the wall following control of AGV mainly depends on delicate control of AGV's rotational increments. The implementation of AGV's rotational increments and the associated rotational dynamics will be further investigated in this section. The rotational dynamics of a nonholonomic AGV is shown in Fig. 2, where Q denotes the center of an AGV and Q' denotes the new position after AGV moving forward from Q for a period of sampling interval T. Let d_l and d_r be the moving distance of AGV's left and right wheel with respect to the Cartesian coordinate centered at the origin O. If r_l and r_r are the rotational radius for the left and right wheel, respectively, then,

$$d_l(k) = r_l \cdot \Delta\theta(k) = V_l(k) \cdot T\ , \tag{10}$$

$$d_r(k) = r_r \cdot \Delta\theta(k) = V_r(k) \cdot T\ . \tag{11}$$

where $V_l(\cdot)$and $V_r(\cdot)$ are AGV's left and right wheel speed, respectively. The speed of AGV can be defined as $V_{avg}(k) = (V_r(k) + V_l(\mathrm{k}))/2$. The moving distance $d_o(k)$ can be considered as the moving distance of AGV's center Q, i.e.,

$$d_o(k) = r \cdot \Delta\theta(k) = V_{avg}(k) \cdot T = (V_r(k) + V_l(k)) \cdot T / 2\ . \tag{12}$$

From (11) and (12), the rotational increment for the *k-th* sampling interval

$$\Delta\theta(k) = (d_r(k) - d_l(k)) / (r_r - r_l) = (d_r(k) - d_l(k)) / 2w\ , \tag{13}$$

where w is the radius of AGV. Substituting $d_l(k)$ and $d_r(k)$ in (10) and (11) into (13),

$$\Delta\theta(k) = (V_r(k) - V_l(k))T / 2w\ . \tag{14}$$

Then,

$$V_r(k) - V_l(k) = 2w\Delta\theta(k) / T\ . \tag{15}$$

From (12),

$$V_r(k) + V_l(k) = 2d_o(k) / T\ . \tag{16}$$

Hence, $V_l(k)$ and $V_r(k)$ can be obtained from both (15) and (16) as following:

$$V_l(k) = (d_o(k) - w\Delta\theta(k)) / T, \tag{17}$$

$$V_r(k) = (d_o(k) + w\Delta\theta(k)) / T. \tag{18}$$

For wall following, AGV's average speed V_{avg} is set as a constant despite that the left and right wheel speed V_l and V_r vary with time. As long as V_{avg} is a constant, AGV's moving distance within every sampling interval, $d_o(k)$, is also a constant according to (12). Referring to (17) and (18), if $d_o(k)$ is set as a constant and $\Delta\theta(k)$ is determined by the type-2 fuzzy controller as in (9), $V_l(k)$ and $V_r(k)$ can be both determined. Since AGV's left and right wheel motor are driven by the voltage-controlled PWM drivers, the left and right wheel can be driven to achieve the calculated speed $V_l(k)$ and $V_r(k)$ by applying corresponding voltages to the PWM drivers.

Referring to Fig. 2 and (10)-(11),

$$r = (r_r + r_l) / 2 = (V_r(k) + V_l(k))T / 2\Delta\theta(k). \tag{19}$$

Substituting (13) into (19) yields

$$r = (V_r(k) + V_l(k))w / (V_r(k) - V_l(k)). \tag{20}$$

Referring to Fig. 2, assume that AGV's rotation angle is $\theta(k)$ at the *k-th* sampling interval with respect to *x*-axis of the global coordinate. Let $\Delta u(k)$ and $\Delta v(k)$ be AGV's displacement increment moving from Q to Q' with respect to the AGV's coordinate. Therefore,

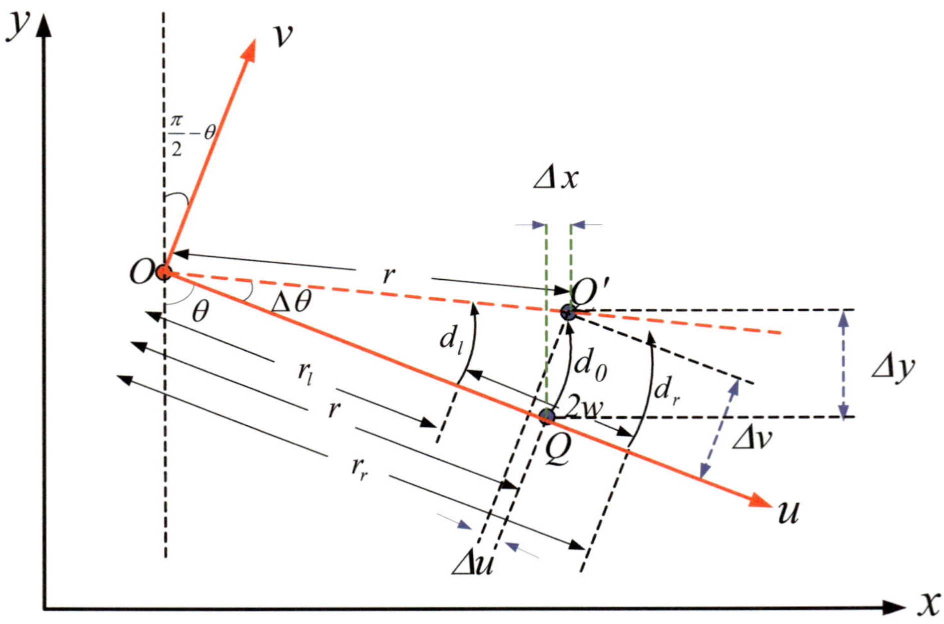

Fig. 2. Rotational dynamics of a holonomic AGV.

$$\Delta u(k) = r \cdot \cos(\Delta\theta(k)) - r\,, \tag{21}$$

and

$$\Delta v(k) = r \cdot \sin(\Delta\theta(k))\,. \tag{22}$$

The *u-v* coordinate is the *x-y* global coordinate with clockwise rotation (π/2 - θ). Therefore,

$$\begin{bmatrix} \Delta x(k) \\ \Delta y(k) \end{bmatrix} = \begin{bmatrix} \cos(\frac{\pi}{2}-\theta) & \sin(\frac{\pi}{2}-\theta) \\ -\sin(\frac{\pi}{2}-\theta) & \cos(\frac{\pi}{2}-\theta) \end{bmatrix} \begin{bmatrix} \Delta u(k) \\ \Delta v(k) \end{bmatrix}. \tag{23}$$

Substituting (21) and (22) into (23),

$$\Delta x(k) = r(\sin(\theta(k) + \Delta\theta(k)) - \sin(\theta(k)))\,, \tag{24}$$

$$\Delta y(k) = r(\cos(\theta(k)) - \cos(\theta(k) + \Delta\theta(k)))\,. \tag{25}$$

With AGV's position and heading angle $[x(k), y(k), \theta(k)]^T$ at Q, the position and heading angle at Q' for the *(k+1)-th* sampling interval can be updated as

$$\begin{bmatrix} x(k+1) \\ y(k+1) \\ \theta(k+1) \end{bmatrix} = \begin{bmatrix} x(k) \\ y(k) \\ \theta(k) \end{bmatrix} + \begin{bmatrix} \Delta x(k) \\ \Delta y(k) \\ \Delta\theta(k) \end{bmatrix}, \tag{26}$$

where $\Delta x(k)$ and $\Delta y(k)$ are determined by (24) and (25), respectively, $\Delta\theta(k)$ is determined by the type-2 fuzzy controller as in (4)-(9).

5. Experiment

The AGV is set to follow a round clump of bushes in the park as shown in Fig. 3. It is obvious that the ultra-sound signals transmitted from the sonar transceivers are easy to be deflected by the flowers, leaves and trigs in the bushes. The distance between the AGV and bushes measured by the sonar systems is contaminated by inevitable noise. Referring to (1), two different interval type-2 fuzzy sets are utilized for $\tilde{A}_1^{(i_1)}$ and $\tilde{A}_2^{(i_1)}$ describing the linguistic terms "negative" and "positive", respectively, i.e., $N_1 = N_2 = 2$. Let $[\underline{\mu}_{\tilde{A}_1^{(1)}}, \overline{\mu}_{\tilde{A}_1^{(1)}}] = [\underline{\mu}_{\tilde{A}_2^{(1)}}, \overline{\mu}_{\tilde{A}_2^{(1)}}]$=[-35, -25], and $[\underline{\mu}_{\tilde{A}_1^{(2)}}, \overline{\mu}_{\tilde{A}_1^{(2)}}] = [\underline{\mu}_{\tilde{A}_2^{(2)}}, \overline{\mu}_{\tilde{A}_2^{(2)}}]$=[25, 35]. Referring (6), a singleton is used to define the centroid of the output fuzzy set $\tilde{B}^{(i_1 i_2)}$ in (1). Let $c_l^{(1,1)} = c_r^{(1,1)}$=-1.25, $c_l^{(1,2)} = c_r^{(1,2)}$=-0.1, $c_l^{(2,1)} = c_r^{(2,1)}$=0.1, $c_l^{(2,2)} = c_r^{(2,2)}$=1.25. To verify the effectiveness and efficiency of the proposed type-2 fuzzy controller, the controller is compared with a type-1 fuzzy controller with similar parameterization. As in the type-2 fuzzy controller, 4 fuzzy rules are defined in the type-1 fuzzy controller. The parameterizations for the type-1 fuzzy controller are set to be as close to the type-2 settings as possible in order to have a fair comparison. The left and right semi-Gaussian function is defined as the membership function for the fuzzy sets describing the linguistic terms "negative" and "positive". Define the left and right semi-Gaussian function, respectively, as following.

$$LG(x;m_l,\sigma_l)=\begin{cases}1, & x\le m_l\\ \exp(-(x-m_l)^2/\sigma_l^2), & x>m_l\end{cases} \tag{27}$$

$$RG(x;m_r,\sigma_r)=\begin{cases}\exp(-(x-m_r)^2/\sigma_r^2), & x\le m_r\\ 1, & x>m_r\end{cases} \tag{28}$$

The left semi-Gaussian function with m_l = -30 and σ_l = 16.5 in (27) is used as the membership function of the fuzzy set describing the linguistic term "negative" for both e_1 and e_2. Similarly, the right semi-Gaussian function with m_r = 30 and σ_r = 16.5 in (28) is used as the membership function of the fuzzy set describing the linguistic term "positive" for both e_1 and e_2. The running paths of the wall-following results using type-2 and type-1 fuzzy controllers are compared in Fig. 3 (a) and (b). It is obvious that the running path due to the type-2 fuzzy controller is smoother than the one due to the type-1 fuzzy controller. The variations of AGV's rotation angle $\theta(k)$ in (26) with respect to time due to type-2 and type-1 fuzzy controller are compared in Fig. 4 (a) and (b). It numerically justifies that the running path due to the type-2 fuzzy controller is smoother because the variations of $\theta(k)$ in Fig. 4(a) due to the type-2 fuzzy controller is much smaller than the one in Fig. 4(b) due to the type-1 fuzzy controller.

(a) (b)

Fig. 3. Comparison of AGV's running paths due to (a) type-2 fuzzy controller, (b) type-1 fuzzy controller.

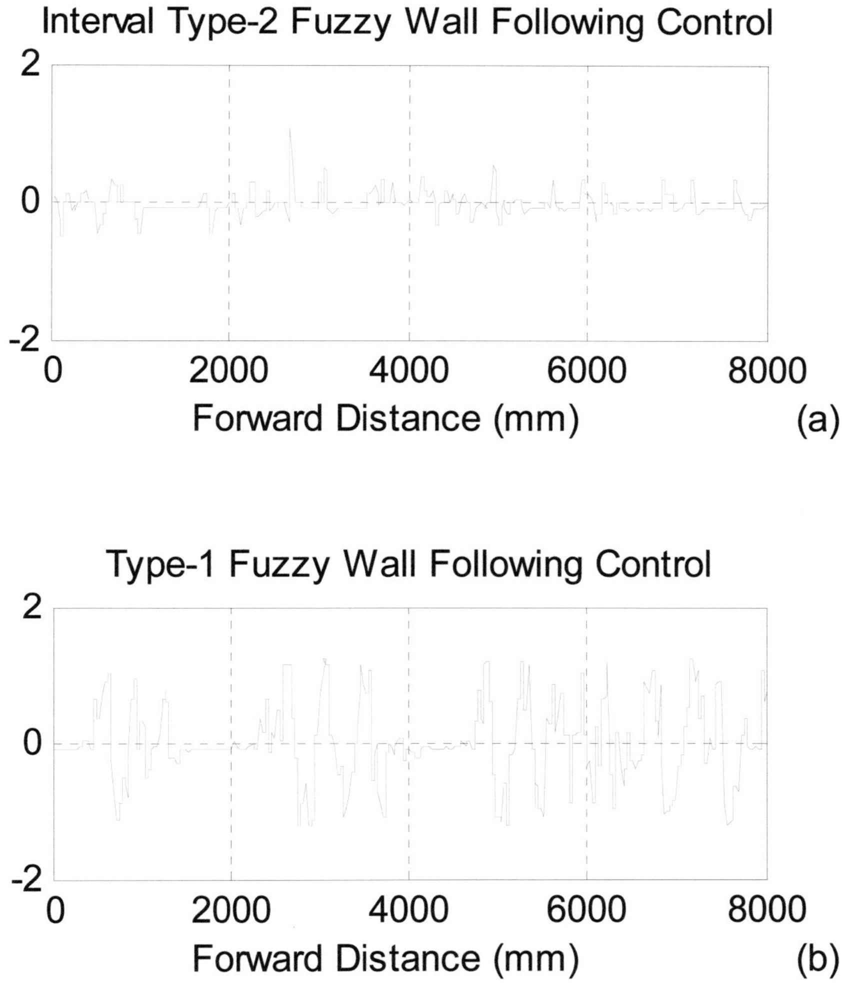

Fig. 4. Comparison of AGV's rotation angle $\theta(k)$ due to (a) type-2 fuzzy controller, (b) type-1 fuzzy controller.

6. Conclusion

A wall-following type-2 fuzzy controller for AGV has been designed in this paper. The proposed type-2 fuzzy controller is especially suitable for the AGV that uses sonar system to measure the distance between the AGV and the wall. The distance measuring scheme used in the sonar system is sensitive to the received ultra-sound signals. The proposed type-2 fuzzy controller features the robustness of the distance measurement. The inevitable noise problem in AGV's sonar-based distance measuring scheme is resolved by using type-2 fuzzy sets to define the distance measurements. Similar approach can also be applied to the sonar-based obstacle avoidance because the surface of obstacle might not be smooth enough to reflect the ultra-sound signals back to AGV's sonar transceivers.

7. References

[1] C.-F. Juang and C.-H. Hsu (2009). "Reinforcement ant optimized fuzzy controller for mobile-robot wall-following control," *IEEE Trans. Ind. Electron.*, vol. 56, no. 10, pp. 3931-3940, Oct. 2009.

[2] C. L. Hwang, L. J. Chang, and Y. S. Yu, "Network-based fuzzy decentralized sliding-mode control for car-like mobile robots," *IEEE Trans. Ind. Electron.*, vol. 54, no. 1, pp. 574-585, Feb. 2007.

[3] D. Wu, W. W. Tan (2005). "Computationally efficient type-reduction strategies for a type-2 fuzzy logic controller," in *Proc. IEEE Int. Conf. Fuzzy Systems*, pp. 353–358, 2005.

[4] H. A. Hagras (2004). "A hierarchical type-2 fuzzy logic control architecture for autonomous mobile robots," *IEEE Trans. Fuzzy Systems*, vol. 12, no. 4, pp. 524–538, Aug. 2004.

[5] H. Wu, J. Mendel (2002). "Uncertainty Bounds and Their Use in the Design of Interval Type-2 Fuzzy Logic Systems," *IEEE Trans. Fuzzy Systems*, vol. 10, no. 5, pp. 622–635, Oct. 2002.

[6] I. Baturone, F. J. Moreno-Velo, V. Blanco, and J. Ferruz (2008). "Design of embedded DSP-based fuzzy controller for autonomous mobile robots," *IEEE Trans. Ind. Electron.*, vol. 55, no. 2, pp. 928-936, Feb. 2008.

[7] J. Godjevac and N. Steele (1999). "Neuro-fuzzy control of a mobile robot," *Neurocomputing*, vol. 28, no. 1, pp. 127-143, Oct. 1999.

[8] J. M. Mendel and R. I. B. John (2002). "Type-2 fuzzy sets made simple," *IEEE Trans. Fuzzy Systems*, vol. 10, no. 2, pp. 117-127, April 2002.

[9] J. M. Mendel (2001). Uncertain Rule-Based Fuzzy Logic Systems: Introduction and New Directions, NJ: Prentice Hall PTR, 2001.

[10] K. C. Ng and M. M. Trivedi (1998). "A neuro-fuzzy controller for mobile robot navigatin and multirobot convoying," *IEEE Trans. Syst., Man, Cyern.-Pt. B: Cybern.*, vol. 28, no. 6, pp. 829-840, Dec. 1998.

[11] M. J. Er and C. Deng (2004). "Online tuning of fuzzy inference systems using dynamic fuzzy Q-learning," *IEEE Trans. Syst., Man, Cyern., Pt. B: Cybern.*, vol. 34, no. 3, pp. 1478-1489, Jun. 2004.

[12] N. N. Karnik and J. M. Mendel (2001). "Centroid of a type-2 fuzzy set," *Inform. Sci.*, vol. 132, no. 1-4, pp. 195–220, Feb. 2001.

[13] S. Nurmaini, S. Z. M. Hashim, and D. N. A. Jawawi (2009). "Environmental recognition using RAM-network based type-2 fuzzy neural network for navigation of mobile robot," in *Proc. Int. Conf. Computer and Automation Engineering*, 8-10 Mar., 2009, pp. 296-301

[14] T.-H. S. Li, S.-J. Chang, and Y.-X. Chen (2003). "Implementation of human-like driving skills by autonomous fuzzy behavior control on an FPGA-based car-like mobile robot," *IEEE Trans. Ind. Electron.*, vol. 50, no. 5, pp. 867-880, Oct. 2003.

[15] W. Tsui, M. S. Masmoudi, F. Karray, I. Song, and M. Masmoudi (2008). "Soft-computing-based embedded design of an intelligent wall/lane-following vehicle," *IEEE/ASME Trans. Mechatronics*, vol. 13, no. 1, pp. 125-135, Feb. 2008.

[16] Z. Liu, Y. Zhang, and Y. Wang (2007). "A type-2 fuzzy switching control system for biped robots," *IEEE Trans. Syst., Man, and Cybern.-Pt. C: App. and Rev.*, vol. 37, no. 6, pp. 1202–1213, Nov. 2007.

14

New Applications of Fuzzy Logic Methodologies in Aerospace Field

Teodor Lucian Grigorie and Ruxandra Mihaela Botez
École de Technologie Supérieure
Canada

1. Introduction

Automatic control can be defined as a way of analyzing and designing a system that can self-regulate with minimal human intervention. It is based on control theory, viewed as an interdisciplinary branch of engineering and mathematics. The device that monitors and modifies the operational conditions of a dynamic system is called a controller.

The global technology evolution has triggered an ever-increasing complexity of applications, both in industry and in the scientific research fields. Many researchers have concentrated their efforts on providing simple control algorithms to cope with the increasing complexity of the controlled systems (Al-Odienat & Al-Lawama, 2008). The main challenge of a control designer is to find a formal way to convert the knowledge and experience of a system operator into a well-designed control algorithm (Kovacic & Bogdan, 2006). From another point of view, a control design method should allow full flexibility in the adjustment of the control surface, as the systems involved in practice are, generally, complex, strongly nonlinear and often with poorly defined dynamics (Al-Odienat & Al-Lawama, 2008). If a conventional control methodology, based on linear system theory, is to be used, a linearized model of the nonlinear system should have been developed beforehand. Because the validity of a linearized model is limited to a range around the operating point, no guarantee of good performance can be provided by the obtained controller. Therefore, to achieve satisfactory control of a complex nonlinear system, a nonlinear controller should be developed (Al-Odienat & Al-Lawama, 2008; Hampel et al., 2000; Kovacic & Bogdan, 2006; Verbruggen & Bruijn, 1997). From another perspective, if it would be difficult to precisely describe the controlled system by conventional mathematical relations, the design of a controller using classical analytical methods would be totally impractical (Hampel et al., 2000; Kovacic & Bogdan, 2006). Such systems have been the motivation for developing a control system designed by a skilled operator, based on their multi-year experience and knowledge of the static and dynamic characteristics of a system; known as a Fuzzy Logic Controller (FLC) (Hampel et al., 2000). FLCs are based on fuzzy logic theory, developed by L. Zadeh (Zadeh, 1965). By using multivalent fuzzy logic, linguistic expressions in antecedent and consequent parts of IF-THEN rules describing the operator's actions can be efficiently converted into a fully-structured control algorithm suitable for microcomputer implementation or implementation with specially-designed fuzzy processors (Kovacic & Bogdan, 2006). In contrast to traditional linear and nonlinear control theory, an FLC is not based on a mathematical model, and it does provide a certain

level of artificial intelligence compared to conventional PID controllers (Al-Odienat & Al-Lawama, 2008).
The objective of the research presented here is to develop a new morphing mechanism using smart materials such as Shape Memory Alloy (SMA) as actuators and fuzzy logic techniques. These smart actuators deform the upper wing surface, made of a flexible skin, so that the laminar-to-turbulent transition point moves closer to the wing trailing edge. The ultimate goal of this research project is to achieve drag reduction as a function of flow condition by changing the wing shape. The transition location detection is based on pressure signals measured by optical and Kulite sensors installed on the upper wing flexible surface. Depending on the project evolution phase, two architectures are considered for the morphing system: open loop and closed loop. The difference between these two architectures is their use of the transition point as a feedback signal. This research work was a part of a morphing wing project developed by the Ecole de Technologie Supérieure in Montréal, Canada, in collaboration with the Ecole Polytechnique in Montréal and the Institute for Aerospace Research at the National Research Council Canada (IAR-NRC) (Brailovski et al., 2008; Coutu et al., 2007; Coutu et al., 2009; Georges et al., 2009; Grigorie & Botez, 2009; Grigorie & Botez, 2010; Grigorie et al., 2010 a; Grigorie et al., 2010 b; Grigorie et al., 2010 c; Popov et al., 2008 a; Popov et al., 2008 b; Popov et al., 2009 a; Popov et al., 2009 b; Popov et al., 2010 a; Popov et al., 2010 b; Popov et al., 2010 c; Sainmont et. al., 2009), initiated and financially supported by the following government and industry associations: the Consortium for Research and Innovation in Aerospace in Quebec (CRIAQ), the National Sciences and Engineering Research Council of Canada (NSERC), Bombardier Aerospace, Thales Avionics, and the National Research Council Canada Institute for Aerospace Research (NRC-IAR).
Recently, morphing wing system studies have branched out into new research directions. Extremely complex and catalogued as inter- and multidisciplinary studies, morphing wing studies continue to 'push' the science to the extreme boundaries of mathematics and physics. These multidisciplinary studies therefore require knowledge of the following disciplines: aerodynamics and computational fluid dynamics, aeroelasticity, automatic control, intelligent materials, signal detection using the latest miniaturized sensors, high computer-time calculations, wind tunnel and flight testing, instruments, and signal acquisition -- these signals have such speed that they are raising serious problems for the existing calculus technology. Consequently, real-time system functioning is conditioned (in addition to other factors) by being able to obtain the best data processing algorithms and employing easy-to-implement software for the command and control unit. Fuzzy logic theories, which offer remarkable facilities, may therefore be used in these algortihms. They facilitate signal processing by allowing empirical models to be designed based on experimental data; thus avoiding the complex mathematical calculus currently in use. In addition, fuzzy logic can be used to model highly non-linear, multidimensional systems, including those with parameter variations, or where the sensors' signals are not accurate enough for other models. This research project included the following: optical sensor selection and testing for laminar-to-turbulent flow transition validation (by use of XFoil code and Matlab), smart material actuator modeling, aeroelasticity wing studies using MSC/Nastran, open loop and closed loop transition delay controller design, and integration and validation on a wing equipped with SMAs and optical sensors (simulation versus experimental test results) (Fig. 1 (Grigorie et al., 2010 b)).

A first phase of this project involved the determination of optimized airfoils available for 35 different flow conditions expressed in terms of five Mach numbers (0.2, 0.225, 0.25, 0.275, 0.3) and seven angles of attack (-1°, -0.5°, 0°, 0.5°, 1°, 1.5°, 2°) combinations. The optimized airfoils, derived from a laminar WTEA-TE1 reference airfoil, were calculated and used as a starting point in the actuation system design. Three steps were completed in the actuation system design phase: optimization of the number and positions of flexible skin actuation points, establishment of each actuation line's architecture, and modeling of the smart materials actuators used in this application with fuzzy logic techniques. The next phase of the project was about the design of the actuation control, for which a fuzzy PD architecture was chosen. In this design, numerical simulations of the open loop morphing wing integrated system, based on an SMA non-linear model, were performed. As subsequent validation methods, a bench test and a wind tunnel test were conducted.

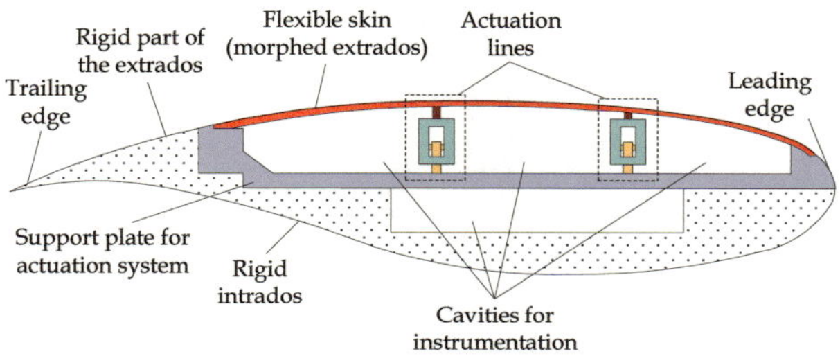

Fig. 1. General architecture of the mechanical model

The shape memory actuator wires were made of nickel-titanium, known as Nitinol, and they contract as muscles do when electrically driven. This ability to flex or shorten is a characteristic of certain alloys that dynamically change their internal structure at certain temperatures. These alloys have the properties of exhibiting martensitic transformation when they deform at a low temperature phase, and may recover their original shape after heating (Popov et al., 2008 a). This phase change, from martensite to austenite, is shown in Fig. 2 (Baron et al., 2003; Thill et al., 2008). The load changes the internal forces between the atoms, forcing them to change their positions in the crystals and consequently forcing the wires to lengthen, which is called the SMA activation or the initial phase. When the wire is heated using a current, the heat generated by the current resistivity causes the atoms in the crystalline structure to realign and force the alloy to recover its original shape. Therefore, any change in the alloy's internal temperature would modify the crystalline structure accordingly and thus the wire's exterior shape. This property of changing the wire length as a function of the electrical current passing through the wire is used for actuation purposes (Popov et al., 2008 a). Another major reason for using Nitinol is that it is the most effective material at withstanding repeated cycles of heating and cooling without exhibiting a fatigue phenomenon (Gonzalez, 2005).

SMA wires can process the deflections obtained using the applied forces and they provide a variety of shapes and sizes that are extremely useful to achieve actuation system goals. For example, SMA wires can provide high forces corresponding to small strains to achieve the correct balance between the forces and the deformations, as required by the actuation system. To ensure a stable system, a compromise or balance must be established and maintained. The structural components of the actuation system should be designed to respect the actuators' capabilities to accommodate the required deflections and forces.

Each of our actuation lines uses three shape memory alloys wires as actuators, and contains a cam, which moves in translation relative to the structure (on the x-axis in Fig. 3 (Georges et al., 2009). The cam causes the movement of a rod related on the roller and on the skin (on the z-axis). The recall employed here is a gas spring. So, when the SMA is heating the actuator contracts and the cam moves to the right, resulting in the rise of the roller and the displacement of the skin upwards. In contrast, the cooling of the SMA results in a movement of the cam to the left, and thus a movement of the skin downwards. The horizontal displacement of each actuator is converted into a vertical displacement at a fixed rate.

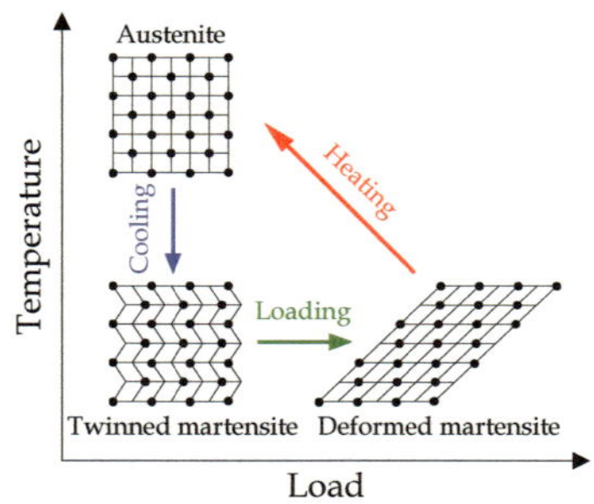

Fig. 2. SMA phase change

SMA wires can execute the deflections resulting from contracting or expanding forces and can provide a variety of shapes and sizes that are extremely useful to achieve actuation system goals. To ensure a stable system, a compromise or balance must be established and maintained. The structural components of the actuation system should be designed to respect the actuators' capabilities to accommodate the required deflections and forces.

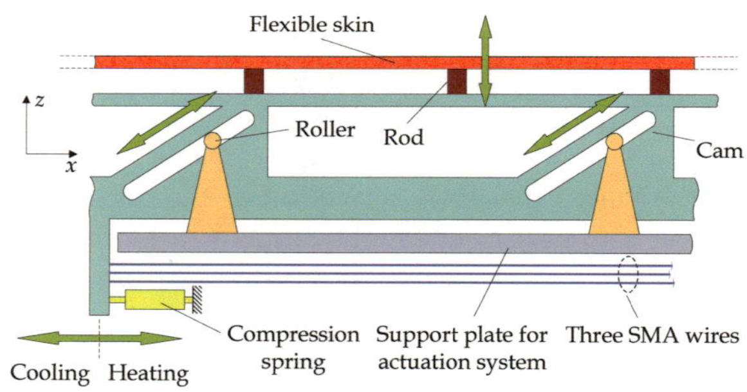

Fig. 3. The actuation mechanism concept

The SMA actuator control can be achieved using any method for position control. However, the specific properties of SMA actuators such as hysteresis, the first cycle effect and the impact of long-term changes must be considered. The operating scheme of our open loop controller can be developed as illustrated in Fig. 4 (Grigorie et al., 2010 b; Grigorie et al., 2010 c).

Based on the 35 studied flight conditions, a database of the 35 optimized airfoils was built. For each flight condition, a pair of optimal vertical deflections (dY_{1opt}, dY_{2opt}) for the two actuation lines is apparent (Fig. 5). The SMA actuators morphed the airfoil until the vertical deflections of the two actuation lines (dY_{1real}, dY_{2real}) became equal to the required

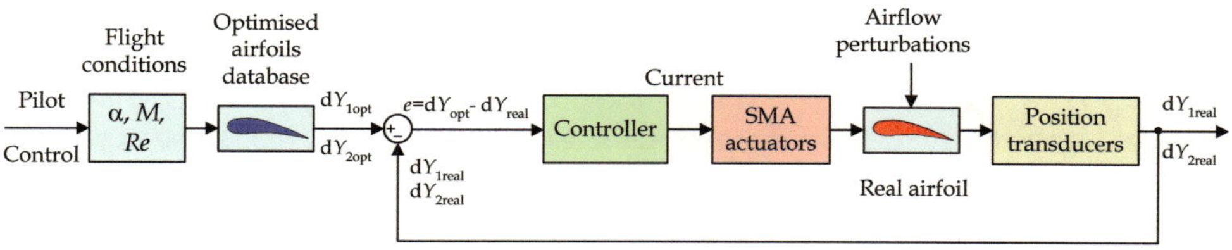

Fig. 4. Operating scheme of the SMA actuators' control

deflections (dY_{1opt}, dY_{2opt}). The vertical deflections of the real airfoil at the actuation points were measured using two position transducers. The controller's role is to send a command to supply an electrical current signal to the SMA actuators, based on the error signals (*e*) between the required vertical displacements and the obtained displacements. The designed controller was valid for both actuation lines, which are practically identical.

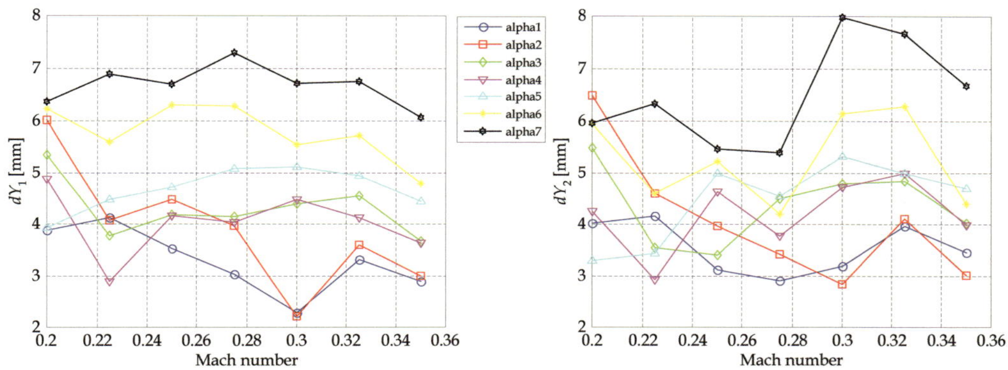

Fig. 5. dY_{1opt} and dY_{1opt}, dY_{2opt} as functions of *M* for various angles of attack

During the first phase of the controller design, numerical simulation of the controlled actuation system was performed; a step which required an SMA actuator model. In the literature, the modeling and control of smart material actuators can be categorized as recent research fields. Technical literature is available in three independent domains: modeling, control and smart materials. A smart actuator is formulated for a large range of smart materials and devices, and can be found in a variety of different configurations. It is common knowledge that all physical systems, including smart actuators, contain nonlinearities. As a consequence, linear modeling of smart material actuators may contain errors, while non-linear modeling remains possible.

In order to conceive such a model, a fuzzy set must be designed, which may be given by the original fuzzy logic theory conceived by Lotfi A. Zadeh (Zadeh, 1965). The most serious problem arises from the determination of a complete set of rules and the membership functions corresponding to each input. The multiple attempts required to reduce errors and to optimize the model are time-consuming and, very often, the results are far from what was expected. A modern design method allows fuzzy model design to be completed in a relatively short time interval. The Adaptive Neuro-Fuzzy Inference System (ANFIS) design technique allows the generation and the optimization of the set of rules and the membership functions' parameters by use of Neural Networks. Moreover, the ANFIS design technique already implemented in Matlab's Neuro-Fuzzy software tools should be relatively easy to use.

Considering the numerical values resulting from the SMA experimental testing (forces, currents, temperatures and elongations), an empirical model can be developed, based on a neuro-fuzzy network. The model can learn the process behavior based on the input-output process data by using a Fuzzy Inference System (FIS), which should model the experimental data.

2. SMA actuator fuzzy model

The general aim of the SMA model is to calculate the elongation of the actuator ($\Delta\delta$) under the application of a thermo-electro-mechanical load for some time (Δt). The load is so-qualified because the actuator can be operated by varying temperature (T_{amb}), by injection of electric current (i) or by applying a force (F). The geometry of the actuator is an SMA wire with constant section and perimeter over the length of the actuator. For these specific model objectives, in the first phase, the SMA actuators were experimentally tested in conditions close to those in which they will be used.

The SMA testing was performed using at T_{amb}=24°C, for six load cases with the forces of 700 N, 850 N, 1000 N, 1100 N, 1250 N and 1500 N. The electrical currents following the increasing-constant-decreasing-zero values evolution were applied to the SMA actuator for each of the six load cases. In each case, the following parameters were registered: time, the electrical current supplied to the SMA, the load force, the material temperature and the actuator elongation.

To model the SMA we will built an integrated controller based on Adaptive Neuro-Fuzzy Inference Systems. The experimental elongation-current curves obtained from the six load cases are indicated in Fig. 6. One can observe that all six of the curves are characterized by four distinct zones: electrical current increase, constant electrical current, electrical current decrease and null electrical current in the cooling phase of the actuator. Therefore, four Fuzzy Inference Systems (FIS's) are used to obtain four neuro-fuzzy controllers: one controller for the current increase, one for a constant current, one for the current decrease, and one controller for the null current (after its decrease). For the first and the third controllers, inputs such as the force and the current are used, while for the second and the fourth controller, inputs such as the force and the time values reflecting the SMA thermal inertia are used (for the four controllers the time values used are those required for the SMA to recover its initial temperature value (approximately 24°C)). Finally, the four obtained controllers must be integrated into a single controller.

The reasoning behind the design of the first and the third controllers is that from the available experimental data, two elongations for the same values of forces and currents are used (see Fig. 6). Due to the experimental data values, this data cannot be represented as algebraic functions, and therefore it is impossible to use the same FIS representation. An interpolation between the two elongation values obtained for the same values of forces and currents can be performed in Matlab, but it is not valid for our application.

Also, the constant values, respectively the null values of the current before, respectively after the current decrease phase are not suggestive to be considered like inputs in the second and in the four controllers. Practically, with these phases the values of the actuator temperature could be used. The time values for these phases do prove very useful, because these values represent a measure of the thermal inertia of the actuator. We use the time value as the second input of the third controller, and therefore, as the second input of the second and of the fourth controllers - since force was considered as the first input (the time values must be considered from the moment when the current becomes constant, or null).

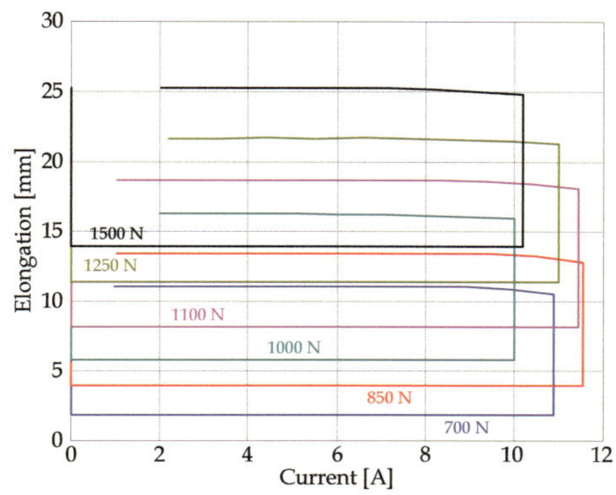

Fig. 6. Elongation versus the current values for different forces values for six load cases

2.1 SMA model architecture based on fuzzy logic controllers

A fuzzy inference system (FIS) can be easily generated using Matlab's "genfis1" or "genfis2" functions. The "genfis1" function generates a single-output Sugeno-type fuzzy inference system (FIS) using a grid partition on the data (no clustering). The FIS thus obtained is used to provide the initial conditions for ANFIS training. The "genfis1" function uses generalized bell-type membership functions for each input. Each rule generated by a "genfis1" function has one output membership function, which is a linear type by default. It is also possible to create the FIS using the Matlab "genfis2" function, which first generates an initial Sugeno-type FIS by decomposition of the operation domain into different regions using the fuzzy subtractive clustering method. For each region, a low order linear model can describe the local process parameters. The non-linear process can then be locally linearized around a functioning point by using the Least Squares method. The obtained model is considered valid in the entire region around this point. To limit the operating regions implies the existence of overlapping among these different regions, whose definition is given in a fuzzy manner. Thus, for each model input, several fuzzy sets are associated with their corresponding definitions of their membership functions. By combining these fuzzy inputs, the input space is divided into fuzzy regions. For each such region, a local linear model is used, while the global model is obtained by defuzzification with the center-of-gravity method (Sugeno), which interpolates the local models' outputs (Sivanandam et al., 2007; MathWorks Inc., 2008).

Based on the concept of finding regions with a high density of data points in the feature space, the subtractive clustering method divides space into a number of clusters. Centers of clusters are selected, starting with the points with the highest number of neighbours. The clusters are identified one by one; for each cluster the data points within a prespecified fuzzy radius are removed (subtracted). After each cluster identification, the algorithm looks for a new one until all of the data points have been examined. If a collection of M data points, specified by l-dimensional vectors u_k, $k = 1, 2..., M$, is considered, a density measure at data point u_k can be defined as follows:

$$\rho_k = \sum_{j=1}^{M} \exp\left(-\frac{|u_k - u_j|}{(r_m/2)^2} \right). \tag{1}$$

where r_m is a positive constant that defines the radius within the fuzzy neighborhood and contributes to the density measure. The point with the highest density is selected as the first cluster center. Let u_{c1} be the point selected and ρ_{c1} its density measure. Next, the density measure for each data point u_k is revised by the formula:

$$\rho_k' = \rho_k - \rho_{c1}\exp\left(-\frac{|u_k - u_{c1}|}{(r_n/2)^2}\right). \tag{2}$$

in which r_n is a positive constant, larger than r_m, and defines a neighborhood to be reduced in its density measure to prevent closely-spaced cluster centers. In this way, the data points near the first cluster center u_{c1} will have significantly reduced density measures, and these points cannot be selected as centers for the next clusters. After the density measure for each point has been revised, the next cluster center u_{c2} is selected and all the density measures are revised again. The process is repeated until all of the data points have been examined and a sufficient number of cluster centers generated. When the subtractive clustering method is applied to an input-output data set, each of the cluster centers are used as the centers for the premise sets in a singleton type of rule base (Khezri & Jahed, 2007).
The Matlab "genfis1" function generates membership functions of a generalized bell type, defined as follows (Kosko, 1992; Kung & Su, 2007):

$$A_q^i(x) = (1 + |(x - c_q^i)/a|^{2b})^{-1}, \tag{3}$$

where c_q^i is the cluster center defining the position of the membership function, a, b are two parameters which define the shape of the membership function, and $A_q^i\,(i=\overline{1,N})$ are associated individual antecedent fuzzy sets of each input variable (N - number of rules).
The Matlab "genfis2" function generates membership functions of the Gaussian type, described by the following expression (Kosko, 1992; Kung & Su, 2007):

$$A_q^i(x) = \exp\{-0.5((x - c_q^i)/\sigma_q^i)^2\}, \tag{4}$$

where c_q^i is the cluster center, and σ_q^i is the dispersion of the cluster.
The Sugeno fuzzy model was proposed by Takagi, Sugeno and Kang to generate the fuzzy rules from a given input-output data set (Mahfouf et al., 1999). For our system, for all four of the FIS's (two inputs and one output) a first-order model is considered, and for N rules is given by (Kung & Su, 2007; Mahfouf et al., 1999):

$$\begin{aligned}
&\text{Rule } 1\text{: If } x_1 \text{ is } A_1^1 \text{ and } x_2 \text{ is } A_2^1, \text{ then } y^1(x_1,x_2) = b_0^1 + a_1^1 x_1 + a_2^1 x_2,\\
&\vdots\\
&\text{Rule } i\text{: If } x_1 \text{ is } A_1^i \text{ and } x_2 \text{ is } A_2^i, \text{ then } y^i(x_1,x_2) = b_0^i + a_1^i x_1 + a_2^i x_2,\\
&\vdots\\
&\text{Rule } N\text{: If } x_1 \text{ is } A_1^N \text{ and } x_2 \text{ is } A_2^N, \text{ then } y^N(x_1,x_2) = b_0^N + a_1^N x_1 + a_2^N x_2,
\end{aligned} \tag{5}$$

where $x_q\,(q=\overline{1,2})$ are individual input variables, and $y^i\,(i=\overline{1,N})$ is the first-order polynomial function in the consequent. $a_k^i\,(k=\overline{1,2},\, i=\overline{1,N})$ are the parameters of the linear function and $b_0^i\,(i=\overline{1,N})$ denotes a scalar offset. The parameters a_k^i, $b_0^i\,(k=\overline{1,2},\, i=\overline{1,N})$ are optimized by Least Square method.

For any input vector, $x = [x_1, x_2]^T$, if the singleton fuzzifier, the product fuzzy inference and the center-average defuzzifier are applied, the output of the fuzzy model y is inferred as follows (weighted average):

$$y = \left(\sum_{i=1}^{N} w^i(\boldsymbol{x}) y^i \right) / \left(\sum_{i=1}^{N} w^i(\boldsymbol{x}) \right), \tag{6}$$

where

$$w^i(\boldsymbol{x}) = A_1^i(x_1) \times A_2^i(x_2). \tag{7}$$

$w^i(\boldsymbol{x})$ represents the degree of fulfillment of the antecedent, that is, the level of firing of the ith rule.

The adaptive neuro-fuzzy inference system adapts the parameters of Sugeno-type fuzzy inference systems using the neural networks. A very simple way to realize the FIS's training is by using the Matlab "ANFIS" function, which use a learning algorithm for the identification of the membership functions' parameters of a Sugeno-type fuzzy inference system with two outputs and one input. As a starting point, the input-output data and the FIS models generated with the "genfis1" or "genfis2" functions are considered. The "ANFIS" optimizes the membership functions' parameters for a number of training epochs; this number is set by the user. The optimization is realized for a better process approximation performed by the neuro-fuzzy model by means of a quality parameter present in the training algorithm (MathWorks Inc., 2008). Following the training phase, the models may be used for elongation value generation corresponding to the parameters at the input.

For training the fuzzy system, ANFIS employs a back-propagation algorithm for the parameters associated with the input membership functions, and a least mean square estimation for the parameters associated with the output membership functions. For the FISs generated using the "genfis1" or "genfis2" functions, the membership functions are of the generalized bell type and gaussian type, respectively. In accordance with equations (3) and (4), in these kinds of membership functions, a, b and c, and σ and c, respectively, are considered variables and must be adjusted. Therefore, the back-propagation algorithm may be used to train these parameters. In this way, we can achieve our goal to minimize a cost function of the form

$$\varepsilon = (y_{des} - y)^2 / 2, \tag{8}$$

where y_{des} is desired output. The output of each rule $y^i(x_1, x_2)$ is defined by:

$$y^i(t+1) = y^i(t) - k_y(\partial\varepsilon / \partial y^i), \tag{9}$$

in which k_y is the step size.

Starting from the Sugeno system's output (eq. (6)), we find:

$$\frac{\partial \varepsilon}{\partial y^i} = \frac{\partial \varepsilon}{\partial y} \cdot \frac{\partial y}{\partial y^i}, \tag{10}$$

with

$$\frac{\partial \varepsilon}{\partial y} = y_{des} - y, \quad \frac{\partial y}{\partial y^i} = w_i(\boldsymbol{x}) / \sum_{i=1}^{N} w^i(\boldsymbol{x}). \tag{11}$$

Therefore, the following equation for the output of each rule is

$$y^i(t+1) = y^i(t) - k_y \cdot (y_{des} - y) \cdot w_i(\boldsymbol{x}) / \sum_{i=1}^{N} w^i(\boldsymbol{x}). \tag{12}$$

If a generalized bell-type membership function is used, for the jth membership function of the ith fuzzy rule the parameters are determined with the relations:

$$a_j^i(t+1) = a_j^i(t) - k_a \frac{\partial \varepsilon}{\partial a_j^i}, \quad b_j^i(t+1) = b_j^i(t) - k_b \frac{\partial \varepsilon}{\partial b_j^i}, \quad c_j^i(t+1) = c_j^i(t) - k_c \frac{\partial \varepsilon}{\partial c_j^i}. \tag{13}$$

For a Gaussian-type membership function, the parameters of the jth membership function of the ith fuzzy rule are calculated with the relations:

$$\sigma_j^i(t+1) = \sigma_j^i(t) - k_\sigma(\partial \varepsilon / \partial \sigma_j^i), \quad c_j^i(t+1) = c_j^i(t) - k_c(\partial \varepsilon / \partial c_j^i). \tag{14}$$

After the four controllers (Controller 1 for increasing current, Controller 2 for constant current, Controller 3 for decreasing current and Controller 4 for null current) have been determined, they must be integrated, resulting in the logical scheme in Fig. 7.
The decision to use one of the four controllers depends on the current vector type (increasing, decreasing, constant or zero) and on the value of variable "**k**". Depending on the "**k**" variable value, we may decide if a constant current value is a part of an increasing vector or a part of a decreasing vector. The initial "**k**" value is equal to 1 when Controller 1 is used, and is equal to 0 when Controllers 2, 3 or 4 are used.

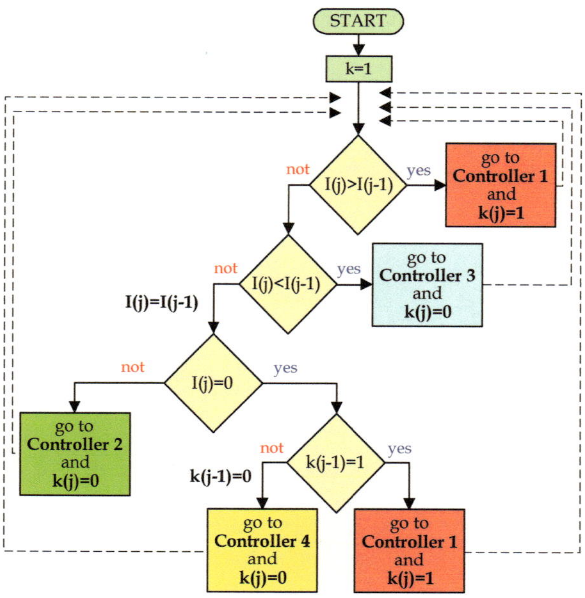

Fig. 7. The logical scheme for the four controller's integration

2.2 The SMA model design and evaluation

In a first phase, the "genfis2" Matlab function (MathWorks Inc., 2008) was used to generate and train the FISs associated with the four controllers in Fig. 7: "Controller1Fis" (for the increasing current phase), "Controller2Fis" (for the constant current phase), "Controller3Fis" (for the decreasing current phase) and "Controller4Fis" (for the null values of the current obtained after the decreasing phase).

The first FIS, with force and electrical current as its inputs, was trained for 5000 epochs using the "ANFIS" Matlab function. The rules were of the type: if (in1 is in1cluster„k") and (in2 is in2cluster„k") then (out1 is out1cluster„k"). For both of these inputs, nine Gaussian-type membership functions (mf) were generated; within the set of rules they are noted by: in„j"cluster„k"; where j is the input number (1÷2), and k is the number of the membership function (1-9). "Controller1Fis" fuzzy inference system thus has the structure shown in Fig. 8, while Controller 1 has the structure indicated in Fig. 9.

The rules of "Controller1Fis" fuzzy inference system, before and after training, are presented in Fig. 10, and Fig. 11 displays the deviation between the neuro-fuzzy models and the experimentally obtained data, defining the quality parameter from the training algorithm, for different training epochs.

Figure 11 shows a rapid decrease in the deviation between the experimental data and the neuro-fuzzy model for the quality parameter within the training algorithm over the first 100 training epochs, from a value of 0.062 to 0.03. Evaluating the FIS before and after training for the experimental data, using the "evalfis" command, the characteristics in Fig. 12 were obtained. The mean of the relative absolute values of the errors decreased from 0.3063% before training to 0.119% after training, while its maximum value decreased from 0.9339% to 0.4342%. Since the error determined for "Controller1Fis" was very small, this FIS was selected to be implemented in the Simulink integrated controller.

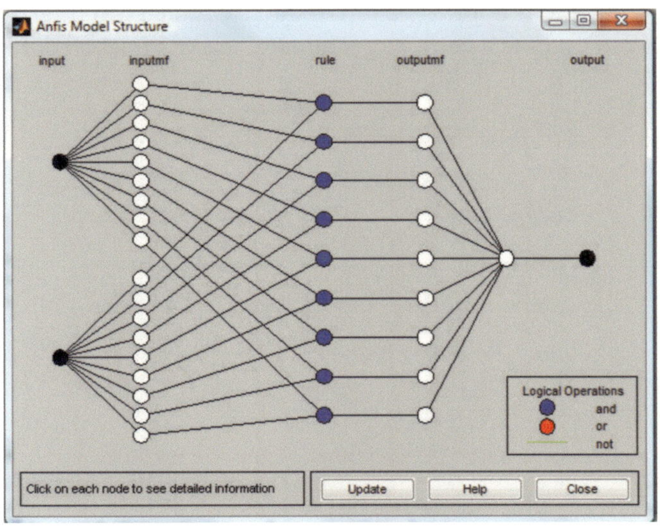

Fig. 8. Structure of the "Controller1Fis" fuzzy inference system

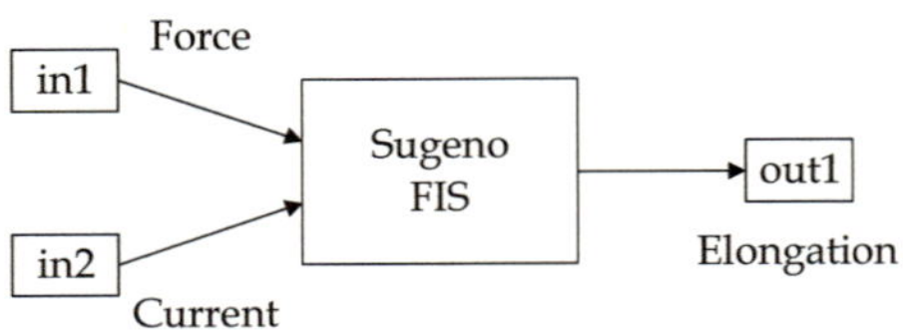

Fig. 9. The structure of Controller 1

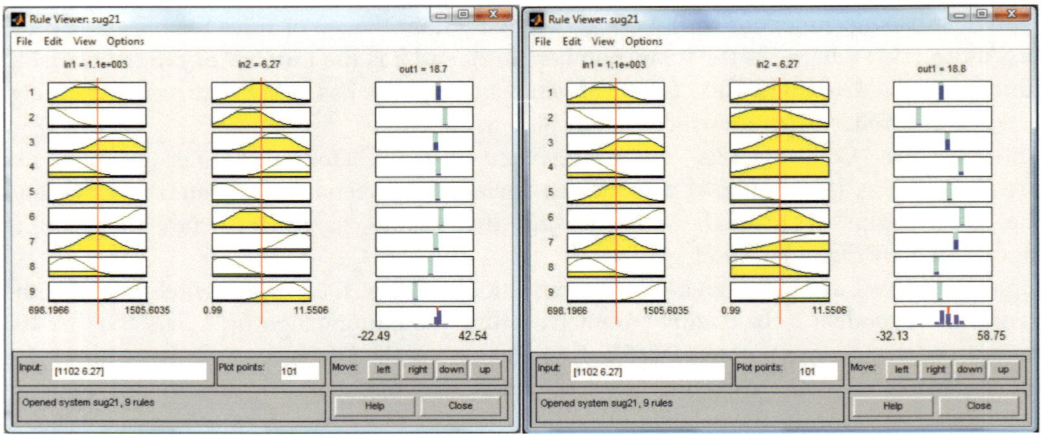

Fig. 10. The "Controller1Fis" rules, before and after training

From Fig. 12 one observes a good overlapping of the FIS model with the elongation experimental data. This superposition is dependent upon the training epochs' number, and improves as the number of training epochs increases. Because the training errors take constant values, an improved approximation of the real model can be achieved with neuro-fuzzy methods only in the case when a larger amount of experimental data is used.

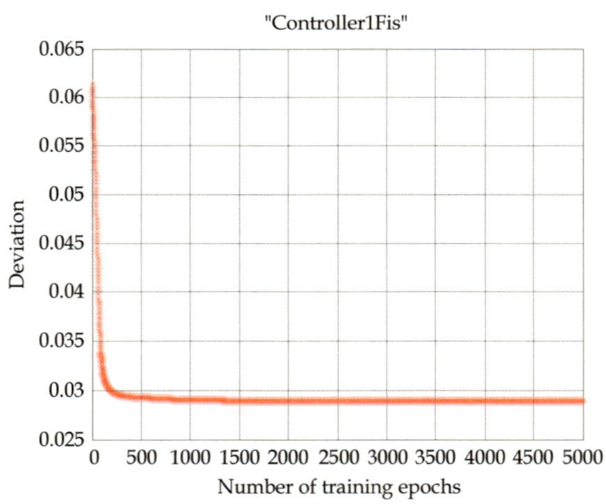

Fig. 11. The training error for "Controller1Fis"

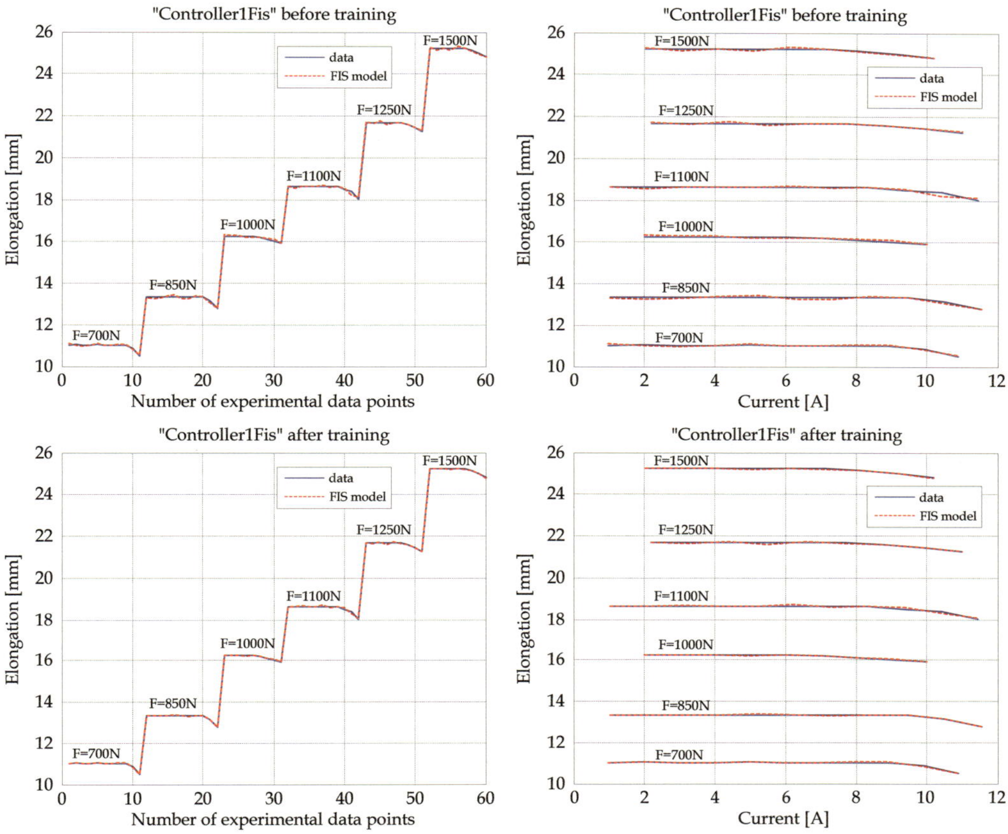

Fig. 12. "Controller1Fis" evaluation, before and after training

The parameters of the input's membership functions for "Controller1Fis", before and after training, are shown in Table 1, while the membership functions' shapes are depicted in Fig. 13. For the Gaussian-type membership functions generated with "genfis2", the parameters are half of the dispersion ($\sigma/2$) and the center for the membership function (c).

Status	Input	Param.	mf1	mf2	mf3	mf4	mf5	mf6	mf7	mf8	mf9
Before training	Force [N]	$\sigma/2$	142.7	142.7	142.7	142.7	142.7	142.7	142.7	142.7	142.7
		c	1003	701.6	1248	851.8	1096	1493	1094	849.3	1498
	Current [A]	$\sigma/2$	1.867	1.867	1.867	1.867	1.867	1.867	1.867	1.867	1.867
		c	6	4.95	7.7	9.45	2.08	5.1	10.4	2.1	9.18
After training	Force [N]	$\sigma/2$	142.8	142.8	142.7	142.7	142.7	142.7	142.7	142.7	142.8
		c	1003	701.6	1248	851.8	1096	1493	1094	849.4	1498
	Current [A]	$\sigma/2$	2.598	3.321	2.328	4.208	2.271	2.252	3.671	2.965	1.885
		c	6.998	4.795	6.942	8.627	0.7952	6.609	10.35	3.194	10.21

Table 1. Parameters of the "Controller1FIS" input's mf, before and after training

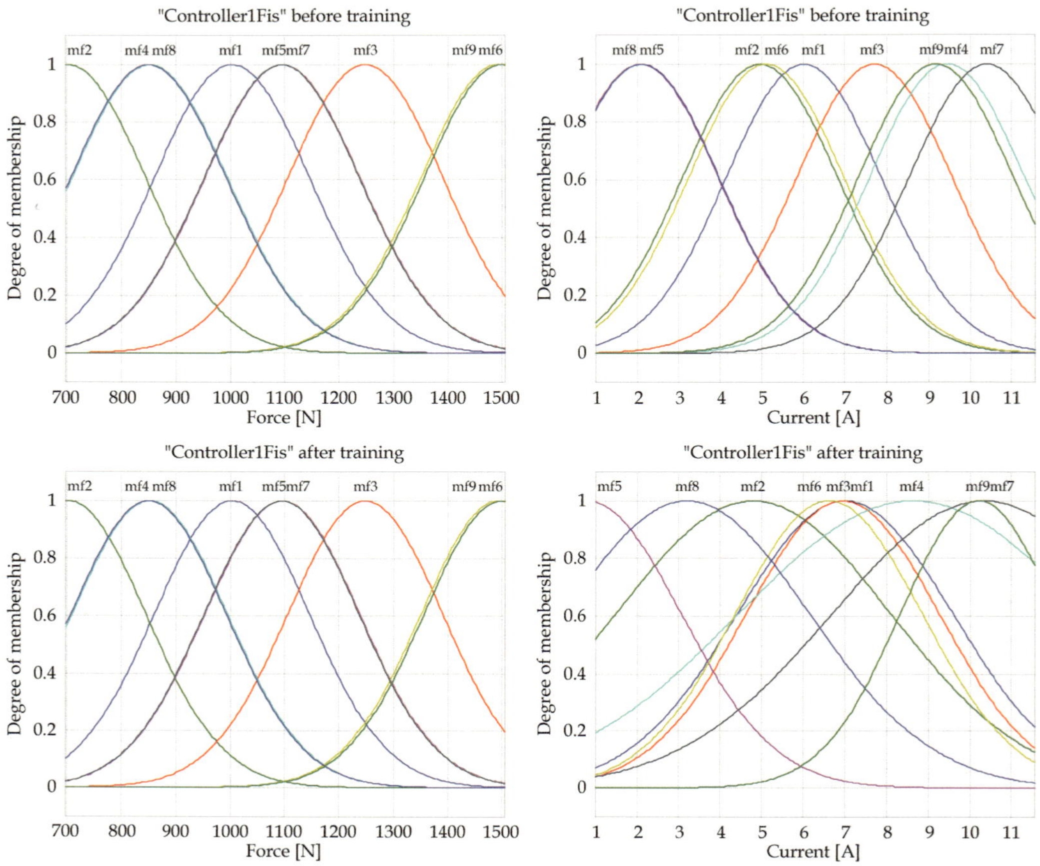

Fig. 13. Membership functions of "Controller1Fis", before and after training

Comparison of the FIS characteristics and the membership function parameters in Table 1, before and after training, indicates a redistribution of the membership functions in the working domain (modification of the *c* parameter) and a change in their shapes by the modification of the σ parameter.

According to the parameter values from Table 1, the FIS's generated with the "genfis2" function give, as a first result, the choice of the same values for the σ/2 parameter, for all membership functions which characterize an input. A second result is the separation of the working space for the respective input, using the fuzzy subtractive clustering method.

Surfaces that reproduce the experimental data before and after the "Controller1Fis" training are presented in Fig. 14.

The second FIS, "Controller2Fis", with inputs of force and time, was trained for the 100000 epochs using the "ANFIS" Matlab function. The rules here were also of the type: if (in1 is in1cluster„k") and (in2 is in2cluster„k") then (out1 is out1cluster„k"). For both of this FIS's inputs, eight Gaussian-type membership functions (mf) were generated. Therefore, "Controller2Fis" fuzzy inference system has the structure shown in Fig. 15, while Controller 2 has the structure given in Fig. 16.

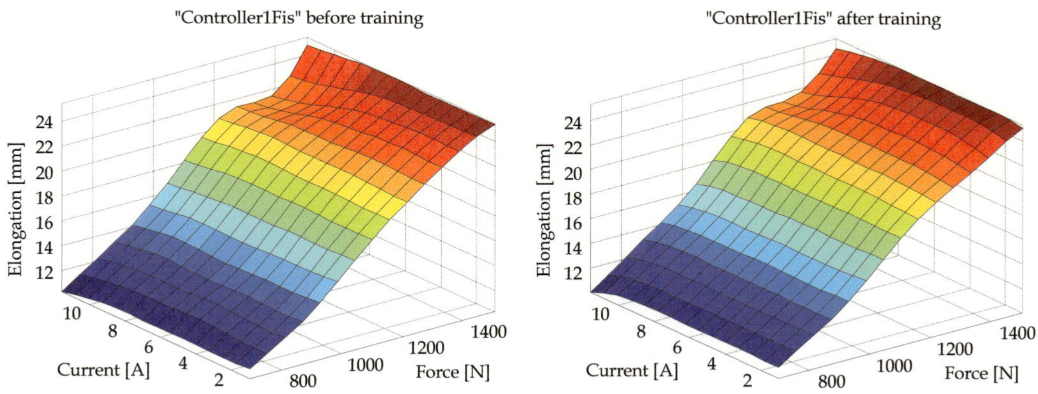

Fig. 14. Control surfaces resulted for "Controller1Fis", before and after training

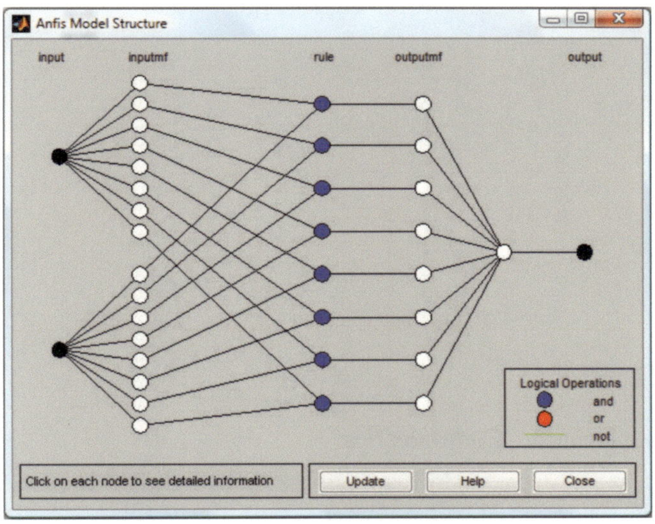

Fig. 15. Structure of the "Controller2Fis" fuzzy inference system

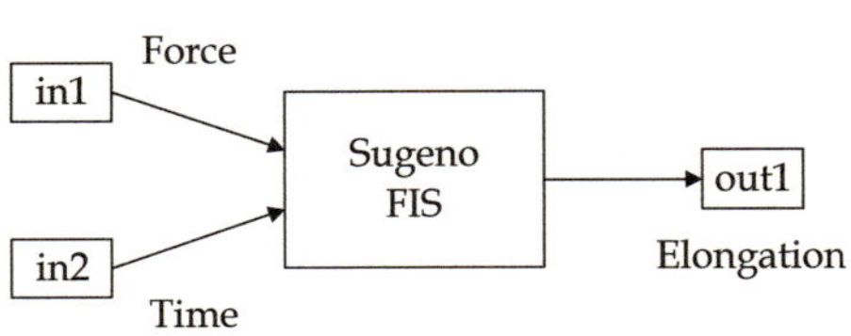

Fig. 16. The structure of Controller 2

The rules of the "Controller2Fis" fuzzy inference system, before and after training, are presented in Fig. 17, while Fig. 18 displays the deviation between the neuro-fuzzy models and the experimentally obtained data, defining the quality parameter from the training algorithm, for different training epochs.

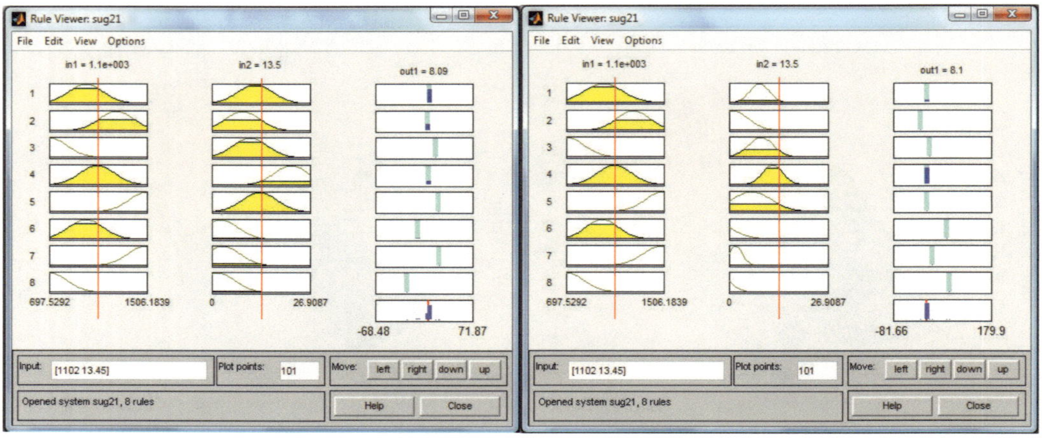

Fig. 17. The "Controller2Fis" rules, before and after training

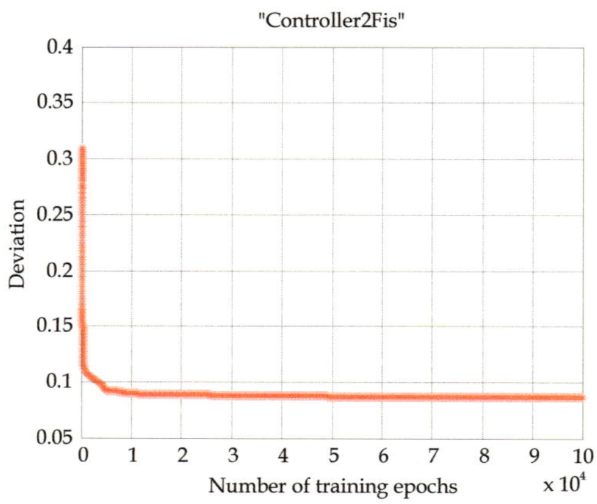

Fig. 18. The training error for "Controller2Fis"

Figure 18 shows a rapid decrease in the deviation between the experimental data and the neuro-fuzzy model for the quality parameter within the training algorithm over the first 5000 training epochs, from 0.31 until a value of 0.09. Evaluating the FIS before and after training for the experimental data, the characteristics in Fig. 19 were obtained. The mean of the relative absolute values of the errors decreased by 3.76 times -- from 3.3503% before training to 0.8902% after training. Considering that the error for the "Controller2Fis" is in the desired limits after 100000 training epochs, this FIS was selected to be implemented in the Simulink integrated controller.

In Fig. 19, a good overlapping of the FIS models' data with the elongation experimental data is clearly visible. As in the previous FIS case, this superposition is dependent on the training epochs' number, and improves as the number of training epochs increases.

The parameters of the input's membership functions for the "Controller2Fis", before and after training, are shown in Table 2, while the membership functions' shapes are depicted in Fig. 20.

Comparison of the FIS characteristics and the membership functions parameters, before and after training, indicates a redistribution of the membership functions in the working domain (modification of the c parameter) and a change in their shapes by modification of the σ parameter (Table 2).

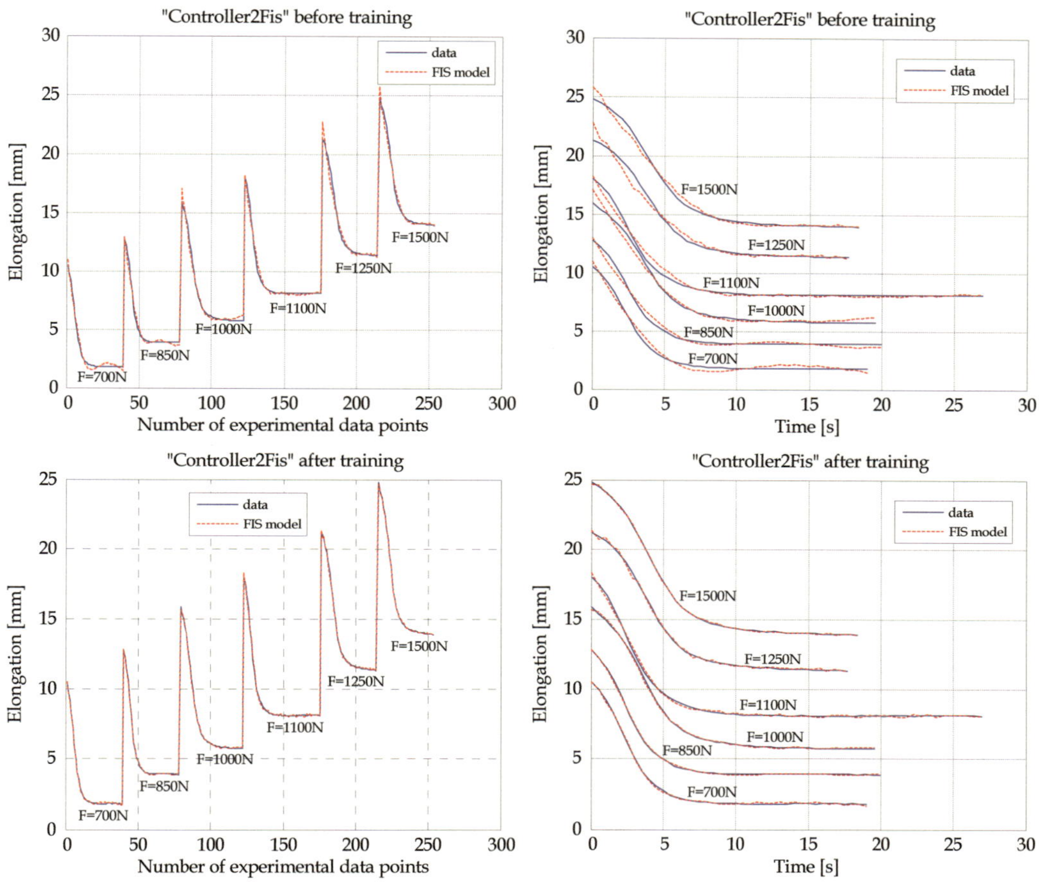

Fig. 19. "Controller2Fis" evaluation, before and after training

Status	Input	Param.	mf1	mf2	mf3	mf4	mf5	mf6	mf7	mf8
Before training	Force [N]	σ/2	143	143	143	143	143	143	143	143
		c	1002	1254	700.9	1096	1503	1002	1492	699.5
	Time [s]	σ/2	4.757	4.757	4.757	4.757	4.757	4.757	4.757	4.757
		c	11.86	8.412	10.46	21.75	13.06	2.355	2.968	1.562
After training	Force [N]	σ/2	159.8	134.6	142.2	137.4	142.1	133.1	150.1	144.6
		c	1007	1254	702.7	1099	1498	997.4	1487	700.3
	Time [s]	σ/2	2.624	4.197	3.393	2.768	5.349	5.261	1.835	3.346
		c	8.244	0.9308	8.639	11.89	6.099	-5.344	1.777	-3.61

Table 2. Parameters of the "Controller2FIS" input's mf before and after training

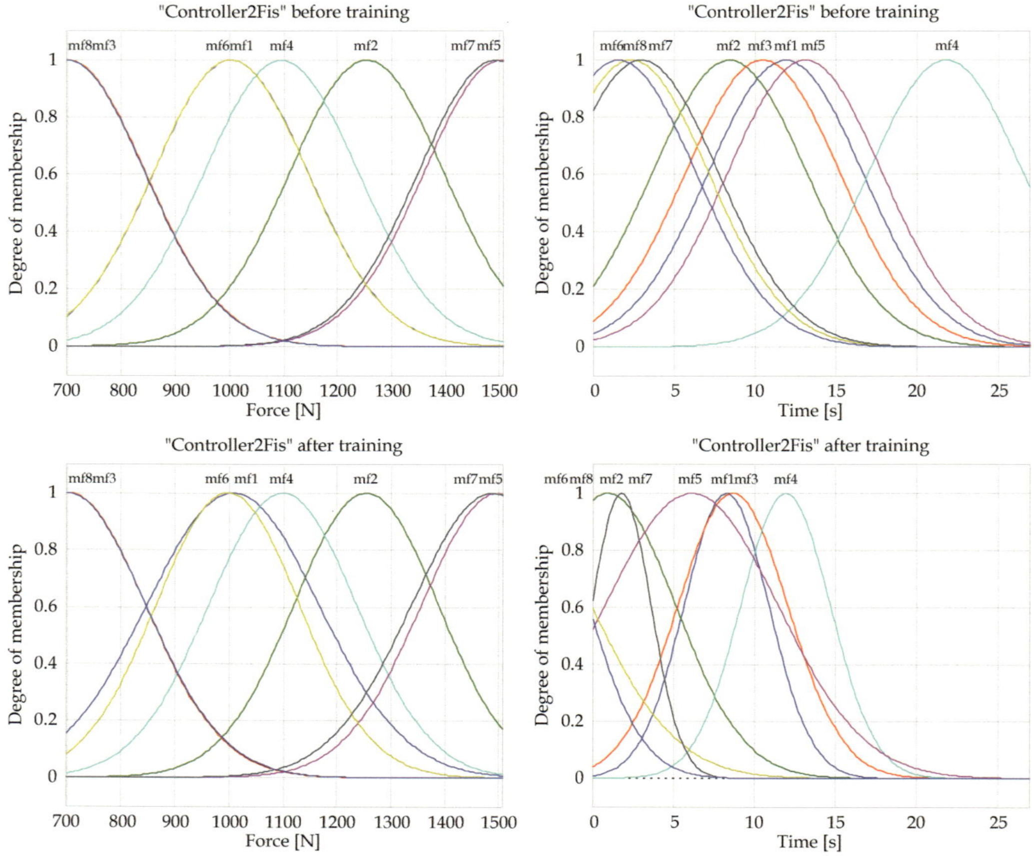

Fig. 20. Membership functions of "Controller2Fis", before and after training

Surfaces which reproduce the experimental data, before and after the "Controller2Fis" training, are represented in Fig. 21.

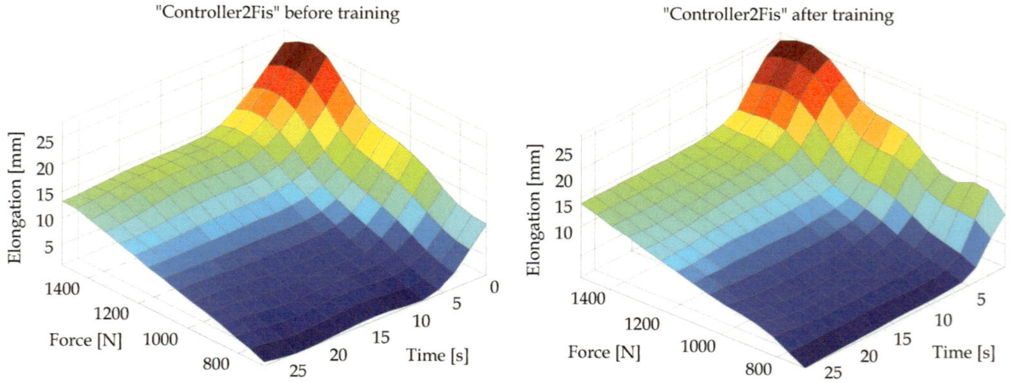

Fig. 21. Control surface resulted for "Controller2Fis", before and after training

The third FIS, "Controller3Fis", which has the force and the current as its inputs, was trained for 20.000 epochs. The rules were also of the type: if (in1 is in1cluster„k") and (in2 is in2cluster„k") then (out1 is out1cluster„k"). For both of this FIS's inputs, seven Gaussian-type membership functions (mf) were generated. Therefore, "Controller3Fis" fuzzy inference system has the structure presented in Fig. 22, while Controller 3 has the same structure as Controller 1, represented in Fig. 9.

The rules of the "Controller3Fis" fuzzy inference system, before and after training, are presented in Fig. 23, and Fig. 24 displays the deviation between the neuro-fuzzy models and the experimentally obtained data for different training epochs, defining the quality parameter from the training algorithm.

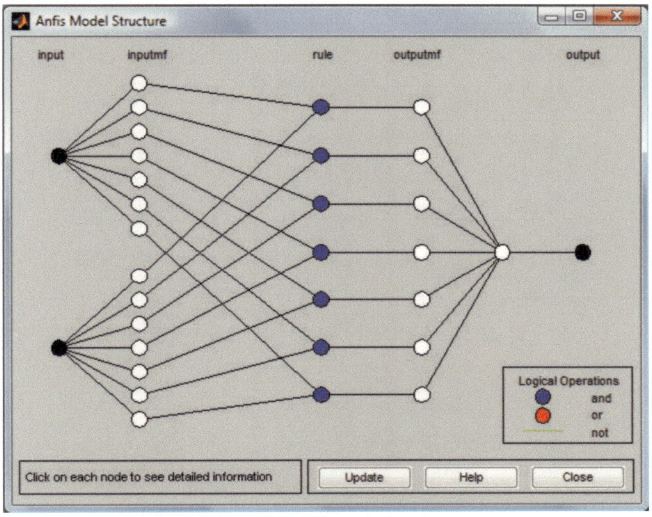

Fig. 22. Structure of the "Controller3Fis" fuzzy inference system

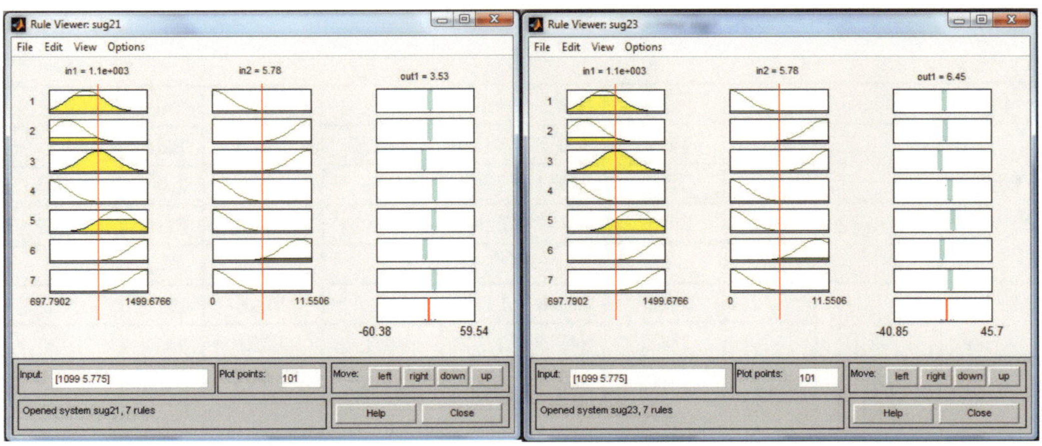

Fig. 23. The "Controller3Fis" rules, before and after training

Figure 24 shows a decrease in the deviation between the experimental data and the neuro-fuzzy model for the quality parameter (with some oscillations) within the training algorithm over the first 3500 training epochs, from the value of $2.52 \cdot 10^{-4}$ to that of $2.05 \cdot 10^{-4}$. Evaluating the FIS before and after training for the experimental data, the characteristics in Fig. 25 were obtained. The mean of the relative absolute values of the errors decreased from $1.5154 \cdot 10^{-3}$ % before training, to $2.3106 \cdot 10^{-13}$ % after training. "Controller3Fis" was selected to be implemented in the Simulink integrated controller because its obtained error was within the desired limits after 20000 training epochs.

From Fig. 25 one observes a good overlapping of the FIS models with the elongation experimental data. As in the previous FISs cases, this superposition is dependent upon the training epochs' number, and is better as the number of training epochs is higher.

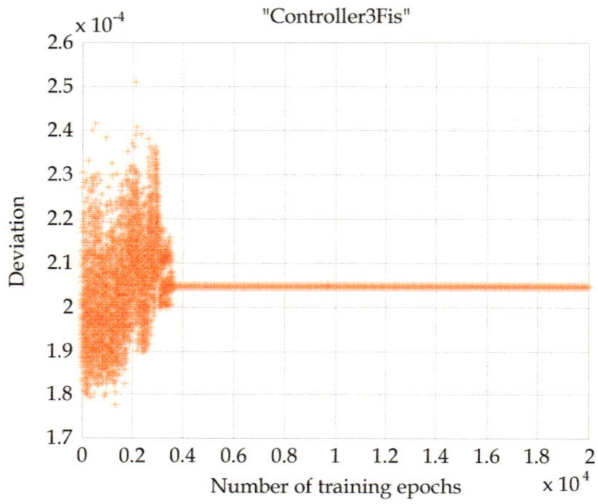

Fig. 24. The training error for "Controller3Fis"

The parameters of the input's membership functions for "Controller3Fis", before and after training, are shown in Table 3, while the membership functions' shapes are depicted in Fig. 26.

Status	Input	Param.	mf1	mf2	mf3	mf4	mf5	mf6	mf7
Before training	Force [N]	σ/2	141.8	141.8	141.8	141.8	141.8	141.8	141.8
		c	1003	847.3	1102	701	1250	1497	1500
	Current [A]	σ/2	2.042	2.042	2.042	2.042	2.042	2.042	2.042
		c	0	11.55	11.44	0	0	10.2	0
After training	Force [N]	σ/2	141.7	141.8	141.8	141.7	141.6	141.8	141.8
		c	1003	847.3	1102	701	1250	1497	1500
	Current [A]	σ/2	2.042	2.165	1.838	2.042	2.042	2.058	2.042
		c	$8.184 \cdot 10^{-5}$	11.3	11.73	$-1.398 \cdot 10^{-6}$	$-4.591 \cdot 10^{-6}$	10.25	$-1.582 \cdot 10^{-7}$

Table 3. Parameters of the "Controller3FIS" input's mf before and after training

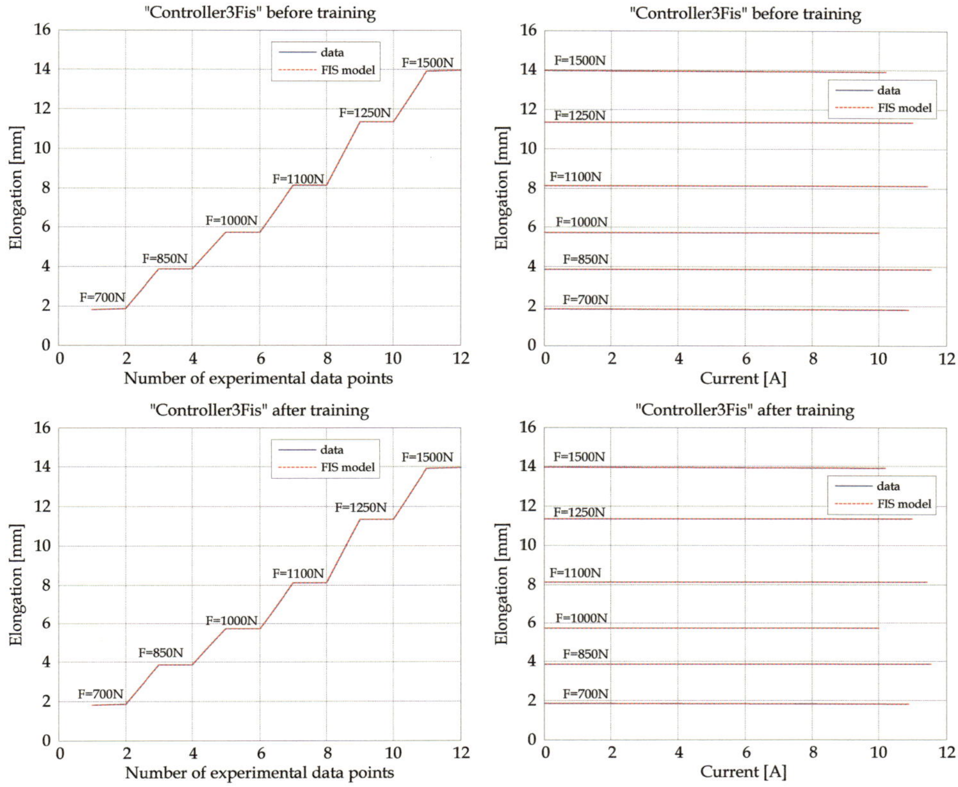

Fig. 25. "Controller3Fis" evaluation, before and after training

Comparison of the FIS characteristics and the membership functions' parameters, before and after training, indicates a redistribution of the membership functions in the working domain (modification of the *c* parameter) and a change in their shapes by modification of the σ parameter (Table 3).

The surfaces reproducing the experimental data, before and after training of the "Controller3Fis", are presented in Fig. 27.

The fourth and last controller FIS, "Controller4Fis", with inputs of force and time, was trained for 250000 epochs. As with the others, the rules were of the type: if (in1 is in1cluster„k") and (in2 is in2cluster„k") then (out1 is out1cluster„k"). Seven Gaussian-type membership functions (mf) were generated for each of the two inputs. Therefore, the "Controller4Fis" fuzzy inference system has the structure given in Fig. 28, while Controller 4 has the same structure as Controller 2, shown in Fig. 16.

The rules of the "Controller4Fis" fuzzy inference system, before and after training, are presented in Fig. 29, while Fig. 30 displays the deviation between the neuro-fuzzy models and the experimentally obtained data, defining the quality parameter from the training algorithm, for different training epochs.

Figure 30 shows a rapid decrease in the deviation between the experimental data and the neuro-fuzzy model for the quality parameter within the training algorithm over the first 50000 training epochs, from the value of 0.67 to that of 0.13. By evaluating the FIS before and after training for the experimental data, the characteristics shown in Fig. 31 were obtained.

The mean of the relative absolute values of the errors decreased from 5.1855% before training, to 1.0316% after training. Since the error found for the "Controller4Fis" was within the desired limits after 250000 training epochs, this FIS was chosen to be implemented in the Simulink integrated controller.

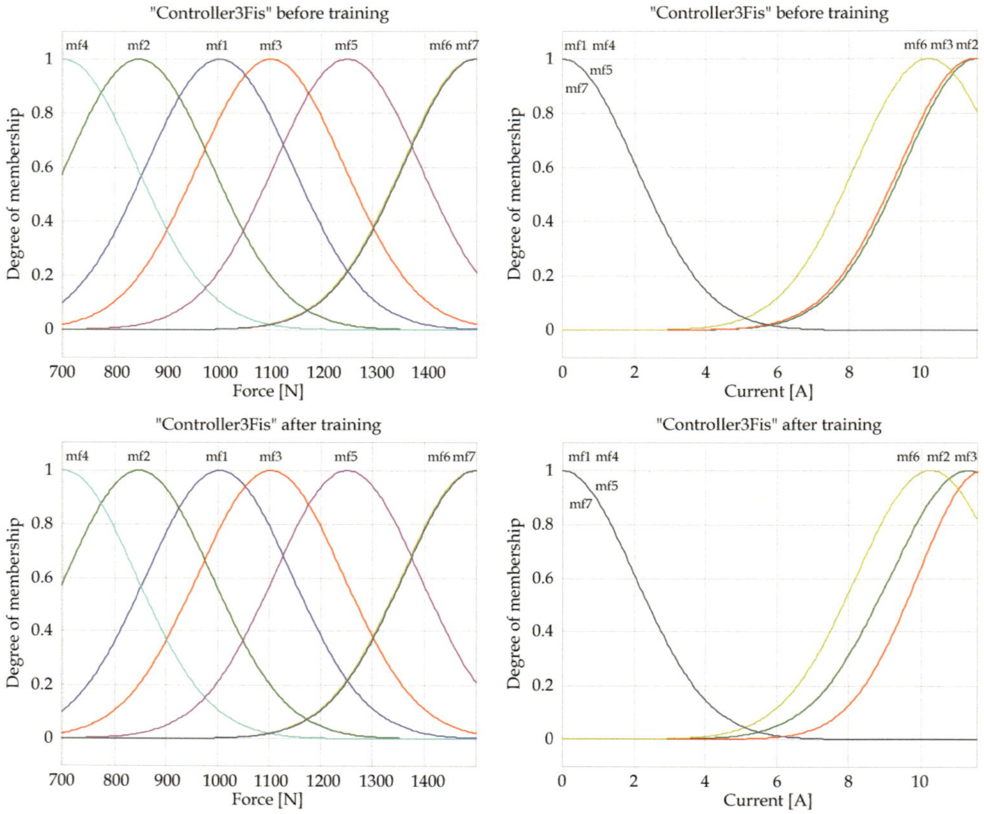

Fig. 26. Membership functions of "Controller3Fis", before and after training

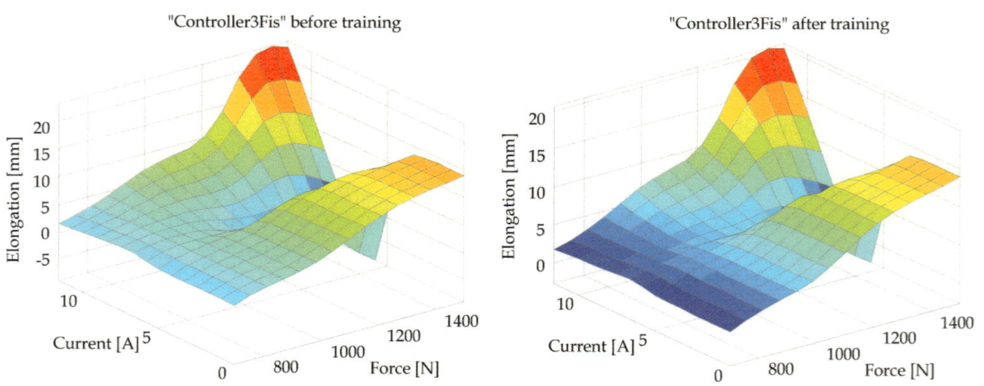

Fig. 27. Control surface resulted for "Controller3Fis", before and after training

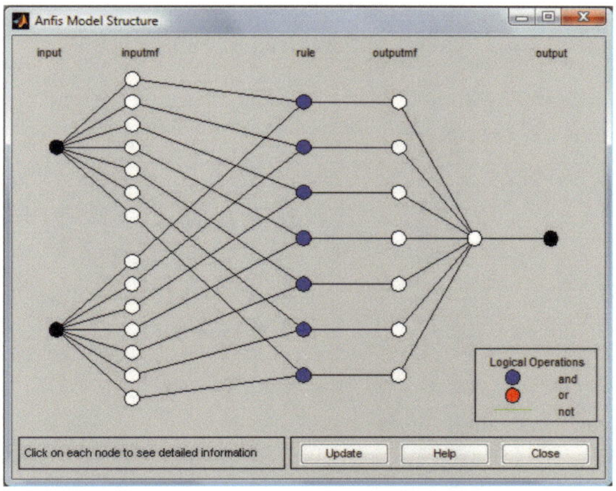

Fig. 28. Structure of the "Controller4Fis" fuzzy inference system

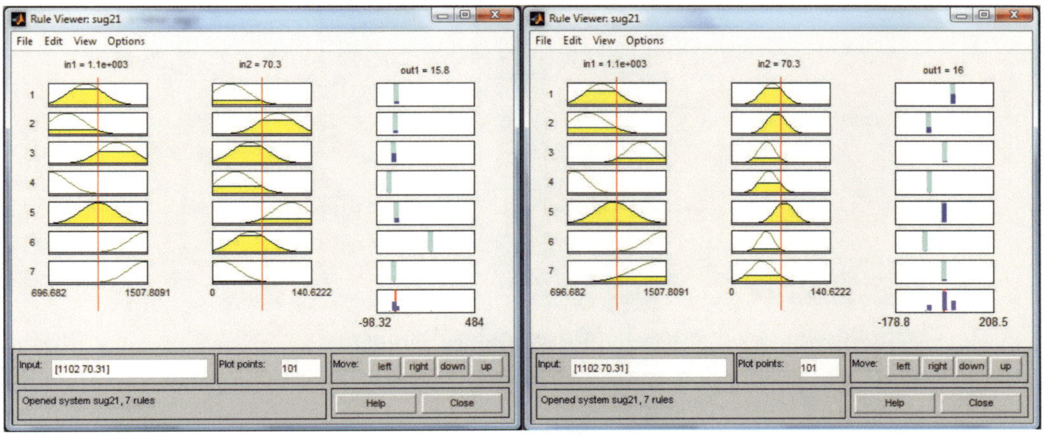

Fig. 29. Rules of the "Controller4Fis" before and after training

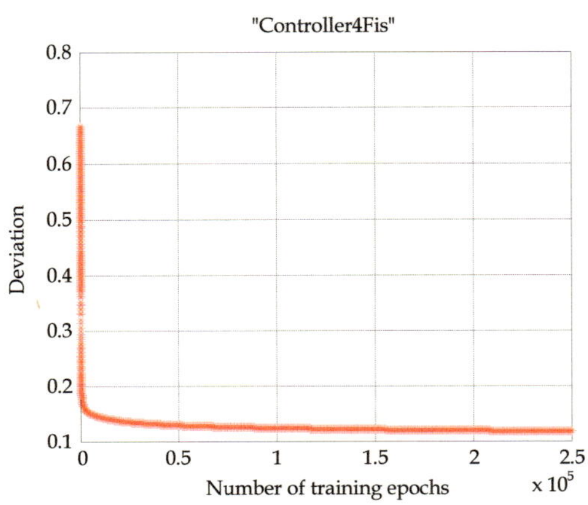

Fig. 30. The "Controller4Fis" training error

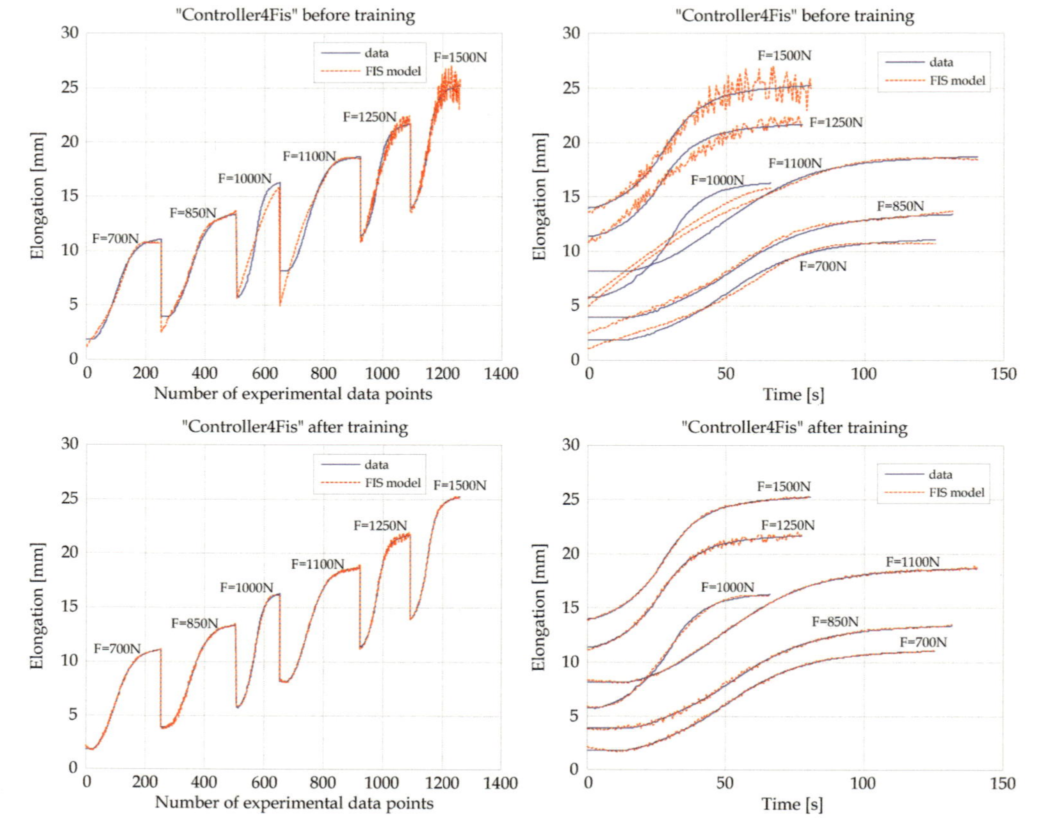

Fig. 31. "Controller4Fis" evaluation, before and after training

From Fig. 31, a good overlapping of the FIS model's output with the elongation experimental data can be observed. As in the previous FIS cases, this superposition is dependent upon the training epochs' number, and is better as the number of training epochs is higher.
The parameters of the input's membership functions for the "Controller4Fis", before and after training, are shown in Table 4, while the membership functions' shapes are depicted in Fig. 32.

Status	Input	Param.	mf1	mf2	mf3	mf4	mf5	mf6	mf7
Before training	Force [N]	σ/2	143.4	143.4	143.4	143.4	143.4	143.4	143.4
		c	1003	847	1255	703	1103	1505	1497
	Time [s]	σ/2	24.86	24.86	24.86	24.86	24.86	24.86	24.86
		c	26.03	92.38	53.75	33.43	112.2	54.45	12.09
After training	Force [N]	σ/2	131.2	154.4	119	107.7	148.2	142.7	216.1
		c	975.6	862	1309	747.9	1077	1493	1462
	Time [s]	σ/2	15.24	13.58	11.41	13.16	13.71	10.4	16.79
		c	59.28	64.99	51.19	54.08	76.06	50.11	44.6

Table 4. Parameters of the"Controller4FIS" input's mf before and after training

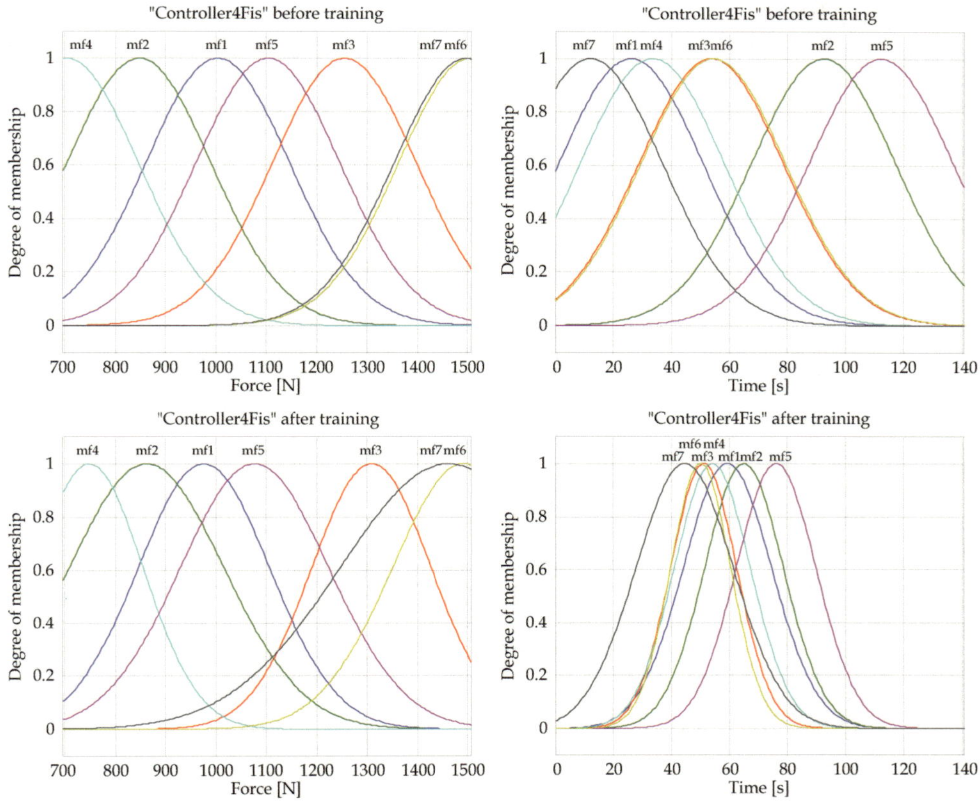

Fig. 32. Membership functions of "Controller4Fis", before and after training

Comparison of the FIS characteristics and the membership functions parameters, before and after training, indicates a redistribution of the membership functions in the working domain (modification of the c parameter) and a change in their shapes by the modification of the σ parameter (Table 4).

The surfaces reproducing the experimental data, before and after training of the "Controller4Fis", are presented in Fig. 33.

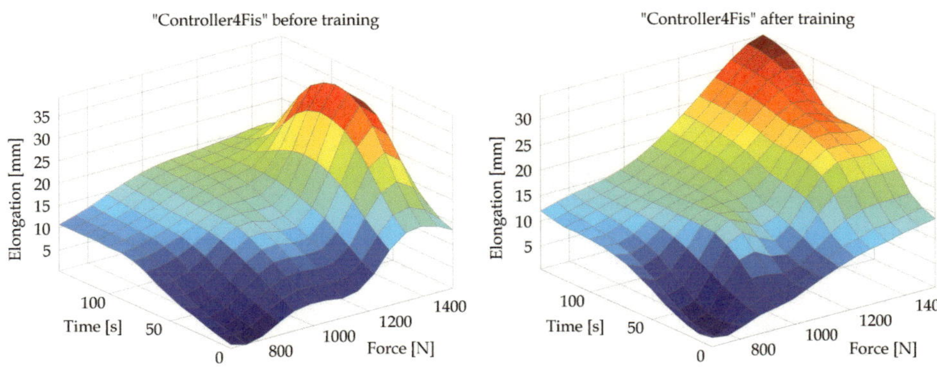

Fig. 33. Control surface resulted for "Controller4Fis", before and after training

Each of the four obtained FISs was imported at the fuzzy controller level, resulting in four controllers: Controller 1 ("Controller1Fis"), Controller 2 ("Controller2Fis"), Controller 3 ("Controller3Fis"), and Controller 4 ("Controller4Fis"). The integration of these four controllers is carried out using the logical scheme given in Fig. 7; resulting in the Matlab/Simulink model below, in Fig. 34.

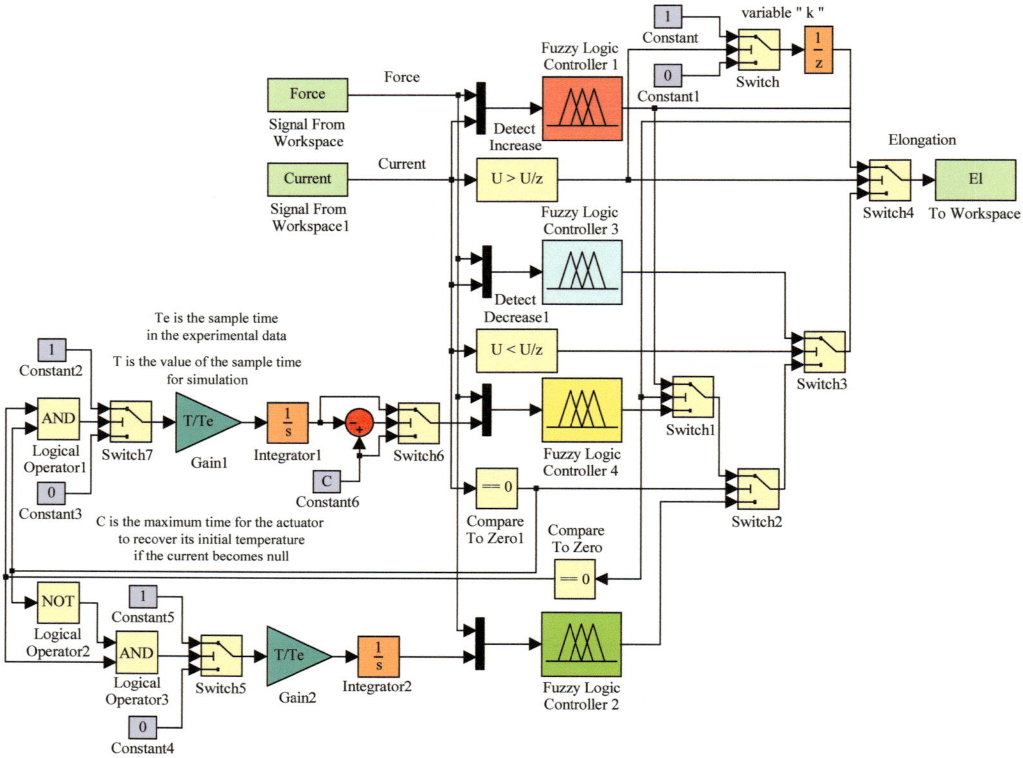

Fig. 34. The integration model schema in Matlab/Simulink

In the Matlab/Simulink model shown in Fig. 34, the second input for Controller 2 and for Controller 4 (Time) is generated by using an integrator, and starts from the moment that either of these controllers is used (the input of the Gain block is 0 if the schema decides not to work with either Controller 2 or 4). Because is possible that the simulation sample time may be different than the sample time used in the experimental data acquisition process, we use the "Gain" block that gives their rapport; "Te" is the sample time in the experimental data and "T" is the simulation sample time. In the scheme, the constant "C" represents the maximum time that it takes for the actuator to recover its initial temperature (approximately 24°C) when the current becomes null.

Evaluating the integrated model for controller (Fig. 34) in all six cases of experimental data, the results in Fig. 35 and Fig. 36 are obtained. These results represent the elongations versus the number of experimental data points and versus the applied electrical current, respectively, using the experimental data and the integrated neuro-fuzzy controller model for the SMA. A good overlapping of the outputs of the integrated neurro-fuzzy controller with the experimental data can be easily observed.

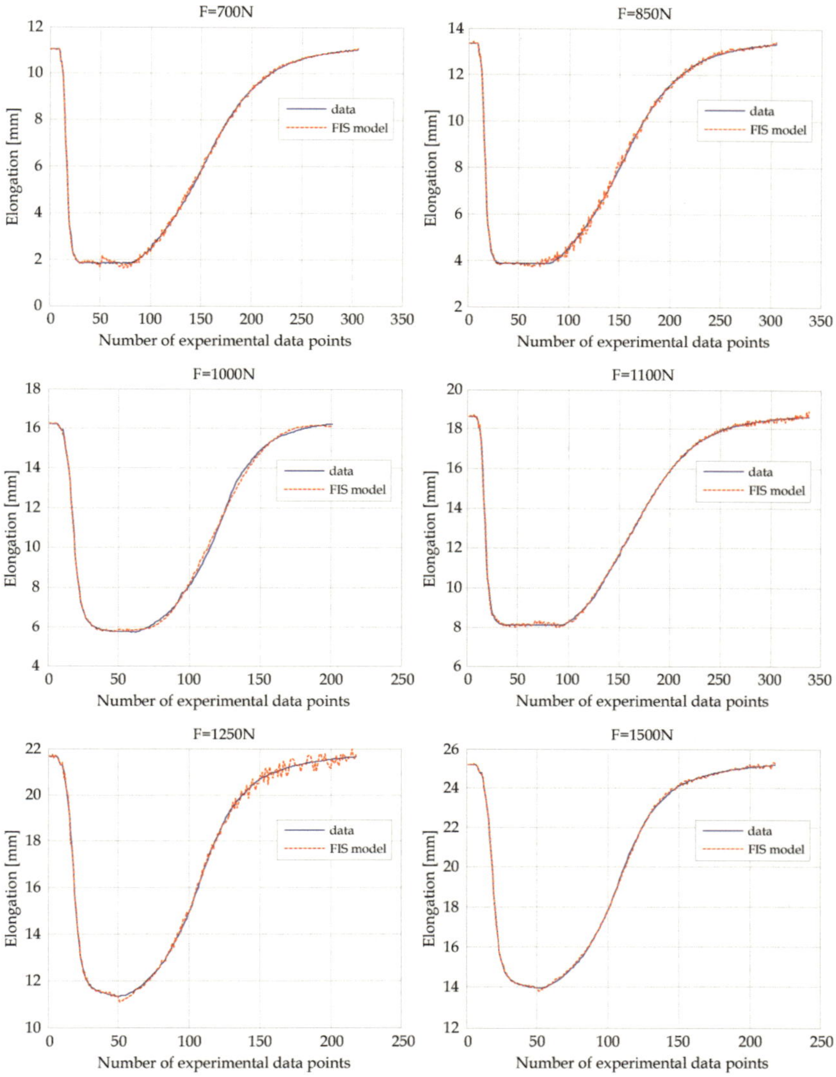

Fig. 35. Elongations versus the number of experimental data points

The same conclusion can be devolved from the 3D characteristics for the experimental data, and for neuro-fuzzy modeled data in terms of temperature, elongation and force, as depicted in Fig. 37 a., and in terms of current, elongation and force, depicted in Fig. 37 b.

The mean values of the relative absolute errors of the obtained model for the six load cases of the SMA actuator, based on adaptive neuro-fuzzy inference systems, are: 1.7538% for 700N, 1.2738% for 850N, 1.0964% for 1000N, 0.5228% for 1100N, 0.7179% for 1250N and 0.2532 for 1250N. Therefore, the mean value of the relative absolute error between the experimental data and the outputs of the obtained model is 0.9363%.

A very important advantage of this new model is its rapid generation due to the "genfis2" and "ANFIS" functions already implemented in Matlab. The user only need assume the four FIS's training performances using the "anfisedit" interface generated with Matlab.

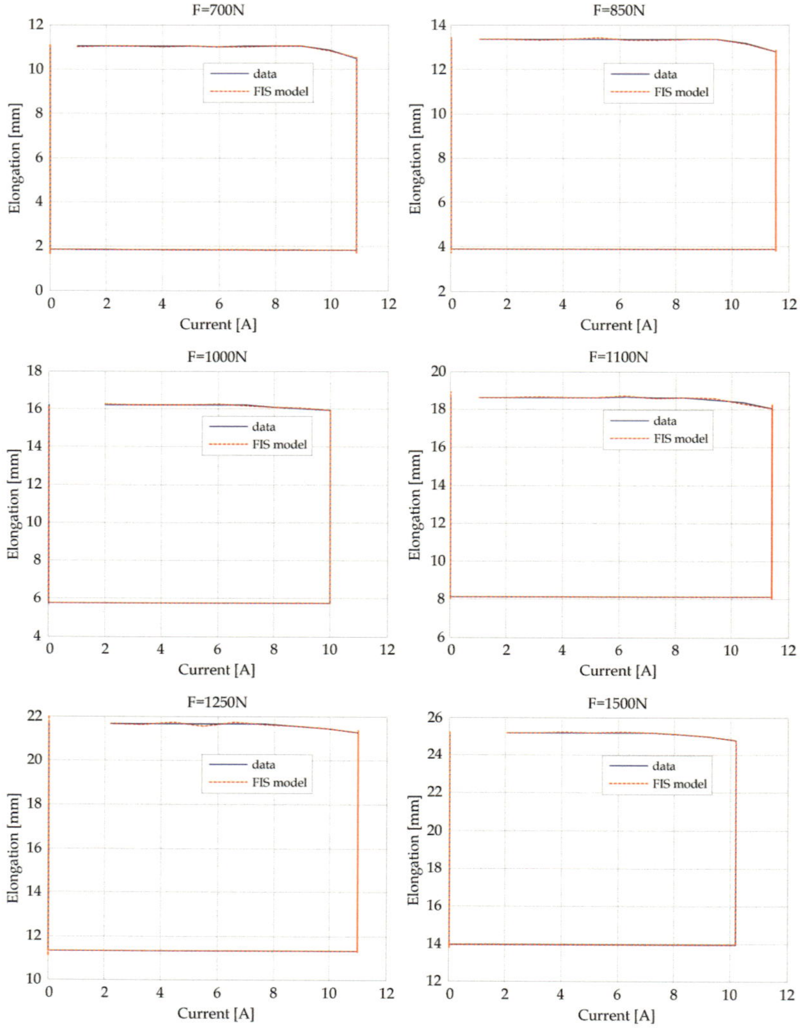

Fig. 36. Elongations versus the applied electrical current

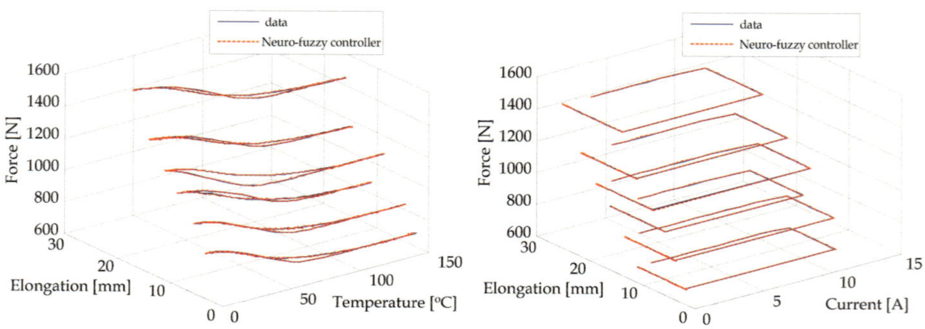

Fig. 37. 3D evaluation of the integrated neuro-fuzzy controller

Another alternative to design the SMA model, necessitating some supplementary work, but also with very good results, uses the "genfis1" Matlab function. In this case, generalized bell-type membership functions are generated for the FISs; within the sets of rules they are noted by: in„j"mf„n"; *j* is the input number (1÷2), and *n* is the number of membership functions. The rules are of the type: if (in1 is in1mf„k") and (in2 is in2mf„p") then (out1 is out1mf„r"). The number of the output membership functions (mf) is $k \times p$ ($r=1 \div (k \times p)$) and is equal to the number of rules; *k* and *p* are the number of mf of the two FIS's inputs. The "genfis1" function allows the membership function number to be chosen for each FIS input (*k* and *p*), while "genfis2" automatically generates the membership function's number.
For example, if $k=6$ and $p=12$ are chosen, the structure of the "Controller1Fis" generated with the "genfis1" function can be organized as in Fig. 38, while Controller 1 has the same structure as that presented in Fig. 9.

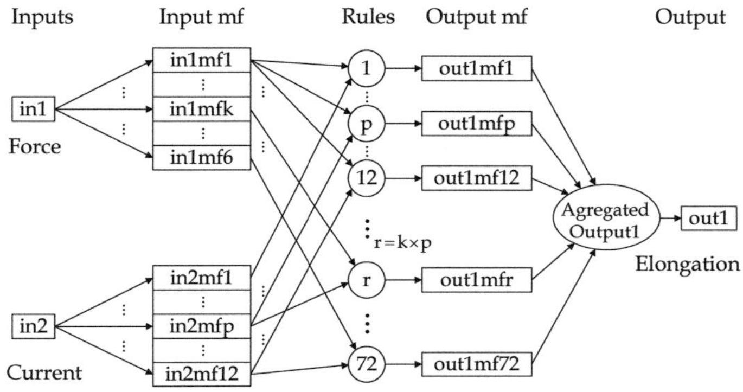

Fig. 38. Structure of „Controller1Fis" if the "genfis1" function is used for $k=6$ and $p=12$

By using the "genfis1" function, generalized bell-type membership functions are generated; their parameters are the membership function center (c) defining their position, and a, b which define their shape (see eq. (3)). Generating FIS's with the "genfis1" function has as a primary result the choice of the same values for the a and b parameters for all of the membership functions that characterize an input, and as a secondary result the separation of the working space for the respective input using a grid partition on the data (no clustering). FIS training with the "ANFIS" function produces an optimized redistribution of the membership functions in the working domain (modification of the c parameter) and a change in their shapes by modification of the a and b parameters.
Usually, for an experimental data set modeling, the "genfis2" function is first used for FIS generation, followed by FIS training with the "ANFIS" function over a different number of training epochs. If the obtained results are not the ones desired, the "genfis1" function will be used to generate the FIS in order to improve the accuracy of the obtained model.

3. Actuation lines' control

3.1 Controller design

Starting from the developed SMA actuators model and based on the operating scheme of the SMA actuators control in Fig. 4, a controller must be designed in order to control the SMA actuators by means of the electrical current supply, in order to cancel the deviation e between the required values for vertical displacements (corresponding to the optimized airfoils) and the real values, obtained from two position transducers. The design of such a controller is difficult due to the strong nonlinearities of the SMA actuators' characteristics. In these conditions, and considering our research team experience in fuzzy logic control systems design, we decided that one variant of control would be developed with fuzzy logic.

The simplest fuzzy logic controller is the Fuzzy Proportional (FP) controller, being relevant for state or output feedback in a state space controller. Its input is the error and the output is the control signal. From another perspective, derivative action helps to predict the error, and the Proportional-Derivative (PD) controller uses further the derivative action to improve closed-loop stability (Jantzen, 1998). The equation of a PD controller can be expressed as follows:

$$i(t) = K_P \cdot e(t) + K_D \cdot \frac{de(t)}{dt} = K_P \cdot \left[e(t) + T_D \cdot \frac{de(t)}{dt} \right], \tag{15}$$

where $i(t)$ is the command variable (electrical current in our case), that is time dependent; e is the operating error (see Fig. 4), K_P is the proportional gain and K_D is the derivative gain. In discrete form, the equation (15) becomes (Kumar et al., 2008):

$$i(k) = K_P \cdot e(k) + K_D \cdot \Delta e(k), \tag{16}$$

$$i(k) = K_P \cdot e(k) + K_D \cdot \frac{[e(k) - e(k-1)]}{T_S}, \tag{17}$$

where k is the discrete step, T_S is the sample period, and $\Delta e(k)$ is the change in error. Therefore, the inputs to the Fuzzy Proportional-Derivative (FPD) controller are the error and its derivative (called change in error in fuzzy control language), while the output is the control signal. We have chosen the structure shown in Fig. 39 for our FLC, where K_D is the change in the output gain.

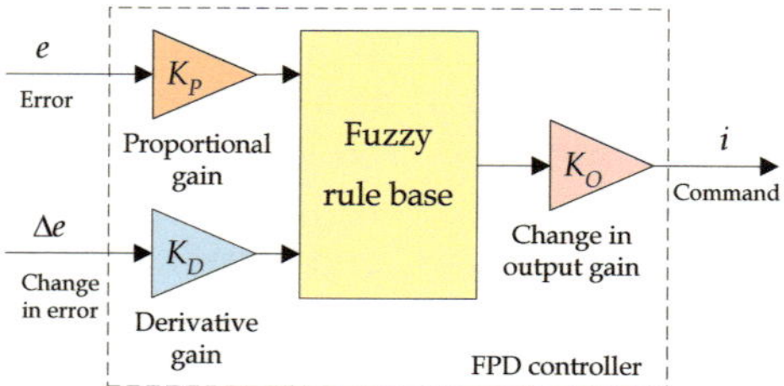

Fig. 39. Fuzzy PD controller architecture

To realize the input-output mapping of the designed controller, we must consider that in the SMA cooling phase the actuators would not be powered or the supplying current would be very small. This cooling phase may occur not only when controlling a long-term phase, when a switch between two values of the actuator displacements is ordered, but also in a short-lived phase, which occurs when the real value of the deformation exceeds its desired value and the actuator wires need to be cooled.

Each of the FLC input or output signals have the real line as the universe of discourse. In practice, the universe of discourse is restricted to a comparatively small interval, many authors and several commercial controllers using standard universes such as [-1, 1], or [-100, 100] corresponding to percentages of full scale. For our system, the [-1, 1] interval was chosen as the universe for inputs signals, and [0, 2.5] interval was chosen as the universe for output signal. Also, following numerical simulations, we have chosen a number of three membership functions for each of the two inputs, and three membership functions for the output. The shapes chosen for inputs membership functions were *s*-functions, п-functions, and *z*-functions. Generally, an *s*-function shaped membership function can be implemented using a cosine function:

$$s(x_{left}, x_{right}, x) = \begin{cases} 0, & \text{if } x < x_{left} \\ \frac{1}{2}\left[1+\cos\left(\frac{x-x_{right}}{x_{right}-x_{left}}\pi\right)\right], & \text{if } x_{left} \le x \le x_{right}, \\ 1, & \text{if } x > x_{right} \end{cases} \tag{18}$$

a *z*-function shaped membership function is a reflection of a shaped *s*-function:

$$z(x_{left}, x_{right}, x) = \begin{cases} 1, & \text{if } x < x_{left} \\ \frac{1}{2}\left[1+\cos\left(\frac{x-x_{left}}{x_{right}-x_{left}}\pi\right)\right], & \text{if } x_{left} \le x \le x_{right}, \\ 0, & \text{if } x > x_{right} \end{cases} \tag{19}$$

and a п -function shaped membership function is a combination of both functions:

$$\pi(x_{left}, x_{m1}, x_{m2}, x_{right}, x) = \min[s(x_{left1}, x_{m1}, x),\ z(x_{m2}, x_{right}, x)], \tag{20}$$

with the peak flat over the $[x_{m1}, x_{m2}]$ middle interval. x is the independent variable on the universe, x_{left} is the left breakpoint, and x_{right} is the right breakpoint (Jantzen, 1998).
To define the rules, a Sugeno fuzzy model was chosen, which for a two input - single output system with N rules is given by eq. (5):

$$\begin{aligned} &\text{Rule 1: If } x_1 \text{ is } A_1^1 \text{ and } x_2 \text{ is } A_2^1, \text{ then } y^1(x_1,x_2) = b_0^1 + a_1^1 x_1 + a_2^1 x_2, \\ &\vdots \\ &\text{Rule } i\text{: If } x_1 \text{ is } A_1^i \text{ and } x_2 \text{ is } A_2^i, \text{ then } y^i(x_1,x_2) = b_0^i + a_1^i x_1 + a_2^i x_2, \\ &\vdots \\ &\text{Rule } N\text{: If } x_1 \text{ is } A_1^N \text{ and } x_2 \text{ is } A_2^N, \text{ then } y^N(x_1,x_2) = b_0^N + a_1^N x_1 + a_2^N x_2. \end{aligned} \tag{21}$$

In the [-1, 1] universe interval, a three range partition, Negative (N), Zero (Z) and Positive (P), were chosen for the inputs e and Δe while in the [0, 2.5] universe interval three-range partition, Zero (Z), Positive-Small (PS) and Positive-Big (PB) were used for the output. According to the values in the Table 5, the membership functions for the inputs are by the form depicted in Fig. 40, and are given by the eq. (18), (19) or (20):

$$A_1^1(x) = z(-0.5, 0, x) = \begin{cases} 1, & \text{if } x < -0.5 \\ \frac{1}{2}[1+\cos(2x+1)\pi], & \text{if } -0.5 \le x \le 0, \\ 0, & \text{if } x > 0 \end{cases} \tag{22}$$

$$A_2^1(x) = z(-1,0,x) = \begin{cases} 1, & \text{if } x < -1 \\ \frac{1}{2}[1+\cos(x+1)\pi], & \text{if } -1 \le x \le 0, \\ 0, & \text{if } x > 0 \end{cases} \tag{23}$$

$$A_1^2(x) = \pi(-1,0,0,1,x) = \min[s(-1,0,x),\, z(0,1,x)] = \begin{cases} 0, & \text{if } x < -1 \\ \frac{1}{2}[1+\cos(\pi x)], & \text{if } -1 \le x \le 1, \\ 0, & \text{if } x > 1 \end{cases} \tag{24}$$

$$A_2^2(x) = \pi(-1,-0.1,0.1,1,x) = \begin{cases} 0, & \text{if } x < -1 \\ \frac{1}{2}\left[1+\cos\left(\frac{10x+1}{9}\right)\pi\right], & \text{if } -1 \le x \le -0.1 \\ 1, & \text{if } -0.1 < x < 0.1, \\ \frac{1}{2}\left[1+\cos\left(\frac{10x-1}{9}\right)\pi\right], & \text{if } 0.1 \le x \le 1 \\ 0, & \text{if } x > 1 \end{cases} \tag{25}$$

$$A_1^3(x) = A_2^3(x) = s(0,1,x) = \begin{cases} 0, & \text{if } x < 0 \\ \frac{1}{2}[1+\cos(x-1)\pi], & \text{if } 0 \le x \le 1. \\ 1, & \text{if } x > 1 \end{cases} \tag{26}$$

Input	mf	mf type	mf parameters			
			x_{left}	x_{m1}	x_{m2}	x_{right}
e	mf1 (A_1^1)	z - function	-0.5	-	-	0
	mf2 (A_1^2)	π -function	-1	0	0	1
	mf3 (A_1^3)	s - function	0	-	-	1
Δe	mf1 (A_2^1)	z - function	-1	-	-	0
	mf2 (A_2^2)	π - function	-1	-0.1	-0.1	1
	mf3 (A_2^3)	s - function	0	-	-	1

Table 5. Parameters of the input's membership functions

For the output membership functions constant values were chosen (Z=0, PS=1.25, PB=2.5), so the values of $a_k^i\,(k=\overline{1,2},\, i=\overline{1,N})$ parameters in eq. (21) were zero. Starting from the inputs' and output's membership functions, a set of 5 inference rules were obtained (N=5):

$$\begin{aligned} &\text{Rule 1: If } e \text{ is } A_1^1 \text{ and } \Delta e \text{ is } A_2^2, \text{ then } y^1(e,\Delta e) = 2.5, \\ &\text{Rule 2: If } e \text{ is } A_1^1 \text{ and } \Delta e \text{ is } A_2^3, \text{ then } y^2(e,\Delta e) = 0, \\ &\text{Rule 3: If } e \text{ is } A_1^2 \text{ and } \Delta e \text{ is } A_2^1, \text{ then } y^3(e,\Delta e) = 1.5, \\ &\text{Rule 4: If } e \text{ is } A_1^2 \text{ and } \Delta e \text{ is } A_2^3, \text{ then } y^4(e,\Delta e) = 0, \\ &\text{Rule 5: If } e \text{ is } A_1^3 \text{ and } \Delta e \text{ is } A_2^2, \text{ then } y^5(e,\Delta e) = 0. \end{aligned} \tag{27}$$

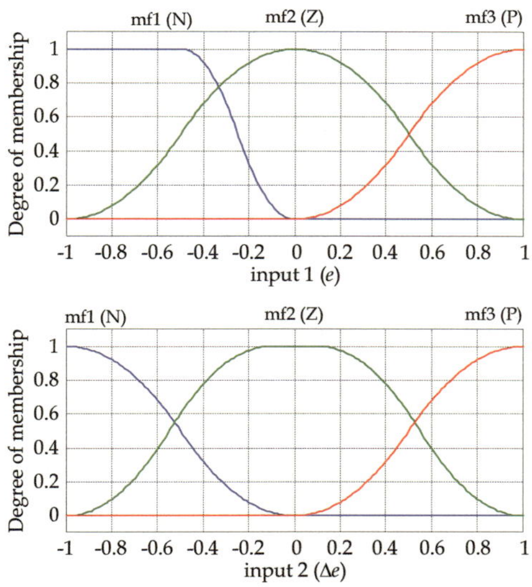

Fig. 40. Membership functions for the fuzzy logic controller inputs

The rule-based inference chosen for each consequent is presented in Table 6. With the previous considerations, the fuzzy control surface results by the form presented in Fig. 41 (two views for different angles).

$\Delta e / e$	N	Z	P
N	-	PS(1.25)	-
Z	PB(2.5)	-	Z(0)
P	Z(0)	Z(0)	-

Table 6. Rule-based inference for the fuzzy logic controller

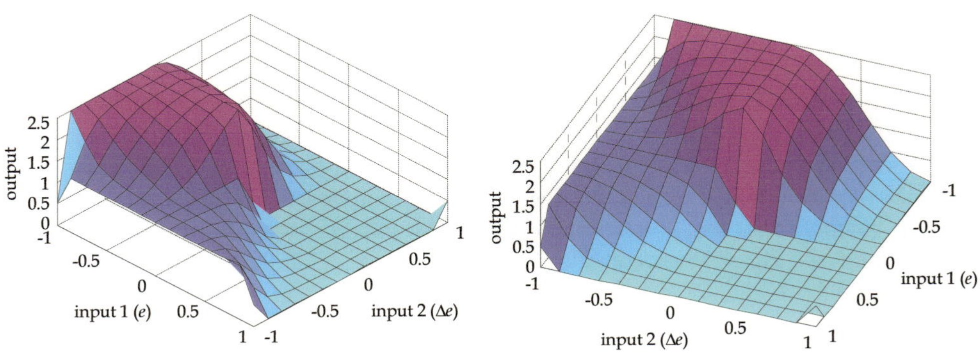

Fig. 41. The fuzzy control surface (two views for different angles)

3.2 Actuation lines' controller implementation and numerical simulation

Implementing the operating scheme of the SMA actuators control (Fig. 4) in Matlab-Simulink, the model shown in Fig. 42 was obtained. The input variable of the scheme is the desired skin deflection, while the output is the real skin deflection.

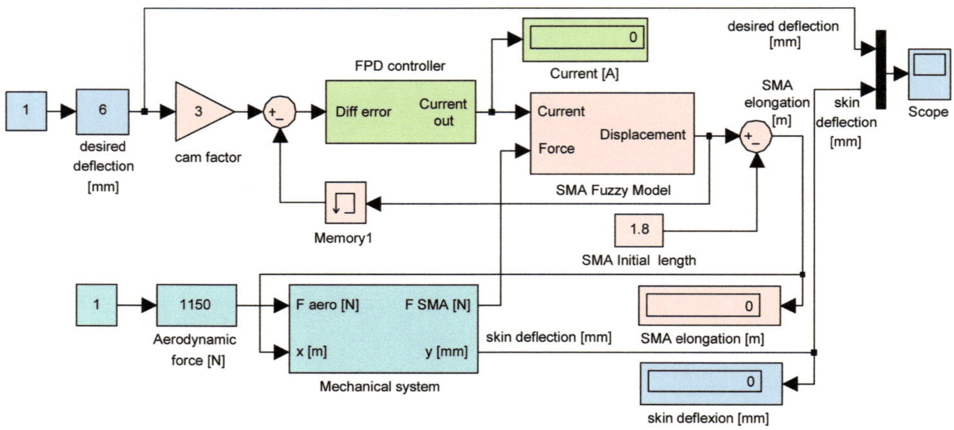

Fig. 42. The simulation model for the controlled SMA actuator with the neuro-fuzzy model

The "FPD controller" block contains the implementation of the controller presented in Fig. 39; the detailed Simulink scheme of this block is shown in Fig. 43. The block has as input the control error (the difference between the desired and the obtained displacements), and the controlled electrical current applied on the SMA actuators as output. The "SMA Fuzzy Model" block has the schema presented in Fig. 34; its inputs are the SMA loading force and the electrical current, while its output is the SMA elongation. The "Mechanical System" block in Fig. 43 models the SMA loading force starting from the aerodynamic force, skin elastic force, gas spring elastic force and gas spring pretension force.

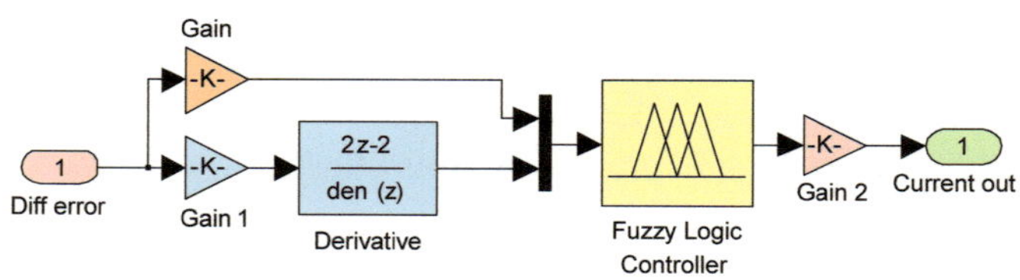

Fig. 43. "FPD controller" block in Simulink

To obtain an automatic control system, the preloaded forces on the gas springs in the two actuation lines must be valid for all 35 studied cases. By estimating the aerodynamic forces for all 35 studied flight conditions and optimized airfoils, a compromise should be done to balance the aerodynamic forces with the preloaded forces of the gas spring. Following estimation calculations, the pretension force of the gas springs in "Mechanical system" Simulink block (see Fig. 42) was considered with the value of 1250 N. In this situation, if the simulated model in Fig. 42 was loaded with an aerodynamic force F_{aero}=1150 N, for a successive steps input signal applied to the controlled actuator, the characteristics shown in Fig. 44 are obtained.

The results shown in Fig. 44 confirm that the obtained FPD controller works very well in both phases (heating and cooling) of the SMA actuators. To see the manner in which the controller works, screenshots were taken at different times of the numerical simulation presented in Fig. 44. The screenshots (Fig. 45) highlighted the fuzzy model input-output mapping of the eight analyzed points (P1÷P8). The chosen time values, shown on Fig. 44, are: 11.67 s (P1), 27.03 s (P2), 29.40 s (P3), 55.32 s (P4), 62.75 s (P5), 108.42 s (P6), 119.12 s (P7)

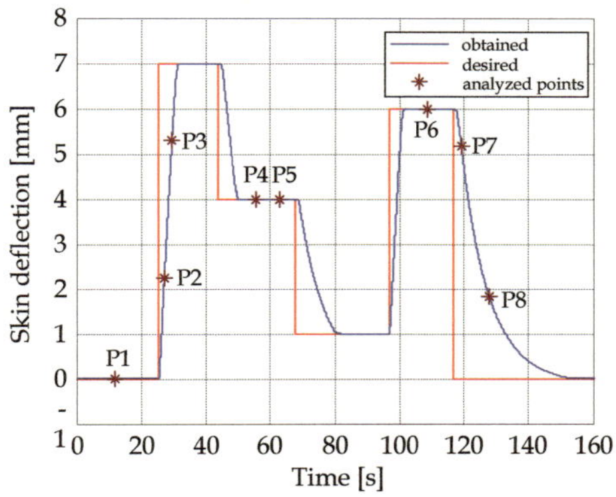

Fig. 44. Response for a successive steps input when F_{aero}=1150 N and $F_{pretension}$=1250 N

127.71 s (P8). Fig. 45 shows that the correspondence between the membership functions of the inputs and the membership functions of the output through the inference engine of the designed fuzzy model was correctly established. The same observation can be found by correlating Fig. 45 with the positions of the analyzed points in Fig. 44 and with the error e and change in error Δe signs and trends.

3.3 Bench test and wind tunnel experimental validation

From the SMA theory and based on the numerical simulations of the morphing wing system, the limits for the electrical current used to drive the actuators, correlated with the SMA temperature and SMA loading force, were estimated. As a consequence, two Programmable Switching Power Supplies AMREL SPS100-33 (Brailovski et al., 2008; Coutu et al., 2007; Coutu et al., 2009), controlled by Matlab/Simulink through a Quanser Q8 data acquisition card (Fig. 46) were chosen to implement the controller model (Austerlitz, 2002; Kirianaki et al., 2002; Park & Mackay, 2003). The AMREL SPS100-33 Power Supplies have RS-232 and GPIB IEEE-488 as standard features, and their technical characteristics include: Power 3.3kW, Voltage (dc) 0-100 V, Current (dc) 0-33 A. The Quanser data acquisition card has 8 single-ended analog inputs with 14-bit resolution, which can be sampled simultaneously at 100 kHz, with A/D conversion times of 2.4 μs/channel, and is equipped with 8 analog outputs, software programmable voltage ranges, that allow the control of the SMA actuators.

The Q8 data acquisition card was connected to a PC and programmed via Matlab/Simulink R2006b and WinCon 5.2 (Fig. 47).

As observed on Fig. 47, all data acquisition card single-ended analog inputs were used: two signals indicating the vertical displacements dY_1 and dY_2 of the SMA actuators are provided by two Linear Variable Differential Transformer (LVDT) potentiometers, and six signals are provided by six thermocouples installed on each of the SMA wires' components. Two of the card output channels were used to control each power supply through analog/external control by means of a DB-15 I/O connector, and other two card output channels were used to start the power supplies with a 5V analog signal. The "SMA1" block had the scheme presented in Fig. 48.

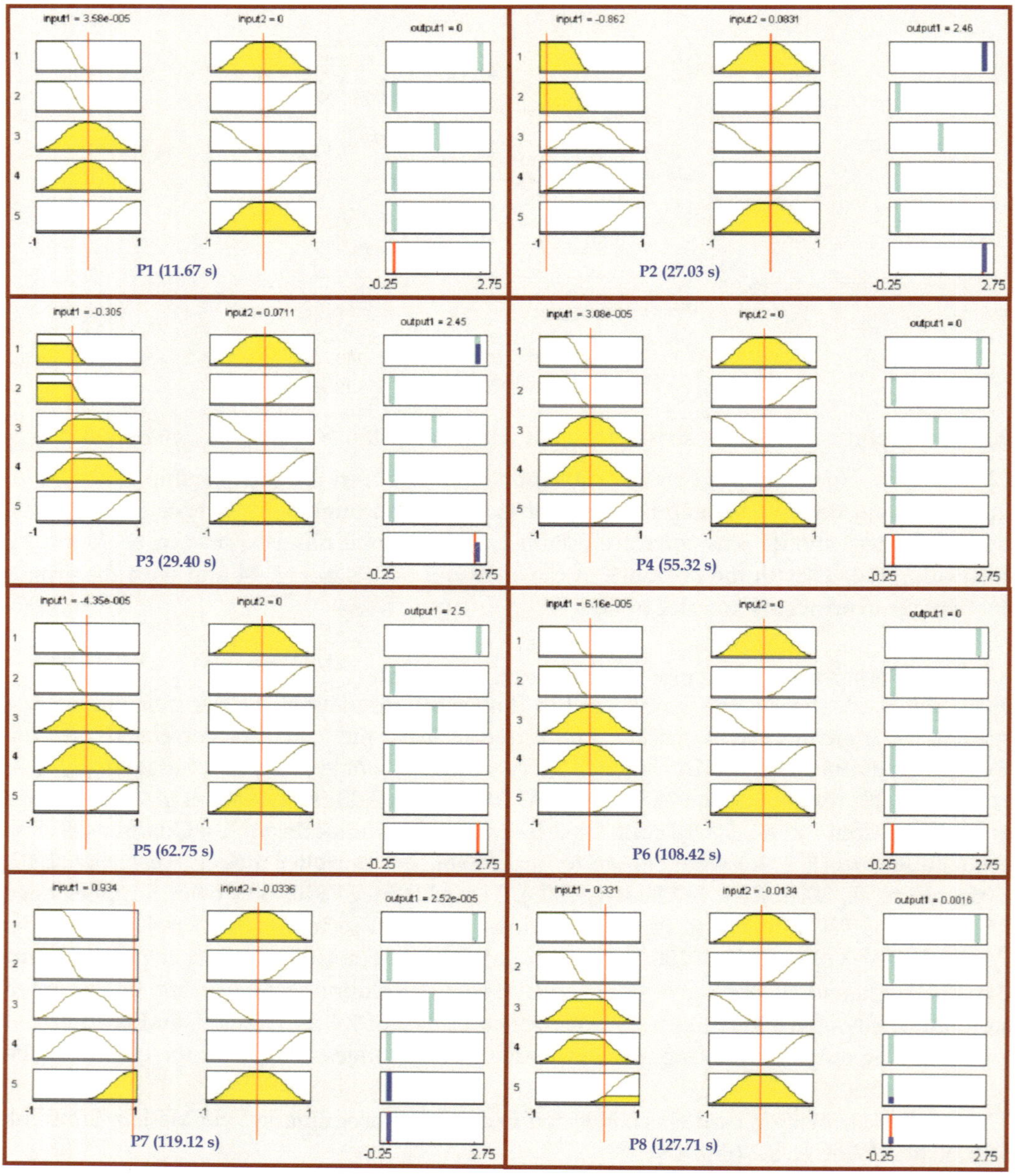

Fig. 45. Fuzzy model input-output mapping of the analyzed points

As seen in Fig. 48, the "SMA1" block, controlling the first actuation line, contains the implementation of the controller presented in Fig. 43 and the observations related to the SMA actuators' physical limitations in terms of temperature and supplying currents. The current supplied to the actuator was limited at 10A, and the control signal was set to be 0-0.606V (maximum voltage for the power supply is 2V for a 33A current supply). The upper limit of the SMA wires temperature in the "Temperature limiter" block was established at

130°C. The control scheme in Fig. 43 was improved with conditioners related to physical model protection. In this way, a software protection of the actuation lines was realized.

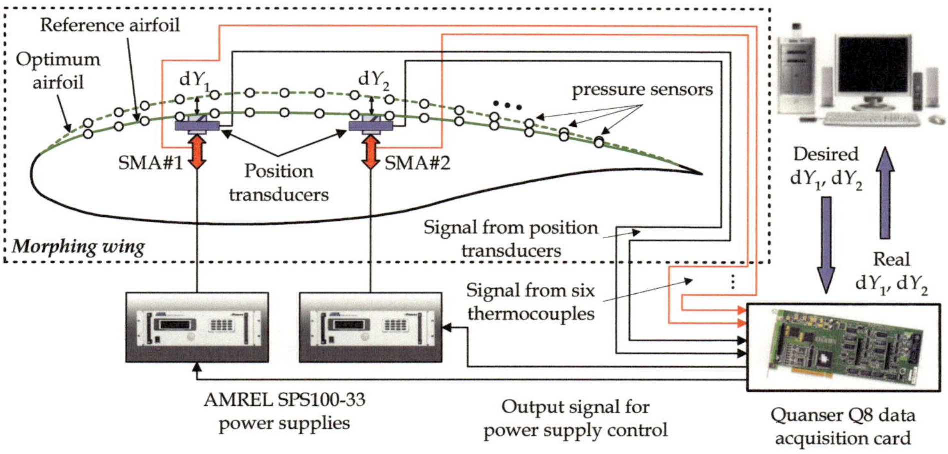

Fig. 46. Bench test physical model operating schema

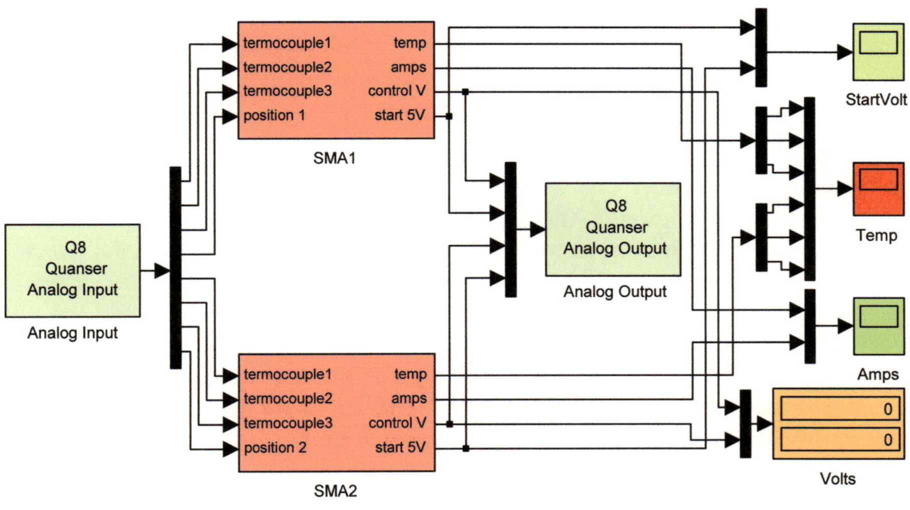

Fig. 47. Q8 data acquisition card using to control the actuators

After some tests with the experimental model, the preloaded force of the gas springs that maintains the SMA wires in tension was chosen to be 1000 N, since in the laboratory the existence of aerodynamic forces could not be considered.

The Matlab/Simulink implemented controller was used in the same way for both actuation lines of the morphing wing system, so the "SMA2" block had a similar scheme to the "SMA1" block, with the exception of the numerical values of the thermocouples calibration gains and constants.

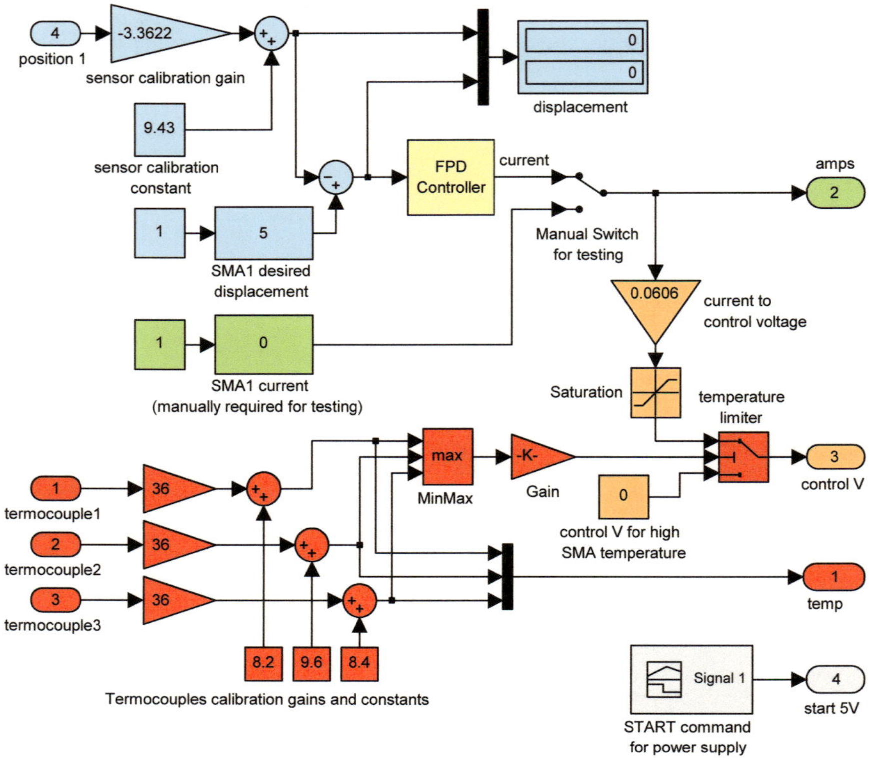

Fig. 48. "SMA1" block, controlling the first actuation line

The validation of the designed controller during bench test runs consisted in two main steps, followed by a secondary one. Firstly, each of the two actuation lines of the morphing system were tested independently, the control prescribed values (the desired displacements dY_1 and dY_2) being presented under the form of successive steps. In this way, the actuation lines responses were obtained in Fig. 49; the characteristics confirmed that the control works very well for both actuation lines. After this first step, the challenge was to test the actuation lines working simultaneously (synchronized commands), for desired displacements (dY_1 and dY_2) under the form of successive steps signals applied at their inputs. A situation acquired during this test is presented in Fig. 50, and validates the good functioning of the designed controller. The obtained results presented in Figs. 49 and 50 show that the controllers, in the two actuation lines, work even at zero values of the desired signal because of the pre-tensioned gas springs. Small oscillations of the obtained displacements are observed around their desired values. The amplitude of the oscillations in this phase is due to the LVDT potentiometers' mechanical link (were not finally fixed because the model was not equipped with the flexible skin in this test - Fig. 51) and to the SMA wires thermal inertia; the smallest amplitude is less than 0.1 mm. In the secondary step of the bench test all pairs of the desired displacements characterizing the 35 optimized airfoil cases were imposed simultaneously as input signals on the two actuation lines, while the skin was provisionally mounted on the model. In this step, we could see if the skin supports both strains simultaneously; the recorded results for all 35 tested cases confirmed the good working of the integrated morphing wing system.

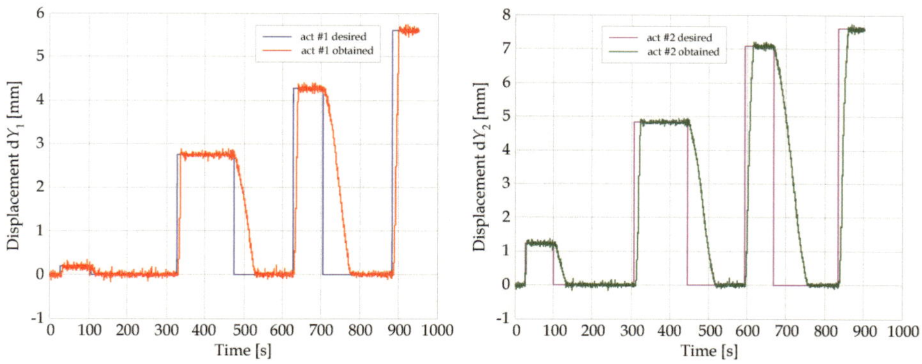

Fig. 49. Actuation lines independent bench test

This secondary step of the bench test was considered in wind tunnel, and get together with the transition point real time position detection and visualization, in order to validate experimentally all of the 35 optimized airfoils theoretically obtained. A typical test for one of the 35 flight conditions consisted in a wind tunnel tare run, followed by a run for the reference (un-morphed) airfoil, and finally by a run for morphed airfoil, reproducing the corresponding optimized airfoil. The morphing wing system during wind tunnel tests is shown in Fig. 52.

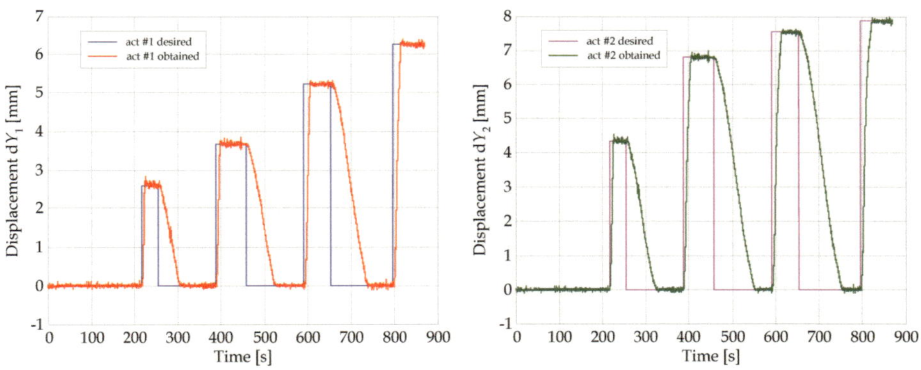

Fig. 50. Actuation lines simultaneously bench test

Fig. 51. Morphing wing system in the bench test

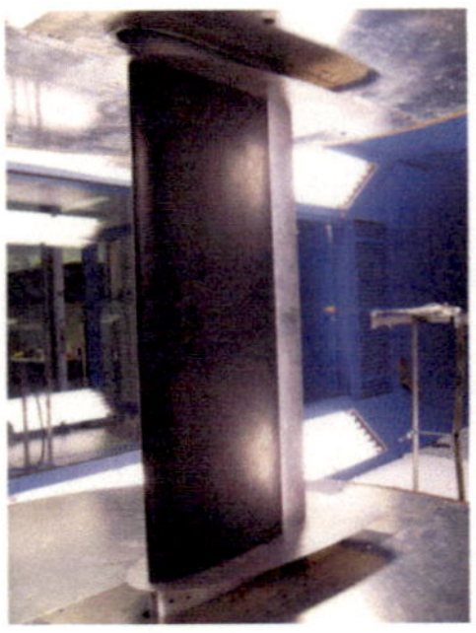

Fig. 52. Morphing wing system in the wind tunnel test runs

Because of the presence of the aerodynamic forces on the flexible skin of the wing for the wind tunnel tests, the preloaded forces of the gas springs were reconsidered at 1500 N. The control results for test run 42, characterized by the angle of attack α=2° and Mach number Mach=0.2 (deflections of both actuators are dY_1=5.73 mm and dY_2=7.45 mm), are shown in Fig 53.

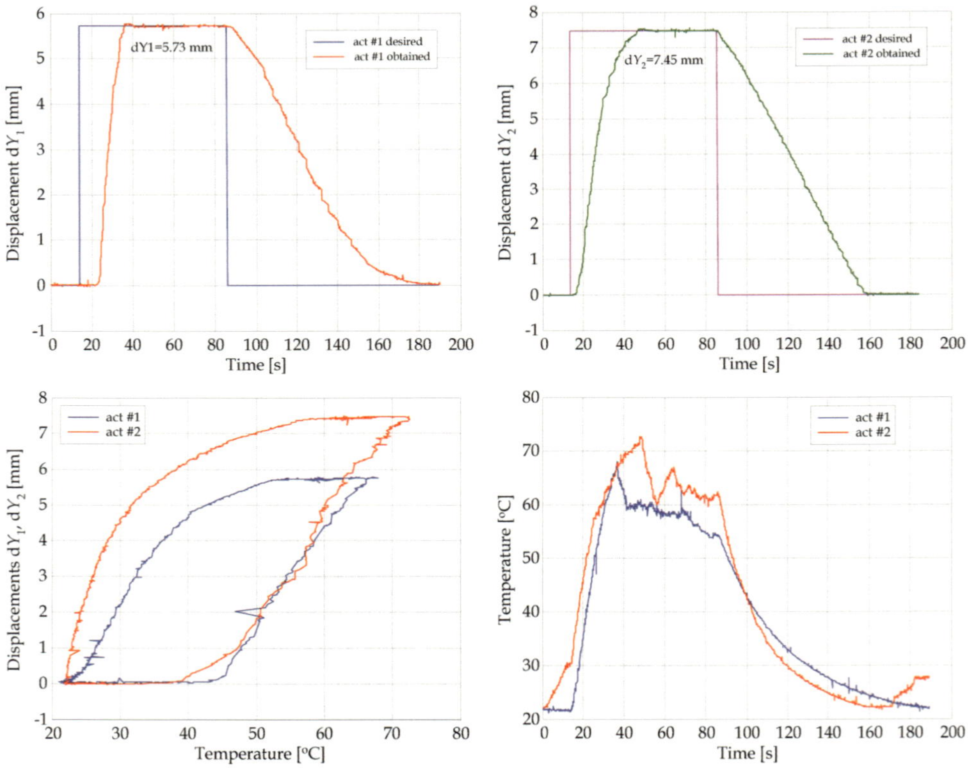

Fig. 53. Wind Tunnel Test for α=2°, Mach=0.2 (dY_1=5.73 mm, dY_2=7.45 mm)

From the experimental results, it can still be observed a high frequency noise influencing the LVDT sensors and thermocouple's instrumentation amplifiers, but with small amplitudes with respect to those for the bench tested cases. A positive impact on the noise amplitude

reduction is the completion of mechanical model by final fixing of the skin on the model; this time, the noise sources are the wind tunnel vibrations, the instrumentation electrical fields and the wind tunnel supplying and monitoring equipments electrical fields.
Fig. 53 and all the tested situations results confirmed that the designed controller works very well in the wind tunnel, being positively influenced by the aerodynamic forces presence.

4. Conclusions

The approaches for the design and to the validation of a morphing wing fuzzy logic application were presented. The developed morphing mechanism used smart materials such as Shape Memory Alloy (SMA) in the actuation control concept.
Two important applications of the fuzzy logic technique were highlighted in this work: the identification of a model for a system starting from some experimental input-output data, and the automatic control of a system. In this way, in our morphing application two directions were developed: smart material actuator modeling and actuation lines' control.
Based on a neuro-fuzzy network and using numerical values resulted from the SMA experimental testing (forces, currents, temperatures and elongations), an empirical model was developed for the SMA actuators that could be used in the design phase of the actuation lines' control. The SMA testing was performed at T_{amb}=24°C for six load cases with the forces of 700 N, 850 N, 1000 N, 1100 N, 1250 N and 1500 N. The electrical currents following the increasing-constant-decreasing-zero values evolution were applied on the SMA actuator in each of the six cases considered. Four Fuzzy Inference Systems (FIS's) were used to obtain four neuro-fuzzy controllers: one controller for the current increase, one for a constant current, one for the current decrease, and one controller for the null current (after its decrease). For the first and for the third controllers, inputs such as the force and the current were used, while for the second and the fourth controllers, inputs such as the force and the time values reflecting the SMA thermal inertia were used. Finally, the four obtained controllers were integrated into a single controller.
The "genfis2" Matlab function was used to generate and train the fuzzy inference systems associated with the four controllers. The four initially obtained fuzzy inference systems were trained for 5000, 100000, 20000, and 250000 training epochs. For the four FISs, the mean of the relative absolute values of the errors decreased from 0.3063%, 3.3503%, $1.5154 \cdot 10^{-3}$ %, and 5.1855%, respectively, before training, to 0.119%, 0.8902%, $2.3106 \cdot 10^{-13}$ %, and 1.0316%, respectively, after training.
Evaluating the model obtained for the SMA actuators (the final, integrated controller) in all six cases of experimental data, the mean values of the relative absolute errors were: 1.7538% for 700N, 1.2738% for 850N, 1.0964% for 1000N, 0.5228% for 1100N, 0.7179% for 1250N, and 0.2532 for 1250N. Therefore, the mean value of the relative absolute error between the experimental data and the outputs of the obtained model was 0.9363%.
A very important advantage of this new model is its rapid generation, since the "genfis2" and "ANFIS" functions are already implemented in Matlab. The user only needs to assume the four FIS's training performances using the "anfisedit" interface generated with Matlab.
The second application of fuzzy-logic techniques in our project (actuation lines' control) supposed the design of an SMA actuators' controller starting from the developed SMA actuators' model. The controller was designed to control the SMA actuators by means of the electrical current supply, in order to cancel the deviation *e* between the required values for

vertical displacements (corresponding to the optimized airfoils) and the real values, obtained from two position transducers. Finally, a fuzzy PD architecture was chosen for the controller. In its design, numerical simulations of the open loop morphing wing integrated system, based on a SMA neuro-fuzzy model, were performed. A bench test and a wind tunnel test were conducted as subsequent validation methods.

A [-1, 1] interval was chosen as the universe for the inputs' signals, and a [0, 2.5] interval was chosen as the universe for the output signal. Also, following numerical simulations, three membership functions for each of the two inputs, and three membership functions for the output were chosen. The experimental validation tests (bench tests and wind tunnel test) confirmed that the designed controller works very well. The wind tunnel tests were quite positive, with their transition point real time position detection and visualization, which experimentally validated all of the 35 theoretically-obtained optimized airfoils.

As a general conclusion, the work presented here has proved the feasibility of using fuzzy logic methodologies in multidisciplinary research studies in the aerospace field, especially for morphing wing or morphing aircraft studies.

5. References

Al-Odienat, A.I. & Al-Lawama, A.A. (2008). The Advantages of PID Fuzzy Controllers Over The Conventional Types, *American Journal of Applied Sciences,* Vol. 5, No. 6, pp. 653-658, June 2008, ISSN: 1546-9239

Austerlitz, H. (2002). *Data acquisition techniques using PCs,* Elsevier, ISBN: 978-0-12-068377-2, USA

Baron, A.; Benedict, B.; Branchaw, N.; Ostry, B.; Pearsall, J.; Perlman, G. & Selstrom, J. (2003). *Morphing Wing (MoW),* ASEN 4018 Senior Projects Technical Report, Department of Aerospace Engineering, University of Colorado, December 2003, Boulder, Colorado, USA, 102 pages

Brailovski, V.; Terriault, P.; Coutu, D.; Georges, T.; Morellon, E.; Fischer, C. & Berube, S. (2008). Morphing laminar wing with flexible extrados powered by shape memory alloy actuators, *Proceedings of ASME 2008 Conference on Smart Materials, Adaptive Structures and Intelligent Systems (SMASIS2008),* pp. 615-623, ISBN: 978-0-7918-4331-4, Maryland, USA, October 28–30, 2008, Publisher ASME, Ellicott City

Coutu, D.; Brailovski, V.; Terriault, P. & Fischer, C. (2007). Experimental validation of the 3D numerical model for an adaptive laminar wing with flexible extrados, *Proceedings of the 18th International Conference of Adaptive Structures and Technologies,* 10 pages, Ottawa, Ontario, Canada, 3-5 October, 2007

Coutu, D.; Brailovski, V. & Terriault, P. (2009). Promising benefits of an active-extrados morphing laminar wing, *AIAA Journal of Aircraft,* Vol. 46, No. 2, pp. 730-731, March-April 2009, ISSN: 0021-8669

Georges, T.; Brailovski, V.; Morellon, E.; Coutu, D. & Terriault, P. (2009). Design of Shape Memory Alloy Actuators for Morphing Laminar Wing With Flexible Extrados, *Journal of Mechanical Design,* Vol. 131, No. 9, 9 pages, 091006, September 2009, ISSN: 1050-0472

Gonzalez, L. (2005). Morphing Wing Using Shape Memory Alloy: A Concept Proposal, *Final research paper in 2005 Summer Research Experience for Undergraduates (REU) on Nanotechnology and Materials Systems,* Texas Institute of Intelligent Bio-Nano

Materials and Structures for Aerospace Vehicles (TiiMS) - NASA Research University, Texas A&M University, July 2005, College Station, Texas, USA

Grigorie, T.L. & Botez, R.M. (2009). Adaptive neuro-fuzzy inference system based controllers for Smart Material Actuator modeling, *Proceedings of the Institution of Mechanical Engineers, Part G: Journal of Aerospace Engineering*, Vol. 223, No. 6, pp. 655-668, June 2009, ISSN: 0954-4100

Grigorie, T.L. & Botez, R.M. (2010). New adaptive controller method for SMA hysteresis modeling of a morphing wing, *The Aeronautical Journal*, Vol. 114, No. 1151, pp. 1-13, January 2010, ISSN: 0001-9240

Grigorie, T.L.; Popov, A.V.; Botez, R.M.; Mébarki, Y. & Mamou, M. (2010 a). Modeling and testing of a morphing wing in open-loop architecture, *AIAA Journal of Aircraft*, Vol. 47, No. 3, pp. 917-923, May–June 2010, ISSN: 0021-8669

Grigorie, T. L.; Popov, A.V.; Botez, R.M.; Mamou, M. & Mebarki, Y. (2010 b). A morphing wing used shape memory alloy actuators new control technique with bi-positional and PI laws optimum combination. Part 1: design phase, *Proceedings of the 7th International Conference on Informatics in Control, Automation and Robotics ICINCO 2010*, pp. 5-12, ISBN: 978-989-8425-00-3, Madeira, Portugal, 15-18 June, 2010, SciTePress - Science and Technology Publications, Funchal

Grigorie, T. L.; Popov, A.V.; Botez, R.M.; Mamou, M. & Mebarki, Y. (2010 c). A morphing wing used shape memory alloy actuators new control technique with bi-positional and PI laws optimum combination. Part 2: experimental validation, *Proceedings of the 7th International Conference on Informatics in Control, Automation and Robotics ICINCO 2010*, pp. 13-19, ISBN: 978-989-8425-00-3, Madeira, Portugal, 15-18 June, 2010, SciTePress - Science and Technology Publications, Funchal

Hampel, R.; Wagenknecht, M. & Chaker, N. (2000). *Fuzzy Control – Theory and Practice*, Physica-Verlag, ISBN-13: 978-3790813272, USA

Jantzen, J. (1998). *Tuning of fuzzy PID controllers*, Technical Report 98-H871, Department of Automation, Technical University of Denmark, September 1998, 22 pages

Khezri, M. & Jahed, M. (2007). Real-time intelligent pattern recognition algorithm for surface EMG signals, *BioMedical Engineering OnLine*, Vol. 6, Paper 45, 12 pages, December 2007, ISSN: 1475-925X

Kirianaki, N.V.; Yurish, S.Y; Shpak, N.O. & Deynega, V.P. (2002). *Data Acquisition and Signal Processing for Smart Sensors*. John Wiley & Sons, ISBN: 978-0470843178, UK

Kosko, B. (1992). *Neural networks and fuzzy systems – A dynamical systems approach to machine intelligence*, Prentice Hall, ISBN: 978-0136114352, New Jersey, USA

Kovacic, Z. & Bogdan, S. (2006). *Fuzzy Controller Design – Theory and applications*, Taylor and Francis Group, ISBN: 978-0849337475, USA

Kumar, V.; Rana, K.P.S. & Gupta, V. (2008). Real-Time Performance Evaluation of a Fuzzy PI + Fuzzy PD Controller for Liquid-Level Process, *International Journal of Intelligent Control and Systems*, Vol. 13, No. 2, pp. 89-96, June 2008, ISSN: 0218-7965

Kung, C.C. & Su, J.Y. (2007). Affine Takagi-Sugeno fuzzy modelling algorithm by fuzzy c-regression models clustering with a novel cluster validity criterion, *IET Control Theory and Applications*, Vol. 1, No. 5, pp. 1255-1265, September 2007, ISSN: 1751-8644

Mahfouf, M.; Linkens, D.A. & Kandiah, S. (1999). Fuzzy Takagi-Sugeno Kang model predictive control for process engineering, *IEE Workshop on Model Predictive Control:*

Techniques and Applications, 4 pages, 29 April, 1999, Printed and published by the IEE, Savoy place, London WCPR OBL, UK

MathWorks Inc. (2008), *Matlab Fuzzy Logic and Neural Network Toolboxes - Help.*

Park, J. & Mackay, S. (2003). *Practical data acquisition for instrumentation and control systems*, Elsevier, ISBN: 978-0750657969, UK

Popov, A.V.; Botez, R.M. & Labib, M. (2008 a). Transition point detection from the surface pressure distribution for controller design, *AIAA Journal of Aircraft*, Vol. 45, No. 1, pp. 23-28, January-February 2008, ISSN: 0021-8669

Popov, A.V.; Labib, M.; Fays, J. & Botez, R.M. (2008 b). Closed loop control simulations on a morphing laminar airfoil using shape memory alloys actuators, *AIAA Journal of Aircraft*, Vol. 45, No. 5, pp. 1794-1803, September-October 2008, ISSN: 0021-8669

Popov, A.V.; Botez, R.M.; Mamou, M.; Mebarki, Y.; Jahrhaus, B.; Khalid. M. & Grigorie, T.L. (2009 a). Drag reduction by improving laminar flows past morphing configurations, *AVT-168 NATO Symposium on the Morphing Vehicles*, 12 pages, 20-23 April, 2009, Published by NATO, Evora, Portugal

Popov, A.V.; Botez, R. M.; Mamou, M. & Grigorie, T.L. (2009 b). Optical sensor pressure measurements variations with temperature in wind tunnel testing, *AIAA Journal of Aircraft*, Vol. 46, No. 4, pp. 1314-1318, July-August 2009, ISSN: 0021-8669

Popov, A.V.; Grigorie, T. L.; Botez, R.M.; Mamou, M. & Mebarki, Y. (2010 a). Morphing wing real time optimization in wind tunnel tests, *Proceedings of the 7th International Conference on Informatics in Control, Automation and Robotics ICINCO 2010*, pp. 114-124, ISBN: 978-989-8425-00-3, Madeira, Portugal, 15-18 June, 2010, SciTePress - Science and Technology Publications, Funchal

Popov, A.V.; Grigorie, T. L.; Botez, R.M.; Mamou, M. & Mebarki, Y. (2010 b). Closed-Loop Control Validation of a Morphing Wing Using Wind Tunnel Tests, *AIAA Journal of Aircraft*, Vol. 47, No. 4, pp. 1309-1317, July–August 2010, ISSN: 0021-8669

Popov, A.V.; Grigorie, T. L.; Botez, R.M.; Mamou, M. & Mebarki, Y. (2010 c). Real Time Morphing Wing Optimization Validation Using Wind-Tunnel Tests, *AIAA Journal of Aircraft*, Vol. 47, No. 4, pp. 1346-1355, July–August 2010, ISSN: 0021-8669

Sainmont, C.; Paraschivoiu, I. & Coutu, D. (2009). Multidisciplinary Approach for the Optimization of a Laminar Airfoil Equipped with a Morphing Upper Surface, *AVT-168 NATO Symposium on the Morphing Vehicles*, 20-23 April, 2009, Published by NATO, Evora, Portugal

Sivanandam, S.N.; Sumathi, S. & Deepa, S.N. (2007). *Introduction to Fuzzy Logic using MATLAB*, Springer, ISBN: 978-3540357803, Berlin, Heidelberg, New York

Thill, C.; Etches, J.; Bond, I.; Potter, K. & Weaver, P. (2008). Morphing skins, *The Aeronautical Journal*, Vol. 112, No. 1129, pp. 117-139, March 2008, ISSN: 0001-9240

Verbruggen, H.B. & Bruijn, P.M. (1997). Fuzzy control and conventional control: What is (and can be) the real contribution of Fuzzy Systems?, *Fuzzy Sets Systems*, Vol. 90, No. 2, pp. 151–160, September 1997, ISSN: 0165-0114

Zadeh, L.A. (1965). Fuzzy sets, *Information and Control*, Vol. 8, No. 3, pp. 339-353, June 1965, ISSN: 00199958

15

Using Fuzzy Control for Modeling the Control Behaviour of a Human Pilot

Martin Gestwa
German Aerospace Center (DLR) - Institute of Flight Systems
Germany

1. Introduction

This chapter presents the use of Fuzzy Control to model the control behaviour of a human pilot during two particular flight tasks. Pilot models are used in different areas of the aeronautical research such as handling qualities, cockpit assistant systems as well as in the area of Human Factors or Human Computer Interaction. Aircraft safety analysis is closely connected with the error analysis of pilot computer interaction (see Enders (1989)). This aspect is also supported by the fact, that 55 % the flight accidents are caused by human factors (see N.N. (2006)). Consequently, knowledge about human factors, for example the pilot workload, during the flight or during a particular flight task is important. For instance significant deviations during a particular fight task of a human pilot from his individual corresponding pilot model could be understood as a modification of his workload.

In general pilot models can be classified into behavioural and biomechanical models (see McRuer & Krendel (1974), McRuer (1988) and Luckner (2010)).The biomechanical models defines the human pilot as a passive biodynamic system and concentrates on the biomechanical and neuromuscular aspects. They emulate the torso, the hip, upper arm and forearm as well as the Stick "feel system" dynamics of a human pilot (see Allan et al. (1973) Köhler (1997), Jex & Magdaleno (1978), von der Vorst (1999) and Höhne (2000))

Behavioural models define the human pilot as a active dynamic control element. They can themsleves also be divided into the *conventional* and *alternative* concepts. Conventional concept makes use of the classical control technology to model a human pilot. Typical example of this approach are the quasi-linear model and the models based on optimal control theory as shown for instance in Hess (1990) and Hosman & Stassen (1999). In Dooyong et al. (2003) an optimal control model of a human pilot was used to simulate pilot control activity for a particular approach trajectory. The pilot model was used to predict pilot workload for shipboard approaches in two different wind-over-deck conditions. Johnson & Pritchett (2002) applied an adaptive control architecture to develop a generic pilot model for inner-loop attitude control.

Alternative concepts are based on soft-computing techniques such as Petri nets, expert systems, decision models, neural networks, or fuzzy-logic. For instance a neural network pilot model was proposed in Amelsberg et al. (2009) for wake vortex recovery of an aircraft during departure. Gestwa & Viet (2009) demonstrate that neural networks can learn from a human pilot to perform a particular flight task during a flight. Furthermore, the knowledge based cockpit assistant system (CASSY) contains a Petri net based reference pilot model.

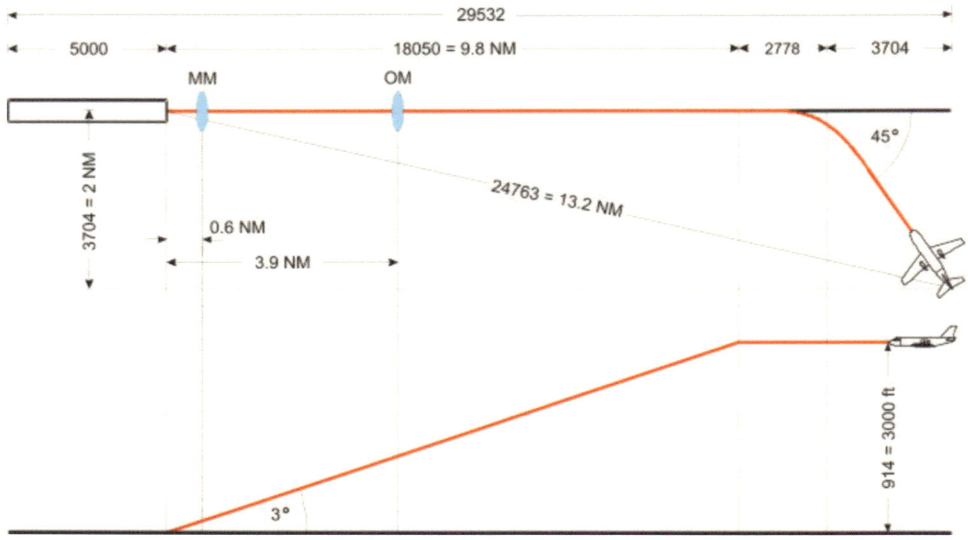

Fig. 1. ILS-Geometry

2. Introduction to flight control during approach

The crucial part of every flight is the approach. In particular pilot workload during approach is significantly higher than during most other phases. For this reason the two scenarios which are considered later are based on this phase.
Fig. 1 shows a typical trajectory for an approach using instrument landing system (ILS). Various types of ILS exist and are very widely used around the world. They are highly accurate means for positioning the aircraft with respect to the runway and this allow operations in poor visibility conditions. This positionings basically constis in determining two angles relatively to the ideal approach path:

- localizer (LOC) which is the lateral deviation to this path
- glide slope (GS) which is the vertical deviation to this path

(see FAA (2009) and Brockhaus (1994)). For each angle exists an corresponding indicator on the cockpit displays. Fig. 2 shows a typical primary flight display (left display) and a typical navigation display (right display).
A precision approach is an approved descent procedure using a navigation facility aligned with a runway where glide slope information is given. When all components of the ILS system

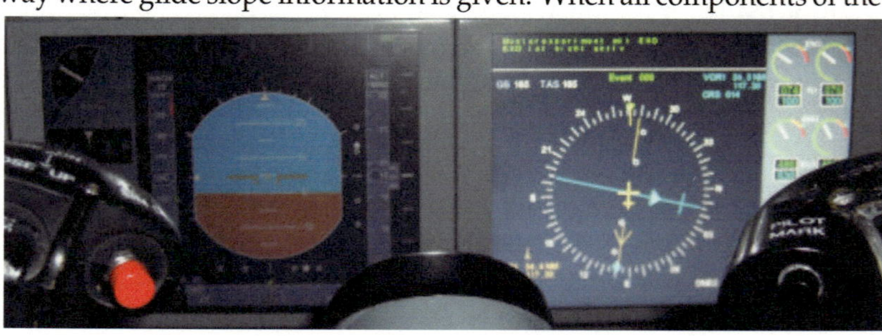

Fig. 2. Typical primary flight display and navigation display

are available, including the approved approach procedure, the pilot may execute a precision approach. FAA (2009) contains a detailed description of an ILS.
A standard ILS-procedure is composed into five parts:

1. The pilot approaches with an offset of 45°to the runway heading.
2. When the aircraft is in the visualised range of the localizer (+2.5°) the pilot initialises the interception. At the end of this maneuver, the aircraft has the right runway heading and the localizer deviation is nearly zero.
3. The next important phase begins when the aircraft is in the visualised range of the glide slope (+0 .5°). Then the pilot changes the aircraft configuration. The landing flaps and slats are set to their maximum position and the gear is extended. The descent initialised and the aircraft declines with an angle of nearly 3°. This angle is called flight path angle.
4. Now the main task of the pilot is to keep the configured aircraft on the glide slope and the localizer with a desired speed. In this state, a slight overshooting of the speed is usually acceptable. However, an significant undershooting of the desired airspeed can lead to a dangerous flight situation. Hence, the pilot observes the speed indicator very carefully during the final approach.
5. At the end of the approach, the landing is performed. In a defined altitude, the pilot initialises the flare. He puts the thrust lever in idle position and commands a pitch up. Afterwards the main gear and a little bit later the nose gear touches down on the runway. Now, the pilot brakes the aircraft and rolls to the final position on the airport.

On order to follow this standard procedure, the pilot has several control actions to perform. Some of them are purely discrete such as flaps and slats configuration or gear extension. Others require quasi-continuous control actions such as longitudinal and lateral control. This control is achieved though a two-axis side stick, pedals and thrust command. All along this chapter the pedals will not be considered because the discussed flight tasks do not require them. The way both side stick and thrust commands change aircraft movement is briefly explained here after. The energy balance of an aircraft is the sum of kinetic and potential energy:

$$E_{total} = E_{pot} + E_{kin} = mgh + \frac{1}{2}mv^2 \quad (1)$$

During a short period of time m is almost constant and can be considered as constant. With this assumption the potential energy only depends on the altitude and the kinetic energy only depends on the speed. If the pilot pushes the side stick, the aircraft reduces the altitude. Potential energy will be transformed in kinetic energy. Without a thrust command the energy balance is quasi constant and consequently the speed increases. According to this the pilot pulls the side stick without a thrust command. The aircraft reduces the speed and increases the altitude. The control strategy of a pilot reflects this fact and can be described as follows:

- If the pilot pulls the side stick, the corresponding thrust command results from the following aspects:
  If the aircraft has a positive speed difference, no thrust is given because the climb reduces the speed difference. If the speed difference is roughly equal zero, a very small amount of thrust has to be set to hold the speed. If the aircraft has a negative speed difference, thrust has to be given because the climb will increase the existing speed difference.

- If the pilot pushes the side stick the thrust command results from the following aspects: If the aircraft has a negative speed difference, no thrust is given because the descent reduces the speed difference. If the speed difference is roughly equal to zero, thrust has to be reduced a little bit to hold the speed. If the aircraft has a positive speed difference, thrust has to be reduced because the descent will increase the existing speed difference.
- The pilot increases only the thrust and with it the airspeed also. The engines of the aircraft, which is consider in this chapter, are beyond the center of gravity. On account of this an increment of the thrust produces a pitch up moment. To compensate this upward movement the pilot gives a small pitch down command.
- The pilot reduces only the thrust and with it the airspeed also. The aircraft pitches down, because a reduction of the thrust produces a pitch down moment. To compensate this downward movement the pilot gives a small pitch up command.

An additional important aspect is that many modern aircraft and in particular the one which is used after are equipped with a flight control system. All pilot commands are inputs of the flight control system. This system compute the necessary displacements of the control surfaces of the aircraft in order to satisfy pilots commands. The later can be differ. Furthermore, a so called rate command attitude hold command system is used. Such a command system stabilises an aircraft on a command attitude, like pitch or roll angle. Side-stick deflection defines a pitch or a roll rate. A consequence of the use of a rate command attitude hold control system is that pilots will only need to perform very short corrections taking the form of short peaks. This will be observed later on Fig. 6 and Fig. 14.

3. The ILS tracking task

The *ILS tracking task* (abbrev. ITT) is based on an instrument landing system of one virtual airport's (see Fig. 1) and focuses only the longitudinal motion of the aircraft. If the aircraft is established on the glide slope and has the required flight conditions, the pilot do not control activities. To compel the pilot to an active control behaviour the ITT was developed and can be described in the following way (see Bauschat (2000)):

> The ITT consists of seven phases. At the beginning the aircraft flies with the target speed and established on the glide slope. After 70 sec the glide slope transmitter shifts to a new position so that the glide slope indicator on the display in the cockpit moves downwards to its minimal deflection (see Subfigure (a) in Fig. 3). Now, the aircraft is above the glide slope, the pilot has to reduce the altitude. For this manoeuvre he has 70 seconds. After this procedure the glide slope transmitter is shifted again so that the glide slope indicator moves upward to its maximal deflection (see Subfigure (b) in Fig. 3). Now the aircraft is under the glide slope and the pilot has to climb with the aircraft. Again the pilot has 70 seconds to compensate the glide slope deviation. In the next phase the glide path indicator moves downward again, afterwards upward again etc. The whole ITT task requires 490 seconds, thereby the glide path indicator moves three times downward and three times upward in a given sequence.

A major aspect for the design of this flight task is to ensure, that the dynamic of the aircraft is sufficient to compensate the resultant altitude difference of the first transmitter shifting. With the typical 3°value for the glide slope tilt angle this would be possible for the aircraft used during this work. Consequently, this tilt angle is later reduced to 1,5°which ensures

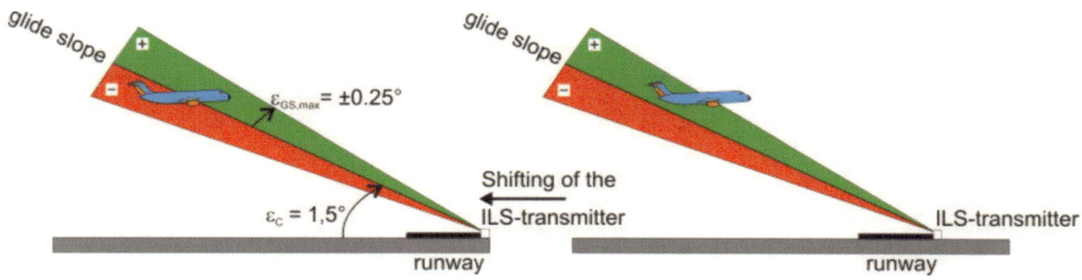

(a) Shifting of the ILS transmitter - aircaft is above the glide slope

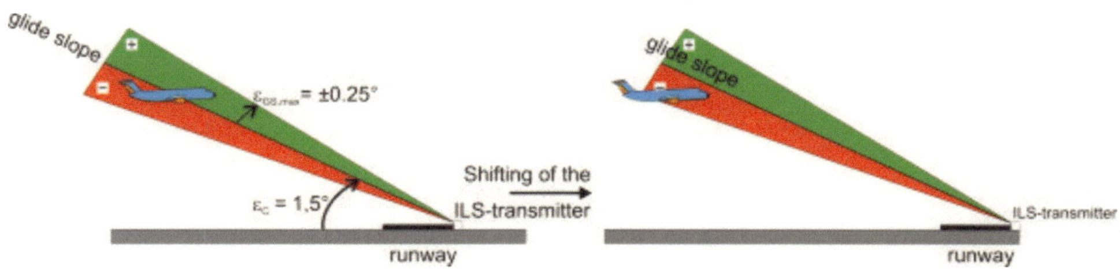

(b) Shifting of the ILS transmitter - aircaft is over the glide slope

Fig. 3. Principle of the ILS tracking Task

the feasibility of the experimental task. Furthermore, this modification implicates that the pilot has to compensate an altitude difference of 196 m instead of 394 m. The shifting of the transmitter raises, that the glide slope display jumps suddenly to its maximum. The pilot senses this behaviour as unrealistic and extremely diverting. Therefore, the shifting rate of the ILS transmitter is attenuated by a first-order filter. This ensures that the glide slope indicator does not jumps but moves continuously in the direction of the current maximum deflection.
To acquire the data basis for the pilot modelling a test pilot has performed three ILS Tracking Task in a flight simulator (see Klaes (2002)). The pilot was instructed to compensate the glide slope deviation as fast as possible and if possible not to deviate from the target speed of 72 m/s (140 kts). Furthermore, the pilot was requested to comment his own control behaviour. These comments were recorded and used for the analysis of his control behaviour as well as for the development of the individual pilot model.

3.1 Development of the ITT-fuzzy pilot

The pilot has to observe many instruments in the cockpit. To find out the information the human pilot uses primarily consciously and unconsciously to perform the ITT, he has to fill a questionnaire (see Rasmussen (1986)). In this questionnaire the pilot describes the priority of the instruments he needed. A given scale is divided into ten priorities, which are subdivided into three classes again (see Table 1).
This information is used to choose the measurements which will be used by the fuzzy pilot. The label numbers in Table 1 are the priorities of a professional pilot who has performed the ITT. His priorities show that for him five indicators are important to perform the ITT. By three of them the signal dynamic is important too. All very important indicators identified by means of the questionnaire in Table 1 is used for the fuzzy pilot model. The dynamics of the indicators is obtained by

$$\Delta \dot{x} = \frac{x_{t+\Delta t} - x_t}{\Delta t} \tag{2}$$

(1) Priority of the instrument										
	very important			important				unimportant		
pitch	1	2	3	4	⑤	6	7	8	9	10
speed trend	1	2	③	4	5	6	7	8	9	10
speed difference	1	2	③	4	5	6	7	8	9	10
glide slope	①	2	3	4	5	6	7	8	9	10
flight path angle	①	2	3	4	5	6	7	8	9	10
altitude	1	2	3	4	5	6	7	8	9	⑩
vertical speed	1	2	3	4	5	⑥	7	8	9	10
Distance	1	2	③	4	5	6	7	8	9	10
(2) Priority of the instrument dynamic										
	very important			important				unimportant		
pitch	1	2	3	4	5	⑥	7	8	9	10
speed trend	1	2	3	4	5	6	7	⑧	9	10
speed difference	1	2	③	4	5	6	7	8	9	10
glide slope	①	2	3	4	5	6	7	8	9	10
flight path angle	1	2	3	④	5	6	7	8	9	10
altitude	1	2	3	4	5	6	7	8	9	⑩
vertical speed	1	2	3	4	5	6	7	8	9	⑩
Distance	1	2	③	4	5	6	7	8	9	10

Table 1. Questionnaire on instrument priority

Between the identified measurements exists a relation which is based on the flight dynamics and physical law. This relation can be used to reduce the number of measurements. For instance, the flight path angle can be derived from the glide slope indicator. If an aircraft is established on the glide slope, the flight path angle is equal the angle of the glide slope. Consequently the flight path angle can be disregarded as a measurement. Similarly, the distance can be derived from the sensitivity the glide slope indicator. Though the pilot consider the label information as important the aforementioned aspects can be used to reduce the numbers of measurements from seven to four. The recorded commentary of the pilot reflects that he also unconsciously reduced the parameter he constantly observe. The four chosen parameters are the glide slope indicator $\Delta\epsilon$, the derivative of the glide slope indicator $\dot{\Delta\epsilon}$, the speed difference Δv and the derivative of the speed difference $\dot{\Delta v}$. Regarding control commands there is no possibility or need to make such a choice: the control commands of the fuzzy pilot are thus simply defined by the control elements in the cockpit. In other words the fuzzy pilot will deliver a side stick command and a thrust command.

3.2 Specification of the linguistic terms and their fuzzy sets

In the following subsection the definition of the linguistic terms and their associated fuzzy sets are described. As examples the glide slope derivative and the side stick command are explained in details. These definitions are based on both pilot comments and recorded flight data.

3.2.1 Derivative of the glide slope indicator

Fig. 4 shows the time evolution of the glide slope indicator derivative. The six movements of the glide slope transmitter are obvious. Except during a few seconds after a move of the

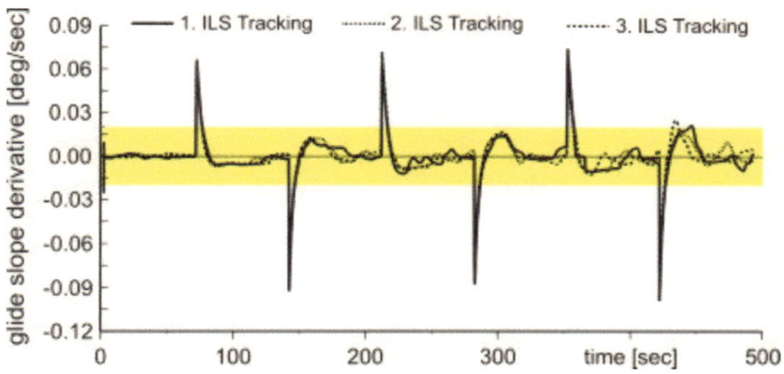

Fig. 4. Time series of the glide slope indicator derivative

glide slope transmitter, the glide slope indicator derivative is in the [-0.02°/sec to 0.02°/sec] interval (identified by the yellow background in Fig. 4).
The investigation of the pilot reaction shows that he does not make any control command immediately after the glide slope transmitter starts to move. The pilot knows that he cannot follow the glide slope directly and that a new phase of the ITT starts. He waits until a quasi-stabilised situation is indicated and then starts to compensate the glide slope deviation. To model this effect the fuzzy pilot will make use of a separate controller to detect the movements of the glide slope transmitter. The measurement of this controller is the glide slope indicator derivative with the universe $[-0.1°/s, 0.1°/s]$ and in agreement with Fig. 4 the three linguistic terms below, zero and above are defined. This fuzzy set overlaps at the begin and end of the the yellow range. The definition points are provided in Table 2.

μ	below	zero	above
0		-0.025	0.015
1	-0.100	-0.015	0.025
1	-0.025	0.015	0.100
0	-0.015	0.025	

Table 2. Definition points of the fuzzy sets for the detection of the glide slope transmitter movement

The control commands of the separate controller are the two linguistic terms *yes* and *no* which indicate that the glide slope transmitter has moved. So, the rule base contains the three rules:

IF	IS above	THEN	shifting IS yes
IF	IS zero	THEN	shifting IS no
IF	IS below	THEN	shifting IS yes

Now the linguistic terms of the glide slope derivative have to be defined in the universe $[-0.025°/s, 0.025°/s]$ (the yellow range in Fig. 4). To describe the strategy of the glide slope derivative the yellow range is enlarged in Fig. 5.
In Fig. 5 six horizontal lines and the zero line can be seen. Based on this classification the universe is divided into seven areas and each area represents a special situation. First the three areas above the zero line will be explained:

– $[0.01°/s, 0.02°/s]$:
  The glide slope transmitter has reached a new position. The motion of the glide slope indicator is normal. The pilot starts to stabilise the aircraft on the glide slope.

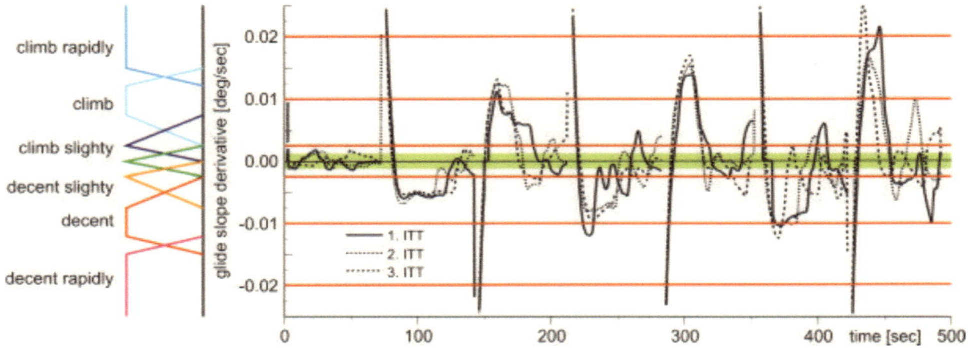

Fig. 5. Zoom of the marked range of Fig. 4

- $[0.0025°/s, 0.01°/s]$:
  The aircraft is in stationary descent or climb. The glide slope deviation is reduced.
- $[0.0°/s, 0.0025°/s]$:
  The aircraft is near to the glide slope and has to be stabilised on the glide slope. According to the commands of the pilot the aircraft oscillates around the glide slope.
- $0°/s$:
  On the glide slope the derivative should have a value of zero. Consequently the aircraft is in a stationary state.

This description can be transfered to the area below the zero line. With the help of the commentaries of the pilot seven linguistic terms can be defined. The terms are:

descent rapidly, descent, descent slightly,
zero,
climb slightly, climb, climb heavily

and the determining points of their fuzzy sets are summarised in Table 3.

μ	descent rapidly	descent	descent slightly	zero	climb slightly	climb	climb rapidly
0		-0.0150	-0.0075	-0.0025	0.0	0.0025	0.0120
1	-0.0250	-0.0120	-0.0025	0.0	0.0025	0.0075	0.0150
1	-0.0150	-0.0075	-0.0025	0.0	0.0025	0.0120	0.0250
0	-0.0120	-0.0025	0.0	0.0025	0.0075	0.0150	

Table 3. Points of the glide slope deviation

3.2.2 Side stick command

The side stick deflections are given as inputs to a rate-command system and Fig. 6 shows the side stick commands of an ITT. It can be seen that the pilot commands have mainly the shape of short peaks. To model this the maximum method will be used for defuzzification because this method tends to cause a pulsed behaviour (see Kruse et al. (1995) and Kahlert & Frank (1994)). With this method the output of the fuzzy pilot is the control action corresponding to the fuzzy set having the greatest value of μ. To determine the control actions an investigation of the pilot side stick commands was made and resulted in the definition of seven actions:

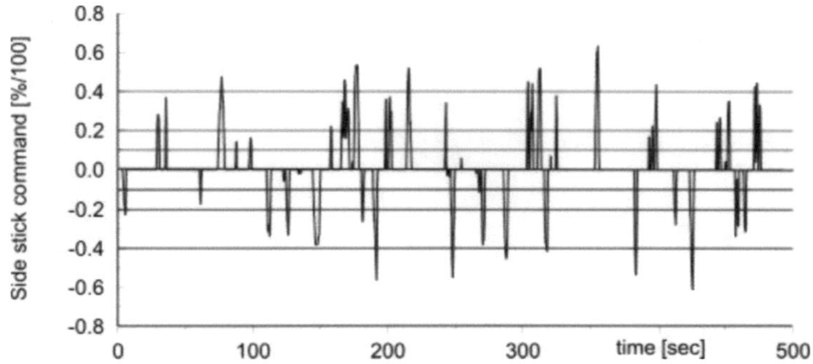

Fig. 6. Side Stick command of the pilot

null, 3 positive and 3 negative. They are represented by the horizontal green and red lines in Fig. 6.
With the values in Fig. 6 and pilot comments the corresponding linguistic terms for the side stick commands can be derived. They are:

pull heavily, pull, pull slightly,
zero,
push slightly, push, push heavily

The universe of the side stick command is defined by the side stick signal with the interval $[-1,1]$. The fuzzy-sets are defined by triangular functions having their maximum exactly at a single point. The linguistic terms and the corresponding fuzzy sets are given in Table 4.

μ	pull heavily	pull	pull slightly	null	push slightly	push	push heavily
0	-1.0	-0.4	-0.2	-0.1	0.0	0.1	0.2
1	-0.4	-0.2	-0.1	0.0	0.1	0.2	0.4
0	-0.2	-0.1	0.0	0.1	0.2	0.4	1.0

Table 4. Points of the side stick command

The control architecture is now complete and is graphically shown in Fig. 7. The ITT rule base must however still be defined.

3.3 Definition of the ITT-rule base

In this section the rule base of the fuzzy pilot will be defined using the specified linguistic terms. For this the basic control strategy of the pilot should be determined from the time histories (see Fig. 8) and the pilot comments.
This strategy can be divided into three phases:

- In the first phase the glide slope transmitter is moving. The absolute value of the glide slope derivative is large. Since he knows that he cannot follow the glide slope indicator, he waits until the indication moves slowly. This behaviour is already modeled by the rule base given in section 3.2.1 on page 7.
- In the second phase the glide slope indicator moves slowly. Now the pilot starts compensating the glide slope deviation. Depending on the actual situation he initiates a descent or climb. In this phase he is reducing the glide slope deviation very fast. He brings

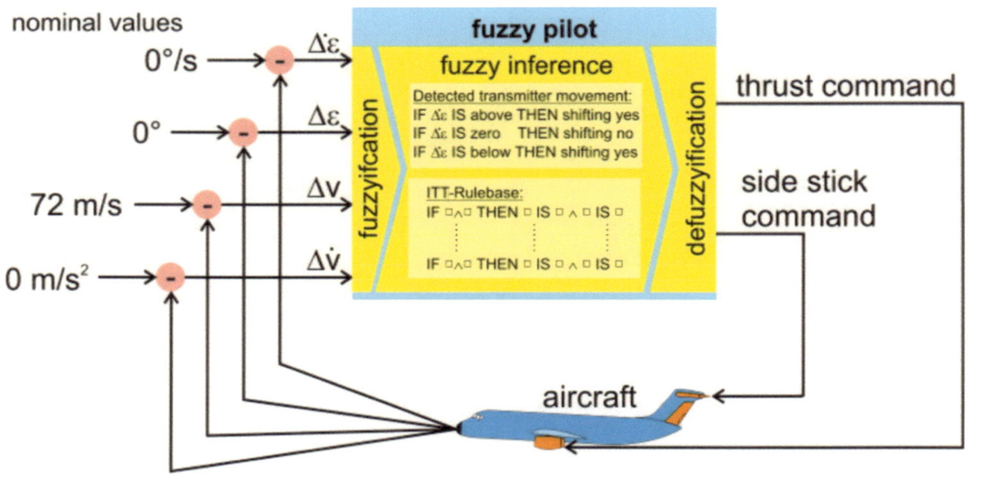

Fig. 7. Structure of the ITT fuzzy pilot

the aircraft as fast as possible close to the glide slope. During the phase of the glide slope movement the pilot only has to wait and to observe.

- In the third phase the aircraft is near the glide slope. Now the pilot has to stabilise the aircraft on the glide slope. For this procedure he stops the descent or climb by pulling or pushing the side stick. Consequently the descent or climb is interrupted and the aircraft will be stabilised on the glide slope as well as possible. Now the aircraft is approximately on the glide slope. The pilot knows that a slight side stick inputs is enough to compensated these deviations it always has except if low frequency component are 0. Furthermore he knows that these slight inputs have no effect to the airspeed.

Evaluating the airspeed difference in Fig. 8 it is remarkable that in some situation the power lever has reached the lower limit but the speed is still too high. In this situation the pilot can reduce the speed difference only with the side stick. If he pulls the side stick the aircraft interrupts the descent and the glide slope deviation is not decreasing. But it is the task of the pilot to compensate the glide slope deviation as quickly as possible. So, he has to accept the

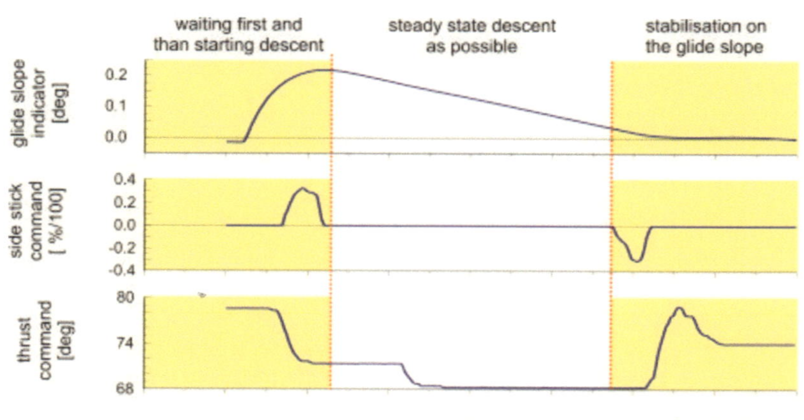

Fig. 8. Strategy of the human pilot

IF	$\Delta\epsilon$ IS zero $\wedge$ $\Delta\dot{\epsilon}$ IS zero $\wedge$ Δv IS zero $\wedge$ $\Delta\dot{v}$ IS zero $\wedge$ shifting IS no
THEN	side stick IS zero $\wedge$ thrust IS hold
IF	$\Delta\epsilon$ IS over $\wedge$ $\Delta\dot{\epsilon}$ IS climb $\wedge$ Δv IS zero $\wedge$ $\Delta\dot{v}$ IS zero $\wedge$ shifting IS no
THEN	side stick IS push heavily $\wedge$ thrust IS raise
IF	$\Delta\epsilon$ IS over $\wedge$ $\Delta\dot{\epsilon}$ IS climb $\wedge$ Δv IS zero $\wedge$ $\Delta\dot{v}$ IS sink $\wedge$ shifting IS no
THEN	side stick IS push heavily $\wedge$ thrust IS raise slightly
IF	$\Delta\epsilon$ IS over $\wedge$ $\Delta\dot{\epsilon}$ IS climb $\wedge$ Δv IS zero $\wedge$ $\Delta\dot{v}$ IS climb $\wedge$ shifting IS no
THEN	side stick IS push $\wedge$ thrust IS raise
IF	$\Delta\epsilon$ IS over $\wedge$ $\Delta\dot{\epsilon}$ IS climb slightly $\wedge$ Δv IS zero $\wedge$ $\Delta\dot{v}$ IS climb $\wedge$ shifting IS no
THEN	side stick IS push $\wedge$ thrust IS raise heavily
IF	$\Delta\epsilon$ IS over $\wedge$ $\Delta\dot{\epsilon}$ IS descent rapidly $\wedge$ Δv IS zero $\wedge$ $\Delta\dot{v}$ IS climb $\wedge$ shifting IS no
THEN	side stick IS null $\wedge$ thrust IS hold
IF	$\Delta\epsilon$ IS over $\wedge$ $\Delta\dot{\epsilon}$ IS descent $\wedge$ Δv IS zero $\wedge$ $\Delta\dot{v}$ IS climb $\wedge$ shifting IS no
THEN	side stick IS null $\wedge$ thrust IS hold

Table 5. Outline of the rule base

interim speed deviation. Here the pilot uses the relation between the side stick and thrust command, which is described in the second section 2 on page 7.
The rule base of the fuzzy pilot has to be designed taking the above mentioned aspects into account. For the development of the rules an iterative approach is applied in order to keep the numbers of rules as low as possible. This iterative process starts with only one rule and the other rules are defined one after the other. If a situation during the ITT occurs for which the fuzzy pilot has no rule the ITT is aborted. A new rule can be defined by analysing the current flight state and this process is repeated until it does not happen anymore. Table 5 contains the result after seven iteration steps.
The control behaviour of these seven rules are shown in Fig. 9 on the base of the first movement of the glide slope transmitter. This method was used to define the whole rule base of the fuzzy pilot.
The development of the fuzzy pilot model based on the information gained from one pilot. This has the consequence, that only his specific control characteristics will be matched.

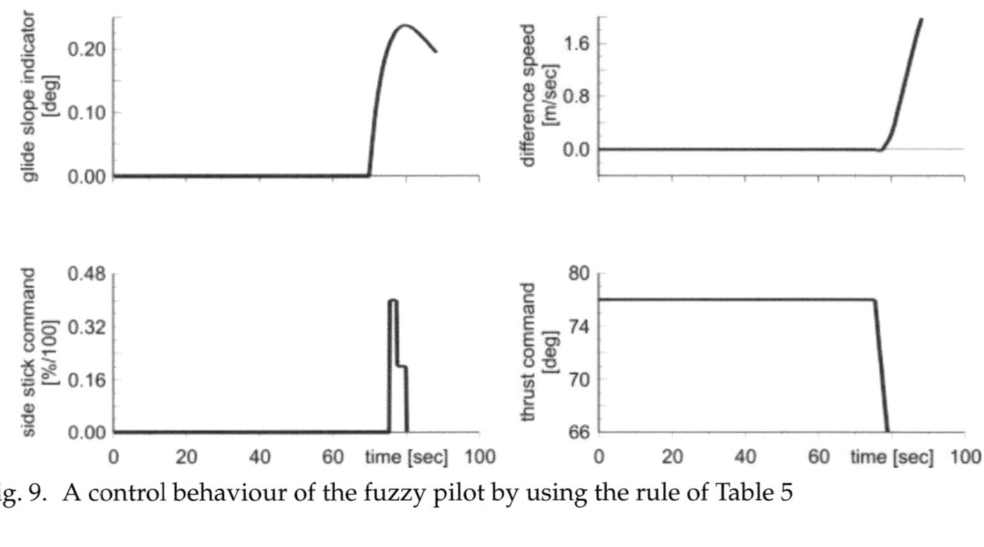

Fig. 9. A control behaviour of the fuzzy pilot by using the rule of Table 5

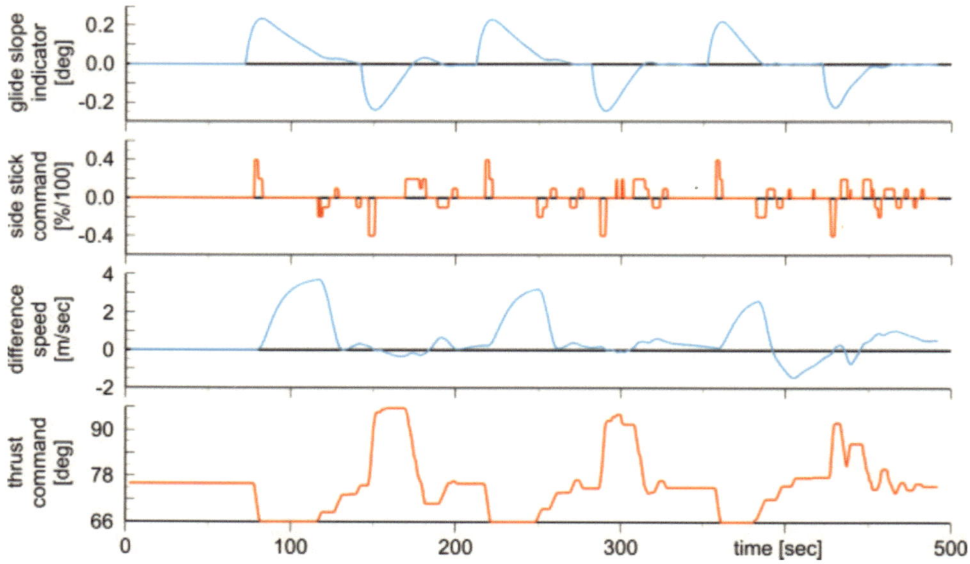

Fig. 10. Control policy of the fuzzy pilot by the ITT

3.4 The fuzzy pilot in comparison with the human pilot

The way the fuzzy pilot performs the ITT is shown in Fig. 10. The fuzzy logic system compensates all glide slope deviations caused by the movements of the transmitter and stabilises the aircraft on it with the demanded target speed. In order to know whether a fuzzy logic control approach is a suitable method to model the human control behaviour an assessment of the control behaviour of the fuzzy pilot in comparison with the control behaviour of the human pilot is necessary. Indeed, many factors may influence the control activities of a human pilot (see Budd (1992)). Therefore the number of experiments which are required to identify the real influence of each one of them is very high. For simplicity, only a simplified comparison is presented here.

3.4.1 Comparison of the glide slope indicator

To compare the glide slope indicator deviations of the human pilot and the fuzzy pilot their time evolution on the same ITT experiment may be analysed. These time evolution are shown in Fig. 11.

During the 2nd, 4th and 5th transmitter movements the two curves are matching acceptably. On the basis of the mean value and the standard deviation of the glide slope deviation it can be assessed, how well the pilot and the fuzzy pilot maintain the glide slope. Table 6 shows that all mean values can be found in the proximity of the ideal mean value zero and all standard

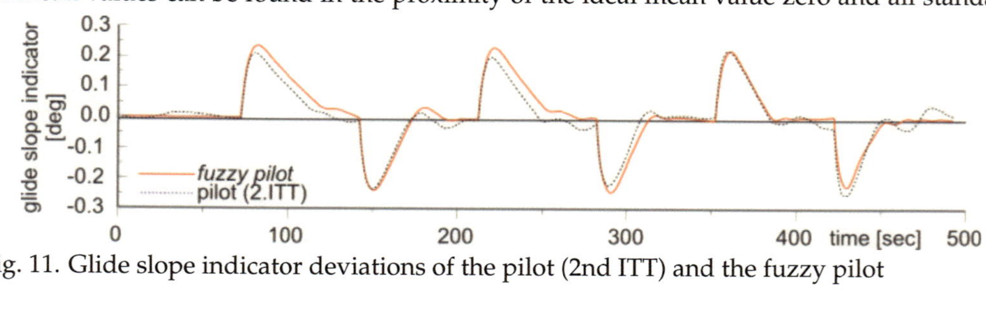

Fig. 11. Glide slope indicator deviations of the pilot (2nd ITT) and the fuzzy pilot

	fuzzy pilot	pilot (1st ITT)	pilot (2nd ITT)	pilot (3rd ITT)
μ	0.00990	0.00083	0.00140	0.00830
σ	0.10100	0.10600	0.09400	0.09700
$\sigma_{\mu=0}$	0.01030	0.01130	0.00880	0.00950

Table 6. Mean value and standard deviation of the glide slope indicator signal

deviations are almost zero, too. Indeed the first and second ITT of the human pilot is better than the fuzzy-pilot. The mean value of fuzzy pilot and the third ITT is very similar. That applies to the standard deviation, also. Consequently, the all values of fuzzy pilot are in the range of the nature bandwidth of the human pilot control activities.

3.4.2 Comparison of the side stick commands

Fig. 12 shows the time series of the side stick commands of the fuzzy pilot and human pilot (2nd ITT).

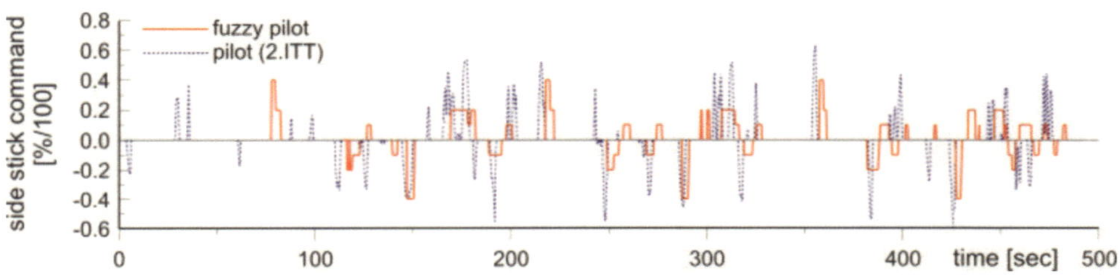

Fig. 12. Side stick command of the pilot and the fuzzy pilot

The maximum values of the side stick commands of the fuzzy pilot are rather acceptable. However, the commands of the human pilot can be characterised as jerky and short inputs in contrast to the fuzzy pilot which prefers weak and long inputs. This difference is based on the defuzzification and is typical for the maximum method. In spite of this difference the reaction of the aircraft is nearly the same (see the last section). Table 7 reflects this result, because the mean value and the standard deviation are in the range of the nature bandwidth of the human pilot control activities

	fuzzy pilot	pilot (1st ITT)	pilot (2nd ITT)	pilot (3rd ITT)
μ	0.00610	0.00680	0.00620	0.00580
σ	0.10200	0.14100	0.13600	0.14700
$\sigma_{\mu=0}$	0.01100	0.02000	0.01800	0.02200

Table 7. Mean values and standard deviations of the side stick command

3.4.3 Comparison of the control strategy

The comparison between the human control strategy and the control strategy of the fuzzy pilot implies that the previously discussed measurements can be seen as an inherent part of a control concept. This concept defines how the pilot has to react in a situation and determine his control behaviour. During the ITT the situation is described by means of the glide slope and the speed. The control strategy is characterised by the side stick command and the thrust command. In the following example one ITT section is evaluated with respect to the control strategy.

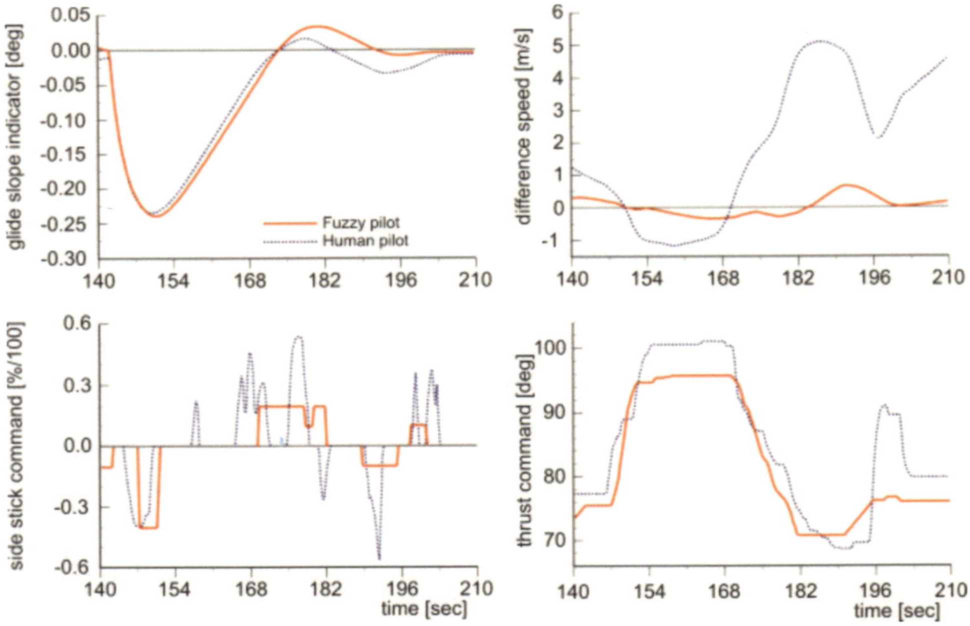

Fig. 13. Control strategy of the fuzzy pilot in comparison with the one of the human pilot

The reaction of the fuzzy pilot is very similar to the reaction of the pilot (see Fig. 13). Both react on a glide slope transmitter shifting with a stationary climb. During the stationary climb, the pilot waits until the aircraft is near the glide slope. Both begin to interrupt the climb so that the aircraft is stabilised on the glide slope. Both pilots stop the climb too late. Consequently, the aircraft overshoots the glide slope. In this situation the pilot as well as the fuzzy pilot push the side stick to return on the glide slope. In the final phase of the ITT both pilots succeed to stabilise the aircraft on the glide slope.

The coupling of the side stick and thrust command can be also observed in this section of the ITT. The commands push and thrust reduction as well as pull and thrust increase define a control unit. It is noticeable that the pilot and the fuzzy pilot has the same strategy to stabilise the aircraft on the glide slope. Both pushes the side stick but the aircraft overshoots the glide slope (see Fig. 13 from 168 to 182 seconds). The flight section in Fig. 13 points out, that the control strategy of both pilots during a negative, maximal movement of the glide slope transmitter is very similar. The previously described control strategy can be observed in every phase of the tracking task. An investigation of all opposed reactions of the fuzzy pilot and the human pilot shows that they are based on different flight states. However, both reactions are traceable and logical. Although some differences between the reaction of the human pilot and the fuzzy pilot exist, the fuzzy pilot reproduce sufficiently well control strategy of the pilot during this particular task.

4. The localizer intercept task

In this section a pilot model for a typical ILS approach should be developed (see Fig. 1). First, a brief description of the ILS approach is given:

The pilot begins the landing with a offset of 45°to the runway. When the localizer indicator starts to move (+2,5°) the pilot initiates the intercept onto the Localizer. At the end of this

manoeuvre the aircraft is approximately on the localizer. The next part starts when the glide slope indicator begins to run downwards (+0.5°). The pilot lowers the landing flaps and landing gear. He changes the aircraft configuration and ensures a descent of approximately -3°. The aircraft is established with target speed on the localizer and on the glide slope. The ILS task ends with the beginning of the flare because the flare is excluded from this study. To develop the pilot model for this flight task a professional human pilot performs this task in a ground simulator.
The ITT can be characterised as a flight task with high control activities of the pilot because the pilot should compensate the deviations as fast as possible. It is a so called high gain task. In contrast to the ITT the ILS task can be characterised with low control activities but with high precision. Therefore, the ILS task is a so called low gain task.
Compared to the experiences with the ITT the structure of the pilot model will be different. By using the theory of the mental models from the cognitive psychology pilot model of the ILS flight task consists of simple, compact controllers (see Dutke (1994)). Each control represents a mental model and they are combined to a complex control. Similarly to classical flight controllers and control laws separate fuzzy controller will be develop for longitudinal and lateral motion. Each movement is separately considered (see Brockhaus (1994)). Furthermore, the fuzzy control of the longitudinal motion contains the thrust controlling (see section 2 on page 2 relation between side stick and thrust command). Consequently, the structure of the control is based on a two-stage controller structure. This structure reflects the strategy of the human pilot in a better way.

4.1 Recording and Preprocessing of the Flight Test Data

To get the knowledge and the control behaviour of a human pilot, a pilot performed ILS approaches in the ground simulator all data of these approaches were recorded. Additionally, the pilot explains his control activities and why he reacts in such a way. The comments of the pilot were recorded as well. This information is the basis for the development of the fuzzy-controller.
An initial analysis of the pilot comments and the general knowledge about the ILS approach permit to identify the measurements which are mainly used by the pilot to perform the ILS flight task:

- time, air speed, pitch angle, and rate as well as roll angle and rate, magnetic heading
- configuration of the landing flaps
- side-stick pitch and roll command as well as position of the right and left power lever
- status of the landing gear, middle, and outer marker
- localizer and glide slope deviation

These measurements can be extracted out of the flight test database.

4.2 Development of a conventional fuzzy controller

The first design step consists in defining the measurements and the control variables. In the case of modeling a human pilot the cockpit indicator, the cockpit input devices and the knowledge of the pilot are information sources to define the input and output variables of the fuzzy controller or rather the cognitive pilot model. All inputs of the pilot are on the primary flight- and navigation display. (see Fig. 2). As mentioned above two separate controllers are developed. The controller of the lateral motion stabilises the aircraft on the localizer whereas

Time [sec]	Comments of the human pilot
9.66	It has been adjusted so far.
	And now, I simply fly until the Localizer comes in.
41.85	Now, the localizer comes in.
44.76	Now, I initialised the turn left, 20°or so.
63.66	Therefore, I finish the turn, in order to reach the desired heading without an overshoot.
120.45	A little correction to the left
124.57	Now, I finish the turn again.
148.35	Intermediate, I check the localizer, it is o.k.
163.95	Localizer is o.k. with a slight tendency to the right

Table 8. Typical comments of the human pilot about the lateral motion

the controller of the longitudinal motion is responsible to keep the aircraft on the glide slope and controls the airspeed.

4.2.1 Fuzzy-controller for the lateral motion

The pilots comments were analysed to identify which indicator on the displays are used by the pilot for the lateral control task. Table 8 summarises some typical comments about the lateral motion.

This analysis showed that the localizer indicator was the primary source of information for the lateral motion during the ILS approach. In addition to the current position the dynamic of the localizer indicator is also important (see the commentary at 41.85 sec in Table 1). Furthermore the pilot derives out of the current localizer indicator position a roll angle, which is qualified for an enhancement of the current fight condition. For the evaluation of a roll command the roll angle gives a good orientation, because the pilot has an accurate idea of the required roll angle. Therefore, the localizer indicator deviation and its derivative as well as the roll angle is used as input for the roll controller. Additional to these inputs the status of the localizer signal is also applied as an input because this controller should only be active when the aircraft receives the localizer signal

The analysis of the flight test data has shown that only the aileron is used to control the lateral motion of the aircraft during the ILS approach and not the rudder. Furthermore, the pilot uses the localizer indicator to perform the intercept. From this fact it follows that the pilot commands only roll input to compensate localizer deviations. Table 9 summarizes the interface of the controller for the lateral motion.

The lateral motion is only controlled by the side-stick roll command. The lateral control strategy of the pilot consists of two parts. First the pilot analyses the localizer deviation. Consequently he derives a set point for the roll angle PHI_new. Then he compares this set point with the current roll angle PHI and compensates a possible difference with an adequate

Measurements:	
Localizer indicator deviation	(DeltaLOC)
Derivation of the localizer indicator deviation	(dDeltaLOC)
Roll angle	(Phi)
Status of the localizer	(LOC_Status)
Control variables:	
Side-stick roll command	(SiStRollCmd)

Table 9. Interface of controller for the lateral motion

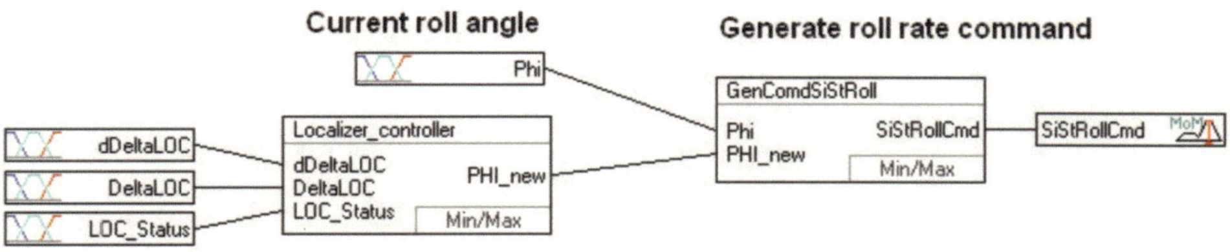

Fig. 14. Fuzzy-Controller of the Lateral Motion

roll command. Fig. 14 shows the resulting structure of the lateral fuzzy-controller.
First the localizer indicator and its derivative are interpreted by the fuzzification interface. Then, the rules of the fuzzy controller transform this information into a target roll angle, which is stored in the internal linguistic variable PHI_new. This linguistic variable and the current roll angle of the aircraft PHI are the inputs of the second fuzzy-controller which generates the corresponding side-stick command. This combination of both controller leads to a classical cascade structure which can easily be identified in Fig. 14.

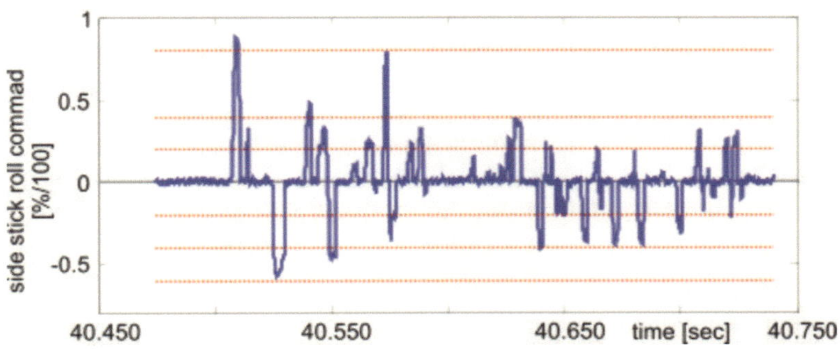

Fig. 15. Analysis of the roll commands of the human pilot

Fig. 15 shows the roll commands of the human pilot during the first ILS approach. The time history exposes that the roll commands have mainly the shape of short peaks. As already seen before this control behaviour is typical for a pilot, using a rate command system (see section 2 on page 2). To model this control behaviour the maximum method is also used for the defuzzification. The fuzzy set of this fuzzy-controler will be defined in the same way like in section 3.2.2 on page 8 describe. The red lines in Fig. 15 represents the tops of the triangle fuzzy-sets.

4.2.2 Fuzzy-controller for the longitudinal motion

The same method as for the lateral motion controller is applied to design the longitudinal controller. Table 10 contains the inputs and the outputs of the controller. Similarly to the lateral motion, the glide slope indicator and its dynamics are the primary information sources which are used by the pilot. Additional the deviation of the target speed is also important.
As seen in section 2 and for the ILS tracking task the control of the longitudinal motion involves the control of both pitch and airspeed. As both are strongly coupled pilots combine both actions and the fuzzy controller has to therefore also work this way. Fig. 16 shows the controller for the longitudinal motion and the airspeed.
The studies in the ground simulator have shown that the human pilot uses the thrust lever rarely. One reason for this behaviour is the knowledge about inertia of the engines. A thrust

command needs a period until the engines reach the new commanded number of revolutions. Therefore, the human pilot moves the thrust lever carefully. In addition, it is possible that a thrust lever command is needless because a pitch command is given.
The controller uses three rule bases. The first rules basis generates an internal thrust lever command out of the difference of the target speed and the current airspeed as well as out of the airspeed tendency or dynamic. The second rule produces an internal pitch command. As inputs this rule basis uses the glide slope deviation and its derivative to model the dynamic of the indicator as well as the glide slope status. The status indicates whether the aircraft receives the glide slope signal or not. In section 2 the relation between pitch and thrust command is explained. This third rule basis combines both commands and generates the ultimate commands. The import aspect of this rule basis is to filter out unnecessary thrust lever commands. Besides, pilots effectively use such a control strategy because they know that it does not make sense to move the thrust lever every second. Thus they adapt themselves by limiting their control bandwidth for the engines which indeed corresponds to what the third rule base does this for the fuzzy-controller.
To defuzzificate the fuzzy control value into a crisp value the maxima of mean method is applied again.
Besides, the fuzzy controller outputs and the changing of aircraft configuration is an important control activity. The trigger of this activity is when the aircraft reaches the reception area of the glide slope. Then the pilot sets the landing flaps and the landing gear. Consequently, this action is a unique event during the flight task and not really a control task. Therefore, this functionality is modeled outside the fuzzy-controller and is a singular discrete procedure.
The studies in the ground simulator have shown that the pilot accepts a slight overshooting of the target speed but on no account a undershooting. Consequently, two fuzzy-sets "null"

Measurements:	
Glide slope indicator deviation	(DeltaGS)
Derivation of the glide slope indicator deviation	(dDeltaGS)
Status of the glide slope	(GS_Status)
Target speed deviation	(DeltaV)
Derivation of the target speed deviation	(dDeltaV)
Control variables:	
Side-stick pitch command	(SiStPitchCmd)
Thrust command	(dDeltaPLA)

Table 10. Interface of controller for the longitudinal motion

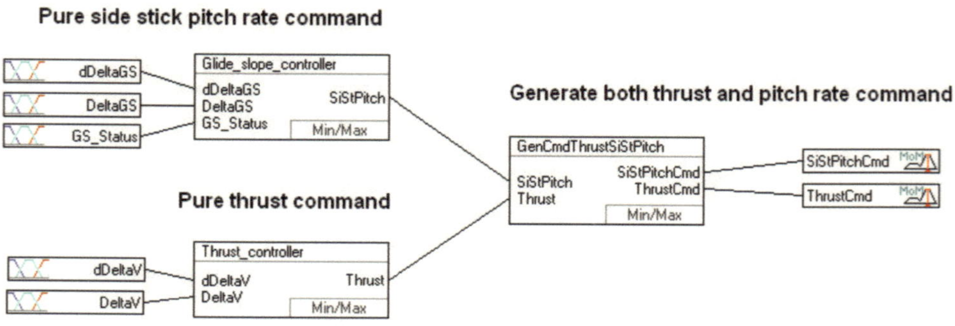

Fig. 16. Fuzzy controller of the longitudinal motion

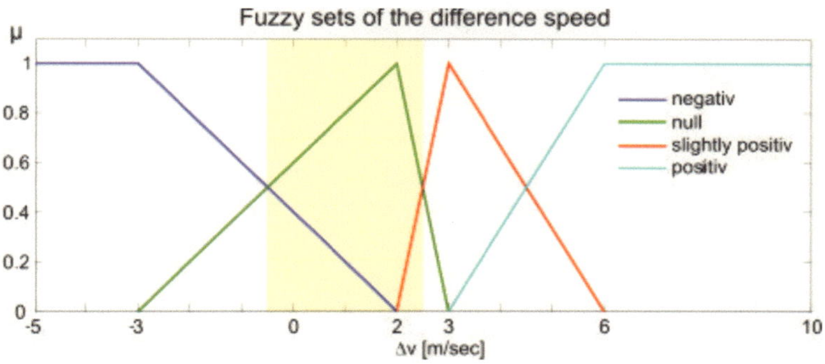

Fig. 17. Fuzzy sets of the difference airspeed

and "slightly positive" were defined to obtain such a strategy (Fig. 17).
It can observe on Fig. 17 that the fuzzy pilot has an asymmetrical tolerance range of [-0.5 m/s, 2.5m/s] which is shown by the yellow sector. -0.5 m/s is the intersection point to the fuzzy set "negative" and 2.5 is the intersection point to "slightly positive". The fuzzy-sets "positive", "slightly positive" and "negative" define an over- and undershooting of the target airspeed. In these cases the aircraft has an undesirable flight state and the pilot has to do some control activities.
To model the control commands of the pilot the recorded flight test data is analysed.
This procedure is also applied to define the other fuzzy-sets of the control variables.
The last design step consists in defining the rule bases. In principal, the rule base of a controller describes the physical process. In the case of modeling the control behaviour of a person or a human pilot the rule base can be interpreted as his mental model of the process or flight task. Additionally, the ILS approach to an airport is a standard flight procedure and all pilots performs it in a quite similar manner.
This knowledge can be used to define an initial subset of rules. The missing rules were defined by using an iterative process (see section 3.3). If all necessary rules were defined to perform the ILS approach the fine tuning of the rule base finished the development of the rule base. Therefore the rule base is analysed to detect gaps or weak points with fewer rules by using a debug-tool. Taking all knowledge about the ILS approach and the flight mechanics as well as flight control into account the rule base is completed. With these rule bases the fuzzy-controller is now defined.

4.2.3 Result of the fuzzy controller

The design fuzzy-controller was used in ILS approach simulations. For one of these simulations Fig. 18 shows the plots of the current airspeed as well as the position with respect to the localizer and glide slope. At the beginning of the simulation, the aircraft is on the left side of the localizer and flying in tis direction: the fuzzy controller has to make a turn left to catch the middle of the localizer signal. For a better understanding the airspeed is plotted against the geodetic y-coordinate as well.The default airspeed of the ILS approach was 140 kts (appr. 72 m/sec). The three time histories show, that the conventional ILS fuzzy-pilot performs the ILS approach. The first plot shows the airspeed. At a y-distance of 17000 m before the runway the ILS-fuzzy-pilot extends the landing gear. In this way he changes the aircraft configuration. Consequently the air drag is increased and the airspeed is reduced. Additionally, the ILS-fuzzy-pilot commands a pitch down command to initialise the descent. According to these control activities the airspeed increases. To keep the default airspeed the

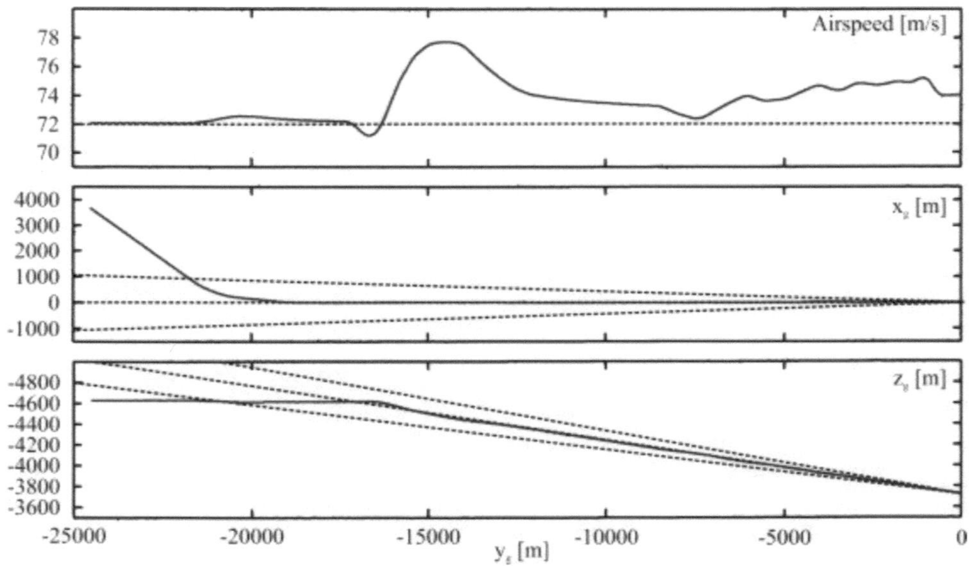

Fig. 18. ILS-approach perform by the conventional fuzzy controller

ILS-fuzzy-pilot has to reduce the thrust. The second and third plot shows the localizer and glide slope deviation. Both plots verify that the ILS-fuzzy pilot perform the ILS approach. The simulation delivers nearly the same results if the aircraft is on right side of the localizer.

4.3 Development of a cognitive pilot model

The aim was to develop a cognitive pilot model for an ILS approach. Therefore the structure of the above fuzzy-controller has to be modified in such a way that the fuzzy controller presumes control characteristics of the human pilot. To realise this aspect the following two modifications are made:

1. The observation of the pilot during the ILS approach in the ground simulator offered that the pilot mostly monitored the cockpit displays. With it, he supervises the flight condition of the aircraft in consideration of the ILS approach. If the current flight condition does not match the desired flight condition well enough the pilot reacts with a corresponding command input at the side stick, the thrust lever or both. This control behaviour can be interpreted as a state switching. The pilot is switching from a monitoring state to a controlling state. Indeed, every pilot has his own tolerances. This fact is the basis of the idea to develop a fuzzy-controller in combination with a finite state machine. The finite state machine is applied to model the state switching of the pilot. As noted below the state machine has the state monitoring and controlling. Between these states the corresponding transitions have to be modeled. The finite state machine starts logically in the state monitoring. In this state the pilot monitors the flight condition and he remains in this state if his evaluation of flight condition is positive. Otherwise he is switching to the state controlling and initialises a control command which is adequately to the current situation. When the control command is finished the finite state machine switch back to the state monitoring.
2. The ILS approach is a standard procedure, but each pilot has his own control characteristic. Typical characteristics are the maximum value or the duration of a control command.

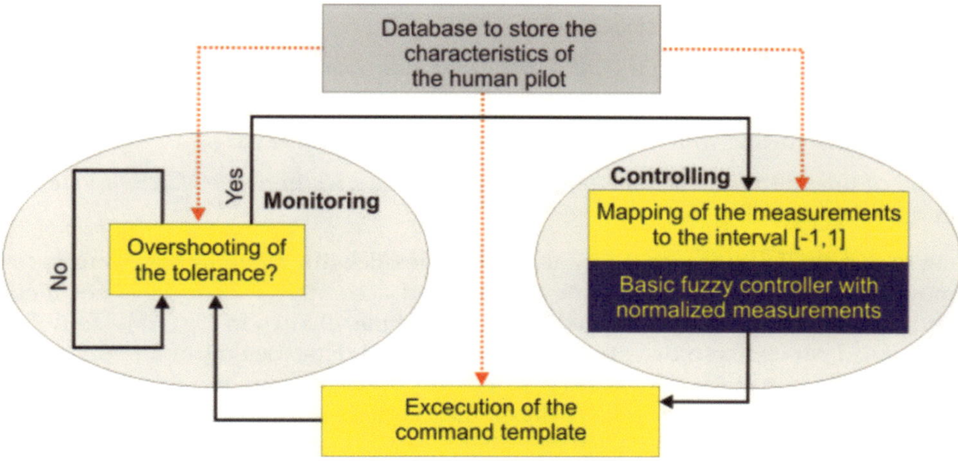

Fig. 19. Structure of the cognitive pilot model for an ILS-approach

To combine clear specified control commands with individual control characteristics the fuzzy-controller generates control command templates instead of a direct control command. These command templates are executed outside the fuzzy-controller. The fuzzy-controller does not generate a new command template as long as the last command is not finished. This technique offers the option to store the control characteristics of each pilot in a database. Furthermore, each pilot has his individual range of permissibility for each measurement. Consequently, the fuzzy-sets of the measurements have to be decoupled from the controller itself. For this purpose the fuzzy-sets are normalised to the interval [-1,+1]. This normalisation has to be adapted for each pilot by defining an individual mapping function.

The combination of a finite state machine with a normalised fuzzy-controller introduces the possibility to adapt the fuzzy-controller to a given control behaviour. The finite state machine models the state switching of the human pilot between monitoring and controlling. During the transition from monitoring into controlling the state machine initialises the control command which is adequately to the current situation. The fuzzy-controller generates a control command template which is corresponding to the standard procedure of the ILS-approach. This output is based on normalised measurements. Afterwards the control command template is executed. The pure fuzzy-controller is transferred to a cognitive pilot model by linking the fuzzy-controller with pilot characteristics database. Fig. 19 shows the final global structure of the cognitive pilot model.

4.3.1 Definition of the control command templates

The definition of the control command templates is based on the idea that all pilot commands can be approximated by triangle or trapezoid signals. These signal types are typical for a rate command system and can be divided into three phases:

1. The pilot moves the side stick from the neutral position to a given value.
2. The pilot holds this value for a time span.
3. The pilot moves the side stick back to the neutral position.

To model this kind of signal the following four parameters are required:

1. Value of the maximum ($MaxSiSt$)
2. Period of time during which the pilot moves the side stick from the neutral position to the $MaxSiSt$ value (ΔT_{up}).
3. Period of time during which the pilot holds the $MaxSiSt$ value (ΔT_{hold}).
4. Period of time during which the pilot moves the side stick from the $MaxSiSt$ value to the neutral position (ΔT_{down}).

During the whole ILS approach the pilot has the sidesstick during in his hand. Furthermore, the movement of the side stick is not constant and accurate. This effect is not modeled and the human pilot corrects it immediately (see at time 40.510 s in Fig. 15). To define all forementioned parameters a two-stage analysis is applied. First the time of the beginning and the end of the command is determined. Afterward the maximum into this time interval is computed. With this method all side-stick commands are approximated. To check the quality of this approximation the integral of the original signal and the approximated signal was computed. $\int(sidestick_{pilot} - sidestick_{fuzzy})^2 dt$ The value of this integrals was small enough to justify the use of this approximation. Additionally, the aircraft flight condition is stored at the beginning and the end of the command as well.
To model the self-limitation of the control bandwidth for the engines the aforementioned method has to be varied a little bit. The human pilot knows that the engines have a delay. For this reason he generates a thrust lever deflection and waits for a moment until the engines react. Consequently, the airspeed changes very slowly. This implicit knowledge of the pilot is the reason, why an additional time delay has to be defined for the thrust lever command. Without such a restriction the fuzzy pilot would move the thrust lever to the maximum, because the slow airspeed change produces a slow reduction of the difference speed. Thereby a hustle and bustle control behaviour of the fuzzy-pilot is avoided. The real thrust control command of the fuzzy pilot is a thrust lever deflection which has to be integrated.

4.3.2 The definition of the pilot database

The structure of the cognitive pilot model is based on the combination of a finite state machine and a normalised fuzzy controller. To adapt this cognitive pilot model to a real human pilot the following parameters of each pilot has to be stored:

- The parameters which are mentioned in the last section
- The tolerances which have an effect on the finite state machine
- The input fuzzy sets which characterised the measurements

To define all above mentioned parameters the same technique as in section 4.2 can be used. To reduce the number of tunable parameters only normalised fuzzy sets are used to model the linguistic terms. Consequently, the apexes of the right and left neighbour fuzzy sets can be used to define the whole fuzzy set. On account of this fact only the apexes of the fuzzy sets have to be defined.
Now all parameters of the cognitive pilot model are defined and Fig. 21 shows the resulting control commands during an ILS approach.

4.3.3 Fine tuning of the cognitive pilot by means of simulations

An important parameter for the tuning of the cognitive pilot model is the tolerance which controls the state transition. To illustrate this three simulations are presented on Fig. 20: for

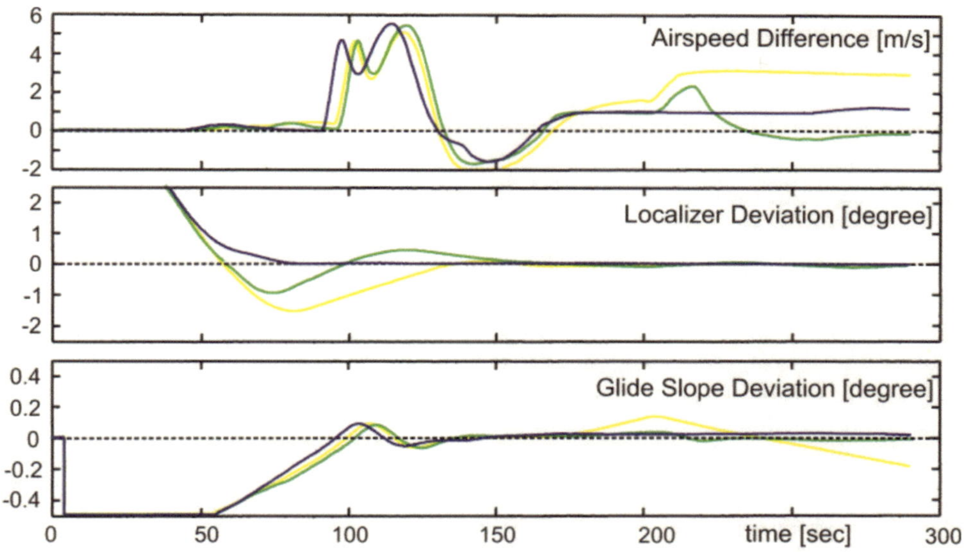

Fig. 20. Cognitive pilot model for the ILS-approach with various tolerances

the blue one the tolerance is set to 0.3, for the green one to 0.7, and finally for the yellow one to 0.9.

First the ILS approach with a tolerance of 0.3 is analysed (blue line in Fig. 20). The corresponding time history of the control commands of the cognitive pilot model are shown in Fig. 21. The localizer deviation has the same behaviour as the conventional fuzzy controller of section 4.2.3. Therefore, the first activity of the cognitive pilot was to initiate the localizer interception with a heavy turn left. Afterwards he compensates the remaining localizer deviation. In the final phase of the approach the cognitive pilot model has stabilised the aircraft on the localizer.

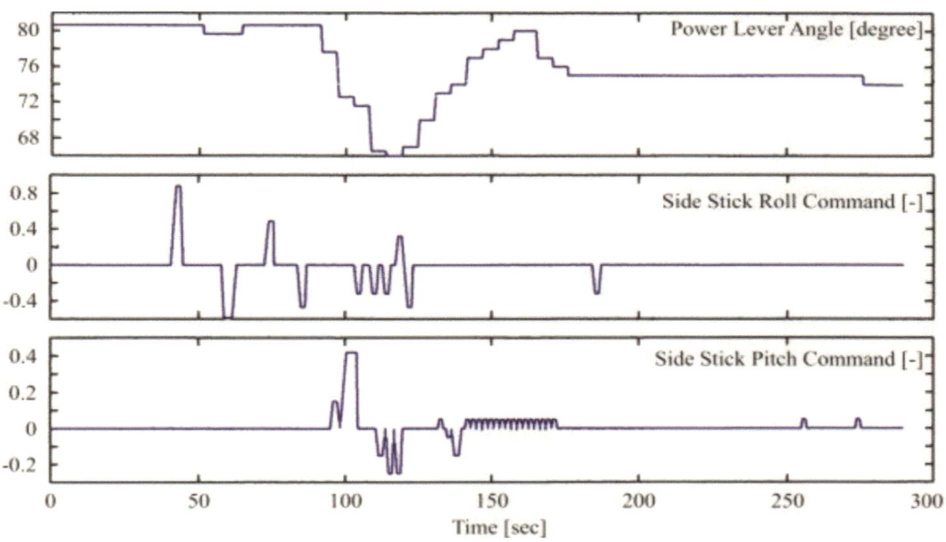

Fig. 21. Control commands of the cognitive pilot model

His first four side stick roll commands can be interpreted as follows:

- Initiates a heavy turn left
- Concludes a heavy turn left
- Initiates a slight turn left
- Concludes a slight turn left

In the last third of the approach the cognitive pilot model makes some slight corrections to stabilise the aircraft definitely on the localizer.
The controlling of the airspeed has the some behaviour as the conventional fuzzy controller. One main aspect of the ILS standard procedure is that the human pilot extends the landing gear when the glide slope starts to move up. When the landing gear is extended the aircraft configuration changes. The new configuration defines a new target speed which is a little bit lower than the previous (in this case 135 kts) and the speed difference increases. Beyond this, the air drag raises and therefore the speed is reduced. After this the cognitive pilot model makes a pitch command to initialise the descent to hold the glide slope. Then again the speed difference increases. To control the speed the cognitive pilot model reduces the thrust by giving a heavy thrust command. To generate no negative difference speed the cognitive pilot model increases the thrust at 150 seconds. During the remaining approach the cognitive pilot model holds the target speed in an acceptable range, a little bit above the target speed.
The control of the glide slope deviation starts with the change of the aircraft configuration. This change is triggered when the glide slope indicator reaches the zero position. As mentioned above the cognitive pilot model makes a side stick pitch down command to initialise the descent on the glide slope. This is necessary because the aircraft is already slightly above the glide slope. The command of the cognitive pilot model was a little bit too heavy and in consequence the glide slope enters zero position too fast. Therefore the fuzzy-pilot gives a pitch up command which finally stabilises the aircraft on the glide slope with a slight deviation.
With tolerances of 0.7 and 0.9 the cognitive pilot model accepts a larger localizer deviation. A greater influence of the tolerance can be obviously observed by the glides slope and the speed difference. Therewith the influence of the finite state machine tolerance is presented clearly.

4.4 Comparison of the cognitive pilot model and the human pilot

The check that a cognitive pilot model can successfully perform a given flight task is relatively easy. For this purpose, only the flight test data have to be analysed, to decide whether the controller can compensate the deviation from the desired value or not (see Fig. 20 for the ILS approach). It is more difficult to decide whether a cognitive pilot model has the same control behaviour as a human controller or at least the same characteristics. One problem is in fact, that there is a fundamental difference between the control behaviour of a fuzzy-system and a human controller. If the fuzzy-system has no random component, it acts deterministically despite all fuzziness. A human pilot cannot reach this high level of determinism, because it is interfered with the following aspects:

- The ability of a human pilot to concentrate depends on his physical and psychological health.
- The environment can also influence the concentration. For instance, disturbing noise or optical stimuli can provoke mistakes.
- It is difficult for a human pilot to concentrate on many things at the same time.

- In the cockpit of an aircraft, the human pilot gets various information at the same time and only a sequential handling can process this information.
- The response time of a human pilot is definitely longer than the response time of a fuzzy-controller.
- A human pilot is adaptive and multiple repeating of a special task improves his performance.
- It is also possible that the routine produces a slinky security feeling which can lead to negligence.

Out of these differences the following problems arise at the interpretation of the pilot behaviour:

- The human pilot can make random faulty control inputs.
- The same human pilot shows different noticeable reactions at several approaches although the same conditions predominate during all these approaches.
- The human pilot uses inadequate commands which forces him to further corrections.

The developed fuzzy-controller and the cognitive pilot model are based on an ILS approach of a human pilot. The rule base, the fuzzy-sets as well as the measurements and the control variables are extracted out of the flight test data of this approach. At first the basic strategy was realised. This strategy was adapted during the further development process to the control behaviour of the human pilot. For instance the moment when the human pilot initiates the localizer interception could be transferred in the fuzzy-pilot very well. The shapes of the command templates are not directly based on the flight test analysis. The templates were tuned during the test of the fuzzy-pilot in such a way that the resulting aircraft dynamics is equal to the dynamics which was induced by the human pilot. Therewith, the artificial pilot gets a similar behaviour like the human pilot. Consequently, the control behaviour of the cognitive pilot model includes yet characteristics of the human pilot. To compare the control behaviour of a human pilot and a cognitive pilot model a method is needed which actually describes their similarity.

In the first instance a direct comparison of their signals can be ruled out due to the non deterministic control behaviour of the human pilot. Therefore, a method has to be applied which uses a no pointwise comparison like the euclid norm or the correlation. The *Dynamic Time Warping* is a method to compare two data series. This method was introduced to the data mining community in Keogh & Pazzani (1999). DTW is still widely used in various fields, e.g. bioinformatics.

Now the DTW is used to compare the control behaviour of the human pilot and the cognitive pilot model. This comparison is made in two steps. Firstly the control strategy of both pilots is intuitively compared. For this reason Fig. 22 shows both roll angle in one time history. Both pilot initialised the intersection obviously at the same time with approximately the same deflection. Furthermore the overshooting of the localizer is compensated in the same manner. It can be summarised that the control strategy of the cognitive pilot model resembled relatively well to the control strategy of the human pilot.

The second step is based on the DTW to compare parts of the ILS approach. Using this a better statement about the adaptation of the cognitive pilot model can be made. For this reason initially the lateral motion is considered, especially the moment where the localizer indicator starts to move. It ends with the stabilisation of the aircraft on the localizer. In the

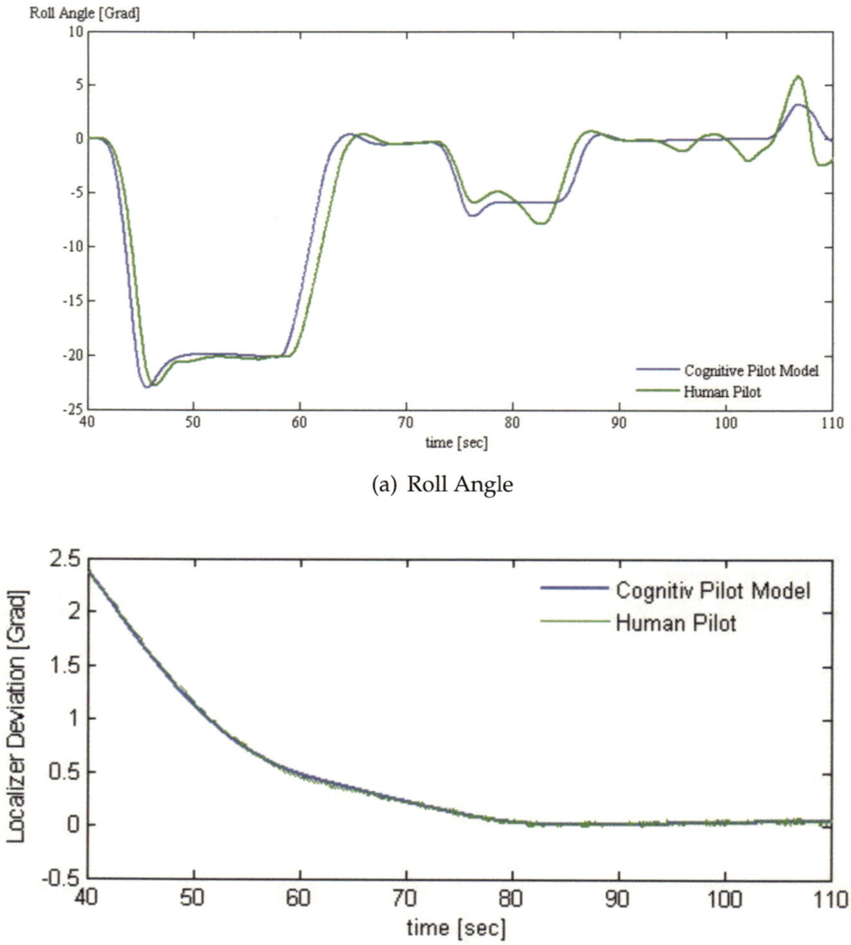

(a) Roll Angle

(b) Localizer deviation

Fig. 22. Comparison of the pilot model and the human Pilot

following 80 seconds, respectively a series with 2000 points, are compared and Fig. 22 shows the time series of localizer deviation of both pilots. Obviously, the cognitive pilot model is able to generate the same localizer deviation as the human pilot. This fact is confirmed by the DTW because the DTW computes the low value 0.00002739. In addition, the reaction of the aircraft to the pilot command is compared, too.

The below time history in Fig. 22 shows the roll angle of both pilot model. These time histories are rather similar and this fact is confirmed by a low DTW value of 0.007351. It can be summarised that the cognitive pilot model has roughly the same control behaviour like the first pilot or the first approach.

This positive result is based on the fact, that the first ILS approach is used to develop the cognitive pilot model. Consequently, both pilots have to have a great similarity. To support this simple fact the fuzzy-pilot is compared with the second ILS-approach. Fig. 23 shows the time histories of the localizer deviation and the roll angle. The intuitive comparison points

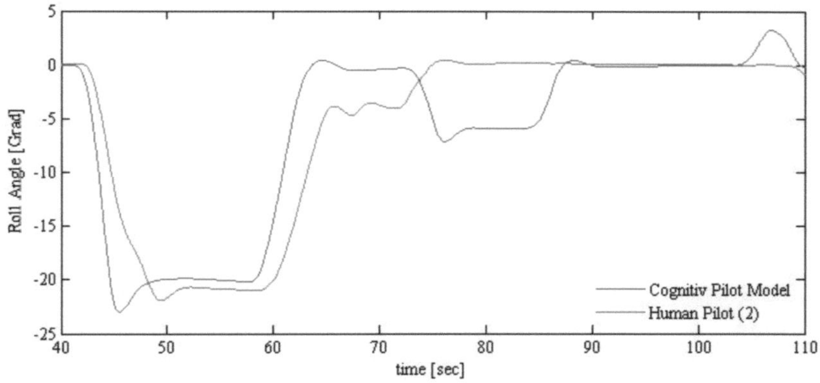

(a) Roll angle

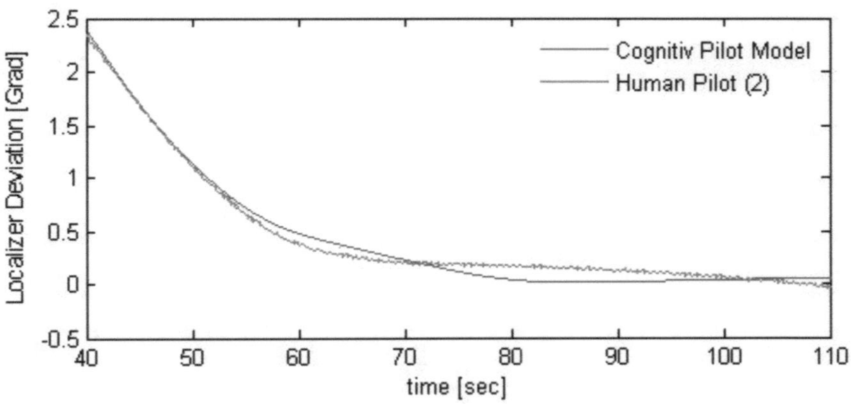

(b) Localizer deviation

Fig. 23. Comparison with the second approach

out that the cognitive pilot model and the second human pilot has slightly different control behaviour. For the localizer deviation the DTW computes a 0.0002011 and for the roll angle a 0.01894. Therefore, the DTW reflects the first visual impression that the both pilots have a slight different control behaviour.

The DTW can be used to prove the similarity of two signals. It is indeed not possible to get direct information on how to modify the parameters of the fuzzy-controller to get a better adaptation. The absolute DTW-value is in any way not that important. Nevertheless, the DTW gives the possibility to show which data series are similar.

5. Conclusion

This chapter presents the use of fuzzy-control to model the control behaviour of a human pilot during a high and a low gain flight task. In both approaches the developed cognitive pilot model reproduced well the characteristics of the human pilot and it could be pointed out that:

- The cognitive pilot models fulfil the requirements of the according flight task
- The measurements and the control commands of the pilot models and the human pilot are very similar in magnitude and trend.
- The control behaviour of the cognitive pilot models are based on the control strategy of the human pilot.
- The cognitive pilot models commands induce a similar aircraft reaction as the human pilot.

Both approaches were based on a fuzzy-controller. The rule base of the controller is an intuitive description of the controlling of the physical process and the rules are to be interpreted easily. The concrete realisation of the fuzzy-sets as a mathematical representation of the linguistic terms is depended from the variations of the individual human control behaviour.

The adaption of the pilot model to another human pilot is not easy because each pilot has to have his individual fuzzy sets. Consequently, the number of tunable parameter is large. Compared with this the pilot model of the ILS Approach based on a finite state machine and a universal fuzzy controller. To adapt this model only the parameters in the pilot database has to be fitted. Nevertheless, the second pilot model profit from the experience of the ITT task. Certainly, in both model the rule base is fixed.

In another research project of the author neural networks are used to model the control behaviour of a human pilot during a clear defined flight task (see Gestwa & Viet (2009)). A great advantage of the neural networks are the automation of the learning. But, on the other hand the neural networks have the disadvantage that they hides their knowledge in a black box. Consequently, their interpretations are very difficult whereas they are easy in combination with a fuzzy-controller.

Based on these aspects future research project of the author will use the neural fuzzy approach or evolution strategies to optimise fuzzy-sets. An other optimisation strategy is the Ants-algorithm. In current and future research activities this work is extended to helicopters as a new platform for pilot modeling investigation.

In the field of pilot modeling the time series comparison is an important subarea. In this context further analyses are necessary. For example instead of the native DTW algorithm the DTW with Sakoe-Chiba band or with Itakura parallelogram could be used (see Salvador & Chan (2007)). Furthermore, the Average Angle Measure could be an adequate criteria to compare two time series.

Thought the rule base is a description of the control activities which are required to perform the ITT. Furthermore, the rules are based on flight mechanic equations and for all pilots these equations are equal. Consequently it can be deduced, therefore, that for an adaption to another pilot only the fuzzy-set has to be modified and the main part of the rule base can be used unmodified.

6. References

Allan, R., Jex, H. & Magdaleno, R. (1973). Manual control performance and dynamic response during sinusoidal vibration, AMRL-TR-73-78.

Amelsberg, S., Bieniek, D. & Luckner, R. (2009). Pilot modelling for departure and wake vortex recovery using neural networks, *Tagungsband - Ausgewählte Manuskripte - Deutscher Luft- und Raumfahrtkongress 2009*, DGLR, Aachen, Germany , 08 - 10 September 2009; Document ID 121153.

Bauschat, J.-M. (2000). An investigation on the dependence of pilot workload and flight simulation fidelity level, *Third International Conference on Engineering Psychology and Cognitive Ergonomics - Edinburgh (25.-27.10.2000)*, Vol. 5, Engineering Psychology and Cognitive Ergonomics, Monterey, California, 05 - 08 August 2002; Paper No. AIAA 2002-4694.

Brockhaus, R. (1994). *Flugregelung*, Springer-Verlag.

Budd, H. (1992). *Menschliche Zuverlässigkeit*, Landsberg/ Lech: ecomed.

Dooyong, L., F., H., Sezer-Uzol, N. & Long, L. N. (2003). Simulation of pilot control activity during helicopter shipboard operation, *Atmospheric Flight Mechanics Conference and Exhibit*, AIAA, Austin, Texas, 11 - 14 August 2003; Paper No. AIAA 2003-5306.

Dutke, S. (1994). *Mentale Modelle Konstrukte des Wissens und Verstehen*, Kognitionspsychologisches Grundlagen für die Software-Ergonomie, Verlag fr Angewandte Psychologie, Göttingen.

Enders, J. (1989). The human element - the key to safe civil operations in adverse weather, *Conference Proceedings Number 470*, Advisory Group of Aerospace Research and Development (AGARD), pp. K2–1 to K2–7.

FAA (2009). Instrument flying handbook - chapter 7, Federal Aviation Administration (FAA), United State of America. `http://www.faa.gov/library/manuals/aviation/instrument_flying_handbook/,cited26September2010.`

Gestwa, M. & Viet, S. (2009). Unschärfe erwnscht soft-computing methoden zur kognitiven pilotenmodellierung, *Tagungsband - Deutscher Luft- und Raumfahrtkongress 2009*, DGLR, Aachen, Germany , 08 - 10 September 2009.

Hess, R. A. (1990). Model for human use of motion cues in vehicular control, *Journal of Guidance, Control and Dynamics* Vol. 13(No. 3): 476–482.

Höhne, G. (2000). Computer aided development of biomechanical pilot models, *Aerospace Science and Technology* 4(1): 57 – 69.

Hosman, R. & Stassen, H. (1999). Pilot's perception in the control of aircraft motions, *Control Engineering Practice* 7(11): 1421 – 1428.

Jex, H. & Magdaleno, R. (1978). Biomechanical models for vibration feedthrough to hands and head for a semisupine pilot, *Aviation, Space, and Environmental Medicine*, Vol. 49(No. 1): 304–316.

Johnson, E. & Pritchett, A. (2002). Generic pilot and flight control model for use in simulation studies, *Modeling and Simulation Technologies Conference and Exhibit*, AIAA, Monterey, California, 05 - 08 August 2002; Paper No. AIAA 2002-4694.

Kahlert, J. & Frank, H. (1994). *Fuzzy-Logik und Fuzzy-Control*, second edn, Braunschweig; Wiesbaden: Vieweg.

Keogh, E. & Pazzani, M. (1999). On the modelling of a human pilot using fuzzy logic control, *in* J. M. Zytkow & J. Rauch (eds), *3rd European Conference on Principles and Practice of Knowledge Discovery in Databases*, Vol. 1704, Springer, Prague, pp. 1–11.

Klaes, S. (2002). Attas and act/fhs system simulation for pre-flight software and hardware testing, *Modeling and Simulation Technologies Conference and Exhibit*, AIAA, Monterey, California, August 5-8, 2002; Paper No. AIAA 2002-4601.

Köhler, R. (1997). A new pilot model for roll ratcheting analysis, Technical Report DLR IB 11-97/32, Braunschweig.

Kruse, R., Gebhardt, J. & Klawonn, F. (1995). *Fuzzy-Systeme*, $2^n d$ edn, Stuttgart: Teubner.

Luckner, R. (2010). Models and methods for wake vortex encounter simulations, *Developments in Wake Turbulence Safety*, WakeNet3 Europa - The 2nd major WakeNet3-Europe

workshop, Airbus Premises in Toulouse on 28th and 29th of June, 2010.
McRuer, D. (1988). Pilot modeling, *AGARD Lecture Series No. 157 'Advances in Flying Qualities'*, AGARD-LS-157, 1988.
McRuer, D. & Krendel, E. (1974). Pilot modeling, AGARD Dografh No. 1988.
N.N. (2006). Statistical summary of commercial jet airplane accidents, worldwide operations 1959 - 2005, *Airplane Safety*, Boeing Commercial Airplanes, Seattle, Washington, USA.
Rasmussen, J. (1986). *Information processing and human-machine interaction. An approach to cognitive engineering*, Elsevier Science Publishing Co., New York, NY, U.S.A., North-Holland Series.
Salvador, S. & Chan, P. (2007). Toward accurate dynamic time warping in linear time and space, *Intelligent Data Analysis* 11(5): 561 – 580.
von der Vorst, J. (1999). A pilot model for helicopter manoeuvres, NLR-TP-98448. URL: *http://www.nlr.nl/id 4639/lang en.pdf*

16

Acquisition and Chaos-Entropy Analysis of Individuality and Proficiency of Human Operator's Skill Using a Fuzzy Controller

Yoshihiko Kawazoe
Saitama Institute of Technology
Japan

1. Introduction

There is an infinite variety of motions ranging from our daily activities to the exceptional movement of an athlete or a musician. Based on his extensive observation of child growth, Gesell (1945) stated some empirical rules. In particular, he noted that the development of motion progresses from a generally integrated state to an individualized state in which individual sections have specialized functions. He also noted that the number of degrees of freedom of the motion increases with development, and that periods of unstabilization and stabilization are repeated to advance development by taking advantage of such fluctuations well. Finally, he observed that chaos plays a very important role in motion. The human process of learning motion can also be studied by focusing on the degrees of freedom. When a person who normally writes with his or her right hand (i.e., their dominant hand) is asked to write with the left hand (i.e., their non dominant hand), the number of degrees of freedom of each joint is initially fixed; but, after training, each joint moves according to a peculiar phase relationship after training (Newell & Van Emmerik, 1989). This implies that we are rigid when we attempt a new motion, but become more relaxed after getting accustomed to it (Taga, 2002).

Machinery and human beings are absolutely of a different nature at the present stage, but most research work on man-machine systems has dealt with the linear characteristics of human behavior (Kawazoe et al., 2008). As an example, many studies on control systems for stabilizing the inverted pendulum as an inherently unstable system have been presented. These studies focus on the linear characteristics of human behavior. There seem to be few studies and a number of unknowns regarding both the nonlinear characteristics of human behavior in an inherently unstable man-machine system as well as the learning process of human operators with objects difficult to control (Kawazoe et al., 2008, 2009).

In order to stabilize an unstable system such as the inverted pendulum, strict judgment of the situation is required. Accordingly, it can be expected that the human operators exhibit complex behaviors or contingencies, that is, the mixture of regular and random actions intermittently.

The behavior during stabilizing control of an inverted pendulum by a human operator exhibits a random-like or limit-cycle like fluctuation, and the stabilizing control by the human operator is robust against the disturbance. This may be because the limit-cycle-like

fluctuation produced by the digital PID computer controller, which means lineally unstable, is more robust against the disturbance than the lineally stable fluctuation according to the experiments. The limit cycle was very stable in the sense of nonlinearity, which means it is robust against the disturbance (Kawazoe et al., 1992, 1994, 1999, 2000, 2001a, 2001b).
This chapter investigates the identification of the chaotic characteristics of human operation from the experimental time series data by utilizing fuzzy inference. It shows how to construct rules automatically for a fuzzy controller of each trial of each human operator. It tries to acquire the individual skill of each operator. Human operators in an experiment were trained so that they were skilled to some extent in stabilizing the pendulum by training, and the data of ten trials per person were successively taken for an analysis. The entropy is estimated from the time series data as a measure of the amount of disorder in a system, and the degrees of freedom of the motion are estimated by the dimensions when curves of the largest Lyapunov exponents are saturated against the embedding dimensions for quantifying the proficiency.

2. Chaos-entropy analysis of human operator's skill during stabilizing control of an inverted pendulum on a cart

2.1 Trials of stabilizing control of an inverted pendulum on a cart by a human operator

Figure 1 shows the experimental setup. An inverted pendulum is mounted on a cart that can move along the line of a sliding rail of limited length. The pendulum is attached to the rail such that the pendulum rotates in one plane. A human operator manipulates the cart directly by hand. Although some time and intensive training are needed in order for a human operator to succeed in stabilizing the pendulum for 60 s, this task becomes less difficult after the first successful instance of stabilization. The human operators in the experiment were trained so that they were skilled to a certain extent in stabilizing the pendulum, and the data obtained in 10 successive trials per person were used for analysis. The angle that the pendulum makes with the vertical axis and the displacement of the cart were measured, and the derivatives and the force that moves the cart can be derived based on these quantities (Kawazoe et al., 2008, 2009).
Figure 2 shows phase plane representations of the chaotic behavior of the inverted pendulum on a cart during stabilizing control by a human operator NK during the first trial after training.

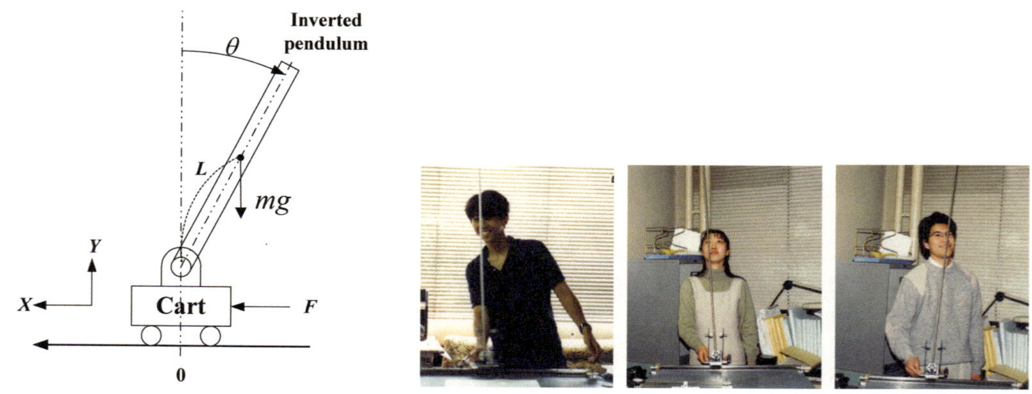

(a) (b)

Fig. 1. Stabilizing control of an inverted pendulum.

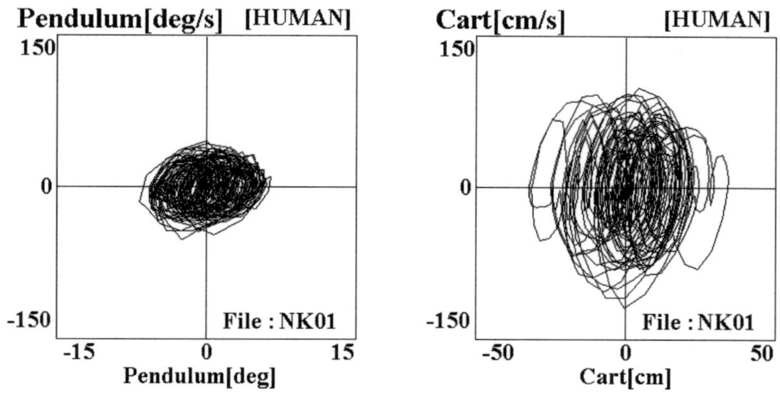

Fig. 2. Behavior of an inverted pendulum in a phase plane.

2.2 Diagnosis of amount of disorder by entropy analysis

Consider a hypothetical statistical system in which the outcome of a certain measurement must be located on a unit interval. If a line is subdivided into N subintervals, then we can associate a probability p_i with the i-th subinterval containing a particular range of possible outcomes. The entropy of the system is then defined as follows:

$$S = -\sum_{i=1}^{Nc} p_i \ln p_i \,. \tag{1}$$

This quantity may be interpreted as a measure of the amount of disorder in the system or as the information necessary to specify the state of the system. If the subintervals are equally probable, so that $p_i = 1/N$ for all i, then the entropy reduces to $S = \ln N$, which can be shown to be the maximum value. Conversely, if the outcome is known to be in a particular subinterval, then $S = 0$ is the minimum value. When $S = \ln N$, the amount of further information needed to specify the result of a measurement is at a maximum, and, when $S = 0$, no further information is required (Baker et al., 1996; Baierlein, 1997). We applied this formulation to the time series data by establishing N bins or subintervals of unit intervals into which the values of the time series data may fall. We define S as the net entropy calculated using Eq. (1) and $S/(\ln\_N)$ as the entropy ratio (Kawazoe et al., 2008, 2009). The ratio of entropy to maximum entropy was estimated at the point at which the ratio saturated as the number of partitioned cells increased.

2.3 Diagnosis of chaotic dynamics by Lyapunov exponent analysis

The detection of the chaotic dynamics and the quantitative characterization of the chaotic dynamics when the model of the entire system is unknown requires the analysis of time series data. Although methods for dynamic analysis of time series data are currently under development, the following two-step process is commonly used at present: (1) reconstruction of the strange attracter of an unknown dynamic system from the time series, and (2) determination of certain invariant quantities of the system from the reconstructed attracter. It is possible to obtain the dynamics from a single time series without reference to other physical variables (Kawazoe, 1999, 2000). A rigorous mathematical basis of this concept has been presented by Takens (1981) and Mane (1981).

Since the attracter dimension is unknown for time series data and the required embedding dimension M is unknown, it is important that the reconstruction be embedded in a space of sufficiently large dimension to represent the dynamics completely. Thus, the dimension of the embedding space is increased by increments of one. The attractor is reconstructed, and its largest Lyapunov exponent is calculated. The process is continued until the largest Lyapunov exponent is saturated with respect to the embedding dimensions, and the dimension, i.e., the degrees of freedom of the system behavior, is estimated. The largest Lyapunov exponent can be obtained from time series data using an algorithm presented by Wolf *et al.* (1985). The Lyapunov exponent can be used to obtain a measure of the sensitivity under the initial conditions. This measure of sensitivity is characteristic of chaotic behavior. If the Lyapunov exponent is positive, nearby trajectories diverge, and so the evolution is sensitive to initial conditions and therefore chaotic.

Consider the time series data $x(t_1)$, $x(t_2)$, ... Successive points in the phase space formed from time-delay coordinates can be written in vector form $\mathbf{X}_i$ as follows:

$$\begin{aligned}
\mathbf{X}_1 &= (x(t_1), x(t_1+\tau), \cdots, x(t_1+(m-1)\tau)) \\
\mathbf{X}_2 &= (x(t_2), x(t_2+\tau), \cdots, x(t_2+(m-1)\tau)) \\
\mathbf{X}_3 &= (x(t_3), x(t_3+\tau), \cdots, x(t_3+(m-1)\tau)) \\
&\vdots \\
\mathbf{X}_i &= (x(t_i), x(t_i+\tau), \cdots, x(t_i+(m-1)\tau)) \\
&\vdots \\
\mathbf{X}_N &= (x(t_N), x(t_N+\tau), \cdots, x(t_N+(m-1)\tau))
\end{aligned} \tag{2}$$

where the symbol τ denotes the time delay, and the symbol m denotes the embedding dimension.

The choice of an appropriate delay τ is important to the success of the reconstruction. If τ is too short, then the coordinates are approximately the same and the reconstruction is useless. If τ is too large, then the coordinates are so far apart as to be uncorrelated. If the system has some rough periodicity, then a value comparable to but somewhat less than that period is typically chosen. Since there is no simple rule for choosing τ in all cases, τ is occasionally adjusted until the results appear to be satisfactory. Time τ is typically some multiple of the spacing between the time series points (Baker,1996). We chose 7 times the spacing between the time series points, i.e., 7×0.0293 s, as the value of τ because the calculated largest Lyapunov exponents were not too sensitive to τ and because the curves of the largest Lyapunov exponents versus embedding dimensions were smooth within a reasonable range, whereas the dominant period of the experimental time series data was 0.5 to 1.0 s.

Since the time series is presumed (by hypothesis) to be the result of a deterministic process, each x_{n+1} is the result of a mapping. In other words, we have

$$x_{n+1} = f(x_n). \tag{3}$$

The differentiation of the above equation is approximated as

$$\frac{df(x_j)}{dx_j} = \frac{dx_{j+1}}{dx_j} = \frac{x_{j+1} - x_j}{x_j - x_{j-1}} = f'(x_j). \tag{4}$$

Thus, the general expression of the Jacobian matrices and the orthogonal vectors $b_{ij}(i=1,2,\cdots,m)$ can be obtained (Kawazoe et al., 2008, 2009). The Lyapunov exponents λ_i for each embedding dimension i are then obtained as (Kawazoe et al., 2008,2009; Baker et al., 1996; Baierlein,1971; Takens, 1981; Mane, 1981; Wolf et al., 1985).

$$\lambda_i = \frac{1}{t_n - t_0}\sum_{j=1}^{n-1}\log_e \mathbf{b}_{ij} \quad (i=1,2,3,\cdots,m). \tag{5}$$

The calculated largest Lyapunov exponent converges at the end of the time series data as the embedded dimensions increase. The number of degrees of freedom of motion are estimated by the dimensions when the curves of the largest Lyapunov exponents are saturated with respect to the embedding dimensions.

3. Generation of a fuzzy controller from time series data during stabilizing control of an inverted pendulum by a human operator

Fuzzy control has a distinguishing feature in that it can incorporate experts' control rules using linguistic expressions. One of the main problems of fuzzy control is the difficulty in acquiring fuzzy rules and tuning the membership functions. The conventional control theory used to design controllers using models of controlled objects has been established. In addition, a number of studies have examined the design of fuzzy control systems using fuzzy models of controlled objects.

To identify the nonlinear characteristics of the human operator from the experimental time series data, we choose the pendulum angle θ_t, angular velocity θ'_t, and the cart displacement X_t and its velocity X'_t as input variables and the force F_t that moves the cart as the output of the fuzzy controller. Furthermore, we choose the combined variables $\theta_t + \beta\theta'_t$ and $X_t + \gamma X'_t$ as inputs so as to reduce the complexity of the control rule table, where β and γ are combination variables.

The method used to obtain the membership functions and the control rules are described in the following. The values of β and γ are identified using the identification of membership functions and control rules by a trial and error method after repeating several simulations. In order to partition the data and determine the border of the data with the fuzzy sets for the assumed values of coefficient β and γ, for example, G_{NB} = 10%, G_{NS} = 25%, G_{ZR} = 30%, G_{PS} = 25%, and G_{PB} = 10% were chosen (Fig.3), and the borders were denoted by $D_{NB\ NS}$, $D_{NS\ ZR}$, $D_{ZR\ PS}$, and $D_{PS\ PB}$ (Fig. 4).

The labels of the membership functions with $\theta + \beta\theta'$ and $X + \gamma X'$ were determined as follows:

NB = minimum of the data: $DMIN$, $NS = (D_{NB\ NS} + D_{NS\ ZR})/2$, ZR = mean of the data: $DAVE$, $PS = (D_{ZR\ PS} + D_{PS\ PB})/2$, PB = maximum of the data: $DMAX$.

The labels of the membership function with F are also determined as follows:

NB = minimum of the data: $DMIN$, $NMB = (NB + NS)/2$, $NS = (D_{NB\ NS} + D_{NS\ ZR})/2$, $NMS = NS/2$, ZR = average of the data: DAVE, $PMS = PS/2$, $PS = (D_{ZR\ PS} + D_{PS\ PB})/2$, $PMB = (PB + PS)/2$, PB = maximum of the data: $DMAX$ (Fig. 5).

Suppose that $\theta_t + \beta\theta'_t$ is G_{NB}, $X_t + \gamma X'_t$ is G_{ZR}, and F_{t+1} is G_{NS}. Then, we count to the cell of label $F = NS$ in the numbered grid to which $\theta + \beta\theta' = NB$ and $X + \gamma X' = ZR$ are given as inputs. Figure 6 shows the fuzzy output grid numbers for generating a control rule. The output is derived using the label frequencies of each grid for each trial and for each human operator and using the following equation (continues to page 334, Eq.(6))

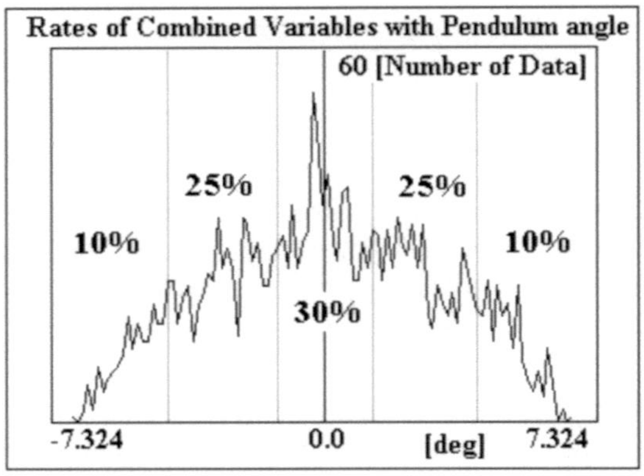

(a) Rates of combined variables with pendulum angle $\theta_t + \beta\theta'_t$

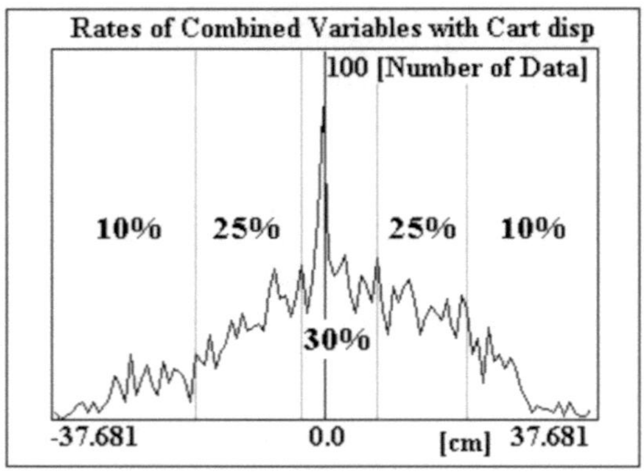

(b) Rates of combined variables with cart displacement $X_t + \gamma X'_t$

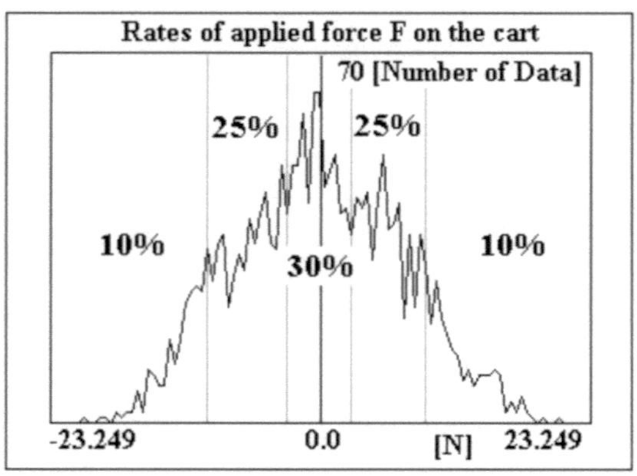

(c) Rates of applied force F on the cart

Fig. 3. Example of rates of inputs and output.

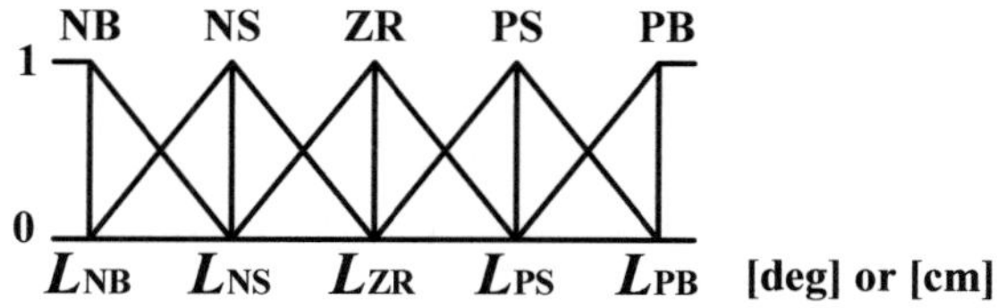

Fig. 4. Membership function for inputs.

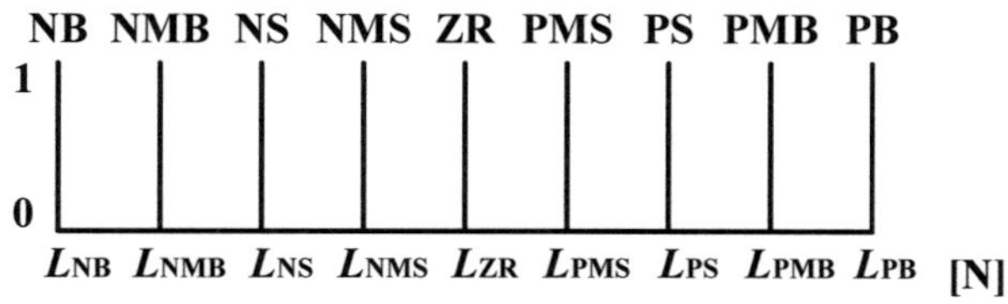

Fig. 5. Membership function (singleton) for output.

		$\theta + \beta\theta'$				
		NB	NS	ZR	PS	PB
$X + \gamma X'$	NB	1	2	3	4	5
	NS	6	7	8	9	10
	ZR	11	12	13	14	15
	PS	16	17	18	19	20
	PB	21	22	23	24	25

Fig. 6. Fuzzy output grid number for generating a control rule.

Output Label	NB	NMB	NS	NMS	ZR	PMS	PS	PMB	PB
F_{OUT}	-3.5	-2.5	-1.5	-0.5	0.5	1.5	2.5	3.5	

Fig. 7. Conformity of output F_{out}.

		$\theta + \beta\,\theta'$				
		NB	NS	ZR	PS	PB
$X+\gamma X'$	NB	PS	PMS	NMS	NMB	ZR
	NS	PMB	PMS	NMS	NMB	ZR
	ZR	PB	PS	ZR	NS	NB
	PS	ZR	PMB	PMS	NMS	NMB
	PB	ZR	ZR	PMS	NMS	NS

Fig. 8. Rule for control of a pendulum on a cart (first trial NK01 of human operator NK).

$$F_{\text{OUT}} = \frac{(-4.4 \cdot \text{NB}) + (-2.0 \cdot \text{NS}) + (0.0 \cdot \text{ZR}) + (2.0 \cdot \text{PS}) + (4.4 \cdot \text{PB})}{\text{NB} + \text{NS} + \text{ZR} + \text{PS} + \text{PB}}. \tag{6}$$

We can determine the output label using Fig.7 and construct the operator's control rule for balancing the inverted pendulum as shown in Fig.8.
Figure 9 shows a block diagram of the stabilizing control simulation of the pendulum on a cart using the constructed fuzzy controller from the time series data of the human operator.
Figure 10 shows the conformity of $\boldsymbol{\theta} + \boldsymbol{\beta\theta'}$, and Fig. 11 shows the conformity of $\boldsymbol{X} + \boldsymbol{\gamma X'}$, if $\theta + \beta\theta'$ = 4.0 degrees and $\boldsymbol{X} + \boldsymbol{\gamma X'}$ = 5.0 cm, as an example. In Fig. 10, the conformity of PS is determined to be 0.70, and that of PB is determined to be 0.30. In Fig. 11 the conformity of ZR is determined to be 0.73, and that of PS is determined to be 0.27. Using the fuzzy rule in Fig. 8, the following rules are found:

$$IF \;\; \theta + \beta\theta' = \textbf{PS} \; and \; X + \gamma X' = \textbf{ZR} \;\; THEN \;\; F = \textbf{NS}$$
$$else$$
$$IF \;\; \theta + \beta\theta' = \textbf{PS} \; and \; X + \gamma X' = \textbf{PS} \;\; THEN \;\; F = \textbf{NMS}$$
$$else$$
$$IF \;\; \theta + \beta\theta' = \textbf{PB} \; and \; X + \gamma X' = \textbf{ZR} \;\; THEN \;\; F = \textbf{NMB}$$
$$else$$
$$IF \;\; \theta + \beta\theta' = \textbf{PB} \; and \; X + \gamma X' = \textbf{PS} \;\; THEN \;\; F = \textbf{NMB}$$

The output values are derived using max-min composition as follows. We use singleton fuzzification as a membership function of output. Figure 12 shows the process called "cutting" by MIN value. Figure 13 shows the process of composition by MAX value. Thus, the membership functions of output referred to as composite fuzzy output are obtained as NMB: 0.30, NS: 0.70, and NMS: 0.27. The output values are calculated using the center of gravity method as follows:

$$F_{\text{OUT}} = \frac{\sum_{i=1}^{9} X_i \cdot Y_i}{\sum_{i=1}^{9} Y_i}, \tag{7}$$

where the term X_i is the X coordinate (-20.46, -13.37, -6.27, -3.14, -0.02, 3.09, 6.18, 14.72, 23.25) of the output membership function, Y_i is the composite conformity, and i denotes an index. The result of fuzzy inference, F = -7.28, is obtained using composite fuzzy output in Fig. 16.
The differential equation of motion of this pendulum-cart system is described as follows:

$$M\ddot{X} - mL\ddot{\theta}\cos\theta + mL\dot{\theta}^2 \sin\theta + \mu_x \dot{X} = F \tag{8}$$

$$I\ddot{\theta} - mL\ddot{X}\cos\theta + \mu_\theta \dot{\theta} = mgL\sin\theta \tag{9}$$

where m denotes the mass of the pendulum; M denotes the mass of the pendulum, the cart, and a human arm; L is the half-pendulum length; I is the inertial moment of pendulum about the supporting point; F is the force that moves the cart, μ_θ is the frictional coefficient of the pendulum support point, and μ_X is the frictional coefficient between the cart and the rail. The coefficients $\mu_\theta$and μ_X are derived from the experiment. The sampling time for control is 0.06 s, and the initial pendulum angle is 3.0 degrees.

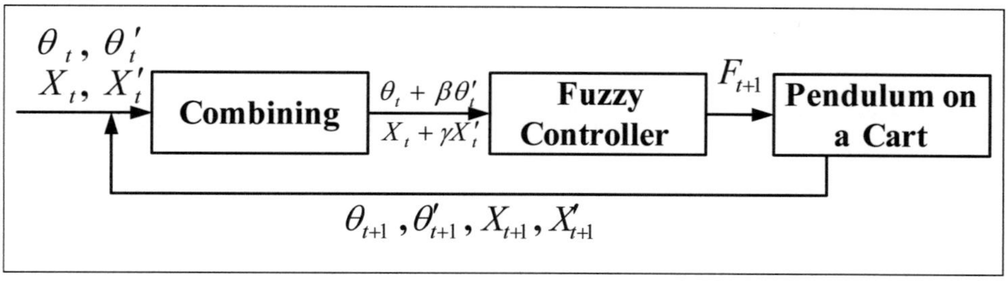

Fig. 9. Stabilizing control simulation of the pendulum using the constructed fuzzy controller from the time series data of a human operator.

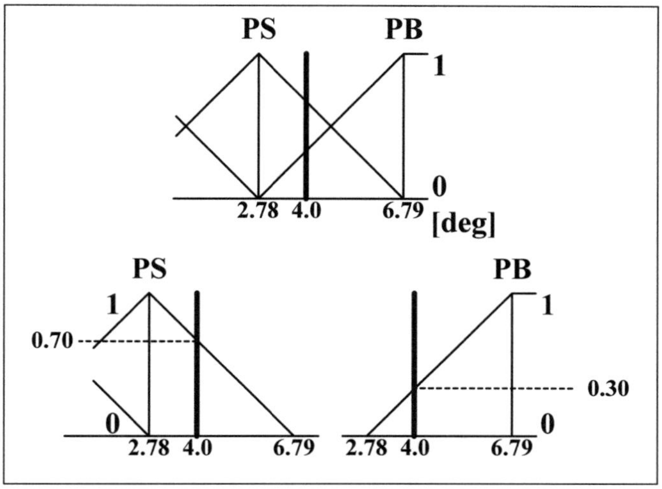

Fig. 10. Conformity of $\theta + \beta\theta'$.

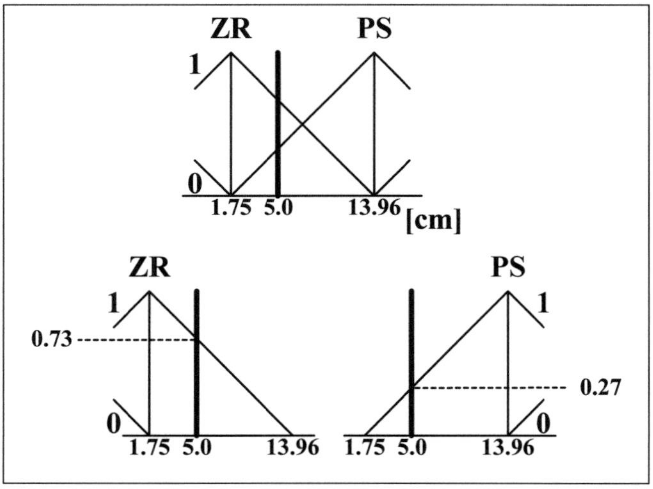

Fig. 11. Conformity of $X + \gamma X'$.

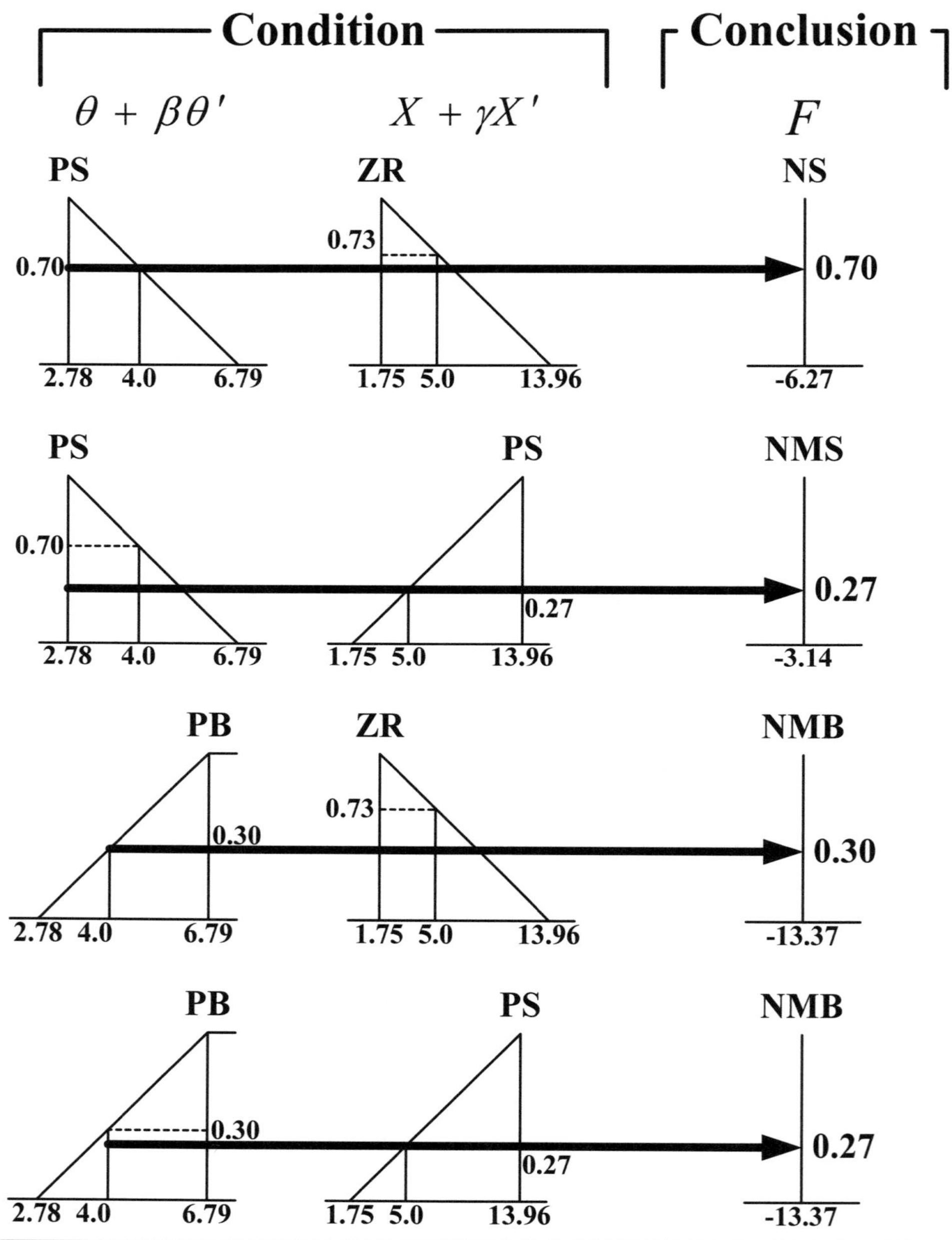

Fig. 12. Cutting by MIN value.

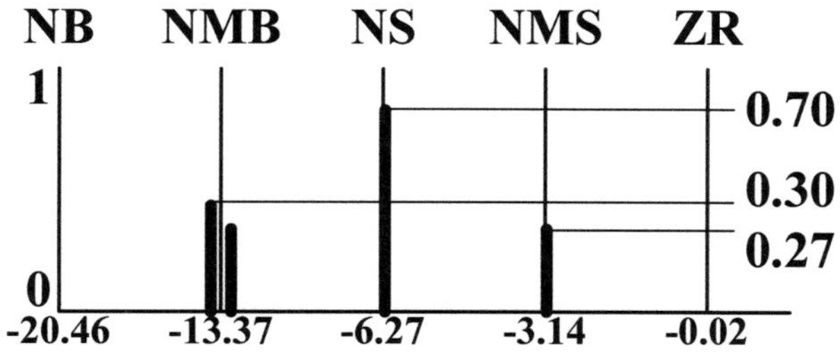

Fig. 13. Composition by MAX value.

We choose the pendulum angle θ_t, angular velocity θ'_t, the cart displacement X_t and its velocity X'_t as input variables, and the force F_t that moves the cart as output of the fuzzy controller, trying to identify the nonlinear characteristics of the human operator from the experimental time series data. Furthermore, we choose the combined variables $\theta_t+\beta\theta'_t$ and $X_t+\gamma X'_t$ as inputs so as to eliminate the complexity of the control rule table. The β and γ are the combination variables.

The values of β and γ are identified with the identification of membership functions and control rules by a trial and error method after repeating many simulations.

We can determine the output label and construct the operator's control rule for balancing the inverted pendulum.

4. Chaos-entropy analysis and acquisition of individuality and proficiency using a fuzzy controller

Figure 14 and Fig.15 show the membership functions of pendulum angle and its angular velocity, the membership function of cart displacement and its velocity, and the

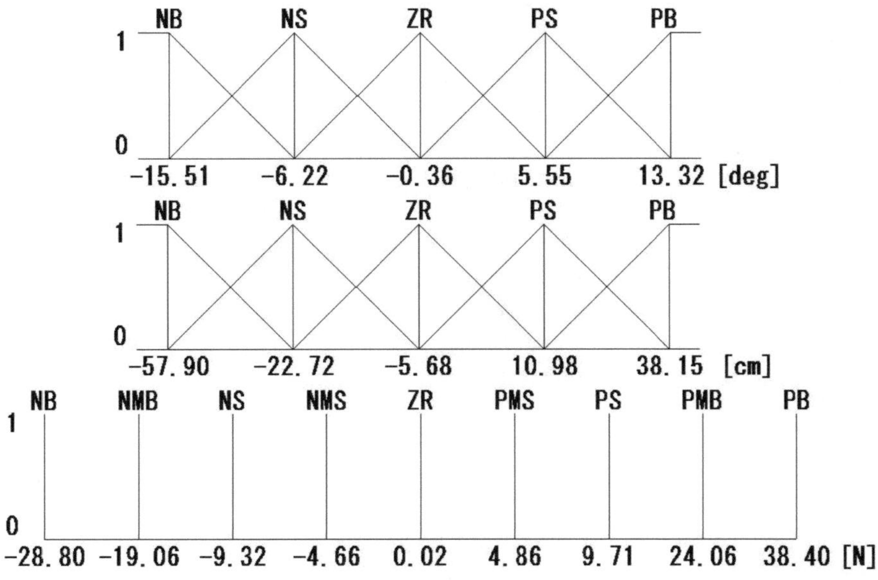

Fig. 14. Identified membership function (operator OT01)

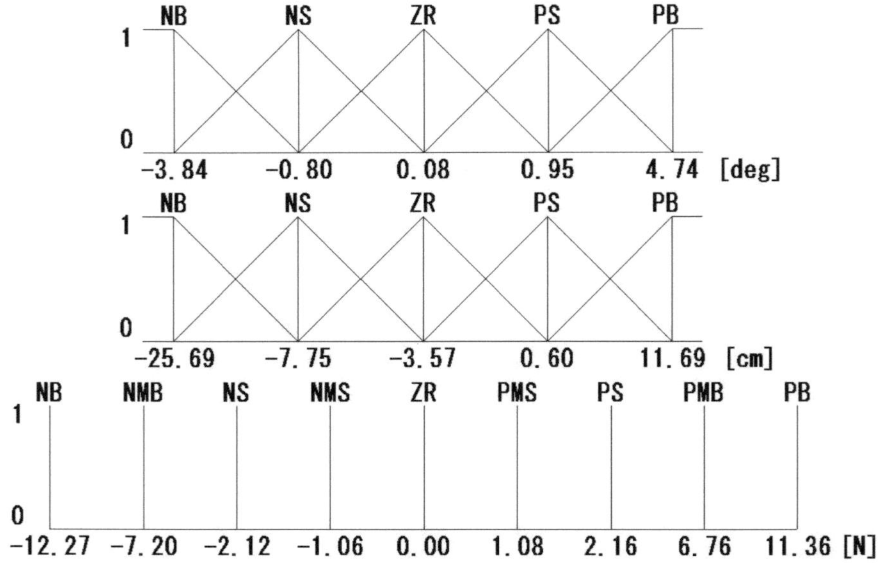

Fig. 15. Identified membership function (operator ME01)

$X+\gamma X'$ \ $\theta+\beta\theta'$	NB	NS	ZR	PS	PB
NB	PS	PMS	NMS	ZR	ZR
NS	PMB	PMS	NMS	NMB	ZR
ZR	PB	PS	ZR	NS	NMB
PS	ZR	PB	PMS	NMS	NMB
PB	ZR	ZR	PS	ZR	NS

(a) Human operator AT01
β=0.0608, γ=0.2280

$X+\gamma X'$ \ $\theta+\beta\theta'$	NB	NS	ZR	PS	PB
NB	PMB	ZR	ZR	NMS	NB
NS	PMB	PMS	ZR	NS	NB
ZR	PMB	PMS	ZR	NMS	NS
PS	PB	PMS	ZR	NMS	NMB
PB	ZR	PS	PS	NMS	NS

(b) Human operator ME01
β=0.0174, γ=0.0797

$X+\gamma X'$ \ $\theta+\beta\theta'$	NB	NS	ZR	PS	PB
NB	PMB	PMS	NMS	ZR	ZR
NS	PMB	PS	NMS	NB	ZR
ZR	PB	PMB	ZR	NMB	NB
PS	ZR	PB	PMS	NMS	NMB
PB	ZR	ZR	PMS	NMS	NMB

(c) Human operator OT01
β=0.0451, γ=0.1619

$X+\gamma X'$ \ $\theta+\beta\theta'$	NB	NS	ZR	PS	PB
NB	PMB	PMS	NMS	NMB	NB
NS	PS	PMS	NMS	NMB	NB
ZR	PMB	PS	ZR	NS	NB
PS	PMB	PB	PMS	NMS	NS
PB	ZR	PB	PS	NMS	NMB

(d) Human operator ST01
β=0.0595, γ=0.6806

Fig. 16. Individual skill of each operator captured in fuzzy rules constructed from the experimental time series data

membership function (Singleton) for output force, which are identified from experimental time series data of Human Operator *OT*'s 1st trial and *ME*'s 1st trial. Figure 16 shows the individual skill of each operator captured in fuzzy rules constructed from the experimental time

series data. It is seen that the fuzzy rules depend on the individual operator and are not symmetrical.
Entropy can be interpreted as a measure of the amount of disorder in the system, and the maximum entropy can be interpreted as a random process with a uniform probability.
Figure 17 shows the entropy ratio vs. number of trial for human operators NK and Ot. According to the results for the estimated entropy ratio, the simulated time series data have a large amount of disorder. The estimated entropy ratio of motion increases with the increase in proficiency.
Figure 18 shows the estimated dimension (degrees of freedom) of motion vs. the number of trials for operators NK and OT. The estimated number of degrees of freedom of motion increases with the increase in proficiency.
Figures 19-1 and 19-2 show examples of simulated waveforms with the identified fuzzy controller and measured waveforms that are similar in appearance for eight human operators.

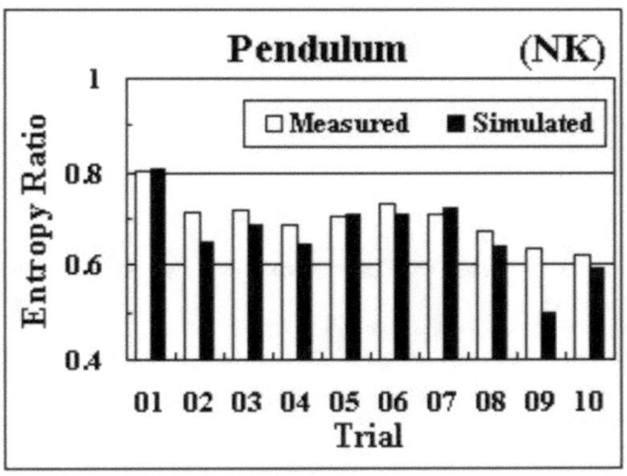

(a) Human operator NK

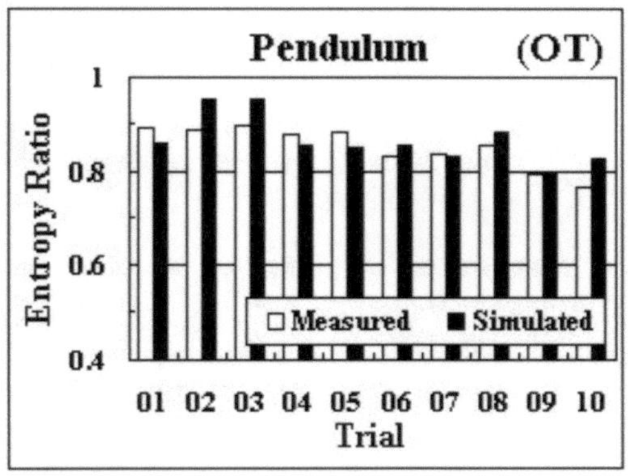

(b) Human operator OT

Fig. 17. Entropy ratio vs. number of trials by human operators (measured and simulated with the identified fuzzy controller).

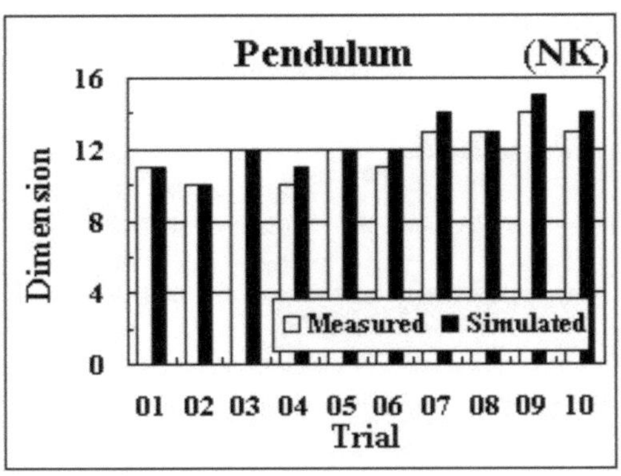

(a) Human operator NK

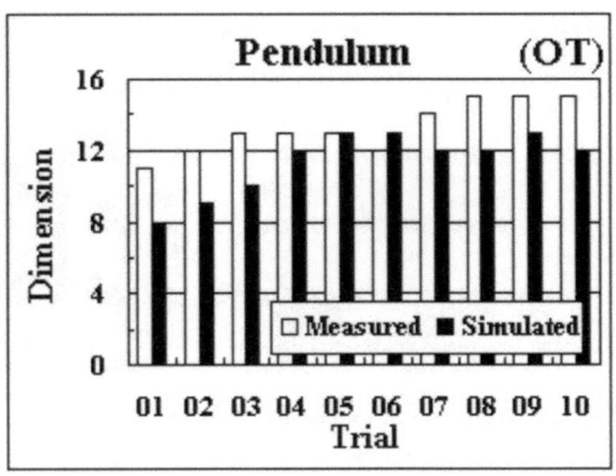

(b) Human operator OT

Fig. 18. Estimated dimension (degrees of freedom) of motion vs. number of trials by human operators (measured and simulated with the identified fuzzy controller).

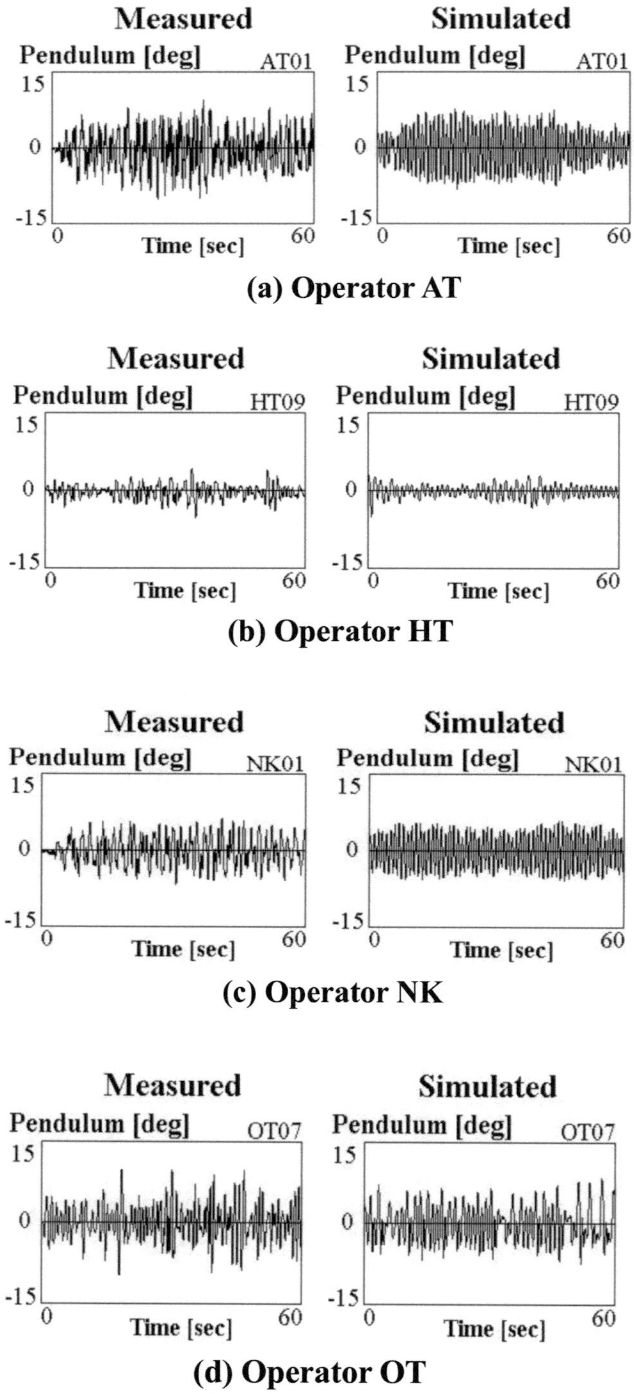

Fig. 19-1. Examples of simulated waveforms with the identified fuzzy controller and measured waveforms that are similar in appearance for eight human operators.

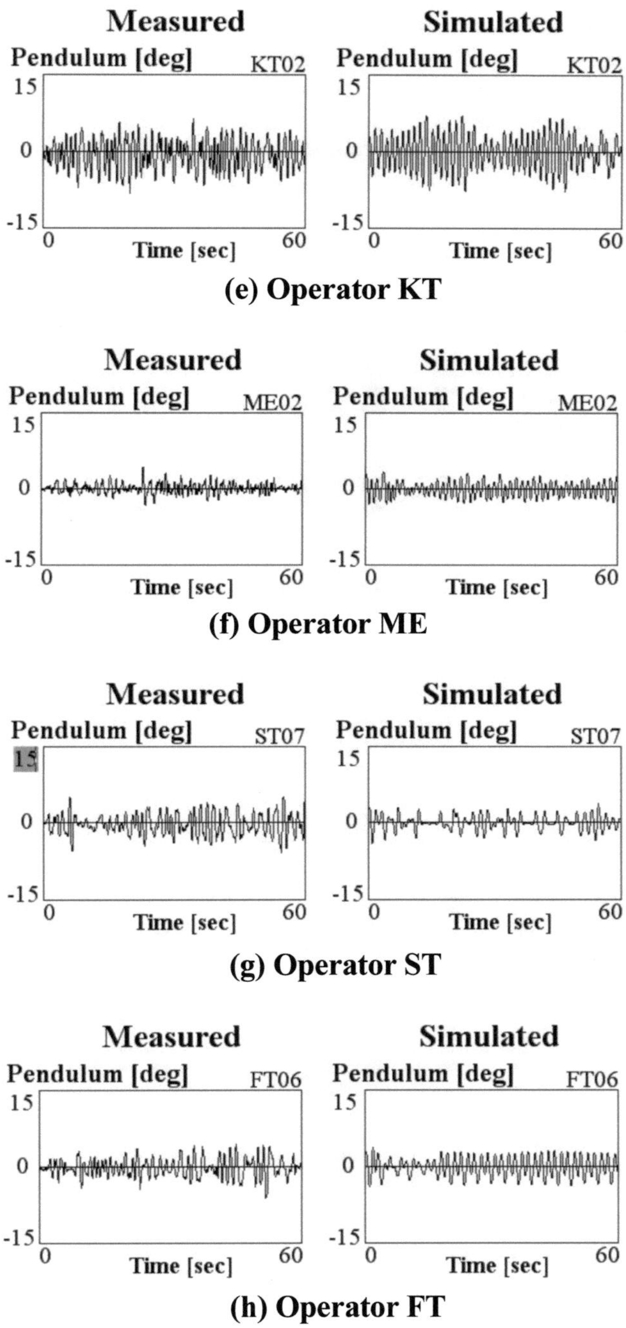

Fig. 19-2. Examples of waveforms simulated with the identified fuzzy controller and measured waveforms that are similar in appearance for eight human operators.

Figure 20 shows the entropy ratios for eight human operators and for simulations using an identified fuzzy controller to produce similar waveforms.
Figure 21 shows the estimated dimension (degrees of freedom) for eight human operators and for simulations using an identified fuzzy controller to produce similar waveforms.
The agreement between the simulated and experimental values for the number of degrees of freedom of motion and the entropy ratio is particularly good when the simulated waveform and the measured waveform are similar in appearance.

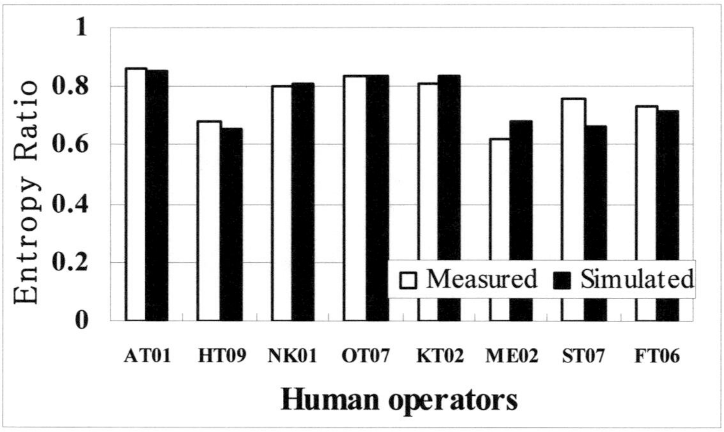

Fig. 20. Entropy ratios for eight human operators and for simulations using an identified fuzzy controller to produce similar waveforms.

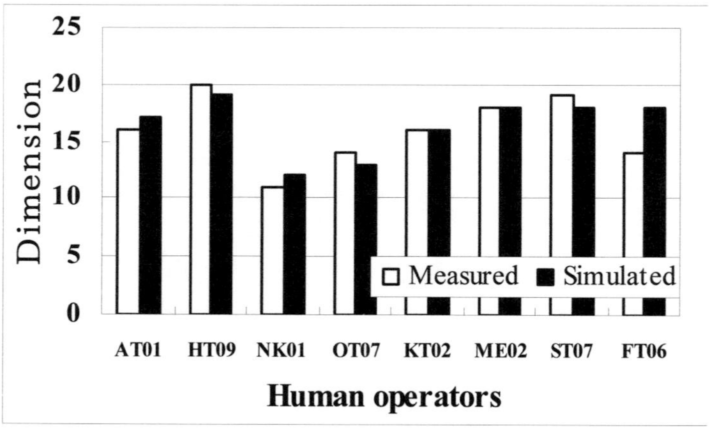

Fig. 21. Estimated dimension (degree of freedom) for eight human operators and for simulations using an identified fuzzy controller to produce similar waveforms.

5. Conclusion

we have demonstrated that the fuzzy controller identified from the measured time series data for each trial for each human operator clearly exhibited the human-generated decision-making characteristics, exhibiting chaos and a large amount of disorder. We have also shown that the estimated number of degrees of freedom of motion increases and the estimated amount of disorder decreases with the increase in proficiency in the fuzzy control simulation. In addition, we have shown that the agreement between the experimental results and the fuzzy simulation for the number of degrees of freedom and for the entropy ratio of motion is particularly good when the measured waveform and the simulated waveform are similar in appearance. Accordingly, it was clarified that a simple fuzzy controller can be very useful for identifying the individuality and proficiency of a human operator when stabilizing an unstable system.

At present, despite notable differences in the behaviors of machinery and human beings, most research on man-machine systems has dealt with the linear characteristics of human behavior. There appear to be few studies and a number of unknowns regarding both the nonlinear characteristics of human behavior in an inherently unstable man-machine system and the learning process of human operators for objects that are difficult to control (Kawazoe et al., 2008, 2009) .

The excessive number of degrees of freedom appears to provide considerable advantages. In several cases, a more flexible instrument, which is certainly much more challenging to work with, has undeniable advantages that provide better results. An experienced master will always prefer an instrument with a greater number of degrees of freedom over an instrument that is easier to use but constrains the worker. For example, a bicycle is harder to control than a tricycle, but anyone who has mastered a bicycle will probably never want to ride a tricycle again. The bicycle is preferred because in the hands of an experienced rider, it is more flexible and maneuverable and becomes more stable than the tricycle. Similarly, lightweight children's skates with their wide blades are less flexible and maneuverable than narrow-bladed speed skates. The practical problem of acquiring dexterity occurs in the early stages of skill development. This fascinating and extremely important area can move us closer to the deepest, concealed caches of knowledge about the human brain and its function (Bernstein, 1996). Real intelligence in autonomous robots appears to be expressed by dexterity in humans or other living creatures as complex systems, and research and development are required to realize intellectual autonomous robots.

Confusion and doubt arise among individuals who are involved in robotics research and development for a long time because numerous robot control theories have been proposed.

Dexterous dynamic actions required for humanoid biped robots, for example, are difficult to achieve through the current standard control strategy for humanoid robots based on the asymptotic convergence to the successive desired states with small fluctuations. Thus, a new and alternative approach is necessary. In the future, we would like to apply the simple nonlinear optimal control of various movements to make full use of instability as a source of driving force.

6. References

Baierlein, R., Atoms and Information Theory, (1971), W. H. Freeman and Co., San Francisco, Chapter 3.

Baker, G. L. and Gollub, J. P., Chaotic dynamics: an introduction, Cambridge University Press, (1996), pp. 86-87.

Bernstein, N. A., Dexterity and its Development, Latash, M. and Turvey, M. (eds.), LEA Publishers, New Jersey, (1996).

Gesell, A., 1945, The embryology of behavior, New York: Harper.

Kawazoe, Y., Manual control and computer control of an inverted pendulum on a cart, *Proc. of the First International Conf. on Motion and Vibration Control*, (1992), pp.930 -935.

Kawazoe, Y. and Ju, D. Y., Nonlinear characteristics of human operator with the stabilizing control of an inverted pendulum on a cart, *Proc. 2nd Int. Conf. on Motion and Vibration Control*, (1994), pp.645- 650.

Kawazoe, Y., Nonlinear characteristics of a human operator during stabilizing control of an inverted pendulum on a cart: Fuzzy identification from experimental time series data and Fuzzy control simulation, *Motion and vibration control in Mechatronics*, Edited by Seto, K., Mizuno, T. and Watanabe, T., (1999), pp.133-138.

Kawazoe Y., Measurement and Analysis of Chaotic Behavior of Human Operator Stabilizing an Inverted Pendulum on a Cart, Proc. *ICMA2000-Human Friendly Mechatronics*, pp.457-462 (2000).

Kawazoe, Y., Fuzzy Identification of Chaotic and Complex Behavior of Human Operator Stabilizing an Inverted Pendulum on a Cart, *Proc. 6th Int. Symposium on Artificial Life & Robotics*, pp.9-12. (2001a)

Kawazoe, Y., Measurement of Chaotic Behavior of Human Operator stabilizing an Inverted Pendulum and Its Fuzzy Identification from Time Series Data, *J. Robotics & Mechatronics*, 13- 1, pp.23- 29.(2001b)

Kawazoe, Y., Ikura, Y., Uchiyama, K., and Kaise, T., Chaos-Entropy Analysis and Acquisition of Individuality and Proficiency of Human Operator's Skill Using a Neural Controller, *Journal of System Design and Dynamics*, Vol. 2, No. 6, (2008), pp. 1351-1363.

Kawazoe, Y., Ikura, Y., Kaise, T., and Matsumoto, J., Chaos-Entropy Analysis and Acquisition of Human Operator's Skill Using a Fuzzy Controller: Identification of Individuality During Stabilizing Control of an Inverted Pendulum, *Journal of System Design and Dynamics*, Vol. 3, No. 6, (2009), pp. 932-943.

Mane, R. On the dimension of the compact invariant sets of certain nonlinear maps, in Rand, D. A. and Young L. S. (eds.), ibid, Vol. 898, (1981), Springer Verlag, Berlin, pp. 230-242.

Newell, K.M.,van Emmerik,R.E.A.,1989,The acquisition of coordination: preliminary analysis of learning to write, Hum Mov Sci., 8, 17-32.

Taga, G., Dynamic Design of Brain and Body, (2002), Kaneko Shobo. (in Japanese)

Takens, F., Detecting strange attracters in turbulence, in Rand, D. A. and Young, L. S. (eds.), Lecture Notes in Mathematics, Vol. 898, pp. 366-381, (1981), Springer-Verlag, Berlin.

Wolf, A., Swift, J. B., Swinney H. L., and Vastano J. A., Determining Lyapunov Exponents From a Time Series, *Physica*, 16D, (1985). pp. 285-317.

17

Fuzzy Logic Deadzone Compensation for a Mobile Robot

Jun Oh Jang
Uiduk University
South Korea

1. Introduction

Mobile manipulators have been introduced as a way of expanding the effective workspace of robot manipulators. Robots with moving vehicle such as macro-micro manipulators, space manipulators, and underwater robotic vehicles can be used for extending the workspace in repair and maintenance, inspection, welding, cleaning, and machining operation. Mobile manipulators possess strongly coupled dynamics of mobile vehicles and manipulators. With the assumption of known dynamics, much research has been carried out. Yamamoto & Yun (1996) addressed the coordination of locomotion and manipulator motion between the base and the arm, and the problem of following a moving surface. Khatib (1999) proposed the coordination and control of the mobile manipulator with two basic task-oriented controls: end-effector task control and platform self posture control. In (Bayle et al., 2003), the concept of manipulability was generalized to the case of mobile manipulators and the optimization criteria in terms of manipulability were given to generate the controls of the system.

Most approaches require the precise knowledge of dynamics of the mobile manipulator, or, they simplify the dynamical model by ignoring dynamics issues, such as vehicle dynamics, payload dynamics, dynamics interactions between the vehicle and the arm, and unknown disturbances such as the dynamic effect caused by terrain irregularity. To handle unknown dynamics of mechanical systems, robust, and adaptive controls have been extensive investigated for robot manipulators and dynamic nonholonomic systems. Dixon et al. (2000) developed a robust tracking and regulation controller for mobile robots. In (Li et al., 2008), adaptive robust output feedback motion/force control strategies were proposed for mobile manipulators under both holonomic and nonholonomic constraints in the presence of uncertainties and disturbances. Impedance control of flexible base mobile manipulator using singular perturbation method and sliding mode control law was presented in (Salehi & Vossoughi, 2008). Because of the difficulty in dynamic modeling, adaptive neural network control has been studied for different classes of systems, such as robotic manipulators (Lewis el al., 1996) and mobile robots (Jang & Chung, 2009). In (Lin & Goldenberg, 2001), adaptive neural network controls have been developed for the motion control of mobile manipulators subject to kinematic constraint. In (Mbede et al., 2005), intelligent navigation is presented for mobile manipulator using adaptive neuro-fuzzy systems. In these schemes, the controls are designed at kinematic level with velocity as input or dynamic level with torque as input, but the actuator dynamics are ignored. Therefore, the actuator nonlinearity deteriorates the system

performance. The actuator nonlinearity compensation techniques are published in (Jang, 2009) for saturation, in (Jang, 2005) for deadzone, and in (Jang & Jeon, 2006) for backlash.
In this paper, we present the deadzone compensation method for a mobile manipulator using fuzzy logic. A rigorous design procedure with proofs is given that results in a kinematic tracking loop with an adaptive FL system in the feed forward loop for deadzone compensation. We derive a practical bound on tracking error from the analysis of the tracking error dynamics and investigate the performance of the FL deadzone compensator in a mobile manipulator through the computer simulations. This paper is as follows. Section 2 provides the mobile manipulator. The FL deadzone compensation is derived in Section 3. The proposed FL deadzone compensation scheme is developed in Section 4. Simulation results of the FL deadzone compensation scheme are given in Section 5. Finally, conclusions are included in Section 6.

2. Mobile manipulator

Consider a mobile manipulator mounted on nonholonomic mobile platform, as shown in Fig. 1. The dynamics of a mobile manipulator subject to kinematics can be obtained using Lagrangian approach in the form (Yamamoto & Yun, 1996)

$$M(q)\ddot{q} + C(q,\dot{q})\dot{q} + F(\dot{q}) + G(q) + \tau_d = B(q)\tau - A^T(q)\lambda \tag{1}$$

where kinematic constraints are described by

$$A(q)\dot{q} = 0\,. \tag{2}$$

and $q \in R^p$ is the generalized coordinates, $M(q) \in R^{p\times p}$ is a symmetric and positive definite inertia matrix, $C(q,\dot{q}) \in R^{p\times p}$ is the centripetal and Coriolis matrix, $F(\dot{q}) \in R^p$ denotes the surface friction, $G(q) \in R^p$ is the gravitational vector, τ_d denotes the bounded unknown disturbances including unstructured unmodeled dynamics, $B(q) \in R^{p\times(p-r)}$ is the input transformation matrix, $\tau \in R^{p-r}$ is the input vector, $A(q) \in R^{r\times p}$ is the matrix associated with the constraints, and $\lambda \in R^r$ is the vector of constraint forces.
In (1), the following properties hold (Lewis et al., 1999).

Property 1 (Skew Symmerricity)

$$\dot{M} - 2C = -(\dot{M} - 2C)^T$$

$$\dot{M} = C + C^T\,. \tag{3}$$

The generalized coordinates q may be separated into two sets $q = [q_v\ q_r]^T$ with $q_v \in R^m$ describes the generalized coordinates appearing in the constraint equations (2), and $q_r \in R^n$ are the free generalized coordinates; $p = m + n$. Therefore, (2) can be simplifed to

$$A_v(q_v)\dot{q}_v = 0 \tag{4}$$

with $A(q_v) \in R^{r\times m}$. Assume that the robot is fully actuated, then (1) can be further rewritten as

$$\begin{bmatrix} M_{11} & M_{12} \\ M_{21} & M_{22} \end{bmatrix}\begin{bmatrix} \ddot{q}_v \\ \ddot{q}_r \end{bmatrix} + \begin{bmatrix} C_{11} & C_{12} \\ C_{21} & C_{22} \end{bmatrix}\begin{bmatrix} \dot{q}_v \\ \dot{q}_r \end{bmatrix} + \begin{bmatrix} F_1 \\ F_2 \end{bmatrix} + \begin{bmatrix} G_1 \\ G_2 \end{bmatrix} + \begin{bmatrix} \tau_{d1} \\ \tau_{d2} \end{bmatrix} = \begin{bmatrix} B_v\tau_v \\ \tau_r \end{bmatrix} - \begin{bmatrix} A_v^T\lambda \\ 0 \end{bmatrix} \tag{5}$$

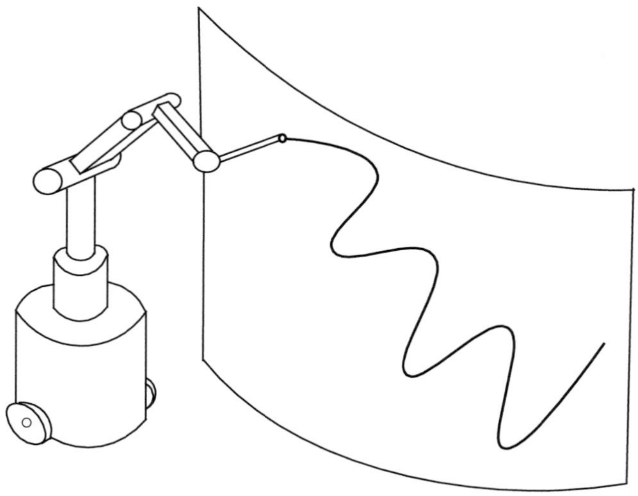

Fig. 1. Trajectory tracking of a mobile manipulator.

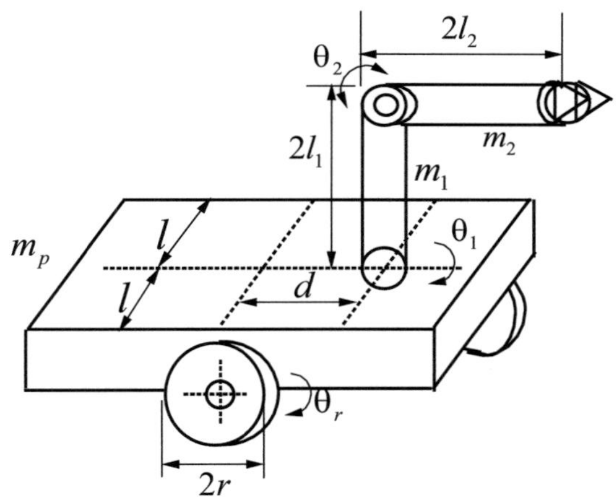

Fig. 2. Two - DOF manipulator mounted on a mobile robot.

where $\tau_v \in R^{m-r}$ represents the actual torque vector of the constrained coordinates, those related to the constrained motion of the wheels, the joints, and the end effector. For simplicity in the theoretical derivation, hereafter we consider only the case where the vehicle motion is constrained. However, the proposed theory can be easily extended to include joint and/or end-effector constraints. $B_v \in R^{m\times(m-r)}$ represents the input transfomation matrix; $\tau_r \in R^n$ the actuating torque vector of the free coordinates; τ_{d1} and τ_{d2} are disturbance torques bounded by $|\tau_{d1}| < \tau_{1N}$ and $|\tau_{d2}| < \tau_{2N}$, with τ_{1N} and τ_{2N} some positive constants.
It is straightforward to show that the following properties hold.

Property 2 :

$$\dot{M}_{21} = C_{21} + C_{12}^T$$

$$M_{12} = M_{21}^T \ . \tag{6}$$

Let $S_v(q_v) \in R^{m\times(m-r)}$ be a full rank matrix formed by a set of smooth and linearly independent vector fields in the null space of $A_v(q_v)$, i.e,

$$S^T(q_v)A_v^T(q_v) = 0 \,. \tag{7}$$

According to (7), it is possible to find an auxiliary vector time function $v(t) \in R^{m-r}$ such that, for all t

$$\dot{q}_v = S(q_v)v(t) \tag{8}$$

and its derivative is

$$\ddot{q}_v = S(q_v)\dot{v} + \dot{S}(q_v)v \,. \tag{9}$$

Equation (8) is called the steering system. $v(t)$ can be regarded as a velocity input vector steering the state vector q in state space.
Let us consider the first m -equations of (5)

$$M_{11}\ddot{q}_v + M_{12}\ddot{q}_r + C_{11}\dot{q}_v + C_{12}\dot{q}_r + F_1 + G_1 + \tau_{d1} = B_v\tau_v - A_v^T\lambda \,. \tag{10}$$

Multiplying both sides of (10) by S^T and using (7) to eliminate the constraint force we obtain

$$S^TM_{11}\ddot{q}_v + S^TM_{12}\ddot{q}_r + S^TC_{11}\dot{q}_v + S^TC_{12}\dot{q}_r + S^TF_1 + S^TG_1 + S^T\tau_{d1} = S^TB_v\tau_v \,. \tag{11}$$

Substituting (8) and (9) into (11) yields

$$S^TM_{11}S\dot{v} + S^TM_{11}\dot{S}v + S^TM_{12}\ddot{q}_r + S^TC_{11}Sv + S^TC_{12}\dot{q}_r + S^TF_1 + S^TG_1 + S^T\tau_{d1} = S^TB_v\tau_v \,. \tag{12}$$

Let us rewrite (12) in a compact form as

$$\overline{M}_{11}\dot{v} + \overline{C}_{11}v + f_1 + \overline{\tau}_{d1} = \overline{\tau}_v \tag{13}$$

where $\overline{M}_{11} = S^TM_{11}S$, $\overline{C}_{11} = S^TC_{11}S + S^TM_{11}\dot{S}$, $\overline{\tau}_{d1} = S^T\tau_{d1}; |\overline{\tau}_{d1}| \le \overline{\tau}_{1N}$ with $\overline{\tau}_{1N}$ some positive constant, and

$$\overline{\tau}_v = S^TB_v\tau_v = \overline{B}_v\tau_v \tag{14}$$

$$f_1 = S^T(M_{12}\ddot{q}_r + C_{12}\dot{q}_r + F_1 + G_1) \,. \tag{15}$$

f_1 consists of the gravitational and friction force, the disturbances on the vehicle base, and the dynamic interaction with the mounted manipulator arm which has been shown to have significant effect on the base motion, thus it needs to be compensated for (Yamamoto, 1994)

Property 3: $\dot{\overline{M}} - 2\overline{C}_{11}$ is skew-symmetric.

Proof:

$$\begin{aligned}\dot{\overline{M}} - 2\overline{C}_{11} &= 2S^TM_{11}\dot{S} + S^T\dot{M}_{11}S - 2S^TM_{11}\dot{S} - 2S^TC_{11}S \\ &= S^T(\dot{M}_{11} - 2C_{11})S\end{aligned} \,. \tag{16}$$

Since $\dot{M} - 2C_{11}$ is skew-symmetric, therefore, $\dot{\bar{M}} - 2\bar{C}_{11}$ is also skew-symmetric.
Let us consider the last n -equations of (5)

$$M_{21}\ddot{q}_v + M_{22}\ddot{q}_r + C_{21}\dot{q}_v + C_{22}\dot{q}_r + F_2 + G_2 + \tau_{d2} = \tau_r \,. \tag{17}$$

Rearrange (17) as follows:

$$M_{22}\ddot{q}_r + C_{22}\dot{q}_r + (M_{21}\ddot{q}_v + C_{21}\dot{q}_v + F_2 + G_2) + \tau_{d2} = \tau_r \,. \tag{18}$$

Equation (18) represents the dynamic equation of the mounted manipulator arm. The terms in the brackets consist of the dynamic interaction term($M_{21}\ddot{q}_v + C_{21}\dot{q}_v$), the gravitational and friction force vector, and the disturbance on the manipulator. Equation (8), (13), and (18) form the complete dynamic model of the mobile manipulator subject to kinematic constraints.
The Lagrange formulism is used to derived the dynamic equation of the mobile manipulator. The dynamical equations of the mobile manipulator in Fig. 2 can be expressed in the matrix form where

$$q_v = \begin{bmatrix} x \\ y \\ \theta \end{bmatrix}, \quad q_r = \begin{bmatrix} \theta_1 \\ \theta_2 \end{bmatrix}$$

$$M_{11} = \begin{bmatrix} m_{p12} + \dfrac{2I_w \sin^2\theta}{r^2} & -\dfrac{2I_w \sin\theta\cos\theta}{r^2} & m_{12}d\sin\theta \\ -\dfrac{2I_w \sin\theta\cos\theta}{r^2} & m_{p12} + \dfrac{2I_w \cos^2\theta}{r^2} & -m_{12}d\cos\theta \\ m_{12}d\sin\theta & -m_{12}d\cos\theta & I_p + I_{12} + m_{12}d^2 + 2I_w\dfrac{l^2}{r^2} \end{bmatrix}$$

$$M_{12} = \begin{bmatrix} 0 & 0 \\ 0 & 0 \\ I_{12} & 0 \end{bmatrix}, \quad M_{21} = \begin{bmatrix} 0 & 0 & I_{12} \\ 0 & 0 & 0 \end{bmatrix}, \quad M_{22} = \begin{bmatrix} I_{12} & 0 \\ 0 & I_{12} \end{bmatrix}$$

$m_{p12} = m_p + m_{12}$, $m_{12} = m_1 + m_2$, $I_{12} = I_1 + I_2$

$$C_{11} = \begin{bmatrix} \dfrac{2I_w\dot{\theta}\sin\theta\cos\theta}{r^2} & \dfrac{2I_w\dot{\theta}\sin^2\theta}{r^2} & m_{12}d\dot{\theta}\cos\theta \\ \dfrac{2I_w\dot{\theta}\cos^2\theta}{r^2} & -\dfrac{2I_w\dot{\theta}\sin\theta\cos\theta}{r^2} & m_{12}d\dot{\theta}\sin\theta \\ 0 & 0 & 0 \end{bmatrix}$$

$$C_{12} = \begin{bmatrix} 0 & 0 \\ 0 & 0 \\ 0 & 0 \end{bmatrix}, \quad C_{21} = \begin{bmatrix} 0 & 0 & 0 \\ 0 & 0 & 0 \end{bmatrix}, \quad C_{22} = \begin{bmatrix} 0 & 0 \\ 0 & 0 \end{bmatrix}$$

$$G_1 = \begin{bmatrix} 0 \\ 0 \\ 0 \end{bmatrix},\ G_2 = \begin{bmatrix} 0 \\ 0 \\ m_2 g l_2 \sin\theta_2 \end{bmatrix},\ \tau_v = \begin{bmatrix} \tau_R \\ \tau_L \end{bmatrix},\ \tau_r = \begin{bmatrix} \tau_1 \\ \tau_2 \end{bmatrix},\ A_v^{\ T} = \begin{bmatrix} -\sin\theta \\ \cos\theta \\ -d \end{bmatrix}$$

$$B_v = \frac{1}{r}\begin{bmatrix} \cos\theta & \cos\theta \\ \sin\theta & \sin\theta \\ -l & -l \end{bmatrix},\quad \lambda = -m_{p12}(\dot{x}\cos\theta + \dot{y}\sin\theta)\dot{\theta}\,. \tag{19}$$

Similar dynamical models have been reported in the literature, for instance in (Yamamoto, 1996) the mass and inertia of the driving wheels and manipulator are considered explicitly.

3. Fuzzy logic deadzone compensation

In this section a FL precompensator is designed for the non-symmetric deadzone nonlinearity. It is shown that the FL approach includes and subsumes approaches based on switching logic and indicator functions (Recker et al., 1991). This brings these references very close to fuzzy logic work in (Kim et al., 1994), and potentially allows for more exotic compensation schemes for actuator nonlinearities using more complex decision (e. g. membership) functions. This section provides a rigorous framework for FL applications in deadzone compensation for a broad class of mobile robot.

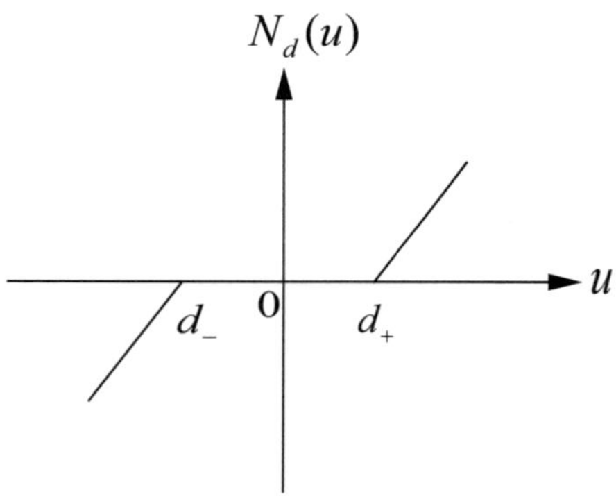

Fig. 3. Deadzone nonlinearity.

If u , $\bar{\tau}$ are scalars, the nonsymmetric deadzone nonlinearity, shown in Fig. 3, is given by

$$\bar{\tau} = N_d(u) = \begin{cases} u - d_-, & u < d_- \\ 0, & d_- \le u < d_+ \\ u - d_+, & d_+ \le u\,. \end{cases} \tag{20}$$

The parameter vector $d = [d_+ \, d_-]^T$ characterizes the width of the system deadband. In practical control systems the width of the deadzone is unknown, so that compensation is difficult. Most compensation schemes cover only the case of symmetric deadzones where $d_- = d_+$.

The nonsymmetric deadzone may be written as

$$\overline{\tau} = N_d(u) = u - sat_d(u) \tag{21}$$

where the nonsymmetric saturation function is defined as

$$sat_d(u) = \begin{cases} d_-, & u < d_- \\ u, & d_- \le u < d_+ \\ d_+, & d_+ \le u. \end{cases} \tag{22}$$

To offset the deleterious effects of deadzone, one may place a precompensator as illustrated in Fig. 4. There, the desired function of the precompensator is to cause the composite throughput from w to $\overline{\tau}$ to be unity. The power of fuzzy logic systems is to that they allow one to use intuition based on experience to design control systems, then provide the mathematical machinery for rigorous analysis and modification of the intuitive knowledge, for example through learning or adaptation, to give guaranteed performance, as will be shown in Section 4. Due to the fuzzy logic classification property, they are particularly powerful when the nonlinearity depends on the region in which the argument u of the nonlinearity is located, as in the non-symmetric deadzone.

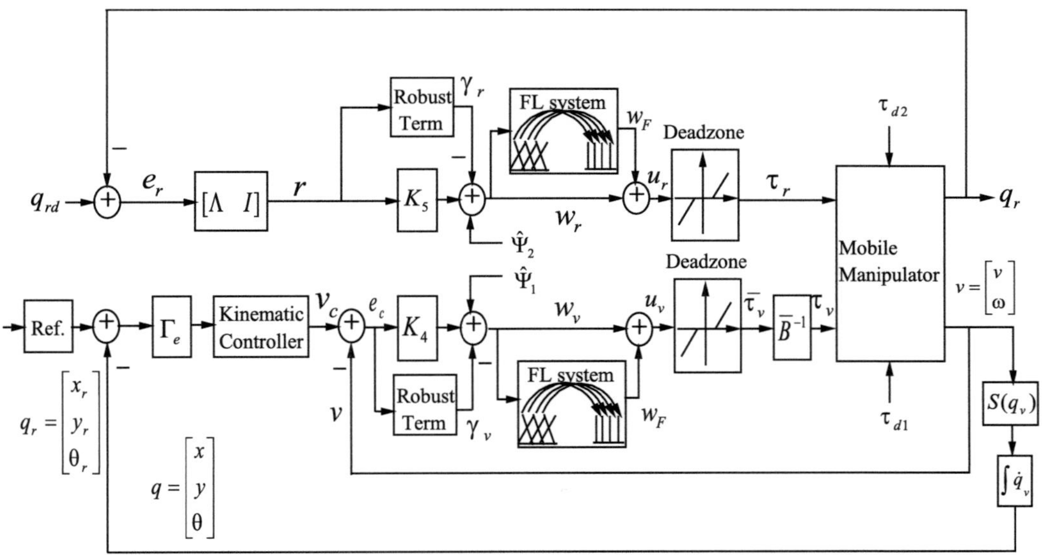

Fig. 4. Fuzzy logic deadzone compensation of a mobile manipulator.

A deadzone precompensator using engineering experience would be discontinuous and depend on the region within which w occurs. It would be naturally described using the rules

$$\text{If } (w \text{ is positive}) \text{ then } (u = w + \hat{d}_+)$$

$$\text{If } (w \text{ is negative}) \text{ then } (u = w + \hat{d}_-) \tag{23}$$

where $\hat{d} = [\hat{d}_+ \ \hat{d}_-]^T$ is an estimate of the deadzone width parameter vector d.

To make this intutive notion mathematically precise for analysis define the membership function's

$$X_+(w) = \begin{cases} 0, & w < 0 \\ 1, & 0 \le w \end{cases}$$

$$X_-(w) = \begin{cases} 1, & w < 0 \\ 0, & 0 \le w \end{cases}. \tag{24}$$

One may write the precompensator as

$$u = w + w_F \tag{25}$$

where w_F is given by the rule base

$$\text{If } (w \in X_+(w)) \text{ then } (w_F = \hat{d}_+)$$

$$\text{If } (w \in X_-(w)) \text{ then } (w_F = \hat{d}_-). \tag{26}$$

The output of the fuzzy logic system with this rule base is given by

$$w_F = \frac{\hat{d}_+ X_+(w) + \hat{d}_- X_-(w)}{X_+(w) + X_-(w)}. \tag{27}$$

The estimates $\hat{d}_+$, $\hat{d}_-$ are, respectively, the control representive value of $X_+(w)$ and $X_-(w)$. This may be written (note $X_+(w) + X_-(w) = 1$) as

$$w_F = \hat{d}^T X(w) \tag{28}$$

where the fuzzy logic basis function vector given by

$$X(w) = \begin{bmatrix} X_+(w) \\ X_-(w) \end{bmatrix} \tag{29}$$

is easily computed given any value of w.
It should be noted that the membership functions (24) are the indicator functions and $X(w)$ is similar to the regressor (Tao & Kokotovic, 1992). The composite through from w to $\overline{\tau}$ of the FL compensator plus the deadzone is

$$\overline{\tau} = N_d(u) = N_d(w + w_F) = w + [w_F - sat_d(w + w_F)]. \tag{30}$$

The FL compensator may be expressed as follows

$$u = w + w_F = w + \hat{d}^T X(w) \tag{31}$$

where $\hat{d}$ is estimated deadzone widths.

Given the FL compensator with rulebase (26), the throughput of the compensator plus deadzone is given by

$$\bar{\tau} = w - \tilde{d}^T X(w) + \tilde{d}^T \delta \tag{32}$$

where the deadzone width estimation error is given by

$$\tilde{d} = d - \hat{d} \tag{33}$$

and the modeling mismatch term δ is bounded so that $|\delta| < \delta_M$ for some scalar δ_M .

4. FL deadzone compensation of a mobile manipulator

In this section, FL deadzone compensation and tuning laws will be derived for the stable joint space tracking of a mobile manipulator described by (8), (13), and (18). The mobile manipulator dynamics is redefined as an error dynamics based on a set of carefully chosen Lyapunov functions. FL deadzone compensators are constructed and new learning laws are proposed. A proof on the tracking stability of the overall closed loop system and the boundedness on FL deadzone estimation errors are provided. The proposed control structure is shown in Fig. 4.

Consider the vehicle dynamics represented by (8) and (13). Tracking control of the steering system (8) has been extensively addressed in the literature (Dixon et al., 2000). For example, for a wheeled mobile robot with two independent actuated wheels, the kinematic parameters in (8) are defined as

$$S(q_v) = \begin{bmatrix} \cos\theta & -d\sin\theta \\ \sin\theta & d\cos\theta \\ 0 & 1 \end{bmatrix}, \; v = \begin{bmatrix} v \\ \omega \end{bmatrix} \text{ and } q_v = \begin{bmatrix} x \\ y \\ \theta \end{bmatrix} \tag{34}$$

where (x, y) represents the Cartesian coordinates of the cart, θ its orientation, v and ω its linear and angular velocities, respectively. Let the reference motion of the vehicle be prescribed as

$$\begin{bmatrix} \dot{x}_r \\ \dot{y}_r \\ \dot{\theta}_r \end{bmatrix} = \begin{bmatrix} \cos\theta & 0 \\ \sin\theta & 0 \\ 0 & 1 \end{bmatrix} \begin{bmatrix} v_r \\ \omega_r \end{bmatrix} \tag{35}$$

where $v_r > 0$ and ω_r are reference linear and angular velocities, respectively. Stable linear and nonlinear velocity feedback laws for (34) can be found in (Kanayama et al., 1990) to achieve the asymptotic tracking. For instance, the following feedback velocity input guarantees that the position tracking of (35) is asymptotically stable [14]:

$$v_c = \begin{bmatrix} v_c \\ \omega_c \end{bmatrix} = \begin{bmatrix} v_r \cos e_3 + k_1 e_1 \\ \omega_r + k_2 v_r e_2 + k_3 v_r \sin e_3 \end{bmatrix} \tag{36}$$

where positive constant k_1 , k_2 and k_3 are control gains, and the position tracking errors are defined as

$$e = \Gamma_e(q_{vd} - q_v)$$

$$\begin{bmatrix} e_1 \\ e_2 \\ e_3 \end{bmatrix} = \begin{bmatrix} \cos\theta & \sin\theta & 0 \\ -\sin\theta & \cos\theta & 0 \\ 0 & 0 & 1 \end{bmatrix} \begin{bmatrix} x_r - x \\ y_r - y \\ \theta_r - \theta \end{bmatrix}. \tag{37}$$

Choosing the following Lyapunov function can prove the stability tracking system

$$V_1 = k_1(e_1^2 + e_2^2) + 2k_3 v_r (1 - \cos e_3). \tag{38}$$

Differentiating yields

$$\dot{V}_1 = 2k_1(e_1\dot{e}_1 + e_2\dot{e}_2) + 2k_3 v_r \dot{e}_3 \sin e_3 . \tag{39}$$

Given the desired velocity $v_c(t)$, define now the auxiliary velocity tracking error as

$$e_c = v_c - v . \tag{40}$$

The velocity tracking error is

$$\begin{aligned} e_c &= \begin{bmatrix} e_4 \\ e_5 \end{bmatrix} = \begin{bmatrix} v_c - v \\ w_c - w \end{bmatrix} \\ &= \begin{bmatrix} v_r \cos e_3 + k_1 e_1 - v \\ \omega_r + k_2 v_r e_2 + k_3 v_r \sin e_3 - \omega \end{bmatrix} \end{aligned} \tag{41}$$

where k_1, k_2, k_3 are positive constants.
Substituting the derivative of the position error in (39), we obtain

$$\dot{V}_1 = 2k_1 e_1 (v_2 e_2 - v_1 + v_r \cos e_3) + 2k_1 e_2(-v_2 e_1 + v_r \sin e_3) + 2k_3 v_r (\omega_r - v_2)\sin e_3 \tag{42}$$

Using (41) and defining $k_2 = (k_1 / k_3 v_r)$ yields

$$\dot{V}_1 = -k_1^2 e_1^2 - k_3^2 v_r^2 \sin^2 e_3 - (k_1 e_1 - e_4)^2 - (k_3 v_r \sin e_3 - e_5)^2 . \tag{43}$$

Differentiating (40), multiplying both sides by M_{11} and substituting (13) into it yields

$$\bar{M}_{11}\dot{e}_c = -\bar{C}_{11} e_c + f_1 + \bar{\tau}_{d1} + \bar{M}_{11}\dot{v}_c + \bar{C}_{11} v_c - \bar{\tau}_v . \tag{44}$$

Equation (44) represents the vehicle dynamics in terms of tracking errors.
Let us choose the Lyapunov function as

$$V_2 = \frac{1}{2} e_c^T \bar{M}_{11} e_c . \tag{45}$$

Differentiating (45) yields

$$\dot{V}_2 = e_c^T \bar{M}_{11}\dot{e}_c + \frac{1}{2} e_c^T \dot{\bar{M}}_{11} e_c . \tag{46}$$

Substituting (44) into (46) we obtain

$$\begin{aligned} \dot{V}_2 &= e_c^T\{f_1 + \bar{\tau}_{d1} + \bar{M}_{11}\dot{v}_c + \bar{C}_{11}v_c - \bar{\tau}_v\} + \frac{1}{2}e_c^T(\dot{\bar{M}}_{11} - 2\bar{C}_{11})e_c \\ &= e_c^T\{f_1 + \bar{M}_{11}\dot{v}_c + \bar{C}_{11}v_c + \bar{\tau}_{d1} - \bar{\tau}_v\} \end{aligned} \quad (47)$$

Now consider the arm dynamics (18). Let us define the arm error as

$$e_r = q_{rd} - q_r \quad (48)$$

and the tracking error as

$$r = \dot{e}_r + \Lambda e_r \quad (49)$$

where $k = k^T > 0$. In (49), tracking error r can be regarded as an input to a linear dynamics system with state variable e_r. Therefore, when $r \to 0$, it can guarantee that $e_r \to 0$ (Lewis et al., 1999).
Differentiating (49) yields

$$\dot{r} = \ddot{e}_r + \Lambda\dot{e}_r = \ddot{q}_{rd} - \ddot{q}_r + \Lambda\dot{e}_r. \quad (50)$$

Therefore, we have

$$\dot{q}_r = \dot{q}_{rd} - (r - \Lambda e_r) \quad (51)$$

$$\ddot{q}_r = \ddot{q}_{rd} - \dot{r} + \Lambda(r - \Lambda e_r). \quad (52)$$

The manipulator dynamics (18) can be formulated in terms of the tracking error as

$$M_{22}\dot{r} = -C_{22}r + f_2 + \tau_{d2} - \tau_r \quad (53)$$

where the nonlinear manipulator function is

$$f_2 = M_{22}(\ddot{q}_{rd} + \Lambda\dot{e}_r) + C_{22}(\dot{q}_{rd} + \Lambda e_r) + M_{21}\ddot{q}_v + C_{21}\dot{q}_v + F_2 + G_2. \quad (54)$$

The nonlinear manipulator function f_2 consists of the manipulator dynamics ($M_{22}(\ddot{q}_{rd} + \Lambda\dot{e}_r) + C_{22}(\dot{q}_{rd} + \Lambda e_r) + F_2 + G_2$) and the dynamics of interaction with the vehicle base ($M_{21}\ddot{q}_v + C_{21}\dot{q}_v$).
To design the manipulator torque input, we choose the Lyapunov function as

$$V_3 = \frac{1}{2}r^T M_{22} r. \quad (55)$$

Notice that M_{22} is a symmetric positive definite matrix. Differentiating (55) yields

$$\begin{aligned} \dot{V}_3 &= r^T M_{22}\dot{r} + \frac{1}{2}r^T\dot{M}_{22}r \\ &= r^T(-C_{22}r - \tau_r + f_2 + \tau_{d2}) + \frac{1}{2}r^T\dot{M}_{22}r \\ &= r^T(-\tau_r + f_2 + \tau_{d2}) + \frac{1}{2}r^T(\dot{M}_{22} - 2C_{22})r \\ &= r^T(-\tau_r + f_2 + \tau_{d2}) \end{aligned} \quad (56)$$

Let us consider the overall dynamics (5) that combines both the arm and vehicle dynamics. Consider the Lyapunov function as

$$V_4 = V_1 + \frac{1}{2}\begin{pmatrix} Se_c \\ r \end{pmatrix} M \begin{pmatrix} Se_c \\ r \end{pmatrix}. \tag{57}$$

In the proposed Lyapunov function V_4, V_1 is used to account for the nonholonomic steering system (8), and the second term accounts for the vehicle base and manipulator arm dynamics, as well as the dynamic couplings between two.
From (57) we have

$$\begin{aligned} V_4 &= V_1 + \frac{1}{2}\begin{pmatrix} Se_c \\ r \end{pmatrix}\begin{pmatrix} M_{11} & M_{12} \\ M_{12}^T & M_{22} \end{pmatrix}\begin{pmatrix} Se_c \\ r \end{pmatrix} \\ &= V_1 + \frac{1}{2}(Se_c)^T M_{11}(Se_c) + \frac{1}{2} r^T M_{12}^T (Se_c) + \frac{1}{2}(Se_c)^T M_{12} r + \frac{1}{2} r^T M_{22} r \\ &= V_1 + \frac{1}{2} e_c^T (S^T M_{11} S) e_c + r^T M_{12}^T (Se_c) + \frac{1}{2} r^T M_{22} r \\ &= V_1 + \frac{1}{2} e_c^T \bar{M}_{11} e_c + r^T M_{12}^T (Se_c) + \frac{1}{2} r^T M_{22} r \\ &= V_1 + V_2 + V_3 + r^T M_{12}^T (Se_c) \end{aligned} \tag{58}$$

Differentiating (58) yields

$$\dot{V}_4 = \dot{V}_1 + \dot{V}_2 + \dot{V}_3 + \frac{d}{dt}\{r^T M_{21}(Se_c)\}. \tag{59}$$

Substituting (43), (47), and (56) into (59) yields

$$\dot{V}_4 \le e_c^T(-\bar{\tau}_v + f_1 + \bar{M}_{11}\dot{v}_c + \bar{C}_{11} v_c + \bar{\tau}_{d1}) + r^T(-\tau_r + f_2 + \tau_{d2}) + \frac{d}{dt}\{r^T M_{21}(Se_c)\} \tag{60}$$

where the four terms in (43) are negative.
From the definition of f_1 in (15) and (51), (52) we have

$$\begin{aligned} f_1 &= S^T(M_{12}\ddot{q}_r + C_{12}\dot{q}_r + F_1 + G_1) \\ &= S^T\{M_{12}(\ddot{q}_{rd} - \dot{r} + \Lambda(r - \Lambda e_r) + C_{12}(\dot{q}_{rd} - (r - \Lambda e_r)) + F_1 + G_1\} \\ &= -S^T\{M_{12}\dot{r} + (C_{12} - M_{12}\Lambda)(r - \Lambda e_r)\} + \bar{f}_1 \end{aligned} \tag{61}$$

where $\bar{f}_1 = S^T(M_{12}\ddot{q}_{rd} + C_{12}\dot{q}_{rd} + F_1 + G_1)$.
From the definition of f_2 in (9) and (54) we have

$$\begin{aligned} f_2 &= M_{21}(\dot{S}v + S\dot{v}) + C_{21}Sv + \{M_{22}(\ddot{q}_{rd} + \Lambda\dot{e}_r) + C_{22}(\dot{q}_{rd} + \Lambda e_r) + F_2 + G_2\} \\ &= (M_{21}S)\dot{v} + (M_{21}\dot{S} + C_{21}S)v + \bar{f}_2 \\ &= (M_{21}S)(\dot{v}_c - \dot{e}_c) + (M_{21}\dot{S} + C_{21}S)(v_c - e_c) + \bar{f}_2 \end{aligned} \tag{62}$$

where $\bar{f}_2 = M_{22}(\ddot{q}_{rd} + \Lambda\dot{e}_r) + C_{22}(\dot{q}_{rd} + \Lambda e_r) + F_2 + G_2$.

Substituting (61) and (62) into (60) and after some collections of them we have

$$\begin{aligned}\dot{V}_4 \le\ & e_c^T(-\bar{\tau}_v + \bar{M}_{11}\dot{v}_c + \bar{C}_{11}v_c) - r^T\tau_r + e_c^T f_1 + r^T f_2 + \frac{d}{dt}\{r^T M_{21}(Se_c)\} \\ & + e_c^T\bar{\tau}_{d1} + r^T\tau_{d2}\end{aligned} \quad (63)$$

First of all, we carry out the following derivation

$$\begin{aligned} & e_c^T f_1 + r^T f_2 + \frac{d}{dt}\{r^T M_{21}(Se_c)\} \\ &= e_c^T\bar{f}_1 + r^T\bar{f}_2 - (Se_c)^T\{M_{12}\dot{r} + (C_{12} - M_{12}\Lambda)(r - \Lambda e_r)\} \\ &\quad + r^T(M_{21}S\dot{v}_c - M_{21}S\dot{e}_c + M_{21}\dot{S}v_c - M_{21}\dot{S}e_c + C_{21}Sv_c - C_{21}Se_c) \\ &\quad + \dot{r}^T M_{21}Se_c + r^T\dot{M}_{21}Se_c + r^T M_{21}\dot{S}e_c + r^T M_{21}S\dot{e}_c \\ &= e_c^T\bar{f}_1 + r^T\bar{f}_2 - (Se_c)^T\{(C_{12} - M_{12}\Lambda)(r - \Lambda e_r)\} \\ &\quad + r^T(M_{21}S\dot{v}_c + M_{21}\dot{S}v_c + C_{21}Sv_c + C_{12}Se_c) \\ &= e_c^T\bar{f}_1 + r^T\bar{f}_2 - (Se_c)^T\{-C_{12}\Lambda e_r - M_{12}\Lambda(r - \Lambda e_r)\} \\ &\quad + r^T(M_{21}S\dot{v}_c + M_{21}\dot{S}v_c + C_{21}Sv_c)\end{aligned} \quad (64)$$

where Properties 2 and 3 have been used in the previous derivations.
Substituting (64) into (63) we obtain

$$\begin{aligned}\dot{V}_4 \le\ & e_c^T(-\bar{\tau}_v + \bar{M}_{11}\dot{v}_c + \bar{C}_{11}v_c) - r^T\tau_r + e_c^T\bar{f}_1 + r^T\bar{f}_2 \\ & + (Se_c)^T\{C_{12}\Lambda e_r + M_{12}\Lambda(r - \Lambda e_r)\} \\ & + r^T(M_{21}S\dot{v}_c + M_{21}\dot{S}v_c + C_{21}Sv_c) + e_c^T\bar{\tau}_{d1} + r^T\tau_{d2} \\ =\ & e_c^T[-\bar{\tau}_v + \bar{M}_{11}\dot{v}_c + \bar{C}_{11}v_c + \bar{f}_1 + S^T\{C_{12}\Lambda e_r + M_{12}\Lambda(r - \Lambda e_r)\}] \\ & + r^T(-\tau_r + \bar{f}_2 + M_{21}S\dot{v}_c + M_{21}\dot{S}v_c + C_{21}Sv_c) + e_c^T\bar{\tau}_{d1} + r^T\tau_{d2}\end{aligned} \quad (65)$$

Therefore

$$\dot{V}_4 \le e_c^T(-\bar{\tau}_v + \Psi_1) + r^T(-\tau_r + \Psi_2) + e_c^T\bar{\tau}_{d1} + r^T\tau_{d2} \quad (66)$$

with unknown nonlinear terms

$$\Psi_1 = \bar{M}_{11}\dot{v}_c + \bar{C}_{11}v_c + \bar{f}_1 + S^T\{C_{12}\Lambda e_r + M_{12}\Lambda(r - \Lambda e_r)\} \quad (67a)$$

$$\Psi_2 = \bar{f}_2 + M_{21}S\dot{v}_c + M_{21}\dot{S}v_c + C_{21}Sv_c\ . \quad (67b)$$

In applications the nonlinear robot function Ψ_1 and Ψ_2 is at least partially unknown. In standard fashion [Jang & Chung, 2009; Lewis et al., 1999], the estimate $\hat{\Psi}_1$, $\hat{\Psi}_2$ may be provided by any means desired. The functional estimation error are defined as $\tilde{\Psi}_1 = \Psi_1 - \hat{\Psi}_1$ and $\tilde{\Psi}_2 = \Psi_2 - \hat{\Psi}_2$. It is assumed that the functional estimation error satisfies

$$|\tilde{\Psi}_1| \le \Psi_{1M}(x) \quad (68a)$$

$$|\tilde{\Psi}_2| \le \Psi_{2M}(x) \quad (68b)$$

for some unknown bounded function $\Psi_{1M}(x)$ and $\Psi_{2M}(x)$.
Therefore, a suitable control input for velocity following is given by the computed torque like control

$$w_v = \hat{\Psi}_1 + k_4 e_c - \gamma_v \tag{69a}$$

$$w_r = \hat{\Psi}_2 + k_5 r - \gamma_r \tag{69b}$$

with k_4 , k_5 are the diagonal positive definite gain matrix. The robustifying signals $\gamma_v(t)$, $\gamma_r(t)$ are required to compensate the unmodeled unstructured disturbances.
Deadzone compensation is provided using

$$u_v = w_v + \hat{d}_v^T X(w_v) \tag{70a}$$

$$u_r = w_r + \hat{d}_r^T X(w_r) \tag{70b}$$

with $X(w_v)$ and $X(w_r)$ given by (29), which gives the overall feedforward throughout (32).
Substituting (69) and (32) into (66)

$$\begin{aligned}\dot{V}_4 &\le e_c^T(-w_v + \tilde{d}_v^T X(w_v) - \tilde{d}_v^T \delta_v + \Psi_1) + r^T(-w_r + d_r^T X(w_r) - \tilde{d}_r^T \delta_r + \Psi_2) \\ &\quad + e_c^T \overline{\tau}_{d1} + r^T \tau_{d2} \\ &\le e_c^T(-\hat{\Psi}_1 - K_4 e_c + \gamma_v + \tilde{d}_v^T X(w_v) - \tilde{d}_v^T \delta_v + \Psi_1) \\ &\quad + r^T(-\hat{\Psi}_2 - K_5 r + \gamma_r + \tilde{d}_r^T X(w_r) - \tilde{d}_r^T \delta_r + \Psi_2) + e_c^T \overline{\tau}_{d1} + r^T \tau_{d2}\end{aligned} \tag{71}$$

Let us define

$$\tau_D = \begin{bmatrix} \overline{\tau}_{d1} \\ \tau_{d2} \end{bmatrix} \quad d = \begin{bmatrix} d_v \\ d_r \end{bmatrix}. \tag{72}$$

Based on the bounds of every element of the vectors and matruces defined above, we may show the following properties hold:

$$\begin{aligned}&|\tau_D| \le |\overline{\tau}_{d1}| + |\tau_{d2}| \le \overline{\tau}_{1N} + \tau_{2N} \equiv \tau_M \\ &|d| \le |d_v| + |d_r| \le d_{vM} + d_{rM} \equiv d_M\end{aligned} \tag{73}$$

The next theorem provides an algorithm for tuning the deadzone precompensator.
Theorem 1: Consider the nonholomic system (13) and (18). Select the tracking control (69) plus deadzone compensator (70), where $X(w)$ is given by (29). Choose the robustifying signal

$$\gamma_v(t) = -(\Psi_{1M} + \tau_M)\frac{e_c}{|e_c|}. \tag{74a}$$

$$\gamma_r(t) = -(\Psi_{2M} + \tau_M)\frac{r}{|r|}. \tag{74b}$$

Let the estimated deadzone widths be provided by the FL system tuning algorithm

$$\dot{\hat{d}}_v = X(w_v)e_c - k_6\hat{d}_v \,|\, e_c \,| \tag{75a}$$

$$\dot{\hat{d}}_r = X(w_r)r - k_6\hat{d}_r \,|\, r \,| \tag{75b}$$

where k_6 is positive definite design parameter. By properly choosing the control gain and design parameter, tracking errors of error dynamics described by (8), (44), (53) and the FL deadzone estimation error $\tilde{d} = (\tilde{d}_v^T, \tilde{d}_r^T)$ evolves practical bounds by the right hand sides of (83) and (84)

Proof) Select the Lyapunov function candidate as

$$V = V_4 + \frac{1}{2}(\tilde{d}_v^T\tilde{d}_v) + \frac{1}{2}(\tilde{d}_r^T\tilde{d}_r). \tag{76}$$

Differentiating yields

$$\dot{V} = \dot{V}_4 + (\tilde{d}_v^T\dot{\tilde{d}}_v) + (\tilde{d}_r^T\dot{\tilde{d}}_r). \tag{77}$$

From (71), (73) and robutifying term (74) it follows that

$$\begin{aligned} \dot{V}_4 &\le -e_c^T k_4 e_c + \tilde{d}_v^T(X(w_v)e_c - \delta_v e_c) + e_c^T(\Psi_1 - \hat{\Psi}_1 + \gamma_v + \overline{\tau}_{d1}) \\ &\quad - r^T k_5 r + \tilde{d}_r^T(X(w_r)r - \delta_r r) + r^T(\Psi_2 - \hat{\Psi}_1 + \gamma_r + \tau_{d2}) \\ &\le -e_c^T k_4 e_c + \tilde{d}_v^T(X(w_v)e_c - \delta_{vM}e_c) - r^T k_5 r + \tilde{d}_r^T(X(w_r)r - \delta_{rM}r) \end{aligned} . \tag{78}$$

where $|\,\delta_v\,| < \delta_{vM}$, $|\,\delta_r\,| < \delta_{rM}$ for some known positive constants δ_{vM} and δ_{rM}.
Using (77), we obtain

$$\begin{aligned} \dot{V} &\le -e_c^T k_4 e_c + \tilde{d}_v^T(X(w_v)e_c - \delta_{vM}e_c) - r^T k_5 r + \tilde{d}_r^T(X(w_r)r - \delta_{rM}r) \\ &\quad + (d_v^T\dot{\tilde{d}}_v) + (\tilde{d}_r^T\dot{\tilde{d}}_r) \\ &\le -e_c^T k_4 e_c + \tilde{d}_v^T(X(w_v)e_c - \delta_{vM}e_c + \dot{\tilde{d}}_v) - r^T k_5 r + \tilde{d}_r^T(X(w_r)r - \delta_{rM}r + \dot{\tilde{d}}_r) \end{aligned} . \tag{79}$$

Since $\dot{\tilde{d}} = -\dot{\hat{d}}$, applying the tuning algorithm (75) yields

$$\begin{aligned} \dot{V} &\le -e_c^T k_4 e_c + \tilde{d}_v^T(X(w_v)e_c - \delta_{vM}e_c - X(w_v)e_c + k_6\hat{d}_v\,|\,e_c\,|) \\ &\quad - r^T k_5 r + \tilde{d}_r^T(X(w_r)r - \delta_{rM}r - X(w_r)r + k_6\hat{d}_r\,|\,r\,|) \\ &\le -e_c^T k_4 e_c + \tilde{d}_v^T(-\delta_{vM}e_c + k_6\hat{d}_v\,|\,e_c\,|) - r^T k_5 r + \tilde{d}_r^T(-\delta_{rM}r + k_6\hat{d}_r\,|\,r\,|) \\ &\le -e_c^T k_4 e_c + \tilde{d}_v^T(\delta_{vM}e_c + k_6(d_v - \tilde{d}_v)\,|\,e_c\,|) - r^T k_5 r + \tilde{d}_r^T(\delta_{rM}r + k_6(d_r - \tilde{d}_r)\,|\,r\,|) \end{aligned} . \tag{80}$$

there results

$$\dot{V} \le -e_c^T k_4 e_c + \tilde{d}_v^T(c_v e_c - k_6\tilde{d}_v\,|\,e_c\,|) - r^T k_5 r + \tilde{d}_r^T(c_r r - k_6\tilde{d}_r\,|\,r\,|) \tag{81}$$

with $c_v = \delta_{vM} + k_6 d_{vM}$ and $c_r = \delta_{rM} + k_6 d_{rM}$. $|\,d_v\,| \le d_{vM}$ and $|\,d_r\,| \le d_{rM}$ with known positive constants d_{vM} and d_{rM}.
Let $\overline{k} = \min(k_4, k_5)$, $E = (e_c^T, r^T)$ and $c = (c_v, c_r)$, we obtain

$$\begin{aligned}\dot{V} &\le -E^T\bar{k}E + E^T c\,|\tilde{d}| - E^T k_6\,|\tilde{d}|^2 \\ &\le -|E|[\bar{k}\,|E| - c\,|\tilde{d}| + k_6\,|\tilde{d}|^2]\end{aligned} \tag{82}$$

This is negative as long as the quantity in the brace is positive. To determine conditions for this, complete the square to see that $\dot{V}$ is negative as long as either

$$|E| > \frac{c^2}{4\cdot\bar{k}\cdot k_6} \tag{83}$$

or

$$|\tilde{d}| > \frac{c}{k_6}. \tag{84}$$

According to the Lyapunov theorem, the tracking error decreases as long as the error is bigger than the right-hand side of Eq. (83). This implies Eq. (85) gives a practical bound on the tracking error

$$|E| \le \frac{c^2}{4\cdot\bar{k}\cdot k_6}. \tag{85}$$

◊

Also, Lyapunov extension shows that the deadzone width bound, $|\tilde{d}|$, is bounded to a neighborhood of the right hand side of Eq. (84). Since a tracking controller, $\bar{k}$, is determined according to the design of a tracking controller, $\bar{k}$ cannot be increased arbitrarily. However, large $\bar{k}$ may decrease the tracking error bound as long as the kinematic controller and the robust term maintain the stability of a control system.

5. Simulation results

In this section, we illustrates the effectiveness of a proposed FL deadzone compenation method for a mobile manipulator. For computer simulations, we took the vehicle and arm parameters as $m_p = 10[Kg]$, $m_1 = 1[Kg]$, $m_2 = 1[Kg]$, $I_1 = I_2 = I_w = 1[Kg\cdot m^2]$, $I_p = 5[Kg\cdot m^2]$, $l_1 = l_2 = 0.05[m]$, $2l = 0.35[m]$, and $r = 0.05[m]$, $d = 0.001[m]$. The controller gains were chosen so that the closed loop system exhibits a critical damping behavior $k_1 = 10$, $k_2 = 5$, $k_3 = 4$, $k_4 = diag\{40,40\}$, $k_5 = diag\{10,10\}$, $k_6 = 1$, and $\Lambda = diag\{5,5\}$. The reference points are constructed by using the kinematic model (35) and the following velocities, as follows:

$$v_r = 1.0[m/\sec]$$

$$\omega_r = -1 + 6\sin(0.0139t)[\deg ree/\sec]. \tag{86}$$

The reference trajectories fo the arm are $\theta_{1d}(t) = \sin(0.0698t)$ and $\theta_{2d}(t) = \cos(0.0698t)$. The departure posture vector is $(-5,-5,0^\circ)$ and the goal is trajectory following. Fig. 5 show the reference trajectory response of a mobile manipulator. Since the deadzone nonlinearity is included in the mobile robot, the performance degraded by the deadzone effects in Fig. 6. The deadzone nonlinearity for mobile platform are $d_+ = 0.33$ and $d_- = -0.3$ for right wheel and $d_+ = 0.31$ and $d_- = -0.3$ for left wheel. The deadzone nonlinearity for manipulator are $d_+ = 0.2$ and $d_- = -0.21$ for arm 1 and $d_+ = 0.19$ and $d_- = -0.2$ for arm 2. In, Fig. 7, the proposed FL deadzone compensation shows an improvement in trajectory response compared with the dynamic controller. The velcocity error, angular velocity error for vehicle, and the estimates of deadzone widths are shown in Fig 7(c)-(e).

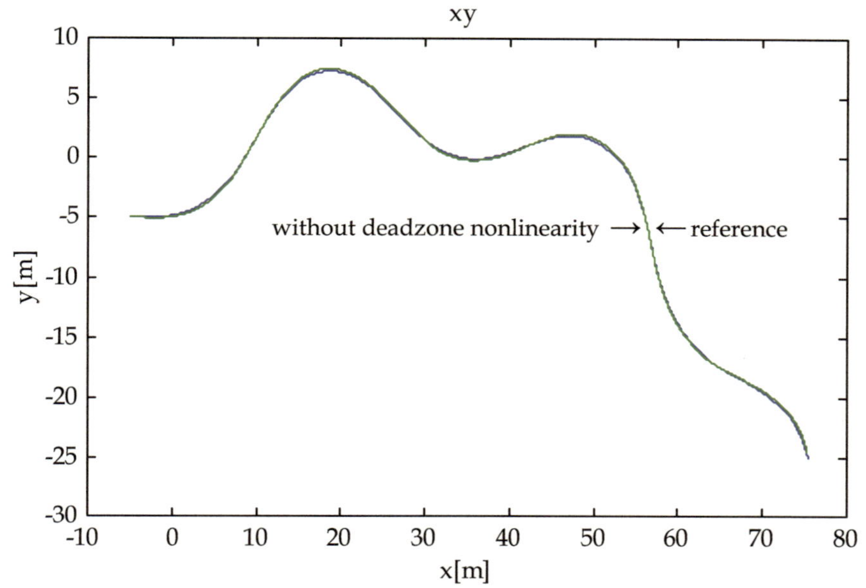

(a)

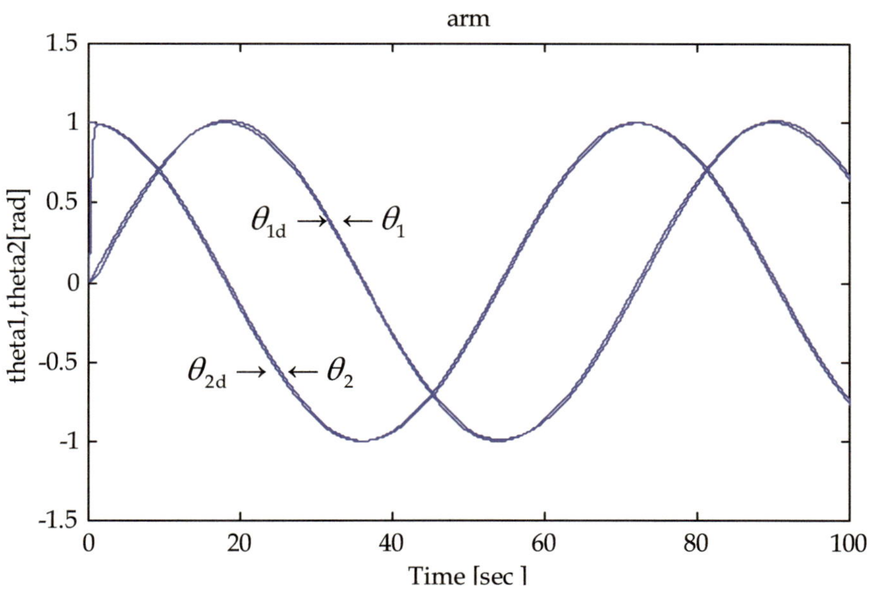

(b)

Fig. 5. Response without deadzone nonlinearity of a mobile manipulator (a) vehicle trajectory and (b) arm position.

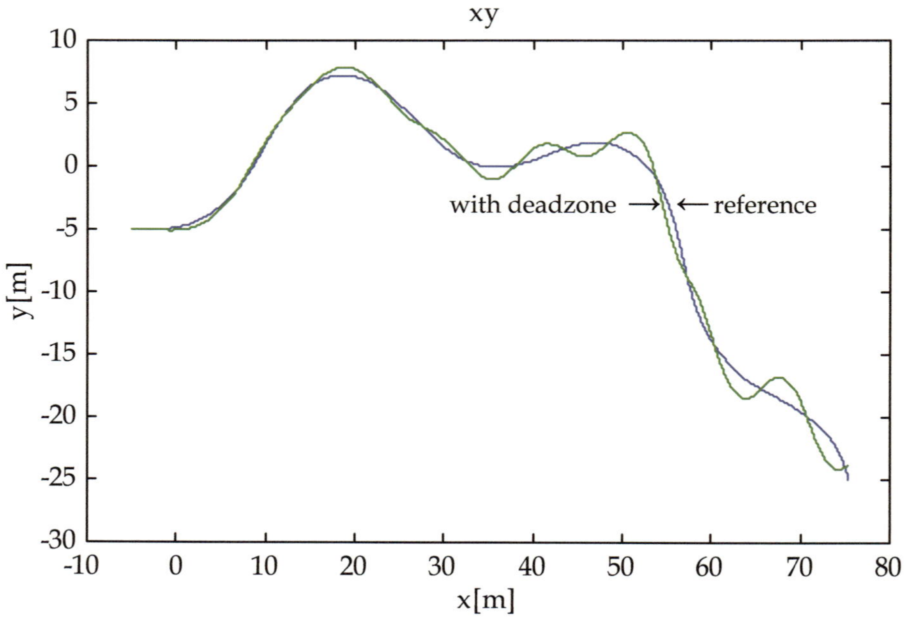

(a)

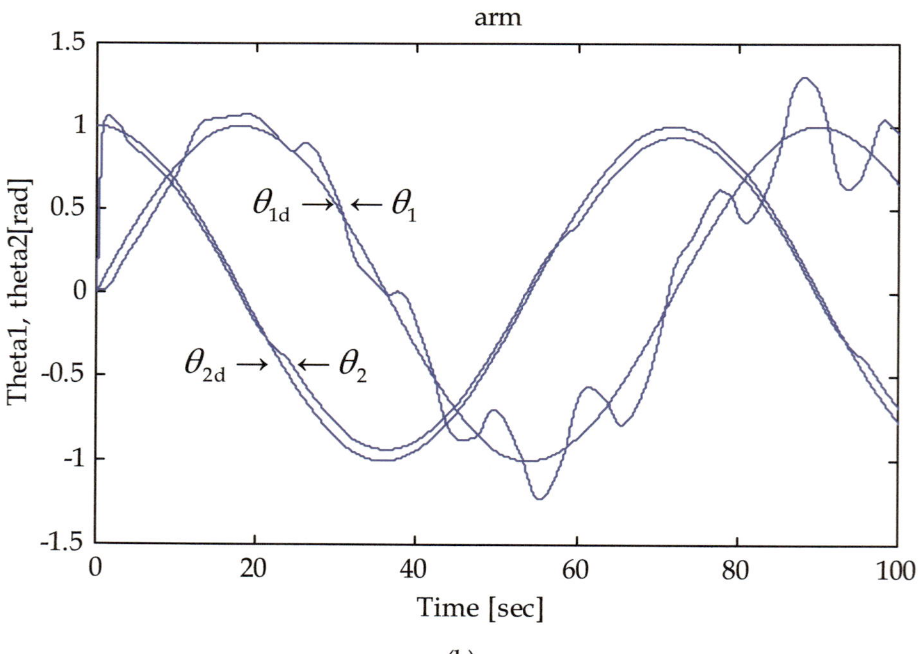

(b)

Fig. 6. Response with deadzone nonlinearity of a mobile manipulator (a) vehicle trajectory and (b) arm position.

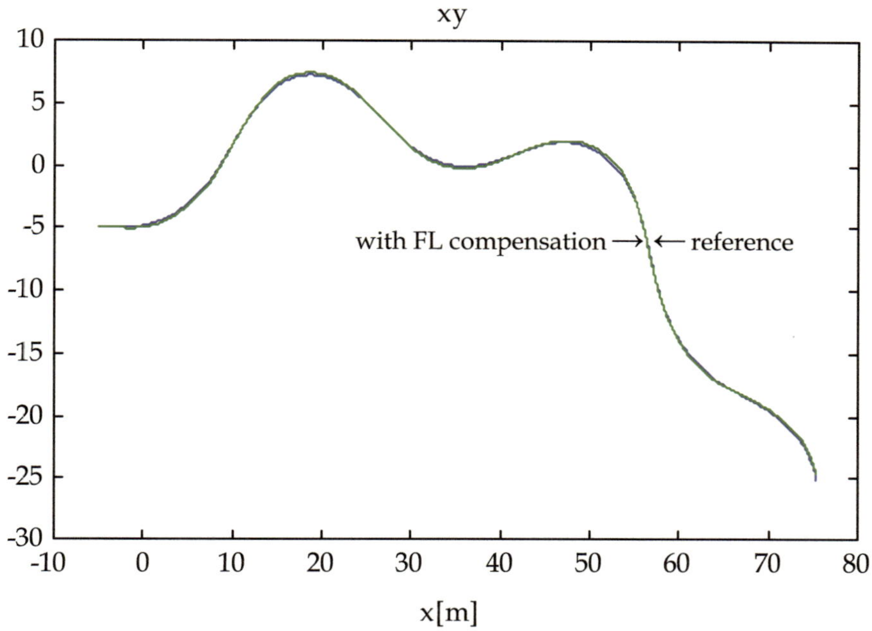
xy
10
5
0
-5
-10
-15
-20
-25
-30
-10
0
10
20
30
40
50
60
70
80
with FL compensation →
← reference
x[m]

(a)

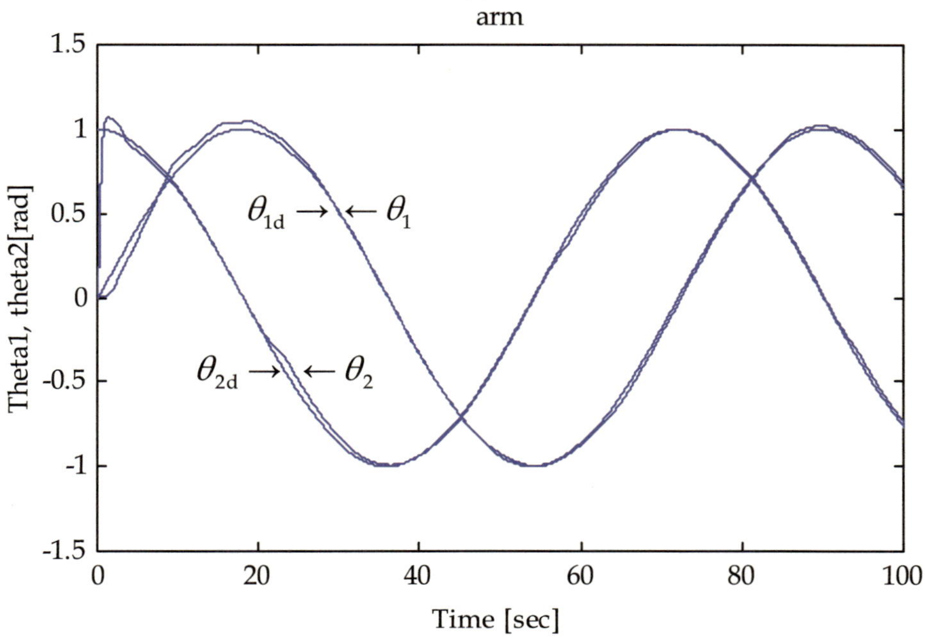
arm
1.5
1
0.5
0
-0.5
-1
-1.5
Theta1, theta2[rad]
θ_{1d} →
← θ_1
θ_{2d} →
← θ_2
0
20
40
60
80
100
Time [sec]

(b)

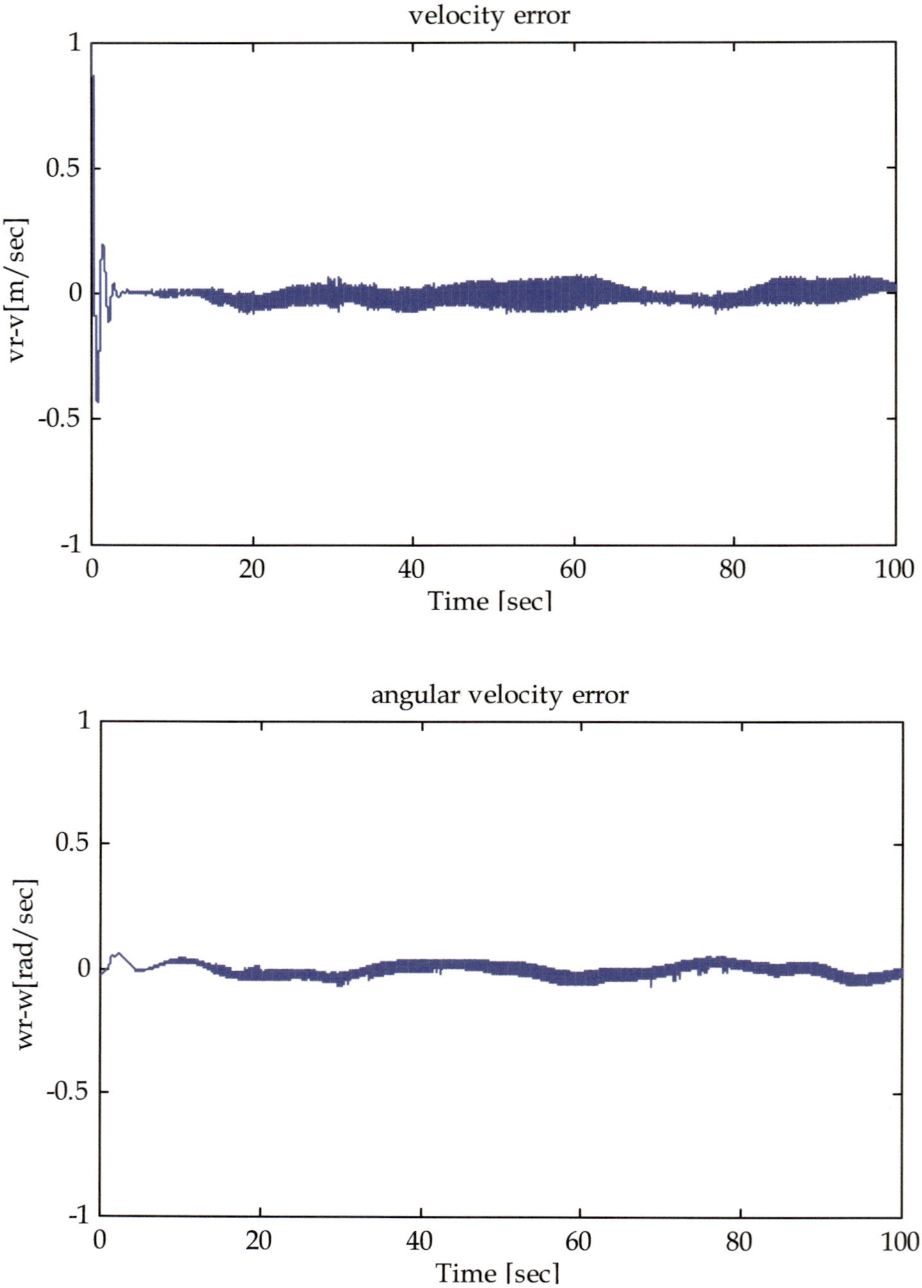
velocity error
vr-v[m/sec]
Time [sec]
1
0.5
0
-0.5
-1
0
20
40
60
80
100
angular velocity error
wr-w[rad/sec]
Time [sec]
1
0.5
0
-0.5
-1
0
20
40
60
80
100

(c)

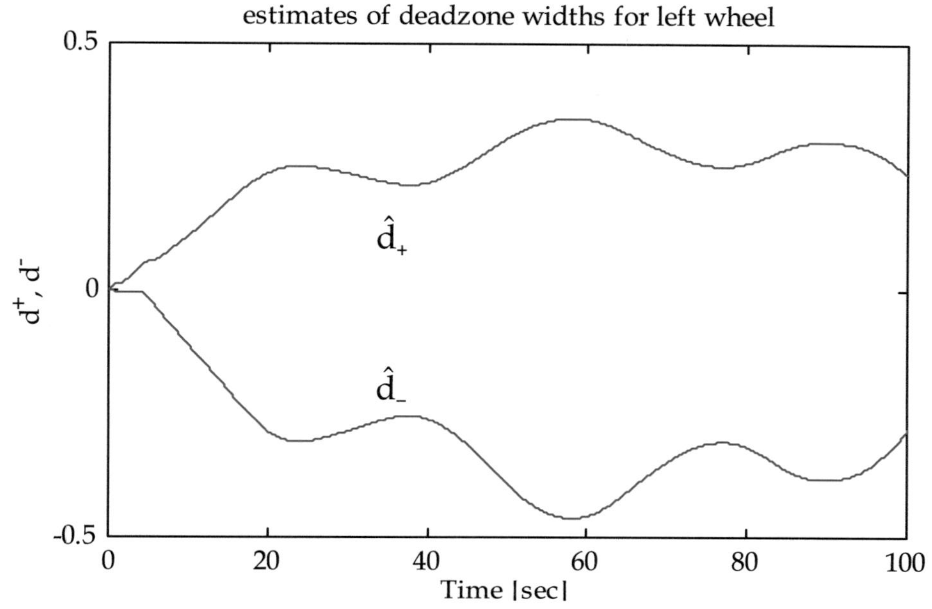
estimates of deadzone widths for left wheel
0.5
0
-0.5
d^+, d^-
$\hat{d}_+$
$\hat{d}_-$
0
20
40
60
80
100
Time [sec]

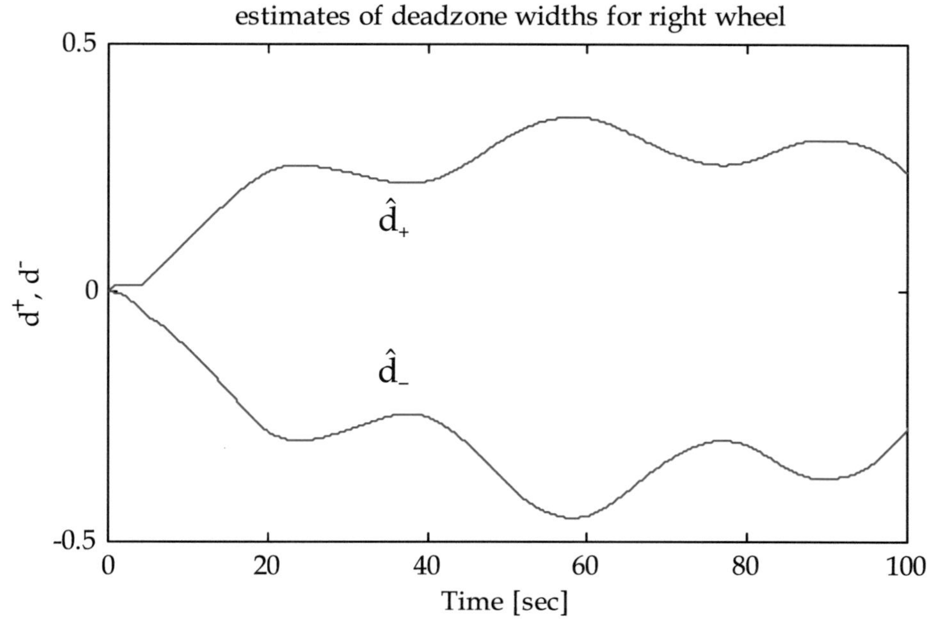
estimates of deadzone widths for right wheel
0.5
0
-0.5
d^+, d^-
$\hat{d}_+$
$\hat{d}_-$
0
20
40
60
80
100
Time [sec]

(d)

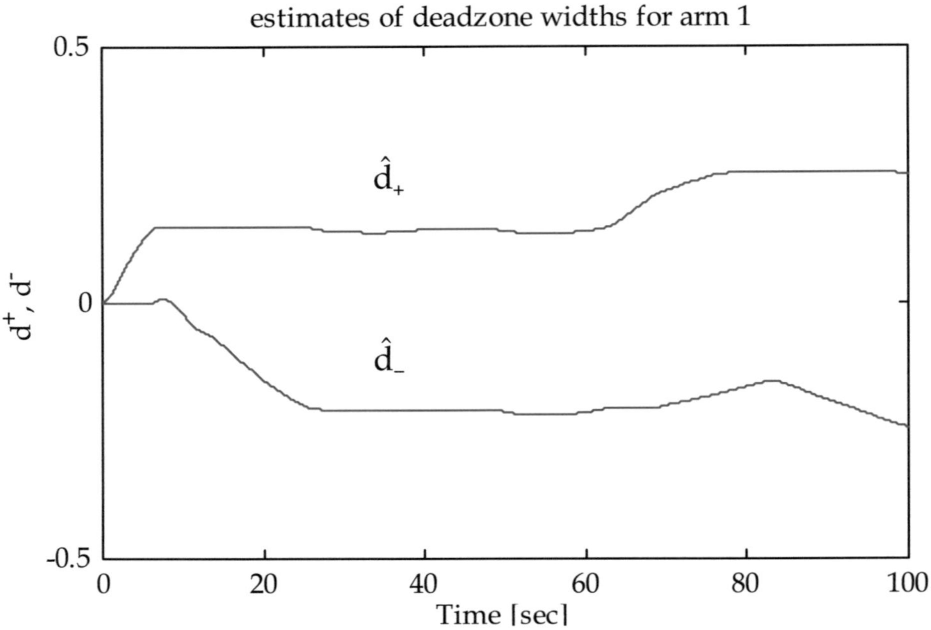

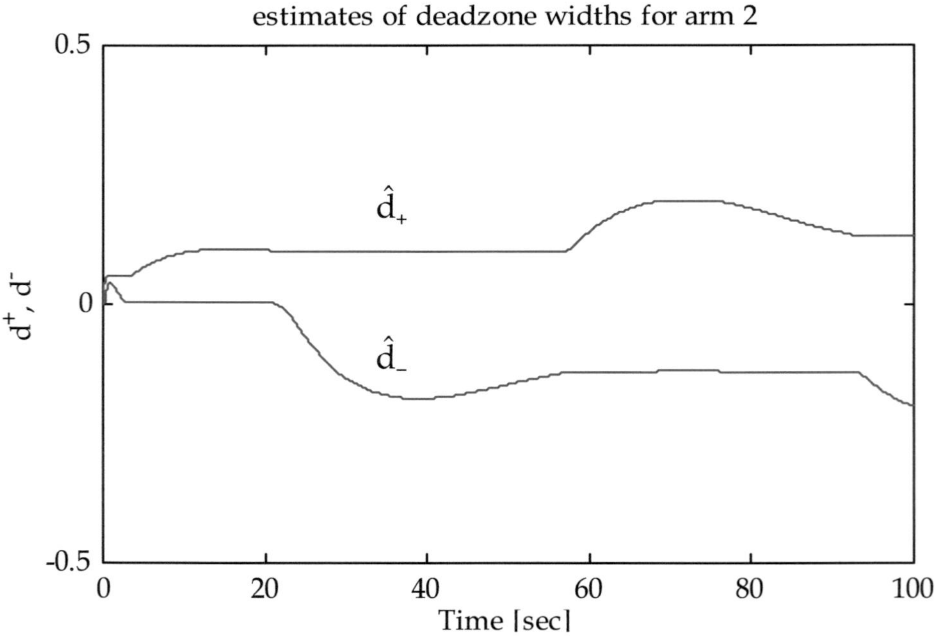

Fig. 7.(Continued).

6. Conclusions

The FL deadzone conpensation with a linear controller for tracking of a mobile manipulators has been developed. In fact, perfect knowledge of the mobile manipulator parameters is unattainable, e.g., the deadzone nonlinearity is very difficult to model by conventional techniques. To confront this, an FL deadzone compensation with guaranteed performance has been derived. The proposed control scheme is shown to be asymptotically stable through theoretical proof and simulation with a mobile manipulator.

7. References

Bayle, B.; Fourquet, J. Y. & Renaud, M. (2003). Manipulability of wheeled mobile manipulators : Application to motion generation, *Int. J. Robot. Res.*, vol. 22, no. 7/8, page numbers (565-581), ISSN 0278-3649.

Dixon, W. E.; Dawson, D. M.; Zergerglu, E. & Zhang, F. (2000) Robust tracking and regulation control for mobile robots, *Int. J. Robust Nonlinear Contr.*, vol. 10, page numbers (199-216), ISSN 1049-8923.

Jang, J. O. (2005). Deadzone compensation of an XY positioning table using fuzzy logic, *IEEE Trans. Ind. Electronics,* vol. 52, no. 6, page numbrs (1696-1701), ISSN 0278-0046.

Jang J. O. & Jeon, G. J. (2006). Backlash compensation of nonlinear systems using fuzzy logic, *Int. J. Systems Science*, vol. 37, no. 7, page numbers (485-492), ISSN 0020-7721.

Jang, J. O. (2009). Neuro-fuzzy network saturation compensation of DC motor systems, *Mechatronics*, vol. 19, no. 4, page numbers (529-534), ISSN 0957-4158.

Jang, J. O. & Chung, H. T. (2009). Neuro-fuzzy network control for a mobile robot, *Proceedings of American Contr. Conf.*, pp. 2928-2933, ISSN 0743-1619, IEEE, St. Louis, MO.

Kanayama, Y.; Kimura, Y.; Miyazaki, F. & Noquchi, T. (1990). A stable tracking control method for autonomus mobile robot, *Proceedings of IEEE Int. Conf. Robot. Automat.*, pp. 384-389, ISBN 0818690615, IEEE, Cincinnati, OH.

Khatib, O. (1999). Mobile manipulation: The robotic assistant, *Robot. Autonomous Syst.*, vol. 26, no. 2/3, page numbers (157-183), ISSN 0921-8890.

Kim, J. H.; Park, J. H.; Lee, S. W. & Cheng, E. K. P. (1994). A two layered fuzzy logic controller for systems with deadzones, *IEEE Trans. Ind. Electron.*, vol. 41, page numbers (155-162), ISSN 0278-0046.

Lewis, F. L.; Jagannathan, S. & Yesildirek, A. (1999). *Neural Network Control of Robot Manipulators and nonlinear Systems,* Taylor and Francis, ISBN 078405968, London, U.K.

Lewis, F. L.; Yesildirek, A. & Liu, K. (1996). Multilayer neural-net robot controller with guranteed tracking performance, *IEEE Trans. Neural Networks*, vol. 7, no. 2, page numbers (388-399), ISSN 1045-9227.

Li, Z.; Ge, S. S.; Adams, M. & Wijesoma, W. S. (2008). Adaptive robut output feedback motion/force control of electrically driven nonholonomic mobile manipulators, *IEEE Trans. Control Systems Tech.*, vol. 16, no. 6, page numbers (1308-1315), ISSN 1063-6536.

Lin, S. & Goldenberg, A. A. (2001). Neural network control of mobile manipulators, *IEEE Trans. Neural Networks*, vol. 12, no. 5, page numbers (1121-1133), ISSN 1045-9227.

Mbede, J. B.; Mveh-Abia, P.; Toure Y.; Graefe, V. & Ma, S. (2005). Intelligent mobile manipulator navigation using adaptive neuro-fuzzy systems, *Information Sciences,* vol. 171, page numbers(447-474), ISSN 0020-0255.

Recker, D. A.; Kokotović, P. V.; Rhode, D. & Winkelman, J. (1991). Adaptive nonlinear control of systems containing a deadzone, P*roceedings of IEEE Conf. Decision and Control*, pp. 2111-2115. ISBN 0780304500, IEEE, Brighton, UK.

Salehi, M. & Vossoughi, G. (2008). Impendance control of flexible mobile manipulator using singular perturbation method and sliding mode control law, *Int. J. Contr., Automat. and Syst.*, vol. 6, no. 5, page numbers (677-688), ISSN 1598-6446.

Tao, G. & Kokotović, P. V. (1992). Adaptive control of plants with unknown dead-zones, *Proceedings of American Control Conf.*, pp. 2710-2714, ISBN 0780302109, IEEE, Chicago, IL.

Yamamoto, Y. (1994). Modeling and control of mobile manipulators, *Ph. D. dissertation,* Univ. Michigan, Ann Arber.

Yamamoto, Y. & Yun, X. (1996). Effect of the dynamic interaction on coordinated control of mobile manipulator, *IEEE Trans. Robot. Autom.,* vol. 12, no. 5, page numbers (816-824), ISSN 1552-3098.